D0501193

America's
TEST KITCHEN

ADDITIONAL COOKBOOKS AND DVD SETS AVAILABLE FROM THE PUBLISHER OF COOK'S COUNTRY INCLUDE:

The *America's Test Kitchen* Family Cookbook

THE BEST RECIPE SERIES
The *Cook's Illustrated* Guide to Grilling and Barbecue
Best American Side Dishes
Cover & Bake
The New Best Recipe
Steaks, Chops, Roasts, and Ribs
Baking Illustrated
Restaurant Favorites at Home
Perfect Vegetables
The Quick Recipe
Italian Classics
American Classics
Soups & Stews

THE AMERICA'S TEST KITCHEN SERIES
(companion cookbooks and DVD sets to our hit public television series)

Cooking at Home with *America's Test Kitchen*: 2006 season companion cookbook
America's Test Kitchen Live! 2005 season companion cookbook
Inside *America's Test Kitchen*: 2004 season companion cookbook
Here in *America's Test Kitchen*: 2003 season companion cookbook
The *America's Test Kitchen* Cookbook: 2002 season companion cookbook
The *America's Test Kitchen* 2005 season 4-DVD boxed set
The *America's Test Kitchen* 2004 season 4-DVD boxed set

THE HOW TO COOK MASTER SERIES
The How to Cook Master Series
How to Make a Pie
How to Make an American Layer Cake
How to Make Salad
How to Grill
How to Make Simple Fruit Desserts
How to Cook Holiday Roasts and Birds
How to Make Stew
How to Cook Shrimp and Other Shellfish
How to Barbecue and Roast on the Grill
How to Cook Garden Vegetables
How to Make Pot Pies and Casseroles
How to Sauté
How to Make Sauces and Gravies
How to Make Muffins, Biscuits, and Scones
How to Cook Chicken Breasts

ADDITIONAL BOOKS FROM THE EDITORS OF COOK'S ILLUSTRATED MAGAZINE INCLUDE:

The Cook's Bible
The *Cook's Illustrated* Complete Book of Pasta and Noodles
The Best Kitchen Quick Tips
The Kitchen Detective
1993–2005 *Cook's Illustrated* Master Index
Cook's Illustrated Annual Editions from each year of publication (1993–2005)

To order any of our cookbooks listed above, give us a call at 800-611-0759 inside the U.S.,
or at 515-246-6911 if calling from outside the U.S. You can order subscriptions, gift subscriptions, and any of our books
by visiting our online store at www.cookscountry.com

$29.95

Copyright 2005 © by The Editors of *Cook's Country*.
All rights reserved, including the right of reproduction in whole or in part in any form.
Published by America's Test Kitchen, 17 Station Street, Brookline, MA 02445
ISBN: 0-936184-94-9   ISSN: 1552-1990

To get home delivery of *Cook's Country*, call 800-526-8447 inside the U.S., or 515-247-7571 if calling from outside the U.S., or subscribe online at www.cookscountry.com

2005 Recipe Index

RC = Recipe card
IBC = Inside back cover

A

Acorn squash ....Oct/Nov 05 — 27
   splitting with little saw.............Oct/Nov 05 — 3
Alfredo Sauce, Artichoke.............Oct/Nov 05 — 5
Allspice ....Dec/Jan 06 — 15
Alsatian Potato Casserole ....Charter Issue — 6
Aluminum foil. See Foil
Angel food cake pans, as
   catchall for corn cob
   kernels............................Oct/Nov 05 — 2
Antipasto Heroes ....Jun/Jul 05 — RC
Appetizer parties (menus) ....Oct/Nov 05 — 18–19
Appetizers and hors
   d'oeuvres ....Oct/Nov 05 — 18–19
   Artichoke Dip, Light and
    Creamy Hot ....Dec/Jan 06 — 7
   Asparagus Puffs ....Oct/Nov 05 — 19
   Beet Spread, Creamy,
    with Endive Leaves ....Oct/Nov 05 — 18
   Brie Cups, Baked ....Oct/Nov 05 — 18
   Cheese Straws (with
    variations) ....Apr/May 05 — 15
   Cherry Tomatoes, Stuffed ....Oct/Nov 05 — 19
   Chutney Cheese Rounds ....Oct/Nov 05 — 19
   Crab Dip, Light and
    Creamy Hot ....Dec/Jan 06 — 7
   Crispy Mexican Bites ....Oct/Nov 05 — 18
   French Dip ....Jun/Jul 05 — 18
   Gingered Shrimp Toasts ....Oct/Nov 05 — 19
   Hot Dip, Light and Creamy ....Dec/Jan 06 — 7
   Jalapeños, Stuffed ....Oct/Nov 05 — 18
   Pineapple Salsa, Fresh ....Oct/Nov 05 — 18
   Roast Beef Canapés ....Oct/Nov 05 — 18
   Sesame Chicken Bites...........Oct/Nov 05 — 19
   Smoked Salmon Pinwheels.....Oct/Nov 05 — 19
   Spinach Dip, Light and
    Creamy Hot ....Dec/Jan 06 — 7
Apple(s). See also Cider
   Bistro Slaw ....Jun/Jul 05 — 24
   Cake, Blue-Ribbon ....Charter Issue — 18
   Candy-Coated Caramel ....Oct/Nov 05 — 10
   Cape Cod Picnic Salad ....Apr/May 05 — 6
   coring with melon baller.........Apr/May 05 — 5
   Cranberry-Orange-, Relish......Dec/Jan 06 — 13
   Harvest Cider-Can Chicken ...Aug/Sep 05 — 19
   Pie, Paper Bag ....Oct/Nov 05 — 16
   Pie Iced Tea ....Jun/Jul 05 — 20
   seeds, cyanide in ....Aug/Sep 05 — 9
   shopping for ....Charter Issue — 29
   Turnovers, Easy ....Oct/Nov 05 — 13
    Sugar and Spice.................Oct/Nov 05 — 13
   varieties of, for baking ....Charter Issue — 19
Apple peelers, electric
   (Speedy-Peel), testing of........Aug/Sep 05 — 9
Applesauce, "doctored":
   Five-Spice ....Apr/May 05 — 21
   Sweet-and-Hot Cinnamon .....Apr/May 05 — 21
Appliances. See also specific
   appliances
   storing receipts and
    product booklets for ....Dec/Jan 06 — 3
Apricot:
   Chicken Salad ....Aug/Sep 05 — 5
   Cream Cheese Spread,
    Zesty ....Aug/Sep 05 — 29
   -Glazed Chicken Breasts ....Jun/Jul 05 — 15
Artichoke:
   Alfredo Sauce ....Oct/Nov 05 — 5
   Hot Dip, Light and Creamy ....Dec/Jan 06 — 7
Arugula..Jun/Jul 05 — 19
Asian Corn and Chicken Soup....Apr/May 05 — RC

B (continued from column)

Asparagus:
   Broiled, with Cheesy Bread
    Crumbs ....Apr/May 05 — 11
   Puffs ....Oct/Nov 05 — 19
Avocado(s):
   and Black Bean Salad ....Jun/Jul 05 — 11
   Crab Louis.............................Aug/Sep 05 — RC
   Monterey Melts ....Oct/Nov 05 — 15

B

Bacon:
   baking short slices of ....Aug/Sep 05 — 2
   "Bring Home the Bacon"
    Tomato Salad ....Aug/Sep 05 — 14
   Cornbread Stuffing with ....Oct/Nov 05 — 12
   Monterey Melts ....Oct/Nov 05 — 15
   oven-frying ....Jun/Jul 05 — 4
   and Roasted Red Pepper
    Sauce (for pasta) ....Oct/Nov 05 — 5
Bahama Mama (winter fruit
   salad) ....Dec/Jan 06 — 23
Bakeware and baking
   supplies:
   angel food cake pans,
    as catchall for corn
    cob kernels ....Oct/Nov 05 — 2
   baking pans
    cutting parchment or
     waxed paper for ....Apr/May 05 — 4
    lining with foil ....Dec/Jan 06 — 3
    square, rating of ....Jun/Jul 05 — 29
   biscuit cutters ....Oct/Nov 05 — 28
   cake pans, flouring ....Apr/May 05 — 4
   cookie cutters
    choosing ....Charter Issue — 29
    drying quickly....................Oct/Nov 05 — 2
   cookie sheets, organizing.......Aug/Sep 05 — 2
   muffin liners, separating
    easily ....Oct/Nov 05 — 2
   muffin tins
    baking meatloaf in ....Dec/Jan 06 — 2
    organizing cookie
     decorations in ....Charter Issue — 26
   parchment paper
    cutting to line baking
     pans ....Apr/May 05 — 4
    holding up pie crust
     during blind
     baking with..................Oct/Nov 05 — 3
    lining baking peel with .....Aug/Sep 05 — 3
    rolling cookie dough
     between ....Charter Issue — 26
   peels, baking or pizza
    lining with parchment
     paper ....Aug/Sep 05 — 3
    makeshift, pizza-delivery
     box as ....Dec/Jan 06 — 3
   rolling pins, tapered ....Oct/Nov 05 — 28
   springform pans, easier
    slicing in ....Charter Issue — 4
Baking soda, cleaning
   drain with ....Charter Issue — 4
Banana(s):
   Bahama Mama (winter
    fruit salad) ....Dec/Jan 06 — 23
   The Elvis Smoothie....................Aug/Sep 05 — 25
   Grilled, and Red Onion Salsa....Jun/Jul 05 — 23
   mashing and measuring
    for baking ....Dec/Jan 06 — 3
   Tutti-Frutti Watermelon
    Boats ....Aug/Sep 05 — 10

B (third column)

Barbecue sauces, bottled,
   tasting of ....Apr/May 05 — 30
Barley Beef Soup with
   Mushrooms ....Charter Issue — 11
Bars. See also Brownie(s)
   Strawberry Pretzel ....Jun/Jul 05 — 7
Basil:
   chopping ahead vs. right
    before use ....Aug/Sep 05 — 28
   Garden Pesto Sauce ....Oct/Nov 05 — 4
Basters, as makeshift funnels
   for very small jars ....Apr/May 05 — 4
Batter Pro, testing of ....Apr/May 05 — 21
BBQ:
   Chicken, Beer-Can.................Aug/Sep 05 — 18–19
   Spareribs, Memphis ....Jun/Jul 05 — 14–15
Bean(s):
   black
    and Avocado Salad ....Jun/Jul 05 — 11
    Crispy Mexican Bites ....Oct/Nov 05 — 18
    Tricolor Mexican Bean
     Salad ....Apr/May 05 — 7
   Boston Baked ....Aug/Sep 05 — 7
   canned, substituting for
    dried beans......................Oct/Nov 05 — 6
   cannellini, in Panzanella
    Salad ....Apr/May 05 — 7
   Cowboy ....Apr/May 05 — 22
   soup, thickening ....Dec/Jan 06 — 2
Beaters, getting last drop of
   batter off ....Aug/Sep 05 — 3
Beef:
   burgers
    shaping quickly.................Dec/Jan 06 — 2
    shaping to prevent bulge ...Jun/Jul 05 — 3
    toppings for (contest) ....Jun/Jul 05 — 27
    Ultimate Hamburger ....Jun/Jul 05 — 26
   Chili con Carne, "Texas Red" ...Jun/Jul 05 — 10–11
   Corned, Hash ....Charter Issue — RC
   Filets Mignons, Bacon-
    Wrapped ....Apr/May 05 — RC
   Meatloaf, Cheesy
    Southwestern ....Apr/May 05 — 23
   pot roast
    Country Style, with
     Gravy ....Charter Issue — 10
    cuts for ....Charter Issue — 10
    leftover, recipes for ....Charter Issue — 11
    skimming fat from............Charter Issue — 29
    in slow cooker.................Charter Issue — 10–11
    Southwestern ....Charter Issue — 11
   roast
    Canapés ....Oct/Nov 05 — 18
    cuts for ....Oct/Nov 05 — 20
    French Dip Sandwiches ...Oct/Nov 05 — 21
    Garlic, Sunday-Best ....Oct/Nov 05 — 20–21
    Jus for, Quick ....Oct/Nov 05 — 21
   sandwiches
    French Dip ....Oct/Nov 05 — 21
    Sloppy Joes (with
     variations) ....Oct/Nov 05 — 17
   short ribs
    Beer-Braised ....Dec/Jan 06 — 8
    English-style vs.
     flanken-style ....Dec/Jan 06 — 29
   soups
    Barley, with Mushrooms ..Charter Issue — 11
    simmering vs. boiling
     broth for ....Dec/Jan 06 — 29
    Vegetable, Hearty.............Dec/Jan 06 — 26–27
   Spicy Noodles and ....Oct/Nov 05 — RC

Beef (CONTINUED)

steak(s)

Flank, Grilled, with
Garlic-Parsley
Sauce ....Charter Issue   **22**

Flank, Stuffed ....Aug/Sep 05   **22**

Grilled, and Onion Salad..Aug/Sep 05   **RC**

lexicon for...........................Dec/Jan 06   **18**

Pan-Seared, with
Balsamic Onions ....Dec/Jan 06   **18**

Stew, Hearty ....Oct/Nov 05   **7**

Stir-Fried, with Snow Peas
and Cashews.....................Dec/Jan 06   **RC**

Taco Salad ....Dec/Jan 06   **RC**

Tortilla Casserole ....Charter Issue   **11**

Beer-Braised Short Ribs.................Dec/Jan 06   **8**

Beer-can chicken:

BBQ...Aug/Sep 05 **18–19**

vertical chicken roasters
and ....Aug/Sep 05   **29**

Beet(s):

Spread, Creamy, with
Endive Leaves....................Oct/Nov 05   **18**

stains, cleaning from
cutting board ....Aug/Sep 05   **9**

Belgian endive ....Jun/Jul 05   **19**

Bench scrapers............................Apr/May 05   **29**

Berry(ies). *See also specific
berries*

storing...................................Jun/Jul 05   **29**

Summer, Bake ....Jun/Jul 05   **RC**

Very, Smoothie ....Aug/Sep 05   **25**

washing.................................Jun/Jul 05   **3**

Beverages. *See also* Smoothies

Hot Chocolate, Mug o'
Minty ....Dec/Jan 06   **10**

iced tea

Sweet (with variations) ....Jun/Jul 05   **20**

tasting of tea bags for.........Jun/Jul 05   **29**

lemonade, tasting of ....Aug/Sep 05   **30**

Mulled Cider, Fireside (with
variations) ....Dec/Jan 06   **14**

straining solids from ....Dec/Jan 06   **28**

Root Beer Floats ....Apr/May 05   **12**

Watermelon Citrus Punch.......Aug/Sep 05   **10**

Bibb lettuce ....Jun/Jul 05   **19**

Birthday Cupcakes, Easy ....Apr/May 05   **26**

Biscuit cutters............................Oct/Nov 05   **28**

Biscuits:

Cheddar ....Dec/Jan 06   **27**

cutting into scone-like
wedges.............................Dec/Jan 06   **29**

Jalapeño Jack ....Dec/Jan 06   **27**

Parmesan Garlic ....Dec/Jan 06   **27**

Quaker Bonnet ....Oct/Nov 05   **8**

Swiss Caraway ....Dec/Jan 06   **27**

Bistro Slaw ....Jun/Jul 05   **24**

Black bean(s):

and Avocado Salad ....Jun/Jul 05   **11**

Crispy Mexican Bites ....Oct/Nov 05   **18**

Tricolor Mexican Bean
Salad.................................Apr/May 05   **7**

Blackberries:

Hollywood Hills (winter
fruit salad) ....Dec/Jan 06   **23**

washing.................................Jun/Jul 05   **3**

Blanching vegetables,
quickly cooling after.............Apr/May 05   **4**

Bleach, soaking plastic
cutting boards in ....Aug/Sep 05   **9**

Blenders, rating of ....Jun/Jul 05   **31**

Blind baking pie shells.................Oct/Nov 05   **28**

with parchment paper
holding up sides of crust ...Oct/Nov 05   **3**

Blueberries:

Hollywood Hills (winter fruit
salad).................................Dec/Jan 06   **23**

Summer Berry Bake ....Jun/Jul 05   **RC**

washing.................................Jun/Jul 05   **3**

Blue cheese:

Creamy Beet Spread with
Endive Leaves....................Oct/Nov 05   **18**

Dressing, Iceberg Lettuce
with....................................Charter Issue   **RC**

Green Salad with Roasted
Pears and ....Dec/Jan 06   **21**

Macaroni and Cheese
after Dark ....Apr/May 05   **8**

"Rhapsody in Blue Cheese"
Tomato Salad ....Aug/Sep 05   **14**

Blue Hubbard squash ....Oct/Nov 05   **27**

Boiled Cake ....Dec/Jan 06   **16**

Boston Baked Beans ....Aug/Sep 05   **7**

Boston lettuce ....Jun/Jul 05   **19**

Bowl covers, mess-free flour
sifting with ....Aug/Sep 05   **3**

Bowl scrapers (dough
scrapers)...............................Apr/May 05   **29**

Brain freeze (ice cream
headache) ....Aug/Sep 05   **27**

Bread. *See also* Biscuits

buttering easily ....Charter Issue   **4**

Cheese Muffins, Savory ....Oct/Nov 05   **22**

Jalapeño Cornbread...........Charter Issue   **21**

Monkey ....Apr/May 05 **9–10**

Panzanella Salad....................Apr/May 05   **7**

Puddings, Individual
Mochaccino ....Oct/Nov 05   **25**

tips and techniques

removing dough stuck
to counter.......................Oct/Nov 05   **2**

rising dough on clothes
dryer ....Apr/May 05   **4**

rising dough with
microwavable
herbal comfort pack ...Aug/Sep 05   **3**

Zucchini..................................Aug/Sep 05   **24**

baking in muffin tin............Aug/Sep 05   **28**

Breaded foods, testing of
Batter Pro for ....Apr/May 05   **21**

Breakfast and brunch fare:

Cloudcakes............................Apr/May 05 **14–15**

Crumb Coffee Cake,
Reduced-Fat........................Jun/Jul 05   **8**

Denver Omelet, Family-Style.....Jun/Jul 05   **21**

Maple Sausage and Waffle
Casserole...........................Dec/Jan 06   **22**

Monkey Bread.........................Apr/May 05 **9–10**

Orange Drop Doughnuts..........Aug/Sep 05   **8**

Brie Cups, Baked ....Oct/Nov 05   **18**

Broccoli:

Calzones, Cheesy ....Aug/Sep 05   **RC**

with Creamy Herb Sauce ....Apr/May 05   **17**

cutting up ....Apr/May 05   **17**

with Lemon and Walnuts........Apr/May 05   **17**

with Mustard–Red Pepper
Vinaigrette ....Apr/May 05   **17**

with Parmesan Bread
Crumbs ....Apr/May 05   **17**

Brown & Crisp Microwave
Cooking Bags, testing of ......Charter Issue   **31**

Brown-Eyed Susan (cake)............Oct/Nov 05   **IBC**

Brownie(s)...............................Charter Issue **24–25**

Basic ....Charter Issue   **24**

Frosted ....Charter Issue   **25**

German Chocolate ....Charter Issue   **25**

Peanut Butter Swirl................Charter Issue   **25**

Pecan Pie ....Charter Issue   **25**

Brownie(s) (CONTINUED)

Peppermint-Surprise, Bites ......Oct/Nov 05   **10**

removing from pan neatly ...Charter Issue   **5**

S'Mores ....Charter Issue   **25**

White Chocolate &
Peppermint ....Charter Issue   **25**

Browning meat, draining
fat from.................................Aug/Sep 05   **3**

Brown sugar, melted, as
last-minute pancake syrup ....Apr/May 05   **5**

Brunch. *See* Breakfast and
brunch fare

Brushes, baby-bottle,
cleaning graters with ....Aug/Sep 05   **3**

Brussels Sprouts, Braised,
with Bacon and Pecans.........Dec/Jan 06   **13**

Burgers:

shaping

to prevent bulge ....Jun/Jul 05   **3**

quickly...............................Dec/Jan 06   **2**

toppings for (contest) ....Jun/Jul 05   **27**

Ultimate Hamburger..................Jun/Jul 05   **26**

Burnt Sugar Cake ....Aug/Sep 05   **16**

Butter:

bringing to room
temperature quickly ....Dec/Jan 06   **29**

Cookies, Chocolate Toffee ....Dec/Jan 06   **4**

melting in microwave neatly ....Jun/Jul 05   **5**

room-temperature, test for ....Dec/Jan 06   **17**

salted vs. unsalted,
cooking with ....Jun/Jul 05   **3**

softening quickly....................Dec/Jan 06   **3**

spreadable, rating of
gadgets for ....Dec/Jan 06   **31**

spreading

on bread ....Charter Issue   **4**

on corn ....Apr/May 05   **5**

Buttercup squash........................Oct/Nov 05   **27**

Buttermilk, makeshift...................Apr/May 05   **29**

Butternut squash ....Oct/Nov 05   **27**

Butterscotch Sauce ....Aug/Sep 05   **27**

C

Cabbage:

leaves, making pliable............Dec/Jan 06   **2**

Red, Slaw ....Charter Issue   **22**

Spicy Peanut Slaw ....Jun/Jul 05   **24**

Cajun Down 'n' Dirty Rice ....Oct/Nov 05   **22**

Cake pans:

angel food, as catchall
for corn cob kernels.........Oct/Nov 05   **2**

flouring ....Apr/May 05   **4**

Cakes:

Apple, Blue-Ribbon ....Charter Issue   **18**

Boiled ....Dec/Jan 06   **16**

Brown-Eyed Susan ....Oct/Nov 05   **IBC**

Burnt Sugar ....Aug/Sep 05   **16**

Chocolate Sheet,
Reduced-Fat.......................Aug/Sep 05   **6**

coffee

Crumb, Reduced-Fat...........Jun/Jul 05   **8**

flavored glazes for.............Dec/Jan 06   **28**

Pecan Sour Cream ....Dec/Jan 06 **17–18**

cupcakes

Birthday, Easy....................Apr/May 05   **26**

decorating (contest) ....Apr/May 05   **27**

Ice Cream ....Charter Issue   **12**

portioning batter for ....Apr/May 05   **26**

decorating supplies for...........Apr/May 05   **29**

determining when done ....Aug/Sep 05   **29**

Icebox Peppermint Yule Log...Dec/Jan 06   **10**

Lady Baltimore ....Dec/Jan 06   **IBC**

Pear, with Ginger Cream,
Western-Slope....................Dec/Jan 06   **13**

Cakes (CONTINUED)

trifles
Strawberry, Quick ....Jun/Jul 05   7
Tipsy Parson ....Dec/Jan 06   9
Calzones, Cheesy Broccoli ....Aug/Sep 05   RC
Camembert, freezing ....Charter Issue   3
Candy. See also Confections
-Coated Caramel Apples ......Oct/Nov 05   10
Candy thermometers, for
frying ....Charter Issue   15
Cannellini beans, in
Panzanella Salad ....Apr/May 05   7
Cantaloupe, in Polka-Dot
Minty Melon Mold ....Aug/Sep 05   10
Cape Cod Picnic Salad ....Apr/May 05   6
Caramel:
Apples, Candy-Coated ....Oct/Nov 05   10
Turtles ....Oct/Nov 05   10
Caraway seeds ....Dec/Jan 06   15
Carbonara, Creamy ....Dec/Jan 06   25
Cardamom ....Dec/Jan 06   15
Carnival squash ....Oct/Nov 05   27
Carrots:
Casablanca Slaw ....Jun/Jul 05   24
Minty Peas and ....Dec/Jan 06   19
Casablanca Slaw ....Jun/Jul 05   24
Casseroles:
Beef Tortilla ....Charter Issue   11
CorningWare AnyWare for .....Oct/Nov 05   29
Maple Sausage and Waffle ...Dec/Jan 06   22
potato
Alsatian ....Charter Issue   6
Cheesy ....Oct/Nov 05   23
Creamy ....Charter Issue   6
Italian Potato Cake ....Charter Issue   6
Mashed Potato and
Herbed Cheese
Bake ....Charter Issue   7
recipe contest ....Charter Issue   6–7
with Spinach and
Sausage ....Charter Issue   7
Sweet Potato ....Dec/Jan 06   13
Tortilla, Easy (with chicken).....Oct/Nov 05   RC
Cast-iron cookware:
Dutch ovens ....Charter Issue   29
Lodge Grill Press, testing of.....Oct/Nov 05   31
Celery "string," tying herb
bundles with ....Jun/Jul 05   4
Cereal box liners, pounding
chicken or meat in ....Dec/Jan 06   3
Charcoal, chimney starters for....Aug/Sep 05   28
lighting ....Aug/Sep 05   28
Cheddar:
Baked Cheese Grits ....Charter Issue   RC
Biscuits ....Dec/Jan 06   27
cutting into scone-like
wedges ....Dec/Jan 06   29
Cape Cod Picnic Salad ....Apr/May 05   6
Chutney Cheese Rounds ....Oct/Nov 05   19
freezing ....Charter Issue   3
reduced-fat, tasting of ....Apr/May 05   29
Cheese. See also Blue cheese;
Cheddar; Cream cheese
biscuits
Cheddar ....Dec/Jan 06   27
cutting into scone-like
wedges ....Dec/Jan 06   29
Jalapeño Jack ....Dec/Jan 06   27
Parmesan Garlic ....Dec/Jan 06   27
Swiss Caraway ....Dec/Jan 06   27
Brie Cups, Baked ....Oct/Nov 05   18
Broccoli Calzones, Cheesy.....Aug/Sep 05   RC
Chutney Rounds ....Oct/Nov 05   19
freezing ....Charter Issue   3

Cheese (CONTINUED)

goat, in Stuffed Cherry
Tomatoes ....Oct/Nov 05   19
grating
freezing before ....Oct/Nov 05   28
with Microplane grater.....Oct/Nov 05   3
Grits, Baked ....Charter Issue   RC
Herbed, and Mashed
Potato Bake ....Charter Issue   7
Macaroni and, Reduced-
Fat (with variations)..........Apr/May 05   8
tasting of cheeses for ......Apr/May 05   29
Mashed Potatoes, Cheesy ...Charter Issue   23
Meatloaf, Cheesy
Southwestern ....Apr/May 05   23
Muffins, Savory ....Oct/Nov 05   22
Potato Casserole, Cheesy......Oct/Nov 05   23
Ravioli Bake, Cheesy ....Oct/Nov 05   RC
Sandwiches, Grilled,
Classic (with variations) ....Oct/Nov 05   15
Straws (with variations) ....Apr/May 05   15
Cheesecake:
Icebox ....Apr/May 05   24–25
Key Lime ....Apr/May 05   25
Peanut Butter ....Apr/May 05   25
Peppermint Chip ....Apr/May 05   25
releasing from pan ....Apr/May 05   25
slicing
neatly ....Apr/May 05   25
in springform pan ....Charter Issue   4
Strawberry Sauce for..............Apr/May 05   25
water bath for ....Dec/Jan 06   28
Cheesecloth, wrapping herbs
or spices in ....Aug/Sep 05   29
Cheese graters, storing ....Charter Issue   5
Cheese slicers, slicing icebox
cookies with ....Charter Issue   4
Chef's knives, rating of ....Aug/Sep 05   31
Cherry:
Chocolate-Covered,
Smoothie ....Aug/Sep 05   25
Lime Rickey Iced Tea ....Jun/Jul 05   20
Pan Sauce (for turkey) ....Apr/May 05   RC
Sauce ....Aug/Sep 05   27
Chicken:
breasts
Apricot-Glazed ....Jun/Jul 05   15
boneless, tasting of ....Oct/Nov 05   30
pounding ....Jun/Jul 05   4
Roast, for Salad ....Aug/Sep 05   5
and Corn Soup, Asian............Apr/May 05   RC
cutlets
with Bacon, Rosemary,
and Lemon...................Oct/Nov 05   RC
cutting ....Dec/Jan 06   28
freezing ....Dec/Jan 06   2
Fried, Extra-Crunchy ....Charter Issue   14–15
Extra-Spicy ....Charter Issue   15
grilled
Apple Harvest
Cider-Can.....................Aug/Sep 05   19
BBQ Beer-Can....................Aug/Sep 05   18–19
Jerk, Easy ....Jun/Jul 05   22–23
Jerk, Sweet 'n' Smoky..........Jun/Jul 05   23
Spicy Lime, with Black
Bean and Avocado
Salad ....Jun/Jul 05   11
livers, in Down 'n' Dirty Rice ...Oct/Nov 05   22
Mahogany ....Aug/Sep 05   RC
with Mushrooms and Leeks ....Dec/Jan 06   RC
Oven-Fried.............................Oct/Nov 05   9
Fiery ....Oct/Nov 05   9
Paprika, Broiled ....Dec/Jan 06   RC
Parmesan, Skillet ....Dec/Jan 06   24

Chicken (CONTINUED)

and Rice, Lemony ....Charter Issue   RC
roast
Crispy, and Potatoes ....Dec/Jan 06   20–21
flipping technique for ....Dec/Jan 06   21
salads
Apricot ....Aug/Sep 05   5
Chinese..............................Aug/Sep 05   5
Curried ....Aug/Sep 05   5
Jalapeño ....Aug/Sep 05   4
recipe contest ....Aug/Sep 05   4–5
Roast Chicken Breasts
for ....Aug/Sep 05   5
Shanghai ....Jun/Jul 05   RC
Waldorf ....Aug/Sep 05   5
Sesame, Bites ....Oct/Nov 05   19
tips and techniques
applying spice rub
underneath skin ....Oct/Nov 05   2
makeshift V-rack.............Dec/Jan 06   28
marinating ahead of
time ....Jun/Jul 05   4
pounding in cereal box
liner ....Dec/Jan 06   3
prepping with
disposable gloves......Charter Issue   5
shredding in food
processor ....Dec/Jan 06   3
washing ....Jun/Jul 05   3
Tortilla Casserole, Easy ....Oct/Nov 05   RC
vertical roasters for,
testing of..........................Aug/Sep 05   29
Chicory ....Jun/Jul 05   19
Children, cutting food into
bite-sized pieces for ....Jun/Jul 05   4
Chiles. See also Jalapeño(s)
canned, chopping with
garlic press ....Aug/Sep 05   2
Chili (seasoning):
-Fried Onion Rings...................Apr/May 05   RC
Salt...Apr/May 05   29
Chili (stew):
con Carne, "Texas Red" ....Jun/Jul 05   10–11
cooling quickly with frozen
vegetables........................Aug/Sep 05   2
Ranch.......................................Charter Issue   20–21
for a Crowd..........................Charter Issue   21
Chimney starters ....Aug/Sep 05   28
lighting ....Jun/Jul 05   5
Chinese Chicken Salad.................Aug/Sep 05   5
Shanghai...................................Jun/Jul 05   RC
Chocolate. See also Brownie(s);
White chocolate
bars, chopping ....Charter Issue   5
Brown-Eyed Susan (cake).......Oct/Nov 05   IBC
chip(s)
Christmas Meringue
Kisses ....Dec/Jan 06   5
cookies, ready-to-bake,
tasting of.....................Apr/May 05   30
tasting of..........................Dec/Jan 06   30
confections
Caramel Turtles ....Oct/Nov 05   10
Confetti Kebabs ....Jun/Jul 05   13
Fudge, Blue-Ribbon...........Aug/Sep 05   23
Rocky Road Bark ....Jun/Jul 05   12
cookies
Fluff.................................Jun/Jul 05   12
Toffee Butter ....Dec/Jan 06   4
Triple-Chocolate................Jun/Jul 05   17
wafers, in Icebox
Peppermint Yule
Log Cake.....................Dec/Jan 06   10
-Covered Cherry Smoothie ....Aug/Sep 05   25

Chocolate (CONTINUED)
  frostings
    Quick.....................Apr/May 05 26
    Reduced-Fat Creamy.......Aug/Sep 05 6
  Glaze, Cup of Cocoa.............Dec/Jan 06 28
  -glazed doughnuts, in
    "Hole-y" Peppermint
    Ice Cream Sandwiches....Dec/Jan 06 10
  Hot, Mug o' Minty....................Dec/Jan 06 10
  ice cream, tasting of.................Jun/Jul 05 30
  Ice Cream Bonbons.............Charter Issue 13
  melting............................Charter Issue 25
    while oven preheats...........Jun/Jul 05 5
  Mochaccino Bread
    Puddings, Individual.........Oct/Nov 05 25
  Mousse, Amazing......................Jun/Jul 05 12
  Peanut Butter Cup Ice
    Cream and Snickers
    Bar Sauce..........................Oct/Nov 05 10
  Peppermint-Surprise
    Brownie Bites.....................Oct/Nov 05 10
  Pudding, Low-Fat.................Charter Issue 8
    Mexican..........................Charter Issue 8
    Orange-Kissed.................Charter Issue 8
  Sauce.......................................Aug/Sep 05 27
    Ginger Ice Cream with.....Apr/May 05 RC
  Sheet Cake, Reduced-Fat.....Aug/Sep 05 6
  Whipped Cream...................Charter Issue 12
Chopping mats (flexible
  cutting mats), testing of.........Aug/Sep 05 31
Christmas cookies. See
  Cookies—Christmas
Chuck wagon cuisine.................Apr/May 05 22
Chutney Cheese Rounds.............Oct/Nov 05 19
Cider:
  -Can Chicken, Apple
    Harvest...............................Aug/Sep 05 19
  Mop.......................................Jun/Jul 05 14
  Mulled, Fireside (with
    variations)...........................Dec/Jan 06 14
    straining solids from...........Dec/Jan 06 28
  vinegar, distilled vinegar vs. ...Dec/Jan 06 6
Cilantro, chopping ahead vs.
  right before use.....................Aug/Sep 05 28
Cinnamon:.....................................Dec/Jan 06 15
  Maple Cream Cheese
    Spread................................Aug/Sep 05 29
  "Toast" Cloudcakes.................Apr/May 05 15
  Toast Glaze.............................Dec/Jan 06 28
Citrus (fruits). See also specific
  fruits
  sectioning...............................Dec/Jan 06 29
  Watermelon Punch.................Aug/Sep 05 10
Cleaning:
  beet stains..............................Aug/Sep 05 9
  cheesy pans............................Apr/May 05 4
  dough stuck to counter..........Oct/Nov 05 2
  food processor blades............Apr/May 05 5
  garbage disposals
    with ice cubes...................Oct/Nov 05 3
    with squeezed lemon
      halves.........................Jun/Jul 05 5
  graters....................................Aug/Sep 05 3
  grill grates..............................Jun/Jul 05 29
  with juiced lemon halves
    garbage disposal.............Jun/Jul 05 5
    greasy pans......................Oct/Nov 05 2
    microwave oven..............Dec/Jan 06 3
  with putty knife......................Aug/Sep 05 3
  removing manufacturer's
    stickers...............................Oct/Nov 05 3
  reusing vinegar from
    to freshen drain...............Charter Issue 4
    to kill weeds......................Oct/Nov 05 3

Cleaning (CONTINUED)
  with rubber spatula...............Charter Issue 4
  scraping pans with
    credit cards.......................Apr/May 05 5
  stainless steel cookware.........Apr/May 05 3
  storage containers.................Apr/May 05 5
Clementines, in Miami
  Vice (winter fruit
  salad)...Dec/Jan 06 23
Cloudcakes.................................Apr/May 05 14–15
  Cinnamon "Toast"...................Apr/May 05 15
  Pucker-Up...............................Apr/May 05 15
Cloves...Dec/Jan 06 15
Club soda, in waffle
  batter..Dec/Jan 06 2
Cocoa (powder):
  Cup of, Glaze..........................Dec/Jan 06 28
  regular (natural) vs.
    Dutched...........................Charter Issue 29
Coconut:
  milk, in Piña Colada
    Smoothie..........................Aug/Sep 05 25
  Piña Colada Mousse.............Apr/May 05 13
Cod, Baked, with
  Crunchy Lemon-Herb
  Topping......................................Dec/Jan 06 RC
Coffee:
  beans, storing.........................Jun/Jul 05 3
  Java Jolt Glaze.......................Dec/Jan 06 28
  Mochaccino Bread
    Puddings, Individual.........Oct/Nov 05 25
  -scented postage stamp
    from Brazil.......................Jun/Jul 05 8
Coffee cakes:
  Crumb, Reduced-Fat................Jun/Jul 05 8
  flavored glazes for.................Dec/Jan 06 28
  Pecan Sour Cream.................Dec/Jan 06 17–18
Coffee filters:
  as makeshift funnel.................Aug/Sep 05 2
  separating easily.....................Oct/Nov 05 2
Coffee grinders, grinding
  spices in....................................Dec/Jan 06 29
Cold food, brain freeze
  and (ice cream
  headache)................................Aug/Sep 05 27
Confections:
  Caramel Turtles.....................Oct/Nov 05 10
  Confetti Kebabs.....................Jun/Jul 05 13
  Fudge, Blue-Ribbon.................Aug/Sep 05 23
  giving away on cheap
    china plates......................Oct/Nov 05 3
  M&M Clusters.......................Oct/Nov 05 10
  Rocky Road Bark.................Jun/Jul 05 12
  Sea Foam Candy.................Charter Issue 9
    mail-order.......................Charter Issue 29
  Wintermint Bark.....................Dec/Jan 06 10
Contests. See Recipe
  contests
Cookbook holders,
  impromptu................................Jun/Jul 05 5
Cookie cutters:
  choosing...............................Charter Issue 29
  drying quickly.........................Oct/Nov 05 2
Cookies:
  chocolate
    Fluff..................................Jun/Jul 05 12
    Toffee Butter....................Dec/Jan 06 4
    Triple-Chocolate.................Jun/Jul 05 17
    wafers, in Icebox
      Peppermint Yule
      Log Cake....................Dec/Jan 06 10
  chocolate chip,
    ready-to-bake,
      tasting of..........................Apr/May 05 30

Cookies (CONTINUED)
  Christmas..............................Charter Issue 26–27
    Best....................................Charter Issue 26
    Chocolate Toffee
      Butter.........................Dec/Jan 06 4
    decorating ideas
      for (contest)...............Charter Issue 27
    Icing for, No-Fuss.............Charter Issue 26
    Macadamia Eggnog
      Creams.......................Dec/Jan 06 5
    Meringue Kisses.................Dec/Jan 06 5
    Molasses Spice Lemon
      Sandwich....................Dec/Jan 06 5
    recipe contest...................Dec/Jan 06 4–5
  and Cream Ice Cream Pie ...Charter Issue 13
  giving away on cheap
    china plates......................Oct/Nov 05 3
  tips and techniques...............Dec/Jan 06 29
    arranging on baking
      sheet..........................Jun/Jul 05 17
    baking one sheet at
      a time.........................Dec/Jan 06 29
    bringing butter and
      eggs to room
      temperature................Dec/Jan 06 29
    freezing dough in
      individual balls.............Apr/May 05 4
      ....Dec/Jan 06 29
    freezing dough portioned
      out as if for baking.........Jun/Jul 05 29
      ....Dec/Jan 06 29
    keeping dough chilled.....Dec/Jan 06 29
    rolling dough on warm
      day.............................Charter Issue 26
    rolling dough without
      flour...........................Charter Issue 26
    shaping slice-and-bake
      dough.........................Dec/Jan 06 3
    slicing icebox dough
      easily..........................Charter Issue 4
    for softer or chewier
      cookies.......................Dec/Jan 06 29
    storing..............................Dec/Jan 06 29
  Washboard.............................Jun/Jul 05 9
Cookie sheets:
  baking one at a time.............Dec/Jan 06 29
  organizing...............................Aug/Sep 05 2
Cookware:
  cleaning
    credit cards as pan
      scrapers.......................Apr/May 05 5
    glued-on cheese...............Apr/May 05 4
    removing grease
      with juiced lemon
      halves.........................Oct/Nov 05 2
    removing manufacturer's
      stickers.......................Oct/Nov 05 3
    with rubber spatula........Charter Issue 4
    stainless steel....................Apr/May 05 3
  Dutch ovens..........................Charter Issue 29
  "large," "medium," and
    "small," measurements
    of..Aug/Sep 05 9
  nonstick....................................Apr/May 05 3
  preventing burns from hot
    handles of..........................Charter Issue 4
  slow cookers
    "hobo pack" for
      vegetables in................Oct/Nov 05 7
    keeping food warm in......Apr/May 05 3
    rating of............................Charter Issue 31
    timer and keep-warm
      features of.................Charter Issue 29
  V-racks, makeshift.................Dec/Jan 06 28

Cooling:
  countertops.................................Oct/Nov 05   3
  kitchen after using electric
    cooktop...............................Aug/Sep 05   2
  large pot of something
    hot quickly with frozen
    vegetables.........................Aug/Sep 05   2
Cordon Bleu Pork Chops.............Apr/May 05 21
Coriander...................................Dec/Jan 06 15
Corks:
  removing pieces of,
    from wine ....Apr/May 05   5
  storing pushpins in ....Aug/Sep 05   3
Corn:
  buttering ....Apr/May 05   5
  and Chicken Soup, Asian.......Apr/May 05 RC
  cob kernels, catchall for ....Oct/Nov 05   2
  Fritters, Farmstand...................Aug/Sep 05 13
  Green Bean Succotash ....Charter Issue 17
  popcorn
    keeping crunchy ....Charter Issue   4
    pan-popped, oil-
      temperature test for....Oct/Nov 05   3
  Pudding, Savory.......................Dec/Jan 06 13
    water bath for....................Dec/Jan 06 28
  Roasted.............................Charter Issue 22
  Sautéed Zucchini and,
    with Chives ....Jun/Jul 05 RC
  Tricolor Mexican Bean
    Salad ....Apr/May 05   7
Cornbread:
  Jalapeño ....Charter Issue 21
  mixes, tasting of ....Oct/Nov 05 12
  stuffing
    with Bacon ....Oct/Nov 05 12
    drying cornbread for ....Oct/Nov 05 12
    with Sausage ....Oct/Nov 05 12
Corned Beef Hash ....Charter Issue RC
CorningWare AnyWare,
  testing of ....Oct/Nov 05 29
Cornstarch, for crispy roast
  chicken.....................................Dec/Jan 06 20
Corn syrup:
  getting last drop of ....Aug/Sep 05   2
  as treacle substitute ....Oct/Nov 05   6
Countertops:
  cleaning dough stuck to ....Oct/Nov 05   2
  cooling down..........................Oct/Nov 05   3
Couscous Salad, Mediterranean ...Jun/Jul 05 RC
Cowboy Beans ....Apr/May 05 22
Crab(meat):
  buying ....Aug/Sep 05 28
  Cakes, Creole ....Aug/Sep 05 21
  Hot Dip, Light and Creamy ....Dec/Jan 06   7
  Louis, Avocado ....Aug/Sep 05 RC
Crackers, keeping crisp...............Apr/May 05   5
Cranberry(ies):
  -Apple-Orange Relish.............Dec/Jan 06 13
  Cape Cod Picnic Salad ....Apr/May 05   6
  Nantucket Iced Tea ....Jun/Jul 05 20
  -raspberry juice, in
    Raz-ma-tazz Iced Tea ....Jun/Jul 05 20
Cream cheese:
  homemade flavored ....Charter Issue   5
  reduced-fat, tasting of ....Dec/Jan 06   7
  spreads
    Apricot, Zesty ....Aug/Sep 05 29
    Lemon-Ginger.....................Aug/Sep 05 29
    Maple-Cinnamon................Aug/Sep 05 29
    Orange ....Aug/Sep 05 29
    Pineapple, Sweet ....Aug/Sep 05 29
Cream Sauce with Sausage
  and Peas (for pasta) ....Oct/Nov 05   5
Creamsicle Smoothie ....Aug/Sep 05 25

Credit cards, scraping pans with ...Apr/May 05   5
Crème brûlée, water bath for......Dec/Jan 06 28
Creole Crab Cakes......................Aug/Sep 05 21
Crochet hooks, deveining
  shrimp with ....Oct/Nov 05   2
Crumb Coffee Cake, Reduced-Fat..Jun/Jul 05   8
Crusts. *See also* Pie crusts
  Graham Cracker Crumb ....Apr/May 05 24
    making even........................Apr/May 05 25
Cucumbers:
  Gazpacho Pasta Salad ....Apr/May 05   7
  pickles, quick........................Aug/Sep 05 19–20
    Bread-and-Butter.................Aug/Sep 05 20
    "Kosher" Double-Dill..........Aug/Sep 05 19
    wrapping spices in
      cheesecloth for ....Aug/Sep 05 29
  slicing thinly ....Dec/Jan 06   3
Cumin seeds ....Dec/Jan 06 15
Cupcakes:
  Birthday, Easy ....Apr/May 05 26
  decorating (contest) ....Apr/May 05 27
  Ice Cream ....Charter Issue 12
  portioning batter for................Apr/May 05 26
Curried:
  Chicken Salad ....Aug/Sep 05   5
  Peas ....Dec/Jan 06 19
Custard:
  Easy ....Dec/Jan 06   9
  water bath for..........................Dec/Jan 06 28
Cutting boards, cleaning
  beet stains from ....Aug/Sep 05   9

D

Decorating and decorations:
  cake-decorating supplies ......Apr/May 05 29
  for Christmas cookies
    contest............................Charter Issue 27
    organizing tip for ....Charter Issue 26
  for cupcakes (contest) ....Apr/May 05 27
Deep-fryers, electric, rating of ....Apr/May 05 31
Deep-frying. *See* Frying
  and deep-frying
Delicata squash...........................Oct/Nov 05 27
Denver Omelet, Family-Style ....Jun/Jul 05 21
  cooking technique for...............Jun/Jul 05 29
Desserts. *See also* Brownie(s);
  Cakes; Confections; Cookies;
  Dessert sauces; Ice cream
  apple(s)
    Candy-Coated Caramel.. Oct/Nov 05 10
    Pie, Paper Bag ....Oct/Nov 05 16
    Turnovers, Easy ....Oct/Nov 05 13
  Berry Bake, Summer ....Jun/Jul 05 RC
  Cheesecake, Icebox ....Apr/May 05 24–25
    Key Lime ....Apr/May 05 25
    Peanut Butter ....Apr/May 05 25
    Peppermint Chip ....Apr/May 05 25
  Chocolate Pudding, Low-
    Fat (with variations).........Charter Issue   8
  gelatin treats ....Apr/May 05 12–13
    Blushing Peach Terrine ......Apr/May 05 13
    Juicy Gelatin Cubes ....Apr/May 05 12
    Piña Colada Mousse........Apr/May 05 13
    Root Beer Floats..................Apr/May 05 12
  Halloween treat makeovers...Oct/Nov 05 10–11
    Candy-Coated
      Caramel Apples ....Oct/Nov 05 10
    Caramel Turtles ....Oct/Nov 05 10
    M&M Clusters ....Oct/Nov 05 10
    Peanut Butter Cup Ice
      Cream and Snickers
      Bar Sauce ....Oct/Nov 05 10
    Peppermint-Surprise
      Brownie Bites ....Oct/Nov 05 10

Desserts (CONTINUED)
  marshmallow treats ....Jun/Jul 05 12–13
    Amazing Mousse ....Jun/Jul 05 12
    Chocolate Fluff Cookies......Jun/Jul 05 12
    Confetti Kebabs ....Jun/Jul 05 13
    Rocky Road Bark ....Jun/Jul 05 12
  Mochaccino Bread
    Puddings, Individual..........Oct/Nov 05 25
  Orange Drop Doughnuts........Aug/Sep 05   8
  Pecan Praline Pie,
    Southern ....Oct/Nov 05 24–25
  peppermint treats ....Dec/Jan 06 10–11
    "Hole-y" Peppermint
      Ice Cream
      Sandwiches................Dec/Jan 06 10
    Icebox Peppermint
      Yule Log Cake.............Dec/Jan 06 10
    Mug o' Minty Hot
      Chocolate ....Dec/Jan 06 10
    Peppermint-Surprise
      Brownie Bites ....Oct/Nov 05 10
    Wintermint Bark................Dec/Jan 06 10
  strawberry(ies)
    with Balsamic Vinegar ....Charter Issue RC
    Pineapple Tart.....................Jun/Jul 05   7
    Pretzel Bars ....Jun/Jul 05   7
    recipe contest ....Jun/Jul 05 6–7
    Scones ....Jun/Jul 05   6
    Trifle, Quick ....Jun/Jul 05   7
  Tipsy Parson ....Dec/Jan 06   9
  watermelon treats
    Polka-Dot Minty
      Melon Mold ....Aug/Sep 05 10
    Tutti-Frutti Watermelon
      Boats ....Aug/Sep 05 10
    Watermelon Ice Pops ....Aug/Sep 05 10
  whipped toppings for
    See also Whipped cream
    tasting of.............................Aug/Sep 05 30
Dessert sauces:
  Butterscotch ....Aug/Sep 05 27
  Cherry ....Aug/Sep 05 27
  Chocolate ....Aug/Sep 05 27
  Marshmallow ....Aug/Sep 05 27
  Peanut Butter ....Aug/Sep 05 27
  Snickers Bar............................Oct/Nov 05 10
  Strawberry...............................Aug/Sep 05 27
Dips:
  French ....Jun/Jul 05 18
  Hot, Light and Creamy ....Dec/Jan 06   7
    Artichoke ....Dec/Jan 06   7
    Crab ....Dec/Jan 06   7
    Spinach................................Dec/Jan 06   7
Dirty Rice ....Oct/Nov 05 22
Dishes:
  serving, warming ....Apr/May 05   3
  thrift-store finds, giving
    away cookies and
    candies on ....Oct/Nov 05   3
  wrapping for moving ....Apr/May 05   5
Dish soap, spraying.....................Oct/Nov 05   2
Dr. Pepper–Glazed Ham.............Dec/Jan 06 12
Doughnuts:
  chocolate-glazed, in
    "Hole-y" Peppermint
    Ice Cream Sandwiches....Dec/Jan 06 10
  Orange Drop.........................Aug/Sep 05   8
Dough scrapers (bowl
  scrapers).................................Apr/May 05 29
Down 'n' Dirty Rice ....Oct/Nov 05 22
Drains, cleaning with vinegar
  and baking soda ....Charter Issue   4
Dried fruit, in Lady Baltimore
  Cake ....Dec/Jan 06 IBC

Dustpans, transferring
   chopped vegetables
   to pot on stove with .... Aug/Sep 05   3
Dutch ovens .... Charter Issue   29
   .... Aug/Sep 05   9
   deep frying in .... Apr/May 05   31

E

Egg(s):
   adding to batter .... Charter Issue   5
   baked dishes with,
     reducing moisture
     in fillings for .... Jun/Jul 05   5
   bringing to room
     temperature quickly .... Apr/May 05   26
     .... Dec/Jan 06   29
   cracking without getting
     pieces of shell in bowl ...... Dec/Jan 06   3
   Denver Omelet, Family-Style ..... Jun/Jul 05   21
     cooking technique for .... Jun/Jul 05   29
   hard-cooked
     peeling .... Jun/Jul 05   4
     retrieving from pot .... Aug/Sep 05   2
   microwave-cooking .... Charter Issue   3
   soft-boiled, cutting open
     shell of .... Charter Issue   3
   storing .... Jun/Jul 05   3
   whites
     beaten, mixing
      batters with .... Oct/Nov 05   3
     Christmas Meringue Kisses .. Dec/Jan 06   5
Eggnog Macadamia Creams ...... Dec/Jan 06   5
Eggplant Salad .... Aug/Sep 05   RC
Egg toppers .... Charter Issue   3
Egg Wave .... Charter Issue   3
Endive Leaves, Creamy
   Beet Spread with .... Oct/Nov 05   18
Equipment and product testing:
   baking pans, square .... Jun/Jul 05   29
   Batter Pro .... Apr/May 05   21
   blenders .... Jun/Jul 05   31
   Brown & Crisp Microwave
     Cooking Bags .... Charter Issue   31
   chef's knives .... Aug/Sep 05   31
   CorningWare AnyWare .... Oct/Nov 05   29
   deep-fryers, electric .... Apr/May 05   31
   Egg Wave .... Charter Issue   3
   flexible cutting mats
     (chopping mats) .... Aug/Sep 05   31
   gadgets to make butter
     more spreadable .... Dec/Jan 06   31
   indoor grills .... Oct/Nov 05   31
   Lodge Grill Press .... Oct/Nov 05   31
   Magic Bullet .... Jun/Jul 05   31
   mandolines .... Aug/Sep 05   23
   mashers .... Charter Issue   23
   Nathan Reversible
     Stovetop Grill & Griddle .. Charter Issue   3
   rolling pins, tapered .... Oct/Nov 05   28
   slow cookers .... Charter Issue   31
   Speedy-Peel apple peeler ..... Aug/Sep 05   9
   toasters .... Dec/Jan 06   31
   vertical chicken roasters .... Aug/Sep 05   29
Escarole .... Jun/Jul 05   19
Everything Straws .... Apr/May 05   15

F

Fat, skimming from gravy .... Charter Issue   29
Fat-separating pitchers,
   pouring pancake batter with .. Oct/Nov 05   5
Fennel:
   Bistro Slaw .... Jun/Jul 05   24
   "Fit as a Fennel" Tomato
     Salad .... Aug/Sep 05   14

Fennel seeds .... Dec/Jan 06   15
Fiesta Slaw .... Jun/Jul 05   24
Filets Mignons, Bacon-Wrapped .. Apr/May 05   RC
First courses. *See* Appetizers
   and hors d'oeuvres; Starters
Fish:
   Cod, Baked, with Crunchy
     Lemon-Herb Topping .... Dec/Jan 06   RC
   Fisherman's Stew, Hearty .... Oct/Nov 05   RC
   Fried, with Pickled Jalapeño
     Mayonnaise .... Charter Issue   22
   salmon
     Glazed, with Dilly
      Mustard Sauce .... Apr/May 05   23
     and Potato Salad, Zesty ...... Jun/Jul 05   23
     Smoked, Pinwheels .... Oct/Nov 05   19
   Swordfish, Grilled, with
     Eggplant Salad .... Aug/Sep 05   RC
   Tuna Sauce, Spicy (for pasta) .. Oct/Nov 05   5
Fisherman's Stew, Hearty .... Oct/Nov 05   RC
Flank steak:
   Grilled, with Garlic-Parsley
     Sauce .... Charter Issue   22
   Stuffed .... Aug/Sep 05   22
Flexible cutting mats
   (chopping mats), testing of .... Aug/Sep 05   31
Floats, Root Beer .... Apr/May 05   12
Flour:
   bleached vs. unbleached,
     tasting of .... Dec/Jan 06   6
   sifting without mess .... Aug/Sep 05   3
Flouring cake pans .... Apr/May 05   4
Foil:
   cleaning grill grates with .... Jun/Jul 05   29
   keeping food hot longer
     with .... Apr/May 05   3
   lining pans with .... Dec/Jan 06   3
Fondue pots, keeping food
   warm in .... Apr/May 05   3
Food processors:
   cleaning blades of .... Apr/May 05   5
   shredding chicken in .... Dec/Jan 06   3
French (cuisine):
   Dip .... Jun/Jul 05   18
   Dip Sandwiches .... Oct/Nov 05   21
   dressing
     All-American .... Jun/Jul 05   18
     Creamy .... Jun/Jul 05   18
   Pork Chops, Country .... Oct/Nov 05   RC
Fries:
   flavored salts for .... Apr/May 05   29
     Chili .... Apr/May 05   29
     Rosemary-Lemon .... Apr/May 05   29
     Warm Spiced .... Apr/May 05   29
   frozen, seasoning before
     cooking .... Oct/Nov 05   3
   Steak, Super-Crisp .... Apr/May 05   18
     oil absorbed by .... Dec/Jan 06   6
Frisée .... Jun/Jul 05   19
Fritters, Corn, Farmstand .... Aug/Sep 05   13
Frostings:
   chocolate
     Quick .... Apr/May 05   26
     Reduced-Fat Creamy .... Aug/Sep 05   6
   Vanilla, Quick .... Apr/May 05   26
Frozen desserts .... Charter Issue   12–13
   See also Ice cream
   Rainbow Sherbet Surprise ..... Charter Issue   12
   Watermelon Ice Pops .... Aug/Sep 05   10
Fruit. *See also* specific fruits
   dried, in Lady Baltimore
     Cake .... Dec/Jan 06   IBC
   frozen, measuring .... Aug/Sep 05   29
   winter, salads .... Dec/Jan 06   23

Frying and deep-frying:
   in Dutch oven .... Apr/May 05   31
   electric deep-fryers for,
     rating of .... Apr/May 05   31
   Lodge Deep Fry Basket for ..... Apr/May 05   31
   monitoring temperature
     of oil in .... Aug/Sep 05   28
   oil absorbed by food in .... Dec/Jan 06   6
   reusing oil for .... Apr/May 05   29
Fudge, Blue-Ribbon .... Aug/Sep 05   23
Fun food:
   gelatin treats .... Apr/May 05   12–13
   Halloween treat makeovers ... Oct/Nov 05   10–11
   ice cream desserts .... Charter Issue   12–13
   with marshmallows and
     chocolate .... Jun/Jul 05   12–13
   peppermint desserts .... Dec/Jan 06   10–11
   watermelon treats .... Aug/Sep 05   10–11
Funnels, makeshift:
   for transferring peppercorns
     into pepper grinder .... Aug/Sep 05   2
   for very small jars .... Apr/May 05   4

G

Garbage, recycling newspaper
   bags for .... Oct/Nov 05   3
Garbage disposals:
   cleaning with ice cubes .... Oct/Nov 05   3
   freshening with juiced
     lemon halves .... Jun/Jul 05   5
Garden Pesto Sauce .... Oct/Nov 05   4
Garlic:
   green shoots in .... Aug/Sep 05   9
   mincing .... Apr/May 05   3
   Parmesan Biscuits .... Dec/Jan 06   27
   peeling
     easily, microwave tip for .. Oct/Nov 05   2
     large quantities .... Charter Issue   4
   removing smell of, from
     hands .... Charter Issue   4
   storing .... Dec/Jan 06   6
Garlic presses, chopping
   canned chiles with .... Aug/Sep 05   2
Gazpacho Pasta Salad .... Apr/May 05   7
Gelatin treats .... Apr/May 05   12–13
   Blushing Peach Terrine .... Apr/May 05   13
   Juicy Gelatin Cubes .... Apr/May 05   12
   Piña Colada Mousse .... Apr/May 05   13
   Polka-Dot Minty Melon Mold .. Aug/Sep 05   10
   Root Beer Floats .... Apr/May 05   12
German Chocolate Brownies .... Charter Issue   25
German Potato Salad, Roasted ...... Jun/Jul 05   RC
Ginger:
   Cream, Western-Slope
     Pear Cake with .... Dec/Jan 06   13
   Ice Cream with
     Chocolate Sauce .... Apr/May 05   RC
   Lemon Cream Cheese
     Spread .... Aug/Sep 05   29
Glazes, flavored, for coffee
   cakes:
   Cinnamon Toast .... Dec/Jan 06   28
   Cup of Cocoa .... Dec/Jan 06   28
   Java Jolt .... Dec/Jan 06   28
   Must Be Maple .... Dec/Jan 06   28
   Tropical Orange .... Dec/Jan 06   28
Gloves:
   dishwashing, opening
     jars with .... Charter Issue   4
   disposable, prepping
     chicken with .... Charter Issue   5
   makeshift, plastic
     sandwich bags as .... Jun/Jul 05   5
   welders', as oven mitts .... Apr/May 05   4

Goat cheese, in Stuffed Cherry
  Tomatoes ....Oct/Nov 05 19
Golden Hubbard squash ....Oct/Nov 05 27
Golden Nugget squash ....Oct/Nov 05 27
Golden syrup (light treacle) ....Oct/Nov 05 6
Graham Cracker Crumb Crust ....Apr/May 05 24
  making even ....Apr/May 05 25
Grapefruit:
  Miami Vice (winter fruit
    salad) ....Dec/Jan 06 23
  sectioning ....Dec/Jan 06 29
Grapes, in The Green
  Monstah (winter fruit salad) ....Dec/Jan 06 23
Grapples, tasting of ....Oct/Nov 05 29
Graters:
  cleaning with baby-
    bottle brush ....Aug/Sep 05 3
  Microplane, containing
    grated zest or
    cheese with ....Oct/Nov 05 3
  rasp-type, transporting
    safely ....Dec/Jan 06 2
Gravy:
  skimming fat from ....Charter Issue 29
  time-saving tip for ....Oct/Nov 05 3
Grease, disposing of ....Aug/Sep 05 3
Greek (cuisine):
  Cheese Straws ....Apr/May 05 15
  "It's All Greek to Me"
    Tomato Salad ....Aug/Sep 05 14
Green bean(s) ....Charter Issue 17
  with Bacon and Onion ....Charter Issue 17
  Garden Potato Salad ....Aug/Sep 05 21
  with Mediterranean Flavors ..Charter Issue 17
  Nutty ....Apr/May 05 RC
  Orange, with Buttered
    Cashews ....Charter Issue 17
  Succotash ....Charter Issue 17
Green leaf lettuce ....Jun/Jul 05 19
The Green Monstah (winter
  fruit salad) ....Dec/Jan 06 23
Greens:
  salad, varieties of ....Jun/Jul 05 19
  washing ....Jun/Jul 05 18
Green Salad with Roasted
  Pears and Blue Cheese ....Dec/Jan 06 21
Griddles: Nathan Reversible
  Stovetop Grill & Griddle,
  testing of ....Charter Issue 3
Grilled:
  Banana and Red Onion Salsa ..Jun/Jul 05 23
  burgers, preventing bulge in .....Jun/Jul 05 3
  Cheese Sandwiches,
    Classic (with variations) ....Oct/Nov 05 15
  chicken
    Apple Harvest Cider-Can ..Aug/Sep 05 19
    BBQ Beer-Can ....Aug/Sep 05 18–19
    Jerk, Easy ....Jun/Jul 05 22–23
    Jerk, Sweet 'n' Smoky ....Jun/Jul 05 23
    Spicy Lime, with Black Bean
      and Avocado Salad ......Jun/Jul 05 11
  flank steak
    with Garlic-Parsley
      Sauce ....Charter Issue 22
    Stuffed ....Aug/Sep 05 22
  Hamburger, Ultimate ....Jun/Jul 05 26
  Pork Tenderloin with Peach
    Salsa ....Aug/Sep 05 RC
  Sausage Sandwiches,
    Open-Faced ....Aug/Sep 05 RC
  Spareribs, Memphis BBQ ....Jun/Jul 05 14–15
  Steak and Onion Salad ....Aug/Sep 05 RC
  Swordfish with Eggplant
    Salad ....Aug/Sep 05 RC

Grill grates:
  cleaning ....Jun/Jul 05 29
  oiling ....Aug/Sep 05 29
Grill Press, Lodge, testing of ....Oct/Nov 05 31
Grills:
  chimney starters for ....Aug/Sep 05 28
    lighting ....Jun/Jul 05 5
  indoor, rating of ....Oct/Nov 05 31
Grits, Baked Cheese ....Charter Issue RC

H

Halloween treat makeovers ....Oct/Nov 05 10–11
  Candy-Coated Caramel
    Apples ....Oct/Nov 05 10
  Caramel Turtles ....Oct/Nov 05 10
  M&M Clusters ....Oct/Nov 05 10
  Peanut Butter Cup Ice
    Cream and Snickers
    Bar Sauce ....Oct/Nov 05 10
  Peppermint-Surprise
    Brownie Bites ....Oct/Nov 05 10
Ham:
  Dr. Pepper-Glazed ....Dec/Jan 06 12
  Split-Pea Soup with ....Oct/Nov 05 26
  Steak with Rhubarb Sauce .....Apr/May 05 11
Hamburgers. See Burgers
Harvest Supper Salad with
  Smoked Turkey and Apples ...Oct/Nov 05 RC
Hash, Corned Beef ....Charter Issue RC
Herb(s). See also specific herbs
  bundles
    tying with celery "string" .....Jun/Jul 05 4
    wrapping in cheesecloth ..Aug/Sep 05 29
  chopping ahead vs. right
    before use ....Aug/Sep 05 28
  growing in kitchen ....Charter Issue 4
Heroes, Antipasto ....Jun/Jul 05 RC
Hobo pack ....Oct/Nov 05 7
"Hole-y" Peppermint Ice
  Cream Sandwiches ....Dec/Jan 06 10
Hollywood Hills (winter fruit
  salad) ....Dec/Jan 06 23
Honey, getting last drop of ....Aug/Sep 05 2
Honeydew:
  The Green Monstah
    (winter fruit salad) ....Dec/Jan 06 23
  Polka-Dot Minty Melon Mold ..Aug/Sep 05 10
Hors d'oeuvres. See Appetizers
  and hors d'oeuvres
Hors d'oeuvres spreaders,
  as makeshift spatulas ....Aug/Sep 05 3
Hot Chocolate, Mug o' Minty ......Dec/Jan 06 10
Hot Dip, Light and Creamy ....Dec/Jan 06 7
  Artichoke ....Dec/Jan 06 7
  Crab ....Dec/Jan 06 7
  Spinach ....Dec/Jan 06 7
Hot food, keeping hot longer ......Apr/May 05 3
"Humble pie" ....Oct/Nov 05 25

I

Iceberg lettuce ....Jun/Jul 05 19
  with Blue Cheese Dressing ...Charter Issue RC
Ice cream:
  Bonbons ....Charter Issue 13
  chocolate, tasting of ....Jun/Jul 05 30
  Cupcakes ....Charter Issue 12
  Ginger, with Chocolate
    Sauce ....Apr/May 05 RC
  Peanut Butter Cup, and
    Snickers Bar Sauce ....Oct/Nov 05 10
  Pie, Cookies and Cream ......Charter Issue 13
  Rainbow Sherbet Surprise .....Charter Issue 12
  Sandwiches, "Hole-y"
    Peppermint ....Dec/Jan 06 10

Ice cream (CONTINUED)
  sauces for
    Butterscotch ....Aug/Sep 05 27
    Cherry ....Aug/Sep 05 27
    Chocolate ....Aug/Sep 05 27
    Marshmallow ....Aug/Sep 05 27
    Peanut Butter ....Aug/Sep 05 27
    Snickers Bar ....Oct/Nov 05 10
    Strawberry ....Aug/Sep 05 27
  sundaes ....Aug/Sep 05 26–27
    recipe contest ....Aug/Sep 05 26
    sauces for ....Aug/Sep 05 27
Ice cream cones, tasting of ....Jun/Jul 05 30
Ice cream headache (brain
  freeze) ....Aug/Sep 05 27
Iced tea:
  Sweet (with variations) ....Jun/Jul 05 20
  tasting of tea bags for ....Jun/Jul 05 29
Ice Pops, Watermelon ....Aug/Sep 05 10
Icings. See also Frostings
  melted peppermint patties as ..Dec/Jan 06 3
Italian (cuisine):
  Cheese Straws ....Apr/May 05 15
  dressings, bottled, tasting of ...Charter Issue 30
  Little Italy Grilled Cheese
    Sandwiches ....Oct/Nov 05 15
  Potato Cake ....Charter Issue 6
  Spinach and Radicchio
    Salad ....Dec/Jan 06 12

J

Jack cheese:
  Jalapeño Biscuits ....Dec/Jan 06 27
  Monterey Jack, grating ....Oct/Nov 05 28
  Monterey Melts ....Oct/Nov 05 15
Jalapeño(s):
  Chicken Salad ....Aug/Sep 05 4
  chopping ....Jun/Jul 05 5
  Cornbread ....Charter Issue 21
  Jack Biscuits ....Dec/Jan 06 27
  Stuffed ....Oct/Nov 05 18
Jars:
  opening
    with dishwashing gloves ..Charter Issue 4
    with thick rubber band .....Dec/Jan 06 3
  spice
    easy pouring from ....Jun/Jul 05 4
    mixing vinaigrette in ....Aug/Sep 05 3
Java Jolt Glaze ....Dec/Jan 06 28
Jerk Chicken, Easy .... Jun/Jul 05 22–23
  Sweet 'n' Smoky ....Jun/Jul 05 23
Juicers, ricers as stand-ins for .....Aug/Sep 05 2
Juniper berries ....Dec/Jan 06 15
Jus, Quick ....Oct/Nov 05 21

K

Kabocha squash ....Oct/Nov 05 27
Kebabs:
  Confetti ....Jun/Jul 05 13
  Luau ....Jun/Jul 05 RC
Ketchups, flavored:
  Five-Alarm ....Jun/Jul 05 29
  Mongolian ....Jun/Jul 05 29
  Passage to India ....Jun/Jul 05 29
  Spicy, Smoky ....Jun/Jul 05 29
  Very Berry ....Jun/Jul 05 29
Kiwis, in The Green Monstah
  (winter fruit salad) ....Dec/Jan 06 23
Knives:
  chef's, rating of ....Aug/Sep 05 31
  plastic vs. metal, for
    cutting lettuce ....Oct/Nov 05 2
  saving edge of ....Charter Issue 4
  transporting safely ....Dec/Jan 06 2

L

Lady Baltimore Cake ....Dec/Jan 06   IBC
Lasagna:
  make-ahead...........................Apr/May 05   3
  Skillet.....................................Jun/Jul 05   25
    with Sausage and Peppers..Jun/Jul 05   25
Lemon(s):
  Ginger Cream Cheese
    Spread ....Aug/Sep 05   29
  juice
    freezing in ice cube tray ..Apr/May 05   5
    tips for maximizing yield....Oct/Nov 05   6
  juiced halves of
    cleaning greasy pans
      with........................Oct/Nov 05   2
    cleaning microwave with ..Dec/Jan 06   3
    freshening garbage
      disposal with...................Jun/Jul 05   5
  Molasses Spice Sandwich
    Cookies.........................Dec/Jan 06   5
  Pucker-Up Cloudcakes...........Apr/May 05   15
  Rosemary Salt........................Apr/May 05   29
  zest, removing ahead and
    freezing............................Jun/Jul 05   4
Lemonade, tasting of....................Aug/Sep 05   30
Lettuce:
  cutting with plastic knife.........Oct/Nov 05   2
  iceberg ....Jun/Jul 05   19
    with Blue Cheese
      Dressing.....................Charter Issue   RC
Lima beans, frozen, adding
  to soups ....Dec/Jan 06   27
Lime:
  juice, freezing in ice cube
    tray...................................Apr/May 05   5
  Key, Icebox Cheesecake.......Apr/May 05   25
  Rickey Cherry Iced Tea.............Jun/Jul 05   20
  sherbet, in Watermelon
    Ice Pops...........................Aug/Sep 05   10
Little Italy Grilled Cheese
  Sandwiches ....Oct/Nov 05   15
Lodge Deep Fry Basket ....Apr/May 05   31
Lodge Grill Press, testing of ....Oct/Nov 05   31
Lost recipes:
  Monkey Bread.........................Apr/May 05   9–10
  Orange Drop Doughnuts........Aug/Sep 05   8
  Quaker Bonnet Biscuits ....Oct/Nov 05   8
  Sea Foam Candy ....Charter Issue   9
  Tipsy Parson ....Dec/Jan 06   9
  Washboard Cookies..................Jun/Jul 05   9
Lovers' Lane (winter fruit salad)...Dec/Jan 06   23
Low-Country Sweet Potato Salad ..Apr/May 05   7
Low-fat recipes. See Reduced-
  fat recipes
Luau Kebabs ....Jun/Jul 05   RC

M

Macadamia (nuts):
  Eggnog Creams......................Dec/Jan 06   5
  Paradise Found (winter
    fruit salad) ....Dec/Jan 06   23
Macaroni:
  and Cheese, Reduced-Fat ....Apr/May 05   8
    after Dark ....Apr/May 05   8
    for Pizza Lovers..................Apr/May 05   8
    tasting of cheeses for ....Apr/May 05   29
  Salad, Cool and Creamy ....Aug/Sep 05   17
Mace ....Dec/Jan 06   15
Mâche ....Jun/Jul 05   19
Magic Bullet................................Jun/Jul 05   31
Magnetic clips, holding
  recipes at eye level with ....Dec/Jan 06   3
M&M Clusters ....Oct/Nov 05   10
Mandolines, rating of...................Oct/Nov 05   23

Mangos:
  Lovers' Lane (winter fruit
    salad)...............................Dec/Jan 06   23
  Paradise Found (winter
    fruit salad) ....Dec/Jan 06   23
  Takes Two to Mango
    Smoothie ....Aug/Sep 05   25
Manufacturer's stickers,
  removing from cookware.......Oct/Nov 05   3
Maple (syrup):
  Cinnamon Cream Cheese
    Spread ....Aug/Sep 05   29
  getting last drop of ....Aug/Sep 05   2
  Glaze ....Dec/Jan 06   28
  Sausage and Waffle
    Casserole..........................Dec/Jan 06   22
  tasting of................................Dec/Jan 06   30
Marinating meat or chicken
  ahead ....Jun/Jul 05   4
Marshmallow(s):
  Amazing Mousse ....Jun/Jul 05   12
  Confetti Kebabs ....Jun/Jul 05   13
  Fluff Chocolate Cookies...........Jun/Jul 05   12
  Rocky Road Bark ....Jun/Jul 05   12
  Sauce...................................Aug/Sep 05   27
  S'Mores Brownies ....Charter Issue   25
  stabilizing whipped cream with ..Jun/Jul 05   5
Mashed potato flakes,
  thickening soups with ....Dec/Jan 06   2–3
Mashers:
  mixing meatloaf with ....Charter Issue   5
  Profi Plus ....Charter Issue   23
Measuring:
  disposable cups for ....Jun/Jul 05   5
  leveling with tongue
    depressors ....Apr/May 05   5
  shortening, reducing mess of..Apr/May 05   5
  wet vs. dry ingredients ....Charter Issue   3
Measuring cups:
  metal vs. glass......................Charter Issue   3
  for shortening, no-stick............Apr/May 05   5
Meat. See also Beef; Pork
  browning, draining fat in ....Aug/Sep 05   3
  marinating ahead ....Jun/Jul 05   4
  pounding in cereal box liner..Dec/Jan 06   3
  resting before serving ....Jun/Jul 05   3
Meatballs, Sausage,
  Spaghetti with ....Dec/Jan 06   RC
Meatloaf:
  baking in muffin tins ....Dec/Jan 06   2
  Cheesy Southwestern ....Apr/May 05   23
  mixing..................................Charter Issue   5
  Sloppy Joe sauce in ....Dec/Jan 06   2
Mediterranean Couscous Salad ....Jun/Jul 05   RC
Melon. See also Watermelon
  honeydew, in The Green
    Monstah (winter fruit
    salad).............................Dec/Jan 06   23
  Mold, Polka-Dot Minty............Aug/Sep 05   10
Melon ballers, coring apples
  with ....Apr/May 05   5
Memphis BBQ Spareribs ....Jun/Jul 05   14–15
Meringue Kisses, Christmas..........Dec/Jan 06   5
Mesclun ....Jun/Jul 05   19
Mexican (cuisine):
  Bites, Crispy..............................Oct/Nov 05   18
  Chocolate Pudding, Low-Fat ..Charter Issue   8
  Tricolor Bean Salad..................Apr/May 05   7
Miami Vice (winter fruit salad) ....Dec/Jan 06   23
Microplane graters, containing
  grated zest or cheese with.....Oct/Nov 05   3
Microwaveable herbal comfort
  packs, keeping bread
  dough warm with.....................Aug/Sep 05   3

Microwave ovens:
  Brown & Crisp Microwave
    Cooking Bags for,
    testing of..........................Charter Issue   31
  preventing splatters in............Apr/May 05   5
Mise en place, disposable
  cups for ....Jun/Jul 05   5
Mixers:
  getting last drop of batter
    off beaters........................Aug/Sep 05   3
  tip for batters with stiffly
    beaten egg whites ....Oct/Nov 05   3
Mochaccino Bread Puddings,
  Individual................................Oct/Nov 05   25
Molasses Spice Lemon
  Sandwich Cookies.................Dec/Jan 06   5
Mongolian Ketchup ....Jun/Jul 05   29
Monkey Bread.............................Apr/May 05   9–10
Monterey Jack cheese:
  grating ....Oct/Nov 05   28
  Monterey Melts ....Oct/Nov 05   15
Mop, Cider ....Jun/Jul 05   14
Mousse:
  Amazing ....Jun/Jul 05   12
  Piña Colada ....Apr/May 05   13
Moving, wrapping dishes for ....Apr/May 05   5
Mozzarella:
  freezing ....Charter Issue   3
  grating ....Jun/Jul 05   4
Muffin liners, separating easily ....Oct/Nov 05   2
Muffins:
  Cheese, Savory......................Oct/Nov 05   22
  Zucchini.................................Aug/Sep 05   28
Muffin tins:
  baking meatloaf in..................Dec/Jan 06   2
  organizing cookie
    decorations in..................Charter Issue   26
Mulled Cider, Fireside ....Dec/Jan 06   14
  straining solids from ....Dec/Jan 06   28
Mushrooms, washing ....Apr/May 05   3
Mustard seeds ....Dec/Jan 06   15

N

Nail files, kitchen uses for...........Charter Issue   5
Nantucket Iced Tea ....Jun/Jul 05   20
Nathan Reversible Stovetop
  Grill & Griddle, testing of.......Charter Issue   3
Neufchâtel reduced-fat
  cream cheese, tasting of ....Dec/Jan 06   7
Newspaper bags, recycling ....Oct/Nov 05   3
Nonstick cooking spray:
  for hands...............................Aug/Sep 05   3
  for mixing spoons...................Aug/Sep 05   3
Nonstick cookware.......................Apr/May 05   3
Noodles. See also Pasta
  Spicy Beef and.......................Oct/Nov 05   RC
Norpro Butter Keeper, testing of..Dec/Jan 06   31
North Carolina Pulled Pork...........Apr/May 05   10–11
Nutmeg..Dec/Jan 06   15
Nuts. See also specific nuts
  chopping...................................Jun/Jul 05   5
  fresh-chopped vs. packaged
    chopped, tasting of..........Oct/Nov 05   6
  toasting.................................Dec/Jan 06   14

O

Odors:
  protecting hands from...............Jun/Jul 05   5
  removing from hands...........Charter Issue   4
Oils:
  buying in large containers
    and transferring ....Aug/Sep 05   2
  as odor barrier for hands...........Jun/Jul 05   5
  reusing in frying ....Apr/May 05   29

Omelet, Denver, Family-Style.........Jun/Jul 05   21
    cooking technique for...............Jun/Jul 05   29
Onion(s):
    Balsamic (caramelized).........Dec/Jan 06   18
    odor of
        protecting hands from ....Jun/Jul 05   5
        removing from hands .....Charter Issue   4
    in potato salad, taming
        harsh taste of ....Dec/Jan 06   2
    Red, and Banana Salsa,
        Grilled ....Jun/Jul 05   23
    Rings, Chili-Fried ....Apr/May 05   RC
    roasting with pork roast ....Oct/Nov 05   14
Orange(s):
    Brown-Eyed Susan (cake).......Oct/Nov 05   IBC
    Cranberry-Apple-, Relish........Dec/Jan 06   13
    Cream Cheese Spread ....Aug/Sep 05   29
    Creamsicle Smoothie.............Aug/Sep 05   25
    Drop Doughnuts ....Aug/Sep 05   8
    Glaze, Tropical ....Dec/Jan 06   28
    juice
        no-thaw frozen ....Apr/May 05   4
        tasting of.........................Charter Issue   30
    juicing with ricer.....................Aug/Sep 05   2
    -Kissed Chocolate Pudding,
        Low-Fat ....Charter Issue   8
    Miami Vice (winter fruit salad)..Dec/Jan 06   23
    sectioning...............................Dec/Jan 06   29
Orangeade Iced Tea.....................Jun/Jul 05   20
Orzo, Spinach ....Jun/Jul 05   21
Oven mitts, welders' gloves as....Apr/May 05   4

P

Pancakes:
    Cloudcakes ....Apr/May 05   14–15
    initials baked into..................Charter Issue   5
        pouring batter with fat-
            separating pitcher.....Charter Issue   5
    syrups for
        last-minute.......................Apr/May 05   5
        maple, tasting of ....Dec/Jan 06   30
Panzanella Salad ....Apr/May 05   7
Papayas:
    Bahama Mama (winter
        fruit salad) ....Dec/Jan 06   23
    Lovers' Lane (winter fruit
        salad) ....Dec/Jan 06   23
Paper plates, containing
    microwave splatters with........Apr/May 05   5
Paradise Found (winter fruit
    salad) ....Dec/Jan 06   23
Parchment paper:
    cutting to line baking pans ....Apr/May 05   4
    holding up pie crust
        during blind baking with ..Oct/Nov 05   3
    lining baking peel with............Aug/Sep 05   3
    rolling cookie dough
        between ....Charter Issue   26
Parmesan:
    Cheese Straws ....Apr/May 05   15
    Chicken, Skillet ....Dec/Jan 06   24
    freezing ....Charter Issue   3
    Garlic Biscuits ....Dec/Jan 06   27
Parsley, storing............................Apr/May 05   4
Parsnips:
    adding to soups.....................Dec/Jan 06   27
    roasting with pork roast ....Oct/Nov 05   14
Passion fruit, in Lovers' Lane
    (winter fruit salad)..................Dec/Jan 06   23
Pasta. *See also* Macaroni
    Carbonara, Creamy ....Dec/Jan 06   25
    cooking basics ....Oct/Nov 05   29
    Couscous Salad,
        Mediterranean ....Jun/Jul 05   RC

Pasta (CONTINUED)
    lasagna
        make-ahead.....................Apr/May 05   3
        Skillet ....Jun/Jul 05   25
    Orzo, Spinach.......................Jun/Jul 05   21
    Ravioli Bake, Cheesy..............Oct/Nov 05   RC
    salad
        Gazpacho ....Apr/May 05   7
        Shrimp, Zesty ....Aug/Sep 05   RC
    sauces
        Artichoke Alfredo ....Oct/Nov 05   5
        Cream, with Sausage
            and Peas ....Oct/Nov 05   5
        Pesto, Garden ....Oct/Nov 05   5
        recipe contest ....Oct/Nov 05   5–6
        Roasted Red Pepper
            and Bacon ....Oct/Nov 05   5
        Tuna, Spicy ....Oct/Nov 05   5
    Shells with Peas and
        Bacon, Creamy ....Charter Issue   RC
    Shrimp Piccata.......................Jun/Jul 05   RC
    Spaghetti with Sausage
        Meatballs........................Dec/Jan 06   RC
    Ziti, Baked, with Sausage ....Apr/May 05   RC
Pasta pots with strainers,
    making stock in......................Apr/May 05   5
Pasta spoons, retrieving
    hard-cooked eggs
    from pot with ....Aug/Sep 05   2
Pastry. *See* Pie crusts; Puff
    pastry
Pea(s) ....Dec/Jan 06   19
    and Carrots, Dilly ....Dec/Jan 06   19
    Cream Sauce with
        Sausage and
        (for pasta) ....Oct/Nov 05   5
    Creamy, with Ham and
        Onion ....Dec/Jan 06   19
    Curried ....Dec/Jan 06   19
    frozen
        adding to soups ....Dec/Jan 06   27
        fresh peas vs., tasting of ...Dec/Jan 06   28
    Smashed Minty ....Dec/Jan 06   19
    Split-, Soup with Ham ....Oct/Nov 05   26
    Sugar Snap, and Cherry
        Tomatoes, Sautéed...........Apr/May 05   23
Peach:
    Salsa ....Aug/Sep 05   RC
    Terrine, Blushing ....Apr/May 05   13
Peanut(s):
    M&M Clusters ....Oct/Nov 05   10
    Slaw, Spicy............................Jun/Jul 05   24
Peanut butter:
    Cup Ice Cream and
        Snickers Bar Sauce ....Oct/Nov 05   10
    The Elvis Smoothie.................Aug/Sep 05   25
    Icebox Cheesecake ....Apr/May 05   25
    natural, keeping
        spreadable ....Charter Issue   5
    Sauce....................................Aug/Sep 05   27
    Swirl Brownies ....Charter Issue   25
Pear(s):
    Cake with Ginger Cream,
        Western-Slope...................Dec/Jan 06   13
    Roasted, Green Salad
        with Blue Cheese and ......Dec/Jan 06   21
    tasting of varieties of..............Dec/Jan 06   28
Pecan(s):
    Caramel Turtles ....Oct/Nov 05   10
    Pie Brownies..........................Charter Issue   25
    Praline Pie, Southern ....Oct/Nov 05   24–25
    Sea Foam Candy ....Charter Issue   9
    Sour Cream Coffee Cake ......Dec/Jan 06   17–18
        flavored glazes for............Dec/Jan 06   28

Peelers:
    apple, electric (Speedy-
        Peel), testing of.................Aug/Sep 05   9
    buttering bread with ....Charter Issue   4
    vegetable
        slicing cucumbers
            thinly with...................Dec/Jan 06   3
        transporting safely ....Dec/Jan 06   2
Peels, baking or pizza:
    lining with parchment paper..Aug/Sep 05   3
    pizza-delivery box as ....Dec/Jan 06   3
Pepper(s) (bell):
    Fiesta Slaw.............................Jun/Jul 05   24
    Gazpacho Pasta Salad ....Apr/May 05   7
    roasted red
        and Bacon Sauce
        (for pasta)........................Oct/Nov 05   5
    Soup ....Charter Issue   RC
Pepper(s), chile. *See* Chiles;
    Jalapeño(s)
Peppercorns...............................Dec/Jan 06   15
    pink.......................................Dec/Jan 06   15
    transferring into pepper
        grinder ....Aug/Sep 05   2
Peppermint:
    Chip Icebox Cheesecake......Apr/May 05   25
    desserts ....Dec/Jan 06   10–11
    "Hole-y" Ice Cream
        Sandwiches.....................Dec/Jan 06   10
    Icebox Yule Log Cake ....Dec/Jan 06   10
    Mug o' Minty Hot Chocolate..Dec/Jan 06   10
    patties, as quick icing ....Dec/Jan 06   3
    -Surprise Brownie Bites ....Oct/Nov 05   10
    and White Chocolate
        Brownies ....Charter Issue   25
    Wintermint Bark.....................Dec/Jan 06   10
Pesto Sauce, Garden...................Oct/Nov 05   4
Pickles, quick...............................Aug/Sep 05   19–20
    Bread-and-Butter ....Aug/Sep 05   20
    "Kosher" Double-Dill ....Aug/Sep 05   19
    wrapping spices in
        cheesecloth for ....Aug/Sep 05   29
Picnic salads:
    Cape Cod ....Apr/May 05   6
    Gazpacho Pasta ....Apr/May 05   7
    Macaroni, Cool and Creamy ..Aug/Sep 05   17
    Panzanella.............................Apr/May 05   7
    recipe contest.......................Apr/May 05   6–7
    Sweet Potato, Low-Country ...Apr/May 05   7
    Tricolor Mexican Bean ....Apr/May 05   7
Pie crusts:
    amount of water in ....Oct/Nov 05   28
    blind baking ....Oct/Nov 05   28
        with parchment paper
            holding up sides
            of crust ....Oct/Nov 05   3
    cutting dough with
        pinking shears ....Aug/Sep 05   3
    Dough (recipe) ....Oct/Nov 05   24
    single, forming......................Oct/Nov 05   24
Pies:
    Apple, Paper Bag..................Oct/Nov 05   16
    Cookies and Cream Ice
        Cream ....Charter Issue   13
    Pecan Praline, Southern ....Oct/Nov 05   24–25
Pie weights:
    parchment paper as
        alternative to ....Oct/Nov 05   3
    pennies as ....Oct/Nov 05   28
Pimento Cheese Sandwiches,
    Grilled....................................Oct/Nov 05   15
Piña colada:
    Mousse ....Apr/May 05   13
    Smoothie...............................Aug/Sep 05   25

Pineapple:
Bahama Mama (winter fruit
  salad) ....Dec/Jan 06   23
Cream Cheese Spread,
  Sweet ....Aug/Sep 05   29
Paradise Found (winter
  fruit salad) ....Dec/Jan 06   23
Piña Colada Mousse ....Apr/May 05   13
Piña Colada Smoothie ....Aug/Sep 05   25
Salsa, Fresh ....Oct/Nov 05   18
Strawberry Tart ....Jun/Jul 05   7
Pinking shears, cutting pie
  crusts with ....Aug/Sep 05   3
Pistachios, in Wintermint Bark ......Dec/Jan 06   10
Pizza cutters, cutting children's
  food into bite-sized pieces
  with ....Jun/Jul 05   4
Pizza peels:
lining with parchment paper ..Aug/Sep 05   3
makeshift, pizza-delivery
  box as ....Dec/Jan 06   3
Plastic wrap:
de-fatting stock with ....Dec/Jan 06   2
keeping from sticking to itself ...Oct/Nov 05   2
Polka-Dot Minty Melon Mold ....Aug/Sep 05   10
Popcorn:
keeping crunchy ....Charter Issue   4
pan-popped, oil-
  temperature test for..........Oct/Nov 05   3
Pork:
chops
  Country French ....Oct/Nov 05   RC
  enhanced vs. unenhanced,
    tasting of.....................Oct/Nov 05   6
  with Spicy Orange Glaze ..Dec/Jan 06   RC
  Tennessee-Whiskey............Aug/Sep 05   12–13
chops, breaded.....................Apr/May 05   20–21
  Cordon Bleu ....Apr/May 05   21
  ideal thickness of
    chops for ....Apr/May 05   29
  Quick and Crunchy ....Apr/May 05   21
  Sesame ....Apr/May 05   21
Cutlets, Pan-Fried, with
  Orange and Green
  Olive Salsa ....Jun/Jul 05   21
Loin, Honey Glazed ....Charter Issue   RC
Luau Kebabs ....Jun/Jul 05   RC
Pulled, North Carolina.............Apr/May 05   10–11
Ranch Chili ....Charter Issue   20–21
  for a Crowd.....................Charter Issue   21
Roast, Marmalade-Glazed,
  with Parsnips and Onions ..Oct/Nov 05   14
Salad Bar Stir-Fry ....Aug/Sep 05   23
Spareribs, Memphis BBQ............Jun/Jul 05   14–15
Tenderloin, Grilled, with
  Peach Salsa ....Aug/Sep 05   RC
Potato(es):
baked, faster............................Dec/Jan 06   6
casseroles
  Alsatian ....Charter Issue   6
  Cheesy...........................Oct/Nov 05   23
  Creamy............................Charter Issue   6
  Italian Potato Cake.........Charter Issue   6
  Mashed Potato and
    Herbed Cheese Bake ..Charter Issue   7
  recipe contest ....Charter Issue   6–7
  with Spinach and
    Sausage.....................Charter Issue   7
fries
  flavored salts for ....Apr/May 05   29
  frozen, seasoning
    before cooking............Oct/Nov 05   3
  oil absorbed by ....Dec/Jan 06   6
  Steak, Super-Crisp ....Apr/May 05   18

Potato(es) (CONTINUED)
mashed
  Cheesy...........................Charter Issue   23
  Cheesy, with Pepper
    Jack and Bacon........Charter Issue   23
  flakes, thickening
    soups with ....Dec/Jan 06   2–3
peeling before vs. after
  cooking ....Dec/Jan 06   6
red, adding to soups...............Dec/Jan 06   27
salads
  Garden (with variations) ..Aug/Sep 05   20–21
  keeping safe ....Jun/Jul 05   3
  Roasted German ....Jun/Jul 05   RC
  taming harsh taste of
    raw onions in ....Dec/Jan 06   2
  and Salmon Salad, Zesty ....Jun/Jul 05   23
  Soup, Rustic ....Dec/Jan 06   RC
  varieties of ....Apr/May 05   19
Potato mashers. *See Mashers*
Pot roast. *See Beef—pot roast*
Poultry. *See also Chicken; Turkey*
applying spice rub
  underneath skin of ....Oct/Nov 05   2
resting before serving ....Jun/Jul 05   3
washing.................................Jun/Jul 05   3
Pretzel(s):
Bars, Strawberry ....Jun/Jul 05   7
M&M Clusters ....Oct/Nov 05   10
Profi Plus Masher........................Charter Issue   23
Puddings:
Chocolate, Low-Fat ....Charter Issue   8
  Mexican.......................Charter Issue   8
  Orange-Kissed ....Charter Issue   8
Corn, Savory.........................Dec/Jan 06   13
  water bath for...................Dec/Jan 06   28
Mochaccino Bread, Individual..Oct/Nov 05   25
Puff pastry:
Apple Turnovers, Easy ....Oct/Nov 05   13
Asparagus Puffs ....Oct/Nov 05   19
keeping cool...........................Oct/Nov 05   29
Strawberry-Pineapple Tart ....Jun/Jul 05   7
straws
  Cheese ....Apr/May 05   15
  Everything..........................Apr/May 05   15
  Greek Cheese ....Apr/May 05   15
  Italian Cheese ....Apr/May 05   15
  Sweet-and-Spicy ....Apr/May 05   15
Pulled Pork, North Carolina..........Apr/May 05   10–11
Pumpkin-carving kits, uses
  for saw blades in ....Oct/Nov 05   3
Punch, Watermelon Citrus............Aug/Sep 05   10
Pushpins, storing in corks ....Aug/Sep 05   3
Putty knives, cleaning
  stuck-on food with.................Aug/Sep 05   3

Q

Quaker Bonnet Biscuits.................Oct/Nov 05   8

R

Radicchio ....Jun/Jul 05   19
  and Spinach Salad, Italian .....Dec/Jan 06   12
Rainbow Sherbet Surprise...........Charter Issue   12
Ranch Chili................................Charter Issue   20–21
  for a Crowd............................Charter Issue   21
Raspberry(ies):
-cranberry juice, in
  Raz-ma-tazz Iced Tea ....Jun/Jul 05   20
Hollywood Hills (winter
  fruit salad) ....Dec/Jan 06   23
Summer Berry Bake ....Jun/Jul 05   RC
Tipsy Parson ....Dec/Jan 06   9
Very Berry Ketchup ....Jun/Jul 05   29
washing...............................Jun/Jul 05   3

Ravioli Bake, Cheesy ....Oct/Nov 05   RC
Recipe cards:
beef
  Corned, Hash...................Charter Issue   RC
  Filets Mignons, Bacon-
    Wrapped ....Apr/May 05   RC
  Spicy Noodles and............Oct/Nov 05   RC
  Steak and Onion Salad,
    Grilled.....................Aug/Sep 05   RC
  Stir-Fried, with Snow
    Peas and Cashews .....Dec/Jan 06   RC
  Taco Salad ....Dec/Jan 06   RC
Calzones, Cheesy Broccoli.....Aug/Sep 05   RC
chicken
  and Corn Soup, Asian ......Apr/May 05   RC
  Cutlets with Bacon,
    Rosemary, and
    Lemon ....Oct/Nov 05   RC
  Mahogany ....Aug/Sep 05   RC
  with Mushrooms and Leeks..Dec/Jan 06   RC
  Paprika, Broiled...................Dec/Jan 06   RC
  and Rice, Lemony...........Charter Issue   RC
  Salad, Shanghai ....Jun/Jul 05   RC
  Tortilla Casserole, Easy ......Oct/Nov 05   RC
Cod, Baked, with Crunchy
  Lemon-Herb Topping ....Dec/Jan 06   RC
Crab Louis, Avocado ....Aug/Sep 05   RC
desserts
  Berry Bake, Summer ....Jun/Jul 05   RC
  Ginger Ice Cream with
    Chocolate Sauce........Apr/May 05   RC
  Strawberries with Balsamic
    Vinegar ....Charter Issue   RC
Fisherman's Stew, Hearty........Oct/Nov 05   RC
grilled
  Pork Tenderloin with
    Peach Salsa................Aug/Sep 05   RC
  Sausage Sandwiches,
    Open-Faced ....Aug/Sep 05   RC
  Steak and Onion Salad ....Aug/Sep 05   RC
  Swordfish with Eggplant
    Salad ....Aug/Sep 05   RC
pasta
  Ravioli Bake, Cheesy.........Oct/Nov 05   RC
  Shells with Peas and
    Bacon, Creamy ....Charter Issue   RC
  Shrimp Piccata ....Jun/Jul 05   RC
  Shrimp Salad, Zesty ....Aug/Sep 05   RC
  Spaghetti with Sausage
    Meatballs....................Dec/Jan 06   RC
  Ziti, Baked, with Sausage..Apr/May 05   RC
pork
  Chops, Country French ....Oct/Nov 05   RC
  Chops with Spicy
    Orange Glaze ....Dec/Jan 06   RC
  Loin, Honey Glazed.........Charter Issue   RC
  Luau Kebabs ....Jun/Jul 05   RC
  Tenderloin, Grilled,
    with Peach Salsa ....Aug/Sep 05   RC
salads, main-course
  Chicken, Shanghai...............Jun/Jul 05   RC
  Harvest Supper, with Smoked
    Turkey and Apples.......Oct/Nov 05   RC
  Shrimp Pasta, Zesty............Aug/Sep 05   RC
  Steak and Onion, Grilled..Aug/Sep 05   RC
  Taco ....Dec/Jan 06   RC
sandwiches
  Antipasto Heroes ....Jun/Jul 05   RC
  Sausage, Open-Faced.....Aug/Sep 05   RC
shrimp
  Pasta Salad, Zesty ....Aug/Sep 05   RC
  Piccata Pasta ....Jun/Jul 05   RC
  and Rice, Skillet ....Apr/May 05   RC
  Spicy Baked ....Oct/Nov 05   RC

Recipe cards (CONTINUED)
side dishes
Couscous Salad,
Mediterranean..............Jun/Jul 05   RC
Eggplant Salad ....Aug/Sep 05   RC
Green Beans, Nutty..........Apr/May 05   RC
Grits, Baked Cheese ....Charter Issue   RC
Iceberg Lettuce with
Blue Cheese
Dressing.....................Charter Issue   RC
Onion Rings, Chili-Fried .....Apr/May 05   RC
Peach Salsa ....Aug/Sep 05   RC
Potato Salad, Roasted
German ....Jun/Jul 05   RC
Zucchini and Corn,
Sautéed, with Chives .....Jun/Jul 05   RC
soups
Corn and Chicken, Asian..Apr/May 05   RC
Potato, Rustic ....Dec/Jan 06   RC
Red Pepper, Roasted......Charter Issue   RC
Swordfish, Grilled, with
Eggplant Salad ....Aug/Sep 05   RC
Tortilla Casserole, Easy ....Oct/Nov 05   RC
Turkey Cutlets with Cherry
Sauce..................................Apr/May 05   RC
Recipe contests:
burger toppings ....Jun/Jul 05   27
chicken salads ....Aug/Sep 05   4–5
Christmas cookies....................Dec/Jan 06   4–5
decorating ideas for ....Charter Issue   27
cupcake decorations ....Apr/May 05   27
ice cream sundaes ....Aug/Sep 05   26
pasta sauces, quick ....Oct/Nov 05   4–5
picnic salads ....Apr/May 05   6–7
potato casseroles ....Oct/Nov 05   6–7
strawberry desserts ....Jun/Jul 05   6–7
Recipe makeovers. See
Reduced-fat recipes
**Recipes, holding at eye
level with magnetic clips** ....Dec/Jan 06   3
Red Cabbage Slaw....................Charter Issue   22
Red leaf lettuce ....Jun/Jul 05   19
Red Turban squash.......................Oct/Nov 05   27
Reduced-fat recipes:
Chicken, Oven-Fried ....Oct/Nov 05   9
Fiery................................Oct/Nov 05   9
Chocolate Frosting, Creamy..Aug/Sep 05   6
Chocolate Pudding ....Charter Issue   8
Mexican.............................Charter Issue   8
Orange-Kissed ....Charter Issue   8
Chocolate Sheet Cake ....Aug/Sep 05   6
Crumb Coffee Cake ....Jun/Jul 05   8
Hot Dip, Light and Creamy ....Dec/Jan 06   7
Artichoke ....Dec/Jan 06   7
Crab ....Dec/Jan 06   7
Spinach...........................Dec/Jan 06   7
Macaroni and Cheese ....Apr/May 05   8
after Dark ....Apr/May 05   8
for Pizza Lovers..............Apr/May 05   8
tasting of cheeses for ....Apr/May 05   29
**Relish, Cranberry-Apple-
Orange**..................................Dec/Jan 06   13
Rémoulade, Quick........................Aug/Sep 05   21
Resting meat before serving...........Jun/Jul 05   3
Rhubarb Sauce (for ham) ....Apr/May 05   11
Ribs:
short
Beer-Braised ....Dec/Jan 06   8
English-style vs.
flanken-style ....Dec/Jan 06   29
Spareribs, Memphis BBQ ....Jun/Jul 05   14–15
Rice:
Chicken and, Lemony ....Charter Issue   RC
Dirty ....Oct/Nov 05   22

Rice (CONTINUED)
fluffy
cooking tip for ....Aug/Sep 05   2
rinsing and.........................Oct/Nov 05   29
long-grain white, basic
cooking directions for.......Oct/Nov 05   6
Shrimp and, Skillet ....Apr/May 05   RC
**Rice Krispie treats, nonstick
handling of** ....Aug/Sep 05   3
Ricers, squeezing oranges with ...Aug/Sep 05   2
Rocky Road Bark..............................Jun/Jul 05   12
Rolling pins, tapered ....Oct/Nov 05   28
Romaine ....Jun/Jul 05   19
Root Beer Floats..........................Apr/May 05   12
Rosemary-Lemon Salt...................Apr/May 05   29

S

Safety concerns:
potato salad, keeping safe ......Jun/Jul 05   3
poultry, washing ....Jun/Jul 05   3
Saffron....................................Dec/Jan 06   15
Salad Bar Stir-Fry ....Aug/Sep 05   23
Salad dressings:
excess, spinning away ....Oct/Nov 05   2
French
All-American ....Jun/Jul 05   18
Creamy.....................................Jun/Jul 05   18
Italian, bottled, tasting of .....Charter Issue   30
vinaigrettes
formula for dressing
leafy salad with ....Apr/May 05   3
mixing in empty spice jar ..Aug/Sep 05   3
tips for ....Aug/Sep 05   20
vinegars for..............................Dec/Jan 06   6
Salads:
bean
Black, and Avocado............Jun/Jul 05   11
Tricolor Mexican ....Apr/May 05   7
Cape Cod Picnic ....Apr/May 05   6
chicken
Apricot.................................Aug/Sep 05   5
Chinese...............................Aug/Sep 05   5
Curried ....Aug/Sep 05   5
Jalapeño ....Aug/Sep 05   4
recipe contest ....Aug/Sep 05   4–5
Roast Chicken Breasts for..Aug/Sep 05   5
Shanghai ....Jun/Jul 05   RC
Waldorf ....Aug/Sep 05   5
Couscous, Mediterranean ....Jun/Jul 05   RC
Eggplant ....Aug/Sep 05   RC
Green, with Roasted Pears
and Blue Cheese ....Dec/Jan 06   21
greens for
varieties of ....Jun/Jul 05   19
washing ....Jun/Jul 05   18
Harvest Supper, with Smoked
Turkey and Apples ....Oct/Nov 05   RC
Iceberg Lettuce with Blue
Cheese Dressing..............Charter Issue   RC
leafy, dressing, formula for .....Apr/May 05   3
Macaroni, Cool and
Creamy...............................Aug/Sep 05   17
Panzanella...........................Apr/May 05   7
pasta
Gazpacho ....Apr/May 05   7
Shrimp, Zesty ....Aug/Sep 05   RC
for picnics (recipe contest) ....Apr/May 05   6–7
potato
Garden (with variations) ..Aug/Sep 05   20–21
keeping safe ....Jun/Jul 05   3
Roasted German ....Jun/Jul 05   RC
taming harsh taste of
raw onions in ....Dec/Jan 06   2
Salmon and Potato, Zesty ....Jun/Jul 05   23

Salads (CONTINUED)
slaws
Bistro ....Jun/Jul 05   24
Casablanca ....Jun/Jul 05   24
Fiesta ....Jun/Jul 05   24
Red Cabbage ....Charter Issue   22
Spicy Peanut ....Jun/Jul 05   24
Spinach and Radicchio,
Italian...............................Dec/Jan 06   12
Steak and Onion, Grilled ....Aug/Sep 05   RC
Sweet Potato, Low-Country ...Apr/May 05   7
Taco....................................Dec/Jan 06   RC
tomato ....Aug/Sep 05   14
"Bring Home the Bacon"..Aug/Sep 05   14
"Fit as a Fennel" ....Aug/Sep 05   14
"It's All Greek to Me" ....Aug/Sep 05   14
"Rhapsody in Blue
Cheese"...........................Aug/Sep 05   14
winter fruit ....Dec/Jan 06   23
Salad spinners:
cooling blanched
vegetables in ....Apr/May 05   4
ridding vegetables and
chopped tomatoes
of excess moisture with ....Jun/Jul 05   5
spinning away extra
dressing in..........................Oct/Nov 05   2
washing greens in ....Jun/Jul 05   18
Salmon:
Glazed, with Dilly Mustard
Sauce...............................Apr/May 05   23
and Potato Salad, Zesty ....Jun/Jul 05   23
Smoked, Pinwheels.................Oct/Nov 05   19
Salsas:
Grilled Banana and Red
Onion ....Jun/Jul 05   23
Peach.................................Aug/Sep 05   RC
Pineapple, Fresh ....Oct/Nov 05   18
Salt(s):
for baking or making candy ..Charter Issue   29
flavored, for fries ....Apr/May 05   29
Chili ....Apr/May 05   29
Rosemary-Lemon ....Apr/May 05   29
Warm-Spiced ....Apr/May 05   29
kosher vs. table ....Aug/Sep 05   9
Sandwiches:
Antipasto Heroes ....Jun/Jul 05   RC
French Dip ....Oct/Nov 05   21
grilled
Cheese, Classic (with
variations) ....Oct/Nov 05   15
Lodge Grill Press for...........Oct/Nov 05   31
no-slide tomatoes for ....Jun/Jul 05   5
Sausage, Open-Faced ....Aug/Sep 05   RC
Sloppy Joes (with variations)..Oct/Nov 05   17
Saucepans:
"large," "medium," and
"small," measurements
of ....Aug/Sep 05   9
nonstick..................................Apr/May 05   3
Sauces. See also Dessert sauces;
Pasta—sauces
barbecue, bottled, tasting of ..Apr/May 05   30
Cherry Pan (for turkey) ....Apr/May 05   RC
Jus, Quick ....Oct/Nov 05   21
ketchups, flavored ....Jun/Jul 05   29
Rémoulade, Quick ....Aug/Sep 05   21
Rhubarb (for ham) ....Apr/May 05   11
Special ....Jun/Jul 05   18
tomato
containing splatters from ....Jun/Jul 05   4
no-stir................................Aug/Sep 05   2
wrapping herbs in
cheesecloth for ....Aug/Sep 05   29

Sausage:
Baked Ziti with ....Apr/May 05 **RC**
Cornbread Stuffing with ....Oct/Nov 05 **12**
Cream Sauce with Peas
and (for pasta) ....Oct/Nov 05 **5**
Meatballs, Spaghetti with.......Dec/Jan 06 **RC**
Potato, and Spinach
Casserole.........................Charter Issue **7**
Sandwiches, Open-Faced .....Aug/Sep 05 **RC**
and Waffle Casserole, Maple...Dec/Jan 06 **22**
Scallions, chopping ahead vs.
right before use........................Aug/Sep 05 **28**
Scones, Strawberry ....Jun/Jul 05 **6**
Scrapers:
bench ....Apr/May 05 **29**
dough (bowl scrapers) ....Apr/May 05 **29**
Sea Foam Candy ....Charter Issue **9**
mail-order ....Charter Issue **29**
Seafood. See Crab(meat);
Fish; Shrimp
Seeds, toasting ....Dec/Jan 06 **14**
Serving dishes, warming................Apr/May 05 **3**
Sesame Chicken Bites.................Oct/Nov 05 **19**
Shallots, measuring ....Dec/Jan 06 **6**
Shanghai Chicken Salad ....Jun/Jul 05 **RC**
Sharp items, transporting safely ..Dec/Jan 06 **2**
Shears, pinking, cutting pie
crusts with ....Aug/Sep 05 **3**
Shellfish. See Crab(meat); Shrimp
Sherbet:
lime, in Watermelon Ice Pops...Aug/Sep 05 **10**
Surprise, Rainbow ....Charter Issue **12**
Shortening, measuring
without mess ....Apr/May 05 **5**
Short ribs:
Beer-Braised ....Dec/Jan 06 **8**
English-style vs. flanken-style ..Dec/Jan 06 **29**
Shrimp:
deveining with crochet hook ..Oct/Nov 05 **2**
Pasta Salad, Zesty....................Aug/Sep 05 **RC**
Piccata Pasta.............................Jun/Jul 05 **RC**
prepping....................................Jun/Jul 05 **4**
and Rice, Skillet......................Apr/May 05 **RC**
Spicy Baked ....Oct/Nov 05 **RC**
Toasts, Gingered ....Oct/Nov 05 **19**
Side dishes:
applesauce, "doctored"
Five-Spice ....Apr/May 05 **21**
Sweet-and-Hot
Cinnamon ....Apr/May 05 **21**
Asparagus, Broiled, with
Cheesy Bread Crumbs .....Apr/May 05 **11**
bean(s)
Black, and Avocado Salad ..Jun/Jul 05 **11**
Cowboy.............................Apr/May 05 **22**
Salad, Tricolor Mexican ....Apr/May 05 **7**
breads
Jalapeño Cornbread .....Charter Issue **21**
Quaker Bonnet Biscuits .....Oct/Nov 05 **8**
Savory Cheese Muffins .....Oct/Nov 05 **22**
broccoli
with Creamy Herb Sauce..Apr/May 05 **17**
with Lemon and Walnuts..Apr/May 05 **17**
with Mustard–Red
Pepper Vinaigrette......Apr/May 05 **17**
with Parmesan Bread
Crumbs ....Apr/May 05 **17**
Brussels Sprouts, Braised,
with Bacon and Pecans...Dec/Jan 06 **13**
Cape Cod Picnic Salad ....Apr/May 05 **6**
corn
Fritters, Farmstand ....Aug/Sep 05 **13**
Pudding, Savory ....Dec/Jan 06 **13**
Roasted ....Charter Issue **22**

Side dishes (CONTINUED)
Couscous Salad,
Mediterranean ....Jun/Jul 05 **RC**
Cranberry-Apple-Orange
Relish..................................Dec/Jan 06 **13**
Eggplant Salad ....Aug/Sep 05 **RC**
Gazpacho Pasta Salad ....Apr/May 05 **7**
green beans
with Bacon and Onion ...Charter Issue **17**
with Mediterranean
Flavors ....Charter Issue **17**
Nutty...................................Apr/May 05 **RC**
Orange, with Buttered
Cashews ....Charter Issue **17**
Succotash ....Charter Issue **17**
Green Salad with Roasted
Pears and Blue Cheese ....Dec/Jan 06 **21**
Grits, Baked Cheese ....Charter Issue **RC**
Iceberg Lettuce with
Blue Cheese Dressing .....Charter Issue **RC**
keeping hot longer.................Apr/May 05 **3**
macaroni
and Cheese,
Reduced-Fat................Apr/May 05 **8**
Salad, Cool and
Creamy ....Aug/Sep 05 **17**
onion(s)
Balsamic (caramelized)....Dec/Jan 06 **18**
Rings, Chili-Fried.................Apr/May 05 **RC**
Panzanella Salad.....................Apr/May 05 **7**
peas
and Carrots, Dilly ....Dec/Jan 06 **19**
Creamy, with Ham
and Onion ....Dec/Jan 06 **19**
Curried ....Dec/Jan 06 **19**
Smashed Minty ....Dec/Jan 06 **19**
pickles
Bread-and-Butter..............Aug/Sep 05 **20**
"Kosher" Double-Dill..........Aug/Sep 05 **19**
potato(es)
Casserole, Alsatian..........Charter Issue **6**
Casserole, Cheesy ....Oct/Nov 05 **23**
Casserole, Creamy ....Charter Issue **6**
Cheesy Mashed ....Charter Issue **23**
Mashed, and Herbed
Cheese Bake..............Charter Issue **7**
Salad, Garden (with
variations) ....Aug/Sep 05 **20–21**
Salad, Roasted German .....Jun/Jul 05 **RC**
Spinach, and Sausage
Casserole ....Charter Issue **7**
Steak Fries, Super-Crisp .....Apr/May 05 **18**
Rice, Down 'n' Dirty ....Oct/Nov 05 **22**
salsas
Banana and Red
Onion, Grilled ....Jun/Jul 05 **23**
Peach ....Aug/Sep 05 **RC**
Pineapple, Fresh ....Oct/Nov 05 **18**
slaws
Bistro ....Jun/Jul 05 **24**
Casablanca ....Jun/Jul 05 **24**
Fiesta ....Jun/Jul 05 **24**
Red Cabbage ....Charter Issue **22**
Spicy Peanut......................Jun/Jul 05 **24**
Spinach Orzo............................Jun/Jul 05 **21**
stuffings
Cornbread and Bacon ....Oct/Nov 05 **12**
Cornbread and
Sausage......................Oct/Nov 05 **12**
Sugar Snap Peas and Cherry
Tomatoes, Sautéed..........Apr/May 05 **23**
sweet potato
Casserole...........................Dec/Jan 06 **13**
Salad, Low-Country..........Apr/May 05 **7**

Side dishes (CONTINUED)
tomato salads
"Bring Home the Bacon"..Aug/Sep 05 **14**
"Fit as a Fennel" ....Aug/Sep 05 **14**
"It's All Greek to Me" ....Aug/Sep 05 **14**
"Rhapsody in Blue
Cheese".......................Aug/Sep 05 **14**
Winter Squash, Brown-
Sugar-Glazed....................Oct/Nov 05 **26**
Zucchini and Corn,
Sautéed, with Chives..........Jun/Jul 05 **RC**
Sifters, keeping flour
contained in ....Aug/Sep 05 **3**
Skewers. See also Kebabs
Sesame Chicken Bites.............Oct/Nov 05 **19**
Skillets:
"large," "medium," and
"small," measurements
of ....Aug/Sep 05 **9**
nonstick..................................Apr/May 05 **3**
Skimmers, mesh or Chinese
(spiders) ....Apr/May 05 **29**
Slaws:
Bistro ....Jun/Jul 05 **24**
Casablanca ....Jun/Jul 05 **24**
Fiesta ....Jun/Jul 05 **24**
Red Cabbage ....Charter Issue **22**
Spicy Peanut ....Jun/Jul 05 **24**
Sloppy Janes ....Oct/Nov 05 **17**
Sloppy Joes................................Oct/Nov 05 **17**
Sloppy Josés ....Oct/Nov 05 **17**
Slow cookers:
"hobo pack" for
vegetables in......................Oct/Nov 05 **7**
keeping food warm in ....Apr/May 05 **3**
rating of ....Charter Issue **31**
recipes for
Beef Stew, Hearty..............Oct/Nov 05 **7**
Boston Baked Beans ....Aug/Sep 05 **7**
Chili con Carne,
"Texas Red" ....Jun/Jul 05 **10–11**
Pot Roast ....Charter Issue **10–11**
Pulled Pork.......................Apr/May 05 **10–11**
Short Ribs, Beer-Braised ....Dec/Jan 06 **8**
timer and keep-warm
features of ....Charter Issue **29**
Smoky Joes..................................Oct/Nov 05 **17**
Smoothies..................................Aug/Sep 05 **25**
brain freeze (ice cream
headache) and ....Aug/Sep 05 **27**
Chocolate-Covered Cherry...Aug/Sep 05 **25**
Creamsicle ....Aug/Sep 05 **25**
The Elvis ....Aug/Sep 05 **25**
measuring frozen fruit for........Aug/Sep 05 **29**
Piña Colada ....Aug/Sep 05 **25**
Strawberry Cream Pie ....Aug/Sep 05 **25**
Takes Two to Mango ....Aug/Sep 05 **25**
Very Berry ....Aug/Sep 05 **25**
S'Mores Brownies......................Charter Issue **25**
Snickers Bar Sauce,
Peanut Butter Cup Ice
Cream and ....Oct/Nov 05 **10**
Soups:
beef
Barley, with
Mushrooms ....Charter Issue **11**
simmering vs. boiling
broth for ....Dec/Jan 06 **29**
and Vegetable,
Hearty ....Dec/Jan 06 **26–27**
Corn and Chicken, Asian.......Apr/May 05 **RC**
Potato, Rustic ....Dec/Jan 06 **RC**
Roasted Red Pepper ....Charter Issue **RC**
Split-Pea, with Ham ....Oct/Nov 05 **26**

Soups (CONTINUED)

thickening

bean soups with refried

beans ....Dec/Jan 06 **2**

with mashed potato

flakes ....Dec/Jan 06 **2–3**

wrapping herbs in

cheesecloth for ....Aug/Sep 05 **29**

Southern Pecan Praline Pie ....Oct/Nov 05 **24–25**

Southwestern (cuisine):

Meatloaf, Cheesy ....Apr/May 05 **23**

Pot Roast ....Charter Issue **11**

Spaghetti squash ....Oct/Nov 05 **27**

Spaghetti with Sausage

Meatballs ....Dec/Jan 06 **RC**

Spareribs, Memphis BBQ ......Jun/Jul 05 **14–15**

Spatulas:

rubber, for cleaning ....Charter Issue **4**

tiny, stand-in for ....Aug/Sep 05 **3**

Special Sauce ....Jun/Jul 05 **18**

Speedy-Peel, testing of ....Aug/Sep 05 **9**

Spice(s). See also specific spices

grinding in coffee grinder ......Dec/Jan 06 **29**

Molasses Lemon Sandwich

Cookies ....Dec/Jan 06 **5**

Rub ....Jun/Jul 05 **14**

applying underneath

poultry skin ....Oct/Nov 05 **2**

tasting of ....Dec/Jan 06 **15**

toasting ....Dec/Jan 06 **14**

wrapping in cheesecloth ......Aug/Sep 05 **29**

Spice jars:

mixing vinaigrette in ....Aug/Sep 05 **3**

pouring easily from ....Jun/Jul 05 **4**

Spiders (mesh or Chinese,

skimmers) ....Apr/May 05 **29**

Spinach ....Jun/Jul 05 **19**

adding to soups ....Dec/Jan 06 **27**

Hot Dip, Light and Creamy ....Dec/Jan 06 **7**

Orzo ....Jun/Jul 05 **21**

Potato, and Sausage

Casserole ....Charter Issue **7**

and Radicchio Salad, Italian ..Dec/Jan 06 **12**

Splatter guards, wire-mesh,

steaming tortillas on ....Dec/Jan 06 **2**

Split-Pea Soup with Ham ....Oct/Nov 05 **26**

Spoons, wooden:

applying spice rub under

poultry skin with

handle of ....Oct/Nov 05 **2**

mixing sticky or pasty

ingredients with ....Aug/Sep 05 **3**

Spreads:

Apricot, Zesty ....Aug/Sep 05 **29**

Beet, Creamy, with Endive

Leaves ....Oct/Nov 05 **18**

Cream Cheese (with

variations) ....Aug/Sep 05 **29**

Lemon-Ginger ....Aug/Sep 05 **29**

Maple-Cinnamon ....Aug/Sep 05 **29**

Orange ....Aug/Sep 05 **29**

Pineapple, Sweet ....Aug/Sep 05 **29**

Springform pans, easier

slicing in ....Charter Issue **4**

Squash (winter):

acorn, splitting with little saw ..Oct/Nov 05 **3**

Brown-Sugar-Glazed ....Oct/Nov 05 **26**

roasting ....Oct/Nov 05 **26**

tasting of varieties ....Oct/Nov 05 **27**

Stainless steel:

cookware, cleaning ....Apr/May 05 **3**

removing smell of garlic and

onions from hands with ..Charter Issue **4**

Star anise ....Dec/Jan 06 **15**

Starters. See also Appetizers

and hors d'oeuvres

Spinach and Radicchio

Salad, Italian ....Dec/Jan 06 **12**

Steak Fries, Super-Crisp ....Apr/May 05 **18**

oil absorbed by ....Dec/Jan 06 **6**

Steaks. See Beef—steak(s)

Steamers, makeshift ....Aug/Sep 05 **3**

Stews:

Beef, Hearty ....Oct/Nov 05 **7**

chili

con Carne, "Texas

Red" ....Jun/Jul 05 **10–11**

Ranch ....Charter Issue **20–21**

cooling quickly with frozen

vegetables ....Aug/Sep 05 **2**

Fisherman's, Hearty ....Oct/Nov 05 **RC**

Sticky ingredients:

getting last drop of ....Aug/Sep 05 **2**

keeping spoon from

sticking to ....Aug/Sep 05 **3**

Stir-fry(ied):

Beef with Snow Peas

and Cashews ....Dec/Jan 06 **RC**

Salad Bar ....Aug/Sep 05 **23**

Stocks:

cooking in large pasta

pot with strainer ....Apr/May 05 **5**

removing fat from ....Dec/Jan 06 **2**

wrapping herbs in

cheesecloth for ....Aug/Sep 05 **29**

Storage containers, cleaning ......Apr/May 05 **5**

Strainers:

alternative to ....Aug/Sep 05 **29**

wire mesh, as makeshift

steamers ....Aug/Sep 05 **3**

Strawberry(ies):

with Balsamic Vinegar ....Charter Issue **RC**

Cream Pie Smoothie ....Aug/Sep 05 **25**

desserts (recipe contest) ....Dec/Jan 06 **6–7**

Ice Cream Cupcakes ....Charter Issue **12**

Pineapple Tart ....Jun/Jul 05 **7**

Pretzel Bars ....Jun/Jul 05 **7**

Sauce ....Apr/May 05 **25**

.............................Aug/Sep 05 **27**

Scones ....Jun/Jul 05 **6**

storing ....Jun/Jul 05 **29**

Trifle, Quick ....Jun/Jul 05 **7**

washing ....Jun/Jul 05 **3**

Straws. See Puff pastry—straws

Stuffings:

cornbread

with Bacon ....Oct/Nov 05 **12**

drying cornbread for ....Oct/Nov 05 **12**

with Sausage ....Oct/Nov 05 **12**

packaged, tasting of ....Oct/Nov 05 **30**

Succotash, Green Bean ....Charter Issue **17**

Sugar:

brown, melted, as last-

minute pancake

syrup ....Apr/May 05 **5**

Burnt, Cake ....Aug/Sep 05 **16**

Sugar Snap Peas and Cherry

Tomatoes, Sautéed ....Apr/May 05 **23**

Sweet Dumpling squash ....Oct/Nov 05 **27**

Sweet potato(es):

adding to soups ....Dec/Jan 06 **27**

Casserole ....Dec/Jan 06 **13**

Salad, Low-Country ....Apr/May 05 **7**

Swiss Caraway Biscuits ....Dec/Jan 06 **27**

Swordfish, Grilled, with

Eggplant Salad ....Aug/Sep 05 **RC**

Syrups:

pancake, last-minute ....Apr/May 05 **5**

Syrups (CONTINUED)

Simple ....Dec/Jan 06 **23**

Cinnamon ....Jun/Jul 05 **20**

for Iced Tea ....Jun/Jul 05 **20**

Orange, Lime, or Lemon .....Jun/Jul 05 **20**

sticky, getting last drop of ......Aug/Sep 05 **2**

T

Taco Salad ....Dec/Jan 06 **RC**

Tangerines, in Miami Vice

(winter fruit salad) ....Dec/Jan 06 **23**

Tart, Strawberry-Pineapple ....Jun/Jul 05 **7**

Tastings:

apple varieties for baking ....Charter Issue **19**

barbecue sauces, bottled ....Apr/May 05 **30**

Cheddar, reduced-fat ....Apr/May 05 **29**

chicken breasts, boneless ......Oct/Nov 05 **30**

chocolate chip cookies,

ready-to-bake ....Apr/May 05 **30**

chocolate chips ....Dec/Jan 06 **30**

chocolate ice cream ....Jun/Jul 05 **30**

cocoa powder, regular

(natural) vs. Dutched ......Charter Issue **29**

cornbread mixes ....Oct/Nov 05 **12**

cream cheese, reduced-fat ..Dec/Jan 06 **7**

flour, bleached vs.

unbleached ....Dec/Jan 06 **6**

Grapples ....Oct/Nov 05 **29**

ice cream cones ....Jun/Jul 05 **30**

Italian dressings, bottled ....Charter Issue **30**

lemonade ....Aug/Sep 05 **30**

maple syrup ....Dec/Jan 06 **30**

nuts, fresh-chopped vs.

packaged chopped ....Oct/Nov 05 **6**

orange juice ....Charter Issue **30**

pear varieties ....Dec/Jan 06 **28**

peas, frozen vs. fresh ....Dec/Jan 06 **28**

pork, enhanced vs.

unenhanced ....Oct/Nov 05 **6**

spices ....Dec/Jan 06 **15**

stuffing, packaged ....Oct/Nov 05 **30**

tea bags for iced tea ....Jun/Jul 05 **29**

tomatoes, conventional

and heirloom varieties ......Aug/Sep 05 **15**

treacle ....Oct/Nov 05 **6**

waffles, frozen ....Dec/Jan 06 **22**

whipped toppings ....Aug/Sep 05 **30**

white chocolate ....Oct/Nov 05 **6**

winter squash varieties ....Oct/Nov 05 **27**

Tea, iced:

Sweet (with variations) ....Jun/Jul 05 **20**

tasting of tea bags for ....Jun/Jul 05 **29**

Teakettles, keeping kitchen

cooler with ....Aug/Sep 05 **2**

Tennessee-Whiskey Pork Chops ..Aug/Sep 05 **12–13**

"Texas Red" Chili con Carne ...Jun/Jul 05 **10–11**

Thermometers:

candy ....Charter Issue **15**

for deep-frying ....Charter Issue **15**

.............................Aug/Sep 05 **28**

location of sensor on ....Aug/Sep 05 **9**

Tipsy Parson ....Dec/Jan 06 **9**

Toasters, rating of ....Dec/Jan 06 **31**

Toasting spices, nuts, and seeds ..Dec/Jan 06 **14**

Toffee Chocolate Butter Cookies ..Dec/Jan 06 **4**

Tomato(es):

cherry

Stuffed ....Oct/Nov 05 **19**

and Sugar Snap Peas,

Sautéed ....Apr/May 05 **23**

chopped, reducing

moisture in ....Jun/Jul 05 **5**

crushing neatly ....Charter Issue **5**

Gazpacho Pasta Salad ....Apr/May 05 **7**

Tomato(es) (CONTINUED)

no-slide, for sandwiches ....Jun/Jul 05   5
Panzanella Salad....................Apr/May 05   7
paste
   freezing in flattened
      plastic bag ....Oct/Nov 05   3
   freezing in individual
      portions ....Charter Issue   5
   removing easily from
      can ....Aug/Sep 05   3
salads ....Aug/Sep 05   14
   "Bring Home the Bacon"..Aug/Sep 05   14
   "Fit as a Fennel" ....Aug/Sep 05   14
   "It's All Greek to Me" ....Aug/Sep 05   14
   "Rhapsody in Blue
      Cheese"......................Aug/Sep 05   14
sauce
   containing splatters from ....Jun/Jul 05   4
   no-stir................................Aug/Sep 05   2
storing and ripening ....Aug/Sep 05   14
tasting of conventional
   and heirloom varieties......Aug/Sep 05   15
Tricolor Mexican Bean
   Salad................................Apr/May 05   7
Tongue depressors, leveling
dry measures with ....Apr/May 05   5
Tortilla(s):
casseroles
   Beef..................................Charter Issue   11
   Easy (with chicken) ....Oct/Nov 05   RC
chips, in Taco Salad ....Dec/Jan 06   RC
Scoops, in Crispy Mexican
   Bites....................................Oct/Nov 05   18
steaming..............................Dec/Jan 06   2
Treacle..Oct/Nov 05   6
Tricolor Mexican Bean Salad.......Apr/May 05   7
Trifles:
Strawberry, Quick ....Jun/Jul 05   7
Tipsy Parson ....Dec/Jan 06   9
Triple-Chocolate Cookies ....Jun/Jul 05   17
Tropical Orange Glaze ....Dec/Jan 06   28
Tuna Sauce, Spicy (for pasta) .....Oct/Nov 05   5
Turkey. *See also* Stuffings
applying spice rub
   underneath skin of ....Oct/Nov 05   2
Cape Cod Picnic Salad ....Apr/May 05   6
Cutlets with Cherry Sauce......Apr/May 05   RC
frozen, thawing ....Oct/Nov 05   28
ground, in Sloppy Janes ....Oct/Nov 05   17
Monterey Melts ....Oct/Nov 05   15
roast
   cooking time for ....Oct/Nov 05   28
   flipping halfway through
      cooking time ....Oct/Nov 05   29
   resting before serving ....Jun/Jul 05   3

Turkey (CONTINUED)

Smoked, Harvest Supper
   Salad with Apples and .....Oct/Nov 05   RC
Turnips, adding to soups ....Dec/Jan 06   27
Turnovers, Apple, Easy ....Oct/Nov 05   13
Turtles, Caramel..........................Oct/Nov 05   10
Tutti-Frutti Watermelon Boats ....Aug/Sep 05   10

V

Vanilla:
beans, storing.........................Oct/Nov 05   2
Frosting, Quick.......................Apr/May 05   26
Vegetable peelers:
slicing cucumbers thinly
   with.....................................Dec/Jan 06   3
transporting safely ....Dec/Jan 06   2
Vegetables. *See also specific*
vegetables
blanching, cooling quickly
   after ....Apr/May 05   4
chopped, transferring to pot
   on stove............................Aug/Sep 05   3
frozen, quickly cooling large
   pot of something hot
   with...................................Aug/Sep 05   2
Vertical chicken roasters,
testing of ....Aug/Sep 05   29
Vinaigrettes:
formula for dressing leafy
   salad with ....Apr/May 05   3
mixing in empty spice jar........Aug/Sep 05   3
tips for..................................Aug/Sep 05   20
Vinegar:
cider vs. distilled......................Dec/Jan 06   6
cleaning with
   drains ....Charter Issue   4
using leftovers to kill
   weeds ....Oct/Nov 05   3
V-racks, makeshift ....Dec/Jan 06   28

W

Waffle(s):
frozen, tasting of ....Dec/Jan 06   22
light and fluffy ....Dec/Jan 06   2
and Sausage Casserole,
   Maple..............................Dec/Jan 06   22
Waldorf Chicken Salad ....Aug/Sep 05   5
Warm-Spiced Salt.......................Apr/May 05   29
Washboard Cookies ....Jun/Jul 05   9
Washington, George,
maxims of ....Apr/May 05   15
Watercress.................................Jun/Jul 05   19
Watermelon:
Boats, Tutti-Frutti ....Aug/Sep 05   10
Citrus Punch ....Aug/Sep 05   10

Watermelon (CONTINUED)

Ice Pops ....Aug/Sep 05   10
Polka-Dot Minty Melon Mold ..Aug/Sep 05   10
Waxed paper, cutting to
line baking pans ....Apr/May 05   4
WD-40, removing
manufacturer's stickers with ..Oct/Nov 05   3
Weeds, killing with vinegar ....Oct/Nov 05   3
Welders' gloves ....Apr/May 05   4
Western (Denver) Omelet,
Family-Style ....Jun/Jul 05   21
cooking technique for ....Jun/Jul 05   29
Whipped cream:
Chocolate ....Charter Issue   12
freezing dollops of ....Apr/May 05   4
Plain ....Charter Issue   12
stabilizing
   with instant vanilla
      pudding ....Oct/Nov 05   3
with marshmallows ....Jun/Jul 05   5
Whipped toppings,
commercial, tasting of...........Aug/Sep 05   30
Whiskey-Glazed Pork Chops ....Aug/Sep 05   12–13
White chocolate...........................Oct/Nov 05   6
M&M Clusters ....Oct/Nov 05   10
and Peppermint Brownies ....Charter Issue   25
tasting of................................Oct/Nov 05   6
Wintermint Bark ....Dec/Jan 06   10
Wine:
Blushing Peach Terrine ....Apr/May 05   13
freezing ....Jun/Jul 05   5
removing cork pieces from ....Apr/May 05   5
Winter fruit salads ....Dec/Jan 06   23
Wintermint Bark ....Dec/Jan 06   10
Wooden spoons, applying
spice rub with handle of ....Oct/Nov 05   2

Y

Yogurt, in Smoothies ....Aug/Sep 05   25
Yule Log Cake, Icebox
Peppermint ....Dec/Jan 06   10

Z

Zest, grated, contained by
Microplane grater ....Oct/Nov 05   3
Ziti, Baked, with Sausage ....Apr/May 05   RC
Zucchini:
Bread..................................Aug/Sep 05   24
   baking in muffin tin............Aug/Sep 05   28
   Cream Cheese
      Spreads for ....Aug/Sep 05   29
   Fruity.................................Aug/Sep 05   24
   Nutty.................................Aug/Sep 05   24
and Corn, Sautéed,
   with Chives.........................Jun/Jul 05   RC

Cook's Country

CHARTER ISSUE

In this issue

Crunchiest-Ever Fried Chicken

S'mores Brownies and More

Best Ranch Chili

BLUE-RIBBON APPLE CAKE
Big Apple Flavor

TASTING ITALIAN DRESSING
Only Two Brands
Worth Buying

EASY POT ROAST
Secrets to Slow-Cooker
Success

CHRISTMAS COOKIE PARTY
Never-Fail Dough with
11 Fun Decorating Ideas

**PRIZE-WINNING
POTATO CASSEROLES**
5 Reader Recipes Take
Top Honors

RATING SLOW COOKERS
Shape, Features, and
Size Matter

**LOW-FAT CHOCOLATE
PUDDING**
Creamy, Rich, and
One-Third the Fat

$4.95 U.S./$6.95 CANADA

Our Recipe Contest Winner!

Christine Puccia of West Roxbury, Massachusetts, sent us a first-place
potato casserole recipe that's been a family favorite on two continents.
See page 6 for her Italian Potato Cake.

Cook's Country

Dear Country Cook,

Many of us at Cook's Illustrated magazine (the sister publication of Cook's Country) grew up in the country and have a great fondness not only for country food but for all that goes with it: nutmeg doughnuts and coffee after church, Fourth of July barbecues, kitchen dances, Old Home Day cookouts, dessert parties, family reunions, and covered-dish suppers. So many of us have grown up on good country cooking—baked beans, baking powder biscuits, pot roast, potato casseroles, molasses cookies—that we felt it was time to start a magazine about what we love most: country folks and country food. Hence the birth of Cook's Country.

For my part, I grew up in a small town in the Green Mountains of Vermont. I ate dinner at noon in an old yellow farmhouse with the farmhands. The milk was from the cow out back, the water was from a hand pump in the sink, and all of the baking was done right in the front parlor on a green Kalamazoo wood cookstove. The food was great, but so was the company: Marie, the cook; Floyd and Junior, the farmers; Herbie and Onie, the farmhands; and Dixie, the collie. Everyone who sat at the table was family.

Today, many of us still enjoy food as the center of our social lives, and that's what this magazine is about. It's not about fancy cooking or expensive restaurants or foods with names you can't pronounce. This is honest country fare.

A word about our recipes. As with Cook's Illustrated, we test recipes 10, 20, 30, even 40 times to make them as foolproof as possible. As we are apt to say in our test kitchen, "We test recipes so you don't have to." We hope you will come to trust both us and our recipes. We know that we have a lot to learn from you, too.

The charter issue you are holding is our invitation to you, a call to join us in the kitchen as well as to share your recipes, your photographs, and your food memories. We are eager to publish what you have to say about food and cooking. Feel free to write to us at Cook's Country, P.O. Box 470739, Brookline, MA 02447, or at cookscountry@bcpress.com.

One last thought. Cooking and eating ought to be fun. In Cook's Country, we remember how to play with our food and have a good time doing it! (Take a peek at the brownie and ice cream stories to see what I mean.)

Welcome to Cook's Country. You're all invited over for supper!

With warm regards,

Christopher Kimball
on behalf of the Cook's Country staff

CHARTER ISSUE

Cook's Country

In every issue

Welcome to Cook's Country   **2**

Ask Cook's Country   **3**

Kitchen Shortcuts   **4**

Simply Supper   **16**

When Things Go Wrong . . .   **28**

Notes from Our Test Kitchen   **29**

Food Shopping   **30**

Equipment Roundup   **31**

Thanks for the Memories   **32**

A tiny rooster, like the one on the front cover, has been hidden somewhere in the pages of this issue. If you find it, write to us with its location (plus your name and address), and you will be entered into a random drawing. The first five winners will receive the Farberware Millennium Slow Cooker (our test winner—see page 31), and the following 25 winners will receive free one-year subscriptions to *Cook's Country*. To enter the contest, write to us at Rooster, Cook's Country, P.O. Box 470739, Brookline, MA 02447, or e-mail us at rooster@bcpress.com.

Founder and Editor Christopher Kimball
Executive Editor Jack Bishop
Art Director Amy Klee
Test Kitchen Director Erin McMurrer
Recipe Editor Eva Katz
Copy Editor India Koopman
Kitchen Assistants Barbara Akins, Tomer Gurantz
Recipe Tester Elizabeth Germain
Contributors Erika Bruce, Matthew Card, Lauren Chattman, Garth Clingingsmith, Julia Collin Davison, Keith Dresser, Rebecca Hays, Bridget Lancaster, Stephanie Lyness, Diane Unger-Mahoney, Nina West
Staff Photographer Daniel J. van Ackere
Proofreader Jean Rogers
Assistant to the Publisher Melissa Baldino

Vice President Marketing David Mack
Sales Director Leslie Ray
Marketing Assistant Connie Forbes
Circulation Director Bill Tine
Circulation Manager Larisa Greiner
Products Director Steven Browall
Direct Mail Director Adam Perry
Customer Service Manager Jacqueline Valerio
Customer Service Representative Julie Gardner
E-Commerce Marketing Manager Hugh Buchan

Vice President Operations James McCormack
Production Managers Mary Connelly, Jessica Lindheimer-Quirk
Production Assistants Jennifer McCreary, Jennifer Power, Christian Steinmetz
Systems Administrator Richard Cassidy
WebMaster Aaron Shuman

Chief Financial Officer Sharyn Chabot
Controller Mandy Shito
Office Manager Saudiyah Abdul-Rahim
Receptionist Henrietta Murray
Publicity Deborah Broide

Editorial Office: 17 Station Street, Brookline, MA 02445; 617-232-1000; fax 617-232-1572. Subscription inquiries: 800-526-8447.

Postmaster: Send all new orders, subscription inquiries, and change-of-address notices to Cook's Country, P.O. Box 8382, Red Oak, IA 51591-1382.

PRINTED IN THE USA

Cover photo: Susie M. Eising/StockFood; illustration: Felix Fu; color photography this page: Keller + Keller; styling: Mary Jane Sawyer

Recipes

6 RECIPE CONTEST: Potato Casseroles
We received more than 150 reader recipes and picked our five favorites.

8 RECIPE MAKEOVER: Chocolate Pudding
Great flavor with half the calories? We were skeptical, but the proof was in the pudding.

9 LOST RECIPES: Sea Foam Candy
We return this old-fashioned confection to its original glory.

10 SLOW COOKING: Pot Roast
Making great slow-cooker pot roast is harder than we thought. The problem? Overcooking. We have the solution, plus two easy recipes for using up leftovers.

12 FUN FOOD: Ice Cream Desserts
We start with store-bought ice cream and end with tasty and entertaining treats.

14 Crispiest, Crunchiest Fried Chicken Ever
Fast-food chicken is a guilty pleasure. Is there a way to re-create its crispy crunch at home?

17 No-Fuss Green Beans
Four new recipes and a forgiving cooking technique make green bean side dishes easy to prepare.

18 Blue-Ribbon Apple Cake
For years, Helen Hanson of Gallatin Gateway, Montana, has been searching for a good apple cake—the kind with lots of apples. We agreed to help.

20 The Best Ranch Chili
The McCrearys of Houston, Texas, serve this spicy version of pork and beans twice a month. The problem was getting the pork fork-tender and the beans just right.

22 Quick Cooking
Two good meals, ready for the table in 30 minutes.

23 Cheesy Mashed Potatoes
Claire Johnston of Newton, Massachusetts, wanted cheesy flavor in her mashed potatoes, but her attempts at home produced gluey disasters. A cheesy recipe with good texture is hard to find.

24 S'mores Brownies and More
Beth Bloomberg of Colchester, Vermont, wanted new flavors for an old favorite. How about S'mores Brownies for starters?

26 Never-Fail Christmas Cookies
A butter cookie dough that can be rolled and cut as many times as needed. Plus favorite cookie-decorating ideas from readers.

Welcome to Cook's Country

We Can Almost Taste Those Crawfish

Frank Bull of Waco, Texas, shared some great photos with us. He writes: "These photos were taken at a crawfish boil that I helped with at First Baptist in Lott, a small community south of Waco. The local youth were raising money for summer activities and mission trips."

Mattituck's 50th Annual Strawberry Festival

Nancy Silverman of Southampton, New York, visited the strawberry festival in the neighboring town of Mattituck with her family this past June and reports that everyone had their fill of juicy local berries. Mattituck is a small farming community on the eastern end of Long Island. The festival is sponsored by the Mattituck Lions Club and raises money for more than 20 local charities. When this celebration of local berries started in 1955, it was a one-day affair attended by about 1,000 people. The event has grown into a three-day festival, and now more than 30,000 people enjoy 9,000 quarts of berries on the Mattituck fairgrounds every year.

Nancy tells us that her husband, Jake, ate plenty of strawberry shortcake (she tried some, too) and that her girls had a great time getting their faces painted and watching the crowning of the Strawberry Festival Queen. Besides shortcake, Nancy's girls tried the chocolate-dipped strawberries and the strawberry shakes. And for entertainment, the whole family enjoyed listening to the Elvis impersonator. Good food and good music—sounds like the perfect summer afternoon.

San Diego Farmers Market

Arlene Dewhurst of San Diego, California, sent us this interesting photo from her local farmers market, held on Wednesday afternoons. We've never seen artichokes that have reached this stage of flowering. She tells us these pretty artichokes are not for eating, but they will look good in her kitchen for a month or so.

Magnificent Melon

Susy DePeyster of Sandgate, Vermont, sent us this photo of a watermelon that was sculpted into the shape of a pig for her annual August ox roast. Two steamship rounds of beef (Susy explained that they don't really cook an ox!) are slow-cooked over a pit of coals that are started the night before. A special homemade rotisserie was built for the occasion years ago—it's made from mattress springs, chicken wire, and rebar (the metal rods used to strengthen concrete foundations). Early birds line up to get the burnt ends.

Take a Chance (on a Cake) at the Rupert Fireman's Carnival

Charlie Sherman from Rupert, Vermont, wrote us to say that the annual fireman's parade and carnival is always successful raising money through the "Wheel of Cakes" contest. Local bakers make dozens of cakes, which are then "won" at the cake booth. Folks put 25 cents down on a number, the wheel is spun, and the winner picks out a cake. A cake can get pretty expensive if you're not feeling lucky! Charlie enclosed a photo of one young winner who looks like he is going to eat the whole thing himself.

Before the carnival starts, there is a fireman's parade that has a different theme each year. This year a woman dressed up as the Statue of Liberty marched proudly in the "God Bless America" parade.

We'd love to hear what's happening in your community. Drop us a note and tell us what's cooking. And please send pictures with those notes. Write to us at Welcome to Cook's Country, Cook's Country, P.O. Box 470739, Brookline, MA 02447. If you'd like to use e-mail, write to us at welcome@bcpress.com.

Ask Cook's Country

WE TRY TO ANSWER ANY QUESTION YOU THROW AT US!

EGGS IN THE MICROWAVE?

Have you seen a product called the Egg Wave? The commercial claims that you can microwave a whole egg with this gadget—something I thought was impossible.

Sari Hunter Glendive, Montana

This product is nothing more than a piece of molded plastic designed to cradle four eggs as they cook. Unfortunately, we wasted $15, as this item was a bust. First we tried to hard-cook four eggs. Placing eggs in the elliptical plastic container was simple enough, but few and far between were the times that the lid was not blown off by an exploding egg. Turning the microwave to half power reduced the mess but also led to either half-cooked eggs or multiple tiny explosions. Either way, the eggs were decidedly rubbery.

The instruction manual also suggests cracking eggs into the cups to make scrambled eggs in the microwave. Scrambled eggs, while still rubbery, at least cooked evenly, but they souffléed up into the top of the Egg Wave, and nothing short of a toothpick or a Q-Tip could get it clean.

Eggs-plosion! Can the Egg Wave do the impossible—cook whole eggs in a microwave without having them explode?

MEASURING MIX-UP

I've never quite understood the difference between metal measuring cups (the kind used to measure flour or sugar) and glass measuring cups (used to measure water or milk). Can I use these different kinds of cups interchangeably?

Marcia Kaplan Charlotte, North Carolina

Not all of the time—let us explain. First of all, 1 cup in a "dry" (usually metal) measuring cup is exactly the same volume as 1 cup in a "wet" (usually glass) measuring cup. The choice, then, of how to measure dry ingredients and wet ingredients comes down to convenience and accuracy. Let's start by defining what we mean by "dry" and "wet" cups. Dry cups are made from metal or plastic and can be leveled off with a straight edge. Wet measuring cups are made of heatsafe glass (such as Pyrex) or plastic and have a pouring spout. Whereas dry measures usually come in sizes from ⅛ or ¼ cup up to 1 cup, wet measures are

If you have a cooking question, are wondering about a product you've seen advertised, or are trying to identify a mystery tool, we'd like to help. Please write to Ask Cook's Country, Cook's Country, P.O. Box 470739, Brookline, MA 02447. If you prefer to use e-mail, write to askcookscountry@bcpress.com.

available in sizes of 1, 2, 4, and 8 cups. When using both dry and wet measuring cups to measure dry ingredients (sugar and flour), we found the dry cups to be much easier to use. It is nearly impossible to get an accurate measure of 1 cup of flour in a liquid measure of any size (even 1 cup) because the top can't be leveled off. Dry ingredients, then, ought to be measured in "dry" cups.

Wet ingredients, on the other hand, ought to be measured in "wet" measuring cups. Measuring liquids in a dry measuring cup is a messy business. You must fill the cup right up to the rim, and spills are likely. It is also important for a wet measuring cup to be transparent. To get an accurate reading of an amount of liquid, you have to stoop down so that the measuring cup is at eye level.

CAN YOU FREEZE CHEESE?

I often buy cheese on sale when I go into town, but then I have to figure out how to use it all up before the cheese turns bad in the refrigerator. What happens if you put cheese in the freezer?

Marilyn Ackerman Mountain Lakes, New Jersey

To see how cheese fares when frozen, we bought blocks of cheddar, Parmesan, Camembert, and mozzarella and placed one of each in the freezer and one of each in the refrigerator. Two days later, we thawed them out, brought all samples to room temperature, and held a blind tasting. We tasted the cheeses raw and melted on toast.

Frozen cheddar and Parmesan were easily identifiable for their off flavors and disagreeable textures. The Parmesan was very dry, with a muted flavor. The cheddar was mealy and grainy, with a flavor several tasters described as "flat." Once melted, the textural differences were gone, but the flavor of the frozen cheeses was still duller than that of their refrigerated counterparts.

Surprisingly, few tasters were able to tell the difference between the frozen and refrigerated Camemberts. In fact, several tasters found the frozen Camembert to be creamier. When the cheese was melted, tasters could discern no textural or flavor differences. When we extended the freezing time to one month, we had similar results.

The cheese that froze the best was the mozzarella. (We tested a low-moisture, shrink-wrapped cheese from the supermarket; fresh mozzarella packed in water should not be frozen.) Tasters found both the frozen and the refrigerated samples to be virtually identical in terms of texture and flavor, whether tasted raw or melted. When we extended the freezing time to one month, we had the same results.

What to do, then, with your leftover cheese? For mozzarella and inexpensive Camembert, go ahead and throw it into the freezer (wrapped tightly in plastic wrap, of course). But store Parmesan and cheddar in the refrigerator. Parmesan should keep for a month or two if tightly wrapped. Cheddar won't last more than a few weeks.

A griddle that also defrosts frozen foods?

A QUICKER WAY TO DEFROST?

Have you seen the TV ad in which a woman defrosts chicken cutlets on a griddle in 20 minutes? If it works, it sure would make cooking dinner during the week a lot easier.

Joey Schipman Gillette, Wyoming

Advertisements for the Nathan Reversible Stovetop Grill & Griddle claim it can cook everything from pancakes to hot dogs. Made of "super high-conductive aluminum" (translation: cast aluminum), it is also supposed to double as a thawing tray. We decided to spend the necessary $20 to find out if it works as advertised.

According to the instruction manual, four 5-ounce frozen boneless chicken breasts should thaw on the tray in just 18 minutes. In our tests, four breasts needed 90 minutes. A single 5-ounce breast took close to an hour to thaw, and two ¾-inch-thick frozen pork chops took nearly two hours.

Cooking performance wasn't much better. The large rectangular griddle is designed to straddle two stovetop burners. The griddle could hold eight pancakes at a time, but the two hot spots directly above the two burners were quite evident. Eleven strips of bacon fit on the griddle, but the rendered fat spilled over its shallow sides before the bacon was crisp. There are certainly better griddles on the market, and you're better off using the microwave on very low power if you need to defrost something in a hurry.

MYSTERY TOOL

I ran across this item in my grandmother's kitchen, but no one seems to remember what it does. Any ideas?

Vickie Neilson New York, New York

Someone in your family probably liked soft-boiled eggs. Called an egg topper, this device is used to cut open the shell neatly and evenly. Just slip the larger hole over the tapered top of a soft-boiled egg

that is sitting in an egg cup. Then put your fingers in the two smaller holes and squeeze. Out will pop four small blades to pierce the shell and separate the top from the rest of the egg.

Kitchen Shortcuts

READERS SHARE CLEVER TIPS FOR EVERYDAY COOKING CHALLENGES

Why Didn't We Think of That?

Buttering Bread Made Easy

Use a Y-shaped peeler to remove slices of butter from the top of a rock-hard stick of butter that's come straight from the refrigerator. The peels can be laid on top of a slice of bread, so there's no need for spreading. That means no more clumps of butter and no more torn, soft bread.

Renee Chiang San Francisco, California

Save Your Knife Edge

After dicing or chopping something, it's common to scrape it across the cutting board into a bowl using the cutting edge of the blade. Unfortunately, this is a great way to dull your knife. To keep it sharp, flip the knife upside down and use the spine to scrape off the board.

Christopher Sadler Washington, D.C.

DOUBLE DUTY

Dishwashing Gloves to the Rescue

Instead of purchasing one of those round rubber jar openers, simply put on a rubber dishwashing glove to get a good grip on the lid of a hard-to-open jar.

Monica Swanson Daly City, California

Smart Thinking!

KEEPING POPCORN CRUNCHY

In our house, popcorn is the snack of choice for our 8- and 3-year-olds. Instead of putting the popcorn in a bowl where the steam can make it soggy, we serve ours in a plastic colander. The popcorn cools quickly (keeping little fingers safe) and stays crunchy longer.

Maria DeVita-Krug Newton, New Jersey

NO MORE SMELLY HANDS

Why spend $20 on a stainless steel bar that is supposed to remove the smell of garlic and onions from your hands? If you have a stainless steel sink, just rub your hands along the inside of the sink. If not, run your hands on a stainless faucet or wash your hands with a teaspoon.

Todd A. Byers Shoreline, Washington

SLICING ICEBOX COOKIES

When baking tons of cookies at Christmastime, I discovered that the easiest way to slice "slice-and-bake" cookies was to use a wire cheese slicer. The wire cuts right through the cold refrigerated cookie dough without distorting the round shape of the log, and the marble base of the slicer keeps the dough nice and cool.

Jeanette Rhile Cornelius, North Carolina

PEELING LARGE QUANTITIES OF GARLIC

To get a good start on peeling a whole head of garlic, I separate it into individual cloves and put the cloves in a Mason jar (or any container with a tight-fitting lid). Then I shake the Mason jar as hard as I can for about three minutes, making sure that the cloves really get banged around on the walls of the jar. Not only does this make it easier to peel the garlic, but it's a great workout for your arms.

Chieu Mai Richardson, Texas

RUBBER SPATULA FOR CLEANING

Keep a rubber spatula (a cheap one—don't waste your best heat-resistant spatula) by the sink. It's great for scraping out pots, pans, and dishes and for getting into the corners of jars and Tupperware. You don't have to worry about scratching your kitchenware, and food doesn't stick to a spatula the way it sticks to a sponge.

Pia Owens Watertown, Massachusetts

NO MORE BURNT HANDS

Some of my recipes call for browning meat in a pan and then putting the pan in the oven to let the meat finish cooking. Whenever I use a pan with a long handle, the same problem occurs: When the meat is finished cooking, I almost always forget the handle is extremely hot and I end up touching it as I finish the meal preparations. As a solution, whenever I take the pan out, I put an oven mitt over the handle. No more burnt hands for me—or anyone else who happens to be in the kitchen.

Hana Zalzal North York, Ontario

KEEPING HERBS IN THE KITCHEN

I plant several kinds of kitchen herbs—such as thyme, oregano, basil, cilantro, rosemary, and dill—in the openings of a strawberry pot and keep it in or near the kitchen. This saves money on fresh herbs and also frees up space in my tiny garden for veggies.

Nathan Keeney San Luis Obispo, California

SWEET-SMELLING DRAIN

Manufacturers recommend that you clean coffee makers with straight vinegar every six months or so. I hated the idea of pouring all of that vinegar down the drain until I discovered that by putting a heaping spoonful of baking soda in my drain first, I could also clean the drain. Let the vinegar and soda sit while you run clean water through the coffee maker, then pour the hot water down the drain. Keeps things fresh and clear!

Elona Cabrera Wichita, Kansas

EASIER SLICING IN A SPRINGFORM PAN

When baking cheesecake in a springform pan, I turn the pan bottom upside down, so that the lip faces downward. This makes it easier to remove the entire cake or even just a slice because the cake server can be slid under the cake without interference from the lip.

Richard Natale Palm Harbor, Florida

If you'd like to submit a tip, please send a letter to Kitchen Shortcuts, Cook's Country, P.O. Box 470739, Brookline, MA 02447, or send an e-mail to shortcuts@bcpress.com. Include your name, address, and phone number. If we publish your tip, you will receive a one-year subscription to *Cook's Country*.

COOL PEANUT BUTTER TRICK

After stirring in the oil on top of the jar, we store natural peanut butter in the refrigerator, where it promptly gets very hard and difficult to spread. We soften it by heating the jar in the microwave for 15 to 30 seconds. When we refrigerate it again, the peanut butter left in the jar does not harden for several days and spreads evenly—even when cold. I'm not sure why this works, but it does.

Ann Renthal
San Antonio, Texas

A GOOD USE FOR DISPOSABLE GLOVES

Prepping uncooked chicken can be difficult with very young children at home. I do the job wearing disposable gloves (available at the dollar store), which can be peeled off in an instant if my toddler needs attention.

S. Hansen
New York, New York

NAIL FILE IN THE KITCHEN

Why ruin a perfectly manicured nail to tear open those pesky plastic packages when a good old-fashioned nail file will do the trick? I keep one handy in the kitchen to break the plastic collars used to seal jar and bottle lids and to puncture the wrapping on packaged supermarket meats. The tip of a metal nail file is even strong enough to pry under jar lids and break the vacuum seal. It's also a neat way to remove the plastic shaker lids from spice jars. And while you're waiting for water to boil, you can always use the file to clean those tiny grooves around the sink and the stovetop that collect gunk. Just wash the file when you're done.

Sandy Mason
White Plains, New York

MIXING MEATLOAF

A potato masher is a natural for incorporating the filler ingredients for meatloaf into the meat. It's a lot easier on your hands, and the masher does a better job anyway. It's also good for breaking up hamburger for chili, tacos, or Sloppy Joes. The masher gets rid of lumps and makes for a more consistent texture.

Ken Weis
Chanhassen, Minnesota

SAVING EXTRA TOMATO PASTE

When I open a new can of tomato paste and use just a small amount, I open the other end of the can (the bottom), discard the bottom, pop the entire can into a plastic sandwich bag, and freeze it overnight. The next day, I remove the can from the bag and run it under hot water for a few seconds, then push the block of frozen tomato paste onto a cutting board. I cut the frozen block quickly into ¼-inch rounds, each of which equals roughly 1 tablespoon of paste. I then put all of the rounds back into the same plastic bag and toss it into the freezer for ready-to-use portions of tomato paste. I can't tell you how many cans of dried-out (or moldy) tomato paste I threw away before I thought of this tip!

Cathy Brenman
San Mateo, California

HOMEMADE FLAVORED CREAM CHEESE

I like making my own flavored cream cheeses. I buy a small tub of softened cream cheese (not the air-puffed stuff), chop up my ingredients (smoked salmon and dried dill, or chives and sun-dried tomatoes), and "cut" them into the lump of cream cheese on a cutting board using two butter or table knives. This saves me the trouble of cleaning out my food processor, and I can make as little or as much as I need and store the rest back in the plastic tub.

Nathan Keeney
San Luis Obispo, California

STORING CHEESE GRATERS

After receiving two flat, rasp-style graters as a gift, I was at a loss as to how to safely store them in my cluttered kitchen tools drawer. Taking a hot pan of lasagna out of the oven gave me an idea. I now keep a pair of the plastic-framed graters (the short squat ones, not the long metal ones) in a square, pocket-style potholder. Just slide them into the pocket, fold the potholder in half, and secure with a rubber band.

Allison Anthony
Pottersville, New Jersey

An Inspired Idea!
CRUSHING TOMATOES NEATLY

Most brands of canned crushed tomatoes contain a fair amount of tomato skin that can detract from (if not ruin) certain dishes. Canned whole tomatoes don't have skins, but when I try to crush them at home with my hands, the juice squirts out every which way from between my fingers and makes a major mess, no matter how deep the bowl or pot. My personal best was an arcing, 8- to 9-foot, right-to-left squirt that sprayed the kitchen window, one whole section of cupboards, and my wife. One way around this, I discovered, is to put the whole tomatoes in a plastic bag (the kind available in the produce section). I then put my right hand in the bag, closing it around my right wrist with my left hand, and crush away, with no fear of making a mess.

Bob Seavers Severn, Maryland

A Cute Idea!
Pancakes for Kids

My young daughter and her friends love to have their initials baked into pancakes. After several disastrous attempts at trying to write by dripping the batter off the end of a spoon, I've found that the easiest way to write a legible initial is to use a plastic syringe-type medicine doser. I draw the batter directly up the barrel and, by slowly depressing the plunger with my thumb, have perfect control when spelling the initials in the pan.

Mark Garvey Concord, Massachusetts

Adding Eggs to Batter

To add several eggs to a batter "one at a time, mixing each egg in thoroughly before adding the next," I break all of the eggs into a measuring cup that has a spout. When I turn on the mixer, I can slowly pour in one egg at a time.

Cathy Brenman
San Mateo, California

A Better Way to Chop Chocolate

Instead of using a knife to chop chocolate before melting it, here's what I do: Hold the wrapped chocolate bar against the side of the counter. Working up the length of the bar, press the chocolate against the countertop. When you're done, the whole bar will be broken into smallish pieces that are perfect for melting—and there's no cleanup.

Kristin Miles
New York, New York

LESS MESS

No More Crumbled Brownies

To make sure brownies come out of the pan neatly, press a large piece of foil into the baking pan, fitting the foil neatly (and squarely) into the corners of the pan. Press the overhanging foil around the exterior of the pan. Grease the foil with cooking spray. Once the brownies have cooled completely, use the foil to move the brownies from the pan to a cutting board.

Kurt Kruger Lenox, Massachusetts

We love potato casseroles, and, evidently, so do you. We received recipes from 152 of you. After weeks of casserole making, everyone in the test kitchen finally agreed on five favorites, including our grand prize–winning recipe from Christine Puccia, who will receive $500. Congratulations to Christine, and thank you to everyone who sent us a recipe.

Our next recipe contest is picnic salads. Please send your entries to us by October 15, 2004. You can reach us at Recipe Contest, Cook's Country, P.O. Box 470739, Brookline, MA 02447; or e-mail your recipe to recipecontest@bcpress.com. Either way, please make sure to include your name, address, and daytime phone number, and tell us what makes your recipe special. The grand prize winner will receive $500. All entries become the property of *Cook's Country*. We look forward to reading (and tasting) your recipes.

Italian Potato Cake

Our Grand Prize Winner!

Christine Puccia West Roxbury, Massachusetts

Christine writes: "I stayed with relatives in Patti, which is in the province of Messina, Sicily, in the summer of 1971. My cousin Nunziata appeared to be making a cake one day. 'It's not cake,' she said to me. It was potatoes!"

Everyone in the test kitchen loved the crisp exterior and delicate interior of this soufflé-like potato casserole that's made with mashed potatoes that have been enriched with eggs. The salami and cheese in the middle make this recipe a real treat.

ITALIAN POTATO CAKE SERVES 10 TO 12

Cut the casserole into wedges and serve with a holiday dinner or brunch.

5	tablespoons unsalted butter, plus extra for greasing pan
5	tablespoons plain bread crumbs
3	pounds russet potatoes (about 6 medium), peeled and cut into 1-inch pieces
½	cup heavy cream
1	teaspoon salt
¼	teaspoon pepper
3	large eggs
6	ounces Italian fontina cheese, sliced thin
¼	pound thinly sliced salami, cut into ½-inch pieces
⅓	cup grated Parmesan or Romano cheese

1. Adjust oven rack to middle position and heat oven to 350 degrees. Butter 9-inch springform pan and sprinkle with ¼ cup bread crumbs, shaking pan to distribute crumbs evenly.

2. Place potatoes in large pot and add enough cold water to cover by 1 inch. Bring potatoes to boil over high heat, then lower heat to maintain gentle simmer. Cook until potatoes are tender, about 15 minutes. Drain potatoes, wipe pot dry, return potatoes to pot, and mash with 4 tablespoons butter until smooth. Stir in cream, salt, and pepper. Cool 5 minutes. Stir in eggs, one at a time.

3. Spoon half of potato mixture into prepared pan. Place slices of fontina over potatoes to cover surface and top cheese with salami pieces. Cover with remaining potatoes. Melt remaining 1 tablespoon butter and mix with remaining 1 tablespoon bread crumbs and Parmesan in small bowl. Sprinkle cheese mixture over top of casserole.

4. Bake until casserole is very hot and puffed and top is golden brown, 35 to 45 minutes. Run paring knife around casserole to loosen. Cool for 10 minutes before unmolding. Serve hot.

Our Runners-Up

 Jone Baley
Roslindale, Massachusetts
CREAMY POTATO CASSEROLE
SERVES 8 TO 10

This casserole is perfect with roast beef.

2½	pounds russet potatoes (about 5 medium), scrubbed, skins left on
1	cup heavy cream
1	cup low-sodium chicken broth
4	medium garlic cloves, minced
4	tablespoons unsalted butter
¾	cup grated Parmesan cheese
¾	teaspoon salt
½	teaspoon pepper
1½	cups shredded sharp cheddar cheese

1. Adjust oven rack to middle position and heat oven to 350 degrees.

2. Place potatoes in large pot and add enough cold water to cover by 2 inches. Bring potatoes to boil over high heat, then lower heat to maintain gentle simmer. Cook until potatoes are just barely tender, 15 to 17 minutes. Drain potatoes. When cool enough to handle (5 to 8 minutes), peel potatoes with paring knife. Shred potatoes using shredding attachment of food processor or large holes on box grater. Place shredded potatoes in large bowl and set aside.

3. Bring cream and broth to simmer in small saucepan. Remove pan from heat and stir in garlic, butter, and Parmesan. Pour cream mixture into bowl with potatoes and stir to combine. Stir in salt and pepper. Scrape potato mixture into 2-quart oval baking dish and sprinkle with cheddar.

4. Cover baking dish with foil and bake for 30 minutes. Uncover and continue cooking until top is nicely browned, 20 to 25 minutes. Cool for 10 minutes before serving.

 Lillian Julow
Gainesville, Florida
ALSATIAN POTATO CASSEROLE
SERVES 6

This French casserole is relatively light, having no cream and very little butter.

1	tablespoon unsalted butter, cut into bits, plus extra for greasing pie plate
2½	pounds russet potatoes (about 5 medium), peeled and cut into ¼-inch-thick rounds Salt
8	slices bacon, chopped
1½	pounds onions (about 5 medium), halved and sliced thin

2 medium garlic cloves, minced
  Pepper
2 cups shredded Gruyère or
  Swiss cheese
½ cup low-sodium chicken broth

1. Adjust oven rack to middle position and heat oven to 400 degrees. Lightly butter 9½-inch deep-dish pie plate.

2. Place potatoes in large pot and add enough water to cover by 1 inch. Add salt to taste. Bring potatoes to boil over high heat, then lower heat to maintain gentle simmer. Cook until potatoes are barely tender but still firm, about 7 minutes. Be careful not to overcook potatoes; they should still hold their shape nicely. Drain.

3. Meanwhile, fry bacon in large skillet over medium heat until crisp, about 10 minutes. Use slotted spoon to transfer bacon to plate lined with paper towels and drain well. Discard all but 2 tablespoons bacon fat in pan. Add onions to skillet and cook over medium-high heat, stirring occasionally, until onions wilt and begin to brown, about 7 minutes. Reduce heat to low and continue to cook until onions are very soft and brown, 25 to 30 minutes. Stir in garlic and remove pan from heat.

4. Cover bottom of prepared pie plate with single layer of potato slices and then sprinkle with salt and pepper to taste. Spread half of onions over potatoes, followed by one-third of bacon and one-third of cheese. Arrange second layer in same manner, seasoning with salt and pepper and topping with remaining onions and half of remaining bacon and cheese. Cover with remaining potatoes, arranging slices slightly overlapping around outside of pan and then filling in open spaces with remaining potato slices. Sprinkle with bits of butter, remaining bacon, and salt and pepper to taste. Pour broth over casserole and sprinkle with remaining cheese.

5. Cover pie plate with foil and bake for 30 minutes. Uncover and continue to bake until cheese has melted and top is golden brown, about 15 minutes.

Alsatian Potato Casserole

Cool for 10 minutes before serving. To serve, cut straight down through all layers into wedges.

3rd **Alice Davis**
Omaha, Nebraska
MASHED POTATO AND HERBED CHEESE BAKE
SERVES 8
Boursin cheese spread, which is flavored with garlic and herbs, is the secret ingredient in this recipe. The casserole can be prepared a day in advance, refrigerated, and then baked, increasing the cooking time by 5 to 10 minutes.

4 tablespoons unsalted butter, plus extra for greasing baking dish
3 pounds russet potatoes (about 6 medium), peeled and cut into 1-inch chunks
2 (5-ounce) packages Boursin cheese spread
½ cup milk
¾ teaspoon salt
¼ teaspoon pepper
3 tablespoons plain bread crumbs
3 tablespoons grated Parmesan cheese

1. Adjust oven rack to middle position and heat oven to 350 degrees. Butter 8-inch-square baking dish.

2. Place potatoes in large pot and add enough water to cover by 1 inch. Bring potatoes to boil over high heat, then lower heat to maintain gentle simmer. Cook until potatoes are tender, about 15 minutes. Drain potatoes, wipe pot dry, put potatoes back into pot, and mash with cheese spread, milk, and 3 tablespoons butter until smooth. Stir

Creamy Potato Casserole

in salt and pepper. Spoon potatoes into prepared pan.

3. Melt remaining tablespoon of butter and toss with bread crumbs and Parmesan in small bowl. Sprinkle bread crumb mixture over casserole. Bake until casserole is very hot and top is golden brown, about 45 minutes. Cool for 10 minutes before serving.

4th **Lynn Zuccarelli Austin**
Brentwood, New Hampshire
POTATO, SPINACH, AND SAUSAGE CASSEROLE SERVES 8
This hearty casserole works with several kinds of sausage, including Italian (sweet or hot), kielbasa, or chorizo. It's really more of a main dish than a side dish.

3 tablespoons unsalted butter, plus extra for greasing baking dish
4 teaspoons olive oil
1 (16-ounce) bag fresh spinach, washed, dried, and stemmed
1 pound sausage, links cut in half lengthwise and then crosswise into ¼-inch-thick pieces
2 large red onions, halved and sliced thin
1 medium garlic clove, minced
3 pounds russet potatoes (about 6 medium), peeled and cut into 1-inch chunks

½ cup heavy cream
¼ cup low-sodium chicken broth
2 tablespoons cider vinegar
⅛ teaspoon nutmeg
¾ teaspoon salt
½ teaspoon pepper
2 cups shredded Gruyère or Swiss cheese

1. Adjust oven rack to middle position and heat oven to 400 degrees. Butter 13 by 9-inch baking dish.

2. Heat 2 teaspoons oil in large skillet over medium-high heat until shimmering. Add spinach and cook, stirring often, until wilted, about 3 minutes. Transfer spinach to strainer and drain. When cool, squeeze out liquid and roughly chop spinach.

3. Wipe skillet clean. Add sausage to skillet and cook over medium-high heat until browned, 5 to 6 minutes. Use slotted spoon to transfer sausage to bowl. Wipe skillet clean. Heat remaining 2 teaspoons oil in skillet. Add onions and cook until golden, about 5 minutes. Add garlic and cook until fragrant, about 1 minute. Scrape mixture into bowl with sausage.

4. Meanwhile, place potatoes in large pot and add enough water to cover by 1 inch. Bring potatoes to boil over high heat, then lower heat to maintain gentle simmer. Cook until potatoes are tender, about 15 minutes. Drain potatoes, wipe pot dry, put potatoes back into pot, and mash with butter, cream, broth, vinegar, nutmeg, salt, and pepper. Stir in spinach and 1 cup cheese.

5. Transfer potato-spinach mixture to prepared baking dish. Top with sausage-onion mixture and sprinkle with remaining 1 cup cheese. Bake until potatoes are very hot and cheese is golden and bubbly, 20 to 25 minutes. Cool for 10 minutes before serving.

OUR RUNNERS-UP FROM LEFT: Jone Baley, Lillian Julow, Alice Davis, and Lynn Zuccarelli Austin.

Mashed Potato and Herbed Cheese Bake

Potato, Spinach, and Sausage Casserole

Recipe Makeover CHOCOLATE PUDDING

Dear Cook's Country,
I love chocolate pudding but hate the fat and calories. I've tried different low-fat versions and found that they really aren't worth eating. Can I make a low-fat pudding that's the real thing—thick, rich, smooth, and chocolatey?

Hilary Tyler, Knoxville, Tennessee

Dear Hilary,
In the test kitchen, we'd much rather have a small portion of something very good (and very rich) than a full-size portion of something not very good (but low in fat). This theory just doesn't work with pudding, though. You might be able to eat just one or two cookies, but you can't (at least we can't) eat just two spoonfuls of pudding. With that in mind, I set out to discover how to arrive at rich chocolate flavor and creamy texture while reducing the fat as much as I possibly could.

All right, so where's the fat? The first place I looked was the chocolate itself since it contains a lot of cocoa butter. Cocoa powder, however, has very little fat, so I thought that the powder would make a good substitute. It turns out that I was only partially correct. Some of the chocolate had to stay to provide the kind of rich flavor that my tasters were looking for. (Low-fat chocolate pudding that tastes like hospital food wasn't going to cut it.) Next, I looked to the sugar to save calories. Not possible: The pudding had to be sweet, and the test kitchen has a permanent ban on artificial sweeteners. Finally, cutting back on the fat in the dairy component of the pudding seemed like a good idea. Before I did

that, however, I wanted to choose the proper thickener.

My tasters quickly rejected a few of the "weird" thickeners used in other recipes, including evaporated milk, gelatin, and vanilla yogurt. Cornstarch was the clear winner of this round of testing, although many tasters complained that the pudding was on the gritty side. After much testing, I figured out a pretty good solution: Once the pudding comes to a boil, continue to simmer it for an additional two minutes. In this short amount of time, the starchy flavor and texture gets cooked off and you get a creamier pudding.

Now I could get back to testing the milk. Pudding made with skim milk required so much cornstarch that even prolonged cooking couldn't remove all of its chalkiness. (I would rather eat an apple than bad chocolate pudding.) To use less cornstarch, I needed richer milk. Although 1 percent milk didn't work, 2 percent milk was pretty good. But my tasters really went for the whole milk version. If you want to count every single calorie, the 2 percent milk is fine, but my tasters and I agreed that the gain in flavor and texture that you get with whole milk is well worth the very few—just 19—extra calories. (See the box, above right, for a complete count of calories and fat in the regular and low-fat recipes.)

Most recipes just throw chopped chocolate into the hot pudding mixture once it comes off the heat (to melt it). This technique was effective, but I could still detect a bit of graininess. On a whim, I tried adding melted chocolate at the beginning—with the cocoa, sugar, and milk—thereby subjecting it to a more strenuous heating and whisking process. This pudding was especially creamy and smooth. Much to my surprise, it also tasted better. Tasters commented that the chocolate flavor was enhanced. "Cooking" the chocolate had intensified its flavor!

The answer to your question, then, is yes, you can make a creamy, chocolatey pudding that has a lot fewer calories—half as many, in fact—than the traditional recipe we usually make in our test kitchen. Is it as good as the real thing? No. But I have to admit that it's a more than respectable second.

–Nina West

LOW-FAT CHOCOLATE PUDDING SERVES 4
To reduce fat and calories further, substitute 2 percent milk for the whole milk; the pudding will have a slightly looser consistency. Don't use 1 percent or skim milk; in our opinion, the pudding won't be worth eating. Once the pudding comes to a boil, make sure to simmer it for a full 2 minutes to cook out the flavor of the cornstarch. To learn more about cocoa powder, see page 29.

- 2 ounces bittersweet chocolate, chopped
- 2 tablespoons cocoa, preferably Dutched
- 2½ tablespoons cornstarch
- ½ cup sugar
- ⅛ teaspoon salt
- 2½ cups whole milk
- 2 teaspoons vanilla extract

1. Melt chocolate over double boiler or in microwave. Cool slightly.

2. Whisk together cocoa powder, cornstarch, sugar, and salt in heavy-bottomed medium saucepan. Add milk all at once and whisk to incorporate. Whisk in melted chocolate.

3. Bring mixture to boil over medium heat, whisking until smooth. Once boiling, reduce heat to low and cook, stirring constantly with heatproof rubber spatula or wooden spoon and making sure to scrape edges of pan, for 2 minutes. (Mixture will become thick and glossy.)

4. Remove pan from heat and stir in vanilla. Pour pudding through fine-mesh strainer and into heatproof bowl, pushing gently with spatula or spoon and leaving any solids in strainer. Place plastic wrap directly on surface of pudding to prevent skin from forming. Refrigerate for 4 hours or until completely chilled. (Pudding will keep for up to 2 days.) Gently stir pudding before transferring to individual bowls and serving.

And the Numbers...
How does our low-fat version stack up against most traditional chocolate pudding recipes? The taste may be similar, but the calorie and fat counts are not. Switching from whole milk to 2 percent milk would trim another 19 calories and 2 grams of fat from our recipe. All numbers are for one serving.

TRADITIONAL HOMEMADE Chocolate Pudding
CALORIES: **581**
FAT: **34 g**
CHOLESTEROL: **202 mg**

COOK'S COUNTRY Low-Fat Chocolate Pudding
CALORIES: **286**
FAT: **13 g**
CHOLESTEROL: **21 mg**

Fun Flavors
Use ingredients you probably have around the kitchen to give chocolate pudding new flavors. Here are two favorites in the test kitchen.

MEXICAN CHOCOLATE PUDDING
Prepare Low-Fat Chocolate Pudding, whisking in 2 teaspoons espresso powder or instant coffee and ½ teaspoon ground cinnamon with other dry ingredients in step 2.

ORANGE-KISSED CHOCOLATE PUDDING
Use vegetable peeler to remove zest (colored skin) from 1 large orange. Prepare Low-Fat Chocolate Pudding, adding strips of orange peel to pan with other ingredients at end of step 2. Proceed as directed, reducing vanilla to 1 teaspoon and adding 1 teaspoon orange liqueur (such as Triple Sec or Grand Marnier) with vanilla.

How to Make
SEA FOAM CANDY

Dear Cook's Country,
When I was a child, we used to visit relatives in Georgia, and I remember eating this sweet, sticky confection called sea foam. It was chewy and filled with pecans. I've never seen a recipe for this candy.
Katherine Pizzarello, New York, New York

Dear Katherine,
No one in the test kitchen had ever heard of sea foam candy, and the first recipes we tried weren't exactly flying off the counter. All were achingly sweet and many were pasty and dense. One batch resembled Spackle—surely memorable but probably not what you had in mind. From our research, we gathered that sea foam should be a light, airy confection that resembles the ocean foam for which it is named. The texture should be similar to meringue, yet softer, with a distinct chew. Clearly, we needed to do some work.

Sea foam is related to divinity candy; the difference is that divinity contains all white sugar, whereas sea foam contains some brown sugar. These candies became popular after the introduction in 1902 of Karo corn syrup—a key ingredient in both divinity and sea foam. We found a recipe for sea foam candy in the original 1931 edition of *Joy of Cooking* and in other cookbooks of this time, but sea foam has all but disappeared from modern cookbooks. We started with these older recipes, most of which feature a base of stiffly beaten egg whites, into which some form of cooked sugar syrup is whipped.

Our first goal was to determine the best ratio of white to brown sugar. Tasters preferred the batch made with roughly half white and half light brown sugar for its even sweetness and rich flavor. Next we went to work on the texture, which had to strike a fine balance between fluffy, creamy, and chewy. We discovered that the corn syrup provided the right chew: Too little corn syrup and the sea foam was too fluffy; too much and the sea foam was dense and puttylike. A total of 3¼ cups sugar and 1 cup corn syrup gave our candies an ideal texture.

Our sea foam was pretty good, but still awfully sweet. We tried adding ingredients to offset the sweetness and found that vinegar, a traditional ingredient included in many older recipes, did the trick; just 1½ teaspoons cut the sweetness without adding a sour bite. A large pinch of salt also helped tame the outrageous sweetness.

In terms of flavor, nuts are the real star in this confection. Toasting the pecans enhances their flavor and is a must-do step. We tried rolling the puffs of sea foam in chopped nuts; this was awkward and the candies looked awful. A single pecan placed atop each piece of sea foam looked best but provided little flavor. Our solution was simple enough. We mixed a lot of chopped nuts into the sea foam before it was shaped and then crowned each candy with a single pecan half.

Early in our recipe testing, most test cooks scattered at the notion of tasting these supersweet candies. With our final version, however, it was the sea foam candies, not the test cooks, that disappeared rapidly from the kitchen.
–Erin McMurrer and Tomer Gurantz

SEA FOAM CANDY

MAKES ABOUT 3 DOZEN 2-INCH CANDIES
You'll need two pieces of equipment to make this confection: a standing mixer and an instant-read thermometer that can read high temperatures. (A candy thermometer is ideal.) These candies must be prepared on a dry day or in a dry, cool environment; they will not set up properly in hot or humid conditions.

3	cups (12 ounces) pecan halves
¾	cup water
1¾	cups granulated sugar
1½	cups packed light brown sugar
1	cup light corn syrup
3	large egg whites
⅛	teaspoon salt
1	teaspoon vanilla extract
1½	teaspoons distilled white vinegar

1. Adjust oven rack to middle position; heat oven to 350 degrees. Spread nuts in single layer on rimmed baking sheet. Toast nuts until fragrant and lightly browned, 10 to 12 minutes, stirring once or twice. Cool nuts to room temperature. Select 40 pecan halves for garnish and set aside; coarsely chop remaining nuts. Place chopped nuts in mesh strainer and shake to remove dust; set chopped nuts aside. Line 2 baking sheets with waxed or parchment paper; set aside.

2. Pour water into 2- to 3-quart heavy-bottomed saucepan; add sugars and corn syrup to center of saucepan, taking care to keep sugar granules from coating sides of pot. Bring to boil over high heat without stirring; reduce heat to medium and cook, without stirring, until syrup registers 255 degrees on instant-read or candy thermometer, about 14 minutes.

3. After reducing heat under sugar syrup, fit standing mixer with whisk attachment and beat egg whites at high speed until mixture forms stiff peaks when whisk is lifted, about 60 seconds; turn off mixer. When sugar syrup is ready and with mixer set at medium speed, pour syrup in slow, steady stream into egg whites; add salt. Increase speed to high and continue beating until mixture loses its sheen and holds medium-stiff peaks when whisk is lifted, 15 to 25 minutes. (Begin checking as soon as thin threads of mixture start to pull away from sides of bowl; see "When Is It Done?" below.) Add vanilla, vinegar, and chopped nuts; beat on medium speed until just combined, about 10 seconds.

4. Working quickly, drop rounded tablespoons of mixture (or use 1¾-inch spring-loaded ice cream scoop) onto prepared baking sheets. Garnish each round with pecan half, pressing gently to adhere. Let stand at room temperature until firm, 2 to 4 hours. Peel candies off paper and transfer to airtight container, sliding fresh sheets of waxed or parchment paper between layers of candies. Sea foam will keep for up to 1 week.

Looking for a lost recipe? We can help. Drop us a note and tell us about the recipe you want to find. Write to Lost Recipes, Cook's Country, P.O. Box 470739, Brookline, MA 02447. Or e-mail us at lostrecipes@bcpress.com.

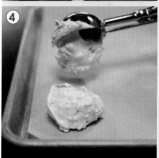

1. Shake chopped nuts in a strainer to remove any dust. **2.** Heat the sugar syrup to 255 degrees. **3.** Pour the hot syrup into the bowl with the whipped egg whites and continue beating. **4.** Form into individual candies and press 1 pecan half into each.

When Is It Done?
The egg white/sugar syrup mixture goes from underbeaten to overbeaten in just a minute or two. When you think you might be close, stop the mixer and lift the whisk to judge the texture. When underbeaten, the mixture will look like molten lava and any peaks will sink slowly back into the bowl. When properly beaten, the mixture will hold medium-stiff peaks and look smooth. If you keep beating the mixture, it will become stiffer and start to look rough.

very good!

Dear Cook's Country,
My family and I love pot roast with gravy, and I'd like to be able to make it in my slow cooker. After many attempts, I have yet to find a recipe that I really like. The meat is usually too dry, and the "gravy" doesn't have much flavor. Worst of all, the roast shrinks to nothing by the time I get home from work. What am I doing wrong?
Loretta Hunt, Kalamazoo, Michigan

Dear Loretta,
The first thing I did was to make a pot roast at home in my own slow cooker and let it cook while I was at work. Guess what? The gravy had no flavor, and the meat had shrunk so much that it might have fed just two people. You were right!

My next step was to bring the recipe into the test kitchen to see what we could come up with. Most of the pot roast recipes I looked at suggested using cuts from the bottom round or top sirloin. Past experience in the test kitchen told me that these cuts would have too little fat and too little flavor, and retesting them only confirmed this point. For best results, I found that a boneless chuck roast is a much better choice. When slow-cooked, it becomes super-tender and tasty.

Most recipes call for a 3½- to 4-pound roast. After cooking close to 100 pounds of pot roast, I found that each hunk of beef lost an average of

2 pounds. If you start with a roast that's only 3½ pounds, well . . . you get the picture. You don't want your family asking, "Where's the beef?"

I had much better luck when I tried a large 5½- to 6-pound roast. The slow cooker was nearly filled to the brim (you must use a slow cooker with a capacity of at least 6 quarts; see page 31 for recommendations), but after a day of cooking there was something substantial left for dinner. At some markets, you will have to special-order a roast this big. If that seems like too much bother, two small roasts (each about 3 pounds) can be used. Either way, this much meat needs six to seven hours on high or nine to 10 hours on low to become tender. The latter regimen is perfect if you want to get dinner going in the morning.

Next I tackled the gravy. To minimize kitchen time, many slow-cooker recipes add ingredients to the pot uncooked. This sure is easy, but you end up with bland gravy. I decided to first brown the meat and vegetables in a skillet to develop some flavor. A slow cooker traps moisture and tends to dilute whatever you are cooking, so you need a strong start for a flavorful finish. To save time in the morning, I found that I could brown the meat and vegetables the night before and refrigerate them overnight.

Adding red wine, broth (not water), tomatoes, and herbs to the base I had created in the skillet gave me a flavorful gravy. But the consistency was too thin. I wanted a gravy that would coat the meat and fill the well in mashed potatoes.

To get that good gravy, when the meat was done, I strained the cooking liquid, discarded the vegetables, and thickened the juices with a mixture of flour and water. This method gave me the consistency I was looking for, but it had two drawbacks. The lumps had to be strained out (I hate lumpy gravy!), and the gravy had to cook over high heat for 30 minutes.

One test cook, bothered by the fact that I was throwing away all of the vegetables in the pot, suggested pureeing them along with the broth. Sure enough, I found this to be both

an economical and a quick way to add substance to the gravy—no starch, no fuss. And if you have children who won't eat their vegetables, this is a good way to sneak them in.

–Diane Unger-Mahoney

COUNTRY-STYLE POT ROAST WITH GRAVY SERVES 6,
WITH ENOUGH LEFTOVERS TO MAKE BEEF BARLEY SOUP WITH MUSHROOMS
Boneless chuck roast is essential in this recipe—other cuts will cook up dry and tough. In most markets, you will have to order a large 5½- to 6-pound chuck roast. Alternatively, use two 3-pound roasts (which are common in most markets). If making Beef Barley Soup with Mushrooms (see recipe on page 11), reserve 6 cups of gravy and 3 cups of meat.

1	large boneless beef chuck roast (5½–6 pounds), tied
	Salt and pepper
4	teaspoons vegetable oil
3	medium onions, chopped
1	large celery rib, chopped
4	medium carrots, chopped
6	medium garlic cloves, minced
1	cup red wine
1	(28-ounce) can crushed tomatoes
2	cups low-sodium chicken broth
½	teaspoon hot red pepper flakes
3	bay leaves
1	teaspoon dried thyme
2	tablespoons chopped fresh parsley

1. Season roast liberally with salt and pepper. Heat 2 teaspoons oil in 12-inch skillet over medium-high heat until shimmering but not smoking. Brown roast thoroughly on all sides, 8 to 10 minutes. Transfer browned roast to slow-cooker insert.

2. Reduce heat to medium. Add remaining 2 teaspoons oil to empty skillet, along with onions, celery, carrots, and garlic. Cook, stirring occasionally, until lightly browned, about 4 minutes. Transfer to slow-cooker insert.

3. Increase heat to high. Add red wine to empty skillet, scraping up any browned bits with wooden spoon, and simmer for 5 minutes. Add tomatoes and broth and bring to boil. Add pepper flakes, bay leaves, and thyme and transfer to slow-cooker insert.

4. Set slow cooker to high, cover, and cook until tender, 6 to 7 hours. (Alternatively, cook on low for 9 to 10 hours.) Transfer roast to carving board; loosely tent with foil to keep warm. Discard bay leaves. Allow liquid in pot to settle, about 5 minutes, then use wide spoon to skim fat off surface (see page 29). Puree liquid and solids in batches in blender or food processor. (Alternatively, use immersion blender and process until smooth.) Stir in parsley and season to taste with salt and pepper.

5. Remove strings from roast and cut into ½-inch-thick slices. Transfer meat to warmed serving platter. Pour about 1 cup gravy over meat. Serve, passing more gravy separately.

Finding the Right Roast
Supermarkets sell dozens of cheap boneless roasts that could in theory be used for pot roast. The roasts fall into three broad categories—chuck roasts (from the shoulder), round roasts (from the leg), and sirloin roasts (from the hip). Here's what we found when we tried various roasts from each of these three parts of the cow.

Chuck Roast
Tender, beefy, rich flavor. The chuck-eye roast is our favorite, but any boneless chuck roast will work. If the butcher has not tied the roast, do this yourself.

Round Roast
Very dry and too chewy. This top round roast needs more fat. We also tested bottom round and eye of round roasts with little success.

Sirloin Roast
The leanest and least tasty choice. This top sirloin roast was very bland and tough. Bottom rump roast was no better.

Slow-Cooker 101: Pot Roast

Here are key points to remember when preparing pot roast in a slow cooker.

1. Start with a boneless chuck roast.
Buy one big or two small roasts—5½ to 6 pounds of meat in total. The meat shrinks a lot as it cooks, so if you want to serve something substantial, you must start with a lot of beef.

2. Brown the meat and vegetables for maximum flavor.
You can do this a day in advance. Prepare either of the recipes through step 3. Instead of transferring the meat, vegetables, and sauce ingredients to the slow cooker, refrigerate them. (Wrap the browned meat in plastic; the browned vegetables and liquid ingredients can be refrigerated together in a container.) In the morning, just transfer everything to the slow cooker. The cooking time will run to the high end of the ranges given in the recipes.

3. Trying to trim the fat from the family diet?
Make the recipe a day ahead. Transfer the roast and gravy to a large bowl and refrigerate overnight. The next day, you can easily remove the fat from the surface of the bowl. Take out the roast, then slice and transfer it to a microwave-safe casserole dish. Puree the gravy as directed, moisten the meat with gravy, and heat until warmed through. More gravy can be heated in a microwave-safe bowl and served on the side.

SOUTHWESTERN POT ROAST

SERVES 6, WITH ENOUGH LEFTOVERS TO MAKE BEEF TORTILLA CASSEROLE

Corn tortillas are used to thicken the gravy for this pot roast. Vary the heat by adjusting the amount of cayenne pepper. Serve with rice or egg noodles. In most markets, you will have to order a large 5½- to 6-pound chuck roast. Alternatively, use two 3-pound roasts (which are common in most markets). If making Beef Tortilla Casserole (see recipe at right), reserve 4½ cups of gravy and 4 cups of meat.

1	large boneless beef chuck roast (5½–6 pounds), tied
	Salt and pepper
4	teaspoons vegetable oil
2	medium onions, chopped
1	medium red bell pepper, chopped
4	medium jalapeño chiles, seeded and minced
8	medium garlic cloves, minced
1	(28-ounce) can crushed tomatoes
2¾	cups low-sodium chicken broth
3	tablespoons chili powder
2	tablespoons ground cumin
1–2	teaspoons cayenne pepper
1	teaspoon dried oregano
6	(6-inch) corn tortillas
2	tablespoons chopped fresh cilantro

1. Season roast liberally with salt and pepper. Heat 2 teaspoons oil in 12-inch skillet over medium-high heat until shimmering but not smoking. Brown roast thoroughly on all sides, 8 to 10 minutes. Transfer browned roast to slow-cooker insert.

2. Reduce heat to medium. Add remaining 2 teaspoons oil to empty skillet, along with onions, bell pepper, chiles, and garlic. Cook, stirring occasionally, until vegetables are lightly browned, about 4 minutes. Transfer vegetables to slow-cooker insert.

3. Increase heat to high. Add tomatoes and 2 cups broth to empty skillet, scraping up any brown bits with wooden spoon. Add chili powder, cumin, cayenne, and oregano and bring to boil. Transfer to slow-cooker insert.

4. Tear tortillas into small pieces and combine in medium microwave-safe bowl with remaining ¾ cup broth. Heat on high power until softened, about 2 minutes. Puree in food processor until smooth. Transfer to slow-cooker insert.

5. Set slow cooker to high, cover, and cook until tender, 6 to 7 hours. (Alternatively, cook on low for 9 to 10 hours.) Transfer roast to carving board; loosely tent with foil to keep warm. Allow liquid in pot to settle about 5 minutes, then use wide spoon to skim fat off surface (see page 29). Puree liquid and solids in batches in blender or food processor. (Alternatively, use immersion blender and process until smooth.) Stir in cilantro and season to taste with salt and pepper.

6. Remove strings from roast and cut into ½-inch-thick slices. Transfer meat to warmed serving platter. Pour about 1 cup gravy over meat. Serve, passing more gravy separately.

When we make pot roast in a slow cooker, we make a lot—enough for two big meals. Reheated pot roast is fine, but there is something about eating the same thing two nights in a row. Here's how to transform leftovers into very different dishes. Our Country-Style Pot Roast becomes a hearty soup with the addition of mushrooms and barley, and our Southwestern Pot Roast becomes the main ingredient in a layered tortilla casserole with pinto beans.

BEEF BARLEY SOUP WITH MUSHROOMS SERVES 6 TO 8

very good

Leftover gravy from the pot roast creates an intensely flavored broth for this soup.

2	teaspoons vegetable oil	2	quarts water
1	large carrot, chopped	⅔	cup pearl barley
10	ounces button mushrooms, sliced	3	cups shredded meat from
6	cups gravy from Country-Style		Country-Style Pot Roast
	Pot Roast		Salt and pepper

1. Heat oil in large stockpot or Dutch oven over medium heat. Add carrot and mushrooms and cook, stirring frequently, until liquid that mushrooms release evaporates, about 4 minutes.

2. Add gravy, water, and barley. Increase heat to high and bring to boil. Reduce heat and simmer, uncovered, until barley is tender, about 45 minutes. Stir in shredded meat and season with salt and pepper to taste. Serve.

BEEF TORTILLA CASSEROLE SERVES 8

This hearty Mexican casserole with beef, beans, tortillas, and cheese makes a complete meal. Just add a salad.

1½	cups shredded sharp cheddar cheese	4	cups meat from Southwestern Pot Roast, torn into 1½-inch chunks
1½	cups shredded Monterey Jack cheese	¼	cup lime juice from 2 limes
4½	cups leftover gravy from Southwestern Pot Roast	¼	cup chopped fresh cilantro
			Salt and pepper
2	(14½-ounce) cans pinto beans, drained and rinsed	18	(6-inch) corn tortillas
		1	cup sour cream
		½	cup chopped scallions

1. Adjust oven racks to upper and lower positions and heat oven to 300 degrees. Spray 13 by 9-inch baking dish with cooking spray. Mix cheeses together and set aside.

2. Bring gravy to boil in large saucepan over medium heat. Stir in pinto beans and meat and warm through. Remove pan from heat, add lime juice and cilantro, and season with salt and pepper to taste.

3. Place tortillas on two baking sheets (some overlapping is fine) and spray both sides of tortillas lightly with cooking spray. Bake until tortillas are very soft and pliable, about 5 minutes. Increase oven temperature to 450 degrees.

4. Spread one-third of beef mixture in greased baking dish. Layer 6 tortillas on top, overlapping as needed. Sprinkle with 1 cup cheese. Repeat to form second layer.

5. Cut remaining 6 tortillas into quarters. Spread remaining beef mixture in baking dish and cover with tortilla pieces. Cover with remaining 1 cup cheese.

6. Bake on bottom oven rack until cheese is golden brown and casserole is bubbling, about 15 minutes. Let rest 5 minutes. Cut casserole into individual portions and transfer to plates. Dollop a heaping tablespoon sour cream in center of each portion and sprinkle with scallions. Serve immediately.

Fun Food ICE CREAM DESSERTS

When was the last time you really had fun with your food? These recipes turn store-bought ice cream into four playful desserts. If you have young kids, these are perfect family projects. The kids will love to lick the bowls clean. And if there are no kids at home, the bowls are all yours.

Rainbow Sherbet Surprise

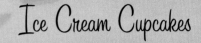

Ice Cream Cupcakes

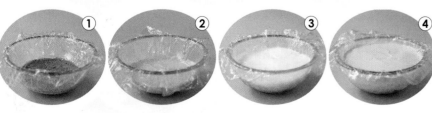

RAINBOW SHERBET SURPRISE

SERVES 8

Other flavors of colorful sherbet or sorbet can be substituted.

- 1 pint raspberry sherbet
- 1 pint orange sherbet
- 1 pint lemon sherbet
- 1 pint lime sherbet

1. First layer Line 2-quart bowl with plastic wrap so that wrap overhangs sides of bowl by at least 1 inch. Let raspberry sherbet stand on counter to soften for 5 minutes. Spoon sherbet into bowl, pressing it along bottom and sides of bowl so it forms smooth layer. Place bowl in freezer for 30 minutes to firm up sherbet.

2. Second layer Let orange sherbet stand on counter to soften for 5 min-utes. Use small spatula to smooth it over raspberry sherbet in even layer. Place bowl in freezer for 30 minutes to firm up orange sherbet.

3. Third layer Repeat process with lemon sherbet.

4. Last layer Let lime sherbet stand on counter to soften for 5 minutes. Spoon lime sherbet into bowl so that it comes to top. Smooth top and cover with plastic. Freeze for at least 6 hours, or until ready to serve, up to 1 week.

5. Unmold and serve Remove bowl from freezer and remove plastic from top. Gently tug at over-hanging plastic lining to loosen sher-bet. (If necessary, briefly dip bowl into hot water.) Place serving platter over bowl, invert bowl, and shake to release sherbet. Peel away plastic. Cut into wedges and serve.

ICE CREAM CUPCAKES

MAKES 12 CUPCAKES

Combination foil/paper cupcake liners (seen in photos) work best in this recipe. Use plain or Chocolate Whipped Cream.

- 1 (10- to 12-ounce) store-bought pound cake
- 4 tablespoons strawberry jam
- 2 pints strawberry ice cream
- 1 cup heavy cream, chilled
- 2 tablespoons sugar
- 1 teaspoon vanilla extract

1. Cut cake and spread jam Arrange 12 cupcake liners in 12-cup muffin tin. Cut pound cake into ½-inch-thick slices. Use 2-inch bis-cuit cutter to cut 12 circles. Reserve remaining pound cake and scraps for another use. Spread 1 teaspoon jam on top of each circle of pound cake. Place circles in cupcake liners.

2. Add ice cream Place nicely rounded scoop of ice cream on top of each pound cake circle. Cover muffin tin with plastic and place in freezer until ice cream is very firm, at least 2 hours and up to 2 days.

3. Frost with whipped cream Beat cream, sugar, and vanilla to soft peaks. Remove muffin tin from freezer and cover ice cream with whipped cream, leaving cakes in tin and spreading whipped cream to form sloped sides with peak.

4. Freeze and serve Return to freezer to allow to set overnight. Remove cupcakes from muffin tin and serve.

CHOCOLATE WHIPPED CREAM

MAKES ABOUT 2 CUPS

- 1 cup heavy cream, chilled
- 2 tablespoons sugar
- 2 tablespoons cocoa, sifted
- 1 teaspoon vanilla extract

Combine ingredients in medium bowl. Using electric mixer fitted with whisk attachment, beat, gradually increasing speed from low to high, until cream just holds stiff peaks. Do not overwhip. Whipped cream will keep, covered with plastic wrap and refrigerated, for up to 6 hours. Whisk whipped cream for a couple of sec-onds before using it.

ICE CREAM BONBONS

MAKES ABOUT 16, SERVING 4 TO 6

Small scoops of ice cream can easily be made to look like bonbons when dipped in melted chocolate. Dust some bonbons with nuts and others with flaked sweetened coconut for variety. The chocolate hardens very quickly, so sprinkle each bonbon with nuts or coconut as soon as it has been coated. Use any flavor ice cream without chunks or nuts. Vanilla, chocolate, and coffee are all good choices.

- 1 pint ice cream
- 12 ounces bittersweet chocolate
- 2 tablespoons vegetable oil
- 3 tablespoons finely chopped nuts
- 3 tablespoons flaked sweetened coconut

1. Scoop ice cream Line two large plates with parchment paper or waxed paper. Place plates in freezer for 15 minutes to chill. Use very small ice cream scoop to make about 16 balls, each with about 2 tablespoons of ice cream, and place them on two chilled plates. Lightly cover plates with plastic wrap and chill until ice cream is very firm, at least 1 hour.

2. Dip ice cream in chocolate Melt chocolate with oil and stir until smooth. Cool completely to room temperature. Remove one plate of ice cream from freezer and, working quickly, use two forks (one in each hand) to dip and roll one ice cream ball in chocolate to cover. Pick up ball by sliding it onto one fork, and let excess chocolate drip back into bowl. Return bonbon to lined plate.

3. Garnish bonbons If desired, immediately sprinkle bonbon with 1 teaspoon nuts or coconut. Repeat dipping and garnishing ice cream balls remaining on plate, one ball at a time. Return first plate to freezer. Remove second plate of ice cream balls from freezer and repeat process to make 8 more bonbons. Freeze bonbons until firm, at least 1 hour or up to 1 day, before serving.

COOKIES & CREAM ICE CREAM PIE

SERVES 6 TO 8

Ice cream pies are more fun (and taste great) when made with a sugar cone (rather than a conventional graham cracker) crust. Adding your own chopped cookies to ice cream allows you to customize the flavor combination. Try Oreos with mint chip ice cream or gingersnaps with peach ice cream.

- 12 sugar cones
- 5 tablespoons unsalted butter, melted
- 2 tablespoons sugar
- 2 pints ice cream, softened
- 2 cups coarsely chopped cookies
- 2 cups plain or Chocolate Whipped Cream (page 12)

1. Make crumbs Adjust oven rack to middle position and heat oven to 350 degrees. Grind sugar cones in food processor to fine crumbs. (You should have 1⅓ cups.)

2. Make crust Stir together crumbs, butter, and sugar in medium bowl until crumbs are moistened. Press crumb mixture evenly against bottom and sides of 9-inch pie plate, compacting it with your fingertips. Bake crust until crisp, 6 to 8 minutes. Let cool completely before filling. (Crust can be wrapped in plastic wrap and frozen for up to 1 month.)

3. Fill pie shell Place ice cream and cookies in bowl and mash mixture with back of spoon until well combined. Turn ice cream mixture into prepared crust and smooth top with spoon. Cover with plastic wrap and freeze until filling is completely frozen, at least 3 hours and up to 1 week.

4. Cut and garnish Cut pie into wedges and dollop each piece with whipped cream. Serve.

–Recipes by **Lauren Chattman**

Ice Cream Bonbons

Cookies & Cream Ice Cream Pie

Crispiest, Crunchiest Fried Chicken Ever

Dear Cook's Country,
My family loves the crunchy coating on fast-food fried chicken, but I think the chicken itself never tastes very good. I've always wanted to make fried chicken at home but have been daunted by the whole process—and the mess. Do you have a no-fuss recipe that produces crispy, crunchy fried chicken?

Mabel McKnight, Lufkin, Texas

Dear Mabel,
Most fast-food fried chicken is certainly crunchy. (Everyone in the test kitchen thinks the chicken from KFC is the crunchiest.) But you're right that the chicken itself, which is often bland and dry, usually plays second fiddle to the coating. With homemade fried chicken, there are two problems: The coating is too thin (or it peels off), and, as you say, the whole process of coating it and frying it makes a huge mess. We wanted just what you asked for: homemade, extra-crunchy fried chicken that doesn't turn your kitchen into a complete disaster area.

Most of my neighbors have given up on homemade fried chicken because it takes too long and is too messy. I wasn't going to be able to make this a simple 10-minute recipe, but I did want to streamline the process as much as possible. The first consideration was the coating. Here recipes fall into two camps: the single dip and the double dip. The former involves a dip in buttermilk and a dredge in flour before the chicken hits the hot oil. The latter adds two steps: a dip in egg wash followed by another dredge in flour. The double-dip method was just

too messy—so for the sake of the kitchen (and my sanity), the single dip seemed like the way to go.

Just plain flour didn't provide enough crunch, so I looked to other ingredients. Crushed Melba toast gave the chicken some crunch, but the crumbs browned too quickly and did not adhere to the chicken very well, leaving more coating in the oil than on the chicken. Cornmeal was another candi-date that didn't fare well. Its fine grains left the coating with a gritty sandiness that was hardly popular in the test kitchen.

I ran across several recipes that called for coating chicken

in store-bought pancake mix. While this idea raised several eyebrows, it seemed worth a shot. Although not perfect, this test was at least partially successful. Because the pancake mix contained baking powder, the coating was light and crisp. The only drawback was that the powder caused the coating to expand slightly, contract, and eventually flake off. I decided to come up with my own version of pancake mix—one with less baking powder. After testing a number of formulas, I found that a mixture of 3 cups flour and 2 teaspoons baking powder was just enough to lighten the crust, but not to the point where it would fall off the chicken.

During testing, a funny thing happened. I noticed that the coating on the pieces of chicken dredged last was thicker than the coating on those dredged first. What was going on? It seems that each time a piece was dredged, the flour absorbed some buttermilk from the chicken. By the time I got around to the last couple of pieces, the flour was almost sticky. This resulted in fried chicken with a crunchier, thicker coating. The obvious next test was to add the buttermilk straight to the flour. Instead of a dip in buttermilk and a dredge in flour, I simply dredged the chicken pieces in the combined mixture. Now I had a sturdy, crunchy coating that didn't fall off.

The next problem was dry, overcooked chicken. We often turn to brining (soaking meat or poultry in a saltwater solution) to solve this problem, but because we were using buttermilk anyway, I wondered if buttermilk would be better than water. Starting with 2 cups buttermilk and 2 tablespoons salt, I soaked the chicken pieces before coating them with the buttermilk/flour mixture. This chicken was not only juicy, it was also more flavorful than the chicken brined in salt water. I did find, however, that you could have too much of a good thing. It's important to take the chicken out of its buttermilk bath after an hour. The longer it sits, the saltier it gets.

The final issue was the mess. One common solution to this problem is to switch from the often-used skillet to a Dutch oven, which tends to keep the oil in the pot rather than let it splatter all over the stovetop. So far so good. I then wondered if covering the pot during some or all of the frying time would help contain the mess. After much testing (and lots of well-fed test cooks), it turned out that covering the pot during the first half of the frying time (before flipping the pieces) worked best. The oil recovered heat more quickly, there was less mess, and there was one other unexpected benefit: The cover trapped steam, which made the chicken more moist. (We found it interesting that the frying oil never gets completely back up to temperature. It starts at 375 degrees, but most of the frying is done between 300 and 315 degrees.)

Until this point, peanut oil had been my choice for frying, and it was performing quite well, lending no off flavors and browning the chicken nicely. But I wanted to test lard and vegetable shortening. Lard, a standby in many Southern kitchens, gave the chicken a deep mahogany color but tinged it with a pork flavor. (We should admit that the supermarket lard in our area is not the best.) Surprisingly, shortening (I used Crisco) was the top performer. Not only did the chicken brown evenly, without even a hint of spottiness, but it tasted like, well, chicken, without a hint of greasiness.

–Keith Dresser

EXTRA-CRUNCHY FRIED CHICKEN

SERVES 4

Keeping the oil at the correct temperature is essential to producing crunchy fried chicken that is neither too brown nor too greasy. Use a candy/deep-fry thermometer to check the temperature of the oil before you add the chicken (see "Gadgets & Gear" below). If you cannot find a chicken that weighs 3½ pounds or less, or if you don't have a pan that is 11 inches in diameter, you will have to fry the chicken in two batches. Follow the recipe, frying the chicken four pieces at a time and keeping the first batch warm in a 200-degree oven while the second batch is cooking. If you want to produce a slightly healthier version of this recipe, you can remove the skin from the chicken before soaking it in the buttermilk. The chicken will be slightly less crunchy.

- 2 **cups plus 6 tablespoons buttermilk**
- 2 **tablespoons salt**
- 1 **whole chicken (about 3½ pounds), cut into 8 pieces, giblets discarded, wings and back reserved for stock**
- 3 **cups all-purpose flour**
- 2 **teaspoons baking powder**
- ¾ **teaspoon dried thyme**
- ½ **teaspoon pepper**
- ¼ **teaspoon garlic powder**
- 4–5 **cups vegetable shortening or peanut oil**

1. Whisk together 2 cups buttermilk and salt in large bowl until salt is dissolved. Add chicken pieces to bowl and stir to coat; cover bowl with plastic and refrigerate for 1 hour. (Don't let chicken soak much longer or it will become too salty.)

2. Whisk flour, baking powder, thyme, pepper, and garlic powder together in large bowl. Add remaining 6 tablespoons buttermilk;

with your fingers rub flour and buttermilk together until buttermilk is evenly incorporated into flour and mixture resembles coarse wet sand.

3. Working in batches of two, drop chicken pieces into flour mixture and turn to thoroughly coat, gently pressing flour mixture onto chicken. Shake excess flour from each piece of chicken and transfer to wire rack set over rimmed baking sheet.

4. Heat oil (it should measure ¾ inch deep) in large heavy-bottomed Dutch oven with 11-inch diameter over medium-high heat until it reaches 375 degrees. Place chicken pieces, skin-side down, in oil, cover, and fry until deep golden brown, 8 to 10 minutes. Remove lid after 4 minutes and lift chicken pieces to check for even browning; rearrange if some pieces are browning faster than others. (At this point, oil should be about 300 degrees. Adjust burner, if necessary, to regulate temperature of oil.) Turn chicken pieces over and continue to fry, uncovered, until chicken pieces are deep golden brown on second side, 6 to 8 minutes longer. (At this point, to keep chicken from browning too quickly, adjust burner to maintain oil temperature of about 315 degrees.) Using tongs, transfer chicken to plate lined with paper towels; let stand for 5 minutes to drain. Serve.

EXTRA-SPICY, EXTRA-CRUNCHY FRIED CHICKEN

Follow recipe for Extra-Crunchy Fried Chicken, adding 4 tablespoons Tabasco sauce to buttermilk-salt mixture in step 1. Replace dried thyme and garlic powder with 2 tablespoons cayenne pepper and 2 teaspoons chili powder in step 2.

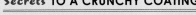

Secrets TO A CRUNCHY COATING

1. Soak the chicken in a buttermilk-salt mixture. **2.** Coat the chicken with the buttermilk-moistened flour.

3. Add the chicken to the hot oil and cover the pot to capture the steam. **4.** Use tongs to flip the chicken and finish cooking with the cover off.

Buying CHICKEN

For a mix of light and dark meat, we like to use a whole cut-up bird for fried chicken. Starting with a whole chicken is inexpensive and not terribly difficult. What's more, you get to keep the neck, backbone, and wings for stock. But if you don't want to wrestle with a whole bird, you do have other options. Just make sure the total weight of the parts doesn't exceed 2¾ pounds.

Whole Legs: Buy four legs and separate them into thighs and drumsticks to yield eight pieces.
Breasts: Buy four split breasts and cut each in half crosswise to yield eight pieces.
Cut-Up Chicken: Buy one cut-up whole chicken (about 3 pounds), save the wings for stock, and cut each breast in half to yield eight pieces.

Gadgets & Gear CANDY THERMOMETER

A $5 candy thermometer isn't just for making candy. When frying chicken or other foods, clip the thermometer to the side of the pot to monitor the temperature of the oil.

MOM'S DELIGHT

I'm Looking for a Recipe . . .

READERS HELP READERS FIND RECIPES

Are you looking for a special recipe? Let other readers of this magazine help. Just send us your requests, and we will print as many of them as we can. We expect you'll be hearing from a lot of new friends.

Send your requests to Looking for a Recipe, Cook's Country, P.O. Box 470739, Brookline, MA 02447, or send an e-mail to lookingforarecipe@bcpress.com. Tell us how you want your new friends to contact you—by regular mail or e-mail or either. If you wish to answer one of the requests below, please contact the reader directly.

Pineapple Pecan Pie
In Hawaii I had one of the best pies I've ever eaten. The filling was fresh pineapple, and the top was like the top of a pecan pie. There was also quite a bit of ginger. I've tried making something up several times but can't quite get it right.

Jennifer Wells, Bluedog1@ak.net

Chocolate Meringue Pie
Back in the late 1950s, I spent the weekend at the home of a high school girlfriend, and her mom made the most delicious chocolate pie. The thing that made it unusual was her use of Hershey's chocolate syrup for the chocolate filling. It was topped with meringue and lightly browned. I have been searching for that recipe ever since.

Norma Nugent, nevnorm@aol.com

Mom's Christmas Cookies
When I was a young boy in Wisconsin, my mother used to make a marvelous cooky at Christmas. It was made up of two disks of dough with a filling made from pitted dates. As I remember, the cooky, even after baking, remained slightly soft and flexible and was oh-so-delicious. Mom attempted to keep them in airtight tins—they may have been airtight, but they were not boy-tight. I look in every baking/cooky book I see and have found only two recipes for a similar cooky; neither produced the soft flexible cooky I remember.

Tony Dunn, osbc@gvtc.com

Brunswick Stew and Pretzel Salad
I would like a recipe for porkless Brunswick stew and an easy recipe for pretzel salad.

Terri Hurt, tphurt@wellingtoninc.com

Yugoslavian Casserole
I have been searching for a recipe for "Yugoslavian Casserole," which was a dish served at Andre's in Houston (also Kansas City). It's a delicious, hearty dish of mostly vegetables with some bacon. They served this dish for many years, until about the late 1980s or early 1990s, when the restaurant was sold to the current owners, who changed the menu. I tried to get the recipe from the chef, without success.

Vivian Weissmann
vivian.weissmann@wholefoods.com

Sour Cream Pancakes
Year ago I made "Sour Cream Pancakes" from an old *McCall's* cookbook. To this day, I have never tasted better pancakes. The cookbook was misplaced, and I have not been able to find a sour cream pancake recipe anywhere.

Teresa Bippen, tbippen1957@yahoo.com

Southern Green Beans
I'm looking for a recipe for "Southern style" green beans. You know, the kind that are cooked until almost leathery, with a bit of ham or other flavoring meat and good pot likker. The key must be the type of beans. Some just get stringy, others stay plump (and are often tasteless). Any leads?

Rick Flynn, 318flynn@bellsouth.net

Cuban Black Beans and Beef
A group of us were vacationing in Florida several years ago. We ate at a little Cuban place and had a wonderful dish of black beans and rice that was served with what I think was round steak. Does anyone have a recipe like that?

Milwaukee Jim, jmskit@tds.net

Simply Supper

We would like to share some of our favorite quick supper recipes with you—the kind of food we make at home during the week to feed our families. We have printed these recipes on cards so that you can collect and organize them. We hope you like these recipes as much as we do.

Iceberg Lettuce and Blue Cheese Dressing

Creamy Shells with Peas and Bacon

Baked Cheese Grits

Roasted Red Pepper Soup

Honey-Glazed Pork Loin

Corned Beef Hash

Strawberries with Balsamic Vinegar

Lemony Chicken and Rice

Simply Supper SALAD

ICEBERG LETTUCE WITH BLUE CHEESE DRESSING

Simply Supper MAIN COURSE

CREAMY SHELLS WITH PEAS AND BACON

Simply Supper SIDE DISH

BAKED CHEESE GRITS

Simply Supper SOUP

ROASTED RED PEPPER SOUP

CREAMY SHELLS WITH PEAS AND BACON SERVES 4

The peas cook right along with the pasta so there's one less pot to clean.

1   cup whole-milk ricotta
½   cup grated Parmesan cheese
2   tablespoons unsalted butter, cut into several pieces
    Salt and pepper
1   tablespoon extra-virgin olive oil
4   slices bacon, cut into ¼-inch strips
1   medium onion, chopped fine
2   medium garlic cloves, minced
1   pound small shells or penne
2   cups frozen peas
1   tablespoon lemon juice

1. Bring 4 quarts water to boil in large pot for cooking pasta.

2. Place ricotta, Parmesan, butter, ¼ teaspoon salt, and ½ teaspoon pepper in bowl large enough to hold cooked pasta.

3. Fry oil and bacon in medium nonstick skillet over medium heat until crisp, 6 to 7 minutes. Transfer bacon to plate lined with paper towels. Add onion to empty pan and cook until lightly golden, about 3 minutes. Add garlic and cook until fragrant, about 1 minute. Transfer onion mixture to bowl with ricotta mixture.

4. Meanwhile, add 1 tablespoon salt and pasta to boiling water. When pasta is about 1 minute shy of al dente, add peas and continue to cook for 1 minute. Reserving 1 cup cooking water, drain pasta and peas. Add ½ cup cooking water and lemon juice to ricotta mixture and whisk until smooth. Add pasta and peas to bowl and toss to coat, adding more reserved cooking water as necessary to moisten pasta. Stir in crisp bacon and adjust seasonings with salt and pepper to taste. Serve.

ICEBERG LETTUCE WITH BLUE CHEESE DRESSING
SERVES 6

If buttermilk is not available, use milk to create a somewhat lighter dressing. To seed the cucumber, cut it in half lengthwise and use a spoon to scoop out the center.

1   medium head iceberg lettuce, cored and cut into 6 wedges
¾   cup crumbled blue cheese
5   tablespoons buttermilk
5   tablespoons sour cream
3   tablespoons mayonnaise
1   tablespoon white wine vinegar
¼   teaspoon sugar
⅛   teaspoon garlic powder
½   teaspoon salt
¼   teaspoon pepper
1   large cucumber, seeded and sliced thin
3   medium ripe tomatoes, cored and cut into 8 wedges each

1. Gently rinse lettuce wedges under cold water. Place them on clean towel to dry.

2. Using fork, mash blue cheese and buttermilk together in small bowl until mixture resembles cottage cheese. Stir in sour cream, mayonnaise, vinegar, sugar, garlic powder, salt, and pepper.

3. Place 1 lettuce wedge on each salad plate. Arrange cucumber slices and tomato wedges around lettuce. Spoon dressing over each wedge of lettuce. Serve.

ROASTED RED PEPPER SOUP SERVES 4 TO 6

Jarred roasted red peppers create a rich soup that requires almost no work. Garnish with croutons. Serve as a first course.

2   tablespoons unsalted butter
4   medium garlic cloves, slivered
1   medium red onion, chopped
     Salt
¼   cup all-purpose flour
3   cups jarred roasted red peppers, drained and rinsed
½   teaspoon hot red pepper flakes
5   sprigs fresh thyme
3½   cups low-sodium chicken broth
1   cup water
¾   cup heavy cream
     Pepper

1. Heat butter in Dutch oven over medium-high heat until just melted. Add garlic and cook, stirring frequently, until lightly browned, 1 to 1½ minutes. Add onion and ½ teaspoon salt and cook until beginning to brown, 4 to 5 minutes. Add flour and stir constantly until flour is lightly toasted, about 45 seconds. Add red peppers, pepper flakes, thyme sprigs, broth, and water and bring to boil. Reduce heat, partially cover, and simmer until peppers are soft, about 20 minutes.

2. Remove and discard thyme sprigs. Working in batches, puree soup in blender until smooth and creamy. Return soup to clean pot over low heat, stir in cream, and adjust the seasonings with salt and pepper. Serve soup when hot.

BAKED CHEESE GRITS SERVES 4 TO 6

Old-fashioned grits are well worth the extra 10 minutes of cooking; instant grits bake up too smooth and have an overprocessed flavor. Grits are ready when they are creamy and smooth but retain a little fine-textured coarseness.

2   tablespoons plus 1 teaspoon unsalted butter
1   small onion, chopped
3   cups water
1   cup heavy cream
½   teaspoon Tabasco sauce
½   teaspoon salt
1   cup plus 2 tablespoons old-fashioned grits
2   cups shredded extra-sharp cheddar cheese
3   large eggs, lightly beaten
     Pepper

1. Adjust oven rack to lower-middle position and heat oven to 350 degrees. Grease 11 by 7-inch baking dish with 1 teaspoon butter.

2. Heat remaining 2 tablespoons butter in large saucepan over medium heat until foaming subsides. Add onion and cook until softened, about 4 minutes. Add water, cream, Tabasco, and salt and bring to boil. Whisk in grits and reduce heat to low. Cook, stirring frequently, until thick and creamy, about 15 minutes.

3. Off heat, stir in 1½ cups cheese, eggs, and pepper to taste. Pour mixture into greased baking dish and smooth top with rubber spatula. Bake for 30 minutes. Sprinkle with remaining ½ cup cheese and continue baking until top is browned, about 15 minutes. Let rest 5 minutes and serve.

HONEY-GLAZED PORK LOIN

CORNED BEEF HASH

STRAWBERRIES WITH BALSAMIC VINEGAR

LEMONY CHICKEN AND RICE

CORNED BEEF HASH SERVES 4

Serve this breakfast classic with ketchup.

- 2 pounds russet potatoes, peeled and cut into ½-inch dice
- Salt
- 4 slices bacon, chopped fine
- 1 medium onion, chopped fine
- 2 medium garlic cloves, minced
- ½ teaspoon minced fresh thyme
- 1 pound corned beef, cut into ¼-inch dice
- ½ cup heavy cream
- ¼ teaspoon Tabasco sauce
- 4 large eggs
- Pepper

1. Bring potatoes, 5 cups water, and ½ teaspoon salt to boil in medium saucepan over medium-high heat. Once boiling, cook potatoes for 4 minutes, then drain and set potatoes aside.

2. Cook bacon in 12-inch nonstick skillet over medium-high heat for 2 minutes. Add onion and cook until browned, about 8 minutes. Add garlic and thyme and cook for 30 seconds. Stir in corned beef. Mix in potatoes and lightly pack mixture with spatula. Reduce heat to medium and pour heavy cream and Tabasco sauce sauce evenly over hash. Cook undisturbed for 4 minutes, then, with spatula, invert hash, one portion at a time, and fold browned bits back into hash. Lightly pack hash into pan. Repeat process every minute or two until potatoes are cooked, about 8 minutes longer.

3. Make four indentations equally spaced on surface of hash. Crack one egg into each indentation and sprinkle eggs with salt and pepper to taste. Reduce heat to medium-low, cover pan, and cook until eggs are just set, about 6 minutes. Cut into four wedges, making sure each wedge contains one egg, and serve.

HONEY-GLAZED PORK LOIN SERVES 4 TO 6

This recipe starts on the stovetop and finishes in the oven, so you will need an ovenproof skillet. Remember that the handle will be blistering hot when you take it out of the oven, so be sure to use a potholder or an oven mitt.

- ⅓ cup honey
- Pinch cayenne pepper
- 1 boneless blade-end pork loin roast (about 2½ pounds)
- 1 teaspoon salt
- ½ teaspoon pepper
- 2 teaspoons vegetable oil

1. Adjust oven rack to middle position and heat oven to 325 degrees. Stir honey and cayenne together in measuring cup. Tie roast at even intervals with 5 pieces of butcher's twine. Rub roast with salt and pepper.

2. Heat oil in heavy-bottomed, ovenproof 10-inch nonstick skillet over medium-high heat until just smoking. Place roast fat-side down in skillet and cook until well browned, about 3 minutes. Using tongs, rotate roast one-quarter turn and cook until well browned, about 2½ minutes. Repeat two more times until roast is well browned on all sides. Pour off fat from skillet. Add honey mixture and cook for 30 seconds, using tongs to turn roast and coat it with glaze.

3. Place skillet in oven and cook until center of roast registers about 135 degrees on instant-read thermometer, 35 to 45 minutes. Transfer roast to carving board and let rest 15 minutes. Meanwhile, set skillet over high heat and boil until glaze reduces to ⅓ cup, about 1 minute. Once reduced to this amount, leave glaze in measuring cup. When ready to carve roast (center should register about 150 degrees on instant-read thermometer), snip off twine and pour glaze over meat. Cut into ¼-inch slices and serve immediately.

LEMONY CHICKEN AND RICE SERVES 4

Use bone-in, skin-on chicken breasts for this recipe.

- 4 split chicken breasts (10 to 12 ounces each)
- Salt and pepper
- 2 teaspoons vegetable oil
- 1 large onion, chopped fine
- 1½ cups long-grain rice
- ⅛ teaspoon hot red pepper flakes
- 3 medium garlic cloves, minced
- 1½ teaspoons grated zest and 2 tablespoons juice from 1 lemon
- 1¾ cups low-sodium chicken broth
- 1 cup water
- 5 medium scallions, sliced thin
- 1 lemon, cut into wedges

1. Adjust oven rack to middle position and heat oven to 350 degrees. Season chicken liberally with salt and pepper. Heat oil in Dutch oven over medium-high heat until just smoking. Add chicken, skin-side down, and cook until golden brown, about 6 minutes. Transfer chicken, skin-side up, to casserole dish and bake until it reaches 160 degrees on instant-read thermometer, 30 to 35 minutes.

2. Meanwhile, remove all but 2 tablespoons fat from pot and return it to medium heat. Add onion and 1 teaspoon salt and cook until soft, 3 to 4 minutes. Add rice and pepper flakes and cook, stirring often, until rice begins to turn translucent, about 3 minutes. Add garlic and lemon zest and cook for 30 seconds. Add broth and water, scraping pan bottom. Bring to full simmer. Turn heat to low, cover, and cook until all liquid is absorbed, 15 to 18 minutes. Remove pot from heat. Let stand for 10 minutes.

3. Fold lemon juice and scallions into rice gently with fork and season with salt and pepper to taste. Serve rice and chicken with lemon wedges.

STRAWBERRIES WITH BALSAMIC VINEGAR SERVES 6

This Italian dessert is elegant but very simple. Serve the berries and vinegar as is or with a small scoop of vanilla ice cream. If you don't have light brown sugar on hand, sprinkle the berries with an equal amount of granulated sugar.

- ⅓ cup balsamic vinegar
- 2 teaspoons granulated sugar
- ½ teaspoon lemon juice
- 3 pints strawberries, hulled and sliced (small berries can be halved or quartered)
- ¼ cup packed light brown sugar
- Pepper

1. Bring vinegar, granulated sugar, and lemon juice to simmer in small saucepan over medium heat. Simmer until syrup is reduced by half (to approximately 3 tablespoons), about 3 minutes. Transfer vinegar syrup to small bowl and cool completely.

2. With spoon, lightly toss berries and brown sugar in large bowl. Let stand until sugar dissolves and berries exude some juice, 10 to 15 minutes. Pour vinegar syrup over berries, add pepper to taste, and toss to combine. Divide berries among individual bowls or goblets and serve immediately.

No-Fuss Green Beans

Dear Cook's Country,

My family is crazy about fresh green beans (even my middle child, who is notoriously picky, gobbles them up!). But we're in a rut—the only way I know how to make them is steamed, with melted butter and toasted almonds. They're tasty, but I get so flustered trying to prepare them at the last minute, and we're ready to try something new. Can you help?

Christine Beder, Andover, Massachusetts

Dear Christine,

I agree that you can't go wrong with steamed green beans, but they do require some last-minute attention, which can be tricky when you're struggling to get dinner on the table. In fact, all of the most common cooking methods for green beans—steaming, stir-frying, and boiling—need to be done just moments before serving. After trying several techniques in the test kitchen, I think a different, more relaxed approach might be the solution to your problem.

In testing a number of cooking methods for green beans, one in particular—braising—stood out as being foolproof and well suited to busy cooks. Braising, or simmering in a small amount of liquid in a covered pan over low heat, requires little attention from the cook. Once the beans, seasonings, and liquid are in the pan, you are free to tend to other matters, returning only to give the beans a quick stir now and then. I found that it takes 20 minutes to braise green beans, give or take a few minutes.

Braising does rob green beans of their brilliant color, but the tradeoff is that the beans pick up tons of flavor during the gentle cooking process. It's difficult, if not impossible, to overcook the beans because they are meant to be cooked well past the crisp-tender point until they are meltingly tender—a nice change of pace from the barely cooked beans many restaurants now serve. It's no big deal if the beans need to be kept warm on the stove for a few minutes while you finish cooking the rest of your meal.

A few more things to consider: Braising is particularly well suited to supermarket green beans, which tend to be relatively thick and sturdy and can stand up to prolonged cooking. If you have ultra-fresh, slender green beans picked from your own garden, stick with one of the quicker techniques, such as steaming.

As for braising liquids, I found several choices that worked well, including orange juice, chicken broth, canned tomatoes, and heavy cream. In each case, just a few additional ingredients are necessary to create rich, satisfying flavors.

I've developed four worry-free recipes for you and your family to try. They should get you out of your green bean rut.

–Rebecca Hays

GREEN BEANS WITH MEDITERRANEAN FLAVORS SERVES 4

If fresh oregano is unavailable, substitute 2 tablespoons minced fresh basil or parsley. Don't use dried oregano—it's too harsh for this recipe.

- 2 tablespoons extra-virgin olive oil
- 3 medium garlic cloves, minced
- 1 (14½-ounce) can diced tomatoes
  Salt and pepper
- 1 pound green beans, stem ends snapped off
- 1 tablespoon minced fresh oregano
- ½ cup pitted kalamata olives, halved

1. Heat oil in large skillet over medium heat. Add garlic and cook until fragrant, about 1 minute. Add tomatoes, ¼ teaspoon salt, and ¼ teaspoon pepper; bring to boil.

2. Add beans, cover, lower heat, and simmer gently, stirring occasionally, until beans are very tender and liquid has reduced, 18 to 22 minutes. Remove lid; simmer briskly to further reduce liquid if necessary.

3. Stir in oregano and olives and adjust seasonings with salt and pepper to taste. Serve.

ORANGE GREEN BEANS WITH BUTTERED CASHEWS SERVES 4

Finely chopping the cashews helps them cling to the beans.

- 2 tablespoons unsalted butter
- ½ cup lightly salted cashews, chopped fine
- ⅛ teaspoon red pepper flakes
- ¾ cup orange juice
  Salt
- 1 pound green beans, stem ends snapped off

1. Heat butter in large skillet over medium-high heat until foaming. Add cashews and pepper flakes and cook, stirring constantly, until butter turns golden brown, about 1½ minutes. Transfer nuts to small bowl and set aside.

2. Wipe out skillet and set over medium-high heat. Add orange juice and ½ teaspoon salt; bring to boil. Add beans, cover, lower heat, and simmer gently, stirring occasionally, until beans are very tender and liquid has reduced, 18 to 22 minutes. Remove lid; simmer briskly to reduce liquid if necessary.

3. Adjust seasonings with salt. Transfer beans to serving dish and sprinkle evenly with cashews. Serve.

GREEN BEANS WITH BACON AND ONION SERVES 4

Serve these Southern-style beans as part of a holiday meal.

- 5 slices bacon, chopped small
- 1 medium onion, halved and sliced thin
- ¾ cup low-sodium chicken broth
- 2 teaspoons dark brown sugar
  Salt and pepper
- 1 pound green beans, stem ends snapped off
- 2 tablespoons red wine vinegar

1. Fry bacon in large skillet over medium-high heat until crisp, about 8 minutes. Using slotted spoon, transfer bacon to plate lined with paper towels.

2. Discard all but 1 tablespoon fat, return skillet to medium heat, and add onion. Cook until onion is translucent, 3 to 4 minutes. Add broth, brown sugar, ¼ teaspoon salt, and ¼ teaspoon pepper; bring to boil.

3. Add beans, cover, lower heat, and simmer gently, stirring occasionally, until beans are very tender and liquid has reduced, 18 to 22 minutes. Remove lid; simmer briskly to further reduce liquid if necessary.

4. Stir in vinegar; adjust seasonings with salt and pepper to taste. Transfer beans to serving dish and sprinkle with bacon. Serve.

GREEN BEAN SUCCOTASH SERVES 4

Green beans replace traditional lima beans in this easy succotash. If you don't have fresh thyme, finish with 2 tablespoons minced fresh parsley or basil.

- 2 tablespoons unsalted butter
- 1 medium onion, chopped fine
- ¾ cup heavy cream
  Salt and pepper
- 1 pound green beans, stem ends snapped off, beans cut into 1-inch pieces
- 1 (10-ounce) package frozen corn
- 1 teaspoon minced fresh thyme
- 2 teaspoons lemon juice

1. Heat butter in large skillet over medium heat until foaming. Add onion and cook until translucent, 3 to 4 minutes. Add cream, ½ teaspoon salt, and ¼ teaspoon pepper; bring to boil.

2. Add beans, cover, lower heat, and simmer gently, stirring occasionally, for 15 minutes. Add corn, cover, and continue to cook, stirring occasionally, until corn is heated through and beans are very tender, 3 to 7 minutes. Remove lid; simmer briskly to further reduce cream if necessary.

3. Stir in thyme and lemon juice and adjust seasonings with salt and pepper to taste. Serve.

Blue-Ribbon Apple Cake

Dear Cook's Country,
For years, my husband and I have been searching for a really good apple cake—you know, one that really has a lot of apples in it! I want a cake that will be the talk of coffee hour after church.

Helen Hanson, Gallatin Gateway, Montana

Dear Helen,
No wonder you've had a hard time finding a good recipe. We tried a half-dozen cakes in our test kitchen, and most of them were nothing more than spice cakes with a few pieces of cubed, raw apples tossed in. We'd rather have a slice of spice cake with a fresh apple on the side! Thinking that apple cakes don't have to be the dessert equivalent of zucchini bread, we got busy in the test kitchen.

Three Cakes, Three Problems

Raw Apples
This cake was baked in a tube pan and contained raw apples, which shed liquid in the oven and made the cake gummy.

Hidden Apples
This layer cake hides the apples beneath a sickeningly sweet frosting and an overabundance of spices.

Sparse Apples
This cake has just a few sad-looking apples on top of a dry yellow cake.

Apple cake recipes call for all sorts of different batters, from a simple American yellow cake to a rich French butter cake, but our favorite was a sour cream cake batter, which produced a fine, tender crumb. I fiddled a bit with the ingredients and ended up with 1 whole egg, 1 yolk, a stick of butter, 1¼ cups all-purpose flour, ¾ cup sugar, ½ cup sour cream, some leavening, and salt. This made for a rich cake that paired off nicely with the apples. The batter is unusual in that room-temperature butter is beaten into the dry ingredients.

The apples were a big problem. Left raw, the cake was so bad that I ended up feeding it to our two pigs. The apples obviously needed some precooking, so I decided to try a quick sauté with sugar in a skillet first. I discovered that the apples must be cooked to the point at which the juices reduce and thicken. Otherwise, the cake ends up sitting in a puddle, hardly the effect I was looking for during coffee hour at our church. But I still wasn't getting enough caramel flavor. The best—and easiest—solution was to use light brown sugar.

Now I had good apple flavor, but I was bothered by the final look of this dessert. I had been treating it like an old-fashioned upside-down cake, adding the batter to the skillet once the apples were caramelized and then putting the whole thing in the oven. This made for a messy cake (it often fell apart during unmolding), so I decided to transfer the cooked apple mixture to a 9-inch cake pan before adding the batter. Now I had a much prettier, more compact cake, and it wasn't much more work.

I also discovered that the cake should be inverted onto a platter about five minutes after it comes out of the oven. This allows enough time for the cake to set slightly but not enough for the caramel to harden. Once it was inverted, I found it best to let the cake sit a bit—gravity helps the cake and apples release without too much banging.

Now our coffee hour is a lot more cheerful. The congregation really appreciates a piece of apple cake that doesn't have to be washed down with three cups of coffee!

–Christopher Kimball

BLUE-RIBBON APPLE CAKE SERVES 8

Granny Smiths are the best choice because they hold their shape nicely and are tart. Other apples that hold their shape when cooked, such as Cortlands, can also be used in this recipe. Serve with whipped cream or vanilla ice cream.

Apples
- 4 tablespoons unsalted butter, plus extra for greasing cake pan
- ½ cup packed light brown sugar
- ⅛ teaspoon salt
- 4 Granny Smith apples, peeled, cored, and cut into ½-inch slices (about 5 cups)

Cake
- ½ cup sour cream
- 1 large egg plus 1 yolk
- ½ teaspoon vanilla extract
- 1¼ cups all-purpose flour
- ¾ cup granulated sugar
- ½ teaspoon baking powder
- ¼ teaspoon baking soda
- ¼ teaspoon salt
- 8 tablespoons (1 stick) unsalted butter, cut into chunks and brought to room temperature

1. Adjust oven rack to center position and heat oven to 350 degrees. Lightly butter 9-inch cake pan.

2. For the apples: Place butter in large heavy-bottomed skillet over medium-high heat. Once butter has stopped foaming, add sugar and stir to combine. Continue to cook until sugar turns dark brown (it should look like dark brown sugar), about 2 minutes, swirling pan occasionally. Add salt and apples and fold with spatula to combine. Cook, stirring often, until apples have softened slightly and juices are thickened and syrupy, 5 to 7 minutes. Remove pan from heat and spoon apples into prepared cake pan.

3. For the cake: In small bowl, whisk together ¼ cup sour cream, egg, yolk, and vanilla until well combined.

4. Place flour, sugar, baking powder, baking soda, and salt in large bowl. Use electric mixer on low speed for 15 seconds to blend. Add butter and remaining ¼ cup sour cream and mix on low speed until dry ingredients are moistened, 1 to 2 minutes. Increase speed to medium and mix for 2 minutes. Add sour cream/egg mixture and beat on medium-high, scraping down sides of bowl, until batter is homogeneous and fluffy, about 1 minute.

5. Spoon batter over apples and gently spread out to thin layer that covers apples. Bake until cake is dark golden brown, feels set, and cake tester comes out clean when inserted in center, 35 to 40 minutes. Transfer pan to wire rack and let cool for 5 minutes.

6. Place serving plate over top of pan and invert. Let cake sit inverted for about 1 minute without tapping or shaking pan. Cake will slowly detach itself. Once cake is on platter, gently remove pan. Serve warm (not hot) or at room temperature.

Getting to Know Apples

The fact that an apple tastes great out of hand does not mean that it will be a good baker. It might be too mushy, or the flavor might not hold up in the oven. We baked 15 varieties in 15 apple cakes to see which ones would be good bakers, and here's what we found. Because our apple cake recipe has so much sugar, when making it we favor tart apples that hold their shape.

Not for Baking
BRAEBURN

This crisp, sweet apple took on an odd flavor and worse texture in our baking tests. Keep this apple out of the oven.

A Favorite
CORTLAND

Traditionally considered a good baker, this mild, slightly tart apple lived up to its reputation. This apple holds its shape well when baked.

On the Sweet Side
GOLDEN DELICIOUS

This popular variety is sweet and buttery and has a nice soft texture when baked. It's not tart enough to work well in sweet recipes such as our apple cake.

Not Recommended
RED DELICIOUS

This lunchbox classic is dry and almost flavorless when eaten out of hand and even worse when baked.

A Good Choice
EMPIRE

This crisp apple is related to the McIntosh and has a nice balance of sweet and tart flavors. It holds its shape fairly well when baked.

Great in Salads
FUJI

This crisp, very sweet apple is a favorite for eating out of hand and for slicing and using in salads. Very fragrant, but loses its appeal (and its shape) in the oven.

Too Sweet
GALA

Another very sweet apple that is better raw than baked.

The Best Baker
GRANNY SMITH

This apple is a great choice for baking. It holds its shape, and its bracing acidity stands up to sugar nicely. It lacks the complex fruity flavor of apples such as the Macoun or even the McIntosh.

Not Recommended
IDA RED

We don't like the vegetal overtones of this tart New England variety. This apple also tends to be very soft.

A Good Choice
JONAGOLD

This apple is related to the Golden Delicious, but it is more tart and complex, with hints of honey and spice. Very juicy and intense.

A Good Choice
MACOUN

This New England apple has a nice balance of sweet and tart flavors. It can be a bit watery. Does not store well and so is available only in the fall and then for only a few weeks.

Too Mushy
McINTOSH

This familiar supermarket apple is refreshingly tart, but in the oven it falls apart and becomes very watery.

Oh, So Sour
NORTHERN SPY

This heirloom variety is very, very tart. In some cases, the flavor can be downright sour. Even so, it used to be considered a pie apple and went into the so-called Northern Pie.

A Bland Beauty
ROME BEAUTY

This firm, sweet apple tastes best when eaten out of hand. Once baked, the flavor becomes one-dimensional and bland.

Not for Baking
WINESAP

Sometimes called Stayman Winesap, this crisp apple can be juicy and crisp when eaten out of hand. Once baked, the sour flavors can dominate.

The Best Ranch Chili

Dear Cook's Country,
I serve ranch chili to my family all the time, but the pork tends to be dried out and the beans are overcooked. What am I doing wrong?

Frank McCreary, Houston, Texas

Dear Frank,
In the test kitchen, we're always happy to take on a chili challenge, and the idea of a spicy, sweet ranch-style chili, brimming with tender pork and creamy beans, appealed to everyone. But you're right—as good as this chili could (and should) be, the recipes I tested turned out batch after batch of tough, bland, dried-out pork and soggy, overcooked beans. What, you ask, were you doing wrong? Probably nothing more than following a bad recipe.

When it comes to making a great chili (with pork, beef, or any other meat), it's easy to take a wrong turn before you even know it. You need to purchase the right cut, one with enough fat in it to cook up nice and tender. For pork chili, many recipes call for pork tenderloin, a lean, dry, and somewhat flavorless cut. (Using tenderloin in a chili recipe is like trying to haul firewood in a Mustang convertible.) Another bad choice—one found in many recipes—is pork loin, which turns out dry, tough cubes of meat. We had much better luck with a cut from the shoulder (also a less expensive cut). A shoulder chop has big flavor and is nicely marbled with fat, but most supermarkets sell only thinly cut shoulder chops, which are too small for chili. A better choice is a pork shoulder roast (often referred to as a Boston butt). It was easy to get 1-inch cubes out of this substantial cut.

Even with the right cut, lots of folks make tough chili (we've done it ourselves plenty of times) because they simply do not cook the meat long enough. A minimum of two hours on the stove makes this tough piece of meat fork-tender. In fact, cooking it even longer makes the meat even silkier and softer.

When it came to adding beans to the chili, I toyed around with the idea of starting out with dried beans, but the extra steps and time involved made me rethink this option (and the allure of ready-to-go, no-work-involved canned beans was just too attractive to ignore). But don't even think about adding canned beans to the chili at the outset. I tried it and got blown-out, mushy beans and an unappetizing chili. It's a much better idea to add these already-tender beans toward the end of the cooking time. Just 30 minutes before serving the chili, gently stir in the beans and they'll soak up flavor and keep their shape.

As for what kind of beans to use, tasters preferred creamy red kidney beans (both light and dark) to starchier pinto beans—the most common choice in this rustic chili. But, honestly, either kind will work.

Now it was finally time to bring in the distinctly sweet, spicy, and smoky flavors that set ranch chili apart from more well-known chili dishes. I had to chuckle when I read other recipes that called for cups (yep, cups) of ketchup, barbecue sauce, and even liquid smoke. I found heat in fresh jalapeños and regular off-the-supermarket-shelf chili powder; when mixed with a little cumin and dried oregano, this made for a great chili blend. Instead of achingly sweet ketchup or barbecue sauce, I used canned tomatoes and a bit of brown sugar to sweeten the chili and balance the spiciness. No liquid smoke was necessary; I got all of the good smokiness and rich flavor I wanted from browned-to-a-crisp bacon.

So the short answer to your question is to buy a piece of Boston butt and cook it until it melts in your mouth (chili can't be rushed!). Forget the supermarket convenience additions—the barbecue sauce, ketchup, and liquid smoke—and stick to honest ingredients—canned tomatoes, brown sugar, and bacon. We serve this chili with sliced scallions and shredded Monterey Jack cheese. And nothing works better than our Jalapeño Cornbread for mopping up the bottom of the chili bowl.

–Bridget Lancaster

RANCH CHILI MAKES ABOUT 2 QUARTS, SERVING 4 TO 6

For spicier chili, boost the heat with a pinch of cayenne or a dash of hot pepper sauce, such as Tabasco. This chili tastes even better when made a day in advance. If you plan to serve it the next day, don't add the beans until you have reheated the chili—this will keep them nice and firm. Good choices for condiments include diced fresh tomatoes, lime wedges, diced avocado, sliced scallions, chopped red onion, chopped cilantro leaves, sour cream, and shredded Monterey Jack or cheddar cheese.

- 3½ pounds boneless Boston butt roast, trimmed of excess fat and cut into 1-inch cubes (see photos at right) Salt and pepper
- 8 slices bacon, chopped fine
- 1 large onion, minced
- 3 large jalapeño chiles (about 2½ inches long), seeded and minced
- 3 tablespoons chili powder
- 1 tablespoon ground cumin
- 1½ teaspoons dried oregano
- 5 medium garlic cloves, minced
- 1 tablespoon brown sugar
- 1 (28-ounce) can diced tomatoes
- 3 cups water
- 2 (16-ounce) cans red kidney beans, drained and rinsed

1. Toss pork cubes with salt and pepper; set aside. Fry bacon in large, heavy soup kettle or Dutch oven over medium heat until fat renders and bacon crisps, about 10 minutes. Remove bacon with slotted spoon to plate lined with paper towels; pour all but 2 teaspoons fat from pot into small bowl; set aside.

2. Increase heat to medium-high, add half of meat to now-empty pot and cook until well browned on all sides, about 5 minutes. Transfer browned meat to bowl. Brown remaining meat, adding another 2 teaspoons bacon fat to pot if necessary. Transfer second batch of meat to bowl.

3. Reduce heat to medium-low and add 3 tablespoons bacon fat to now-empty pot. Add onion, jalapeños, chili powder, cumin, and oregano; cook, stirring occasionally, until vegetables are beginning to brown, 4 to 5 minutes. Add garlic and brown sugar; cook until just fragrant, about 15 seconds. Add diced tomatoes and scrape pot bottom to loosen browned bits. Add reserved bacon, browned pork, and water; bring to simmer. Continue to cook, uncovered, at slow simmer until meat is tender and juices are dark and starting to thicken, about 2 hours.

4. Add beans, reduce heat to low, and simmer, uncovered, stirring occasionally, for 30 minutes. Adjust seasoning with additional salt and serve with condiments.

RANCH CHILI FOR A CROWD

Our recipe can be doubled, but if you try to brown four batches of the meat in the same pan, the drippings will burn. We recommend that you brown the extra meat (in two batches) in a separate skillet. You can pick up the recipe from step 3, cooking twice as many vegetables in the large pot. Don't let the browned bits in the extra skillet go to waste. Use 1 cup of the water to deglaze the empty skillet, then add this liquid to the stew.

Secrets TRIMMING THE MEAT

Supermarkets combine uneven scraps from various parts of the animal in their packages of "stew meat." We prefer to cut up a Boston butt. If you start with a 3½-pound roast, you will end up with about 2½ pounds of trimmed meat.

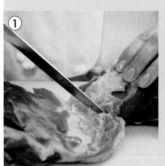

1. With your hands, pull the roast apart at the fatty seams and then separate the muscles with a knife. **2.** Trim the thick pieces of fat from each piece of meat.

3. Using an upward sawing motion, remove the smaller pieces of fat and the translucent membrane called silver skin. **4.** Cut the trimmed meat into rough 1-inch cubes.

sides JALAPEÑO CORNBREAD

Nothing quite makes chili a meal like fresh cornbread. And for spice lovers, jalapeño cornbread is the best choice. As any Southerner will tell you, an extremely hot cast-iron skillet is the secret to a crisp, golden-brown crust. If you don't already own one, seasoned cast-iron skillets can be found at some garage sales for very reasonable prices. Pick one up, even if it is only for cornbread. Most Southern cornbread recipes instruct you to preheat the pan in the oven. Although in this recipe the skillet is already heated through from cooking the peppers, it's a good idea to keep it hot in the oven while you finish mixing the batter. We've found that if the batter sizzles when it is added to the pan, a perfect, golden crust should result.

JALAPEÑO CORNBREAD
SERVES 6

The texture of the cornbread will vary according to your cornmeal. Very fine-grained meal will result in a dense, uniform texture, while coarser-grained meal will have a bit more bite. The stone-ground cornmeal typically sold in supermarkets is the best choice.

- 2 tablespoons plus 1 teaspoon vegetable oil
- 2 medium jalapeño chiles, seeded and minced
- 1 medium red bell pepper, seeded and minced
- 1 cup yellow cornmeal, preferably stone-ground
- 2 teaspoons packed light brown sugar
- ¾ teaspoon salt
- 1 teaspoon baking powder
- ¼ teaspoon baking soda
- ¼ teaspoon pepper
- ½ cup boiling water
- ¾ cup buttermilk
- ⅛ teaspoon Tabasco sauce
- 1 large egg, lightly beaten
- ½ cup shredded sharp cheddar cheese

1. Adjust oven rack to lower-middle position and heat oven to 450 degrees. Heat 2 tablespoons oil in 10-inch cast-iron skillet over medium-high heat until shimmering. Add chiles and bell pepper and cook, stirring occasionally, until softened and beginning to brown, about 5 minutes. Transfer peppers to small bowl and set aside. Add remaining 1 teaspoon oil to empty skillet and swirl to coat. Set skillet, uncleaned, in oven.

2. Measure ⅓ cup cornmeal into medium bowl. In separate larger bowl, whisk together remaining cornmeal, brown sugar, salt, baking powder, baking soda, and pepper. While whisking, pour boiling water in slow, steady stream into ⅓ cup cornmeal, followed by buttermilk, Tabasco, and egg. Pour wet mixture into dry ingredients and stir until just combined. Mix in cooked peppers and cheese.

3. Carefully remove skillet from oven and quickly pour batter into heated skillet. Bake until light golden brown, about 10 minutes. Remove skillet from oven, invert cornbread onto wire rack, and cool for 5 minutes. Flip bread right-side up and serve warm or at room temperature. For moister texture, let cornbread cool in skillet.

Quick Cooking

A new twist on old Southern favorites

FRIED FISH WITH PICKLED JALAPEÑO MAYONNAISE SERVES 4

A nonstick skillet makes it possible to pan-fry fish in a thin film of oil supplemented with butter to improve browning of the crust. Look for cans of pickled jalapeños in the aisle with Mexican ingredients at your supermarket.

- ½ cup mayonnaise
- 2 tablespoons chopped pickled jalapeño chiles
- 6 tablespoons chopped scallions
- 2 teaspoons lime juice
  Salt and pepper
- 1½ cups plain bread crumbs
- 2 large egg whites
- 4 skinless trout, catfish, or flounder fillets (5 to 7 ounces each)
- 5 tablespoons olive oil
- 3 tablespoons unsalted butter, cut into 2 pieces
  Lime wedges for serving

1. Combine mayonnaise, pickled jalapeños, 2 tablespoons scallions, and lime juice in small bowl. Season with salt and pepper and set aside.

2. Adjust oven rack to lower-middle position, set heatproof serving platter on rack, and heat oven to 200 degrees.

3. Combine bread crumbs, 1 teaspoon salt, pepper to taste, and remaining ¼ cup scallions in shallow bowl. Whisk egg whites in another bowl until slightly foamy. Season fish with salt and pepper. One at a time, dip fillets first in egg whites and then in bread crumb mixture, pressing down to adhere coating. Set breaded fillets aside in single layer on large plate.

4. Heat 3 tablespoons oil and 1 piece butter in 12-inch nonstick skillet over medium-high heat. When butter stops foaming, place 2 fillets in skillet and cook until browned and crisp, about 3 minutes. Flip and cook on second side until thickest part of fillet easily separates into flakes when pierced with paring knife, about 2 minutes. Transfer fillets to heated platter. Wipe out skillet and repeat with remaining oil, butter, and fish. Serve immediately with mayonnaise and lime wedges.

ROASTED CORN SERVES 4

Roasting ears of corn in the oven highlights their sweetness, and there's no bothering with a big pot of boiling water.

- 4 ears corn, husked
- 2–3 tablespoons unsalted butter, at room temperature
  Salt and pepper

Adjust oven rack to middle position and heat oven to 475 degrees. Place corn on rimmed baking sheet, spacing ears out so they do not touch. Use knife to spread corn with butter. Sprinkle corn with salt and pepper to taste. Roast, turning corn once or twice, until just tender, 15 to 17 minutes. Place corn on serving dish and pour any remaining melted butter from baking sheet over corn. Serve.

Steak and slaw, Italian style

GRILLED FLANK STEAK WITH GARLIC-PARSLEY SAUCE SERVES 4

Don't waste hours marinating flank steak before cooking it. Coating the grilled steak with a potent sauce adds just as much flavor—and takes just 5 minutes.

- ½ cup minced fresh parsley
- ¼ cup minced red onion
- 2 medium garlic cloves, minced
- ¼ cup red wine vinegar
- ¼ cup extra-virgin olive oil
- ⅛ teaspoon hot red pepper flakes
  Salt and pepper
- 1½ pounds flank steak

1. Combine parsley, onion, garlic, vinegar, oil, pepper flakes, and salt and pepper to taste in small bowl. Season steak with salt and pepper to taste.

2. Grill steak over very hot fire until browned on both sides and slightly less done than you want, about 10 minutes.

3. Place steak in baking dish and coat with parsley sauce. Cover dish with foil and let rest for 5 minutes. Slice steak thinly against grain and serve with sauce remaining in baking dish.

RED CABBAGE SLAW SERVES 4

An Italian-style dressing and fresh basil breathe new life into an easy slaw. Use a chef's knife or the shredding disk on a food processor to prepare the cabbage.

- ½ medium head red cabbage, shredded (about 6 cups)
- 1 red bell pepper, seeded and sliced thin
- ½ cup fresh basil leaves, cut into strips
- 2 tablespoons balsamic vinegar
- 1 teaspoon honey
  Salt and pepper
- 2 tablespoons extra-virgin olive oil

Combine cabbage, pepper, and basil in large bowl. Whisk vinegar, honey, ½ teaspoon salt, and ⅛ teaspoon pepper together in small bowl until honey has dissolved. Whisk in oil, pour dressing over cabbage, and toss well. Adjust seasonings with salt and pepper. Serve.

–Recipes by
Eva Katz and **Stephanie Lyness**

Cheesy Mashed Potatoes

Dear Cook's Country,
For a change of pace, I recently stirred some cheese into my mashed potatoes. Boy, was that a bad idea. The cheese turned the mashed potatoes into a stiff, gluey mess and didn't even add much flavor. What went wrong?

Claire Johnston, Newton, Massachusetts

Dear Claire,
I never thought about the problem of "cheesy" potatoes before, but when I mashed shredded cheese into just-boiled potatoes, I discovered that you were absolutely right. I got an awful bowlful of gluey spuds. What a waste.

Next, I tried adding chunks of cheese to one batch of potatoes and melted cheese to another. No luck either time. Rather than melting into gooey pockets, as I had hoped, the chunks of cheese turned into mushy lumps. And the melted cheese gave the potatoes a grainy texture. Even worse, neither approach added much cheese flavor. Just "winging it" wasn't going to work. I needed to rethink this recipe.

Here's what I knew. The best regular mashed potatoes contain only a few ingredients: potatoes, butter, and half-and-half (milk makes watery mashed potatoes and cream is far too rich). I like russet potatoes best, as do most cooks in our test kitchen, because they make very fluffy mashed potatoes. Yukon Golds, another test kitchen favorite, are pretty dense when mashed. Because texture is clearly a problem when cheese is added to the mix, I decided to stick with the russets, just to be safe.

Once the potatoes have been simmered and drained, I usually mash 'em with a fair amount of butter and just enough half-and-half to give the potatoes a nice consistency. So how should I add cheese to this formula?

Given the weak flavor that you experienced at home (and that I repeated in the test kitchen), I figured only strong cheeses need apply. Extra-sharp cheddar and spicy Monterey Jack varieties, such as Pepper Jack and Horseradish Jack, topped the list of tasters' favorites. Adding ounce after ounce of cheese to 2 pounds of russets, we couldn't taste the cheese until I had worked in a whopping 6 ounces. Rule number one: Use a strong cheese and don't be stingy.

By now, my cheesy potatoes were tasting pretty good, but the texture was still pasty. I thought maybe I needed to pay more attention to my technique. Dumping everything into the pot with the drained potatoes and mashing away—what I had been doing—certainly wasn't working. I set up some tests, adding the butter, half-and-half, and cheese in different sequences. This turned out to be the key to success.

If I mashed cheese with the potatoes, they became unbelievably gluey. But if I mashed the potatoes into small bits, added the butter and half-and-half, and then—and only then—gently folded in the cheese, my mashed potatoes were smooth and creamy. Rule number two: Beating up the cheese with the masher is a big no-no.

Everyone in the test kitchen thought the potatoes tasted very good, but were they super-cheesy? Not really. I decided to sprinkle more cheese over the finished mashed potatoes, throw the lid on the saucepan, and wait for five minutes. This last batch of cheese melted into pleasing, gooey pockets. Now you could taste and see the cheese. One last trick: I found that a few tablespoons of sour cream boosted the tangy flavor of the cheese. I now had the cheesiest mashed potatoes ever. I hope you think so, too. **–Julia Collin Davison**

Secrets BUILDING SUPER-CHEESY FLAVOR

If you don't handle the cheese properly, the potatoes can become gluey. Here's how to keep the texture fluffy and light while packing the potatoes with lots of cheese flavor.

1. Start with a strong cheese and use lots of it. **2.** Gently fold in most of the cheese after mashing the potatoes. **3.** Sprinkle the rest of the cheese over the potatoes, cover the pot, and let the cheese melt.

CHEESY MASHED POTATOES SERVES 4 TO 6

The amount of half-and-half needed to achieve the correct consistency will depend on the potatoes you use and how well you drain them. It is important for both the butter and the half-and-half to be hot when added to the potatoes to make sure that the cheese melts.

- 2 pounds russet potatoes, peeled, quartered, and cut into 1-inch chunks
- 4 tablespoons unsalted butter, melted
- ½ teaspoon salt
- ⅛ teaspoon pepper
- ½–¾ cup half-and-half, hot
- 3 tablespoons sour cream
- 2 cups shredded extra-sharp cheddar cheese

1. Cover potatoes with 1 inch water in large saucepan. Bring to simmer over high heat (this should take about 10 minutes). Reduce heat to medium and continue to simmer until potatoes are tender and dinner fork can be slipped easily into center, about 20 minutes longer.

2. Drain potatoes in colander, tossing gently to remove any excess water. Wipe saucepan dry and return potatoes to pan off heat. Using masher, work potatoes into uniform consistency. (Alternatively, push potatoes through ricer or food mill and back into dry saucepan.)

3. Using large wooden spoon or rubber spatula, stir melted butter into potatoes until just combined. Sprinkle salt and pepper over potatoes and add ½ cup hot half-and-half and sour cream. Stir until just combined. Stir in remaining half-and-half as needed to achieve desired consistency. Gently fold in 1½ cups cheese. Taste and adjust seasonings. Sprinkle remaining ½ cup cheese over potatoes and cover pot with lid. Let sit for 5 minutes and then partially stir in cheese. Transfer potatoes to serving bowl and serve.

MASHED POTATOES WITH PEPPER JACK AND BACON

Cook 4 slices bacon until crisp. Drain and crumble to yield about ½ cup. Follow recipe for Cheesy Mashed Potatoes, substituting either Pepper Jack or Horseradish Jack cheese for cheddar. Sprinkle crumbled bacon over potatoes before serving.

Equipment Pick: Our Favorite Masher

The Profi Plus Masher (about $16) beat out seven other models in a head-to-head mash-off. With its small holes, this masher yields soft, silky spuds. We like the easy-to-grip, rounded handle, too.

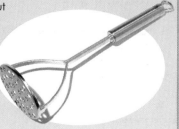

S'mores Brownies and More

Dear Cook's Country,
I make pretty good brownies (at least that's what my son says). But I'm tired of making plain brownies all the time—and adding some nuts just isn't exciting enough. Do you have any new ideas for brownies?

Beth Bloomberg, Colchester, Vermont

Dear Beth,
Here in the test kitchen, we're pretty serious about brownies and usually stick with tradition. Cream cheese brownies are as adventurous as it gets with the kitchen crew. But at home, my two daughters are always clamoring for something other than "plain old brownies." They beg me to sprinkle M&Ms over the batter, and I resist. Thanks to your prodding, I began to think I was a stick-in-the-mud. Why can't brownies be more fun?

To make things simple, I decided to use the same basic brownie as the base for all of my recipes. I knew I needed fairly sturdy brownies (you can't frost crumbly brownies), but they had to taste great on their own. Luckily, the test kitchen had already developed the perfect recipe, so it was time to let loose with brownie add-ons. I started slowly, not wanting to "shock" any of my kitchen colleagues.

Chocolate Frosting
Who doesn't like a thick, creamy chocolate frosting? I figured this variation would be easy to develop. Unfortunately, melted chocolate alone wouldn't set up correctly. After experimenting with various additions (including cream and butter), I found that a little vegetable oil helped to create a shiny glaze that firmed up quickly.

White Chocolate and Peppermint
I assumed that a white chocolate frosting could be made the same way as regular chocolate frosting, but time after time the white chocolate frosting cracked as it cooled. White chocolate is pretty fickle. Some brands contain cocoa butter, but others do not. I thought that white chocolate chips, which are made with emulsifiers and other stabilizers, might work better. Sure enough, these chips melted perfectly on their own, without any other ingredients.

A dusting of crushed peppermint candies gave these brownies a festive appearance. They were soon dubbed "Jack's Christmas brownies."

Caramel and Pecans
I didn't want to make real caramel sauce (no thanks to a thermometer or tricky timing). Instead, I improvised with brown sugar and butter, but the mixture was grainy. I tried adding some cream, but in the end a little corn syrup gave my quick caramel sauce a nice smooth texture. Tasters said the caramel called out for nuts, so I obliged with pecans.

Peanut Butter
The people at Reese's are onto something, and I planned to follow their lead. Would I have to add other ingredients (butter, cream cheese, or sugar) to the peanut butter, or could I just dollop some over the brownie batter and then swirl in it? As long as I chose a sweetened peanut butter (rather than an old-fashioned variety with oil on top), the peanut butter was fine on its own. A few tasters (who were now really getting into the spirit) wanted me to top these brownies with chocolate frosting. I wasn't about to argue.

Butterscotch and Coconut
German chocolate cake was the inspiration for brownies topped with melted butterscotch chips and toasted sweetened coconut. Simple and delicious.

Marshmallows and Graham Crackers
I had developed five brownie variations and thought I was done having fun. But then I spied some mini-marshmallows in the pantry, and my thoughts turned to campfire meals and my favorite childhood dessert: s'mores. Could I use brownies in place of the chocolate bar? I baked a simple graham cracker crust and then poured the brownie batter on top. Once the brownies were done, I arranged mini-marshmallows in the pan and set the oven to broil. Tasters in the kitchen were nearly giddy with anticipation. One bite transformed my normally adult colleagues into ravenous kids fighting for seconds. If this recipe can't beat the plain old brownie blues, nothing will.

–Jack Bishop

BASIC BROWNIES
MAKES 16 BROWNIES
These brownies are moist and packed with chocolate flavor, but they won't crumble when you cut them. In fact, they hold up well enough to pack in a child's lunchbox or bring to a picnic or bake sale. They're pretty good at home, too, with a tall glass of milk. And these sturdy brownies are the perfect base for all kinds of fun variations.

- 3 ounces unsweetened chocolate, chopped
- 8 tablespoons (1 stick) unsalted butter, cut into chunks
- 1 cup sugar
- ½ teaspoon baking powder
- ¼ teaspoon salt
- 2 large eggs
- 1 teaspoon vanilla extract
- ⅔ cup all-purpose flour

1. Adjust oven rack to middle position and heat oven to 350 degrees. Line 8-inch baking dish with foil (see photo on page 5) and coat foil with cooking spray.

2. Melt chocolate and butter in small bowl in microwave or in heatproof bowl set over pan of simmering water, stirring occasionally to combine. Cool mixture for several minutes.

3. Whisk sugar, baking powder, salt, eggs, and vanilla together in medium bowl until combined, about 15 seconds. Whisk in chocolate mixture until smooth. Stir in flour until no streaks of flour remain. Scrape batter evenly into prepared pan.

4. Bake until toothpick inserted halfway between edge and center of pan comes out clean, 22 to 27 minutes. Cool brownies on wire rack to room temperature, about 2 hours. Using foil, lift brownies from pan to cutting board. Slide foil out from under brownies and cut brownies into 2-inch squares. (Brownies can be stored in airtight container for several days.)

S'mores Brownies

Knowing When Brownies Are Done
The toothpick test is only moderately reliable. If you stick a toothpick in the center of a pan of brownies and it comes out completely free of crumbs or batter, you've probably overcooked the brownies. Try sticking the toothpick halfway between the center and the edges of the pan. Here's where the toothpick should come out clean. When stuck in the center, the toothpick should come out with some moist batter or crumbs. Better to undercook brownies than to overcook them. Not only are overcooked brownies dry, but they have less chocolate flavor.

FROSTED BROWNIES

Semisweet chips are fine for this frosting. If you're anxious to firm up the frosting, pop the tray of frosted brownies into the refrigerator for 15 minutes.

Basic Brownies (page 24)
- 4 ounces semisweet or bittersweet chocolate, chopped
- 1 tablespoon vegetable oil

Prepare Basic Brownies as directed. When brownies have cooled for 1 hour, heat chocolate and oil in microwave or in bowl set over pan of simmering water, stirring occasionally until chocolate has melted and mixture is smooth. Cool until barely warm, about 5 minutes. Pour chocolate mixture over brownies and spread evenly with spatula. Continue cooling brownies until glaze sets, 1 to 2 hours. Cut brownies as directed.

WHITE CHOCOLATE & PEPPERMINT BROWNIES

Make sure to use chips rather than bar chocolate in this recipe. Use a food processor to chop the peppermint candies.

Basic Brownies (page 24)
- 6 ounces white chocolate chips
- 1/3 cup finely chopped peppermint candies

Prepare Basic Brownies as directed. When brownies come out of oven, sprinkle white chocolate chips over brownies and let sit until they are softened but not melted, about 5 minutes. Using spatula or table knife, smooth chocolate evenly over top of brownies. Sprinkle with ground peppermint candies. Cool brownies on wire rack until topping firms up, about 2 hours. Cut as directed.

PECAN PIE BROWNIES

Sprinkling the nuts over the brownie batter (rather than folding them into the batter) ensures that they toast and become crisp in the oven. A quick caramel topping makes these brownies irresistible.

Basic Brownies (page 24)
- 1/2 cup coarsely chopped pecans
- 1/3 cup packed dark brown sugar
- 4 tablespoons unsalted butter
- 2 tablespoons corn syrup

Prepare Basic Brownies as directed, sprinkling pecans over batter just before placing pan in oven. Bake and cool as directed. Bring brown sugar, butter, and corn syrup to simmer in small saucepan over medium heat. Cook until sugar dissolves and mixture is smooth, 1 to 2 minutes. Remove pan from heat and cool until barely warm, about 10 minutes. Pour caramel mixture over brownies and spread evenly with spatula. Refrigerate until topping firms up, about 40 minutes. Cut brownies as directed.

PEANUT BUTTER SWIRL BROWNIES

To gild the lily, cover these brownies with chocolate frosting, following the recipe for Frosted Brownies. Use either creamy or chunky peanut butter, but avoid old-fashioned brands with oil on top.

Basic Brownies (page 24)
- 1/3 cup peanut butter, at room temperature

Prepare Basic Brownies through step 3. Drop peanut butter in 10 small dollops over batter. Without touching foil lining, run paring knife through batter to create swirls. Bake as directed.

GERMAN CHOCOLATE BROWNIES

The cake of the same name inspired this recipe.

Basic Brownies (page 24)
- 1/2 cup sweetened shredded coconut
- 6 ounces butterscotch chips

Prepare Basic Brownies as directed. While brownies are baking, heat medium skillet over medium heat and toast coconut until lightly browned, 5 to 8 minutes. Remove from pan and set aside. When brownies come out of oven, sprinkle butterscotch chips over brownies and let sit until they are softened but not melted, about 5 minutes. Using spatula or table knife, smooth chips evenly over top of brownies. Sprinkle with toasted coconut. Cool brownies on wire rack until topping has firmed up, about 2 hours. Cut as directed.

S'MORES BROWNIES

You will need 6 whole graham crackers to yield 3/4 cup crumbs when finely ground in a food processor. Prepare the brownie batter while the crust bakes. This recipe will not work in an oven with a separate broiler compartment.

Basic Brownies (page 24)
- 3/4 cup graham cracker crumbs
- 1 tablespoon sugar
- 4 tablespoons unsalted butter, melted
- 2 cups mini-marshmallows

1. Preheat oven and prepare pan according to step 1 of Basic Brownies. With fingers, combine graham cracker crumbs, sugar, and melted butter in bowl until evenly moistened. Firmly pat crumbs into prepared pan and bake until firm and lightly browned, 8 to 10 minutes. Remove pan from oven and set aside if brownie batter is not yet ready. Scrape brownie batter over crust and gently push batter into corners to cover crust. Bake as directed (don't sink toothpick into crumb crust). Remove pan from oven and turn oven to broil.

2. Sprinkle brownies evenly with single layer of marshmallows. Return pan with brownies to oven and broil until marshmallows are lightly browned, 1 to 3 minutes. (Watch oven constantly. Marshmallows will melt slightly but should hold their shape.) Immediately remove pan from oven. Cool brownies to room temperature, about 2 hours. When cutting brownies, coat knife with cooking spray to prevent marshmallows from sticking to knife.

Now That's Easy MELTING CHOCOLATE

Most brownie recipes start by melting chocolate and butter together. There are two good ways to do this.

A. In a Microwave:
Place the chocolate and butter in a microwave-safe bowl and microwave for 45 seconds. Stir (the chocolate won't liquefy unless you stir) with a spatula and keep microwaving until the mixture is smooth, checking and stirring at 15-second intervals.

B. On the Stovetop:
Bring a pan of water to a gentle simmer. Set a heat-proof bowl (metal is perfect) over the pan (but not touching the water) and add the chocolate and butter. Heat the chocolate and butter, stirring from time to time, until smooth.

Pecan Pie Brownies

White Chocolate & Peppermint Brownies

Basic Brownies

Peanut Butter Swirl Brownies

Frosted Brownies

German Chocolate Brownies

Never-Fail Christmas Cookies

Kitchen Helper
THREE TIPS FOR EASIER CHRISTMAS COOKIES

Rolling on a Warm Day
If your kitchen is extraordinarily warm, you can ice down the countertop prior to rolling. Fill a rimmed baking sheet with ice cubes and let it sit on the counter for 10 minutes.

Organizing Decorations
During the holidays, you may find yourself making cookies several times over a period of several weeks. Use a muffin tin to keep sprinkles and such organized. It's easy to move the tin around. When you're done, just cover the tin in plastic wrap.

Rolling without Flour
Use too much flour while rolling out cookie dough and the baked cookies will be tough. To avoid this problem, sandwich the dough between two sheets of parchment paper. Parchment paper can be found in the supermarket baking aisle or next to the plastic wrap.

Dear Cook's Country,
For the past 10 years, I've made Christmas cookies from my mother's old recipe, which I've enclosed for you to try. They taste good and the kids love them, but the cookies are really difficult to roll out. The dough is very soft and sticks to the rolling pin and countertop, which causes it to rip. And the rerolled cookies don't have the same texture as the first batch. Can you help?

Jennifer Tantum, Olney, Maryland

Dear Jennifer,
Sticky cookie dough is the last thing a busy baker wants to encounter around the holidays. But it seems like all the best-tasting recipes are a real challenge to roll out. More butter equals more flavor and more fuss. And it's absolutely true that baking rerolled scraps of dough makes for one tough cookie! There's no way I would ever throw out these scraps, but no one on my list deserves tough cookies. To solve this problem once and for all, I went into our test kitchen and started at the very beginning.

Most Christmas cookies are a simple combination of butter, flour, sugar, vanilla, and baking powder. Your mother's recipe has two somewhat unusual ingredients—eggs and sour cream. The eggs make your mother's cookies extra-rich, and the sour cream adds a nice tang that balances the sugary decorations. But there's a downside to these flavor-boosting ingredients. Your mother's dough is quite wet, and a wet dough is a sticky dough. I hoped to keep the great flavor that makes your mother's cookie dough so special while getting rid of the excess moisture that makes it so hard to roll out.

My first thought was to use less sour cream. Not a good idea. Less sour cream meant less flavor. I quickly turned my attention to the eggs. Your mother's recipe has two eggs, so I tried to use just one, but the cookies didn't taste as good. I wondered if I could keep both yolks (which have most of the fat and flavor) but lose the whites (which have much of the moisture). The dough made with two yolks was much drier. In fact, the dough was so dry it was a bit hard to mix. But when I cut out and baked some cookies, everyone in the test kitchen agreed that they tasted great. Best of all, I found that the scraps could be kneaded together and rerolled without toughening. I was onto something!

Most cookie dough is mixed via the "creaming" method. The butter and sugar are blended with an electric mixer until fluffy, after which the remaining wet and dry ingredients are added. But now there was so little moisture in your mother's recipe that the creaming method wasn't working.

I wondered if melting the butter—in effect, turning it from a solid to a liquid ingredient—would make the dough less dry and easier to handle. The melted butter mixed easily with the egg yolks, sour cream, and vanilla, and it took just moments to stir the mixture into the flour. Once chilled, the dough rolled out very easily without any sticking. So far, so good. The real test came once everyone tasted the cookies. They were as delicious as your mother's and a whole lot easier to make. I didn't even need a mixer. Two bowls, a whisk, and a spatula did the job.

To make rolling out the dough completely foolproof, I took the extra precaution of sandwiching it between two sheets of parchment paper (see the photo at right). Because the dough won't stick to the paper, I didn't have to add much flour during rolling, and this also helped to keep the scraps from becoming tough when rerolled.

One more thought: The dough must also be cool and very firm to the touch before you start to roll it out. If the dough gets too soft to handle easily, slide it into the refrigerator for a few minutes. When making cookies, patience really is a virtue.

I hope these ideas help. Drop me a note this Christmas and let me know if the dough was easy to roll out and if the cookies tasted as good as your mom's. **–Matthew Card**

BEST CHRISTMAS COOKIES

MAKES 2 TO 3 DOZEN COOKIES, DEPENDING ON SHAPE
This dough can be rerolled repeatedly without getting tough. If it becomes too soft to roll out or cut without sticking, return it to the refrigerator until firm. Resist the urge to add more flour. Rolling the dough between sheets of parchment paper is key to prevent sticking.

- 2¾ cups all-purpose flour
- 1¼ cups sugar
- 1 teaspoon baking powder
- ¼ teaspoon salt
- 2 large egg yolks
- 6 tablespoons sour cream
- 1 tablespoon vanilla extract
- 12 tablespoons (1½ sticks) unsalted butter, melted and slightly cooled

1. Whisk flour, sugar, baking powder, and salt together in large bowl. Whisk yolks, sour cream, and vanilla in second smaller bowl until well combined. Whisking constantly, gradually pour butter into sour cream mixture; whisk until incorporated. Pour wet mixture into dry mixture and stir with rubber spatula until combined. Knead dough by hand in bowl until flour is completely incorporated and dough has formed ball. Turn dough out onto lightly floured work surface and divide in half. Shape each half into ¾-inch-thick rectangle and wrap in plastic wrap. Refrigerate until firm, about 1 hour (can also freeze for 30 minutes).

2. Adjust oven racks to upper- and lower-middle positions and heat oven to 325 degrees. Line two baking sheets with parchment paper. Roll out 1 rectangle of dough between 2 sheets of lightly floured parchment paper to an even ⅛-inch thickness. (If dough seems soft, slide rolled dough, still between parchment, onto baking sheet and refrigerate until firm, about 15 minutes.) Cut into desired shapes using cookie cutter(s) and place cookies on parchment-lined baking sheets, spacing them about 1 inch apart.

3. Bake until cookies are lightly browned around edges, 16 to 18 minutes, rotating baking sheets halfway through baking time. Repeat process with remaining dough. (Dough scraps can be kneaded together and rerolled.) Cool cookies on wire rack to room temperature before glazing and decorating.

NO-FUSS ICING

MAKES ENOUGH TO GLAZE SEVERAL DOZEN COOKIES
Flavor this icing with vanilla, peppermint, or almond extract, if desired. It can also be dyed with food coloring. If glaze hardens over time, add a bit of milk or water and mix until smooth.

- 1–2 tablespoons milk
- 1 cup confectioners' sugar
  Food coloring (optional)
- 2–3 drops flavored extract (optional)

With small whisk or fork, combine 1 tablespoon milk and confectioners' sugar in small bowl to make soft, smooth icing. Stir in optional food coloring and flavored extracts. If mixture is too stiff, add milk in very tiny increments until desired consistency is reached.

Decorating Ideas for Christmas Cookies

Our call for decorating ideas for Christmas cookies was met with hundreds of responses from readers. Here are some of our favorites. Congratulations to our grand prize winner, Naomi Pardaz, who will receive $500. Six second-prize winners will receive $100.

Grand Prize Winner
Candy Canes
Naomi Pardaz
Minnetonka, Minnesota

Naomi spreads melted white chocolate (use white chocolate chips, if you like) over cooled cookies and sprinkles them with crushed candy canes. You can also use peppermint candies. Naomi's decoration is simple, tasty, and clever.

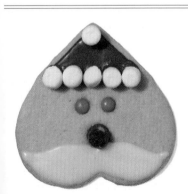

Second Prize Holly Leaves
Alice Shapiro of Solebury, Pennsylvania, makes cookies in the shape of holly leaves. Before baking, she places three red mini-M&M candies at the base of the leaf to represent berries. After baking the cookies and letting them cool, she paints each leaf with green icing.

Second Prize Almond Christmas Trees
Fran Baker of Rockledge, Florida, bakes her cookies in the shape of Christmas trees. Once they are cool, she lightly glazes the cookies, then shingles unpeeled almond slices up the tree. She sometimes sprinkles the cookies with confectioners' sugar, which looks like snow on the tips of the branches.

Second Prize Glittering Stars
Laura Speer of Fredericksburg, Virginia, mixes confectioners' sugar with a little water and spoons this glaze over star cookies. She then sprinkles brownish Demerara sugar (Sugar in the Raw works, too) or white decorating sugar over the glaze. The sugar dissolves only slightly, and the cookies really sparkle.

Second Prize
Rudolph the Red-Nosed Reindeer
Lynda North of Wallis, Texas, uses a large heart-shaped cookie cutter. Before baking, she presses mini-pretzels into each side of the "crown" of each heart for antlers. She then uses two brown mini-M&M candies for the eyes and a gum drop for that famous red nose.

Second Prize Stained Glass Stars
Sandy Casella of Bentonville, Arkansas, uses a small cutter to make a hole in each cookie before it goes into the oven. Three-quarters of the way through the baking time, she fills the center with crushed hard candies and then continues baking until the candies have melted. Wait 10 minutes before transferring them to a rack. Dust the cooled cookies with confectioners' sugar.

Second Prize Winter Snowmen
Susan Przybylo of South Holland, Illinois, cuts three circles of descending size and gently presses them together to form a snowman. When the baked cookies are cool, she covers them with white glaze and dusts them with sweetened shredded coconut. Pieces of licorice work as lumps of coal for the snowmen's eyes and as buttons. A candy corn doubles for the nose.

Honorable Mention
Santa Claus
Susan Haran of Boulder, Colorado, uses a large heart-shaped cutter, turning the heart upside down. Before baking, she uses green mini-M&Ms for Santa's eyes and a red gum drop for his nose. After baking and cooling the cookies, she uses red icing and mini-marshmallows for his hat and plain white icing for his beard.

Honorable Mention
Colored Christmas Trees
Dana Bourne of Chestertown, Maryland, pipes or drizzles colored frosting in lines back and forth across cooled tree-shaped cookies. The "ornaments" are brightly colored mini-M&M candies. For something fancier, try the tiny silver balls (called dragées) sold in many markets during the holidays.

Honorable Mention
Wreaths
Lisa Fiebig of Columbus, Ohio, uses fluted round cutters to create holiday wreaths. She pipes a ring of white frosting in the center of each one and then decorates with green sprinkles or sanding sugar (baker's decorating sugar). She adds a bow by cutting red licorice (Twizzlers are perfect) into small triangles.

Honorable Mention
Wrapped Boxes
Jenny Bernasconi of Newtown, New York, bakes square cookies and frosts them to create pretty gift boxes. Coat cooled cookies with one colored glaze, let it dry, and then use a second glaze to create a pretty ribbon. Or just spread white icing on the cookies and sprinkle with colored sugar to create a ribbon.

When Things Go Wrong in the Kitchen

Every cook has a favorite story about a kitchen disaster. We asked readers to share those stories with us and were inundated with letters—more than 850 funny, touching, harrowing, and instructive tales. We were struck by the stories about husbands and wives and the funny things we do to try to please our spouses. Here are some of the more unusual stories that made us chuckle. Who says cooking isn't love?

PEELING THE EEL

Years ago, I came across a recipe for *anguille au vert*, a spinach soufflé crowned with slices of eel, a recipe only the French could have invented. My French husband had put a star next to the recipe. "This is not simple," he warned. Undeterred, the next day I searched for a whole, fresh eel—in Albuquerque, N.M. I found a frozen specimen. It was nearly 3½ feet long and looked like a walking stick.

At home, I washed away the sand frozen into the eel and set it to thaw while my 2-year-old daughter watched. An hour later, the eel began to exhibit more eel-like properties and lay coiled in the sink. The recipe was on a tear-out card from *Elle* magazine. Reading the French instructions was the easy part.

Step A instructed me to pound a nail into the windowsill above my kitchen sink. I followed step B and tied a cord to the head of the nail, the end dangling to the floor. For step C, I had to cut a slit around the eel's neck. To conduct this surgery, I placed the eel on the kitchen table, where, as slippery in morbidity as in life, it thrashed its tail end over the table's edge and onto the kitchen chairs. My daughter was strapped into her highchair, out of harm's way.

To follow step D, I retrieved pliers from my toolbox. "Tie the eel to the cord so that you can grab the skin at the neck and pull it off." The recipe mentioned that I could put my foot against the counter for leverage. I pulled, I slipped, and the eel still clung to its skin. I tried again. The floor was getting dangerously slippery, and I fell against a chair. My daughter looked a little concerned.

I gathered up the skin and bone, wrapped it in paper, and set it on the floor. I'd run out of counter-space. It was now 7 o'clock. I wasn't obsessive about having everything ready when my husband got home, but the sight that greeted him would have crumpled lesser men. He first spotted the eel head nailed to the sill. Taking in the rest took a moment. "Oh, la, laaaaa! What happened, Mina?"

Eventually, dinner turned out fine. My husband applauded my efforts. Have I ever made that recipe again? Not on your life.

Mina Yamashita Albuquerque, New Mexico

PURPLE GRAVY

The first weekend after our honeymoon, I decided to cook a big Sunday dinner for my new husband. He mentioned that he liked "brown" gravy. The only gravy I knew how to make was milk gravy, so I thought I would just make that and get the brown color by browning the flour that went into it. I was not successful, so, with everything else hot and ready, I quickly tried to figure out what to do. Then a light bulb went on in my head. Food coloring! One can make all sorts of colors out of the primary colors, yes?

I tried a little yellow, a little red, and then some blue to darken it. No go. I had good gravy alright, but I wasn't about to ladle that shade of purple over mashed potatoes.

Diana Stevens Danville, Indiana

HELP! THERE'S A VOLCANO IN MY KITCHEN!

When my parents came back from their honeymoon, they moved in with my father's parents while he, a World War II vet, went to college. My mother knew nothing about cooking but decided to surprise my father by making fried chicken.

She sequestered herself in the kitchen and began to "cook." She filled a large pot with a gallon of oil, put the heat on high, and, when the oil came to a rolling boil, threw in the chicken. And then the fun began. The pot boiled over, and it kept on boiling over, like an erupting volcano, making an incredible mess. (My mother did not think to turn off the burner.) The stove was covered with a thick coating that oozed onto the floor. The whole kitchen was filled with smoke. My father was pounding on the kitchen door, wanting desperately to be let in, and my mother was crying. She fled the room, leaving behind her a mess of gargantuan proportions.

Here's the kicker. It wasn't a gallon of oil that my mother had used—it was a gallon of maple syrup. My grandparents were up all night cleaning kitchen.

Deirdre Nicholson South Burlington, Vermont

THE CASE OF THE EXPLODING CHICKEN

Several months before I was married, I was at my fiancé's house. He decided to cook some chicken and dumplings. Hey, I was impressed. My future husband was actually going to cook something other than a frozen pizza.

Being a bachelor, he didn't have all of the right kitchen equipment, so he decided to boil the chicken in a pressure cooker. As you might imagine, the cooker exploded with a large bang. I mean to tell you there was chicken everywhere, and the place was chaos! Dogs were slurping chicken and bones off the floor. I was chasing dogs with chicken bones in their mouths. My fiancé was splashing cool water on himself, as he was burned on his face and chest—

luckily, not too terribly. It looked like a bad sunburn.

To cool off, my fiancé had changed into a robe and was sitting in front of a fan. That's when my parents arrived unannounced. I opened the door and they asked, "Did we come at a bad time?" They peered inside and saw my red-faced fiancé in his robe. "Oh, my goodness, we diiiiid come at a bad time."

Danielle Simoneau Lakewood, Colorado

MY, WHAT SMALL BREASTS!

As a young bride (who had never cooked anything more difficult than a box cake), I had the regular task of cutting up whole chickens. They were a lot less expensive than chicken parts, and we were on a budget. For six months, my husband complained that although we were saving money by buying whole chickens, the breasts were seriously lacking in white meat.

At that point, I decided to check a cookbook—only to find out that after cutting off the wings and the legs, I apparently hadn't been able to tell the front from the back; I had been throwing out the breasts and serving him the BACKS!!! This has become a favorite family story and is especially funny now that I've remarried. My new husband abhors white meat and will only eat legs, thighs, and wings. What goes around comes around.

Karen Knegten Lincolnshire, Illinois

HOMEMADE SHRIMP JERKY

Back in 1972, my husband and I were living in an apartment in San Francisco, and my mother visited for the day. My husband, despite being severely challenged in the kitchen, offered to make us lunch. I had planned a lunch of shrimp salad and sourdough French bread and made the dressing in advance, so I figured it would be easy enough for him to put things together while my mother and I chatted.

The afternoon was getting on and we hadn't been served. My husband repeatedly said he didn't need any help with the cooking. The kitchen door was closed. Then we heard the strangest noise. I recognized it as my old-fashioned pressure cooker, which emitted a pfsst, pfsst, pfsst sound. I said to my mother, "I wonder why he is using the pressure cooker." A little while later, we again heard the pfsst, pfsst sound. Still no lunch.

Finally, my husband came out of the kitchen. He said apologetically, "I've tried and tried. I've boiled them and baked them and even pressure-cooked them twice, but I just can't get the shrimp to cook. They are still pink!" He had accidentally invented shrimp jerky, which did nothing to improve his culinary status with me or my mother.

Karen Buckter Mill Valley, California

Send us your funniest kitchen disaster stories. Please write to us at Kitchen Disasters, Cook's Country, P.O. Box 470739, Brookline, MA 02447. If you'd like to use e-mail, write to us at kitchendisasters@bcpress.com.

Notes from Our Test Kitchen

TIPS, TECHNIQUES, AND TOOLS FOR BETTER COOKING

Tasters evaluate chocolate pudding made with different kinds of cocoa. Now that's hard work!

TWO KINDS OF COCOA POWDER
Cocoa powder delivers strong chocolate flavor with a minimum of fat and calories, making it an essential ingredient in our Low-Fat Chocolate Pudding (page 8). That's because cocoa powder is unsweetened chocolate with about three-quarters of the cocoa butter removed. What's left behind are the potent cocoa solids. When shopping for cocoa powder, you have two basic choices.

Regular (or natural) cocoa powder is naturally acidic and has a sharp flavor. Many American cocoa powders, including Hershey's basic cocoa powder, fall into this category. We found that regular cocoa powder gives our pudding a light brown color and good flavor.

Dutched cocoa has been treated with an alkali, which mellows the harsher, acidic notes in cocoa. European cocoas have traditionally been processed this way, and now many American companies offer Dutched versions of their cocoa. We found that Dutched cocoa gives our pudding a deep brown—almost black—color and rich flavor.

While we prefer Dutched cocoa in our pudding recipe, regular cocoa will work fine. It's worth noting that it's not advisable to substitute one type of cocoa for another in recipes that use a leavener (usually baking soda or powder). For instance, cakes often won't rise if you use the wrong kind of cocoa powder.

SHOPPING FOR APPLES
We love to bake with Granny Smith apples—they are tart (so they work well with sugary cakes) and hold their shape. As versatile as they are, shopping for Grannies can be tricky. The color of most fruits intensifies as it ripens. Not so with Grannies. Yellowish or light green Grannies are riper (and better tasting) than dark green Grannies.

MAIL-ORDER SEA FOAM CANDY
When researching sea foam candy (see page 9), we ordered some samples from a number of small companies around the country. Our favorite version of this old-fashioned candy came from McCrackin Street Sweets (458 McCrackin Street, Juliette, GA 31046; 478-994-4498; www.mccrackinstreetsweets.com). You want to order what this family-run company calls Seafoam Divinity. It's not too sweet, chewy yet light, and loaded with pecans. The candy costs $9.95 per pound, plus shipping and handling.

SLOW-COOKER TIMER
When testing slow cookers (see page 31), we found that a timer and keep-warm function were valuable features, especially if you like to use your slow cooker when you're at work. Without these features, a traffic jam might mean overcooked pot roast or bloated baked beans. Unfortunately, several of our favorite models did not have these features. But Rival (inventor of the original Crock-Pot) sells a separate timer that works with most slow cookers, including the one you may already own.

Here's how the Smart-Part Programmable Module (model #SP100, $9.95) works. Simply plug your slow cooker into the Smart-Part, plug the Smart-Part into a wall outlet, and then program the Smart-Part. Cooking times are limited to four and six hours on high and eight or 10 hours on low. Still, a restrictive timer is better than no timer at all, and this device will automatically turn the slow cooker to "warm" once the set time has elapsed. The Smart-Part is available at many kitchenware shops and on the Web at amazon.com and cooking.com.

This handy timer can adjust the temperature of your slow cooker when you're not home.

DON'T FORGET THE SALT
Most cooks know that salt makes food taste better. It's hard to imagine a steak, chicken, or vegetable dish without it. But many good cooks we know forget the salt when baking. Just a pinch of salt makes countless baked goods—everything from apple cake (page 18) to brownies (pages 24–25)—taste better. And salt serves a crucial function in our sea foam candy (page 9), helping to cut the sweetness and intensify the nut flavor. Although you can use almost any kind of salt when making savory recipes, table salt (with its fine, easily dissolved crystals) is best when baking or making candy.

A Cut Above
Although you may be tempted by cute designs, we suggest you buy cookie cutters based on material and sharpness. We've found that heavy-duty metal cutters are more likely to have sharp edges that can cut neatly through cookie dough. Avoid plastic cutters, which often have quite dull edges, as well as flimsy metal ones that can make for sloppy cutouts. Cheap metal cutters also rust easily.

Everyone Should Have...
A Dutch Oven

Many cooks probably know the Dutch oven as a lidded casserole. This pot was originally manufactured with "ears" on the side (small, round tabs used to pick up the pot); the lid had a wire handle that stayed cooler than the lid itself and a lip around its edge. Before the advent of cooking stoves, hot coals were placed on the lid (and held in place by the lip), in effect turning this pot into an oven for baking everything from beans to biscuits. That explains why it's called an "oven." As for the "Dutch" part of the name, the best cast iron used to come from Holland. In early America, almost every home had a Dutch oven, and these durable pots were also used by cooks on chuck wagons in the 19th century.

Today, a cast-iron Dutch oven is just as useful. It's relatively affordable (expect to spend $50), but it must be seasoned regularly with oil. More expensive Dutch ovens made from other metals or from enameled cast iron are also good choices. We've found that 7 to 8 quarts is the best size.

SKIMMING FAT FROM GRAVY
Our favorite cut of meat for pot roast (see page 10) is the chuck roast. Its flavor and texture are superior to those of other cuts of beef, at least when it comes to this recipe. But there is one problem with chuck roasts. They tend to be fatty (that's why they taste good), and the gravy you get from them for your pot roast can be very greasy by the time the roast has finished cooking. The easiest way to remove excess fat is to wait. If you put the gravy and roast in the refrigerator overnight, the fat will rise to the surface and harden, where it can be easily scooped away.

But what if you want to serve the pot roast as soon as it has finished cooking? The answer is simple—combine a little patience with a big spoon. Here's what to do: Remove the roast from the gravy and set it aside on a cutting board under a piece of foil. Wait at least 5 minutes (10 minutes is even better). The fat should separate and float to the surface. You can see it—it will be clear. Use a large, wide spoon to skim off the fat. You might lose a bit of gravy, too, but don't worry, there's a lot of gravy in the pot.

O il and vinegar make the simplest salad dressing, one that's easy enough to put together yourself: Just whisk oil, vinegar, salt, and pepper, then serve. So why would anyone purchase a bottled salad dressing? We can think of a couple of reasons. Sometimes you are just too tired to do it yourself. But the better reason is that sometimes you want something with more personality and zip. Italian dressing, for example, contains not just oil and vinegar but garlic, red pepper, oregano, and other herbs and spices. Sounds good, but several of those ingredients need to be finely chopped, which can add up to a lot of work. All of a sudden, the commercial stuff in the bottle starts to look attractive.

Still, if the supermarket Italian dressing tastes awful, we'd just as soon stick with plain old oil and vinegar. To find out if any of the Italian dressings out there are worth buying, we rounded up seven leading brands. Of the dressings we selected (all available nationwide), most had similar ingredient lists: oil, vinegar, water, sugar, and salt, along with garlic, onion, red bell pepper, various herbs and spices, stabilizers, and preservatives. (A key ingredient in these dressings is xanthan gum, a stabilizer that gives them their signature thickness.)

Were any of these dressings good enough to buy? We found two that were up to snuff. The winner, Good Seasons, requires that you add your own oil and vinegar at home, so it was closest to homemade. In second place, Kraft Seven Seas Italian was OK but on the sweet side. Each dressing was sampled on a piece of iceberg lettuce by 20 panelists, who did not know which brands were being tasted. The dressings are listed in order of preference.

–Erika Bruce

Top Picks

1. GOOD SEASONS Italian All Natural Salad Dressing Mix $2.39 (includes cruet and
2 packets with dried seasonings; each packet yields 8 ounces of dressing)
Comments: It is easy to understand why this brand came out on top. Adding our own oil and vinegar (plus a little bit of water, per packet instructions) made this dressing taste "most like homemade." The packet provides the right balance of herbs and spices, especially in the garlic and black pepper departments, as well as the right amount of sugar, resulting in a dressing that was "not too tart or sweet."

2. KRAFT Seven Seas Viva Italian Dressing $2.79 for 16-ounce bottle
Comments: A close second (and requiring no extra steps), this zesty dressing brought many tasters back to their childhood, with comparisons to "lunchroom cafeteria Italian dressing." Several tasters thought it would be a "good dressing for kids" because it had a sweet garlic and red pepper flavor to balance out the vinegar. This "light and spicy" dressing had the right amount of herbs and zip.

Also-Rans

3. WISH-BONE Italian Dressing $2.79 for 16-ounce bottle
Comments: "Tart," "tangy," and "garlicky" were the words most often used to describe this dressing. While tasters appreciated its sharp and assertive flavor, they complained about its texture, which was described as "too thick," "unnaturally viscous," and "too stabilized."

4. NEWMAN'S OWN Family Recipe Italian $3.19 for 16-ounce bottle
Comments: This dressing includes a healthy dose of Romano cheese and, in smaller amounts, anchovies. It was no surprise that tasters mistook this dressing for Caesar. They liked the strong garlic and black pepper flavors but not the overabundance of oil and the weak vinegar kick. A little fancier than the usual Italian dressing.

5. KRAFT House Italian Dressing $2.79 for 16-ounce bottle
Comments: Like Newman's Own, this dressing contains cheese, both Parmesan and Romano. Combined with a "dried herb" and "strong garlic" flavor, it reminded tasters of "bad pizza." The assertive flavors seemed "more suited for a marinade" than a salad dressing.

6. KEN'S STEAKHOUSE Italian Dressing and Marinade $2.69 for 16-ounce bottle
Comments: This bare-bones dressing contains few of the herbs and spices found in the other dressings sampled. Beyond oil, vinegar, salt, garlic, and onion, it featured only a long list of stabilizers and preservatives. The dressing was pale yellow and acidic, with lemony undertones. Some tasters appreciated the lack of particulate matter; others felt that this dressing did not have enough personality to qualify as Italian.

7. CAINS Italian Dressing $2.79 for 24-ounce bottle
Comments: Tasters were hard-pressed to say anything nice about this exceedingly sweet dressing. The flavor of "freeze-dried herbs" and "stale oregano" predominated; the red pepper "floaties" tasted "artificial."

Buyer's Guide Orange Juice

You can spend a little or a lot for orange juice, but does more money always buy a better product? To find out, we tasted several dozen juices that fall into five basic categories. Here's what we found.

Fresh-squeezed juice is the best (that's no surprise), but store-bought fresh-squeezed juice requires no work and tastes nearly as good. If your supermarket carries fresh squeezed, give it a try. The juices from our local markets were very good, but they were also expensive—more than 60 cents a glass.

Among the chilled juices, the not-from-concentrates have a fresher flavor than the made-from-concentrates. That's because juices made from concentrate are pasteurized twice—once when the concentrate is made and again when the juice is packaged. Not-from-concentrates are pasteurized just once, when the juice is packaged. Because pasteurization destroys some flavor, you want to buy a juice that's been pasteurized only once. In our markets, both juices cost about the same (42 cents per glass), so why not buy the one that tastes better?

If price is your top concern, frozen orange juice concentrate is your best buy. It's been pasteurized just once (when the concentrate was made) and tastes almost as good as chilled not-from-concentrate juice that costs nearly twice as much. Here are some highlights from our tasting, with our choices listed in order of preference. –Erika Bruce

① **Fresh Squeezed**
65 cents/serving
"Like eating an orange," "balanced flavor."

② **Store-Bought Fresh Squeezed**
62 cents/serving
"Tastes like fresh squeezed."

③ **Chilled, Not from Concentrate**
42 cents/serving
"Not too acidic" and "sweet."

④ **Frozen, from Concentrate**
25 cents/serving
"Too tart" but "not bad for not fresh."

⑤ **Chilled, from Concentrate**
42 cents/serving
"Sour," "too bitter," and "stale."

Best Value
Frozen concentrate has a surprisingly good flavor and costs less than the other options.

Best Taste
Juice squeezed at the supermarket tastes nearly as good as juice you squeeze yourself.

Slow cookers (better known as Crock-Pots, a name trademarked by the Rival company) may be the only modern kitchen convenience that saves the cook time by using more of it rather than less. But gone are the days of merely picking out what size you need. We found 40 different models online, which begs the question: Is one slow cooker better than another? To find out, we rounded up eight leading models and put them through some very slow tests.

We prepared a simple beef chili on the low temperature setting for six hours in each model, and, frankly, each chili was pretty good. We also prepared pot roast (see the recipe on page 10) on the high temperature setting in each model, leaving the meat in the cooker until the roast maintained an internal temperature of 200 degrees for an hour. All but one slow cooker managed this task, albeit at different lengths of time, ranging from seven to nine hours. Time, however, is not really the name of this game. It turns out that what matters is size, at least with our pot roast recipe. We recommend buying a slow cooker with a minimum capacity of 6 quarts. Anything smaller and a modest 5-pound roast or brisket won't fit.

Shape also matters. We found the round crock styles to be deeper than the oval crocks, and they heated more evenly. That said, while the depth and shape of these round cookers made them perfect for submerging a roast in braising liquid, it proved a hindrance with recipes requiring bulky, layered ingredients, such as chicken parts or ribs. Oval-shaped slow cookers, such as the Farberware Millennium and the West Bend Versatility, have more surface area for cooking and are better suited to these kinds of recipes. Because oval cookers also work with chilis or roasts, they are more versatile.

In addition to differences in size and shape, we noted a variety of features on slow cookers, some of which are quite helpful. A "keep warm" setting is sensible (it turns the heat down once the food is done), but only when paired with a timer. This way, if you are late getting home from work, dinner will still be fine. Without a timer, the keep warm function seems useless. (See page 29 for information about a separate timer that can be plugged into almost any slow cooker.)

–Garth Clingingsmith

Recommended
FARBERWARE Millennium FSC600
Capacity: 6 quarts
Price: $29.99
Features: Low and high settings; power light

Comments: The largest usable capacity (among the 6-quart models) gave the pot roast plenty of room. The oval shape is also well suited to recipes with bulky ingredients, such as chicken parts and ribs. A good cooker for a fair price.

Recommended
WEST BEND Versatility Cooker #84716
Capacity: 6 quarts
Price: $39.99
Features: Variable thermostat; "crock" is actually a lightweight pot that is stovetop-safe and ovensafe to 350 degrees

Comments: Not your standard slow cooker, the Versatility Cooker lives up to its name. Instead of a ceramic crock enveloped by heating elements, a lightweight metal pot gives you the option of jumpstarting recipes on the stovetop and then transferring the "crock" to its griddle-like base to finish cooking. Heat output struggles at lower settings.

Recommended
PROCTOR SILEX #33627
Capacity: 7 quarts
Price: $39.95
Features: Low and high settings; dishwasher-safe crock and lid

Comments: Huge capacity and most even heating. An efficient round shape is perfect for roasts, but not well suited to bulky chicken parts or ribs. This bare-bones slow cooker could use some bells and whistles, especially a power light so you'd know if it was working.

Recommended with Reservations
RIVAL Recipe Smart Pot #4865
Capacity: 5.5 quarts
Price: $79.99
Features: Low and high settings; keep warm function; power light; timer; dishwasher-safe crock and lid; digital display with recipes

Comments: The "ultimate" in slow cookers is not without serious faults. Most troublesome was the small size of the crock, which could barely contain a big pot roast. On the plus side, the timer could be set at half-hour increments to one of three temperatures. Including recipes with the pot is intriguing, but the small digital screen is not easy to read.

Recommended with Reservations
RIVAL Smart Pot #38601
Capacity: 6 quarts
Price: $49.99
Features: Low and high settings; keep warm function; power light; timer; dishwasher-safe crock and lid

Comments: The timer was frustrating to use because it can be set only to four and six hours on high and to eight or 10 hours on low. The pot roast also swelled enough during cooking to pop the lid open.

Not Recommended
Toastmaster #1320
Capacity: 6 quarts
Price: $24.99
Features: Low and high settings; power light

Comments: Same features as the Farberware (both are produced by Salton), but this cooker had a harder time maintaining even heat on the low setting. Chili ranged from a barely-safe-to-eat 165 degrees in the center to a full simmer at the edge of the crock. Using the high temperature setting eliminated this problem, allowing us to produce a well-cooked pot roast. For identical features and better performance, spend the extra $5 on the Farberware cooker.

Not Recommended
HAMILTON BEACH Meal Maker #33575
Capacity: 6 quarts
Price: $35.99
Features: Low and high settings; keep warm function; dishwasher-safe crock and lid

Comments: Exceptionally even heat, but food sputtered onto the wall because the lightweight lid could not contain the huffing and puffing of either the chili or the pot roast.

Not Recommended
WEST BEND Crockery Cooker #84346
Capacity: 6 quarts
Price: $31.99
Features: Low and high settings; keep warm function; power light; dishwasher-safe crock and lid

Comments: The most uneven slow cooker at low temperature, and high temperature failed to push the internal temperature of the pot roast much over 190 degrees; the other cookers easily got the pot roast up to 200 degrees.

Does It Work? Brown & Crisp Bags

Can you really brown foods in the microwave? According to the manufacturer of Brown & Crisp Microwave Cooking Bags, you can. We checked out this claim by using the bags to microwave bacon, frozen hot pockets, popcorn, frozen pizza, a whole potato, and a boneless, skinless chicken breast. These bags (a package of 12 costs $10) do not live up to their promise of taking baking, broiling, steaming, frying, and barbecuing to the microwave. You are more likely to flame-broil with these bags; we set two of them on fire in the test kitchen microwave during normal use.

This product's patent, as registered with the U.S. Patent and Trademark Office, reads as follows: Wherever food "does not cover the susceptor material"—that is, the bag— "the susceptor will get extremely hot, often hot enough to cause damage to the package. Indeed, it has been reported that susceptor packages have caught fire in consumer microwave[s] often." This warning should appear on the packaging, but it doesn't.

–Garth Clingingsmith

Thanks for the Memories

For this charter issue, we asked readers to share some of their favorite food memories with us; we heard from hundreds of you. We were particularly touched by the power of cakes, cookies, breads, and other baked goods to evoke strong images from the past. Here's a sampling of the letters we received.

Priceless Bread and Butter
Bobbie Somerville,
Tualatin, Oregon

When I think about Grandma Lawson's homemade bread long enough, I can actually smell that wonderful yeasty aroma that filled her tiny farm kitchen in Douds, Iowa. She baked it in an old wood-burning stove, and she thought that was part of the reason why it was so tasty. She always made round loaves instead of the usual rectangle shape. She'd put a little lard on her fingers and rub the tops of the loaves just after they came out of the stove, which put a nice shine on them.

She and Grandpa had cows, so her butter was made fresh. Sometimes, on the days we visited, she would milk one of the cows and bring the metal pail up to the kitchen doorstep, where she let it sit until the cream rose to the top. Then she would take an old white enameled spoon and slowly skim off the layer of thick, rich cream to put in the butter churn. She'd let us kids churn the butter for her, and we would get fresh butter on our bread. It's funny, but the only food I remember eating at her house was her homemade bread. I would pay $100 today for a loaf of her bread and a pound of her butter.

The Wedding Cake
Joan Perry Morris, Tallahassee, Florida

I was a member of the secretarial staff of the Florida State University Library in the early 1960s. A group of us began taking turns bringing home-baked goodies to the staff gatherings. We were sometimes joined by a professional journalist named Allen.

One day I brought a chocolate cake that I thought was pretty good, and I did receive several compliments. Except from Allen, who said, "Almost as good as my father used to make." Thinking I could make a chocolate cake better than anyone's father, I asked, "How was your father's chocolate cake better than mine?" Allen answered, "He used to make a devil's food chocolate cake."

Well, the next time it was my turn to bring a "goodie," I made a devil's food chocolate cake. Allen was there, and I expected to receive a compliment. But again, I heard instead, "Almost as good as my father used to make." Again I asked, "How was your father's chocolate cake better than mine?" "He used to make a three-layer devil's food chocolate cake," he answered.

Spurred on by the competition, I didn't even wait for my turn but made a three-layer devil's food chocolate cake for the next gathering. After receiving high praise from most of the group, I turned to Allen, again expecting a "well done."

Instead, he said, "Almost as good as my father used to make." Between almost gritted teeth, I responded again, "How was your father's chocolate cake better than mine?" "He

used to frost it with a dark fudge frosting," Allen lightheartedly replied.

After that exchange, Allen felt guilty about having teased me into baking more often than I ordinarily would and gave one of the group enough money to reimburse me for the cost of the ingredients.

Still incensed, I baked a three-layer devil's food chocolate cake, frosted it with dark fudge frosting, and placed the money, wrapped in plastic wrap, under a marked section of the cake. I told everyone else what I had done and, when I served the cake, made sure that Allen got the right piece. We talked and laughed and only when we were cleaning up did we realize that Allen had made no comment about the added ingredients in his piece of cake.

Only later did I learn what Allen had done with the chocolate-cake-covered, plastic-wrapped money. He had hidden it in his suit pocket. That was the beginning of a beautiful friendship—and 37 years of marriage.

The Taste of Freedom
Jayne Rizz, New York, New York

I was maybe 2 or 3 years old when my mother was taken to a concentration camp in Germany. My father managed to escape but was then taken by the Russians to forced labor. I was placed in an orphanage, under an assumed name. My father, who was very resourceful and daring, managed to get away from the Russians. He was concerned about the Nazis closing in on the city, so he made arrangements to get me out of the orphanage. Of course, I was very young and did not really recognize him as my father, so I didn't want to go with him. From his pocket he then took out something in a greasy paper and gave it to me, with the following words: "You know what it is? This is your favorite pastry with poppy seeds. I have only this one piece and wanted to give it to you when we got home, but I just changed my mind."

As I looked at this cake my eyes lit up, and I could not wait to bite into it. But I did not. I wanted to look at it, touch it, just savor the fact that I had not enjoyed anything like it for months. At that point, it all came back to me that this must be my father. I must go with him; perhaps he had more pastries. My father and his pastry saved my life. The next day the Nazis executed all the kids at the orphanage.

Watch Out for Green Cakes!
Jill Sevier, Houston, Texas

One summer when I was 8 years old, my big sister and I decided to bake a cake. For some reason that I no longer recall, we decided to put green food coloring in the cake. It looked rather sickening, but it tasted fine! The day after making the colorful

concoction, my parents sat my sister and me down and proceeded to inform us that my mother was pregnant with our soon-to-be younger brother. Unfamiliar at that point with the facts of life and not knowing what else might be the cause of the happy event, I assumed the green cake must be the culprit!

More than 40 years later, my sister's kids are grown, and my brother and I both have teenagers, but the legend of the green cake lives on in our family and always brings a chuckle and a smile.

Cookies Not Fit for a Dog
Nevada Coleman, Dallas, Texas

When I was 8 years old and a new cook, I decided to make my mom's favorite cookies, Molasses Crinkles. Owing to a miscalculation, my 12 drop cookies melded into one giant cookie with a smell that woke my mother out of a dead sleep through a closed door. Trying not to laugh at my dismayed expression, she told me to offer it to the dog. Replying with tears in my eyes, I explained that I had tried, but he took one sniff and retreated to his doghouse, refusing to come out until I had removed the disaster from the area. Needless to say, I made sure I double-checked ingredients and amounts from then until now. I still remain a bit paranoid when making cookies.

A Christmas Present
Melissa Flynn, Andover, Massachusetts

I was pregnant and had a desire for a big warm pretzel. As soon as I put the frozen pretzel in the oven, my sister called to say her twins were born! I was so excited that I rounded up the family for the two-hour drive to Maine to meet our new nieces. Right in the middle of the celebration, I realized what I had left in the oven! It was the quickest goodbye and the quietest ride home.

The house was fine. The pretzel was black as coal, with a beautiful shiny patina—just waiting for us. It was such a relief that nothing caught on fire that I shellacked the pretzel and gave it to my sister to use as a Christmas ornament!

Please share a food memory that includes your parents. Parents shape our lives in countless ways, even in the kitchen. For our next issue, we'd love to hear food memories about your mother or father. Write to us at Food Memories, Cook's Country, P.O. Box 470739, Brookline, MA 02447. If you'd like to use e-mail, write to us at foodmemories@bcpress.com.

Postcards from Home

COOK'S COUNTRY READERS SHOW US WHAT'S COOKING AT HOME!

Fun Cake

Chrissy Olson Marshfield, Massachusetts

Chrissy writes: "My husband, John, is a very creative man whose sense of humor astounds us all. This cake was for our cousin, whose nickname is Dana Bug!"

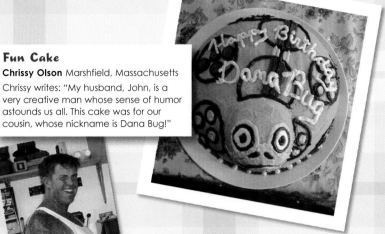

Cooking Together

Donna Knoth
Holland, Michigan

Donna writes: "What a great way to share warm memories. Here's my dear husband in the kitchen with me!"

A Special Thanksgiving

Patrick & Anne Gomes
Guatemala City, Guatemala

Patrick and Anne write: "For Thanksgiving, we had 32 guests— Mexicans, Argentines, a Brazilian, an Australian, and several Guatemalans joined 10 American Peace Corps volunteers stationed here in Guatemala— making the holiday even more special."

CUTE BABY of the MONTH!

Go, Kid, Go!

John Engemann
Chapel Hill, North Carolina

John writes: "I love this picture of our son with a tomato salad because it reminds me of when he just started crawling and realized there's nothing better than big juicy tomatoes picked at their peak."

What a Good Friend

Heather Mader
Portland, Oregon

Heather writes: "I might be the only woman on the planet who wants to make her own birthday cake! It's my sweet way of saying thank you to my friends. This one was a giant chocolate cake layered with creamy coconut filling and covered in chocolate ganache. I made the gold dragonflies by dusting gold powder over a homemade stencil."

ONE SPOOKY CAKE!

Halloween Surprise

Brett Roach
San Jose, California

Pig Out

John Baker Noblesville, Indiana

John writes: "This cake was made for a pig roast party. The pig is entirely edible and was made using three chocolate cakes and two white cakes. The round red object was an apple, also made of cake."

WOW!

Steven Adashek Baltimore, Maryland

Steven writes: "This was my first attempt at making *croquembouche*, the classic French wedding cake. I worked for two days, and then our family had a wonderful time breaking it apart to eat the individual éclairs filled with Grand Marnier–flavored pastry cream."

We love to see what you're growing, cooking, and eating at home. Send your digital photos to postcards@bcpress.com. If we publish your photo, you will receive a complimentary one-year subscription to *Cook's Country*. Make sure to include your name, address, and daytime phone number in the e-mail along with your photo. And tell us a little bit about what makes your photo special.

Recipe Index

main courses

Beef Barley Soup with Mushrooms 11
Beef Tortilla Casserole 11
Corned Beef Hash RC
Country-Style Pot Roast with Gravy 10
   Southwestern Pot Roast
Creamy Shells with Peas and Bacon RC
Extra-Crunchy Fried Chicken 15
   Extra-Spicy, Extra-Crunchy Fried Chicken
Fried Fish with Pickled Jalapeño
   Mayonnaise 22
Grilled Flank Steak with Garlic-Parsley
   Sauce 22
Honey-Glazed Pork Loin RC
Lemony Chicken and Rice RC
Ranch Chili 21
   Ranch Chili for a Crowd

starters, salads, and side dishes

Baked Cheese Grits RC
Cheesy Mashed Potatoes 23
   Mashed Potatoes with Pepper Jack
   and Bacon
Green Beans 17
   Green Bean Succotash
   Green Beans with Bacon and Onion
   Green Beans with Mediterranean Flavors
   Orange Green Beans with Buttered
   Cashews
Iceberg Lettuce with Blue Cheese
   Dressing RC
Jalapeño Cornbread 21
Potato Casseroles 6
   Alsatian Potato Casserole
   Creamy Potato Casserole
   Italian Potato Cake
   Mashed Potato and Herbed Cheese Bake
   Potato, Spinach, and Sausage Casserole
Red Cabbage Slaw 22
Roasted Corn 22
Roasted Red Pepper Soup RC

desserts

Best Christmas Cookies 26
   No-Fuss Icing
Blue-Ribbon Apple Cake 18
Brownies 24
   Basic Brownies
   Frosted Brownies
   German Chocolate Brownies
   Peanut Butter Swirl Brownies
   Pecan Pie Brownies
   S'mores Brownies
   White Chocolate & Peppermint Brownies
Fun with Ice Cream Desserts 12
   Chocolate Whipped Cream
   Cookies & Cream Ice Cream Pie
   Ice Cream Bonbons
   Ice Cream Cupcakes
   Rainbow Sherbet Surprise
Low-Fat Chocolate Pudding 8
   Mexican Chocolate Pudding
   Orange-Kissed Chocolate Pudding
Sea Foam Candy 9
Strawberries with Balsamic Vinegar RC

RC = Recipe Card

Cook's Country

APRIL/MAY 2005

Super-Crisp Steak Fries
You Can Hear the Crunch!

Marshmallow Daisy Cupcakes
And 11 More Fun Designs

The Best Breaded Pork Chops
Crispiest Coating Ever

NORTH CAROLINA PULLED PORK
Real BBQ Flavor from a Slow Cooker

MACARONI 'N CHEESE LITE
Less Fat, but Not Less Flavor

CLOUDCAKES
The Fluffiest, Lightest Pancakes Ever

TASTING BOTTLED BARBECUE SAUCE
Two Brands Get Thumbs Up

SOUTHWESTERN MEATLOAF
New Spin on an Old Favorite

ICEBOX CHEESECAKE
No Bake, No Fuss

$4.95 U.S./$6.95 CANADA

0 3>

0 74470 05251 7

Our Picnic Salad Contest Winner!

Lisa Keys of Middlebury, Connecticut, sent us a first-place picnic salad recipe that combines local New England ingredients such as cranberries, maple-glazed turkey, and cheddar cheese.
See page 6 for her Cape Cod Picnic Salad.

Cook's Country

Dear Country Cook,

Most of us can still remember when an ice cream cone loomed large on a hot summer day. Shoeless. In a pickup. Driving on a dusty back road. Wherever we tasted that first cold, creamy lick, it didn't matter. It always transported us to a place that was pretty much perfect.

I remember drinking ice-cold sodas in the cab of a green Ford; Charlie, the farmer at the wheel, Dixie, the collie in between, and me, leaning out the window, trying to gulp the cool air. I can still feel the hay in my T-shirt and taste the cold, sweet soda going down quick. Grape. Orange. Cream. Root beer.

All good cooks know the secret. "Give us the simple pleasures," we say. An unexpected kiss. A shy smile. Sitting on a bag of cement eating an ice cream cone with your brother. That's plenty good enough for us.

Welcome to Cook's Country.

Christopher Kimball
Founder and Editor, Cook's Country Magazine

Farm Boys Eating Ice Cream Cones, Washington, Indiana, July 1941. Photographer: John Vachon.
Library of Congress, Prints & Photographs Division, FSA-OWI Collection, LC-USF347-016109-M3-B-Q.

APRIL/MAY 2005

Cook's Country

departments

6 RECIPE CONTEST: **Picnic Salads**

8 RECIPE MAKEOVER: **Macaroni and Cheese**

9 LOST RECIPES: **Monkey Bread**

10 SLOW COOKING: **Pulled Pork**

11 QUICK COOKING: **Casual Spring Supper**

12 FUN FOOD: **Gelatin Desserts**

15 EASIER THAN YOU THINK: **Party Straws**

16 SIMPLY SUPPER: **Recipe Cards**

21 ON THE SIDE: **Applesauce**

23 QUICK COOKING: **Fancy Spring Supper**

23 REGIONAL FAVORITES: **Southwestern Meatloaf**

30 FOOD SHOPPING: **Barbecue Sauce**

31 EQUIPMENT ROUNDUP: **Electric Deep Fryers**

in every issue

Welcome to Cook's Country   **2**

Ask Cook's Country   **3**

Kitchen Shortcuts   **4**

I'm Looking for a Recipe . . .   **16**

When Things Go Wrong . . .   **28**

Notes from Our Test Kitchen   **29**

Thanks for the Memories   **32**

features

14 Lighter-Than-Air Pancakes
Buttermilk and two extra beaten egg whites make pancakes so light and fluffy they nearly float off the plate.

17 A New Way with Broccoli
Four quick recipes show you how to cook stalks and florets together and add pizazz with easy sauces.

18 Super-Crisp Steak Fries
Tired of soggy fries? We use an unusual technique (microwaving) and a surprise ingredient (cornstarch) to give fries an audible crunch.

20 Shaking Up Shake 'n Bake
Kathleen McKeown of East Haddam, Connecticut, wanted a homemade recipe like Shake 'n Bake. Our coating is tastier and crunchier—and it's almost as quick and easy to prepare as the boxed version.

22 Rustle Up Some Beans!
What's the secret ingredient in Texas-style barbecued baked cowboy beans?

24 Icebox Cheesecake
Our one-bowl, no-bake recipe is nearly goofproof—with tasty variations using peanut butter, mint, and limes.

26 Happy Birthday Cupcakes
Jenny Williamson of Marblehead, Massachusetts, was looking for an easy cupcake recipe for her daughter's birthday. Our recipe, plus 12 creative decorating ideas from readers, should make for quite a party.

Founder and Editor Christopher Kimball
Executive Editor Jack Bishop
Deputy Editor Dan Rosenberg
Senior Editor Bridget Lancaster
Test Kitchen Director Erin McMurrer
Copy Chief India Koopman
Associate Editors Keri Fisher, Eva Katz
Assistant Editor Melissa Baldino
Assistant Test Cook Cali Todd
Kitchen Assistants Sara Borcherding, Katie Henderson
Contributors Erika Bruce, Matthew Card, Lauren Chattman, Garth Clingingsmith, Julia Collin Davison, Rebecca Hays, Charles Kelsey, Sean Lawler, Jeremy Sauer, Diane Unger-Mahoney, Nina West
Proofreader Dawn Carelli

Design Director Amy Klee
Designer Heather Barrett
Staff Photographer Daniel J. van Ackere

Vice President Operations James McCormack
Production Manager Mary Connelly
Production Assistants Jeanette McCarthy, Jennifer Power, Christian Steinmetz
Systems Administrator Richard Cassidy
WebMaster Aaron Shuman

Vice President Marketing David Mack
Sales Director Leslie Ray
Marketing Assistant Connie Forbes
Circulation Director Bill Tine
Circulation Manager Larisa Greine
Fulfillment Manager Carrie Horan
Products Director Steven Browall
Direct Mail Director Adam Perry
Customer Service Manager Jacqueline Valerio
Customer Service Representative Julie Gardner
E-Commerce Marketing Manager Hugh Buchan

Chief Financial Officer Sharyn Chabot
Controller Mandy Shito
Staff Accountant Maya Santoso
Office Manager Saudiyah Abdul-Rahim
Receptionist Henrietta Murray
Publicity Deborah Broide

Editorial Office: 17 Station Street, Brookline, MA 02445; 617-232-1000; fax 617-232-1572. Subscription inquiries: 800-526-8447.
Postmaster: Send all new orders, subscription inquiries, and change-of-address notices to Cook's Country, P.O. Box 8382, Red Oak, IA 51591-1382.

PRINTED IN THE USA

Cover photo: StockFood/Carrier.
Cover illustration: John Burgoyne.
Color photography this page: Keller + Keller.
Styling: Mary Jane Sawyer.

Welcome to Cook's Country

Stalking the Farmers Market

Dot Ferrero of Culpeper, Virginia, took this beautiful photo at the Fredericksburg Farmers Market. She writes: "I loved the gentleman with the checkered shirt. I took several photos of him while he was shopping. I hope he didn't think I was stalking him!"

'Fresh Native Ice Cubes'

Jennifer Cox wrote to us about her local convenience store, the Town Landing Market in Falmouth, Maine. Lobsterman Danny Groves is the owner of the market, but he prefers to be called its caretaker. Jennifer tells us that while no one knows exactly when it was built, locals believe the building dates back to the 1890s. It has served as a gas station (with gravity-fed pumps), and at one point it was the only grocery store between Portland and Yarmouth. Today it is "a simple market that has everything," according to Danny. Jennifer and her family make at least one visit a day, whether to pick up some chili, tapioca pudding, or "Fresh Native Ice Cubes."

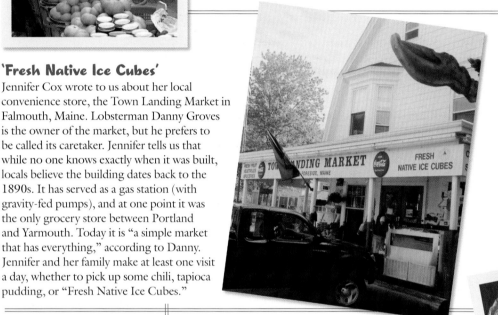

Prairie Piecemakers

Cindy Sanger from Panora, Iowa, is part of a quilters' group that calls itself the Prairie Piecemakers. The group meets every other week to sew and to share ideas, tips, fabric scraps, and, most important, friendship. For the past two years, the community of Panora has been working to raise enough money to build a new library. The Piecemakers have contributed to the fundraising in several ways. On the suggestion of member Novie Martin, they sponsored a chicken-and-noodle dinner at the library committee's annual auction. Member Lyn Watson offered a quilt top that she had just completed for auction, and Trisha Rutledge, who had recently opened a quilt store, offered to finish the quilt. Several members called on local businesses to ask for their support, and the whole crew sewed aprons to wear while serving the dinner. The quilt was auctioned for $325 and the dinner event raised $1,700.

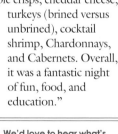

Community Taste Test

Carol Turner from Southborough, Massachusetts, is the program director for the Southborough Community House. Every year, she organizes events that help educate the community. She sent us this photo of Ron Kolodziej and John Sullivan from their latest event, the "Community Test Kitchen." She writes: "We had 12 different tables, each manned by town residents with a passion for good food, and each table featured a different type of food. For example, one table featured various salmons, all smoked on a Cajun smoker grill. We compared farm-raised salmon with warehouse-store salmon, Alaskan wild salmon, and frozen salmon. We also taste-tested apple crisps, cheddar cheese, turkeys (brined versus unbrined), cocktail shrimp, Chardonnays, and Cabernets. Overall, it was a fantastic night of fun, food, and education."

What's the Hurry?

Elena Battista visited the Cumberland County Fair in Cumberland, Maine, and sent us this photo. The week-long fair has been held every year for the past 133 years! There's lots of good food—none of it very fast. Elena tells us that she particularly loves the doughnuts and the freshly made fries.

We'd love to hear what's happening in your town. Drop us a note and send us a photo. Write to Welcome to Cook's Country, P.O. Box 470739, Brookline, MA 02447. If you'd like to use e-mail, write to us at welcome@bcpress.com. If your submission is published, you'll receive a complimentary one-year subscription to *Cook's Country*.

Prize-Winning Apple Pie

Patricia Evans of Seabrook, New Hampshire, won third prize in the 2004 Topsfield (Massachusetts) Fair apple pie contest. Patricia explained that the judges liked her pie's flaky crust, the texture of the cooked apples, the freshly grated spices, and the pastry leaf decorations. The judges also liked her selection of apples: two Cortland, two McIntosh, two Granny Smith, one Jonagold, and one Macoun. The first prize went to a man who entered an apple pie with a crumb crust. Patricia writes: "He won first prize with a lazy pie! It must have been spectacular, because the judges gave it 26 points more than the second-place pie and raved about the delicious and buttery flavor. I wish we'd been able to sample a little, or at least see the recipe." Patricia won a big white ribbon, $25, a bag of apples from Cider Hill Farms, and, of course, bragging rights.

Ask Cook's Country

MAKE-AHEAD LASAGNA

With my big family, make-ahead dinners are a help. I like to have a lasagna or two in the freezer at all times. But sometimes the edges of the pasta dry out by the time the frozen lasagna is heated through. How do you heat up a frozen lasagna?

Michelle Tardy, Oakland, California

Here's what we do in the test kitchen. Wrap the lasagna tightly with plastic and then foil and freeze it for up to three months. Thaw the lasagna for 24 hours in the refrigerator and then let it sit for one hour at room temperature. (If the center is icy cold when the lasagna goes into the oven, the edges are more likely to dry out, so don't skip these steps.) Remove the foil and plastic wrap and rewrap the dish with foil that has been sprayed with cooking spray (so it won't stick to the melted cheese). Bake for 25 to 30 minutes at 375 degrees, remove the foil, and continue to bake until the cheese is spotty brown and the sauce is bubbling, another 25 to 30 minutes. To test the lasagna, insert a knife into the center of the dish and hold it there for five seconds. When you pull out the knife blade, test it against your hand—it should feel hot. Make sure to let the lasagna cool and solidify for 10 minutes before you dig in.

WASHING MUSHROOMS

I've heard that you shouldn't wash mushrooms. But how do you remove the dirt? The mushroom brushes I've seen in stores seem silly, and the task of wiping each mushroom clean with a towel is tedious.

Suzie Alderman, Stony Creek, Connecticut

In the wild, mushrooms grow in damp forests where it rains all the time, so it makes no sense to proclaim that one should "never wash mushrooms." You just want to avoid overdoing it. At some point, mushrooms can soak up water and become soggy. In the test kitchen, we place whole mushrooms in a colander, rinse them gently under cool running water, and then immediately pat them dry with towels. Because water beads up on the exterior of mushrooms, washing whole specimens is fine. Cut mushrooms are another story. The exposed flesh will soak up water like a sponge, so clean mushrooms before slicing them.

BUYING NONSTICK COOKWARE

My mother wants to buy me some cookware for my first apartment. I want nonstick everything, but she says that's a mistake.

Catherine Palmer, Denver, Colorado

Listen to your mother. Nonstick is great for certain dishes—such as sautéed fish fillets or steamed rice. But a nonstick coating isn't always the best choice because it inhibits browning. For example, you can't sear a steak and make a pan sauce in a nonstick skillet.

We think three nonstick pans are useful. A large nonstick skillet (about 12 inches) is great for cooking fish. (You should ask your mother to buy you a conventional—not nonstick—large skillet as well to cook any foods you want to brown.) A small nonstick skillet (8 or 10 inches) is perfect for egg dishes—everything from fried eggs to omelets. Finally, a medium nonstick saucepan (about 2 quarts) is good for preparing foods that tend to stick, such as rice, oatmeal, and puddings. For all other pots (a large saucepan, a Dutch oven, a stockpot), we'd much rather have a conventional surface.

MINCING GARLIC

I was watching a chef on TV the other day, and he said you should never use a garlic press. This chef always minces garlic with a knife. He says it tastes better. Is he right?

Chopin Rabin, New York, New York

You can't always believe what you hear on TV. A garlic press often produces better-tasting garlic than a knife. That's because a press guarantees that the garlic will be broken down into small, even bits. In contrast, garlic minced with a knife often has irregular pieces—some large, some small. The large bits are more likely to scorch and taste bitter when cooked. Of course, a TV chef might be able to create a smooth, fine mince of garlic with a knife every time. For the rest of us, though, a garlic press is the better choice. In the test kitchen, we like the Zyliss garlic press, which costs just $13—a modest price to pay for insurance against burnt, bitter garlic.

RESCUING A BEAT-UP PAN

I have a couple of stainless steel pans that are really dirty. They were expensive, and I should have taken better care of them over the years. But I didn't, and now the exteriors are covered with burnt black spots. Is there any way to make them shine like new?

Sheila Stevens, Tamarac, Florida

For regular cleaning of stainless steel cookware, we use Cameo and Bar Keepers Friend. These powdered cleansers will remove most stubborn messes, especially when used in combination with a copper or nylon scrubber. We use oven cleaner to remove blackened stains that are immune to powdered cleansers. Note that oven cleaner is suitable only for the exterior of a pan, but that's usually where the problems are anyway.

Take the offending pan outdoors and place it on several layers of newspaper in a shady spot. Wearing rubber gloves, spray the exterior of the pan with oven cleaner and let the pan sit for about 20 minutes. Still wearing gloves, use an old damp cloth or sponge to wipe off the oven cleaner. Discard the newspaper and cloth, then bring the pan back inside, wash it with dishwashing liquid, and rinse thoroughly. This should be a one-time treatment; you don't want to rely on it to clean pans on a regular basis. It is truly the method of last resort.

DRESSING A SALAD

My salads often turn out too dry or too soggy. Is there an easy formula to follow when dressing a leafy salad?

Meri Soloman, Westin, Florida

There's nothing worse than an improperly dressed salad. To prevent mishaps, in the test kitchen we measure the greens and, when using a vinaigrette, the dressing. Lightly pack the greens into a 4-cup measuring cup. Figure on 2 cups of lightly packed, washed, torn greens for each person. As for the vinaigrette, you will need 1 tablespoon for every 2 cups of greens.

Here's how the math works. For four people, you will need 8 cups of greens and 4 tablespoons (or ¼ cup) of vinaigrette. For eight people, you will need 16 cups of greens and 8 tablespoons (or ½ cup) of vinaigrette. This formula does not apply to creamy dressings, which don't coat greens nearly as well; generally, you will need more. Whether you're using a thick or thin dressing, remember to add it gradually, toss, and taste. You can always add more dressing, but once a salad is soggy there's no turning back.

GETTING EVERYTHING TO THE TABLE HOT

I like my food hot. But if I'm serving a roast plus two or three side dishes for Sunday supper, at least one dish is always tepid. Any suggestions?

Beth Richman, Portland, Oregon

Getting everything done at just the right moment is nearly impossible. But if you take us up on the following strategies to keep side dishes warm, precise timing will be unnecessary.

Warm serving dishes in a cool oven (150 to 200 degrees) or by filling them with very hot tap water, waiting a minute, then dumping out the water and wiping the dishes dry. This is great for vegetables—everything from broccoli to green beans. Warm bowls will keep food hot for five or 10 minutes.

To keep food hotter longer, use a slow cooker (set to low) or fondue pot (finally, a use for that wedding gift). Creamy or thick side dishes, such as mashed potatoes, candied sweet potatoes, creamed onions, and macaroni and cheese, will stay hot for an hour or more in either device. Over time, these side dishes may start to dry out. If necessary, adjust their consistency with a little warm milk, cream, broth, juice, or water.

Keep fried foods warm in a 250-degree oven for up to 20 minutes. Place the food on a wire rack set over a rimmed baking sheet so hot air can circulate around it.

Keep dinner rolls, biscuits, and corn on the cob warm by wrapping them in foil. For extra protection, nestle the foil-wrapped items in a paper grocery bag and then roll the bag shut. These items should remain hot for 30 minutes.

To send us a cooking question, write to Ask Cook's Country, P.O. Box 470739, Brookline, MA 02447. If you prefer to use e-mail, write to askcookscountry@bcpress.com. See if you can stump us!

Kitchen Shortcuts

Hot Tip!
Heavy-Duty

I've bought every kind of oven mitt available, but the ones that work best and are the cheapest are welders' gloves. They are absolutely heatproof, and they are more flexible than most mitts, making it easier to pick things up.

Elizabeth Harbison
Germantown, Maryland

A Cool Idea!
Whipped Cream Anytime

I drop rounded spoonfuls of leftover whipped cream on a cookie sheet and freeze them, then drop the frozen dollops in a zipper-lock plastic bag and return them to the freezer. They're just the thing for topping pudding cups or mugs of hot cocoa.

Lillian Julow Gainesville, Florida

A Neat Way to Line Baking Pans

Most new baking pans come with a manufacturer's label that is an exact fit for the inside of the pan. Instead of throwing the labels away, I fold them up and put them in the pocket at the back of my recipe file. I use them as templates for cutting just-the-right-size parchment or waxed paper to fit the pan.

Jennifer Maslowski New York, New York

TIME SAVER

Talk about Multitasking!
QUICK BREAD RISING

When baking bread, I try to do a load of laundry at the same time. The top of the dryer is a perfect place to let the bread rise in an otherwise cold house. I make sure to wrap the bowl tightly with plastic, which also helps speed things along. **–Tim Knight** Corvallis, Oregon

CLEANING CHEESY PANS

My husband has a great method for removing the glued-on cheese from a stovetop dish like macaroni and cheese. After the meal is over and the food has been removed from the pan, he adds a little water along with several tablespoons of inexpensive white vinegar and brings it to a boil. He lets it sit for a few minutes and then cleans it out easily with the scrubber. The vinegar releases the gluey residue.

Cecilia Slay
Camptonville, California

MAKESHIFT FUNNEL

When I need a very small funnel, I simply pull the rubber bulb off a baster and use the plastic tube. Works great for filling a very small jar.

Kathy Johnson
Ava, Missouri

MANAGING PARSLEY

The best way to store leftover parsley is not in a plastic bag stuffed in the back of the refrigerator vegetable drawer. (That's what I used to do.) Now I've got a much better technique. I keep the parsley tied in a bunch and take what I need by placing the bunch on a cutting surface, pinching the leaves together, and trimming off thin slices, starting at the top. I then store what remains—still tied—in a jar of cold water in the refrigerator, covered with a plastic bag. I keep trimming the leaves this way, from the top down, until all that remains are the stems. Then I divide the stems into bundles of six or eight and freeze them for adding to soups and stews for a fresh, bright flavor.

Lillian Julow
Gainesville, Florida

NO-THAW FROZEN OJ

I never wait for a can of frozen orange juice to thaw. Instead, I empty the can into a pitcher, pour in one or two containers of water, and then use a potato masher to break up the frozen juice. Once the juice has completely melted, I add the rest of the water and mix.

Darwin Richardson
Ukiah, California

SPIN DOCTOR

When blanching vegetables, I like to use the bowl of a salad spinner to hold the water and ice cubes. I drain the blanched vegetables in the spinner basket and then plunge the basket into the ice-cold water in the bowl to quickly cool the vegetables. After a minute or two, I remove the basket, pour out the cold water, replace the basket, and spin the blanched vegetables dry.

Lorraine Shank
Summit, New Jersey

FLOURING A PAN

Long ago I learned that when the instructions on a boxed cake mix tell you to "grease and flour" the pan, it's better to use a bit of the dry mix instead of plain flour. The resulting cake tastes better, and there's no white mess left behind (an especially good thing if you're making a chocolate cake). Anyone who doesn't use ready mixes for baking can try the same thing by dusting the greased pan with a bit of the combined dry ingredients instead of the flour. This makes for a sweeter, more pleasant-tasting crust on the cake.

Valerie Follet
Hayward, California

FRESH-BAKED COOKIES AT THE READY

When making a batch or two of cookies, shape the dough into balls and freeze them on a baking sheet or plate. Once firm, place the frozen balls in a freezer bag. When you're in the mood for some cookies, just place some frozen balls on a baking sheet; they will be ready to pop into the oven by the time your oven has heated up to the correct baking temperature. Warm cookies whenever you want them!

Carolyn Beverley
Kleinburg, Ontario

If you'd like to submit a tip, please send a letter to Kitchen Shortcuts, Cook's Country, P.O. Box 470739, Brookline, MA 02447. Or e-mail us at shortcuts@bcpress.com. Include your name, address, and phone number. If we publish your tip, you will receive a one-year subscription to *Cook's Country*.

NO-STICK SHORTENING

Before measuring shortening for a recipe, I rinse the measuring cup with water. When I turn the cup upside down, the shortening slips right out, leaving not a trace in the cup—a "slick trick" in the true sense of the word! I do hate extra work, and this is so easy.

Jeanette Wagner
Aylett, Virginia

LAST-MINUTE PANCAKE SYRUP

Run out of pancake syrup? Melt brown sugar by microwaving it. Add water to get a consistency you like. You can also add butter or a flavoring such as almond or vanilla.

Betsy Branstetter
Jefferson City, Missouri

STOCK MAKING, SIMPLIFIED

When making stock, I put everything—meat, bones, celery, carrots, and onions—in my large pasta pot, which comes with a strainer. I fill the pot with water, simmer the whole thing for a few hours, then lift out the strainer to remove the solids. This is great! No more bones falling from the pot to the strainer and causing the contents to splatter everywhere. And the stock left behind is pretty well strained, with just a few small shreds of meat and vegetables.

Louise Gagnon
Toronto, Ontario

KEEPING FOOD PROCESSOR BLADES SAFE

When washing the parts of my food processor in the dishwasher, I always place the workbowl directly over the blade in the upper rack. This keeps my hands out of harm's way during unloading, when the blade might otherwise hide under a bowl or cup.

Molly Hays
Kenmore, Washington

WRAPPING DISHES FOR MOVING

Don't use printed newspaper for packing and storing dishes—the ink will rub off and you'll have to wash them again. Instead, go straight to the source to get the end of the roll of newspaper (without print) and use it for packing. The plant changes rolls before the end runs out and saves the leftover rolls. These rolls are also great for kids' art projects.

Nancy M. Bertha
Carrboro, North Carolina

CRISP CRACKERS, EVEN IN SUMMER

To keep crackers, potato chips, corn chips, and pretzels crisp during a hot and humid summer, my mother would clip the bags shut and store them in the freezer. Any big clip, including one for papers, really works well.

Sandra Harrisson
Kennett Square, Pennsylvania

STORAGE CONTAINER CLEANUP

I can't tell you how many times I've tried to remove that grungy, dirty look from the lids of plastic storage containers. Even scrubbing with dishwashing liquid doesn't remove the grime. Then one day I was using baking soda to remove stains from teacups (as I have for years), and it occurred to me that I might also get good results with those stubborn plastic lids. I rubbed the lids with baking soda and then scrubbed them using the rough green surface of a sponge. It worked perfectly.

Cecilia Slay
Camptonville, California

NO MORE MICROWAVE SPLATTERS

I keep a stack of cheap paper plates near my microwave oven. Anytime I use the microwave, I place a paper plate on top of the bowl or plate of food. It's a quick and easy way to prevent splatters and help the food heat more evenly.

Pan Bookstaber
New Canaan, Connecticut

GOOD CREDIT

Unsolicited and out-of-date credit cards make great disposable pan scrapers. They have nice sharp edges and are easy to rinse clean.

Daniel Kleine
via e-mail

DOUBLE DUTY

Tipsy Tip!
Removing Cork Pieces from Wine

The best way to remove pieces of cork from a poorly opened bottle of wine is to line a funnel with a paper coffee filter and pour the wine through the funnel into a clean bottle or pitcher.

Kristen Arent
Boston, Massachusetts

Apple Sense

If I can get to an orchard in the fall, I buy a bushel of apples and have an applesauce marathon when

I get home. In the midst of all this cooking and pureeing, I have found that a melon baller is the ideal tool for removing the core of the apples after quartering them. Unconventional, yes, but it works much better than a paring knife.

Alice Ammons
McComb, Mississippi

Say Ahhhhh

I ask my doctor for extra tongue depressors and put one in each of my dry goods containers. When it comes time to scoop out and level off a cup of flour or sugar,

I don't have to fumble around for something with a straight edge. The depressors are sanitary and they never wear out (but if you absolutely must replace them, you can't beat the price!). I always keep extras in a drawer, just in case.

Kendra Knight
Spring Valley, California

Better Buttering

Tired of chasing that little pat of butter around your plate while trying to butter an ear of corn? I was, too, until I discovered this speedy method: Put several ears of corn and a piece of butter in a 1-gallon zipper-lock plastic bag and toss. The heat from the corn melts the butter, and tossing ensures an even coat on each ear. Pour any leftover melted butter into a gravy boat to pass at the table.

Fritz Wilger
Cincinnati, Ohio

Penny Pinching
SQUEEZING THE MOST FROM EVERY LEMON

I use lots of lemon and lime juice in recipes and so like to buy them in bulk whenever they go on sale. I juice all of them, pour the juice into an ice cube tray, and freeze. Once the cubes are frozen, I transfer them to a freezer bag. Each cube is about 2 tablespoons. When I need the juice, I just remove the amount I need from the bag and defrost in the microwave. I also use them frozen in drinks.

Cecilia J. Bessette Berthoud, Colorado

Recipe Contest PICNIC SALADS

Readers toss up five great salads that go anywhere you want

Wow! We were inundated with a huge variety of recipes—everything from Brocco-Berry Burst to California Roll Seven-Layer Salad. Who says that American home cooking is dead? Our five favorite recipes were less adventurous but still contained a healthy pinch of culinary fireworks. Congratulations to the winners, and many thanks to everyone who shared their recipes and stories.

Our Grand Prize Winner!

Lisa Keys, Middlebury, Connecticut

Lisa writes: "Years ago, when my children were little, we spent many summers vacationing on Cape Cod. On rainy days we enjoyed shopping in the quaint stores, and often I would purchase interesting cranberry products like the chutney in this salad. I thought it would be nice to combine it with other New England foods, like the maple turkey, crisp apples, cheddar, and walnuts."

The test kitchen was most impressed with the mix of flavors in this picnic salad. With tart, crisp apples, sweet cranberries, and satisfying walnuts, turkey, and cheese, this thematic salad tasted just as delicious as it looked.

CAPE COD PICNIC SALAD
SERVES 8 TO 10

Lisa's secret ingredient is cranberry chutney, but we found that apricot preserves will work, too. Make sure to ask for a single piece of unsliced turkey breast at the deli counter.

- 1   red apple, quartered, cored, and cut crosswise into ¼-inch-thick slices
- 3   tablespoons lime juice
- ¼   cup cranberry chutney or apricot preserves
- 2   teaspoons Dijon mustard
- ½   cup extra-virgin olive oil
-      Salt and pepper
- 2   heads romaine lettuce
- 1   bunch watercress
- ½   pound piece unsliced deli maple-glazed turkey breast, diced
- ½   cup diced sharp cheddar cheese
- ¼   cup chopped walnuts, toasted
- ¼   cup dried cranberries

1. Toss apples with 1 tablespoon lime juice in small bowl. Whisk remaining 2 tablespoons lime juice, chutney, and mustard together in large bowl. Gradually whisk in oil until incorporated. Season with salt and pepper to taste, and reserve ¼ cup dressing in measuring cup.

2. Toss lettuce and watercress with remaining dressing in large bowl and arrange on large platter. Arrange apples, turkey, cheddar, walnuts, and cranberries on top of lettuce. Drizzle salad with remaining dressing. Serve or refrigerate for up to 1 hour.

Low-Country Sweet Potato Salad

Gazpacho Pasta Salad

Panzanella Salad

Tricolor Mexican Bean Salad

Veronica Callaghan
Glastonbury, Conn.

LOW-COUNTRY SWEET POTATO SALAD SERVES 6 TO 8

Sweet potatoes and sesame seeds are an important part of cooking along the South Carolina coast, otherwise known as the Low Country.

2¾	pounds sweet potatoes, peeled and cut into 1½-inch pieces
1½	pounds russet potatoes, peeled and cut into 1-inch pieces
½	cup olive oil
4	slices bacon, cut into ½-inch pieces
1	large shallot, minced
1	teaspoon cayenne pepper
	Salt and pepper
1	tablespoon lemon juice
1	teaspoon Tabasco sauce
2	tablespoons toasted sesame seeds
2	tablespoons chopped fresh parsley

1. Adjust oven racks to upper-middle and lower-middle positions and heat to 375 degrees. Spray two rimmed baking sheets with cooking spray. Set aside.

2. Toss potatoes with ¼ cup oil, bacon, shallot, cayenne, 1 teaspoon salt, and ¼ teaspoon pepper in bowl. Divide between prepared pans and bake until tender, 30 to 40 minutes, stirring potatoes every 10 minutes and switching positions of pans halfway through cooking. Cool potatoes for 20 minutes.

3. Whisk together lemon juice, Tabasco, and remaining ¼ cup olive oil in small bowl. Season dressing with salt and pepper to taste. Transfer cooled potatoes to large serving bowl, add lemon juice mixture and 1 tablespoon each of sesame seeds and parsley, and toss gently to coat. Sprinkle remaining sesame seeds and parsley on top. (Salad can be refrigerated for up to 1 day.) Serve chilled or at room temperature.

Debra Jenkins
Sylvania, Ohio

GAZPACHO PASTA SALAD SERVES 8 TO 10

Gazpacho, the classic chilled summer soup, gets a new look as a dressing for this zesty pasta salad. Use any curly pasta in this recipe.

1	(14½-ounce) can diced tomatoes (do not drain)
3	medium garlic cloves, minced
1	teaspoon hot red pepper flakes
¼	cup packed fresh basil
1	tablespoon red wine vinegar
	Salt
1	pound rotini pasta
1	medium cucumber, peeled, halved lengthwise, seeded, and cut into ¼-inch pieces
1	medium red bell pepper, chopped
1	medium yellow bell pepper, chopped
2	cups cherry tomatoes, halved
¼	cup chopped fresh parsley
3	scallions, thinly sliced
¼	cup extra-virgin olive oil
½	cup crumbled feta cheese
½	cup pitted black olives, quartered

1. Puree diced tomatoes, garlic, red pepper flakes, basil, vinegar, and ½ teaspoon salt in blender until smooth. Transfer to bowl (don't use metal), cover, and refrigerate for at least 2 hours or overnight.

2. Bring 4 quarts of water to boil in large pot. Add 1 tablespoon salt and pasta and cook until al dente. Drain pasta, rinse with cold water, and set aside.

3. Place cucumber, red and yellow peppers, cherry tomatoes, parsley, scallions, and oil in large serving bowl and toss well to combine. Add pasta and pureed dressing and toss again. (Salad can be refrigerated overnight.) Scatter cheese and olives over top. Serve chilled or at room temperature.

Michaela Rosenthal
Woodland Hills, Calif.

PANZANELLA SALAD SERVES 6 TO 8

Thanks to prepared basil pesto from the supermarket, this Italian bread salad is easy to make. The bread croutons will soften as they sit in the salad, so add them just 10 minutes before serving.

2	cups 1-inch cubes Italian bread
½	cup olive oil
2	cups cherry tomatoes, halved
1	(14-ounce) can cannellini beans, drained and rinsed
1	medium cucumber, peeled, halved lengthwise, seeded, and cut into 1-inch pieces
1	medium shallot, minced
½	cup pesto
¼	cup red wine vinegar
	Salt and pepper
2	tablespoons thinly sliced fresh basil

1. Adjust oven rack to middle position and heat to 375 degrees. Toss bread cubes with ¼ cup olive oil on rimmed baking sheet. Spread bread cubes on pan and bake until golden brown, 12 to 15 minutes, shaking pan halfway through to prevent bread from sticking. Remove from oven and cool completely. (Bread cubes can be stored in zipper-lock bag for one or two days.)

2. Meanwhile, mix tomatoes, beans, cucumber, and shallot in large bowl. Whisk pesto, vinegar, and remaining ¼ cup oil together in small bowl, and season with salt and pepper to taste. Drizzle pesto dressing over vegetables, toss well, and refrigerate for at least 2 hours or overnight.

3. Ten minutes before serving, add bread cubes to vegetables and toss well. Transfer to serving bowl and sprinkle basil on top. Serve.

Sally Sibthorpe
Shelby Township, Mich.

TRICOLOR MEXICAN BEAN SALAD SERVES 6

Full of color and big on flavor, this salad gets better as it sits.

3	tablespoons lemon juice
3	tablespoons lime juice
2	large garlic cloves, crushed
1	tablespoon chili powder
1	teaspoon ground cumin
	Salt
¼	teaspoon hot red pepper flakes
½	cup olive oil
2	ears corn, boiled and kernels cut off
1	(16-ounce) can black beans, drained and rinsed
1	large yellow bell pepper, chopped
½	celery rib, minced
3	scallions, thinly sliced
⅓	cup fresh parsley leaves
2	tomatoes, seeded and chopped

1. Puree lemon and lime juices, garlic, chili powder, cumin, 1 teaspoon salt, and red pepper flakes in blender until smooth. Turn blender back on and add oil in steady stream until incorporated.

2. Place corn, beans, bell pepper, celery, scallions, and parsley in serving bowl. Pour dressing over salad and toss well to combine. Cover and refrigerate for at least 2 hours or overnight.

3. Just before serving, stir in tomatoes. Season with salt to taste.

We are looking for holiday cookie recipes for an upcoming contest. Please send us entries by May 1, 2005. Write to us at Recipe Contest, Cook's Country, P.O. Box 470739, Brookline, MA 02447, or e-mail us at recipecontest@bcpress.com. Either way, please make sure to include your name, address, and daytime phone number, and tell us what makes your recipe special. The grand prize winner will receive $500. All entries become the property of *Cook's Country*. We look forward to reading (and tasting) your recipes.

Recipe Makeover MACARONI AND CHEESE

This American classic has an awful lot of butter and cheese—that's why it tastes so good. Is slimming down mac and cheese a lost cause?

We usually don't worry too much about fat and calories here in the test kitchen, but when I ran the numbers on our favorite macaroni and cheese recipe, I was shocked. A main-course serving contained more than 1,100 calories and 40 grams of fat. A slimmed-down version was looking more attractive.

I started by trying out a variety of "low-fat" recipes, and what I ended up with was "macaroni and milk"—they were trimming the fat by trimming the cheese. While certainly low fat, these recipes were also "low flavor." Other recipes substituted low-fat cheese for the real thing, and they produced dishes with rubbery clumps of curdled cheese. I was clearly on my own here.

I went back to our favorite full-fat recipe, which is built on a classic French white sauce. Butter is melted, flour is whisked in, milk is added, and the sauce is stirred until thickened. When cheese is added to this mixture, it is much less likely to curdle. My first thought was to substitute skim milk for whole milk. This worked fine, and I had found my first reduction in fat and calories.

The next obvious ingredient to tackle was the cheese. I tested a half-dozen brands of low-fat cheddar and found two that were pretty good, especially when I added some grated Parmesan, which is high in flavor but low in fat. Now the sauce tasted good, but the texture was stringy and rubbery. It would have to be a whole lot creamier.

I thought a creamier low-fat cheese might help. I tested everything from cottage cheese to cream cheese and finally settled on part-skim ricotta. To make it smoother, I gave it a few whirls in the food processor. Now the sauce was creamier, but the cheddar was still stringy.

It was time for a brainstorm. I had to process the ricotta anyway; what if I processed the cheddar right along with it? I mixed up another batch and hit pay dirt. The sauce had a smooth, creamy texture with good body.

It was time to run the numbers again (see "And the Numbers . . ."). I had trimmed more than half the calories and fat from the test kitchen's favorite full-fat macaroni and cheese recipe. Granted, this is no low-cal, low-fat recipe, but it's certainly a reduced-cal, reduced-fat recipe. What's more, everyone enjoyed eating it. In our kitchen, that's what counts most.

–Nina West

Help yourself to seconds. Our macaroni and cheese tastes great—and it's less filling.

REDUCED-FAT MACARONI AND CHEESE SERVES 4 AS A MAIN COURSE OR 6 TO 8 AS A SIDE DISH

See page 29 for information on the test kitchen's favorite reduced-fat cheddars.

Bread Crumb Topping
- ⅓ cup plain bread crumbs
- 1 tablespoon unsalted butter, melted

Macaroni and Cheese
- ½ cup shredded reduced-fat sharp cheddar cheese (3 ounces)
- ½ cup grated Parmesan cheese
- ½ cup part-skim ricotta cheese
- 1 tablespoon plus ½ teaspoon salt
- ½ pound elbow macaroni
- 1 tablespoon unsalted butter
- 1½ tablespoons all-purpose flour
- 1 teaspoon powdered mustard
- 2½ cups skim milk
- ½ teaspoon Tabasco sauce (optional)

1. For the topping: Toss bread crumbs with butter in small bowl until combined. Set aside.

2. For the macaroni and cheese: In food processor or blender, process cheddar, Parmesan, and ricotta until no large pieces of cheese remain, 1 to 2 minutes. Transfer to bowl and set aside.

3. Adjust oven rack to lower-middle position and heat broiler. Bring 4 quarts water to boil in Dutch oven over high heat. Add 1 tablespoon salt and macaroni and cook until tender, 7 to 9 minutes. Drain macaroni and leave in colander.

4. In now-empty Dutch oven, heat butter over medium-high heat until foaming. Add flour and mustard and cook, whisking to combine ingredients, until mixture is smooth, about 1 minute. Whisking constantly, slowly add milk and Tabasco, if using, and bring to full boil. Reduce heat to medium and simmer, whisking frequently, until mixture becomes slightly thicker than heavy cream, 2 to 4 minutes. Remove pan from heat. Whisk in cheese mixture and ½ teaspoon salt until cheese is melted. Add pasta and cook, stirring constantly, over medium-low heat, until mixture is steaming, 2 to 3 minutes.

5. Transfer mixture to broilersafe 8-inch-square baking dish and sprinkle with bread crumbs. Broil until crumbs are deep golden brown, 2 to 4 minutes, rotating pan if necessary for even browning. Cool 2 minutes. Serve.

And the Numbers . . .

All numbers are for a main-course serving.

TRADITIONAL Macaroni and Cheese
CALORIES: 1,118
FAT: 41 g
SATURATED FAT: 25 g

COOK'S COUNTRY Reduced-Fat Macaroni and Cheese
CALORIES: 493
FAT: 15 g
SATURATED FAT: 10 g

Fun Flavors

It's easy enough to jazz up this all-American dish with an extra ingredient or two. Here are two test kitchen favorites.

MACARONI AND CHEESE AFTER DARK

This grown-up variation uses a small amount of blue cheese— perfect for when the kids have gone to bed.

Follow recipe for Reduced-Fat Macaroni and Cheese, replacing Parmesan cheese with ⅓ cup crumbled blue cheese.

MACARONI AND CHEESE FOR PIZZA LOVERS

Fresh tomatoes, garlic, and basil give this American favorite an Italian twist.

Follow recipe for Reduced-Fat Macaroni and Cheese, adding 2 tablespoons chopped fresh basil to bread crumb mixture in step 1. In step 4, add 1 teaspoon minced garlic to pot with flour and mustard. After stirring pasta into cheese sauce and cooking 2 to 3 minutes, add 1 cup chopped fresh tomato and 3 tablespoons chopped fresh basil, and stir well to combine. Proceed as directed.

Pull this gooey, sweet yeast bread apart with your hands, and let the fun begin.

Dear Cook's Country,
Growing up, my brothers and I would help our mom make something called monkey bread. As we pulled apart the hot hunks of gooey bread with our hands, Mom would joke that we looked more like a pack of wolves than monkeys. Now that I have two young kids of my own, I'd like to revive this tradition. Can you help?

Heather Wilding
Bedford, New Hampshire

Dear Heather,
Monkey bread was a family affair in my household, too, and I always thought that making it was a little bit of magic. My mother would start with homemade bread dough that we kids would pick apart and roll into many, many balls. The balls were dipped in butter, rolled in cinnamon-sugar, stacked in a tube or Bundt pan, and baked. The pieces of dough seemed to melt together, with the sugar and butter transformed into a thick, caramel goo that oozed into every nook and cranny. And because the balls of dough were piled one on top of another, the end result was a crowning confection of the softest, sweetest, stickiest, most cinnamony bread I ever tasted. I thought my mom was a genius.

I still think my mom's a smart cookie, but I have since found out that she didn't invent monkey bread! Its origins date back at least a century, and the super-soft Parker House roll is surely a close relation. The name "monkey bread" is enigmatic. Some say it comes from the bread's resemblance to the prickly monkey-puzzle tree. Others (myself included) think it refers to the way we eat it—that is, using our hands to pull apart the sticky clumps of bread and stuff them in our mouths, just like happy little monkeys. And for those who think monkey bread may be lacking panache, consider that former First Lady Nancy Reagan served monkey bread at the White House.

The oldest monkey bread recipes I found in my research were two-day affairs. The dough was started the night before, refrigerated, and shaped and baked the next day. Contemporary recipes have taken the road of convenience; in most cases, they use store-bought biscuit dough. I tried it, and, believe me, the time saved wasn't worth it. The biscuit dough was too lean, too dry, and too bland.

I looked to the few contemporary recipes that could be made in one day and then made a few adjustments. To provide plenty of lift and yeasty flavor, I used a whole envelope of rapid-rise yeast, which also made this a same-morning operation; no need to plan ahead. Milk and melted butter went in to keep the dough rich and moist, and a little sugar made the bread sweet enough to eat on its own. To compensate for the sweet dough, I changed the granulated sugar normally used to coat the dough balls to the mellower light brown sugar.

Rolling and shaping the many balls of dough was always half the fun of making monkey bread, so at this point I took a cue from my mother and set up my own assembly line in the test kitchen. My fellow workers and I dipped, rolled, and baked dozens of monkey breads until the right one came out of the oven. After a few cruel minutes of waiting, I released the bread from its pan and reverted back to my childhood, watching the hot caramel drip down the sides. Some recipes call for drizzling a simple confectioners' sugar glaze over the monkey bread, which may seem gratuitous, but I didn't think the glaze made the monkey bread too sweet. In fact, I thought that with the glaze the bread was now just perfect.

–Bridget Lancaster

MONKEY BREAD
SERVES 6 TO 8
The dough should be sticky, but if you find that it's too wet and not coming together in the mixer, add 2 tablespoons more flour and mix until the dough forms a cohesive mass. Make sure to use light brown sugar in the sugar mix; dark brown sugar has a stronger molasses flavor that can be overwhelming. After baking, don't let the bread cool in the pan for more than 5 minutes or it will stick to the pan and come out in pieces. Monkey bread is at its best when served warm.

Dough
- 2 tablespoons unsalted butter, softened, plus 2 tablespoons melted
- 1 cup warm milk (about 110 degrees)
- 1/3 cup warm water (about 110 degrees)
- 1/4 cup granulated sugar
- 1 package rapid-rise or instant yeast
- 3 1/4 cups all-purpose flour, plus extra for work surface
- 2 teaspoons salt

Brown Sugar Coating
- 1 cup packed light brown sugar
- 2 teaspoons ground cinnamon
- 8 tablespoons (1 stick) unsalted butter, melted

Glaze
- 1 cup confectioners' sugar
- 2 tablespoons milk

1. For the dough: Adjust oven rack to medium-low position and heat oven to 200 degrees. When oven reaches 200 degrees, turn it off. Butter Bundt pan with 2 tablespoons softened butter. Set aside.

2. In large measuring cup, mix together milk, water, melted butter, sugar, and yeast. Mix flour and salt in standing mixer fitted with dough hook. Turn machine to low and slowly

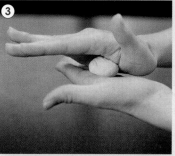

1. After patting the dough into an 8-inch square, cut the square into quarters. **2.** Cut each quarter into 16 pieces. **3.** Roll each piece of dough into a rough ball. **4.** Coat the balls with melted butter and sugar and place in buttered Bundt pan, staggering the balls as you build up the layers.

Looking for a lost recipe?
We can help. Drop us a note and tell us about the recipe you want to find. Write to Lost Recipes, Cook's Country, P.O. Box 470739, Brookline, MA 02447. Or e-mail us at lostrecipes@bcpress.com.

continued from page 9

add milk mixture. After dough comes together, increase speed to medium and mix until dough is shiny and smooth, 6 to 7 minutes. Turn dough onto lightly floured counter and knead briefly to form smooth, round ball. Coat large bowl with nonstick cooking spray. Place dough in bowl and coat surface of dough with cooking spray. Cover bowl with plastic wrap and place in warm oven until dough doubles in size, 50 to 60 minutes.

3. For the sugar coating: While dough is rising, mix brown sugar and cinnamon together in bowl. Place melted butter in second bowl. Set aside.

4. To form the bread: Gently remove dough from bowl, and pat into rough 8-inch square. Using bench scraper or knife, cut dough into 64 pieces. (See photos 1 and 2 on page 9.)

5. Following photo 3 on page 9, roll each dough piece into ball. Working one at a time, dip balls in melted butter, allowing excess butter to drip back into bowl. Roll in brown sugar mixture, then, following photo 4 on page 9, layer balls in Bundt pan, staggering seams where dough balls meet as you build layers.

6. Cover Bundt pan tightly with plastic wrap and place in turned-off oven until dough balls are puffy and have risen 1 to 2 inches from top of pan, 50 to 70 minutes.

7. Remove pan from oven and heat oven to 350 degrees. Unwrap pan and bake until top is deep brown and caramel begins to bubble around edges, 30 to 35 minutes. Cool in pan for 5 minutes, then turn out on platter and allow to cool slightly, about 10 minutes.

8. For the glaze: While bread cools, whisk confectioners' sugar and milk in small bowl until lumps are gone. Using whisk, drizzle glaze over warm monkey bread, letting it run over top and sides of bread. Serve warm.

Monkey Bread without a Mixer

In step 2, mix flour and salt in large bowl. Make well in flour, then add milk mixture to well. Using wooden spoon, stir until dough becomes shaggy and is difficult to stir. Turn out onto lightly floured work surface and begin to knead, incorporating shaggy scraps back into dough. Knead until dough is smooth and satiny, about 10 minutes. Shape into taut ball and proceed as directed.

Slow Cooking PULLED PORK

Use a slow cooker to make this North Carolina barbecue classic while you're at work.

With a slow cooker, you can enjoy real barbecue flavor at any time of the year.

Authentic North Carolina pulled pork begins with a dry spice rub that coats the meat. The spice-rubbed meat is then smoked over hickory or mesquite, low and slow, for hours (tended all the while by a devoted pitmaster). When cool enough to handle, the meat is "pulled," or "picked," into tender, bite-sized shreds and served with a vinegar-based sauce. This fairly thin sauce is nothing like the gooey molasses-based barbecue sauces most of us know and love.

Could I get all of this from a slow cooker? I had my doubts but was willing to give it a shot. Although the slow cooker abides by the same low-and-slow mantra as the barbecue, the cooking mediums (dry and smoky versus wet and watery) couldn't be more different. My first test, which produced pork that tasted more boiled than barbecued, had me worried. It also had an odd pickled taste that I found distressing.

Most slow-cooker recipes for pulled pork simply simmer the meat in bottled barbecue sauce. I decided to try a more traditional route. First, I rubbed dry spices (a mix of paprika, chili powder, cumin, salt, and pepper) into my favorite cut, a Boston butt. This gave the meat more flavor, but not enough. Next time I decided to cut open the roast, spread the spices all over, and then close up the roast. This was much better, with

the flavor of the spices penetrating deep into the meat. Letting the rubbed roast "cure" overnight in the refrigerator also intensified the flavor.

I decided early on that barbecue sauce, whether homemade or bottled, was the wrong cooking medium for the pork. The vinegar in these sauces was making the meat taste pickled. Given the 10-hour cooking time, this shouldn't have been much of a surprise. In a slow cooker, some sort of cooking liquid is a must, but what should I use in place of the sauce? Chicken broth added a neutral, meaty flavor. Just 2 cups did the job, in part because the pork gave up so much moisture as it cooked. By the time the meat was tender, I had 6 cups of super-flavorful liquid. Unfortunately, the meat itself was a bit bland. What the slow cooker had stolen from the pork in 10 hours, I had to put back.

I skimmed the fat from the liquid and reduced it down to 1 cup while the pork was cooling. To transform

the liquid into the characteristic vinegar-based BBQ sauce, I added cider vinegar, brown sugar, and some ketchup. I now had 3 cups of rich, tangy, pork-flavored sauce. After shredding the pork, I poured 1½ cups of the sauce onto the pork and watched as the meat drank it up like a thirsty pitmaster. The elusive pork flavor was back where it belonged, but something was still missing: the smoke flavor that makes pulled pork so appealing.

I tried adding liquid smoke to the cooking liquid, with disastrous results. The smell was reminiscent of a campfire drenched by a summer rainstorm. Next I tried throwing bacon into the slow cooker as the pork cooked, but it brought little flavor to the party. Ham steak tasted fine, but it cost almost as much as the pork butt and was quickly ruled out. I finally hit on terrific smoky flavor when I tried smoked ham hocks. It may sound like a strange addition to a pulled pork

Secrets SEASONING TO THE MAX

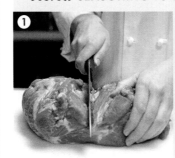   

1. Using a sharp knife, slice lengthwise down the center of the roast and pull the two sides apart. **2.** Cut a horizontal slit into each lobe of meat so the roast will sit flat on the cutting board. **3.** Apply the spice rub with your hands, massaging the spices deep into the meat. **4.** Loosely reshape the meat back to its original size so it will fit in the slow cooker.

recipe, but the hocks became meltingly tender (I shredded them with the pork) and added an authentic smoke flavor. Although super-concentrated liquid smoke didn't work in the cooking liquid, it worked well in the finished sauce. (I guess you shouldn't cook liquid smoke for 10 hours!) Piled high on a soft white bun, this pulled pork had an authentic outdoor flavor.

–Diane Unger-Mahoney

NORTH CAROLINA PULLED PORK SERVES 8 TO 10

Ham or pork hocks are available smoked and cured or just smoked. Although either will work in this recipe, smoked and cured hocks (which are deep red) will provide the best flavor. We prefer to use Boston butt for this recipe, but a picnic roast can be used instead. You will need a 6-quart slow cooker for this recipe. Don't be tempted to speed up the process by turning the cooker to the high setting—the pork will have a decidedly boiled texture. Serve the pork piled high on white bread or hamburger buns, with plenty of coleslaw and pickle chips on top. To warm up leftovers, add 1 tablespoon water for every cup of pork and heat in a large skillet over medium-low heat until warmed through.

Spice Rub
- 4   tablespoons paprika
- 3   tablespoons dark brown sugar
- 2   tablespoons chili powder
- 1   tablespoon ground cumin
- 1   tablespoon pepper
- 2   teaspoons salt

Pork
- 3   smoked ham hocks
- 1   boneless pork butt (Boston butt), 5 to 6 pounds, prepared as shown in photos 1 and 2 on page 10
- 2   cups low-sodium chicken broth

Sauce
- 1   cup cider vinegar
- ¾   cup ketchup
- 3   tablespoons dark brown sugar
- 1½ teaspoons hickory or mesquite liquid smoke
    Salt and pepper
    Tabasco sauce for serving

1. For the spice rub: In small bowl, combine paprika, brown sugar, chili powder, cumin, pepper, and salt.

Make Ahead

If you're worried about getting home in time to check on your slow cooker, start the pulled pork before going to bed. In the morning (if the intoxicating barbecue aroma doesn't wake you earlier), transfer the meat and liquid to a large bowl and refrigerate until ready to proceed (up to three days). To finish the recipe, remove the solidified fat on top of the cooking liquid, transfer the defatted liquid and pork to a Dutch oven, and cook over medium-low heat until warmed through. Proceed with the recipe from step 4.

---

2. For the pork: Place ham hocks in bottom of slow-cooker insert. Set aside. Following photo 3 on page 10, thoroughly coat pork butt with spice rub. Following photo 4, reshape pork butt and place on top of ham hocks, tucking meat down into slow cooker as far as possible. Cover insert with plastic wrap and refrigerate overnight.

3. The next morning, discard plastic wrap and set insert into slow-cooker base. Pour chicken broth over pork, cover with lid, and cook on low until pork is very tender, 8 to 10 hours.

4. Using 2 large spoons, carefully transfer pork butt and ham hocks to rimmed baking sheet. Using two forks, separate pork butt into large chunks. Set aside to cool slightly. When cool enough to handle, shred pork butt and ham hocks, discarding excess fat from both as well as small bones from ham hocks.

5. For the sauce: While pork is cooling, pour cooking liquid through strainer into medium saucepan. (You should have 5 to 6 cups.) Using large spoon, skim excess fat from surface. Bring to boil over medium-high heat and cook until liquid is reduced to 1 cup, 30 to 40 minutes. Whisk in vinegar, ketchup, and brown sugar, and simmer for 1 minute. Off heat, stir in liquid smoke. (You will have about 3 cups.)

6. Pour 1½ cups sauce over meat, tossing to combine, and let stand until meat has absorbed most of sauce, 10 to 15 minutes. Season with salt and pepper to taste. Serve, passing remaining sauce and Tabasco separately.

Casual spring supper with ham and asparagus

HAM STEAK WITH RHUBARB SAUCE SERVES 4 TO 6

Look for a bone-in ham steak that is cut crosswise from a whole ham. These steaks are far superior to individual (and sometimes processed) ham steaks.

- 1   pound rhubarb, leaves discarded, stalks cut into ½-inch pieces
    Salt
- 1   tablespoon unsalted butter
- 1   thick-cut, bone-in ham steak (about 2½ pounds), patted dry with paper towels
- 2   tablespoons water
- 1   tablespoon cider vinegar
- ¼   cup sugar
- 1   tablespoon minced fresh ginger
    Pepper

1. Toss rhubarb with 1 teaspoon salt in medium bowl and let sit for 20 minutes. Rinse rhubarb in colander and drain well. Set aside.

2. Heat butter in large skillet over medium-high heat until foaming subsides. Add ham steak and cook without moving until browned, about 5 minutes. Using tongs and large spatula, flip steak and cook on second side until browned, about 4 minutes. Transfer ham steak to serving platter, tent with foil, and set aside.

3. Return skillet to medium heat and add water, vinegar, sugar, and ginger. Simmer until sugar has dissolved, about 30 seconds. Stir in rhubarb and cook until tender but not mushy, 5 to 8 minutes. Season with salt and pepper to taste. Spoon sauce over ham steak and serve.

BROILED ASPARAGUS WITH CHEESY BREAD CRUMBS SERVES 4

Peppered Boursin cheese also works well in this recipe.

- ¼   cup plain bread crumbs
- 2   tablespoons unsalted butter, melted
    Salt and pepper
- ⅓   cup Boursin cheese with garlic and herbs
- 3   tablespoons heavy cream
- ½   teaspoon grated lemon zest
- 2   pounds asparagus, tough ends snapped off

1. Adjust oven rack so that it sits 6 inches below heating element and heat broiler. Toss bread crumbs with 1 tablespoon melted butter in bowl and season with salt and pepper. Using fork, mix cheese, cream, and lemon zest in another bowl until paste forms.

2. Toss asparagus with remaining 1 tablespoon melted butter on large rimmed baking sheet and season well with salt and pepper. Spread asparagus in single layer on baking sheet and broil, shaking pan halfway through, until asparagus is tender and lightly browned, 8 to 10 minutes.

3. Transfer asparagus to broilersafe baking dish. Spoon cheese mixture over asparagus and toss to coat. Sprinkle with bread crumbs and broil until lightly browned, 30 to 60 seconds. Serve.

Rhubarb for dinner? Along with ginger, it creates a tasty sauce for ham steak.

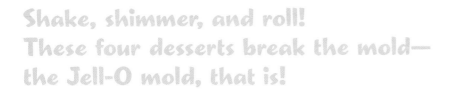

Fun Food

Shake, shimmer, and roll!
These four desserts break the mold—
the Jell-O mold, that is!

Root Beer Float

JUICY GELATIN CUBES SERVES 4

Make either the pink lemonade or cranberry juice squares and serve separately, or make both (yielding 8 servings) and stack together for a pretty presentation. Garnish each serving with a sprig of fresh mint, if desired.

4$^{1}/_{2}$ cups pink lemonade or cranberry juice cocktail

3 envelopes unflavored gelatin
$^{1}/_{4}$ cup sugar

1. Soften gelatin Place 1 cup lemonade or cranberry juice cocktail in small bowl and sprinkle gelatin over liquid. Let stand 5 minutes to soften gelatin.
2. Heat liquid Bring 2$^{1}/_{2}$ cups lemonade or cranberry juice cocktail and sugar to boil in medium saucepan. Remove from heat and whisk in gelatin mixture until all lumps dissolve. Stir in remaining 1 cup lemonade or cranberry juice cocktail. Pour into 8-inch-square baking dish. Refrigerate until firm, at least 3 hours or up to 1 day.
3. Cut and layer cubes Cut gelatin into 1-inch squares. Divide squares among 4 dessert goblets or sundae dishes. Serve.

Juicy Gelatin Cubes

ROOT BEER FLOATS SERVES 4

Layers of bubbly root beer–flavored gelatin and soft whipped cream make up this malt-shop classic. To preserve as many bubbles as possible, use two 12-ounce bottles of root beer, opening the second bottle just before stirring it into the gelatin mixture. For special effect, save the bubbly top of the root beer gelatin to crown the float.

2 (12-ounce) bottles or cans cold root beer
2 envelopes unflavored gelatin
$^{1}/_{4}$ cup plus 2 tablespoons sugar
1 cup heavy cream

1. Soften gelatin Place $^{1}/_{2}$ cup root beer in small bowl and sprinkle gelatin over root beer. Let stand 5 minutes to soften gelatin.
2. Heat liquid Bring 1 cup root beer and $^{1}/_{4}$ cup sugar to boil in small saucepan, stirring to dissolve sugar. Remove from heat and whisk in gelatin mixture until all lumps dissolve. Pour into bowl and cool to room temperature. Gently stir in remaining 1$^{1}/_{2}$ cups root beer, taking care not to deflate bubbles. Refrigerate until firm, at least 6 hours or up to 1 day.
3. Beat cream Using electric mixer, beat cream and remaining 2 tablespoons sugar in medium bowl until cream holds soft peaks.
4. Layer float Spoon one-eighth of root beer mixture into each of 4 mugs or sundae dishes. Top with one-eighth of whipped cream. Repeat with remaining root beer mixture and whipped cream. Top with cap of bubbly root beer gelatin and serve.

Piña Colada Mousse

BLUSHING PEACH TERRINE SERVES 6 TO 8

Any way you slice it, this elegant "loaf" of peaches and blush wine makes a stunning presentation. For a bubbly variation, substitute an equal amount of pink champagne for the wine.

- 1 (29-ounce) can sliced peaches in heavy syrup, drained
- 1/2 cup cold water
- 2 envelopes unflavored gelatin
- 1 1/2 cups white Zinfandel or rosé wine
- 1/2 cup sugar

1. Arrange fruit Arrange fruit in even layer in 1 1/2-quart nonstick loaf pan.

2. Soften gelatin Place water in small bowl and sprinkle gelatin over water. Let stand 5 minutes to soften gelatin.

3. Heat liquid Bring 1 cup wine and sugar to boil in small saucepan, stirring to dissolve sugar. Remove from heat and whisk in gelatin mixture until all lumps dissolve. Pour into bowl and stir in remaining 1/2 cup wine. Let cool to room temperature.

4. Add wine to peaches Pour wine mixture over peaches. Cover with plastic wrap and refrigerate until set, at least 6 hours or up to 1 day.

5. Unmold Dip loaf pan in hot water for 30 seconds. Place serving platter over loaf pan, invert, and tap gently to unmold. Serve.

Blushing Peach Terrine

PIÑA COLADA MOUSSE SERVES 6 TO 8

"If you like piña coladas . . ." you'll love this frozen mousse made from pineapple juice and cream of coconut; add the optional rum, and it's perfect for grown-up gatherings. Fill the center with a blend of fresh pineapple, oranges, limes, and strawberries, or, for a more elegant presentation, use raspberries all by themselves.

- 1/4 cup cold water
- 1 envelope unflavored gelatin
- 1 (6-ounce) can pineapple juice
- 1 (15-ounce) can cream of coconut (such as Coco Lopez brand)
- 1/4 cup light rum (optional)
- 1 1/3 cups heavy cream
- 2 cups mixture of fresh sliced strawberries, pineapple chunks, orange segments, and lime slices

1. Soften gelatin Place water in small bowl and sprinkle gelatin over water. Let stand 5 minutes to soften gelatin.

2. Heat liquid Cook pineapple juice and cream of coconut in small saucepan over medium heat until mixture is warm to touch. Remove from heat and whisk in gelatin mixture until all lumps dissolve. Whisk in rum, if using. Place pan over large bowl of ice water and let stand, whisking occasionally, until mixture is chilled and begins to thicken but is not yet solidifying, 15 to 20 minutes.

3. Beat cream Using electric mixer, beat cream in medium bowl until it just holds stiff peaks. Using large spatula, gently fold pineapple-coconut mixture into whipped cream. Scrape mousse into 1-quart ring mold. Cover with plastic wrap and freeze until completely set, at least 6 hours or up to 1 day.

4. Unmold Dip ring mold in hot water for 30 seconds. Place serving platter over mold, invert, and tap gently to unmold. Let stand on counter for 30 minutes. Fill center with 1 1/2 cups fruit. Scatter remaining 1/2 cup fruit around base of mousse. Serve.

–Recipes by **Lauren Chattman**

Whisking Wisdom

To get the fluffiest and lightest pancakes, beat the egg whites to the soft peak stage. Beating the eggs to stiff peaks will cause the batter to deflate and result in flat pancakes.

Lighter-Than-Air Pancakes

Whipped egg whites make especially fluffy pancakes that nearly float off the plate.

Folding Ever So Gently

For the fluffiest texture, you must avoid deflating the egg whites when folding them into the batter. Using a rubber spatula, gently fold the whipped egg whites into the batter. A few visible streaks of egg white should remain.

Dear Cook's Country,

While staying at a bed and breakfast in Vermont, my husband and I ate pancakes that were incredibly light and fluffy, even after we poured the local maple syrup all over them! The pancakes were also nice and tangy. The innkeepers called them Angel Cakes. How can I make pancakes like this?

Sue Howard, Boulder, Colorado

Dear Sue,

Recipes for super-fluffy pancakes have lots of nicknames. In addition to Angel Cakes, we have also seen recipes for Cloudcakes (the name we think best describes their texture), Heavenly Hotcakes, and even Zeppelin Pancakes. You get the idea. What do these recipes have in common? Almost all of them rely on separated rather than whole eggs. The yolks are mixed into the batter, while the whites are beaten into a foam that expands during cooking and makes the pancake rise like a soufflé.

tried several recipes with beaten egg whites, and they all produced fairly light pancakes. But you also asked for fluffy and tangy pancakes, and these recipes didn't come through on those counts. My first thought was to substitute buttermilk for regular milk. Sure enough, the pancakes rose higher and they tasted a bit tangier. Many of the recipes I tried used a lot less flour than liquid, but my tasters found that these variations lacked structure and height. I found that a batter made with about the same amount of flour and buttermilk made pancakes with good structure that sat up nicely in the skillet.

So where was I? Well, I had good hearty pancakes that were thick and pretty light, but I was after a griddle cake that really lived up to the name Cloudcake. My first clue came from a recipe from the Campton Place Hotel in San Francisco, which makes the world's best fluffy pancakes. The hotel chefs use extra whites. I followed their lead, using 4 whites and 2 yolks. Now I was getting close to ethereal.

Once in a while, my pancakes wouldn't rise enough, and I figured that the problem was likely overmixing. Now that I was adding egg whites to the batter in a separate step, I was mixing twice. I learned (the hard way) to stop mixing the wet and dry ingredients when they were just barely combined, with lots of lumps and dry flour visible. The act of folding in the egg whites finished the job.

I had one last concern. Were my pancakes truly "tangy," as you described in your letter? I had seen recipes with sour cream. Maybe that would help.

I added ¼ cup and held my breath as the batter almost rose out of the pan. Besides giving the pancakes great flavor, the sour cream reacted with the baking soda in the batter to create tremendous lift. My pancakes finally lived up to the name Cloudcakes. I hope you agree. –Sean Lawler

CLOUDCAKES

MAKES TWENTY-FIVE 3-INCH PANCAKES, SERVING 4 TO 6

These very light pancakes are best served with maple syrup. Home stovetops vary, so you may need to adjust the burner setting between medium-low and medium. For maximum rise, allow the eggs and buttermilk to come up to room temperature before using them. Low-fat buttermilk works best here; if using fat-free buttermilk, reduce the amount to 1 cup plus 2 tablespoons. Although these pancakes are at their puffiest when served in batches, they can be kept warm on a cooling rack coated with cooking spray and placed over a sheet pan in a 200-degree oven for up to 20 minutes.

1¼	cups all-purpose flour
1½	tablespoons sugar
1	teaspoon baking soda
¾	teaspoon salt
1¼	cups low-fat buttermilk (see note)
¼	cup sour cream
2	large eggs, separated, plus 2 extra egg whites
2	tablespoons unsalted butter, melted and cooled
1–2	tablespoons vegetable oil

1. Whisk flour, sugar, baking soda, and salt together in large bowl. Stir buttermilk and sour cream together in medium bowl until combined.

Easier Than You Think:

Party Straws

Fancy gourmet shops sell cheese straws for top dollar. But you can make something even better at a fraction of the cost—and in just 20 minutes. The secret? Purchase frozen Pepperidge Farm Puff Pastry, sprinkle both sides with cheese, cut the dough into thin strips, and then bake for 10 minutes in a hot oven. We also played around with different flavor variations, including chili powder, cinnamon, poppy and sesame seeds, olives, feta, basil, garlic, sun-dried tomatoes—you name it. We stand the baked straws straight up in a tall glass and serve them with drinks when company calls. But guard them with your life: Kids love these crunchy twists and will eat them up before the adults have a chance to try one.

Cheese and a variety of seeds and spices transform supermarket frozen puff pastry into quick party fare.

Add egg yolks and butter to buttermilk mixture, and stir well to combine. With electric mixer or balloon whisk, beat all 4 egg whites in large bowl to soft peaks. Pour buttermilk mixture over dry ingredients and whisk until just combined. (Batter should be lumpy, with visible streaks of flour.) Using spatula, carefully fold whites into batter until just combined. Do not overmix—a few streaks of whites should be visible.

2. Heat 2 teaspoons oil in large nonstick skillet over medium-low heat for 5 minutes. Using ⅛-cup measure or small ladle, spoon batter into pan. Cook until bottoms are evenly browned, 2 to 3 minutes. Flip pancakes and cook until golden brown on second side, 2 to 3 minutes longer. Serve, cooking remaining batter and using more vegetable oil as needed to grease pan.

CINNAMON "TOAST" CLOUDCAKES

Cinnamon and sugar make these pancakes reminiscent of homemade cinnamon toast. They are perfect served with apple butter.

Follow recipe for Cloudcakes, increasing sugar to 3 tablespoons and adding 1 teaspoon ground cinnamon to other dry ingredients in step 1.

PUCKER-UP CLOUDCAKES

Serve these lemon-scented pancakes with blueberry sauce or syrup.

Follow recipe for Cloudcakes, replacing ¼ cup of flour with equal amount of yellow cornmeal and adding 1 teaspoon grated lemon zest to dry ingredients in step 1.

CHEESE STRAWS

MAKES 14 STRAWS

Pepperidge Farm Puff Pastry, sold in the supermarket freezer case, works well with this recipe. Thaw the puff pastry on the counter as you preheat the oven and grate the cheese. This recipe requires parchment paper, available next to the plastic wrap in the market. Completely cooled cheese straws can be stored in an air-tight container at room temperature for up to 3 days—but they won't last that long.

  1 **sheet frozen puff pastry (½ box), thawed on counter for 10 minutes**
  1 **cup grated Parmesan cheese**
  ¼ **teaspoon salt**
  ¼ **teaspoon pepper**

1. Adjust two oven racks to upper-middle and lower-middle positions and heat oven to 425 degrees. Line 2 baking sheets with parchment paper and set aside. Place puff pastry on sheet of parchment and sprinkle with ½ cup cheese and ⅛ teaspoon each salt and pepper. Place another sheet of parchment over cheese and, using rolling pin, press cheese into dough by gently rolling pin back and forth. Without removing parchment, carefully flip dough over, cheese side down. Remove top layer of parchment and sprinkle pastry with remaining cheese, salt, and pepper. Cover pastry with parchment and continue to roll out, if necessary, to form 10½-inch square.

2. Remove top sheet of parchment and, using sharp knife or pizza cutter, cut dough into fourteen ¾-inch-wide strips. Holding each end, gently twist strips of dough in opposite direction and transfer to parchment-lined baking sheets, spacing strips about 1 inch apart.

3. Bake immediately, until fully puffed and golden brown, about 10 minutes, reversing positions of baking sheets from top to bottom halfway through baking time. Cool on wire rack for 5 minutes before serving.

SWEET-AND-SPICY STRAWS

Replace Parmesan, salt, and pepper with 2 teaspoons chili powder, ⅛ teaspoon cinnamon, and 1 tablespoon sugar.

EVERYTHING STRAWS

Replace Parmesan and salt with 1 teaspoon sesame seeds, ½ teaspoon poppy seeds, ½ teaspoon dehydrated minced garlic, ½ teaspoon kosher salt, and ¼ teaspoon caraway seeds.

GREEK CHEESE STRAWS

Replace Parmesan with ½ cup minced black olives, ¼ cup crumbled feta cheese, and 1 tablespoon minced fresh oregano.

ITALIAN CHEESE STRAWS

Replace Parmesan with ¼ cup minced sun-dried tomatoes, 2 tablespoons minced capers, 1 tablespoon minced fresh basil, and 2 teaspoons minced garlic.

The American Table: Founding Father Knows Best

The historical papers of our first president include two books of school exercises that offer insight into the man and his times. (Just imagine what your high school homework might tell future historians about you?) Besides mathematics, poetry, and legal treatises, Washington wrote out by hand the *Rules of Civility and Decent Behaviour in Company and Conversation*. Historians believe these 110 maxims, which originated in France in the 1600s, had a profound effect on Washington's character development. Many of the maxims applied to table manners, and they still make sense today. Here are some of our favorites, with Washington's original spelling and punctuation.

91st **maxim:** *Make no Shew of taking great Delight in your Victuals, Feed not with Greediness; cut your Bread with a Knife, lean not on the Table neither find fault with what you Eat.*

94th **maxim:** *If you Soak bread in the Sauce let it be no more than what you Put in your Mouth at a time and blow not your broth at Table but Stay till Cools of it Self.*

97th **maxim:** *Put not another bit into your Mouth til the former be Swallowed let not your Morsels be too big for the Gowls.*

105th **maxim:** *Be not Angry at Table whatever happens & if you have reason to be so, Shew it not but on a Chearfull Countenance especially if there be Strangers for Good Humour makes one Dish of Meat a Feast.*

MOM'S DELIGHT

I'm Looking for a Recipe . . .

Minute Rice

There used to be a recipe on the Minute Rice box for something that resembled chicken chow mein. The commercial for the recipe featured a young girl making the dish, which was served over Minute Rice, for her father. I contacted the Minute Rice company years ago, but no one ever got back to me. I would love to re-create this recipe for my 77-year-old mother.

Liz Sorrentino
Brooklyn, New York

Harvest Apple Pie

Years ago, I made a "Harvest Apple Pie" with shredded apples, carrots, zucchini, and nuts in a double pastry. When we moved into our new house, the recipe disappeared. It was a great pie for fall.

Patsy Fazio
North Pole, Alaska

Mocha Rum Cheesecake

More than 30 years ago, my mom cut out a recipe for Mocha Rum Cheesecake from the *New York Times* magazine. The cake was to-die-for wonderful, and she made it for every special occasion. One time, she even made it with 151-proof rum, as that was all we had in the house! At some point the recipe disappeared, and no one has a copy. My mom had a stroke, and she can't remember the recipe. If I could find it, a piece of my childhood would be recovered and I could make it for my mom.

Ellen Feibel
Garwood, New Jersey

Pineapple Pudding

I am looking for a recipe for a pineapple rice pudding that was served at my school in Georgetown, Ohio, when I was growing up. Sometimes it was served slightly warm, sometimes cold. I have found some recipes, but none of them match the creamy, fruity pudding that exists in my memory.

Melissa Winterod
Burlington, Kentucky

Apple Pie in a Bag

I am looking for a recipe for Apple Pie in a Bag. The pie had a crumb topping, and it was printed in a magazine 20 to 25 years ago. The pie could also be baked without the bag, but it was not as juicy.

Shelley Arrigoni
Asheville, North Carolina

Apricot-Filled Cookies

I am looking for a cookie recipe that had a filling of dried apricots, spices, and a jigger of vodka. The dried apricots were cooked in vodka, water, lemon juice, and spices, and the dough had cream cheese in it. The dough was rolled out and cut into squares, and a dollop of the filling was placed between two cookies.

Yvonne Quiring
Stockton, California

Butter Mints

My mother and I have lost contact with some neighbors who used to make butter mints every winter. Our neighbors would place a frozen marble slab outside, and, after boiling the sugar, they would pour the steaming mass onto the slab. My father would go over and play "tug of war," helping to pull and stretch the sugar until it turned satiny. The mints would then be snipped with scissors. The unique thing about these mints was that they contained butter; when eaten, they melted on your tongue. They were not crunchy, like hard candy, but light and airy, more like a meringue.

Robin Smith
Berryville, Virginia

Burnt Sugar Cake

My grandmother once made a cake that I could not stop eating. Only my mother's threatening looks kept me from making a complete pig of myself. When I asked what kind of cake it was, my grandmother replied that it was "just an old burnt sugar cake." I have never tasted anything like it since.

Jacquelyn Clymer
Santa Maria, California

Sage's Honey Whole Wheat Bread

In the 1970s, Sage's, the small, quirky supermarket chain in the Boston area, made a wonderful honey whole wheat bread. I have tried various recipes that seemed similar, but I have never come close to Sage's version. It was sold as a fairly small loaf with a soft crust. The interior was shiny, chewy, and dark brown, with large air holes. The taste was slightly sweet.

Joan M. Corr
West Newton, Massachusetts

Are you looking for a special recipe? Let other *Cook's Country* readers help. Just send us your requests, and we will print as many of them as we can. Write to Looking for a Recipe, Cook's Country, P.O. Box 470739, Brookline, MA 02447, or send an e-mail to lookingforarecipe@bcpress.com. If you can help with one of the above requests, contact us at the same postal or e-mail address. We will post responses on www.cookscountry.com.

Find the Rooster! A tiny version of this rooster has been hidden somewhere in the pages of this issue. If you find it, write to us with its location (plus your name and address), and you will be entered into a random drawing. The first winning entry drawn will receive the Rival Cool Touch Deep Fryer (our test winner—see page 31), and the next five winners will each receive a free one-year subscription to *Cook's Country*. To enter the contest, write to us at Rooster, Cook's Country, P.O. Box 470739, Brookline, MA 02447, or e-mail us at rooster@bcpress.com. Entries are due by May 15, 2005.

Did you find the rooster in the charter issue? It was hidden in the pot roast picture on page 10. Sue Zega of Bridgewater, New Jersey, spotted it, and she won a Farberware slow cooker.

Simply Supper

We would like to share some of our favorite quick supper recipes with you—the kind of food we make at home to feed our families. We have printed these recipes on cards so that you can collect and organize them. We hope you like these recipes as much as we do.

Baked Ziti with Sausage

Nutty Green Beans

Ginger Ice Cream with Chocolate Sauce

Bacon-Wrapped Filets Mignons

Skillet Shrimp and Rice

Asian Corn and Chicken Soup

Chili-Fried Onion Rings

Turkey Cutlets with Cherry Sauce

BAKED ZITI WITH SAUSAGE

NUTTY GREEN BEANS

GINGER ICE CREAM WITH CHOCOLATE SAUCE

BACON-WRAPPED FILETS MIGNONS

NUTTY GREEN BEANS SERVES 4

Marinating the onions in the hot vinaigrette mellows their flavor. These beans pair nicely with our Turkey Cutlets with Cherry Sauce.

- ½ cup red wine vinegar
- 1 tablespoon sugar
  Salt
- ½ medium red onion, sliced thin
- ½ cup walnuts, roughly chopped
- 1 pound green beans, ends snapped off
- 2 teaspoons extra-virgin olive oil
- 1 tablespoon minced fresh tarragon
  Pepper

1. Bring vinegar, sugar, and ¼ teaspoon salt to boil in small saucepan over high heat. Add onion and return mixture to boil. Immediately remove pan from heat and transfer mixture to small bowl to cool.

2. Toast walnuts in small skillet over medium heat until golden and fragrant, about 5 minutes. Transfer to plate.

3. Meanwhile, bring 2½ quarts water to boil in large saucepan. Add beans and 1 teaspoon salt and cook until tender, about 5 minutes. Drain beans and transfer to large serving bowl. Strain onions through sieve and discard liquid. Add onions, walnuts, oil, and tarragon to bowl with beans and toss well. Season with salt and pepper to taste. Serve.

BAKED ZITI WITH SAUSAGE SERVES 4 TO 6

Make this family favorite with sweet or hot sausage.

- 2 tablespoons extra-virgin olive oil
- 1 pound Italian sausage, cut into ½-inch pieces
- 2 medium garlic cloves, minced
- 1 (28-ounce) can crushed tomatoes
- 1 (14½-ounce) can diced tomatoes
  Salt
- 1 pound ziti or penne
- 2 cups shredded mozzarella cheese
- ¼ cup grated Parmesan cheese
- 2 tablespoons minced fresh parsley

1. Adjust oven rack to middle position and heat oven to 400 degrees. Brush 13 by 9-inch baking dish with 1 tablespoon oil. Cook sausage in large skillet over medium heat until browned, 5 to 6 minutes. Transfer sausage to bowl.

2. Drain all but 1 tablespoon fat from skillet, add remaining 1 tablespoon oil and garlic, and cook until fragrant but not brown, about 1 minute. Add crushed and diced tomatoes, return sausage to skillet, and simmer until thickened, 15 to 18 minutes. Season with salt to taste.

3. Meanwhile, bring 4 quarts water to boil in large pot. Add 1 tablespoon salt and pasta. Cook until slightly underdone. Reserve ¼ cup cooking water, drain pasta, and return to pot along with reserved water. Stir in tomato sauce.

4. Pour half of pasta into prepared baking dish. Sprinkle with half of each cheese. Pour remaining pasta into dish, sprinkle with remaining cheeses, and sprinkle with parsley. Bake until golden brown, about 20 minutes. Remove from oven and let rest for 5 minutes. Serve.

BACON-WRAPPED FILETS MIGNONS SERVES 4

This is company food, perfect for a Saturday-night dinner party. The filets are seared on the stovetop and then cooked through on a preheated baking sheet in the oven, which gives you time to attend to side dishes.

- 4 tablespoons unsalted butter, at room temperature
- 2 tablespoons minced fresh parsley
- 1 teaspoon grated lemon zest
- 1 medium garlic clove, minced
  Salt and pepper
- 4 slices bacon
- 4 center-cut filets mignons, each about 1½ inches thick
- 4 teaspoons olive oil

1. With fork, beat butter, parsley, lemon zest, garlic, ¼ teaspoon salt, and ¼ teaspoon pepper together in small bowl until smooth. Set aside.

2. Wrap 1 bacon slice around each filet, overlapping ends and securing ends to filet with toothpick. Adjust oven rack to lower-middle position, place rimmed baking sheet on rack, and heat oven to 450 degrees.

3. Heat 2 teaspoons oil in medium skillet over high heat until just smoking. Sprinkle filets with salt and pepper. Place 2 filets in skillet and cook, without moving, until browned and nice crust has formed, 2 to 3 minutes. Using tongs, turn filets and cook on second side, 2½ minutes longer. Hold filets on their sides and crisp bacon slightly all around. Set filets aside on plate. Heat remaining 2 teaspoons oil in empty skillet and sear remaining 2 filets.

4. Transfer all 4 seared filets to preheated baking sheet in oven. Roast 4 to 6 minutes for rare, 6 to 8 minutes for medium-rare, or 8 to 10 minutes for medium. Transfer filets to large plate, tent with foil, and let rest for 5 minutes. Spoon some parsley-lemon butter onto each filet. Serve.

GINGER ICE CREAM WITH CHOCOLATE SAUCE SERVES 4

Regular vanilla ice cream can be quickly dressed up with the flavors of ginger and orange. Look for crystallized ginger in the spice aisle of the supermarket.

- 1 pint vanilla ice cream
- 3 tablespoons chopped crystallized ginger
- 1 teaspoon grated orange zest
- ½ cup heavy cream, or more as needed
- 2 tablespoons light corn syrup
- 2 tablespoons unsalted butter
  Pinch salt
- ⅔ cup semisweet chocolate chips

1. Transfer ice cream to medium bowl. Let stand at room temperature until soft, 5 to 15 minutes.

2. Stir in ginger and orange zest. Place piece of plastic wrap directly on top of ice cream, and cover top of bowl tightly with another piece of plastic wrap. Freeze until ice cream is firm, at least 30 minutes.

3. While ice cream is in freezer, bring ½ cup heavy cream, corn syrup, butter, and salt to boil in small saucepan over medium-high heat. Remove from heat and add chocolate chips while gently swirling saucepan. Cover and let stand until chocolate melts, about 5 minutes. Uncover and whisk gently until combined. If necessary, adjust consistency by stirring in another 1 or 2 tablespoons cream.

4. Scoop ice cream into 4 individual bowls. Spoon warm chocolate sauce over each portion. Serve.

SKILLET SHRIMP AND RICE

ASIAN CORN AND CHICKEN SOUP

CHILI-FRIED ONION RINGS

TURKEY CUTLETS WITH CHERRY SAUCE

ASIAN CORN AND CHICKEN SOUP SERVES 4 TO 6

Coconut milk and ginger give this creamy American classic an Asian twist. Simmer the soup gently, as strong heat will cause the coconut milk to break. Serve as a first course or a light main course.

- 1 pound frozen corn kernels
- 1 (14-ounce) can coconut milk
- 2 tablespoons vegetable oil
- ½ teaspoon hot red pepper flakes
- 4 medium garlic cloves, minced
- 2 tablespoons minced fresh ginger
- 3 cups low-sodium chicken broth
- 1 pound boneless, skinless chicken thighs or breasts, trimmed of fat and cut into ½-inch pieces
- 3 tablespoons minced fresh cilantro
- 1 tablespoon lime juice
  Salt and pepper
  Lime wedges for serving

1. Place corn in large bowl and microwave on high until completely defrosted but not hot, 1 to 2 minutes. Process corn and coconut milk in blender on high speed until creamy, 1 to 2 minutes. Set aside.

2. Combine oil, pepper flakes, garlic, and ginger in large Dutch oven. Cook, stirring often, over medium heat until fragrant but not browned, 1 to 3 minutes. Add broth and corn mixture and bring to gentle simmer. As soon as soup simmers, reduce heat to medium-low and cook, stirring occasionally, until flavors combine, about 15 minutes. Add chicken and continue cooking until chicken is no longer pink, 7 to 10 minutes. Stir in cilantro and lime juice and season with salt and pepper to taste. Serve with lime wedges.

SKILLET SHRIMP AND RICE SERVES 4 TO 6

If you don't own a skillet that can go from stovetop to oven, transfer the mixture to a covered baking dish in step 2.

- 1½ pounds extra-large shrimp, peeled and deveined
- 2 tablespoons plus 1 teaspoon extra-virgin olive oil
- 1 teaspoon paprika
  Salt
- 4 ounces chorizo or kielbasa sausage, cut into ¼-inch pieces
- 1 medium onion, chopped fine
- 6 medium garlic cloves, sliced thin
- 1½ cups medium-grain rice
- 1 (14½-ounce) can diced tomatoes, drained
- 2 cups water
- 1 (8-ounce) bottle clam juice
- 1 cup frozen peas
  Pepper

1. Adjust oven rack to middle position and heat oven to 350 degrees. Toss shrimp with 1 tablespoon oil, paprika, and ¼ teaspoon salt in medium bowl. Heat 1 teaspoon oil in large ovenproof skillet over medium-high heat until smoking. Add half of shrimp and cook until lightly browned, 30 to 40 seconds. Turn shrimp and cook 30 seconds longer. Transfer shrimp to clean bowl. Repeat with remaining shrimp. Cover bowl and set aside.

2. Reduce heat to medium and add remaining 1 tablespoon oil, chorizo, onion, and garlic. Cook until sausage begins to brown, 5 to 6 minutes. Add rice and cook 1 minute. Stir in tomatoes, water, clam juice, and ½ teaspoon salt. Bring to boil over high heat, cover, and transfer skillet to oven. Cook until rice is tender and liquid is absorbed, about 20 minutes. Remove skillet from oven, stir in peas, and scatter shrimp over top. Cover and set aside until shrimp and peas are heated through, about 5 minutes. Season with salt and pepper. Serve directly from hot skillet.

TURKEY CUTLETS WITH CHERRY SAUCE SERVES 4

One cutlet per person makes a skimpy serving, so we call for a total of six to serve four people. Add rice pilaf or mashed potatoes and a green vegetable, such as our Nutty Green Beans.

- 6 turkey cutlets (each weighing about 4 ounces), rinsed and patted dry
  Salt and pepper
- 2 tablespoons vegetable oil
- ½ cup minced shallots
- ½ cup dried cherries
- 1 teaspoon minced fresh rosemary
- ½ cup port
- ½ cup orange juice
- 2 tablespoons unsalted butter, cut into 2 pieces

1. Adjust oven rack to middle position, set large heatproof plate on rack, and heat oven to 200 degrees. Sprinkle both sides of cutlets with salt and pepper.

2. Heat 1 tablespoon oil in large skillet over medium-high heat until just smoking. Place 3 cutlets in pan and cook without moving, until golden, about 2 minutes. Turn and cook until meat feels firm when pressed, about 1 minute. Transfer cutlets to warm plate in oven. Cook remaining cutlets and place them on plate in oven.

3. Add remaining 1 tablespoon oil to empty skillet and return to medium heat. Add shallots, cherries, and rosemary and cook until shallots become softened, about 1 minute. Add port and orange juice, and, using wooden spoon, scrape any browned bits from bottom of pan. Increase heat to high and simmer until liquid becomes thickened and syrupy, 3 to 4 minutes. Whisk in butter, 1 piece at a time, along with any accumulated juices from cutlets. Season sauce with salt and pepper to taste. Arrange cutlets on platter or individual plates and spoon sauce over them. Serve.

CHILI-FRIED ONION RINGS SERVES 4

Hot and spicy as well as crispy, these onion rings are addictive. They partner perfectly with steaks. Use a deep-fry thermometer to monitor the temperature of the oil.

- 1 cup buttermilk
- 1¼ cups all-purpose flour
- ¾ cup cornstarch
- 3 tablespoons chili powder
- 1 teaspoon cayenne pepper
- 1 teaspoon sugar
- 1½ teaspoons salt
- 1 teaspoon pepper
- 6 cups peanut or vegetable oil
- 2 large yellow onions, sliced into ¼-inch rounds and separated into rings

1. Adjust oven rack to middle position and heat oven to 250 degrees. Line rimmed baking sheet with paper towels and set aside.

2. Place buttermilk in medium bowl. Whisk flour, cornstarch, spices, sugar, salt, and pepper together in another bowl.

3. Heat oil in large Dutch oven over medium-high heat to 400 degrees. Meanwhile, dip one-third of onion rings in buttermilk and shake off excess liquid. Dredge rings in flour mixture, shake off excess, and place on large plate. When oil reaches proper temperature, scatter battered onions in single layer in oil and cook, stirring gently, until golden brown, 1 to 2 minutes (oil temperature should not dip below 375 degrees). Using tongs, transfer onions to prepared baking sheet. Place baking sheet in oven.

4. Repeat battering and frying process with remaining two batches of onions, making sure oil temperature returns to 400 degrees before adding each batch. Serve.

A New Way with Broccoli

I hate to throw away food, even broccoli stalks. I especially hate to throw away food that tastes good, and broccoli stalks are sweeter than the florets and have a nice creamy texture. But cooking an entire bunch in one pot is tricky. Mushy florets and crunchy stalks are the rule. How do you avoid this problem?

First, you have to peel the fibrous outer layer from the stalks. Don't bother trying this with a vegetable peeler. It won't be strong enough. You need a knife to slice away the tough exterior. Even when trimmed, the stalks cook more slowly than the delicate florets. Cutting the stalks into much smaller pieces than the florets helps erase some of this difference in cooking time.

I tried steaming the florets and stalks together in a basket set in a covered pot of simmering water. But even with the stalks cut very small, they took a long, long time to cook. By then, the florets were mushy. I thought the microwave might work, but I found the difference between crunchy and overcooked broccoli was, quite literally, a matter of split-second timing, which seemed to vary from one microwave to the next.

I returned to the stovetop and tried cooking the stalks right in the simmering water, with the florets still in the steamer basket. Success! Boiling cooks food faster than steaming, so the stalks and florets were now done at the same time. I would have stopped there if not for a colleague's question: "Why bother with that steamer contraption?" She was right. Broccoli florets become waterlogged when boiled—that's why I had been using the basket. But the stalks in the water were now forming their own "basket" that I could use to elevate the florets above the simmering water—without any extra "contraptions." I just set the timer for four minutes and the broccoli—both stalks and florets—was perfectly cooked every time. Once it's tender, give the broccoli a thorough draining (watery broccoli is not very appealing) and then toss it with flavorful ingredients. –Rebecca Hays

BROCCOLI WITH PARMESAN BREAD CRUMBS SERVES 4

Shred the Parmesan on the large holes of a box grater.

- 3 tablespoons unsalted butter
- 1 cup plain bread crumbs
- 2 medium garlic cloves, minced
  Salt and pepper
- 1½ pounds broccoli, prepared as shown in photos
- 1½ cups shredded Parmesan cheese

1. Heat butter in large nonstick skillet over medium-high heat. When foaming, add bread crumbs and cook, stirring frequently, until dark golden brown, about 2 minutes. Add garlic and cook until fragrant, about 30 seconds. Season with salt and pepper.

2. Meanwhile, bring 1 cup water and ½ teaspoon salt to boil in large saucepan over high heat. Add broccoli stalks, then place florets on top of stalks so that they sit just above water. Cover and cook until broccoli is bright green and just tender, 3 to 4 minutes. Drain thoroughly.

3. Toss hot broccoli with Parmesan in large bowl until cheese melts. Transfer to serving dish, sprinkle with bread crumbs, and adjust seasonings with salt and pepper. Serve.

BROCCOLI WITH MUSTARD-RED PEPPER VINAIGRETTE SERVES 4

Serve hot or at room temperature, with chicken or fish.

- 3 tablespoons extra-virgin olive oil
- 1 tablespoon red wine vinegar
- 2 teaspoons Dijon mustard
- 2 tablespoons diced jarred roasted red peppers
- 1 small garlic clove, minced
  Salt and pepper
- 1½ pounds broccoli, prepared as shown in photos

1. Whisk oil, vinegar, mustard, red peppers, and garlic in large bowl until combined. Season with salt and pepper.

2. Bring 1 cup water and ½ teaspoon salt to boil in large saucepan over high heat. Add broccoli stalks, then place florets on top of stalks so that they sit just above water. Cover and cook until broccoli is bright green and just tender, 3 to 4 minutes. Drain thoroughly.

3. Toss hot broccoli with vinaigrette until evenly coated. Adjust seasonings with salt and pepper. Serve.

BROCCOLI WITH CREAMY HERB SAUCE SERVES 4

When mixed with hot broccoli, the goat cheese melts to form a tangy sauce.

- 3 tablespoons goat cheese
- 3 tablespoons heavy cream
- 2 tablespoons minced fresh parsley
- ¼ teaspoon hot red pepper flakes
- 2 teaspoons lemon juice
  Salt and pepper
- 1½ pounds broccoli, prepared as shown in photos

1. Use fork to whip together goat cheese, cream, parsley, red pepper flakes, and lemon juice in large bowl. Season with salt and pepper.

2. Bring 1 cup water and ½ teaspoon salt to boil in large saucepan over high heat. Add broccoli stalks, then place florets on top of stalks so that they sit just above water. Cover and cook until broccoli is bright green and just tender, 3 to 4 minutes. Drain thoroughly.

3. Toss hot broccoli with cheese mixture until evenly coated. Adjust seasonings with salt and pepper. Serve.

BROCCOLI WITH LEMON AND WALNUTS SERVES 4

Chopping the walnuts finely will help them cling to the broccoli. Prepare the walnuts while the broccoli is cooking.

- 3 tablespoons unsalted butter
- ½ cup walnuts, chopped fine
- 1 teaspoon grated zest and 2 teaspoons juice from 1 lemon
  Salt and pepper
- 1½ pounds broccoli, prepared as shown in photos

1. Heat butter in medium nonstick skillet over medium heat until foaming. Add walnuts and cook, stirring constantly, until butter turns golden brown, 1½ to 2 minutes. Stir in lemon zest and juice. Scrape into large bowl and season with salt and pepper.

2. Meanwhile, bring 1 cup water and ½ teaspoon salt to boil in large saucepan over high heat. Add broccoli stalks, then place florets on top of stalks so that they sit just above water. Cover and cook until broccoli is bright green and just tender, 3 to 4 minutes. Drain thoroughly.

3. Toss hot broccoli with nut mixture until evenly coated. Adjust seasonings with salt and pepper. Serve.

Now That's Easy
CUTTING UP BROCCOLI

1. Hold the broccoli upside down on a cutting board. Trim the florets from the stalk, separating the larger florets into 1-inch pieces, if necessary. **2.** Trim the top and bottom from the stalk. Cut away ⅛ inch of the tough outer peel. **3.** Cut the stalk in half lengthwise and then into ½-inch pieces.

Broccoli with Lemon and Walnuts

Jim Dionese love to ride his motorcycle in the country, but his wife prefers it when he spends time on his other hobby—cooking.

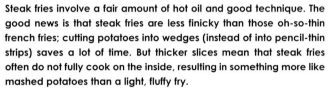

Super-Crisp Steak Fries

Dear Cook's Country,
My steak fries are never crisp enough on the outside. Even worse, they are soggy in the middle. Can you help?

Jim Dionese, East Lansing, Michigan

Dear Jim,
Steak fries involve a fair amount of hot oil and good technique. The good news is that steak fries are less finicky than those oh-so-thin french fries; cutting potatoes into wedges (instead of into pencil-thin strips) saves a lot of time. But thicker slices mean that steak fries often do not fully cook on the inside, resulting in something more like mashed potatoes than a light, fluffy fry.

Secrets to SUPER-CRISP FRIES

1. Using potholders, shake the bowl of potatoes halfway through microwaving to ensure even cooking.
2. Stirring a little cornstarch into the cooking oil will help to crisp the fries.
3. After frying the second batch, add the first batch of steak fries back to the pot to heat through and crisp up.

To come up with the best possible steak fry, I started by testing different kinds of potatoes. It was no surprise that russet potatoes turned out to be the best choice. No matter their size, russets are relatively light, dry potatoes that cook up fluffy, not heavy.

Now I hit the "double-fried" wall. Most recipes call for cooking fries twice: once to cook through the insides and a second time to crisp the outsides. Not only is this a time-consuming and messy process, but I found it produced only fair results. Even fried twice, relatively thin steak fries were too thick to cook through. I was just as stumped as you were.

Then I remembered a trick I use for baked potatoes when I'm running short on time. I start them in a microwave and then move them to the oven to finish. I threw a handful of potato wedges with a bit of oil into a bowl, covered it, and zapped them on high until tender. Then I followed up with a quick dip in hot oil. The result? A creamy, fluffy interior, but the exterior was still not perfectly crisp.

For my next trick, I stole an idea from a restaurant chef friend. When she wants fried foods to be extra-crispy, she dusts them with a bit of cornstarch. Well, to say that this didn't work would be kind. The cornstarch fell off in the oil, and the texture of the fries was sandy, not crispy. But—and here comes the good news—when I threw the remaining potato wedges (with no cornstarch coating) into the same hot oil (now laced with cornstarch), I hit a home run. I could actually hear the "crunch" when I bit into one! So the secret was to add a tablespoon of cornstarch to the hot oil just before frying. I found that it also helped to fry the potatoes in two batches; tossing them into the oil all at once caused the oil to cool down too much.

To fine-tune the process, I cooked some more fries for everyone in the test kitchen. I discovered that I could reheat the batch fried first by adding it to the pot with the second batch during the last minute of frying. Now all the fries were ready at the same time.

–Julia Collin Davison

SUPER-CRISP STEAK FRIES
SERVES 4 TO 6

Do not let the potatoes cool completely on paper towels in step 1; they may stick. Keeping the oil at the correct temperature is essential for producing crisp fries. Use a deep-fry thermometer to check the temperature of the oil before you add the potatoes.

- 3 **large russet potatoes, each one scrubbed and cut into 16 wedges**
- 5 **cups peanut or vegetable oil**
- 1 **tablespoon cornstarch**
   Salt and pepper

1. In large microwave-proof bowl, toss potato wedges with ¼ cup oil. Cover bowl tightly with plastic wrap and microwave on high until potatoes are completely tender but not falling apart, 8 to 12 minutes, tossing them (without removing the plastic) halfway through cooking time. (Microwave times vary, so check potatoes for doneness at 6 minutes.) Carefully remove plastic wrap (beware of steam) and drain. Gently spread potatoes out over several layers of paper towels. Pat dry and let cool 10 minutes. Gently peel potatoes from paper towels and transfer to large plate. (Potatoes can be held at room temperature for up to 2 hours.)

2. Heat remaining 4¾ cups oil (it should measure about 1 inch deep) in large Dutch oven or other wide, deep pot over high heat to 375 degrees.

3. When oil is ready, add cornstarch and stir to disperse. Add half of potatoes and fry, stirring and prodding to keep them from sticking together, until golden brown, 5 to 6 minutes. Remove fries from oil using slotted spoon or wire spider (see page 29) and transfer to baking sheet lined with paper towels. Lightly pat potatoes dry with paper towels. Return oil to 375 degrees and repeat with remaining potato wedges. When second batch is golden brown, return first batch to pot and continue to fry until all potatoes are deeply golden with dark brown edges, 1 to 3 minutes longer. Transfer fries to fresh layers of paper towels, pat dry, and season with salt and pepper (or one of the flavored salts on page 29) to taste. Serve.

Believe it or not, the microwave plays an important role in our recipe for extra-crisp steak fries.

One Potato, Two Potato, Four Potato, More!

For the best steak fries, buy large, uniform russet potatoes and cut each one into 16 thin, even wedges.

Getting to Know Potatoes

Looks can be deceiving. Although many potato varieties look alike, their cooking properties can be very different. Starch content determines how various potatoes should be cooked. Potatoes can generally be divided into three categories: high starch, medium starch, and low starch. High-starch potatoes, such as russets, are best baked, mashed, or fried. Medium-starch potatoes, such as Yukon Golds, are the most versatile and can be baked, mashed, roasted, or used in soups. Low-starch varieties, such as red potatoes, are best boiled or roasted and used in soups, salads, or other dishes in which you want the potatoes to hold their shape. Here are 15 popular varieties and our recommendations on how to use them, based on our experience in the test kitchen.

Russet
BEST BAKED POTATO

This popular high-starch potato bakes up to light and fluffy perfection. Also known as an Idaho, this potato is equally satisfying when turned into a creamy mash or a crispy fry.

All Blue
EARTHY BAKE OR MASH

This unique tuber is, as its name suggests, blue inside and out. Because it is fairly high in starch, baking or mashing produces the best results.

All-Purpose
PANTRY STAPLE

The name says it all. Although this medium-starch spud isn't quite as fluffy as a russet when baked or as sturdy as a red potato when boiled, it is an excellent stand-in for almost every potato dish.

Fingerling
TRULY BUTTERY

The novelty of this medium-starch variety is its miniature size. We like to sauté or boil these potatoes whole to bring out their sweet, buttery flavor.

Purple Peruvian
BUYER BEWARE

Don't be fooled by the interesting color. This medium-starch potato is fine in a pinch, but the flavor is a bit flat and the flesh is mushy when overcooked.

Yukon Gold
GOLDEN BEAUTY

This versatile medium-starch spud has a delicious, buttery flavor. It can be boiled or mashed with great results but is especially good sautéed (for home fries) or roasted in a casserole.

Yellow Finn
GOLDEN TWIN

This medium-starch variety is very similar to the Yukon Gold, with yellow flesh and a creamy, buttery taste. A great choice for mashed potatoes, soups, and stews.

Bintje
YELLOW ROASTER

This yellow potato is popular in Europe but is also sold in the United States. We like to roast this medium-starch variety.

Klondike Rose
YELLOW IN DISGUISE

Although its skin is red, this medium-starch variety has all of the properties of a yellow potato. Like the Yukon Gold, it's very versatile.

Red Potato
STURDY SPUD

These low-starch potatoes are terrific boiled with or without their fiber-rich skin. They hold their shape well in moisture-laden dishes like casseroles, soups, and salads.

Red Creamer
SMASHING STAR

This low-starch spud is ideal for boiling or steaming. Our favorite to smash, skin-on, for a colorful rustic look.

White Creamer
LIKE THEIR RED RIVALS

Similar to the red variety, this potato produces a great smashed potato, and its low starch content makes it ideal for boiling or steaming.

Ruby Crescent
UNIQUE LOOK

We like to preserve the curved, finger-like shape of this low-starch fingerling by boiling or steaming it whole.

Russian Banana
RICH FLAVOR

This sturdy low-starch variety is similar to other fingerlings, with an especially good flavor. Visually appealing when served boiled or roasted whole.

French Fingerling
GREAT TASTE

This plump fingerling has a nutty flavor and is best when boiled, steamed, or roasted whole.

Shaking Up Shake 'n Bake

Kathleen McKeown serves pork chops at least once a week. During the summer, chops are rubbed with spices and grilled. For the rest of the year, breaded pork chops are a family favorite.

Dear Cook's Country,
My husband loves pork chops coated with Shake 'n Bake. Breaded pork chops are quick and easy (that's why I like them), but I do wish the coating tasted better and had more crunch. Do you have a good recipe?

Kathleen McKeown, East Haddam, Connecticut

Dear Kathleen,
As someone who grew up on Shake 'n Bake, I can relate to your husband. My mom fed us kids a steady diet of breaded pork chops, chicken cutlets, and fish fillets. But I must confess—I hadn't tried Shake 'n Bake pork chops in a long time. When I did, they weren't as good as I remembered. In fact, the coating was bland and soggy.

In my homemade version of Shake 'n Bake pork chops I wanted two things above all: good flavor and a thick, crunchy crust. I wasn't very worried about flavor—I figured it wouldn't be too hard to do better than a box from the supermarket—but I was worried about the crunch. I looked through a bunch of cookbooks and found recipes that coated the chops with corn-flake crumbs, flour, matzo meal, bread crumbs, cornmeal, and more. You name it, I tried it. But these crusts were all too thin and gummy. I realized I needed coarser, sturdier crumbs.

With a heavy-duty freezer bag and a mallet, I found I could turn almost any cracker into crumbs. And I could control their texture. I tried Ritz crackers, saltines, and oyster crackers, but Melba toasts were the test kitchen favorite. Everyone liked their dense, hearty crunch and subtle, toasted flavor. What's more, a 5-ounce box of Melba toasts, once crushed, produced the perfect amount of crumbs to coat four chops.

Up until this point, I had been using the Shake 'n Bake method: Moisten the chops with water, pile them into the bag with the crumbs, and shake them up. Although mess-free, this method didn't produce the thick, crunchy crust I had envisioned. Too many crumbs fell off. I discovered that getting my hands dirty—by pressing the crumbs into the chops—was more effective. But I still needed something stickier than water to support a super-thick crust.

I tried beaten eggs, buttermilk, heavy cream, sour cream, and milk. All were acceptable in flavor, but none contributed to that elusive crunch. After doing some thinking (and eating yet another pork chop dinner), I realized that everything I had used to adhere the crumbs to the chops was water based; no wonder the crust was sodden! Plain vegetable oil worked better, but the coating was a bit thin. The winner turned out to be— believe it or not—mayonnaise!

By coating each chop with a tablespoon of mayonnaise (which stuck to the meat like frosting on a cake), I was able to build a thick crust. The Melba mixture stuck to the chop like a champ and staunchly defended its territory. Seasoning the Melba crumbs was easy. Pantry staples such as garlic powder, onion powder, paprika, and dried thyme did the trick.

Now I worked on the cooking method. I started with a 425-degree oven, the temperature recommended on a box of Shake 'n Bake. This part of the recipe was dead on. One part that wasn't was the advice to cook the chops on a baking sheet; the underside of the chops always turned out soggy. I solved this problem by placing the breaded chops on a wire rack set over a rimmed baking sheet. Finally, I had figured out homemade Shake 'n Bake. Of course, "Press 'n Bake" would be more like it, as there wasn't a whole lot of shakin' going on.

–Jeremy Sauer

You'll never guess the secret ingredient in the coating for this juicy breaded pork chop. It's Melba toast.

QUICK AND CRUNCHY PORK CHOPS SERVES 4

For a substantial crust, don't break up the Melba toasts too much, and coat the chops well with mayonnaise. Although an instant-read thermometer takes the guesswork out of determining when the meat is done, you can use the "nick-and-peek" method: Use a paring knife to make a slit in the top of the pork chop and take a look at the meat's interior. The Melba crumbs can be made weeks in advance and stored in the freezer. Applesauce is a natural with these chops.

- 1 (5-ounce) box Melba toast, broken into rough pieces
- 1/2 teaspoon salt
- 1/2 teaspoon garlic powder
- 1/2 teaspoon onion powder
- 1/2 teaspoon paprika
- 1/2 teaspoon dried thyme
- 1/8 teaspoon sugar
- 6 tablespoons mayonnaise
- 4 center-cut boneless pork chops, 3/4 inch to 1 inch thick (each 6 to 7 ounces), patted dry with paper towels

1. Adjust oven rack to middle position and heat oven to 425 degrees. Place Melba toast pieces, salt, garlic powder, onion powder, paprika, thyme, and sugar in heavy-duty zipper-lock freezer bag. Seal bag and pound with heavy blunt object (such as a rolling pin) until Melba toasts are crushed but still have some crumbs the size of small pebbles. Add 2 tablespoons mayonnaise to bag and work mayonnaise evenly into crumb mixture by gently squeezing outside of bag. Transfer Melba crumb mixture to large plate.

2. Using your fingers, coat 1 chop with 1 tablespoon mayonnaise. Transfer to plate with Melba crumbs, sprinkle top of pork chop with some Melba mixture, and press down firmly on chop to adhere crumbs. Flip chop and repeat, making sure that thick layer of crumbs coats both sides and edges. Transfer breaded pork chop to baking rack set over rimmed baking sheet. Repeat with remaining chops.

3. Bake pork chops until juices run clear and instant-read thermometer inserted into center of chop registers 145 to 150 degrees, 16 to 22 minutes. Remove chops from oven and let rest on rack for 5 to 10 minutes. Serve immediately.

SESAME PORK CHOPS

This variation is a great match with our Five-Spice Applesauce.

Toast 1/4 cup sesame seeds in small skillet over medium-low heat, stirring frequently, until fragrant and golden, 4 to 5 minutes. Follow recipe for Quick and Crunchy Pork Chops, substituting sesame-flavored Melba toast for regular Melba toast and adding toasted sesame seeds to Melba crumb mixture in step 1.

CORDON BLEU PORK CHOPS

In this variation, ham and cheese top the pork chops before they are breaded.

Place 4 thin slices provolone cheese on top of each pork chop (pile of cheese should be no more than 1/4 inch thick) and tear cheese to leave 1/8-inch border on all sides. Top with 1 slice deli ham large enough to cover cheese completely, and press down on ham to adhere to pork chop. Follow recipe for Quick and Crunchy Pork Chops, reducing salt to 1/4 teaspoon and increasing cooking time by one or two minutes.

Secrets to BREADED PORK CHOPS

1. Thoroughly coat each pork chop with 1 tablespoon of mayonnaise. **2.** Use your fingers to press the crumbs into each chop.

3. Bake the breaded chops on a rack set over a baking sheet. **4.** Insert an instant-read thermometer into the side of the chop to determine when it's done.

Does It Work? THE BATTER PRO

Fans of late-night television will undoubtedly be familiar with the Batter Pro ($24.95, plus shipping and handling). The thought of breaded foods without messy hands seemed too good to be true, so we picked one up and got shakin'.

Is this space-age breading gadget worth $25?

The Batter Pro (which looks like a UFO from a 1950s B movie) consists of two clear plastic lids that connect to opposite sides of a sifting tray. The concept is simple: Place the breading and raw food inside, cover, and shake. After shaking, the Batter Pro is inverted, allowing the excess breading to fall through the perforated sifting tray, leaving a light coating on the raw food.

To be fair, the Batter Pro can easily handle up to four pork chops, four chicken breasts, or 1½ pounds of shrimp in one shaking. Unfortunately, the Batter Pro does not deliver on its "no mess, no waste" promise: The raw food must still be transferred by hand into and out of the sifting apparatus, and so many crumbs are needed to bread the food that there is also quite a bit of waste. So roll up your sleeves and save your money. –J.S.

on the side PAGING DOCTORED APPLESAUCE

Nothing goes better with pork chops than applesauce. Breathe new life into store-bought brands with these simple recipes that rely on two unlikely ingredients: Red Hot cinnamon candies and Chinese five-spice powder. Both recipes can be served immediately or refrigerated for up to three days.

SWEET-AND-HOT CINNAMON APPLESAUCE
MAKES 3 CUPS

Red Hots—that's right, the candies—add both sweetness and heat to this applesauce.

- 3 cups prepared applesauce
- 8 Red Hot candies

Combine applesauce and Red Hots in medium saucepan. Cover and cook over low heat, stirring often, until candies have completely dissolved and applesauce has turned light pink, about 15 minutes. Serve warm or at room temperature.

FIVE-SPICE APPLESAUCE
MAKES 3 CUPS

Look for five-spice powder in the spice aisle of the supermarket. This Chinese blend usually contains cinnamon, cloves, fennel seed, star anise, and Sichuan peppercorns.

- 3 cups prepared applesauce
- 1/4 teaspoon Chinese five-spice powder

Combine applesauce and five-spice powder in saucepan. Cover and cook over low heat, stirring often, until applesauce is heated through, about 10 minutes. Serve warm or at room temperature.

Rustle Up Some Beans!

A mug of strong black coffee gives cowboy beans a swift kick in the pants

Dear Cook's Country,

At a local barbecue joint, I ate beans that looked like baked beans but tasted much better. They were sweet, spicy, and smoky. The pit-master called them cowboy beans, and, when I asked for his recipe, he grinned and said it was "top secret." Can you help me out?

Jessica Derby, Andover, Massachusetts

Dear Jessica,

I contacted a pitmaster on my own and, despite a lot of pleading, he wouldn't give me his recipe, either. But he was willing to hand over a few hints. He cooks pinto beans really slowly with browned onions, barbecue sauce, "odds and ends" of smoked meat, and a few "secret" seasonings. One ingredient, he said, "was pretty out there." I wasn't sure what he meant by that, but I was certainly intrigued.

Cowboy beans seem to be a cattle-country spin on Boston baked beans. In Boston baked beans, navy beans are stewed with salt pork, onion, mustard, and molasses; cowboy beans have pinto beans and barbecued beef or pork as well as a laundry list of various seasonings. I found dozens of recipes for cowboy beans, each a little different from the last. My goal was to create the robust flavor you liked but with commonly available ingredients. That meant no barbecued beef or pork, which might be sitting around in a restaurant kitchen but not in a home kitchen.

First things first. I had to decide on the best method for cooking the beans. As much as I like canned beans, they can't survive a lengthy simmer: Dried beans were a must. I liked both pinto and navy beans.

Most cowboy bean recipes bring the beans and flavorings to a boil on the stovetop and then slide the pot into the oven. Rush this process, and the beans break apart. I found that the beans needed to cook in a 300-degree oven for about four hours. Some things are worth the wait, and good beans are one of them.

With a basic cooking method in hand, I tackled flavor. I first cooked a chopped onion in oil, but then thought better of the oil. Why not cook the onion in something more robust, like rendered bacon? The smoky meat and rich fat might be the perfect replacement for the "odds and ends" of barbecued meat. I browned a few slices of chopped bacon and then added the onion to soften in the fat. While I was at it, I added a few cloves of minced garlic. These beans were beginning to taste pretty good already.

The pitmaster undoubtedly adds home-brewed barbecue sauce, but I went with bottled sauce and had good results. A couple of tablespoons of spicy brown mustard—common to a lot of recipes—added a zip that tasters appreciated. I'm willing to wager that the brown mustard is one of the pitmaster's "secret" ingredients.

The beans were now good but still lacked that special something. What was that "pretty out there" ingredient the pitmaster had hinted at? I scoured more recipes for anything I might have missed and, lo and behold, I found it: A couple of them added a mugful of coffee. Now that is out there.

I stirred some coffee into the beans before they went into the oven, and what a difference it made! Its roasted, mildly bitter flavor tied all of the other flavors together. Who would have thought that the secret to great-tasting beans was a cup of coffee? **–Matthew Card**

COWBOY BEANS
SERVES 4 TO 6

A heavy-bottomed Dutch oven prevents the beans from cooking too rapidly or scorching. If you're thinking ahead, you can soak the beans in 6 cups of water overnight (then skip step 1). Adjust the heat, smoke, or salt by stirring in more Tabasco or barbecue sauce at serving time.

- 1 pound dried pinto or navy beans, washed and picked clean of any debris
- 4 slices bacon, chopped fine
- 1 medium onion, chopped fine
- 4 medium garlic cloves, minced
- 4½ cups water
- 1 cup strong black coffee
- ⅓ cup packed dark brown sugar
- 2 tablespoons prepared brown mustard (such as Gulden's)
- ½ cup plus 2 tablespoons barbecue sauce
- ½ teaspoon Tabasco sauce
  Salt and pepper

1. Place beans and 6 cups water in large Dutch oven. Bring to boil over high heat and cook for 5 minutes. Remove pot from heat, cover, and allow beans to sit for 1 hour. Drain beans. Clean and dry pot.

2. Adjust oven rack to lower-middle position and heat oven to 300 degrees. Add bacon to pot and cook over medium heat until lightly browned, 6 to 8 minutes. Stir in onion and cook until beginning to brown, 6 to 8 minutes. Add garlic and cook until fragrant, about 30 seconds. Add drained beans, water, and coffee. Bring to simmer over high heat and cook for 10 minutes. Add brown sugar, mustard, ½ cup barbecue sauce, Tabasco sauce, and 2 teaspoons salt. Return to boil over high heat, cover pot, and transfer to oven.

3. Cook until beans are just tender, 2 to 2½ hours. Remove lid and continue to cook, stirring occasionally, until liquid has thickened to syrupy consistency, 1 to 1½ hours. Remove from oven, stir in remaining 2 tablespoons barbecue sauce, and season to taste with salt and pepper. (Beans can be refrigerated for several days.)

The American Table:

Chuck Wagon Cuisine

The fabled chuck wagons of Old West fame first hit the trail shortly after the Civil War. Charles Goodnight, a larger-than-life cattle baron of the Texas Panhandle, had a surplus army cart outfitted with reinforced fittings and enough cabinetry to store the requisite dry goods, equipment, and fuel for a crew of cowboys on the trail. A back flap flipped down to serve as the cook's countertop, on which he prepared a never-ending stream of beans, biscuits, steaks, and coffee.

Chuck wagon cooks—always called Cookie by the cowboys—led as hard a life as those they fed. Cooks were up for hours before the sun rose, whipping up breakfast, and stayed up long into the night cleaning dishes. They also had to keep the wagon stocked with food, fuel, and water—easier said than done on the open plains.

To keep on the good side of Cookie, cowboys followed an unwritten code. If riding close to the wagon, they always stayed downwind so the dirt and dust they kicked up wouldn't get into the food. The same rule applied when it came to dismounting their horses. Cowboys never crowded the cooking fires for warmth, and under no circumstances would they ever help themselves to the last serving without an OK from Cookie. –M.C.

Quick Cooking

GOOD MEALS IN ABOUT 30 MINUTES

Fancy spring supper with salmon and fresh sugar snap peas

GLAZED SALMON WITH DILLY MUSTARD SAUCE

SERVES 4

Broilers vary in heat output, so cooking times can vary dramatically. When you are broiling, it is best not to walk away from the oven. Keep a close watch on your food, and start checking after a few minutes.

- 2 tablespoons Dijon mustard
- 2 tablespoons honey
- 1 tablespoon white wine vinegar
- 3 tablespoons olive oil
- 1 tablespoon soy sauce
- 1 tablespoon chopped fresh dill, plus a few sprigs for garnish
- 4 salmon fillets, each about 6 ounces
  Salt and pepper

1. Adjust oven rack so that it sits about 6 inches from heating element and heat broiler. Line rimmed baking sheet with foil for easy cleanup.

2. Whisk mustard, honey, and vinegar in medium bowl. Whisk in oil, then transfer 3 tablespoons mustard mixture to small bowl and stir in soy sauce. Whisk dill into mustard mixture in medium bowl.

3. Arrange salmon fillets on baking sheet. Season with salt and pepper and brush top and sides with mustard-soy glaze. Broil salmon until tops are just browned and a peek at inside of fish with paring knife shows that they are just cooked through, 5 to 8 minutes. Transfer salmon to serving platter, garnish with dill sprigs, and serve with mustard-dill sauce.

SAUTÉED SUGAR SNAP PEAS & CHERRY TOMATOES SERVES 4

A little sugar intensifies the flavor of the tomatoes and helps balance the acidity of the lemon juice.

- 1 tablespoon olive oil
- ½ pound sugar snap peas, ends snapped off and strings removed
- 2 cups cherry tomatoes, cut in half
- 1 teaspoon sugar
- 1 medium garlic clove, minced
- 1 teaspoon grated zest and 1 tablespoon juice from 1 lemon
  Salt and pepper

Heat oil in large nonstick skillet over medium heat until just shimmering. Add peas and cook, stirring occasionally, until crisp/tender, 2 to 3 minutes. Transfer peas to medium serving bowl. Add cherry tomatoes, sugar, garlic, and lemon zest to skillet and cook for 30 seconds. Add lemon juice, toss well, then transfer tomatoes to bowl with sugar snap peas. Toss to combine and season with salt and pepper to taste. Serve.

Regional Favorites: South-of-the-Border Supper

From barbecue sauce to soy sauce, it's easy to give meatloaf a new twist. But meatloaf variations can spin out of control. I recently ran across a recipe that called for canned peaches. Another used bananas and mustard! I prefer something a bit more traditional and stick with bold south-of-the-border flavors. –**Eva Katz**

CHEESY SOUTHWESTERN MEATLOAF SERVES 6 TO 8

Use either medium or hot salsa for the glaze. Ground pork adds tenderness and sweetness to the meatloaf, but you can use 2 pounds of ground beef if you prefer.

- 1 cup prepared salsa
- 3 tablespoons brown sugar
- 4 (6-inch) corn tortillas
- 1½ pounds ground beef chuck
- ½ pound ground pork
- ½ cup sour cream
- 3 large eggs
- 1 (4-ounce) can green chiles, drained and finely chopped
- ¾ cup chopped scallions
- ¼ cup minced fresh cilantro
- 1 tablespoon chili powder
- 1 teaspoon ground cumin
- 1 teaspoon salt
- ½ teaspoon pepper
- 1 cup grated pepper Jack cheese

1. Adjust oven rack to middle position and heat oven to 350 degrees. Line rimmed baking sheet with foil.

2. Combine salsa and brown sugar in small saucepan and set aside.

3. Tear tortillas into small pieces, grind in food processor or blender until they resemble cornmeal, and transfer to large bowl. Add beef, pork, sour cream, eggs, chiles, scallions, cilantro, chili powder, cumin, salt, and pepper, and mix with fork until evenly blended. Turn mixture onto foil-lined baking sheet and, using moistened hands, pat into 9 by 5-inch loaf shape. Brush with ¼ cup salsa mixture.

4. Bake for 40 minutes. Scatter cheese on top and continue baking until center of loaf registers 160 degrees on instant-read thermometer, about 30 minutes. Set aside to cool slightly.

5. While meatloaf cools, simmer remaining salsa mixture over medium-high heat until thickened, 3 to 5 minutes. Slice meatloaf and serve with salsa mixture passed separately at table.

Magic Ingredients

Most meatloaf recipes call for sautéing onion and garlic. Thanks to canned green chiles, our meatloaf gets plenty of spice and flavor with no precooking required. Ground corn tortillas take the place of the more traditional bread crumbs or oatmeal, and the resulting flavor is unquestionably southwestern.

Emmy Lam is originally from New York and prides herself on being a cheesecake fanatic.

Icebox Cheesecake

Gelatin and whipped cream help our creamy no-bake cheesecake set up in the refrigerator—but this cool trick will take at least six hours.

Dear Cook's Country,
Over the years, I've tried several no-bake cheesecake recipes that call for gelatin. These recipes are really easy, but the cheesecake is always kind of rubbery. I once tried using a lot less gelatin, but the filling never set up. Is there something between cheesecake soup and cheesecake so stiff you can bounce a quarter off the top?

Emmy Lam, Kissimmee, Florida

Dear Emmy,
I grew up on no-bake cheesecake, but my family called it icebox cheesecake because it set up in the refrigerator. In essence, this cheesecake is a sweetened mixture of cream cheese and heavy cream held together not by eggs but by gelatin—the source of the "no-bake" magic. This recipe eliminates the oven and messy water bath that are standard with other cheesecakes.

When I started testing recipes, I had the same experience you did. The majority called for too much gelatin, which does indeed create a rubbery texture. On the other end of the spectrum were recipes that relied on the stabilizers in the cream cheese and the stiffness of an artificial whipped topping, such as Cool Whip, to hold the shape of the filling. But the gelatin-free recipes I tried were soft, gummy, and messy. (They didn't taste very good, either.) It became apparent that gelatin was a must-have ingredient.

After testing various ratios of ingredients, I hit upon the following formula: 1 pound cream cheese, 1½ cups heavy cream, ⅔ cup sugar, and 1 envelope (or 2 teaspoons) gelatin. The filling was set and there was no jiggle or bounce, but it was a bit too dense and heavy. Although no one in the kitchen had liked the fake flavor

of the recipe made with Cool Whip, I had an idea: Maybe I should whip the heavy cream in my recipe to lighten the texture of the filling. It took me a couple of tries to figure out that I needed to whip almost all of the cream. I used the rest to soften and dissolve the gelatin.

My no-bake cheesecake now had great texture; it was light, creamy, and sliceable. But one thing still bothered me. Up until this point in my testing, I had been using two bowls, one to whip the cream and sugar until stiff, and another to beat the cream cheese until smooth. Could I make the recipe even simpler and use just one bowl? I tried whipping the cream and sugar to soft peaks (instead of stiff peaks), adding chunks of cream cheese, and whipping the filling until thoroughly aerated. The results were the same, except that I had one less bowl to wash. Not quite magic, but this truly was the icing on the cake. **– Charles Kelsey**

ICEBOX CHEESECAKE
SERVES 12

Don't rush the softening of the cream cheese. If microwaved, the cream cheese will cook slightly and eventually cause the entire cheesecake mixture to break. To speed up the process, cut the cream cheese into chunks and then let it stand at room temperature for at least half an hour. When the cream cheese is no longer cold and gives easily under pressure, it's ready to use.

Crust
- 1 cup graham cracker crumbs (crushed from 8 whole crackers)
- 1 tablespoon sugar
- 5 tablespoons unsalted butter, melted and kept warm

Filling
- 1½ cups heavy cream
- 1 envelope unflavored gelatin
- ⅔ cup sugar
- 1 pound cream cheese, cut into 1-inch chunks and

softened 30 to 45 minutes at room temperature
- 2 tablespoons juice and 1 teaspoon grated zest from 1 lemon
- 1 teaspoon vanilla extract
  Pinch salt

1. For the crust: Adjust oven rack to middle position and heat oven to 325 degrees. Stir graham cracker crumbs and sugar together in medium bowl, then add butter and stir well with fork until mixture resembles wet sand. Transfer crumbs to 9-inch springform pan and, following photo at top of page 25, use bottom of measuring cup to firmly press crumbs into even layer over bottom of pan. Bake crust until fragrant and beginning to brown, about 13 minutes. Cool completely on wire rack, at least 30 minutes.

2. For the filling: Pour ¼ cup heavy cream into microwave-safe measuring cup. Add gelatin and whisk to combine. Let stand until gelatin

is softened, about 5 minutes, then microwave on high power for about 30 seconds, or until cream is bubbling and gelatin is completely dissolved. Set aside.

3. Using electric mixer, beat remaining 1¼ cups heavy cream and sugar in large bowl at medium-high speed until soft peaks form, about 2 minutes. Add cream cheese and beat at medium-low speed until combined, about 1 minute (a few coffee bean–sized lumps may remain). Scrape bottom and sides of bowl well with rubber spatula. Add lemon juice, vanilla, and salt and continue to beat at medium-low speed until combined, about 1 minute. Scrape bottom and sides of bowl again. Increase speed to medium-high and beat until mixture is smooth, about 3 minutes. Add dissolved gelatin mixture and lemon zest and continue to beat at medium-high until smooth and airy, about 2 minutes.

4. Pour filling into cooled crust and, using offset or icing spatula dipped in hot water, spread filling out evenly. Refrigerate for at least 6 hours, but for best results refrigerate overnight.

5. To serve, wrap hot, damp kitchen towel around springform pan, as shown in photo 1, below right. Unlock pan and carefully lift off sides. Slip thin metal spatula under crust and carefully slide cheesecake onto serving platter.

STRAWBERRY SAUCE
MAKES ABOUT 2½ CUPS

This strawberry sauce pairs perfectly with our basic Icebox Cheesecake, but it also goes nicely with the Key lime variation. Frozen strawberries work well in this recipe, but if you can find fresh, very ripe berries, by all means, use them instead. Be sure to stir the strawberries gently so that they do not break down completely—large chunks of strawberries are very appealing. You can make this sauce up to 2 days in advance.

1	**pound frozen strawberries, whole**
½	**cup seedless strawberry jam**
¼	**cup sugar**
	Pinch salt
2	**teaspoons lemon juice**

Combine strawberries, jam, sugar, and salt in medium saucepan. Cook, stirring frequently, over medium heat, until sauce has thickened, about 8 minutes. Remove from heat, stir in lemon juice, and transfer to medium bowl. Cool for 30 minutes, then loosely cover with plastic wrap and refrigerate until chilled, about 2 hours.

PEPPERMINT CHIP ICEBOX CHEESECAKE

To make the crust for this cheesecake, place 16 Double Delight Oreo Mint 'n Creme cookies in a food processor or blender and pulse until ground.

1. Prepare Icebox Cheesecake crust, substituting 1¼ cups Oreo mint cookie crumbs (see note) for graham cracker crumbs. Omit sugar and reduce melted butter to 2 tablespoons.

Proceed to make, bake, and cool crust as directed.

2. Prepare filling as directed, reducing sugar to ½ cup, substituting 2 tablespoons crème de menthe for lemon juice and vanilla, omitting lemon zest, and folding 1 cup mini semisweet chocolate chips into finished filling. Proceed as directed.

KEY LIME ICEBOX CHEESECAKE

Regular limes are just fine in this refreshing variation.

1. Prepare Icebox Cheesecake crust, substituting 1 cup animal cracker crumbs for graham cracker crumbs. Increase sugar to 3 tablespoons, add 1 teaspoon grated lime zest, and reduce butter to 4 tablespoons.

2. Prepare filling as directed, substituting 3 tablespoons lime juice for lemon juice and vanilla, and 2 tablespoons grated lime zest for grated lemon zest. Proceed as directed.

3. After removing chilled cheesecake from pan, top with sugared lime slices.

PEANUT BUTTER ICEBOX CHEESECAKE

Creamy peanut butter, Nutter Butter cookies, and chopped salted peanuts pack a triple peanut punch in this cheesecake. To make the crust, you'll need 16 Nutter Butter cookies, broken into rough pieces and processed in a food processor or blender until ground. Serve this cheesecake drizzled with melted chocolate.

1. Prepare Icebox Cheesecake crust, substituting 1¼ cups Nutter Butter cookie crumbs (see note) for graham cracker crumbs. Omit sugar and reduce melted butter to 2 tablespoons. Proceed to make, bake, and cool crust as directed.

2. Prepare filling as directed, reducing sugar to ½ cup, omitting lemon juice and lemon zest, and beating ½ cup creamy peanut butter into finished mixture. Proceed as directed.

3. After removing chilled cheesecake from pan, press ½ cup chopped salted peanuts into sides of cheesecake.

How to Make
AN EVEN CRUST

Mix graham cracker crumbs with melted butter and sugar, and use the bottom of a dry measuring cup to press the mixture firmly into the pan.

Secrets
CUTTING CLEAN EDGES

Even the greatest cheesecake isn't much good if you can't get it out of the pan and slice it neatly.

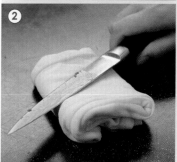

1. To release the cheesecake, wrap a hot, damp kitchen towel around the pan for 20 seconds. Unlock the pan and remove the sides. Slide a thin spatula under the crust and transfer the cheesecake to a serving platter.
2. For neat, clean slices, wipe the knife on a damp towel between each cut.

No More Crummy Crusts

A good cheesecake filling deserves a great crust. Store-bought graham cracker crusts are made with shortening—and taste like it. Take 15 minutes to make a homemade crust with butter. And, yes, because the crust must be baked, our cheesecake recipe isn't 100 percent "no-bake." But if you skip this step, the crumb crust will be soft and messy, not crisp and neat.

Happy Birthday Cupcakes

EASY BIRTHDAY CUPCAKES
MAKES 24 CUPCAKES

Store unfrosted cupcakes in an airtight container at room temperature for up to three days. Cupcakes are best served the day they are frosted. This recipe can easily be cut in half to yield 12 cupcakes.

3	cups cake flour
1	teaspoon baking powder
½	teaspoon baking soda
1	teaspoon salt
4	large eggs, at room temperature
2	teaspoons vanilla extract
1⅓	cups sugar
12	tablespoons (1½ sticks) unsalted butter, melted and cooled slightly
1¼	cups buttermilk

1. Adjust oven rack to middle position and heat oven to 325 degrees. Line 2 standard muffin/cupcake tins with paper or foil cupcake liners.

2. Whisk flour, baking powder, baking soda, and salt in medium bowl until combined. Whisk eggs and vanilla in large bowl until well blended. In steady stream, pour sugar into eggs, whisking constantly. Gradually whisk in melted butter, then add buttermilk. Add one-third of dry ingredients to bowl with wet ingredients. Using whisk, gently combine; a few streaks of flour should remain. Repeat twice with remaining dry ingredients. Continue to gently stir batter with whisk until most lumps are gone. Do not overmix.

3. Fill cupcake liners about two-thirds full. Bake, with tins side by side on middle rack, until cupcakes just begin to color and toothpick inserted into center comes out clean, 18 to 22 minutes. Cool pans on wire racks for 5 minutes, then remove cupcakes from pans, place back on rack, and cool to room temperature before frosting, about 1 hour.

QUICK VANILLA FROSTING
MAKES ABOUT 4 CUPS, ENOUGH TO GENEROUSLY FROST 24 CUPCAKES

If the frosting gets too soft while you ice the cupcakes, put the frosting back in the fridge for about 10 minutes.

¾	pound (3 sticks) unsalted butter, at room temperature
3	cups confectioners' sugar
2	tablespoons milk
2	teaspoons vanilla extract
⅛	teaspoon salt

Using electric mixer, beat butter in large bowl until fluffy, about 30 seconds. With mixer on low speed, add sugar, 1 cup at a time, and mix to combine. Increase speed to high and beat until pale and fluffy, about 1 minute. Reduce speed to medium-low and add milk, vanilla, and salt. Increase speed to high and beat until fluffy, 30 more seconds.

QUICK CHOCOLATE FROSTING

Melt 1 cup semisweet chocolate chips in small bowl and set aside to cool slightly. Follow recipe for Quick Vanilla Frosting, reducing butter to 2½ sticks and replacing ¼ cup confectioners' sugar with ¼ cup unsweetened cocoa powder. Once sugar and cocoa have been added, beat in melted chocolate and proceed as directed.

Dear Cook's Country,

I am a busy mother of a 1-year-old daughter named Tenley. As you can imagine, her birthday celebration is quite a big deal in my family. I don't want to make cupcakes from a boxed mix, but I don't have a lot of time, either. Do you have a simple recipe for birthday cupcakes?

Jenny Williamson, Marblehead, Massachusetts

Dear Jenny,

I have to be honest. I don't like cupcakes made from a boxed cake mix. They are too sweet and artificial tasting. Of course, I don't have children running around at home, so I have the time to make cupcakes from scratch. But I know time is precious, especially with a 1-year-old underfoot. With that in mind, I've created a really simple homemade recipe. It's almost as easy as a boxed mix and requires no fancy techniques or special equipment. Let me know what you and Tenley think. I know kids can be the toughest critics.

Erika Bruce

Jenny Williamson sent us this photo of her daughter, Tenley, at her first birthday party. Jenny writes: "Tenley loved the cupcakes, and the party was a great success. Thanks for your easy recipe."

Kitchen Helper
QUICKER CUPCAKES

These tips will help you get cupcakes in the oven in no time.

Taking the Chill Off Eggs

Forget to pull the eggs from the fridge ahead of time? Just put them in a bowl and fill with hot tap water. They should reach room temperature in 10 minutes.

Quicker Batter Portioning

We found it took a long time to spoon batter into each of the cupcake liners. Using a spring-loaded ice cream scoop to portion out the batter saved us a lot of time and made for more even cupcakes.

Cupcake-Decorating Contest

Our call for decorating ideas was met with hundreds of reader responses. Here are our favorites. Congratulations to our grand prize winner, Amanda Weber, who will receive $500. All 11 runners-up will receive a complimentary one-year subscription to the magazine.

Grand Prize Winner

Marshmallow Daisies
Amanda Weber of Sheboygan Falls, Wisconsin, uses large marshmallows to create whimsical daisies. Using 1½ to 2 marshmallows per cupcake, she cuts each into 5 or 6 pieces crosswise (the pieces will pinch and form petal shapes) and then places them in a circle on top of each frosted cupcake (sticky side down), leaving a hole in the center. She uses a yellow gumdrop as the flower's center.

Cracker Jack Balls
Sarah Finnegan of Oakland, California, frosts a cupcake with vanilla icing and covers it with Cracker Jack popcorn and peanuts. She then inserts a prize in the top of the cupcake.

Ice Cream Cones
Andrea Dyan Wyant of Phillipsburg, New Jersey, bakes her cupcakes in flat-bottomed ice-cream cones. When the cupcakes are cool, she frosts them and then decorates them with multicolored sprinkles.

Clown Cakes
Michelle Youngblood of Fort Worth, Texas, ices a cupcake with vanilla frosting, then tops it with a sugar cone. She pipes colored frosting to make a ruffled collar and uses dots to decorate the hat and gumballs and licorice for the face.

Apples-of-My-Eye
Christine Sapp of Columbus, Ohio, ices cupcakes with red-tinted frosting. She cuts leaves out of fruit leather and inserts one into the top of each cupcake. For a stem, she uses a ½-inch piece of a pretzel stick.

Earthworms in "Dirt"
Amy Odum Fothergill of Half Moon Bay, California, ices cupcakes with chocolate frosting and dips them in Oreo cookie crumbs to coat. She then cuts gummy worms in half and sticks the pieces into the "dirt."

Spring Birds' Nests
Katie Suarez of Broken Arrow, Oklahoma, tints vanilla frosting and sweetened coconut with green food coloring and nestles three malted milk chocolate eggs in the center.

Hot Fudge Sundaes
Elizabeth Jackson of Carmel, California, generously pipes white frosting on a cupcake, using a pastry bag fitted with a plain tip. She drizzles a little chocolate sauce on top and garnishes with a maraschino cherry.

Cappuccino Cakes
Racelle Rosett of Studio City, California, dissolves instant espresso in the milk used to make chocolate frosting. Whipped cream, candied coffee beans, powdered cocoa mix, and a white chocolate pretzel complete her design.

Batter Up!
Tara Bishop of Boston, Massachusetts, celebrates her son's love of baseball by baking cupcakes. After icing a cupcake with white frosting, she cuts up strings of red licorice to make the laces.

It's a Boy!
Juliana Goodwin of Springfield, Missouri, tints frosting bright blue (or pink) and then frosts each cupcake in spiky patterns that look like waves. She sets a yellow marshmallow chick or toy rubber duck on top.

Almond Flowers
Karen Blandini of Wakefield, Massachusetts, uses sliced almonds to decorate her chocolate frosted cupcakes. She arranges several almond slices into simple flowers and places silver ball candies (dragées) in their centers.

When Things Go Wrong in the Kitchen

READERS SHARE FUNNY STORIES ABOUT COOKING MISHAPS

SMOKY PUMPKIN PIE

At Thanksgiving, I always make pumpkin pies, usually eight or 10. One Thanksgiving, some 20 years ago, I had this big pot of pumpkin ready for pies. The very last thing I do is add some Southern Comfort as additional flavoring. I took the cap off the bottle of Southern Comfort, poured in a healthy amount, and suddenly this terrible odor hit my nose. It was certainly not the smell of bourbon. It was the smell of liquid smoke! Well, I immediately knew who the culprits were. At the time, my three sons were teenagers, 19, 17, and 15 years old. They had thrown a party some time when my husband and I were away and had consumed the entire bottle of Southern Comfort. Needless to say, I was one angry mom. I went ahead and baked the pies anyway, and guess who were the guinea pigs when it came time to eat them? All these years later, we still get a big laugh out of it every Thanksgiving.

Mary Montoya Coeur d'Alene, Idaho

FIVE-ALARM POTATOES

My husband, Todd, and I hosted a cookout for two friends who were moving. Todd is fantastic with the grill, so I am always responsible for the side dishes. Baked potatoes are the de facto starch for our cookouts. I usually "bake" them in the microwave, but Todd requested that I use the oven this time. That seemed a simple enough request. I dutifully consulted the *Joy of Cooking* for instructions on oven temperature and baking time. Now, I must confess, I love butter. I remembered that as a girl I had rubbed butter on the outside of potatoes before baking them. Out came the butter, and the rubbing began.

The oven was ready, so I popped the potatoes in and moved on to other things. Soon afterward, smoke was rolling out of the oven. I rushed to open doors and windows, but it was too late. Our smoke alarm was sounding. I dashed to the control panel and entered the code. Sweet silence. Todd was in the shower. Then, in the distance, I heard sirens. Fire truck sirens. I looked out through our front door and saw a big fire truck parked in front of the house. I ran out and began explaining what had happened. The firemen were chuckling (and not in a very subtle manner), and the sirens were still sounding (also not terribly subtle).

Dejected, I went back inside. Todd had just finished with his shower. "Did I hear the alarm go off?" he asked. I told him, "I can't even cook baked potatoes. What kind of idiot can't bake potatoes? It's so embarrassing that I set off the alarm." Todd interrupted, trying to console me. "Well, honey, it could have been worse; the fire department could have shown up."

Laura Snedegar Broken Arrow, Oklahoma

YANKEE GARLIC APPLE PIE

The first time I made an apple pie from scratch, I used a recipe that took the trouble to specify the use of a clean cutting board, designated only for fruits and such, to slice the apples, the idea being to prevent the transfer of unwanted flavors to the apples. I thought my usual cutting board would be just fine. So I sliced the apples, tossed them with sugar, dumped them into a pie pan, dotted the filling with butter, and baked the pie.

As the pie baked, I was surprised to detect the scent of garlic. Well, I thought, it must be only a little from the cutting board. But when I served the pie that evening to some guests, it was more than just a little garlicky. It tasted like garlic bread! Wow! All of that flavor from a cutting board? I apologized to my guests, but they said that the pie was still good and quite distinctive. The next day, I noticed a container of leftover green beans from two days earlier, and I realized where all of the garlic flavor must have come from. I had made too much garlic butter for the beans and had saved the remainder in the refrigerator. It was that leftover butter, solidified from its stay in the fridge, that I had used to dot the pie with butter. So much for Yankee thrift.

Andrew Garland Lexington, Massachusetts

PIZZA PERFECT ROMANCE

After being divorced for about a year, I joined a divorce recovery group. We were going to have a potluck, and I wanted to make something special. I decided on a fruit pizza since there was a man in the group I was interested in and I thought the fruit pizza would interest him in my cooking. I took special care in gathering only the freshest fruit so it would turn out extra-yummy. About an hour before preparing the pizza, I received an e-mail from this man telling me how beautiful and wonderful he thought I was! After that I became distracted and left out several key ingredients. The pizza was a horrible flop. But a second pizza turned out great—and so did the relationship. Now we're married!

Susan Abrahamse Oak Harbor, Washington

JUST A SPOONFUL OF FUDGE

My mother was not one for making dessert, so on the occasion when she did make one, it was a special treat. One time she decided to make a batch of fudge. After she prepared the fudge, and it had finally cooled, she allowed us children to have a taste. We tried a bite and told her that it didn't taste very good. She just thought we were being smart alecks until she tried a piece herself. It seems that instead of putting vanilla in the fudge, she had grabbed a similar large brown bottle that contained a vile-tasting liquid tonic. For years afterward, we teased Mom about her "medicinal" fudge.

Rebecca Loach Greenville, South Carolina

TRIPLE-DECKER BISCUITS

My husband and his family are from the South, and he was raised eating biscuits. Being a newlywed, I thought I would surprise him with homemade biscuits. I love to cook, and making homemade biscuits didn't seem like it would be that hard. I started to follow a recipe, and then I had an idea. I thought that if I rolled out the dough a little thinner, I could easily layer three biscuits on top of one another to get a flaky effect. The outcome, I imagined, would be big, flaky, beautiful biscuits with three layers.

Well, needless to say, when I opened the oven door, I was shocked. Instead of seeing those big beautiful biscuits that I'd hoped my husband would brag about to others, I saw an oddly shaped mass; the biscuits had tipped over and spread out on the baking sheet. I began laughing because they truly looked bad, and they were as hard as rocks. My husband just looked at them and calmly said, "It's OK, just keep practicing." He then proceeded to butter and eat one.

Celia B. Gibbar Phoenix, Arizona

Send us your funniest kitchen disaster stories. Please write to us at Kitchen Disasters, Cook's Country, P.O. Box 470739, Brookline, MA 02447. If you'd like to use e-mail, write to us at kitchendisasters@bcpress.com. If your story is published, you'll receive a complimentary one-year subscription to *Cook's Country*.

CHUNKY CARROT CAKE

I have too many disasters to list them all. When making cookies, I once forgot to add the sugar. Another time, I made fried chicken but couldn't find anything in the kitchen to coat the chicken pieces with, so I used raisin bran. I think the topper came when I attempted to make carrot cake for the first time. I used my sister's handwritten recipe. She didn't specify how to prepare the carrots, so I sliced them. It seemed strange, but I couldn't imagine any other way to prepare them. When the cake was baked and frosted, I triumphantly started to slice it, despite the wisecracks of my brother (who was still reminding me of my recent fiasco with raisin bran chicken). Then there was a "thunk"! The knife had hit the sliced carrots. My sister asked, incredulously, why I hadn't grated the carrots. I had no answer except to say that she didn't put it down in her recipe. **Marina Krefft** Darien, Illinois

Notes from Our Test Kitchen

TIPS, TECHNIQUES, AND TOOLS FOR BETTER COOKING

Teamwork Once we use frying oil three times in the test kitchen, we dispose of it—but not down the sink, where it can clog pipes. Two members of our kitchen staff demonstrate our preferred method for dealing with spent oil. Katie holds open two plastic grocery bags while Cali carefully pours in the cooled oil. Just tie the doubled bags shut, and the oil is ready for the garbage.

Make Room in Your Kitchen Drawer for a ...

Spider A spider in the kitchen? We're not talking the eight-legged variety. A spider (also known as a mesh, or Chinese, skimmer) is the test kitchen's favorite tool of retrieval. Its wide face lets us remove vegetables from boiling water or steak fries from hot oil by the bushel, and its open, web-like design allows every bit of water or oil to drip right back inside the pot where it belongs. When shopping for spiders, look for one that will allow the maximum amount of drainage; those with an open wire-mesh face work best. Although you can buy spiders or skimmers made with a bamboo handle and brass wire basket, we prefer stainless steel. They are dishwasher-safe and usually come with a long 12-inch handle, perfect for keeping an arm's distance from hot oil or water. The test kitchen drawers are packed with several brands, but most of us reach first for the Johnson-Rose 6-Inch Round Mesh Skimmer. You can buy this restaurant-grade tool for just $3.25 from Ace Mart Restaurant Supply, item #JRC3156 (888-898-8079; www.acemart.com).

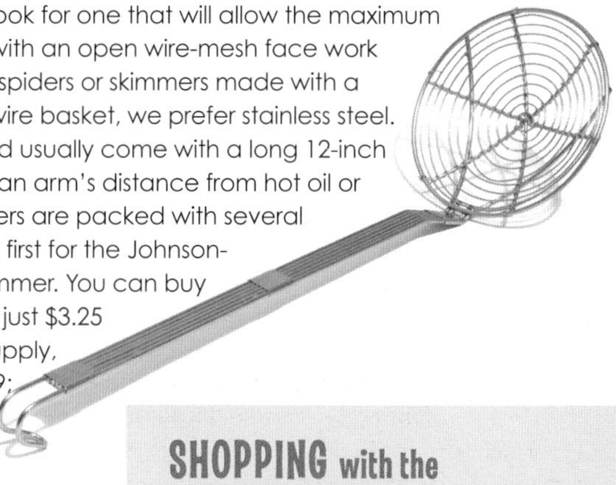

SHOPPING with the TEST KITCHEN

Top Choice

CHEESE WIZ

When developing our recipe for Reduced-Fat Macaroni and Cheese (page 8), we tested several reduced-fat cheddar cheeses and found two brands that were surprisingly good. Cracker Barrel Reduced Fat Sharp Cheddar Cheese makes an excellent macaroni and cheese and is our first choice. Cabot 50% Light Sharp Cheddar also works well and cuts even more fat from this recipe.

CHOP SHOP

When testing our recipe for Quick and Crunchy Pork Chops (page 21), we discovered that thickness really matters. Paper-thin chops will go from juicy to jerky in a New York minute. And super-thick chops never seem to cook all the way through. Chops about 3/4 inch thick are ideal for this recipe. But just because one edge is the proper thickness, don't think good results are guaranteed. We purchased a number of misshapen chops that had been cut on an angle by the butcher. Often one side would measure 3/4 inch thick, while the other side was just 1/4 inch thick. Our advice? Inspect chops carefully, and choose flat—not slanted—ones.

Watch Out for Slanted Chops

OIL CONSERVATION

Deep-frying our steak fries (page 18) requires a fair amount of oil. And once the frying is over, it seems a shame to throw it all away. In the test kitchen, we've found that it's perfectly fine to save frying oil for another use—with a little cleanup, that is.

After the oil has cooled completely, use a slotted spoon (or a spider, see photo, above right) to remove any large particles of food. Line a mesh sieve (the finer the mesh, the better) with two layers of paper towels, then slowly pour the oil through the lined sieve into a plastic or glass airtight container. Seal the container and refrigerate the oil for up to one month.

The oil can be used up to two more times, as long as it is filtered and refrigerated between uses. One caveat: Don't try this trick with oil that has been used to fry seafood. Pungent foods will flavor the oil, and you don't want your next batch of steak fries to taste like last Friday's fish.

SCRAPING BUY

Making bread or other baked goodies is easy if you have the right tools. In the test kitchen, our bakers rely on two inexpensive items. A dough, or bowl, scraper is made of flexible plastic that conforms to the shape of the bowl as you scrape out every last sticky bit. A metal bench scraper slips under rolled pie dough and can be used to divide elastic bread dough into individual loaves or rolls. (It does a great job with the dough for our Monkey Bread on page 9.) And if that weren't reason enough to own one, the bench scraper will also remove every last piece of stuck-on dough from your countertop.

MAKESHIFT BUTTERMILK

Buttermilk is a key ingredient in many recipes—everything from pancakes to cupcakes—and for good reason. Being acidic, it not only gives baked goods a smooth tang but will also give them lift when combined with a basic (or alkaline) ingredient such as baking soda. We can't imagine a kitchen without a carton in the fridge.

But even in the test kitchen we occasionally find ourselves without buttermilk. Luckily, a great substitute can be made with ingredients we usually have on hand. Take 1 cup of milk (any kind will do), stir in 1½ tablespoons lemon juice, and let sit for a good five minutes; the mixture will begin to thicken to a buttermilk-like consistency. Use this mixture as you would buttermilk, and you'll never be without fluffy pancakes again.

COOL SPRINKLES

Our party cupcakes (see page 27) show that when it comes to decorating, imagination is the only limit. When it came time to duplicate all the fanciful cupcake submissions from our readers, we found that our local supermarket sufficiently supplied the basics (sprinkles, candies, and such).

For harder-to-find items, we found a great resource in Wilton Industries (630-963-1818/800-794-5866; www.wilton.com). Long known for its vast array of cake-decorating supplies, Wilton carries such goodies as edible glitter, food-coloring pastes and gels in every color of the rainbow, and sprinkles in the shapes of leaves, flowers, animals, and stars (just to name a few). You can order most of these products right off the Wilton Web site, but they are also available at most large craft supply stores, such as Michael's and A.C. Moore.

Kitchen Creations
Flavored Salts for Fries

It's easy to jazz up plain fries (or almost anything) by flavoring the salt. We prefer to use kosher salt because its larger crystals add crunch.

ROSEMARY-LEMON SALT

Combine 1 tablespoon kosher salt (or 1½ teaspoons table salt) with 1 teaspoon minced fresh rosemary and ½ teaspoon grated lemon zest.

WARM SPICED SALT

Combine 1 tablespoon kosher salt (or 1½ teaspoons table salt) with ½ teaspoon ground cumin, ½ teaspoon ground coriander, ¼ teaspoon paprika, and ⅛ teaspoon cayenne.

CHILI SALT
Combine 1 tablespoon kosher salt (or 1½ teaspoons table salt) with 1 teaspoon chili powder, ¼ teaspoon garlic powder, ¼ teaspoon pepper, and ⅛ teaspoon cayenne (or more, if you like).

Food Shopping

BOTTLED BARBECUE SAUCES: Are Any as Good as Homemade?

Homemade barbecue sauce is a project recipe requiring a laundry list of ingredients and a good chunk of time. No wonder bottled barbecue sauce is so popular—in just one local supermarket, we found more than 30 varieties! To make sense of all these options, we conducted a blind taste test of eight leading national brands.

We chose tomato-based sauces that were labeled "original" and tasted them as a dipping sauce for homemade chicken fingers. While tasters' personal preferences varied, we found a few sauces that were universally liked—and a few that were universally disliked. Sauces that tasted like tomatoes rather than tasting just plain sweet were the clear favorites. A good balance of smoke and spice was also appreciated; the several sauces judged out of whack in one or both areas received low scores. Texture was another important issue, with tasters objecting to very thin sauces as well as sauces with an overly thick, gloppy consistency, which seemed artificial. Odd colors (one sauce was bright red from the use of food dye) and jarring flavors (one sauce reminded us of spicy Red Hot candies) were not appreciated.

Our conclusion: You don't have to make your own barbecue sauce, but the one you buy should taste—and look—like homemade. The sauces below are listed in order of preference. –Erika Bruce

Top Picks

1. TEXAS BEST Barbecue Sauce, Original Rib Style, $2.79 for 19 ounces

> **Comments:** This sauce topped the charts because of its emphasis on tomatoes. Tasters liked the "thick, coarse texture," which seemed "unprocessed." They also praised the "good sweet/tart balance" with "lots of spices."

2. BULL'S-EYE Original BBQ Sauce, $1.79 for 18 ounces

> **Comments:** Leaning heavier on the smoke, this second-place sauce was still deemed "well balanced," although a few tasters thought the heavy smoke "hit you in the back of the throat." Bull's-Eye gained points for its "great dark color" and "thick consistency."

Runners-Up

3. HUNT'S BBQ Original Recipe Barbecue Sauce, $1.19 for 18 ounces

> **Comments:** You can't beat the price of this "sweet and tangy" sauce. Heavy on tomato, light on smoke and spice, this "mild" sauce had the perfect balance of vinegar and molasses. Tasters also appreciated its "thick," "smooth," texture.

4. SWEET BABY RAY'S Original Barbecue Sauce, $1.99 for 18 ounces

> **Comments:** True to its name, this sauce came through as "ultra-sweet," with an emphasis on "malty caramel" and tomato flavors. Tasters liked its "subtle spiciness" but found the texture "goopy" and "gluey."

5. KC MASTERPIECE Original Barbecue Sauce, $1.79 for 18 ounces

> **Comments:** "Very sweet," "very thick," and "a lot of smoke" summed up tasters' comments. Tasters also found that the "gloppy," "gluey" texture of the sauce detracted from its "meaty depth."

6. STUBB'S Original Bar-B-Q Sauce, $3.69 for 18 ounces

> **Comments:** This sauce placed more emphasis on spice and vinegar. While some tasters found it favorably "tangy," "with a good kick," others objected to the lack of sweetness. This sauce was also the thinnest, even "watery," according to one taster.

7. KRAFT Original Barbecue Sauce, $1.39 for 18 ounces

> **Comments:** On top of its disagreeable texture, deemed "corn syrupy," and its "processed" flavor, this sauce was also criticized for an "artificial smoke flavor." Still, some likened it to a sweet-and-sour sauce with "good tang."

8. OPEN PIT Original Barbecue Sauce, $1.99 for 18 ounces

> **Comments:** This "super-sour" sauce was heavy on the vinegar and light on the tomato (the fifth ingredient listed). Several tasters pointed out the unnaturally bright red color and odd "Red Hot cinnamon" flavor. "Not BBQ sauce," wrote one.

Buyer's Guide
Ready-to-Bake Chocolate Chip Cookies

Nothing beats a good homemade cookie straight from the oven, right? Or can you cheat and buy ready-to-bake cookie dough? To find out if our tasters could tell the difference, we baked up three batches of cookies: one homemade recipe taken from the back of a bag of Nestlé semisweet chips; one from Nestlé Toll House Chocolate Chip Cookie Dough, sold in the traditional log shape; and one from a new product, Nestlé Toll House Chocolate Chip Cookie Dough Bar. No need to slice or measure the dough—it's already been cut into individual pieces. Just break off as many as you like and bake.

Our results were, well, surprising: The homemade batch didn't win. It seems that when it comes to chocolate chip cookies, the number of chips per cookie is what counts. Both types of ready-to-bake cookies were chock full of tiny chips, and one (the winner) had more chips than our homemade cookies. While tasters praised the homemade cookies for being light and chewy and having great butterscotch flavor, they criticized their sparse dotting of chips. Granted, the chips were larger than those in the ready-to-bake doughs, but tasters wanted more chocolate in every bite.

Of the two types of ready-to-bake cookies, the slice-and-bake won not only for having the most chips but also for their more natural, craggy appearance. How much does the convenience of ready-made dough cost? The slice-and-bake cookies cost $3.59 and give you about 24 cookies. The ingredients for our homemade cookies cost about $4.50, but the recipe makes at least four dozen cookies—certainly a better value. Personally, I'd rather save some money and make my own cookies. I'll just add more chips next time. –Erika Bruce

① **Nestlé Toll House Chocolate Chip Cookie Dough**
$3.59 for about 2 dozen cookies

"Loaded with chips," "nice craggy top and crisp edges."

② **Homemade cookies (made with Nestlé Toll House Semi-Sweet Morsels)**
$4.50 for about 4 dozen cookies
"Crunchy and chewy, with the best flavor," but "low chip-to-cookie ratio."

③ **Nestlé Toll House Refrigerated Chocolate Chip Cookie Dough Bar**
$3.69 for 20 cookies
"Flat and compact," and "too uniform."

Equipment Roundup

ELECTRIC DEEP FRYERS: Do They Really Work?

We ordered 10 deep fryers, all priced under $65 (who wants to spend more on an infrequently used kitchen item?), and noticed that they fell into two distinct camps. In the first were the traditional round models. In the second were some newer models styled in the fashion of the sleek stainless steel fryers you might see in a fast-food restaurant. These professional-style models also have a larger capacity.

For our first test, we noted how long each fryer took to heat the oil to 375 degrees. We then measured heat loss when we dumped frozen fries into the heated oil. Whereas the temperature in the top-rated Oster, a professional-style model, dropped just 40 degrees, the temperature in the Black & Decker, a home-style fryer, plummeted more than 130 degrees. What does this mean in practical terms? It means that the Oster produced super-crisp fries, whereas the fries cooked in the Black & Decker absorbed a lot of oil and emerged pale, limp, and soggy.

We also measured the time it took the oil to recover between batches of fries. Ultimately, we ignored the thermostats and fried two batches of chicken tenders back to back, without waiting for the oil to reheat. (Something you might do when kids are begging for more food, fast.) Only the professional-style models could manage this daunting task.

Ten gallons of oil later, what had we learned? The "professional" fryers, with their powerful heating elements, were best able to keep the oil up to temperature, especially in the frozen french fry test, which some of the home-style models failed. The latter hide the electric heating coil inside a stay-cool plastic housing, whereas in professional-style models the heating coil sits at the bottom of the cooking chamber and is in direct contact with the oil. But there's a price to pay for this performance. Professional models are real oil hogs, calling for an extra quart or so.

So which model should you buy? On points, the professional-style fryer from Oster was the champ. If you'd like to save money on oil, though, the Rival Cool Touch is our favorite home-style fryer. It holds on to heat nearly as well as the "professional" models—and, more important, it turns out fried foods every bit as addictive.

–Garth Clingingsmith

HOME-STYLE DEEP FRYERS

Recommended
RIVAL Cool Touch Deep Fryer CF275
Capacity: 2.5 liters Price: $49.99
Comments: This model maintained heat as well as the "professional" fryers. The only model with a window in the lid that did not steam over. Because the built-in timer will turn off the heat when the set time expires, use the "stay on" setting and rely on a separate timer.

AROMA Cool Fry Deep Fryer ADF-172D
Capacity: 2 quarts Price: $59.99
Comments: Body and lid remained the coolest of any fryer tested. Results equaled the top-rated Rival and Oster fryers, but the fry basket is smallish and the window fogs immediately.

Recommended with Reservations
DELONGHI Cool Touch Deluxe Fryer D650-UX
Capacity: 2 quarts Price: $62.99
Comments: A drain allows for easy oil removal, but to clean bowl and lid (which are not removable) we had to lug the fryer to the sink. Lack of thermostat is a serious shortcoming.

PRESTO Dual Daddy Electric Deep Fryer 05450
Capacity: 2 quarts Price: $37.70
Comments: This rudimentary fryer lacks all bells and whistles. No basket, no thermostat, and no lid to control the mess, but it cranks out intense heat.

Not Recommended
PRESTO Cool Daddy Cool-Touch Electric Deep Fryer 05444
Capacity: 2 liters Price: $49.99
Comments: This model failed our heat loss test, and both preheat and recovery times exceeded acceptable limits. The shallow bowl made it impossible to submerge chicken.

T-FAL Maxi Fry Deep Fryer FF100100
Capacity: 3 quarts Price: $39.99
Comments: Required a very long 20 minutes to preheat the oil. The frying chamber is not removable, so cleanup is a slippery mess.

BLACK & DECKER Fry Mate DF200
Capacity: 2 liters Price: $54.99
Comments: Painfully slow to preheat and recover temperature between batches. The oil temperature plummeted 130 degrees during the frozen food test, leading to greasy, pale fries.

PROFESSIONAL-STYLE DEEP FRYERS

Recommended
OSTER Immersion Deep Fryer ODF540
Capacity: 3 liters Price: $59.99
Comments: The top performer among the sleek restaurant-style fryers. Excels at maintaining heat, but not everyone will want to deal with 3 liters of used oil. On the bright side, only the heating element and control box are not dishwasher-safe.

GENERAL ELECTRIC Professional Style Deep Fryer 106770
Capacity: 3.5 liters Price: $54.84
Comments: The huge basket matches the excessive capacity of this fryer. Only for the serious deep-fry enthusiast. Identical results can be achieved with other fryers that use much less oil.

Recommended with Reservations
RIVAL Commercial Style Deep Fryer CZF610
Capacity: 3 liters Price: $59.99
Comments: Preheating and recovery times are excellent. However, the too-smart-for-its-own-good timing system cuts the heat once the set time has expired, and there is no way to bypass this safety system.

Gadgets & Gear
LODGE DEEP-FRY BASKET

Frugal fryers don't bother with an electric deep fryer; they simply use a heavy Dutch oven. It offers the ultimate in heat control and easy access to the food being fried, and it can multitask as, well, a Dutch oven. Of course, you don't get a thermostat (a big drawback) or fry basket. But one company has attempted to deal with the second issue. For years, we've used (and liked) Lodge's cast-iron Dutch ovens in the test kitchen. They do not break the bank, and an occasional deep-fry is a great way to keep them seasoned. We recently noticed that Lodge was selling chrome frying baskets for use with its Dutch ovens. Was this option worth considering?

The Lodge Deep Fry Basket (about $25) saves you time spent fishing around for that last onion ring, and the tailor-made fit utilizes the space efficiently. The basket handle collapses for easy storage. The mess on the stove is unavoidable, but you have fewer parts to wash than with an electric deep fryer. Also, the flame on a stovetop offers much more control than the thermostats on an electric fryer. For $75, you can own both a 7-quart Dutch oven and the deep-fry basket. Sounds like a bargain to us.

–Garth Clingingsmith

Thanks for the Memories

For this issue, we asked readers to share food memories about their mothers and fathers (a few snuck in stories about grandparents and brothers). Our favorite story is about a father from Illinois who rigged up Hershey bar and malted milk ball trees in the middle of the night. It's funny how the smallest traditions started when we were children loom so large later in life.

Moms and Apple Pies
Eunice Johnson Odin, Minnesota

The setting for making apple pie has changed over the years in my family. The first was in my mother's house, where I made faltering attempts at mastering the tricky business of the pie crust. We used home-rendered lard, and that was an advantage. However, the oven was part of a 1940s model combination gas and wood range with an unreliable thermostat. The apples came from our own trees, but the trees had not always been sprayed for insects. That meant that the person doing the peeling often had do to some pretty fancy knife work around the invaders. But the pies were delicious, and they were eagerly eaten by our big Minnesota farm family.

Shift to the years of my own family on a farm. Mother would come for the day, and we would try to beat the number of pies we had made in one day the year before. By now the home freezer was part of daily life, and we would store pies for the winter to come—that is, any we could rescue from our hungry men and the kids off the school bus.

The next shift was in my mother's staying power. She suffered from arthritis but never let herself be conquered by it. Because of her stiff and sore hands, she was an early advocate of dough made in a processor, and she perfected that technique. She needed more breaks now, but the fellowship was still good and the pies were still delicious.

When the scene eventually shifted to my daughter's house, I was the chief pie maker while she tended to her young children and quickly peeled apples from her backyard. I relished the task of rolling dough on the marble counter in her kitchen and the help from her boys, who were interested in baking, too.

Now another shift has occurred, as I have become the one who must sit with a pan in my lap and be the assistant. And how it makes me think of my mother, her discomfort, her determination to be part of the team, and all of those fragrant, warm apple pies.

A Fourth of July to Remember
Jeanette Hermann Fairmont, West Virginia

One year, my family attended a wedding reception for one of my second cousins. Everyone was having a wonderful time, especially my elderly Scottish grandmother, who was drinking more than she should have been.

All of a sudden, all of our relatives, neighbors, and people we didn't even know started to come up to my mother to tell her how much they were looking forward to attending our Fourth of July get-together to taste her homemade enchiladas. My mother just smiled kindly and said, "See you then." It didn't take long to track down the cause of my mother's confusion. Nana was bragging about her daughter's homemade enchiladas and had invited more than 100 people to our house for the Fourth of July. Bear in mind that we lived in Davis, California, in the middle of the hot Central Valley, in a tiny house with no air conditioning.

I still remember that holiday. It was 114 degrees, one of the hottest days on record, and my mom was in the hot, hot kitchen making hundreds of tortillas and enchiladas. The house was packed, with guests overflowing into the front and backyard. In spite of all of this, the sound of laughter could be heard from the kitchen as my mother said, "For God's sake, someone take that beer away from Mom, or who knows how many people I will have to cook for this Thanksgiving."

Thanksgiving All Year-Round
Bonnie Dodson Robbinsville, North Carolina

My best food memories are based on an ongoing tradition that started when I became a stepmom to three young children. I wanted to make sure that their weekend visits with their father and me were enjoyable, and I figured the best way to their hearts was through good food. We cooked a lot, but the favorite meal quickly became what we called the Thanksgiving Feast, even though we ate it year-round. About every six weeks, we would do the entire thing: roast turkey breast, mashed potatoes, rice, gravy, dressing, sweet potato casserole, green beans, and homemade yeast rolls. The kids loved working with me in the kitchen, getting everything prepared. The best part is that all three of them have become good cooks now that they are grown. They call me to ask questions about food, and they share their successes and failures in the kitchen and in their lives. Good food became the basis of three wonderful and long-lasting relationships.

Salty Toast and Crisp Pink Sheets
Amy Cooper Arlington, Massachusetts

Having three sisters to compete with for attention made it a special treat to stay overnight at Grandma and Grandpa's when we were kids. First, I got to pack all of my stuff in Mom's tiny, old green alligator suitcase. Then, I'd get all of Grandma and Grandpa's attention to myself for a whole evening of relaxation, which included reading Dad's old Disney comics. The night would end early, with me tucked into one of Grandma's amazingly comfy beds made with crisp pink sheets. In the morning, you got to eat

crunchy granola and, if you were lucky, some home-canned plums on salted toast. Salted toast! I never could believe they salted their toast.

Does Candy Really Grow on Trees?
Sue Hennelly Phoenix, Arizona

Each spring, when my brother and I were small, my dad would take us out to the backyard of our home in Illinois and show us the "buds" on the Hershey bar tree and the malted milk ball tree. Dad would sneak out in the dark of night and hang tiny Hershey bars—individually wrapped, of course—on one tree and malted milk balls on another tree, pretending it was their growing season. All the neighborhood kids would come over and we would pick the harvest! Dad also "grew" gum in the garden; when the bulb flowers came up each spring, they would magically "sprout" sticks of Wrigley's Doublemint and spearmint gum.

I have assumed the job of gardener now and "grow" the same sorts of things for my nieces and nephews.

Earthquake Cake
Rita Sotelo Sinclair Bellingham, Washington

In southern California, where I grew up, earthquakes were a part of life. As a teenager, I already did quite a bit of the family cooking, and, in the late 1960s, when my brother was in Vietnam, he often wrote to us about how he missed home cooking and my desserts, especially my brownies and various cookies. When it was announced that he was finally coming home, he wrote to us and asked me to make a "special" dessert for his arrival.

I decided to make a chocolate cake. I had the whole project timed and was right on schedule until we got word that he was arriving home earlier than expected. I hurried along and ended up frosting the two-tiered cake too early. By the time I brought it into the dining room, the whole cake had cracked open and exposed crevasses as deep as the San Andreas fault! We had a lot of laughs that day. Since then, I've always frosted this cake while it is still warm and call it Earthquake Cake. Some mistakes make wonderful memories.

Send us your food memories. Write to us at Food Memories, Cook's Country, P.O. Box 470739, Brookline, MA 02447. If you'd like to use e-mail, write to us at foodmemories@bcpress.com. If we publish your story, you'll receive a complimentary one-year subscription to Cook's Country.

Postcards from Home

COOK'S COUNTRY READERS SHOW US WHAT'S COOKING AT HOME

Pols Picnic in Portsmouth
Grace Lessner
Portsmouth, New Hampshire
Grace writes: "About twice a year I get together with three of my former colleagues from the New Hampshire State Legislature and our spouses. For last summer's celebration, we set a picnic table in my backyard with a view of the Piscataqua River and the Portsmouth Naval Shipyard. The lobsters were cooked in a pot of sea water on an outdoor propane burner. We loaded the table with homemade salads, bread, and beverages, and savored the company, the food, and the view. Two of us are not lobster lovers, so I also made salmon with a mustard sauce. As I was serving the salmon to Carol, it flopped onto the grass instead of her plate! We had a good laugh and invoked the 30-second

KITCHEN WIT
Joe Paterson Norwood, Ontario
Joe writes: "Thought you might enjoy this old limerick."

Parker House Rolls
A corpulent lady named Dole
Had a humor exceedingly droll,
To a masquerade ball,
She wore nothing at all,
And backed in as a
Parker House roll.

Dangerously Delicious Turkey
Craig Shoenbaum Culver City, California
Craig writes: "This Thanksgiving, all 15 of our guests said that my deep-fried turkey was the best they had ever eaten. We brined the 20-pound turkey for about 18 hours in salt and herb water, and then deep-fried it for 1 hour in 35 pounds of peanut oil. It was incredibly juicy, with an herb flavor and a dangerously delicious, nutty flavored skin."

Pupcakes
Rebecca Pearson Mid Levels, Hong Kong
Rebecca writes: "On the first birthday of my dog, Gao Ho, which means 'good dog' in Cantonese, my boyfriend and I wanted to do something special. We came up with the perfect solution: dog-friendly cupcakes, aka pupcakes! The recipe went over quite well. So well, in fact, that I had to convince my boyfriend not to try one for himself!"

a Reader Worth Meeting

Lora writes: "I decided to send you pictures of some special cakes I've been baking up. It all started when I made a special cake for each of my co-workers for their birthdays. I found something they enjoyed in their life and made a cake to reflect that. Now people are requesting cakes left and right! Last year, I baked birthday cakes for all 16 of my co-workers. I think this year will be more difficult, as I have to come up with new ideas for all of them.

Lora Pfluger of Southold, New York, has a way with cakes.

Tamale Tutor
Andrea Beesley Norman, Oklahoma
Andrea writes: "I recently started a business called The Culinary Tutor. I go to people's homes and cook with them. In my first session, we made spicy mushroom tamales. Only two of the four burners on my client's stove were working, and we had to use pliers (instead of the missing knobs) to turn them on. Her kitchen also lacked a steamer and a pot lid, so we had to improvise by placing a ring of foil under a colander for the steamer and an upside-down bowl for the lid. The results made us both proud!"

From left to right: A cake Lora made for a friend who likes to quilt; the largest cake she has ever made—a 13-layer chocolate cake with strawberries; a cake for a co-worker who loves pugs; and an igloo cake complete with penguins.

We love to see what you're growing, cooking, and eating at home. E-mail your photos to postcards@bcpress.com or send them to Postcards, Cook's Country, P.O. Box 470739, Brookline, MA 02447. If we publish your photo, you will receive a complimentary one-year subscription to *Cook's Country*. Make sure to include your name, address, and daytime phone number along with your photo. And tell us a little bit about what makes your photo special.

Recipe Index

main courses

Bacon-Wrapped Filets Mignons RC
Baked Ziti with Sausage RC
Cheesy Southwestern Meatloaf 23
Glazed Salmon with Dilly Mustard Sauce 23
Ham Steak with Rhubarb Sauce 11
North Carolina Pulled Pork 11
Quick and Crunchy Pork Chops 21
　Quick and Crunchy Cordon Bleu Pork Chops
　Quick and Crunchy Sesame Pork Chops
Reduced-Fat Macaroni and Cheese 8
　Reduced-Fat Macaroni and Cheese
　　after Dark
　Reduced-Fat Macaroni and Cheese for
　　Pizza Lovers
Skillet Shrimp and Rice RC
Turkey Cutlets with Cherry Sauce RC

starters, soups, salads, and sides

Asian Corn and Chicken Soup RC
**Broiled Asparagus with Cheesy
　Bread Crumbs** 11
Cheese Straws 15
　Everything Straws
　Greek Cheese Straws
　Italian Cheese Straws
　Sweet-and-Spicy Straws
Chili-Fried Onion Rings RC
Cowboy Beans 22
"Doctored" Applesauce 21
　Five-Spice Applesauce
　Sweet-and-Hot Cinnamon Applesauce
Flavored Salts for Fries 29
　Chili Salt
　Rosemary-Lemon Salt
　Warm Spiced Salt
Nutty Green Beans RC
Picnic Salads 6-7
　Cape Cod Picnic Salad
　Gazpacho Pasta Salad
　Low-Country Sweet Potato Salad
　Panzanella Salad
　Tricolor Mexican Bean Salad
**Sautéed Sugar Snap Peas and
　Cherry Tomatoes** 23
Super-Crisp Steak Fries 18
Tasty Broccoli Dishes 17
　Broccoli with Creamy Herb Sauce
　Broccoli with Lemon and Walnuts
　Broccoli with Mustard–Red Pepper
　　Vinaigrette
　Broccoli with Parmesan Bread Crumbs

desserts and breakfast

Cloudcakes 14-15
　Cinnamon "Toast" Cloudcakes
　Pucker-Up Cloudcakes
Easy Birthday Cupcakes 26
　Quick Chocolate Frosting
　Quick Vanilla Frosting
Gelatin Treats 12-13
　Blushing Peach Terrine
　Juicy Gelatin Cubes
　Piña Colada Mousse
　Root Beer Floats
**Ginger Ice Cream with
　Chocolate Sauce** RC
Icebox Cheesecake 24-25
　Key Lime Icebox Cheesecake
　Peanut Butter Icebox Cheesecake
　Peppermint Chip Icebox Cheesecake
　Strawberry Sauce
Monkey Bread 9

 = Recipe Card

Cook's Country

JUNE/JULY 2005

Steakhouse Burgers at Home
Try Our Secret Ingredients!

Triple-Chocolate Cookies
Better Than Brownies

Skillet Lasagna
Really Easy, Really Good

MEMPHIS BBQ RIBS

SOUR CREAM COFFEE CAKE
This 'Lite' Recipe Is No Lightweight

RATING CHOCOLATE ICE CREAMS

TEXAS CHILI
The Real Deal in a Slow Cooker

NEW SLAWS FOR SUMMER

GRILLED JERK CHICKEN
Our Molasses-Spiked Marinade Is a Winner

FINDING THE BEST BLENDER

DENVER OMELET
Ham, Eggs, and Cheese for a Crowd

APRICOT-GLAZED CHICKEN

$4.95 U.S./$6.95 CANADA

0 74470 05251 7   07>

Our Strawberry Dessert Contest Winner!

Jennifer Wickes of Pine Beach, N.J., won our hearts and taste buds with her easy-to-bake **Strawberry Scones**. See page 6 for her recipe.

Cook's Country

Dear Country Cook,

Most of us bake a dozen or so biscuits at a time—but not a navy cook, like the young recruit below. Danny, one of our Vermont neighbors, cooked for the navy during World War II, and he once explained how he prepared Thanksgiving dinner for the whole ship: two dozen turkeys roasted in just two ovens plus the pies, mashed potatoes, gravy, and other fixings. It was a nightmare of menu planning.

For years, Danny used to show up at Tom and Nancy's farmhouse for Friday dinner. He'd stop and leave groceries in the morning, and Nancy was supposed to cook whatever he left. To return the favor, Danny reprised his famous Thanksgiving dinner once a year.

Danny never said a word about Normandy, Anzio, or Sicily. And he never bragged about his cooking, even though he is one of the best cooks I know. That's the country for you. Good food and good neighbors with an extra spoonful of humility. You can never tell a good country cook by his cover.

Welcome to Cook's Country.

Christopher Kimball
Christopher Kimball
Founder and Editor, Cook's Country Magazine

Biscuits being baked by a Cooks and Bakers School enrollee at the U.S. Maritime Service Training Station in St. Petersburg, Fla., 1944.
Photographer unknown. Library of Congress, Prints & Photographs Division, FSA-OWI Collection LC-USW33-026130-C.

JUNE/JULY 2005

Cook's Country

departments

6 RECIPE CONTEST: **Strawberry Desserts**

8 RECIPE MAKEOVER: **Crumb Coffee Cake**

9 LOST RECIPES: **Washboard Cookies**

10 SLOW COOKING: **Texas-Style Chili**

11 QUICK COOKING: **Spicy Dinner from the Grill**

12 FUN FOOD: **Marshmallow Desserts**

15 DRESSING UP: **Split Chicken Breasts**

16 SIMPLY SUPPER: **Recipe Cards**

19 GETTING TO KNOW: **Salad Greens**

21 REGIONAL FAVORITES: **Denver Omelet**

21 QUICK COOKING: **Easy Mediterranean Meal**

23 QUICK COOKING: **Salmon and Potato Salad**

27 RECIPE CONTEST: **Burger Toppings**

30 FOOD SHOPPING: **Chocolate Ice Cream**

31 EQUIPMENT ROUNDUP: **Blenders**

in every issue

Welcome to Cook's Country   **2**

Ask Cook's Country   **3**

Kitchen Shortcuts   **4**

I'm Looking for a Recipe   **16**

When Things Go Wrong . . .   **28**

Notes from Our Test Kitchen   **29**

Thanks for the Memories   **32**

features

14 Memphis BBQ Spareribs
How do you make ribs good enough to pass muster in Tennessee? It's all about the rub and the mop.

17 Triple-Chocolate Cookies
Two kinds of chips—one melted, one not—are the secret to these intense, chewy cookies.

18 All-American French Dressing
Long before Julia Child, Americans were tossing salads with this sweet-and-sour dressing made with ketchup, of all things.

20 A New Twist on Sweet Tea
Forget sugary bottled teas. We take an old Southern favorite, sweet tea, and pair it with fresh, modern flavors.

22 A Spicy Taste of the Tropics
After his honeymoon in Jamaica, Aaron Oppenheimer of Gaithersburg, Md., wanted to grill authentically spicy jerk chicken at home. We show him how.

24 Sassy Summer Slaws
Plain Jane mayonnaise isn't the only way to dress a slaw. And cabbage isn't the only vegetable choice, either.

25 Skillet Lasagna
Can you make a 45-minute lasagna without fussy layering? Yes, if you cook the noodles right along with the sauce.

26 The Ultimate Steakhouse Burger
Is it possible to start with regular supermarket ground beef and produce a great steakhouse-style burger?

Founder and Editor Christopher Kimball
Executive Editor Jack Bishop
Senior Editor Bridget Lancaster
Test Kitchen Director Erin McMurrer
Copy Chief India Koopman
Associate Editors Keri Fisher, Eva Katz
Assistant Editor Melissa Baldino
Test Cooks Stephanie Alleyne, Jeremy Sauer
Assistant Test Cook Cali Todd
Kitchen Assistant Nadia Domeq

Contributors Erika Bruce, Lauren Chattman, Garth Clingingsmith, Julia Collin Davison, Keith Dresser, Rebecca Hays, Charles Kelsey, Sean Lawler, Diane Unger-Mahoney, Nina West
Proofreader Dawn Carelli

Design Director Amy Klee
Designer Heather Barrett
Staff Photographer Daniel J. van Ackere

Vice President Operations James McCormack
Production Manager Mary Connelly
Production Assistants Jeanette McCarthy, Jennifer Power, Christian Steinmetz
Systems Administrator Richard Cassidy
Internet Technology Director Aaron Shuman

Vice President Marketing David Mack
Sales Director Leslie Ray
Marketing Assistant Connie Forbes
Circulation Director Bill Tine
Circulation Manager Larisa Greiner
Fulfillment Manager Carrie Horan
Products Director Steven Browall
Direct Mail Director Adam Perry
Customer Service Manager Jacqueline Valerio
Customer Service Representative Julie Gardner
E-Commerce Marketing Manager Hugh Buchan

Chief Financial Officer Sharyn Chabot
Controller Mandy Shito
Staff Accountant Maya Santoso
Office Manager Saudiyah Abdul-Rahim
Receptionist Henrietta Murray
Publicity Deborah Broide

Editorial Office: 17 Station Street, Brookline, MA 02445; 617-232-1000; fax 617-232-1572. Subscription inquiries: 800-526-8447.
Postmaster: Send all new orders, subscription inquiries, and change-of-address notices to Cook's Country, P.O. Box 8382, Red Oak, IA 51591-1382.

Cover photo: StockFood/Susie Eising.
Cover illustration: John Burgoyne.
Color photography this page: Keller + Keller.
Styling: Mary Jane Sawyer.

Cook's Country magazine (ISSN 1552-1990), number 03, is published bimonthly by Boston Common Press Limited Partnership, 17 Station Street, Brookline, MA 02445. Copyright 2005 Boston Common Press Limited Partnership. Application to mail at periodical postage rates pending at Boston, MA, and additional mailing offices. POSTMASTER: Send address changes to Cook's Country, P.O. Box 8382, Red Oak, IA 51591-1382. For subscription and gift subscription orders, subscription inquiries, or change-of-address notices, call 800-526-8447 in the U.S. or 515-247-7571 from outside the U.S., or write us at Cook's Country, P.O. Box 8382, Red Oak, IA 51591-1382..   PRINTED IN THE USA

Welcome to Cook's Country

The Connecticut River Shad Fish Bake

ESSEX, CONN. John Mulligan is a member of the Essex Rotary Club, which has been hosting the Connecticut River Shad Fish Bake every June since 1960 to raise funds for local charities. Feeding as many as 600 people, the club boasts a menu of Connecticut River shad, cherrystone clams, corn on the cob, salad, assorted pies, coffee, and other beverages.

The shad fillets, with a couple of strips of salt pork placed on each fillet, are nailed to large cedar planks (far left) and slathered with a "secret sauce." The fish-laden planks are then placed around the edges of a huge bonfire (center top), which cooks the fish. When the fish is done, the boards are removed from the fire and taken to the "denailing station" (center left).

John also sent photos of two other custom-designed contraptions. The first is a big burner used to boil corn (center right), the second, a coffee pot made from a hot water tank (far right). John tells us that we are all invited this year to "grab a beer, stand by the fire, watch the fish bake, and have a good time!"

Now That's Fast!

DARDENDELLE, ARK. J. P. Morgan wrote to us about the Crain Island Ranch Chuck Wagon Races held once a year in Dardanelle, Ark. J.P. refers to the race as Amish Nascar. There is also a watermelon-eating contest that J.P. has won for the past three years. He tells us, "The first year, I was able to eat a quarter of a watermelon in 28 seconds. Last year, I whittled that down to 26 seconds. This year, I did it in 24 seconds. That's a quarter of a whole melon down the hatch in 24 seconds! And it's all in me, none on the ground or on the table. Maybe one day I will share my secret on how to eat a quarter of a melon in 24 seconds." And, yes, J. P. Morgan really is his name, though he claims no relation to the famous financier.

Oyster Farms

OLD FIELD, N.Y. Ted Rosenberg likes to grow more than just fruits and vegetables: He also cultivates oysters. He tells us, "These delicious bivalves are grown in floating cages in Conscience Bay in Old Field, N.Y. The infant oysters, called spat, are placed inside the floating cages around mid-July. The spat are roughly the size of the fingernail on your pinky. The oysters grow rapidly throughout the summer and fall, and during the winter they are basically dormant. By the end of the next summer, they are perfect eating size. There are about a dozen of us growing oysters in our village. We place half of our crop back into the surrounding waters to replenish the local stock and consume the balance. Each of us raises 2,000 to 4,000 oysters per year." As far as we're concerned, you can never have too many oysters.

An International Festival

HOUSTON, TEXAS Virginia Stautinger is a teacher at the Northwood Montessori School in Houston. She describes the school as a "micro–United Nations." There are 75 students, and all but 17 have first- or second-generation ties to another country. Every year they organize an event called the Festival of Nations. The children dress in costumes from their countries of origin, and the families bring homemade ethnic dishes. During the festival, there is also a "parade of nations" in which the participants carry flags and play national music. Virginia tells us, "We are dedicated to providing an atmosphere of understanding, peace, and joy."

We'd love to hear what's happening in your town. Drop us a note and send us a photo. Write to Welcome to Cook's Country, P.O. Box 470739, Brookline, MA 02447. If you'd like to use e-mail, write to us at welcome@bcpress.com. If your submission is published, you will receive a complimentary one-year subscription to *Cook's Country*.

Ask Cook's Country

STORING COFFEE BEANS

I store coffee beans in the freezer, but the clerk at my local coffee shop recently told me that I should keep the beans at room temperature. Who's right?

Jay Barry Brooklyn, N.Y.

You're both right. In taste tests, we've found that fresh, room-temperature beans make coffee with slightly more flavor than frozen beans. That's because the oils on the chilled beans congeal and don't release their flavor as readily. However, other factors come into play as the beans hang around your kitchen. Exposure to oxygen begins to take its toll on coffee beans almost immediately after roasting. Eventually, coffee beans will lose much of their flavor. Storing beans in the freezer (it offers more protection than the refrigerator without any additional risk) will slow down this process. After a month, we found that beans stored in the freezer made better-tasting coffee than beans stored on the counter during the same period. Therefore, if you buy freshly roasted beans every week or two, keep them on the counter in an airtight container away from direct sunlight. If you buy beans less often, store them in the freezer. To prolong their freshness, drop the bag of beans into a zipper-lock bag, press out the air, and seal tightly.

BERRY CLEANING

Is it necessary to wash fresh berries?

John Stone Calistoga, Calif.

Washing berries before you use them is always a good idea. Unless you've picked them from your backyard, you don't know if the berries have been sprayed. Also, most berries hide bits of dirt. We've found that strawberries and blueberries are easy enough to wash. Just place the berries in a colander and rinse them gently under running water for at least 30 seconds, then blot dry with paper towels. Raspberries and blackberries are more problematic because they are so delicate. In the test kitchen, we swish these berries in a bowl of water and then dry them in a salad spinner lined with paper towels. (Even the light pressure from blotting the berries with paper towels can crush them.) Don't spin the raspberries or blackberries too long or too fast, or they will bruise. And don't wash any berries until you want to use them.

KEEPING POTATO SALAD SAFE

I have a great potato salad recipe that includes mayonnaise in the dressing, so I worry about bringing it to picnics and letting it sit out on the table. Should I make potato salad with an oil-and-vinegar dressing instead?

Judi Greenbaum Tamarac, Fla.

Poor mayonnaise! It has a bad reputation, blamed for spoiled potato salads and upset stomachs after many picnics and barbecues. Mayonnaise is rarely the problem. Despite what you've heard, it's actually the potatoes that are more likely to go bad. The bacteria usually responsible for spoiled potato salad are found in soil and dust, and they thrive on starchy foods like potatoes. No matter what kind of dressing you use, don't leave any potato salad out for more than two hours (one hour if the temperature is above 90 degrees), and promptly refrigerate any leftovers in a covered container.

RINSING CHICKEN

My mother always washes raw chicken before she cooks it. I don't think it's necessary. Who's right?

Bonnie Mason Marlboro, N.J.

Both the U.S. Department of Agriculture and the Food and Drug Administration advise against washing poultry. According to their research, while rinsing may remove some bacteria, the only way to ensure that all bacteria are killed is through proper cooking. Moreover, splashing bacteria around the sink can be dangerous, especially if water lands on food that is ready to be served. All the same, some people will argue that chicken should be rinsed for flavor—not safety—reasons. After sitting in its own blood and juices for days, they argue, chicken should be unwrapped and refreshed under running water. To find out if rinsing had any impact on flavor, we roasted four chickens—two rinsed, two unrinsed—and held a blind tasting. Tasters couldn't tell the difference. Our conclusion? Skip the rinsing.

BULGING BURGERS

My burgers always bulge when I grill them, looking more like tennis balls than hamburger patties. Is there any way to prevent this?

Eliza Turnbull Jamaica Plain, Mass.

Burgers bulge when the connective tissue at the edges contracts during cooking, tightening like rubber bands and forcing the interior meat to puff up and out into a ball shape. For burgers that cook up flat, press the center of each patty down with your fingertips before grilling. You're basically forming a divot in the top of each patty. On the grill, the divots will still "puff" but form relatively flat burgers.

RESTING MEAT

I often see recipes that tell me to allow steaks to "rest" before serving. What does this mean?

Declan Murphy Boston, Mass.

In the test kitchen, we rest most meat and poultry after cooking. The theory is that resting—or allowing the meat to sit undisturbed for a time before serving—allows the juices, which are driven to the center of the meat during cooking, to redistribute themselves more evenly throughout the meat. As a result, meat that has rested will shed much less juice than meat sliced straight from the grill or the oven. To test this theory, we grilled four steaks and let two rest while slicing into the other two imme- diately. The steaks that had rested for 10 minutes shed 40 percent less juice than the steaks sliced right after cooking. The meat on the unrested steaks also looked grayer and was not as tender.

A thin steak or chop should rest for 5 to 10 minutes, a thicker roast for 15 to 20 minutes. And when cooking a huge turkey (18 pounds or more), the bird should rest for 30 minutes before it is carved. To keep meat warm while it rests, tent it loosely with foil. But don't crimp the foil around the edges of the pan or plate; this can trap steam and soften the crust or skin.

COOKING WITH SALTED BUTTER

Why do so many recipes call for unsalted butter but then add salt? Can I just use salted butter and not add any extra salt?

Peter Stephens Portland, Maine

We find that salt often masks the sweet creaminess associated with butter. In the test kitchen, we always develop recipes with unsalted butter. We think it tastes better.

If you want to use salted butter in savory recipes that call for unsalted, you will need to reduce the total amount of salt in the recipe. A stick of salted butter contains the equivalent of ⅓ to ½ teaspoon of table salt, so adjust recipes accordingly.

In baking, we strongly recommend using unsalted butter. Given its sodium content, salted butter will make many recipes inedible. For instance, our favorite butter frosting calls for just a pinch of salt and our sugar cookies need only ¼ teaspoon salt. Each recipe calls for two stick of butter, so if you were to use salted butter (rather than unsalted), each would contain about ¾ teaspoon of salt—an amount easily detected.

STORING EGGS

I read somewhere that you should never store eggs in the plastic tray on the inside of the refrigerator door. Is this true?

Beth Miller Hamden, Conn.

Eggs should be kept off the refrigerator door and in their original carton for several reasons. Most important, the door is probably the warmest spot in your refrigerator. We placed thermometers in the doors of six test-kitchen refrigerators and found that the temperature averaged 45 degrees. The temperature on the shelves is between 35 and 40 degrees, an ideal temperature for prolonging the shelf life of eggs. Even if your refrigerator door is cold enough, we suggest keeping eggs in the carton. Believe it or not, eggs can dry out, and the carton offers them some protection against this. Eggs can also readily absorb flavors from pungent foods, such as onions, and the carton helps to keep these stinky odors at bay.

To send us a cooking question, write to Ask Cook's Country, P.O. Box 470739, Brookline, MA 02447. If you prefer to use e-mail, write to askcookscountry@bcpress.com. See if you can stump us!

Kitchen Shortcuts

Don't See Red!
Taming Tomato Sauce

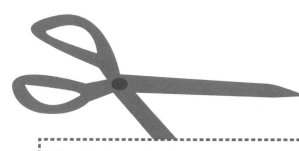

I make a lot of spaghetti sauce, and my stovetop used to look like a red polka-dotted mess from simmering the sauce uncovered. To avoid a massive kitchen scrub-down, I now top my saucepan with a large mesh strainer. It keeps the splattering sauce contained, and the strainer goes right into the dishwasher.

Fran Coppola Boston, Mass.

Marinating Ahead

A lot of recipes call for marinating meat or chicken over-night. When I go grocery shopping and bring home meat or chicken that I intend to freeze for later use, I do the following: Before putting the chicken in the freezer, I unwrap it, put it in a sealable freezer bag, and add the marinade that I would like to cook it in. Then, when the meat or chicken thaws out, it will already be marinated, and I've saved myself some time.

TIME SAVER

Lesley Pew Lynn, Mass.

Quick Cuts!
Not Just for Pizza

I use a rotary pizza cutter to cut my children's food into bite-sized pieces. If you give the cutter a quick spritz or two with nonstick cooking spray, you can even use it on warm cheese toast, grilled cheese, and que-sadillas—not to mention pizza—without having the cheese stick to the blade.

Amy Pearson Beaumont, Texas

All Tied Up!
STRINGS ATTACHED

I was making chicken stock one day and discovered that I did not have any twine to tie together my herb bundle. So I improvised: I decided to "string" a celery stalk—cut the tip of the stalk at an angle and peel away the fibrous string—and use the string to tie my herbs together. It worked!

Twyla Olmeda Austin, Texas

COOL GRATING

My family's favorite cheese is mozzarella, and we grate it for almost everything (which is less expensive than buying packages of already-grated cheese). Grating the mozzarella was difficult until I tried putting it in the freezer for 10 to 15 minutes first. Now it isn't so much of a chore for me, and the cheese doesn't break into clumps when my children grate their own cheese.

Carol Fowler Prescott Valley, Ariz.

THE SCOOP ON EGGS

My husband and I have a small farm in North Carolina. We have lots of very fresh eggs to make egg salad, but I find peeling them to be time-consuming and tedious, and I often end up with lots of eggshell bits on the eggs. Then one day I came up with this very easy way to tackle the job.

After letting the hard-boiled eggs cool, I place them on a cutting board and whack them in the middle with the blunt edge of a butter knife. Then I cut the eggs in half with the sharper edge. After all the eggs are cut, I use a teaspoon to scoop out the egg, running the spoon between shell and the egg white. The egg releases easily, coming out in one piece and with no bits of shell attached.

Dale R. Fluke Oxford, N.C.

POUNDING CHICKEN BREASTS

Most recipes advise you to cover chicken breasts with plas-tic wrap when you pound them into cutlets. I recently tried a zipper-lock freezer bag instead of plastic wrap, and what an im-provement. The heavier-gauge zipper-lock bag was easier to manipulate, didn't tear apart the way plastic wrap sometimes does, made for easier cleanup, and even allowed for easier rotation of the breast for more evenly pounded meat.

Mark Monjot Avon Lake, Ohio

OVEN-FRYING BACON

Oven-frying is a great way to cook bacon, and now that I've figured out a way to keep it out of the rendering fat while it cooks, I like it even more. I simply place a cooling rack in a rimmed baking sheet and arrange the bacon on top. The bacon doesn't need to be turned while it cooks, the fat doesn't need to be drained off, and the bacon needs just a quick blot with a paper towel before serving. And as a bonus, the fat can easily be poured into a container and then stored and used for cooking.

Virginia Lake Lakeland, Fla.

EASY SHRIMP PREP

I use a pair of stainless-steel hair-cutting scissors (reserved just for this task) to snip along the back of a shrimp to peel and devein it in one easy step. Once the cut is made, the vein is exposed and the shell peels off easily. And the scissors, which can be purchased at any drug-store, are dishwasher-safe.

Greg Perlstein Overland Park, Kan.

ZEST AT THE READY

Whenever a recipe calls for lemon juice, I remove the peel with a zester before squeezing the lemon, place the peel in a small resealable container, and freeze it. I always have lemon zest whenever I need it, and don't need any fresh lemons just for zesting. And it's easy to chop the peel finely and measure it when it is frozen.

Mary Ellen Gran Shelter Island, N.Y.

EASIER SPICE POURING

Instead of tearing off the "seal-ing" paper placed under the lid of new spice jars, I use the tip of a paring knife to cut a small triangle in the paper. This makes it is easy to pour the spices into measuring spoons.

Joyce Sikora Edwardsville, Ill.

If you'd like to submit a tip, please send a letter to Kitchen Shortcuts, Cook's Country, P.O. Box 470739, Brookline, MA 02447. Or e-mail us at shortcuts@bcpress.com. Include your name, address, and phone number. If we publish your tip, you will receive a one-year subscription to *Cook's Country*.

MEASURING INGREDIENTS

I keep small plastic portion cups (available at warehouse-club stores and restaurant-supply stores) or small paper cups in a drawer in my kitchen. I use these for mise en place—the French phrase for measuring out all of the ingredients you need for a recipe before cooking it. Their small size is perfect, and, when I'm done, I simply discard the cups. Keeps my kitchen a lot cleaner at "crunch" time.

Deb Rouse
Houston, Texas

DON'T GO NUTS CHOPPING NUTS

It's difficult to chop nuts without having them fly all over the place. My solution is to put them in a heavy-duty zipper-lock bag and tap them with a meat-pounding mallet or soup can until they are the desired size.

Rebecca Biddle
Fort Bragg, N.C

WINE SLUSH

I often need wine for a recipe when I don't have any on hand. I read that you can freeze wine without harming its flavor, so I keep at least 2 cups of it, both red and white, frozen in jars in my freezer. When I need some wine for a recipe, it's always there. I open the jar and scoop out whatever amount I need —large or small—which is easy to do because the wine doesn't freeze completely.

Tricia Finley
Burnaby, British Columbia

OIL BARRIER STOPS ODOR

Whenever I prepare to cut up onions or other foods that cause lingering odors on my fingers, I "wash" my hands well with salad oil and then dry them well on a towel. The salad oil soaks into the skin and creates a barrier that odors can't penetrate. After cutting up the produce, I just wash my hands with soap and water, then put on another coat of oil to keep them from drying out. I have been using this trick since 1964 and have never had problems with smelly hands!

Thomas Miller
East Lansing, Mich.

STABILIZING WHIPPED CREAM

My mother-in-law was the cook in a small-town restaurant many years ago. She knew lots of kitchen tricks, one of which was to soak some marshmallows in whipping cream a few hours before whipping. The soft marshmallows would dissolve and beat easily into the cream, stabilizing and sweetening it.

Marlene Evans
Inlay City, Mich.

NO MORE SOGGY FILLINGS

I often make baked egg and vegetable dishes like strata and quiche, but the moisture from the vegetables can make the fillings wet. To get rid of excess moisture, I give the cooked veggies a turn in the salad spinner before adding them to the eggs. This also works great for seeding chopped tomatoes and removing some extra juice. When I make tomato salad recipes that call for salting and draining the tomatoes, I do the salting in the spinner basket. After a few minutes, I give them a spin or two.

Annalisa Rengenfuss
La Habra Heights, Calif.

A NEW WAY TO MELT CHOCOLATE

I melt chocolate (or chocolate and butter) in an ovenproof bowl that I place in the oven just before I turn it on to pre-heat. When I think the chocolate has melted, I remove it from the oven and whisk it. If there are still a few lumps, I simply put it back in the oven for a minute or two. The chocolate melts slowly and evenly, and it never burns.

Louise Fox
Coconut Creek, Fla.

SQUEEZING TWO MORE USES OUT OF A LEMON

After juicing lemons for use in recipes, I place the spent lemon halves in a zipper-lock bag and freeze them. When my in-sink garbage disposal starts to take on some unpleasant odors, I simply grab some lemon halves, place them in the disposal with a cup of ice, and turn on the faucet and the disposal. This freshens the garbage disposal and sharpens the blades at the same time.

Michelle Fisher
Satsuma, Fla.

In the Bag!
Chopping Jalapeños

I rarely have a glove handy to protect my hands when I need to dice a jalapeño or two. So I grab a small plastic sandwich bag, turn it inside out, and hold the pepper with my hand wrapped in the bag. Leftover pepper can be pulled right into the bag, sealed, and popped into the freezer for later use.

Deb Scheider Gloucester, Ohio

Keeping Cookbooks Open

DOUBLE DUTY

Having never purchased a cookbook stand, I have found a suitable substitute that all cooks are likely to have in their cupboards. I take a clear glass Pyrex pie plate or dish and place it over the open cookbook. The weight holds the book open, and I can read the recipe clearly through the glass.

Kristin Miles New York, N.Y.

No-Fail Chimney Starting

I keep vegetable oil nearby when I grill. I use it when I clean the hot grates with oil-dampened paper towels (held by tongs, of course). I've found that if I drizzle a little of the oil on newspapers before wadding them up and placing them in my chimney starter, the chimney fire never goes out.

Kurt Moyer Fishers, Ind.

Sandwich Solution!
No-Slide Tomatoes

Every once in a while I have a good supply of Roma or other small tomatoes. But when I slice them for use in a

sandwich, the small slices tend to squeeze or slide out of the sandwich. One way to prevent this is to slice the tomatoes like folding screens. The tomatoes will open out, and one or two small tomatoes will sit in a sandwich very nicely.

Mina Yamashita
Albuquerque, N.M.

Time-Honored Trick!
NO MORE SPLATTERING BUTTER

No matter how low the power level, I can't seem to keep the milk solids in butter from boiling and splattering in the microwave. Now when a recipe calls for melted butter, I microwave it in my 2-cup Pyrex measuring cup covered with the wrapper from the butter stick. The residue from the butter adheres the wrapper to the rim of the cup, containing the splatters.

Becky Flanagan Loveland, Ohio

Four great summer recipes with strawberries and cream

We received hundreds of strawberry recipes and spent weeks (and had lots of fun) making them. When we looked at our favorites, we noticed a common theme: Fresh strawberries and cream are an unbeatable combination. Congratulations to the winners, and many thanks to everyone who shared their recipes.

Our Grand-Prize Winner!

Jennifer Wickes
Pine Beach, N.J.

Jennifer writes: "This recipe reminds me of my heritage. My family is of British descent, and when I discovered scones I was in heaven! I devised this recipe after tasting the most fantastic strawberry scones at an Amish bake sale in western New York. I did my best to duplicate the recipe, and this is my final result." We think Jennifer has done a great job of re-creating this bake sale winner.

STRAWBERRY SCONES MAKES 8

Serve with a dollop of clotted cream (and a cup of tea, of course) for an elegant afternoon snack. For tender scones, avoid overhandling the dough.

2	large eggs
1	tablespoon plus 1/4 cup heavy cream
1/4	cup buttermilk
1	teaspoon vanilla extract
2	cups all-purpose flour, plus extra for dusting work surface
1/3	cup plus 1 tablespoon sugar
2	teaspoons baking powder
1/4	teaspoon salt
6	tablespoons unsalted butter, cut into 1-inch pieces
2/3	cup strawberries, hulled and chopped

1. Adjust oven rack to middle position and heat oven to 375 degrees. Line baking sheet with parchment paper. Beat 1 egg with 1 tablespoon cream in small bowl. Set aside. Whisk remaining egg, remaining 1/4 cup cream, buttermilk, and vanilla together in medium bowl.

2. Pulse flour, 1/3 cup sugar, baking powder, and salt in food processor until blended. Add butter and pulse into flour until mixture resembles coarse cornmeal, about ten 1-second pulses. Transfer mixture to large bowl and make well in center. Add buttermilk mixture and stir until batter forms moist clumps. Carefully stir in strawberries.

3. Transfer dough to lightly floured work surface and knead gently until dough comes together and is smooth, about 10 seconds. Pat dough into 7-inch circle about 1 inch thick. Using sharp knife, cut circle into 8 wedges. With pastry brush, remove excess flour from wedges. Transfer wedges to prepared baking sheet, brush tops with egg and cream glaze, and sprinkle with remaining 1 tablespoon sugar.

4. Bake until lightly browned and toothpick inserted in center of scones comes out with a few crumbs attached, about 15 minutes. Transfer scones to wire rack. Serve warm or at room temperature. (Cooled scones can be stored in airtight container for up to 2 days.)

Our Runners-Up

Patricia Harmon Baden, Pa.

STRAWBERRY-PINEAPPLE TART SERVES 8

To prevent the puff pastry from cracking when opened, defrost the pastry in the refrigerator overnight. To avoid a soggy crust, top with the cream cheese and fruit just before serving.

1 (1-pound) box frozen puff pastry, thawed
   in refrigerator overnight
   Flour for dusting work surface
1 large egg, beaten
5 tablespoons sugar
1/2 teaspoon cinnamon
1 quart strawberries, hulled and thinly sliced
1/2 teaspoon grated lemon zest
8 ounces cream cheese, cut into 1-inch pieces and
   softened at room temperature for 30 to 45 minutes
1/4 teaspoon almond extract
1 1/2 cups 1-inch-chunks fresh pineapple
   Mint leaves for garnish (optional)

1. Adjust oven rack to lower-middle position and heat oven to 425 degrees. Line baking sheet with parchment.

2. Unfold both pieces of puff pastry onto floured work surface. Brush egg along one edge of one sheet of pastry. Overlap with second sheet by 1 inch and press to seal together. (Two sheets should form large rectangle.) Cut two 1-inch-wide strips from long side of dough rectangle and two 1-inch-wide strips from short side. Brush dough rectangle with egg. Place strips on top of edges of dough rectangle, creating raised border, and brush with egg. Transfer tart shell to parchment-lined baking sheet.

3. Mix 2 tablespoons sugar and cinnamon in small bowl and sprinkle over tart shell, leaving outer border plain. Using fork, poke entire bottom of shell. Bake 12 to 14 minutes, reduce oven temperature to 350 degrees, and continue to bake until golden brown and crisp, 13 to 15 minutes. (If shell rises in middle, pierce with fork to deflate.) Transfer shell to wire rack to cool. (Cooled shell can be wrapped in plastic and stored at room temperature for up to 2 days.)

4. Stir strawberries, 2 tablespoons sugar, and lemon zest together in medium bowl. Set aside. Beat cream cheese, remaining 1 tablespoon sugar, and almond extract with electric mixer at high speed until light and fluffy, about 1 minute.

5. Spread cream cheese mixture onto cooled pastry shell. Scatter strawberries and pineapple on top. If desired, garnish with mint leaves. Serve immediately.

Judith Liebman Urbana, Ill.

STRAWBERRY PRETZEL BARS MAKES 20 BARS

Getting the gelatin to just the right consistency before spooning it over the cream cheese is key. Look for the bowl of gelatin to ripple slightly when jiggled. If it wobbles in one mass, it is too solidified and will clump when layered on top of the fruit and cheese. Use a rubber mallet to make the pretzel crumbs in a sealed plastic bag.

2 1/2 cups finely crushed pretzel crumbs
12 tablespoons (1 1/2 sticks) unsalted butter, melted
3 tablespoons brown sugar
2 envelopes unflavored gelatin
3 cups white grape juice
1 cup plus 3 tablespoons granulated sugar
1 cup heavy cream
8 ounces cream cheese, cut into 1-inch pieces and
   softened at room temperature for 30 to 45 minutes
3 cups strawberries, hulled, thinly sliced, and chilled

1. Adjust oven rack to middle position and heat to 350 degrees. Coat bottom of 13 by 9-inch baking dish with cooking spray.

2. Toss pretzel crumbs, butter, and brown sugar together in medium bowl until evenly combined. Press firmly into even layer on bottom of baking dish. Bake until fragrant and slightly deepened in color, about 10 minutes. Cool completely.

3. Meanwhile, sprinkle gelatin over 1 cup grape juice in small bowl. Let stand 5 minutes to soften.

4. Bring another 1 cup grape juice and 1 cup granulated sugar to boil in medium saucepan over medium-high heat. Remove pan from heat, add gelatin mixture, and whisk to dissolve any lumps, about 1 minute. Stir in remaining 1 cup grape juice. Transfer mixture to medium bowl and refrigerate until mixture just begins to set, about 1 hour.

5. Meanwhile, beat heavy cream and remaining 3 tablespoons granulated sugar in medium bowl with electric mixer at medium-high speed until cream just holds soft peaks, about 2 minutes. With mixer running, gradually add cream cheese, then whip until mixture is well blended, scraping down sides of bowl as necessary, about 3 minutes. Spread mixture evenly over cooled pretzel crust and top with strawberries. Let chill in refrigerator until gelatin is ready to use. Carefully spoon gelatin over strawberries, cover with plastic wrap, and refrigerate until completely set, at least 4 hours or overnight. Cut into 20 squares and serve. (Bars can be refrigerated for up to 2 days.)

Carol Forcum Marion, Ill.

QUICK STRAWBERRY TRIFLE SERVES 12 TO 14

Grand Marnier adds a hint of orange, but the liqueur can be omitted if desired.

2 quarts strawberries, hulled and thinly sliced
2 tablespoons granulated sugar
2 (10-ounce) packaged angel food cakes,
   cut into 1/2-inch slices
1/4 cup Grand Marnier (optional)
1 1/2 cups heavy cream
1 cup confectioners' sugar
1 pound low-fat cream cheese, cut into 1-inch pieces
   and softened at room temperature for 30 to 45 minutes
1 cup low-fat sour cream, at room temperature
1/2 teaspoon almond extract
1/4 teaspoon vanilla extract
   Pinch salt

1. Toss strawberries and granulated sugar together in medium bowl. Set aside, stirring once or twice to help sugar dissolve. Brush cake slices with Grand Marnier, if using. Set cake slices aside.

2. Beat heavy cream and confectioners' sugar in medium bowl with electric mixer at medium-high speed until soft peaks form, about 2 minutes. Add cream cheese and beat at medium-low speed until combined, about 1 minute. Scrape bottom and sides of bowl well with rubber spatula. Add sour cream, almond extract, vanilla extract, and salt, and continue to beat at medium-low until combined, about 1 minute. Scrape bottom and sides of bowl again. Increase speed to medium-high and beat until mixture is smooth and thoroughly combined, about 3 minutes.

3. Place one-third of cake slices into bottom of 3 1/2-quart (or larger) glass bowl or trifle dish. Set 1/2 cup strawberries aside in small bowl. Spread one-third of cream cheese mixture on cake and top with one-third of remaining strawberries. Repeat layering of cake, cream cheese mixture, and berries two more times. (Cover with plastic wrap and refrigerate for up to 8 hours.) Arrange reserved strawberries on top and serve.

We are looking for pasta casserole recipes for an upcoming contest. Please send us entries by July 1, 2005. Write to us at Recipe Contest, Cook's Country, P.O. Box 470739, Brookline, MA 02447, or e-mail us at recipecontest@bcpress.com. Either way, please make sure to include your name, address, and daytime phone number, and tell us what makes your recipe special. The grand-prize winner will receive $500. All entries become the property of *Cook's Country*. We look forward to reading (and tasting) your recipes.

Recipe Makeover CRUMB COFFEE CAKE

Low-fat sour cream and a surprise mixing method yield a tender, moist cake.

Can this Sunday-brunch treat be slimmed down and still taste good?

I make my prized crumb coffee cake recipe for Sunday brunch when company is coming. The brown sugar topping perfectly complements the rich, buttery yellow cake. Although it is lightly flavored with cinnamon and vanilla, this cake gets most of its appeal from the two main ingredients: butter and sugar. That's why almost everyone who tastes my coffee cake asks for the recipe.

To my surprise, my sister Kiersten recently called and asked for a lighter version. Yes, a modest serving of my coffee cake contains nearly 450 calories and 20 grams of fat. Not too rich for my taste, but Kiersten apparently disagrees.

Never one to shirk a culinary challenge (or some sibling rivalry), I decided to see if I could develop a lower-fat crumb coffee cake for my number-crunching sister. But I was willing to go only so far in the name of sisterhood. If a revised recipe was going to bear my name, it would have to taste good.

My original coffee cake is very sweet. It calls for white sugar in the cake and a mix of white and brown sugars in the topping. My first step was to reduce the total amount of crumb topping. So far, so good. But when I tried to reduce the white sugar in the cake, it turned horribly dry. The simple solution—an idea borrowed from the topping recipe—was to use a combination of brown and white sugars. Brown sugar added back plenty of moisture, making a big improvement in the texture of the cake. In the end, I was able to trim ½ cup of sugar from my recipe.

I knew I had to reduce the amount of butter, too, but this would be tricky. Fat tenderizes baked goods, and with less butter my cake baked up tough. I would have to look elsewhere for moisture and tenderness. I tried applesauce, low-fat buttermilk, and low-fat yogurt, but low-fat sour cream contributed the most richness (as well as a tangy flavor).

My recipe was now very good—at least most of the time. The problem was that sometimes the cake still turned out tough. Why? My reduced-fat batter was really thick—more like a sticky bread dough—and I was having trouble blending all the ingredients together with a spoon or spatula. I had a feeling that when the cake baked up tough, it was probably because I was overworking the batter. Was there a more reliable way to mix this batter?

An electric mixer wasn't much better, but the food processor showed promise. The batter came together in seconds, and the baked cake was very tender. Although this seems counterintuitive, it's hard to overwork batter in a food processor. The pulse button works very efficiently, and it's easy to stop mixing the moment the batter is ready.

My reduced-fat coffee cake, with just two-thirds the calories and half the fat, is quite good. I'm not sure if it would win a head-to-head competition against my original version, but I've served my new coffee cake to unsuspecting guests, and several have even asked for the recipe. Maybe my sister had a point after all.

–Nina West

REDUCED-FAT CRUMB COFFEE CAKE SERVES 8 TO 10

It's best to serve this cake the same day you make it; the crunchy crumb topping will soften if covered or stored for more than a day. Low-fat cakes are prone to toughness, especially if overmixed. Once the ingredients just come together, stop mixing. Low-fat cakes are also prone to dryness, especially if overbaked—even slightly. Pull the cake out of the oven just *before* you think it's done. Residual heat from the pan will finish the baking.

- 2 cups all-purpose flour
- ¾ cup packed light brown sugar
- ½ cup granulated sugar
- ½ teaspoon salt
- ½ teaspoon baking powder
- ¼ teaspoon baking soda
- 4 tablespoons unsalted butter, melted and cooled slightly
- 1 cup low-fat sour cream, at room temperature
- 1 large egg, at room temperature
- 1 teaspoon vanilla extract
- 1 teaspoon cinnamon

1. Adjust oven rack to center position and heat oven to 350 degrees. Coat 8-inch-square pan with nonstick cooking spray.

2. Pulse flour, ½ cup brown sugar, granulated sugar, salt, baking powder, and baking soda in bowl of food processor until blended. With food processor running, add 3 tablespoons melted butter and blend until flour mixture looks sandy. Transfer ¼ cup flour mixture to medium bowl and set aside. Add sour cream, egg, and vanilla to flour mixture in food processor. Pulse until mixture just comes together. Do not overmix. Using rubber spatula, scrape batter into prepared pan and smooth top.

3. Stir remaining ¼ cup brown sugar and cinnamon into bowl with reserved flour mixture. Add remaining 1 tablespoon butter and toss gently with fork or hands until butter is evenly distributed, creating some larger pea-sized crumbs. Sprinkle crumb mixture evenly over batter.

4. Bake until crumbs are golden brown and toothpick inserted in center of cake comes out with a few crumbs attached, 30 to 35 minutes. Transfer to wire rack to cool. Serve warm or at room temperature.

Scratch and Sniff

A cup of fragrant coffee is the perfect accompaniment to a piece of coffee cake. Or is it? How about a postage stamp? This limited-edition scented stamp was produced in Brazil to promote the coffee industry in 2001. Microcapsules of coffee aroma were mixed with clear varnish and applied to the surface of the stamp. To release the aroma of freshly roasted beans, you would just rub the stamp. Nearly four years after production, this rare stamp still smells strong. Not to be outdone, the Swiss have created chocolate-scented stamps. The U.S. Postal Service might consider honoring our nation's greatest culinary achievements. We wouldn't mind taking a whiff of a barbecue-scented stamp.

And the Numbers...

All nutritional information is for one serving.

TRADITIONAL HOMEMADE Coffee Cake
CALORIES: **434**
FAT: **20 g**
SATURATED FAT: **9 g**

COOK'S COUNTRY Reduced-Fat Crumb Coffee Cake
CALORIES: **297**
FAT: **9 g**
SATURATED FAT: **6 g**

Lost Recipes WASHBOARD COOKIES

IT'S A FACT: *Before the advent of electric washing machines, the washboard was the tool of choice for scrubbing clothes clean. Today, you are more likely to see a washboard up on stage being played by a folk or jazz musician. Check out the International Washboard Festival held every June in Logan, Ohio.*

Modern washing machines made washboards a thing of the past, but these cookies are too good to forget.

Dear Cook's Country,
My grandmother Mavis often held tea parties for the ladies of our local garden club. Along with crustless sandwiches and canapés, she offered her guests a plate of homemade cookies. When we thought that the ladies weren't looking, my sisters and I would creep down the kitchen stairs to steal the cookies—plate and all! Grandmother would catch us in this act of thievery and then stage a fuss, but we later learned that she would prepare an extra "decoy" plate of cookies so the ladies would get their fair share. My favorite cookie on the plate was called a washboard. The name referred to the fork-indented ridges on top of each cookie. These cookies were crisp and not too sweet, with the distinct flavor and aroma of coconut; I can still smell them baking. Any chance that you can replicate this stolen treat from my youth?
Andrew J. Budrow, Thibodaux, La.

Dear Andrew,
I, too, love tea cookies. I'm sure that we both agree that a good "tea" cookie is not too sweet, not too greasy, and not too filling. In other words, it is a modest cookie perfectly suited to white gloves and good manners.

That being said, I had never heard of washboards. Cookbooks of recent vintage yielded few clues, and my inquiries around the office were met with glazed stares. Turning to the Internet, I punched in "washboard cookies" and found some promising recipes. When I baked these cookies, however, they were distinctly different from the ones that you describe. These rich cookies were decidedly moist and chewy, not a bad thing as cookies go, but much too sweet and greasy for the garden club set. As for the coconut, these recipes used so little that if I hadn't made the cookies myself, I never would have guessed that coconut was involved.

My luck improved when I turned to our collection of old and out-of-print cookbooks. Many dating back to the early 1900s made mention of crisp coconut cookies, but I first saw the name "washboards" in midcentury cookbooks, such as *Betty Crocker's Picture Cookbook* (1950). That book described washboards as "coconut-taffy bars." I whipped up a batch, and here indeed were cookies that actually tasted of coconut and were snappy-thin and crisp, just as a tea cookie should be. The word *bars* seemed to refer to the cookies' rectangular shape (they

continued on page 10

These old-fashioned ridged cookies pack a big coconut and brown sugar crunch.

WASHBOARDS
MAKES 3 DOZEN COOKIES

The dough can be made ahead of time. Simply shape the dough into the rectangular log, wrap the log in plastic wrap, and refrigerate for up to 2 days or freeze for up to 1 month. If frozen, defrost dough on counter for 20 minutes before slicing.

- 2 cups all-purpose flour
- 1/2 teaspoon baking powder
- 1/4 teaspoon baking soda
- 1/4 teaspoon salt
- 1/4 teaspoon nutmeg
- 1 large egg
- 2 tablespoons milk
- 8 tablespoons (1 stick) unsalted butter, softened but still cool
- 1 cup packed light brown sugar
- 1 cup sweetened shredded coconut

1. Whisk together flour, baking powder, baking soda, salt, and nutmeg in medium bowl. Whisk together egg and milk in small bowl. Place butter and brown sugar in large bowl and beat with electric mixer on medium-high speed until light and fluffy, about 2 minutes. Add egg mixture and beat on medium-high, scraping down sides of bowl, until well combined, about 30 seconds. Add flour mixture and coconut, and mix on low speed until just incorporated, 15 to 30 seconds.

2. Turn dough out onto lightly floured surface and, using floured hands, shape into 15-inch log (see photo 1, above right). Flatten top and sides of log so that it measures 1 inch high and 3 inches wide (photo 2). Wrap tightly with plastic wrap and refrigerate until firm, about 45 minutes.

3. Adjust oven racks to upper- and lower-middle positions and heat oven to 350 degrees. Line two baking sheets with parchment paper. Remove chilled dough from refrigerator, unwrap, cut into 1/4-inch-thick slices (photo 3), and arrange slices 1 inch apart on baking sheets. Dip dinner fork in flour, then make crosswise indentations in dough slices (photo 4). Bake until cookies are toasty brown, 15 to 18 minutes, rotating baking sheets halfway through baking time. Cool cookies on baking sheets for 10 minutes, then transfer to racks to cool to room temperature. Serve.

How to Make WASHBOARDS

1. Using floured hands, shape the cookie dough into a 15-inch log. **2.** Flatten the top and sides of the log so that it measures 1 inch tall and 3 inches wide. Wrap dough in plastic wrap and chill at least 45 minutes. **3.** Cut chilled log crosswise into 1/4-inch-thick slices and transfer to parchment-lined baking sheets, arranging slices 1 inch apart. **4.** Use the floured tines of a fork to gently press crosswise indentations into the dough slices.

Looking for a lost recipe?
We can help. Drop us a note and tell us about the recipe you want to find. Write to Lost Recipes, Cook's Country, P.O. Box 470739, Brookline, MA 02447. Or e-mail us at lostrecipes@bcpress.com.

continued from page 9

were not at all like "bars" of the brownie and blondie variety).

Step by step, I played with the recipe to get closer to Grandmother Mavis's ideal. Away went the saccharine taste of white sugar and in went light brown sugar, which gave the cookie a toastier flavor and enhanced the coconut. Knowing when enough brown sugar was enough was important, for, as every society lady knows, a good tea cookie should not give one a toothache. I reduced the amount of butter to keep the cookie lean, and I loved the flavor of nutmeg that I found in one recipe. When it came to the coconut, well, I am a coconut hound and knew that some self-restraint was in order. I added just enough to make it the star of the show without turning the cookie into a macaroon. Absolutely delicious.

Antique recipes had me painstakingly shaping each washboard by hand. After I had shaped more than a hundred this way, the task began to lose its charm. In search of an easier method, I took a cue from refrigerator cookies and rolled the dough into a log. I bashed the top and sides, making a rough rectangular box, then cut very thin slices of cookie dough and spaced the slices on baking sheets. Talk about easy!

Other parts of the process, I decided, were best left untouched. I'm sure there's an electric supermatic cookie-ridge-digger out there somewhere, but if Grandma Mavis used a fork to make the washboards' ridges, then a fork is good enough for me.

In the oven they went, and out of the oven they came: beautiful, toasty little coconut cookies—just perfect with my cup of tea—and my white gloves. Thank you, Andrew, for the cookie idea. I hope this recipe does justice to your fond recollections of your grandmother.

–Bridget Lancaster

How about a slow-cooker chili that is thick, not watery, and has big, beefy Texas flavor?

My favorite chili features big chunks of tender beef in a thick, fiery red sauce. In Texas, this chili is called a bowl of red. I wondered if I could adapt this Lone Star classic to my slow cooker. I certainly wouldn't mind having a big bowl of red to come home to after a long day at work.

Your typical Texas chilihead believes there is one and only one true recipe for chili, and that is one in which large pieces of cubed beef are browned and then simmered with dried chiles in stock or water. Many authentic chili recipes demand a mix of dried chiles—which must be toasted, seeded, and ground—in place of the all-purpose supermarket chili powder. Tomatoes and onions are a matter of local preference, although the former are not accepted in true Texas chili circles. And beans are strictly for amateurs. Let's get this straight: This dish is about meat.

In the test kitchen, we've found that ready-cut stew meat usually makes dry, dull chili. These scraps often come from pretty lean parts of the cow, and for chili you want something with some fat and flavor. A chuck-eye roast is our top choice for chili; it takes just 10 minutes to cut up the meat.

Most slow-cooker chili recipes just dump the meat and other ingredients into the pot, throw on the lid, and hope for the best. You would

We confess that we've messed with Texas chili just a bit by adding red beans. Garnishes of minced red onion and shredded cheese should be less controversial.

never make Texas chili this way on the stovetop. The beef is always browned. Just to make sure this extra step was worth the mess and time, I made two batches of chili—one with raw beef, the other with beef browned in a hot skillet filmed with oil. There was no comparison. The chili made with browned beef tasted much, much beefier. It was also less watery.

With my beef browned and waiting in the slow cooker, I sautéed onions and jalapeño chiles. Instead of taking the trouble to toast and grind dried chiles, I was hoping to use commercial chili powder and cumin, but they tasted bland. Cooking these spices with the

onions and some fresh chiles brought out their flavor. It was like wiping away the fog from a windshield. Canned chipotle chiles (dried, smoked jalapeños) added more complexity, and tasters preferred chili made with—that's right—tomatoes. I often find that herbs are best added when a slow-cooker recipe is basically done. Texas chili was no exception. When I added oregano at the outset, its flavor disappeared.

At this point I was more than happy with the taste of the chili, but the sauce was still on the thin side. Pureed corn tortillas (see box, below) turned out to be part of the solution, but I still needed help. I got that help quite by accident one morning when I was rushed for time and used unevenly cut pieces of beef, some large and some quite small. By the end of the day, the smaller chunks had cooked to the point of falling apart, while the larger chunks held their own. Now I had a meaty chili with a varied texture and a sauce that had just the right beefy thickness.

Beans helped to extend the pot (I am a frugal cook), and their starch helped balance the heat. If, like me, you elect to mess with what for many Texans is the chili code of honor, stir in the beans during the last minutes of cooking so they'll retain their shape and texture.

–Diane Unger-Mahoney

Secrets to THICK CHILI IN A SLOW COOKER

Beef Chunks in Two Sizes

How the meat is cut changes the texture of the chili. Cut one roast into 3/4-inch pieces that will break down during cooking and thicken the chili. Cut the other roast into 1 1/4-inch pieces to give the chili its chunky heft.

Pureed Tortillas

Because food must cook with the lid on in a slow cooker, watery sauces are a recurring problem. Conventional slow-cooker recipes add flour or cornstarch, but these ingredients can impart a starchy flavor. We had better results with corn tortillas, blistered in a hot skillet to accentuate their flavor, and then pureed in a blender with chicken broth to create a thick paste.

"TEXAS RED" CHILI CON CARNE

**SERVES 10 TO 12 WITHOUT BEANS,
12 OR MORE WITH BEANS**

Chuck-eye roasts are fatty, so don't be surprised if you trim off a pound or more from each one. You should have 5 to 6 pounds of trimmed meat when you start the recipe. Chipotle chiles are smoked jalapeños canned in a red sauce called adobo. They are available in the international aisle of the supermarket. If you cannot find them, use 8 jalapeños. This chili is authentically spicy; for milder chili, reduce the chipotles and jalapeños by half.

- 6 (6-inch) soft corn tortillas
- 3 cups low-sodium chicken broth
- 1 (28-ounce) can diced tomatoes, with juice
- 5 chipotle chiles in adobo sauce
- 1½ tablespoons dark brown sugar
- 2 (3½- to 4-pound) boneless beef chuck-eye roasts, trimmed and cut as shown in photo on page 10
  Salt and pepper
- 5 tablespoons vegetable oil
- ¼ cup plus 2 tablespoons water
- 3 medium onions, chopped medium
- 4 medium jalapeño chiles, stemmed and minced
- 6 tablespoons chili powder
- 2 tablespoons ground cumin
- 8 medium garlic cloves, minced
- 3 (16-ounce) cans pinto or kidney beans, drained and rinsed (optional)
- 1 teaspoon dried oregano

1. Heat large skillet over medium-high heat. Add 3 tortillas, overlapping them as necessary, and cook until blistered on both sides, about 2 minutes per side. Transfer to plate and repeat with remaining tortillas. Tear tortillas into 2-inch pieces and combine with 2 cups chicken broth in microwave-safe bowl. Heat in microwave on high until tortillas are saturated, 2 to 3 minutes. Puree mixture in blender or food processor until smooth, then transfer to slow-cooker insert. Add tomatoes and chipotles to blender or processor and blend until smooth. Transfer to slow-cooker insert along with remaining 1 cup chicken broth and brown sugar.

2. Dry beef thoroughly with paper towels, then season with salt and pepper. Heat 2 teaspoons oil in skillet over medium-high heat until just smoking. Brown one-third of beef thoroughly on all sides, 8 to 10 minutes. Transfer browned beef to slow cooker, return skillet to medium-high heat, and repeat with 2 more teaspoons oil and second batch of beef. Transfer to slow-cooker insert and repeat with 2 more teaspoons oil and remaining beef. Transfer to slow-cooker insert. Add ¼ cup water to skillet, scraping up any browned bits, and return skillet to medium-high heat. Cook until almost all water has evaporated, about 3 minutes. Transfer skillet contents to slow-cooker insert, and wipe skillet dry with paper towels.

3. Heat remaining 3 tablespoons oil over medium heat until shimmering. Add onions, jalapeños, and ¼ teaspoon salt and cook until onions are softened, about 5 minutes. Stir in chili powder and cumin and cook, stirring occasionally, until spices are deeply fragrant, about 2 minutes. Add garlic and cook until fragrant, about 30 seconds longer. Transfer vegetables to slow-cooker insert. Add 2 tablespoons water to skillet, scrape up any spices, and transfer contents to slow-cooker insert. Stir ingredients to combine thoroughly.

4. Set slow cooker to high, cover, and cook until tender, 6 to 7 hours. (Alternatively, cook on low for 9 to 10 hours.) Stir in beans (if using) and cook 15 minutes. Stir in oregano and adjust seasoning with additional salt and pepper. Leftovers can be refrigerated for several days or frozen for several months.

Make Ahead

To bring out their full flavor, we found that you must brown the meat and sauté the vegetables and spices before they go into the slow cooker. If you'd rather not do this in the morning (say, on a busy weekday), you can complete this step the night before. Prepare the recipe through step 3. Instead of transferring the meat, vegetables, and other chili ingredients to the slow cooker, refrigerate them in airtight containers. The browned meat should go into its own container; the tortilla mixture, tomato mixture, and sautéed vegetables and spices can be refrigerated together. In the morning, just transfer everything to the slow cooker. The cooking time will run to the high end of the ranges given in the recipe.

The American Table: Chili Champions

Chili is serious business—just ask the chiliheads who participate in the International Chili Society's World Championship Chili Cookoff. Since 1967, one lucky home cook has been crowned king or queen of the chili world. Last year's prize was $25,000. Not bad for a bowl of red. Here are some past winners and their fancifully named creations.

Year	Name	Chili
2004	Kathleen Hipskind	Dago Reds Wop 'n' Good Chili
2003	Bob Wetzel	Bronco Bob's Chili
2002	Ron Burt	Warning Shot Chili—Runs for Your Life
1998	Kathy LeGear	24-Karat Chili
1993	Cathy R. Wilkey	Puppy's Breath Chili
1991	Randy Robinson	Road Meat Chili
1989	Philip M. Walter	Tarantula Jack's Thundering Herd Buffalo Tail Chili
1980	Bill Pfeiffer	Capitol Punishment

Quick Cooking

GOOD MEALS IN ABOUT 30 MINUTES

The sauce in this recipe works double-duty as marinade and dressing.

GRILLED SPICY LIME CHICKEN WITH BLACK BEAN AND AVOCADO SALAD SERVES 4

To determine when chicken is done, peek into the thickest park with the tip of a small knife. The chicken should be opaque at the center.

- ⅓ cup lime juice
- ½ cup chopped fresh cilantro
- ¼ cup olive oil
- 2 chipotle chiles, roughly chopped, plus 2 tablespoons adobo sauce
- 1 tablespoon honey
- 3 medium garlic cloves, minced
- 2 teaspoons ground cumin
  Salt and pepper
- 8 boneless, skinless chicken thighs or breasts
- 2 (16-ounce) cans black beans, drained and rinsed
- ½ cup chopped scallions
- 1 red bell pepper, sliced thin
- 1 ripe avocado, sliced thin
  Lime wedges for serving

The combination of lime juice, cilantro, chiles, garlic, and cumin gives a boost to both the chicken and the black bean salad.

1. Light grill. Whisk lime juice, cilantro, oil, chiles and sauce, honey, garlic, cumin, ½ teaspoon salt, and ¼ teaspoon pepper together in small bowl.

2. Toss chicken with ¼ cup lime juice mixture in separate large bowl. Season with salt and pepper. Marinate chicken in refrigerator while grill continues to preheat.

3. Toss beans, scallions, red pepper, and avocado with ¼ cup lime juice mixture in serving bowl. Season with salt and pepper to taste.

4. Grill chicken over very hot fire until well browned on both sides and cooked through, 8 to 13 minutes. Transfer chicken to serving platter and drizzle with remaining lime juice mixture. Serve immediately with black bean and avocado salad.

Fun Food

What can you do with marshmallows and chocolate when there's no campfire nearby? These four fanciful creations prove that s'mores are just the beginning when it comes to this dynamic duo. Serve these desserts at a kid's birthday party or a backyard barbecue. Our Amazing Mousse is even grand enough for a Saturday-night dinner party. RECIPES BY LAUREN CHATTMAN

AMAZING MOUSSE SERVES 4

Mousse without eggs or fuss? This super-quick mousse relies on melted marshmallows for its airy texture. For a whimsical garnish, top mousse with a few toasted mini-marshmallows.

- 3/4 cup milk
- 4 cups mini-marshmallows
- 3 ounces bittersweet chocolate, finely chopped
- 3/4 cup heavy cream
- 1 teaspoon vanilla extract

1. Melt marshmallows and chocolate Combine milk, marshmallows, and chocolate in medium saucepan over low heat, whisking constantly, until marshmallows and chocolate are melted. Pour into medium bowl and set bowl over larger bowl of ice water. Let stand, whisking often, until mixture is cool and thickened, 15 to 20 minutes.

2. Beat cream Using electric mixer, beat cream and vanilla in bowl until cream just holds stiff peaks.

3. Finish mousse and chill Fold chocolate mixture into whipped cream, leaving a few streaks. Spoon into dessert cups or goblets and refrigerate for at least 6 hours or up to 2 days.

CHOCOLATE FLUFF COOKIES MAKES 12 COOKIES

These cookies are inspired by Mallomars but taste much better. Freezing the Fluff-topped cookies before coating them with chocolate prevents the Fluff from losing its shape. We like Carr's biscuits in this recipe for their round shape, crisp texture, and gentle sweetness.

- 12 Carr's Wheatmeal Biscuits
- 1 1/2 cups Marshmallow Fluff
- 8 ounces bittersweet chocolate, finely chopped
- 2 tablespoons vegetable oil

1. Make cookies Place biscuits on wire rack set over rimmed baking sheet. Top each biscuit with 1 rounded heaping tablespoon Marshmallow Fluff. Place baking sheet in freezer until Fluff has firmed up, about 10 minutes.

2. Coat with chocolate Melt chocolate and oil in small saucepan and stir until smooth. Cool to room temperature. Spoon chocolate evenly over each cookie to coat Fluff completely. Return baking sheet to freezer until chocolate is set, about 10 minutes. Refrigerate for at least 1 hour or up to 2 days.

ROCKY ROAD BARK MAKES SIXTEEN 2-INCH SQUARES

On the odd chance that you have some leftover Rocky Road Bark, it will keep in an airtight container in the refrigerator for up to 1 week.

- 6 whole graham crackers
- 6 tablespoons unsalted butter
- 1/4 cup packed light brown sugar
- 1/2 teaspoon salt
- 1 cup milk chocolate chips
- 3/4 cup mini-marshmallows
- 1/2 cup chopped pecans, walnuts, or almonds

1. Make graham cracker layer Adjust oven rack to center position and heat oven to 375 degrees. Line 8-inch-square baking pan with heavy-duty aluminum foil, making sure that foil is tucked into all corners and that at least 1 inch of foil overhangs top of pan on all sides. In single layer, line bottom of pan with graham crackers, breaking them if necessary to fit tightly.

2. Make caramel Combine butter, brown sugar, and salt in small saucepan and cook over low heat, stirring constantly, until butter is melted and sugar has dissolved. Scrape mixture onto graham crackers and smooth with small spatula so that mixture covers crackers completely. Bake until caramel is bubbling, about 10 minutes.

3. Add chocolate Remove pan from oven, sprinkle with chocolate chips, and return to oven to soften chocolate, 1 to 2 minutes. Remove from oven and, using spatula, smooth chocolate into even layer.

4. Garnish and freeze Sprinkle marshmallows and then nuts over chocolate. Press lightly with fingertips to adhere to chocolate. Cool on wire rack 30 minutes, then freeze until chocolate hardens, 30 minutes.

5. Cut and serve Grabbing overhang, lift foil from pan onto cutting board and use sharp chef's knife to cut bark into 2-inch-squares.

CONFETTI KEBABS SERVES 4

12 marshmallows
4 ounces bittersweet, semisweet, or
milk chocolate, melted
2 tablespoons finely chopped toasted nuts
1 tablespoon sprinkles or nonpareils
2 tablespoons toasted flaked coconut

1. Skewer marshmallows Using scissors, snip off pointed ends of 4 bamboo skewers (remove any splintered wood). Thread 3 marshmallows onto each skewer. Place skewers on baking sheet lined with parchment or waxed paper and freeze until firm, about 15 minutes.

2. Coat with chocolate Spoon melted chocolate onto each marshmallow. Use back of spoon to spread chocolate evenly around entire marshmallow.

3. Garnish Working over individual bowls of nuts, sprinkles, and coconut, sprinkle one side of each chocolate-coated marshmallow with garnishes. Set skewer back on baking sheet, plain chocolate side down, and repeat with remaining skewers. Freeze at least 30 minutes or up to 2 days.

Greetings from Memphis!

No sweet, sticky sauces need apply. These ribs are all about the spice rub, which is applied before the meat hits the grill—and again just before serving.

Tommy Littlejohn is the father of six children. Luckily, he enjoys grilling for a crowd.

Dear Cook's Country,
For this year's Fourth of July party, I want to try my hand at something special: Memphis-style barbecued pork spareribs. My father-in-law is coming over and he's from Tennessee, so I want the real thing.

Tommy Littlejohn, Winston-Salem, N.C.

Dear Tommy,
In Memphis, traditional barbecue sauce has no place. The ribs get their flavor from a dry spice rub, applied before the ribs go on the grill. As they smoke for hours, the ribs develop a crispy, crusty exterior, or "bark." Why cover up all that flavor with a gooey sauce?

Pitmasters in Memphis aren't the only ones to rub ribs with dry spices. But in Memphis they take this idea a step further by sprinkling some of the rub over the ribs just before they come off the grill. This double hit of spices is a hallmark of authentic Memphis ribs.

I experimented with almost everything on my spice rack and along the way discovered three essential rules when assembling barbecue rubs. First, salt is a must. Second, sugar is essential to mellow the flavor of the more potent spices and to balance the salt. It's common to see salt and sugar in equal amounts, but this formula was too salty for me. I think 3 parts brown sugar (its light molasses flavor is welcome) to 1 part salt is just about right. Third, because some of the rub is sprinkled over the ribs just before they come off the grill, it's best to avoid spices that taste harsh straight from the jar. Cumin, which appears in many recipes, falls into this category.

The spice rub is key, but do the rubbed ribs really need to "cure" overnight, as many recipes suggest? No. I found that ribs absorb plenty of flavor in just one hour—basically, the time it takes to soak wood chips and fire up the grill. I also discovered that overnight soaks in salty brines, another step recommended by several sources, gave the meat a firm, spongy texture that I didn't care for. Parboiling was the most puzzling approach taken by some older recipes. This messy technique robbed the ribs of their meaty flavor and toughened them as well.

Although Memphis ribs should never be shellacked with a sticky sauce, they are usually brushed with a thin liquid, called a mop, as they cook. What goes into the mop is open to debate, although vinegar is pretty much a constant. Other common choices include beer, juice, and water.

My favorite mop is a mixture of apple cider and cider vinegar. Brushed onto the ribs whenever the cover is lifted off to turn them, this simple mixture adds a pleasing balance of sweetness and acidity.

Like most Memphis barbecue chefs, I thought it a shame to throw out the leftover mop. Instead, I simmered the mop down to make a dipping sauce for the table. I even added a pinch of my spice rub, along with Tabasco sauce, for an extra hit of flavor.

No doubt about it: Real Memphis ribs take a good piece of time. But the combination of smoke, spice, and pork is unbeatable. I hope you—and your father-in-law—agree.

–Sean Lawler

MEMPHIS BBQ SPARERIBS
SERVES 4 TO 6

These ribs are moderately spicy—adjust the cayenne and Tabasco as you wish. To reheat leftovers, place the ribs in an ovenproof dish, add a few tablespoons of water, cover with foil, and place in a 250-degree oven for 20 to 30 minutes.

Spice Rub
- 4 tablespoons paprika
- 3 tablespoons light brown sugar
- 2 tablespoons chili powder
- 2 tablespoons black pepper
- 1 tablespoon salt
- 2 teaspoons garlic powder
- 2 teaspoons onion powder
- 1 teaspoon cayenne pepper

Cider Mop
- 3 cups apple cider
- 1 cup cider vinegar

- 2 cups wood chips, hickory or mesquite
- 2 full racks pork spareribs, preferably St. Louis cut, trimmed of any large pieces of excess fat, membrane removed (see photos on page 15), and patted dry
- 2 teaspoons Tabasco sauce

Tickle Your Ribs

Barbecuing shouldn't be rocket science, but for great ribs, a little care and dedication are necessary. To make things easy, we've come up with a barbecue schedule that will give you tender, smoky, flavorful ribs off the grill every time.

Turning the ribs: Turn the two racks every 30 minutes, switching their position and rotating them 180 degrees.

Adding fuel and smoke: Add 1/2 cup of wood chips to the coals every 30 minutes (whenever you turn the ribs). Once every hour, add 12 unlit briquettes, sliding the top and bottom vents completely open after the first addition.

"Mopping" the ribs: After the first hour, baste the ribs every 30 minutes (when turning them) with the warm mop. Use a pastry brush or spray bottle to apply the mop.

1. For the spice rub and mop: Mix spice rub ingredients together in small bowl. Stir cider and vinegar together in small saucepan.

2. One hour before cooking ribs: Place wood chips in bowl with enough water to cover. Reserve 2 tablespoons plus 1 teaspoon spice rub. With fingers, work remaining rub into both sides of rib racks. Let ribs stand at room temperature until ready to cook.

3. Thirty minutes before cooking ribs: Light about 45 charcoal briquettes. When coals are covered with thin layer of gray ash, stack them 2 to 3 briquettes high on one side of grill. Set cooking grate in place, open top and bottom vents halfway, cover grill, and let heat for 5 minutes. Drain wood chips.

4. Position ribs on side of grill without coals. Drop 1/4 cup wood chips through grate onto coals. Cover grill, positioning lid so that vents are opposite coals to draw smoke through grill. Meanwhile, bring mop to simmer; cover and keep warm.

5. Barbecue ribs until meat starts to pull away from bones and has rosy glow on exterior, 3 to 4 hours. You will need to flip ribs and baste them with mop, as well as replenish charcoal and wood chips, according to

schedule in "Tickle Your Ribs," above. At all other times, keep grill covered.

6. Before removing ribs from grill, sprinkle each rack with 1 tablespoon reserved spice rub. One at a time, place each rack of ribs on grate directly over mound of coals, cooking about 30 seconds on each side, then transfer to cutting board. Tent ribs with foil and let rest for 20 to 30 minutes.

7. While ribs rest, add remaining 1 teaspoon spice rub to remaining mop and simmer, uncovered, until liquid has reduced to about 2 cups, 10 to 15 minutes. Add Tabasco and more salt and pepper to taste, if desired. Slice ribs between bones and serve with sauce on side.

MEMPHIS RIBS ON THE GAS GRILL

Follow recipe for Memphis BBQ Spareribs, placing 2 cups soaked wood chips in small disposable aluminum foil pan. In step 3, place pan directly on primary burner in gas grill, turn all burners to high, and preheat with lid down until chips are smoking heavily, 15 minutes. In step 4, turn primary burner down to medium and shut off other burners. Position ribs over cool part of grill. Proceed with recipe as directed.

How to READ RIBS FOR THE GRILL

Removing the papery membrane on the underside of the ribs will help the fat render more quickly. Removing the membrane also lets the spices better penetrate the meat. The membrane itself is very thin, so removing it should not expose the rib bones.

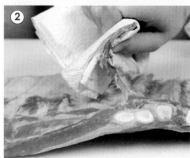

1. At one end of the rack, loosen the edge of the membrane with the tip of a paring knife or your fingernail.
2. Grab the membrane with a paper towel to keep it from slipping. Pull slowly—it should come off in one piece.

Shopping MEAT ME IN ST. LOUIS

Got your map out? "Memphis" and "Kansas City" refer to a style of cooking spareribs. "St. Louis," however, refers to a particular cut of spareribs. A full rack of spareribs contains the brisket bone and surrounding breast meat and usually weighs about 3 1/2 pounds. The brisket bone and breast meat are often trimmed off to produce a narrower, rectangular rack. These are St. Louis spareribs, and each rack weighs about 2 3/4 pounds.

We prefer the St. Louis ribs because they fit side by side on the grill, they cook more quickly, and they are easier to slice and eat. That said, regular spareribs work fine. You may need to overlap the racks on the grill, and you can count on a cooking time that's closer to four, rather than three, hours.

Dressing Up: Split Chicken Breasts

A sweet and sticky glaze made with apricot preserves and orange juice is just the thing to chase away the weekday chicken blues. But no one likes roast chicken breasts with soggy skin, a common problem with this recipe. And excessive sweetness is no good either. How do you avoid these pitfalls? Brown the chicken breasts in a skillet before roasting them, so the skin is crisp, not flabby. Add a healthy dose of lemon juice to make the glaze bright and lively. And, since apricots are the real star, add chopped dried apricots along with the preserves. Perfection was never so easy or so fast. **–Keith Dresser**

APRICOT-GLAZED CHICKEN BREASTS SERVES 4

To make sure that the chicken cooks evenly, buy large, split chicken breasts that are similar in size—about 12 ounces apiece. Stovetops vary, so check the chicken after about 6 minutes to make sure it isn't browning too quickly.

1	(10- to 12- ounce) jar apricot preserves
1/2	cup orange juice
3	tablespoons lemon juice
1/4	cup quartered dried apricots
	Salt and pepper
4	split bone-in, skin-on chicken breasts
2	teaspoons vegetable oil

1. Adjust oven rack to middle position and heat oven to 425 degrees. Whisk apricot preserves, orange juice, lemon juice, apricots, 1/8 teaspoon salt, and 1/8 teaspoon pepper together in medium bowl. Season both sides of chicken breasts with salt and pepper.

2. Heat oil in large skillet over medium-high heat until just smoking. Place chicken breasts, skin side down, in skillet, and cook until well browned and most fat has rendered, 8 to 10 minutes. Turn chicken and lightly brown on second side, 2 to 3 minutes longer.

3. Transfer chicken to medium baking dish and set aside. Discard fat in skillet and add apricot mixture. Simmer vigorously over high heat, stirring constantly, until thick and syrupy, 3 to 4 minutes. Pour glaze over chicken and turn chicken skin side down.

4. Bake, turning chicken skin side up halfway through cooking, until thickest part of breast registers 160 degrees on instant-read thermometer, 12 to 16 minutes. Transfer chicken to platter and let rest 5 minutes. Meanwhile, transfer glaze remaining in baking dish to small bowl. Serve chicken, passing extra glaze separately.

I'm Looking for a Recipe

Pineapple Upside-Down Carrot Cake

I had a recipe for pineapple upside-down carrot cake that I foolishly loaned to someone instead of making her a copy. It was made with a boxed spice cake mix, grated carrots, pineapple slices, and maraschino cherries in an 8-inch-square pan. My kids really enjoyed the cake, and I'd like to make it for them again.

Kathleen Kenna
La Cañada, Calif.

Mung Bean Pudding

I once ate a dessert at a Vietnamese restaurant that was served in a glass with beans on ice flakes, with a small glass of coconut milk on the side. The ice and beans were stirred until smooth, and then the milk was poured over the mixture. I have been trying to find a recipe for this for almost 10 years.

John Elder
White Bear Lake, Minn.

Monte Cristo Cookies

When visiting my sister-in-law in southern California several years ago, we visited a cute boutique that sold cards and small gifts and had a coffee and dessert area. It made the most marvelous cookies, two layers of a shortbread-type cookie with a creamy layer, with a hint of lemon, and a raspberry filling in the middle. The store has since changed owners, and the cookies are not quite as good. We think the cookies are called Monte Cristo cookies. The recipes we've found to date come close but don't measure up to the originals.

Trudee Billo
Galion, Ohio

Crisco Cake

In the mid-1950s, I had a favorite cake. It was the "special" cake that I took to potlucks, gave to families in bereavement, and baked for birthdays. Somehow, in the haste of cleanup, I lost the recipe! It came from a magazine advertisement for Crisco oil and consisted of a beautiful chocolate chiffon cake that turned out magnificently. The frosting was a "boiled" frosting made with egg whites and boiled syrup that was flavored with a little mint extract and tinted green. The crowning glory was a square of bittersweet chocolate melted with a tablespoon of Crisco and drizzled down the sides of the green frosting. It was a beauty to behold and tasted as good as it looked.

June Coady
Via e-mail

Dixon's Chili

We moved a lot when I was growing up, and I remember each place by a special restaurant we went to or a meal that we ate. When we lived in Kansas City, Mo., we often went to Dixon's for chili. Dixon's chili was made with finely ground beef with little, if any, tomato in it. The beans, as I recall, were served separately. It was also very greasy. I would love to find the original recipe.

Miranda Page
Eugene, Ore.

Zucchini Crisp

About two years ago I found a recipe for a zucchini crisp that was made just like an apple crisp but used small cubes of zucchini instead. I brought it to a potluck, and it was a great hit. I have looked high and low for this recipe but to no avail. It's a great way to use up zucchini. If anyone can locate this recipe, I would very much like to have it.

Evie O'Brian
Portland, Ore.

Tosca Board

I made a recipe at least 10 years ago called Tosca Board, but I don't remember where I found it. Tosca Board started with a crust shaped into three rectangles. The crust pieces were baked for a few minutes while a filling of sugar, cream, butter, and slivered almonds was prepared. The filling was divided among the three layers of crust and then baked. I am hoping that someone can help me.

Carol Doyle
Surrey, British Columbia

Are you looking for a special recipe? Let other *Cook's Country* readers help. Just send us your requests, and we will print as many of them as we can. Write to Looking for a Recipe, Cook's Country, P.O. Box 470739, Brookline, MA 02447, or send an e-mail to lookingforarecipe@bcpress.com. If you can help with one of the above requests, contact us at the same postal or e-mail address. We will post responses on www.cookscountry.com.

Find the Rooster! A tiny version of this rooster has been hidden somewhere in the pages of this issue. If you find it, write to us with its location (plus your name and address), and you will be entered into a random drawing. The first winning entry drawn will receive the Braun PowerMax Blender (our test winner—see page 31), and the next five winners will each receive a one-year subscription to *Cook's Country*. To enter the contest, write to us at Rooster, Cook's Country, P.O. Box 470739, Brookline, MA 02447, or e-mail us at rooster@bcpress.com. Entries are due by July 15, 2005.

Did you find the rooster in the April/May 2005 issue? It was hidden in the Cracker Jack cupcake pictured on page 27. Christine Owen of Shorewood, Ill., spotted it, and she won a Rival Cool Touch Deep Fryer.

Simply Supper

We would like to share some of our favorite quick supper recipes with you—the kind of food we make at home to feed our families. We have printed these recipes on cards so that you can collect and organize them. We hope you like these recipes as much as we do.

Luau Kebabs

Sautéed Zucchini and Corn with Chives

Shanghai Chicken Salad

Antipasto Heroes

Summer Berry Bake

Roasted German Potato Salad

Mediterranean Couscous Salad

Shrimp Piccata Pasta

Simply Supper MAIN COURSE

LUAU KEBABS

Simply Supper SIDE DISH

SAUTÉED ZUCCHINI AND CORN WITH CHIVES

Simply Supper MAIN COURSE

SHANGHAI CHICKEN SALAD

Simply Supper MAIN COURSE

ANTIPASTO HEROES

SAUTÉED ZUCCHINI AND CORN WITH CHIVES SERVES 4

Zucchini need a good squeeze to rid them of excess moisture. Look for smaller zucchini at the supermarket; they are much more flavorful and less watery than their larger counterparts. This recipe also works with frozen corn. Simply defrost the corn and add it during the last minute or two of cooking time.

- 4 medium zucchini, ends trimmed
- 3 tablespoons unsalted butter
- 1 medium shallot, minced
- 2 medium ears sweet corn, kernels cut away with a knife
- 1 tablespoon minced fresh chives
  Salt and pepper

1. Shred zucchini on large holes of box grater or with shredding disk of food processor. Wrap shredded zucchini in triple layer of paper towels and squeeze out excess liquid.

2. Heat butter in large nonstick skillet over medium-high heat. When foaming subsides, add shallot and cook, stirring occasionally, until soft, 2 to 3 minutes. Add zucchini and corn and cook, stirring occasionally, until tender, 6 to 8 minutes. Stir in chives and season to taste with salt and pepper. Serve.

LUAU KEBABS SERVES 4 TO 6

You can configure the kebabs any way you like, but be sure to skewer the cubes of pork between two pieces of pineapple. The pineapple helps to tenderize and flavor the pork.

- 1¾ pounds boneless center-cut pork chops, about 1¼ inches thick
- ¼ cup plus 2 tablespoons extra-virgin olive oil
- 3 medium garlic cloves, minced
- 2 tablespoons soy sauce
  Salt and pepper
- 1 large pineapple, peeled, cored, and cut into 1-inch chunks
- 2 red bell peppers, stemmed, seeded, and cut into 1-inch pieces
- 1 large red onion, peeled and cut into 1-inch pieces

1. Cut pork chops into 1¼-inch cubes. Combine ¼ cup oil, garlic, soy sauce, ¾ teaspoon salt, and ½ teaspoon pepper in medium bowl. Add pork cubes, toss to coat, and marinate for 15 minutes. Toss pineapple, peppers, and onion with remaining 2 tablespoons oil in medium bowl and season with salt and pepper.

2. Thread pork, pineapple, peppers, and onion onto eight 12-inch metal skewers. Brush skewers with any remaining marinade.

3. Grill kebabs over high heat, turning skewers, until pork is well browned and cooked through, 8 to 10 minutes. Serve.

ANTIPASTO HEROES SERVES 4

Traditional Italian antipasto ingredients make a hearty sandwich filling. Weighting the sandwiches makes these filled-to-the-brim heroes easier to eat, but if you're really hungry, you can omit this step. If your market sells very long baguettes, use just one.

- 1 (14-ounce) can artichoke hearts, drained, rinsed, and patted dry
- 1 medium garlic clove, peeled
- 4 tablespoons extra-virgin olive oil
  Salt and pepper
- ¾ cup jarred roasted red peppers, chopped
- 5 pepperoncini, rinsed and finely chopped
- ½ cup chopped black olives
- 2 (12-inch-long) baguettes
- 2 cups arugula leaves
- ½ pound thinly sliced hard salami or cappicola
- 8 ounces fresh mozzarella, thinly sliced

1. In food processor or blender, puree artichokes, garlic, and 2 tablespoons oil until smooth paste forms. Transfer to small bowl and season with salt and pepper.

2. Combine red peppers, pepperoncini, black olives, and remaining 2 tablespoons oil in medium bowl.

3. Slice baguettes in half lengthwise and pull out most of soft crumb from tops and bottoms. Spread artichoke paste on both sides of bread.

4. Fill bottom cavities of bread with pepper mixture. Layer with arugula, meat, and cheese, place tops of bread over bottom, and press firmly. Wrap each sandwich tightly in foil and weight down using heavy object (canned tomatoes are perfect) for 1 to 3 hours. Unwrap sandwiches, cut each in half, and serve.

SHANGHAI CHICKEN SALAD SERVES 4

Chow mein noodles, hoisin sauce, and toasted sesame oil can all be found in the international aisle of the supermarket.

- ½ cup rice vinegar
- 3 tablespoons plus ⅓ cup soy sauce
- ⅓ cup hoisin sauce
- 1½ tablespoons grated fresh ginger
- ¼ cup toasted sesame oil
- 1½ pounds boneless, skinless chicken breasts, trimmed, with tenderloins removed
  Salt and pepper
- ½ head Napa or Chinese cabbage, shredded
- 1 large red bell pepper, stemmed, seeded, and thinly sliced
- 1 bunch scallions, thinly sliced on diagonal
- 1 cup chow mein noodles

1. Whisk vinegar, 3 tablespoons soy sauce, hoisin sauce, ginger, and sesame oil together in medium bowl. Place chicken in single layer in Dutch oven. Pour ½ cup vinegar mixture over chicken breasts; reserve remaining vinegar mixture to use as dressing. Add remaining ⅓ cup soy sauce and 3 cups water to pot. Bring to boil over high heat. Cover, reduce heat to low, and simmer chicken until cooked through, 7 to 10 minutes.

2. Transfer chicken to plate, cover loosely with plastic wrap, and refrigerate until cool enough to handle. Shred chicken into long, thin strands using two forks or fingers.

3. Transfer chicken to large serving bowl, toss with 2 tablespoons dressing, and season with salt and pepper. Add cabbage, bell pepper, scallions, and remaining dressing and toss to combine. Sprinkle with chow mein noodles and serve.

SUMMER BERRY BAKE

ROASTED GERMAN POTATO SALAD

MEDITERRANEAN COUSCOUS SALAD

SHRIMP PICCATA PASTA

ROASTED GERMAN POTATO SALAD SERVES 4 TO 6

This bacon-dressed potato salad tastes best when served warm or at room temperature and makes a natural accompaniment to grilled pork. If your bacon does not render 1/4 cup of fat, add olive oil to get to 1/4 cup.

- 2 pounds red potatoes, scrubbed and cut into 1-inch pieces
- 3 tablespoons extra-virgin olive oil
- Salt and pepper
- 8 strips bacon, chopped
- 1 medium onion, finely chopped
- 1/2 teaspoon sugar
- 1/2 cup white vinegar
- 1/2 cup water
- 1 tablespoon whole-grain German-style mustard
- 1/4 cup chopped fresh parsley

1. Adjust oven rack to middle position and heat oven to 425 degrees. Toss potatoes with oil in medium bowl and season generously with salt and pepper. Roast potatoes in single layer in shallow roasting pan, tossing potatoes once or twice, until golden brown and skins are wrinkled, 30 to 40 minutes. Transfer to large serving bowl.

2. Meanwhile, fry bacon in large skillet over medium heat until crisp, about 7 minutes. Using slotted spoon, transfer bacon to plate lined with paper towels. Discard all but 1/4 cup fat, return skillet to medium heat, and add onion. Cook until onion is softened and just beginning to brown, about 4 minutes. Add sugar and stir until dissolved, about 30 seconds. Add vinegar and water, increase heat to high, bring to boil, and cook until mixture is reduced to about 3/4 cup, 6 to 8 minutes. Off heat, whisk in mustard and 1/4 teaspoon pepper. Pour dressing over warm potatoes. Add parsley and bacon and toss to combine; adjust seasonings with salt and pepper. Serve warm or at room temperature.

SUMMER BERRY BAKE SERVES 4

Prepared lemon curd can be found on the supermarket shelves near the jams and preserves. If you haven't removed your cream cheese from the refrigerator to bring it to room temperature, you can microwave it for 10 seconds on full power to soften.

- 4 ounces (1/2 package) cream cheese, at room temperature
- 1/4 cup lemon curd
- 1/4 cup sour cream
- 2 cups fresh raspberries
- 1 cup fresh blueberries
- 1/4 cup packed light brown sugar

1. Adjust oven rack to sit 7 inches below broiler element and heat broiler.

2. Whisk cream cheese, lemon curd, and sour cream in medium bowl until smooth.

3. Scatter berries in 1-quart broilersafe gratin dish or tart pan. Spoon cream mixture over berries and gently spread so that mixture covers berries completely. Sprinkle brown sugar evenly over surface, place in oven, and broil until sugar is bubbly and caramelized, 2 to 4 minutes. Serve warm.

SHRIMP PICCATA PASTA SERVES 4

Be sure to toss the shrimp and sauce with the pasta immediately after draining. The hot pasta will heat the shrimp and melt the butter.

- 2 tablespoons extra-virgin olive oil
- 1 pound large shrimp, peeled, deveined, and halved lengthwise
- 4 medium garlic cloves, minced
- 1/8 teaspoon red pepper flakes
- 1/2 cup dry white wine
- 1 (8-ounce) bottle clam broth
- 3 tablespoons lemon juice
- Salt
- 1 pound linguini
- 3 tablespoons drained small capers
- 1/3 cup chopped fresh parsley
- 4 tablespoons unsalted butter, softened
- Pepper

1. Bring 4 quarts water to boil in pot for cooking pasta. Meanwhile, heat 1 tablespoon oil in large skillet over high heat. Add shrimp and cook, stirring, until just opaque, about 1 minute. Transfer to large plate. Heat remaining tablespoon oil in empty skillet over medium heat. Add garlic and pepper flakes and cook until fragrant but not browned, about 30 seconds. Add wine, increase heat to high, and simmer until liquid is reduced and syrupy, about 2 minutes. Add clam broth and lemon juice, bring to boil, and cook until mixture is reduced to 1/3 cup, about 8 minutes.

2. As the sauce cooks, add 1 tablespoon salt and pasta to boiling water and cook until al dente. Reserving 1/2 cup cooking water, drain pasta, then transfer to large serving bowl. Toss with sauce, shrimp, capers, parsley, and butter until butter melts and shrimp is warmed through. (Add reserved cooking water if sauce seems dry.) Adjust seasonings with salt and pepper. Serve.

MEDITERRANEAN COUSCOUS SALAD SERVES 4

A soft and porous pasta, couscous absorbs the lemon and olive oil in this inviting salad. Serve this summery side dish with grilled chicken or fish.

- 2 cups water
- 1 1/2 cups couscous
- Salt
- 3 tablespoons lemon juice
- 1 medium garlic clove, minced
- 1/3 cup extra-virgin olive oil
- 1 (16-ounce) can chickpeas, drained and rinsed
- 1/2 cup chopped fresh parsley
- 3 medium scallions, chopped
- 4 ounces feta cheese, crumbled
- Pepper

1. Bring water to boil in medium saucepan. Remove from heat, add couscous and 3/4 teaspoon salt, and stir. Cover and let stand 10 minutes. Transfer couscous to serving bowl and fluff with fork.

2. Meanwhile, whisk together lemon juice, garlic, and oil in small bowl. Add lemon juice mixture and chickpeas to couscous, toss well to combine, and cool to room temperature, about 20 minutes. Toss in parsley, scallions, and feta. Adjust seasonings with salt and pepper. Serve at room temperature.

Triple-Chocolate Cookies

Dear Cook's Country,
The triple-chocolate cookies from a nearby bakery are really chewy and have an intense chocolate flavor. But when I have tried to make these cookies at home, I've gotten chocolate overkill—a gooey, sugary thing closer to fudge than a cookie. Can you help?

Dottie Naylor, Durango, Colo.

Dear Dottie,
The most common trio of chocolates used to make triple-chocolate cookies consists of unsweetened, bittersweet, and semisweet. The unsweetened chocolate adds intense, earthy chocolate flavor (think brownies); the bittersweet adds a sophisticated, rich chocolate flavor; and the semisweet balances the two more bitter chocolates.

At least that's the theory behind this recipe. In reality, many recipe writers seem to believe this cookie is an excuse for excess. A triple-chocolate cookie shouldn't be a case of death by chocolate. All the same, this cookie ought to be rich and intense. But how do you build in so much chocolate and not end up with—as you say—a piece of fudge?

Most cookies are made by creaming butter and sugar, then adding eggs and the dry ingredients. This method simply won't work with triple-chocolate cookies—there's no place to add all of that melted chocolate. The brownie method—melt chocolate and butter, add sugar, then eggs, then flour—was the most common choice in the recipes I found, but I had trouble getting the cookies to hold their shape.

I had better luck beating the eggs and sugar together until fluffy, then adding the melted chocolate along with the melted butter, and adding the dry ingredients last. Beating the eggs and sugar for four minutes gave the batter more structure. When baked, the cookies had a crisp shell, kind of like a meringue cookie, that tasters really liked.

Tasters liked a relatively small amount of unsweetened chocolate (too much was overpowering) balanced by equal amounts of bittersweet and semisweet. I found that premium bittersweet bar chocolates were actually too rich (and too greasy) for this recipe. I had better luck with bittersweet chocolate chips, which contain less fat than bittersweet chocolate bars. The melted chips improved the batter by making it less fluid, yet they also added the same grown-up, not-to-sweet flavor as the bittersweet bar chocolates.

The semisweet chocolate is the buffer that rounds out the harsh edges of the bittersweet and unsweetened. But when I added even a small amount of melted semisweet chocolate, the cookies became gooey and cloying. After much trial and error, I hit upon a novel idea. I added the semisweet chocolate in chip form once the batter was assembled. Because the chips softened but did not melt in the oven, they added chocolate flavor without increasing the fluidity of the batter or harming the texture of the cookies.

My final recipe contains 1⅓ pounds of chocolate. Although most kids will like these cookies with a glass of milk, the grown-ups in the test kitchen enjoyed them straight up. Talk about chocolate decadence!

–Stephanie Alleyne

TRIPLE-CHOCOLATE COOKIES MAKES 26 COOKIES

The key to the fudgy texture of these cookies is letting them cool directly on the baking sheets. Avoid using bittersweet bar chocolate—the cookies will be too rich and won't hold their shape.

- 3 ounces unsweetened chocolate, chopped
- 1½ cups bittersweet chocolate chips
- 7 tablespoons unsalted butter, cut into pieces
- 2 teaspoons instant coffee
- 2 teaspoons vanilla extract
- 3 large eggs, at room temperature
- 1 cup sugar
- ½ cup all-purpose flour
- ½ teaspoon baking powder
- ½ teaspoon salt
- 1½ cups semisweet chocolate chips

1. Melt unsweetened chocolate, bittersweet chips, and butter in heatproof bowl set over saucepan of simmering water, stirring frequently, until completely smooth and glossy. Remove bowl from pan and set aside to cool slightly.

2. Stir coffee powder and vanilla extract together in small bowl until dissolved. Beat eggs and sugar in large bowl with electric mixer at medium-high speed until very thick and pale, about 4 minutes. Add vanilla-coffee mixture and beat until incorporated, 20 seconds. Reduce speed to low, add chocolate mixture, and mix until thoroughly combined, about 30 seconds.

3. Whisk flour, baking powder, and salt together in medium bowl. Using large rubber spatula, fold flour mixture and semisweet chips into batter. Cover bowl with plastic wrap and let stand at room temperature for 20 to 30 minutes until batter firms up (it will more closely resemble thick brownie batter than cookie dough).

4. Meanwhile, adjust two oven racks to upper- and lower-middle positions and heat oven to 350 degrees. Line two large baking sheets with parchment paper. Using 1 heaping tablespoon batter per cookie, place cookies 2 inches apart on prepared baking sheets (see photo, right). Bake until cookies are shiny and cracked on top, 11 to 14 minutes, rotating baking sheets top to bottom and front to back halfway through baking time. Transfer baking sheets to racks and cool cookies completely, on baking sheets, before serving.

With their crackled tops and chewy texture, these cookies are similar to brownies.

How to ARRANGE COOKIES

By staggering the rows of cookie batter, it's easy to fit 13 cookies on a single large baking sheet.

Hold Your Horses
Right from the mixer, my test recipes were a bit messy to portion out. I thought about using the refrigerator to stiffen the batter. Happily, as I weighed my options, the solution emerged before my eyes. Letting the batter sit on the counter for 20 to 30 minutes did the trick. Although not as dry as regular cookie dough, this batter could now be scooped neatly onto a baking sheet.

All-American
French Dressing

Linda Smith's favorite hobbies are gardening, spending time outdoors, and painting. She is always looking for new recipes to serve with her garden-fresh vegetables.

Dear Cook's Country,
My husband, Andy, loves good restaurant versions of French dressing. Not vinaigrette, but the creamy red dressing he grew up with. He thinks bottled French dressing is too sweet and doesn't have enough zip. I've tried some recipes at home, but none have worked just right.

Linda Smith, Ithaca, N.Y.

Dear Linda,
Before Julia Child taught us about real French cooking, generations of Americans grew up on a sweet-and-sour red dressing made with ketchup and oil. Despite its name, this French dressing has its roots in America. I did some sleuthing in old cookbooks, and the earliest recipe I could find dated back to 1930 and appeared in the *Heinz Book of Salads*. (Even then, food companies were developing recipes so consumers would use their products). Hundreds of French dressing recipes filled cookbooks in the ensuing decades.

A their core, these recipes share a base of tomato (usually ketchup), vegetable oil, vinegar, and sugar. Most of the ones that I tried were too sweet and too bland. I decided to examine each ingredient to improve the overall flavor of this simple salad dressing.

I found recipes calling for everything from chili sauce to tomato paste. The version made with chili sauce tasted, not surprisingly, like chili sauce, and neither tomato juice (not tomatoey enough) nor tomato paste (too tomatoey) tasted right. Ketchup it was. I guess there's no arguing with Heinz.

Ketchup is already sweet, so adding more sugar can be problematic. Many recipes measure the sugar by the cupful. I found that 2 tablespoons was plenty. The typical recipe also calls for distilled white vinegar, but I sought something more flavorful. Lemon juice made the dressing taste like a Bloody Mary—not bad served in a frosty glass but less than ideal when tossed over greens. A batch made with cider vinegar had a distinctive apple flavor that tasters either loved or hated. White wine vinegar, which provided fruitiness with a kick, was the favorite.

I wanted to keep prep work to a minimum, but grated onion, an ingredient in several older recipes I found, added a sweet, sharp depth. A little Tabasco sauce perked up the other flavors. Although these changes are fairly simple, they yield a dressing with more personality than anything you can buy.

–Keri Fisher

ALL-AMERICAN FRENCH DRESSING
MAKES 1 CUP
Odds are that you have everything you need in the pantry to make this quick and easy salad dressing. Use the large holes of a box grater to grate the onion, and remember that a little bit of grated onion goes a long way. This dressing is traditionally served with iceberg or other mild lettuces such as green leaf, red leaf, romaine, Boston, or Bibb. We think its sweet-and-sour punch also works well with bitter greens, such as Belgian endive, radicchio, and watercress.

- 1/2 cup ketchup
- 1/2 cup vegetable or canola oil
- 1/4 cup white wine vinegar or distilled white vinegar
- 2 tablespoons sugar
- 1 teaspoon grated onion
- 1/4 teaspoon Tabasco sauce (or more to taste)

Add all ingredients to lidded container and shake vigorously until combined. (Dressing can be refrigerated in airtight container for 1 week.)

This sweet-and-sour red dressing may have a foreign name, but its origins date back 75 years to Pittsburgh.

Washing Greens 101

Simply rinsing greens under running water doesn't always remove the dirt that collects in crevices and folds. That's why we use a salad spinner for both washing and drying salad greens. Place the greens in a salad spinner, with the basket in its bowl. Fill the bowl with water, swirl the greens, and then lift the basket out of the bowl, leaving the sediment behind. If your greens are especially dirty, do this several times. Be sure to rinse the bowl before returning the basket to spin the greens dry. After spinning, we like to blot greens dry with paper towels because we have found that even the best salad spinners don't dry greens completely. If you don't plan on using the greens immediately, you can refrigerate them in the spinner bowl with the lid firmly in place for several days.

The French Connection

Enjoy our All-American French Dressing over your favorite salad greens, or make it work overtime as a base for other recipes. –K.F.

CREAMY FRENCH DRESSING
MAKES 1 1/4 CUPS
Mayonnaise tones down the kick of the vinegar and makes this creamy orange dressing more kid-friendly.

- 1 cup All-American French Dressing
- 1/4 cup mayonnaise

Whisk dressing and mayonnaise together in bowl until smooth. (Dressing can be refrigerated in airtight container for 1 week.)

FRENCH DIP
MAKES ABOUT 2 1/2 CUPS

- 8 ounces cream cheese, at room temperature
- 1 cup sour cream
- 1/2 teaspoon Tabasco sauce
- 1 cup All-American French Dressing

Whisk cream cheese, sour cream, and Tabasco together in bowl until smooth. Add dressing and whisk to combine. Cover and refrigerate until thick, 1 to 2 hours. (Dip can be refrigerated in airtight container for 1 week.)

SPECIAL SAUCE
MAKES 1 1/2 CUPS
Sweet pickle relish is the secret to our "special" sauce, which is a natural topping for sandwiches or our Ultimate Hamburger (page 26). Be sure to drain the pickle relish in a mesh sieve so that the sauce is not too thin.

- 1 cup mayonnaise
- 1/2 cup All-American French Dressing
- 1/4 cup sweet pickle relish, drained well

Whisk all ingredients in bowl until combined. (Sauce can be refrigerated in airtight container for 1 week.)

Getting to Know Salad Greens

Even the most basic supermarket now stocks an array of lettuces and salad greens. Here's our take on today's most popular choices. When matching greens with a specific dressing, keep two factors in mind: texture and flavor. While thin dressings (such as vinaigrettes) can work with almost any salad green, thick, creamy dressings are best with sturdier greens—romaine and iceberg rather than baby spinach or watercress. As for flavor, you can serve milder dressings with any kind of green, but bolder dressings should be matched with something spicy.

Arugula
ROCKET POWER
Long a staple of Italian cuisine, arugula (also known as rocket) is sold in small bunches with the roots still attached. Bitter and peppery, it's best in modest quantities.

Bibb
LIKE BUTTER
This butterhead lettuce is characterized by a loose head and bright green leaves. Bibb is smaller than Boston, but they are interchangeable. Both have a mild, almost sweet flavor that makes them very adaptable.

Boston
WICKED SWEET
This butterhead lettuce is similar to Bibb, with the same mild, sweet flavor but with larger, looser, more tender leaves.

Chicory
NOT SHY
Chicory, related to the endive family, has a strong, assertively bitter flavor, especially in the larger outer leaves. We like the mellower, more tender inner leaves. Use in combination with a sweeter, milder green.

Belgian Endive
CLASSY CONTINENTAL
Crisp and refreshing, these spear-shaped leaves have a bitter but not pungent flavor. To keep it white, Belgian endive is grown without light. Purchase when the tips have just started to yellow.

Escarole
EARTHY, WITH A BITE
Escarole is mildly bitter, but less so than chicory or Belgian endive. Often cooked in Italian soups and pasta dishes, escarole makes a fine salad green, especially when matched with an assertive vinaigrette.

Frisée
FEATHERED FRIEND
From the French for "curled," this aptly named green, which is a member of the chicory family, has a very subtle peppery kick and a festive shape. Mix with mild lettuces to make this pricey green go further.

Green or Red Leaf
SANDWICH STAPLE
Mild and somewhat sweet, this widely available supermarket green is great on sandwiches or as the base for a salad. Use green and red leaf lettuces interchangeably.

Iceberg
COMEBACK KID
Iceberg has been enjoying a renaissance, thanks to its clean, slightly sweet flavor and crisp texture. The leaves hold a lot of water, which some cooks don't like, but others find iceberg refreshing, especially in summer. It works well with thick, creamy dressings.

Mâche
A BUTTERY ACCENT
Small, delicate, and pricey, this restaurant darling, also known as lamb's lettuce, has a mildly nutty flavor and a very tender texture. It's quite perishable and so must be used quickly. Don't overwhelm its mild flavor by matching it with bold-tasting greens.

Mesclun
MIX IT UP
This blend of baby greens (the name derives from the French for "mixture") varies by producer and retailer but typically includes some mix of baby spinach, radicchio, arugula, mâche, baby oak leaf, frisée, and herbs. Look for mixes with a variety of greens.

Radicchio
COLORFUL AND ASSERTIVE
Another member of the chicory family, radicchio looks like a miniature red cabbage. It is assertive, with hints of onion or cabbage and a peppery bitterness. Use with other greens to add a burst of color and flavor.

Romaine
DRESSES WELL
Best known for its starring role in Caesar salad, romaine lettuce is crisp, like iceberg, but with a sweeter flavor. Its many ridges and channels hold creamy dressings well. When freshest, heads will be firm and relatively light in color.

Spinach
STURDY STANDARD
Popeye's favorite is pungent, grassy, and, of course, full of iron. Spinach is fine as a stand-alone or as an accent to other greens. Buttery and sweet baby spinach is best in salads; save larger leaves with thicker stalks for cooking.

Watercress
A TASTE OF GREEN
This grassy-tasting green is slightly peppery, with hints of citrus and mustard. Small round leaves and crisp stems make watercress perfect for sandwiches. Pairs nicely with less assertive lettuces, but can stand on its own.

A New Twist on Sweet Tea

No More Bitter Tea

Boiling water makes iced tea that's bitter and cloudy. For the smoothest flavor and clearest appearance, use room-temperature water to brew the tea. Knot the tea-bag strings together for easy removal and don't squeeze the bags before discarding them; doing so releases bitter tannins. Plain Lipton tea bags are the test kitchen favorite.

Pitchers of chilled, sweet iced tea were as much a part of my North Carolina childhood as the constant humidity. Iced tea should be perfectly clear and extra-smooth, without any bitterness. When I tried conventional brewing methods, using boiling or near-boiling water, my iced tea often came out bitter and cloudy. When I was a kid, my mother always started her iced tea by making sun tea. Could I make smooth, clear tea more quickly and without the sun?

Steeping tea overnight in the refrigerator produced beautifully clear results, but the flavor was too weak. I had better luck with room-temperature water on the counter. The trick was to use more tea bags than usual. Instead of 6 bags for 4 cups of water (a standard ratio), I found I had to use 10 bags.

I tried adding fruit juice to the brewed tea, but the flavor was one-dimensional and the tea barely sweet. I solved the problem by adding simple sugar syrup (white sugar heated with water), along with the fruit juice. And, to add some pizazz, I infused my syrup with citrus zest (lemon, lime, or orange) or cinnamon sticks. This is key to making flavored sweet teas that really sparkle.

I think my teas taste much better than sugary bottled brews, with their artificial flavors and ingredients. Best of all, you can mix and match fruit juices and simple syrups to make your own fun flavors. **–Cali Todd**

Iced tea with wild flavor combinations doesn't have to come from a bottle. You can make your own sweet tea using homemade sugar syrups and fruit juices.

SWEET ICED TEA
MAKES 2 QUARTS

- 10 tea bags
- 4 cups water, at room temperature
- 2 cups juice
- 6–9 tablespoons Simple Syrup (see box, below)

1. Submerge tea bags in water in serving pitcher. Steep for 45 minutes. Remove and discard tea bags.

2. Stir juice and Simple Syrup (adjust amount depending on desired sweetness) into tea. Serve over ice.

CHERRY LIME RICKEY ICED TEA
Make Sweet Iced Tea with 2 cups cherry juice and Lime Syrup.

APPLE PIE ICED TEA
Make Sweet Iced Tea with 2 cups apple juice and Cinnamon Syrup.

NANTUCKET ICED TEA
Make Sweet Iced Tea with 2 cups cranberry juice and Lime Syrup.

ORANGEADE ICED TEA
Make Sweet Iced Tea with 2 cups lemonade and Orange Syrup.

RAZ-MA-TAZZ ICED TEA
Make Sweet Iced Tea with 2 cups cranberry-raspberry juice and Lemon Syrup.

SIMPLE SYRUP FOR ICED TEA
MAKES ABOUT 1 CUP

In the test kitchen, we keep sugar syrup in the refrigerator at all times during the summer. This recipe makes enough syrup for two pitchers of iced tea and can be doubled if you go through a lot of iced tea in your household.

Heat 1 cup sugar, 1 cup water, and flavorings (see below) in small saucepan over medium-high heat until sugar completely dissolves, about 5 minutes. Cool to room temperature. Strain and discard zest or remove and discard cinnamon stick, if using. Syrup can be refrigerated for 1 week.

ORANGE, LIME, OR LEMON SYRUP
Add 1 tablespoon grated citrus zest.

CINNAMON SYRUP
Add 1 cinnamon stick.

Regional Favorites: Denver Omelet

No one wants to be a short-order cook at home, making one omelet after another. But can you make a single omelet big enough to feed four? My "eight-egg monster," as my test kitchen colleagues dubbed it, has a lacy, browned exterior and soft, tender center filled with ham steak, sautéed peppers and onions, and melted Jack cheese. The trick to cooking a super-sized omelet involves the skillet lid and low heat. To perfect your omelet-shaping skills, see the photos on page 29. – Charles Kelsey

FAMILY-STYLE DENVER OMELET
SERVES 4

Make sure to chop the filling ingredients finely; if you don't, the eggs won't set properly and the omelet will fall apart.

- 4 tablespoons unsalted butter
- 4 ounces ham steak, trimmed and finely chopped
- 1/2 red bell pepper, finely chopped (about 1/2 cup)
- 1/2 green bell pepper, finely chopped (about 1/2 cup)
- 1 small onion, minced
- 8 large eggs, well beaten
  Salt and pepper
- 1 cup shredded Monterey Jack cheese
  Tabasco sauce, for serving

1. Melt 1 tablespoon butter in large nonstick skillet over medium-high heat. Add ham steak and cook until lightly browned, about 3 minutes. Add peppers and onion and cook until browned around edges, 6 to 7 minutes.

2. Reduce heat to medium and stir in 2 tablespoons butter. Once butter melts, pour in eggs, and season with salt and pepper. Cook, without stirring, until edges just begin to set, about 5 seconds, then, with rubber spatula, stir in circular motion until slightly thickened, 30 to 60 seconds. Using spatula, pull cooked edges toward center of pan, tilting pan to one side so that uncooked egg runs to edge of pan. Repeat until bottom of omelet is just set but top is still very runny, about 1 minute.

3. Cover skillet with lid, reduce heat to low, and cook until top of omelet is beginning to set but still moist, 3 to 5 minutes. Remove pan from heat and sprinkle omelet with cheese. Cover and let pan sit off heat until cheese is partially melted, about 1 minute.

4. Tilt pan and, using spatula, push half of omelet onto serving platter. Tilt pan so omelet flips onto itself and forms half-moon. Spread remaining tablespoon butter on omelet and let rest 1 minute before serving with Tabasco.

...e American Table: You Say Denver, I Say Western

People who live in the West usually call this hearty diner staple a Denver omelet, but in the East it's often called a Western omelet. Whatever you call it, this omelet has a filling that is traditionally mixed in with the eggs, a technique carried over from the dish's origins as a sandwich filling between slices of buttered white bread. If you want to avoid the whole Denver versus Western issue, just order "a cowboy with spurs" the next time you're eating out. If the waitress knows her diner lingo, she'll serve your omelet (Denver or Western) with a side of fries.

Quick Cooking
GOOD MEALS IN ABOUT 30 MINUTES

An exotic but easy meal from the Mediterranean

PAN-FRIED PORK CUTLETS WITH ORANGE AND GREEN OLIVE SALSA SERVES 4
A vibrant orange and green olive salsa adds sparkle to breaded pork cutlets.

- 2 seedless oranges, peeled, pith removed with knife, and orange segments cut into 1/4-inch pieces
- 1 cup pimento-stuffed olives, chopped
- 1 medium garlic clove, minced
- 2 tablespoons chopped fresh parsley
- 1 tablespoon olive oil
  Salt and pepper
- 1/2 cup all-purpose flour
- 1 cup plain bread crumbs
- 2 large eggs
- 4 boneless pork chops, about 1/2 inch thick
- 1/2 cup vegetable oil

1. Toss oranges, olives, garlic, parsley, and olive oil in small bowl. Season salsa with salt and pepper.

2. Place flour and bread crumbs in separate shallow bowls. Beat eggs with fork in third bowl.

3. Season pork chops with salt and pepper. One at a time, dip chops first in flour, then in egg, and finally in bread crumbs, pressing down to adhere crumbs. Set pork chops aside in single layer on large plate.

4. Heat vegetable oil in large nonstick skillet over medium-high heat until shimmering. Place chops in skillet, lower heat to medium, and cook until crisp on both sides, 4 to 6 minutes. Drain chops on paper towels, transfer to platter, and serve with salsa.

SPINACH ORZO SERVES 4
Add the orzo to the boiling water a couple of minutes before slipping the pork chops into the hot oil.

- Salt
- 1 cup orzo
- 4 cups baby spinach
- 2 tablespoons olive oil
- 1 medium garlic clove, minced
- 1/2 teaspoon grated lemon zest
  Pepper

1. Bring 3 quarts water to boil in large pot over high heat. Add 1 teaspoon salt and orzo and cook until al dente. Reserve 1/4 cup cooking water and drain orzo.

2. Meanwhile, place spinach, oil, garlic, and lemon zest in large serving bowl. Add drained orzo and toss to coat, adding reserved cooking water as necessary, until spinach is wilted. Adjust seasonings with salt and pepper. Serve.

Aaron Oppenheimer played in a band before he began working full-time. Aaron still plays the banjo, and he likes to impress his new wife with his cooking.

A Spicy Taste of the Tropics

Dear Cook's Country,

My wife, Virginia, and I returned a month ago from our honeymoon in Jamaica, and I'm already in jerk chicken withdrawal. I've tried recipes from cookbooks and the Internet, but they either called for ingredients I couldn't find or were just plain bland—not hot enough for me. Is there a way to make spicy jerk chicken at home, or do I have to go back to Jamaica for a second honeymoon?

Aaron Oppenheimer, Gaithersburg, Md.

Dear Aaron,

I'm a jerk junkie, too. The marriage of hot chiles, warm spices, and a cool Red Stripe beer is my vision of island paradise. Jerk paste is a combination of ground chiles, herbs, and spices. This centuries-old preparation is believed to have first been used by escaped Jamaican slaves to cook wild boar. Nowadays, jerk is popular around the world, especially when the paste is used to flavor grilled chicken.

All of the recipes I found called for either jalapeño or habanero chiles. Both have great flavor, but I was surprised by the differences in the ways they carry their heat. The jalapeños would smack you in the lips and then fade, while the habaneros would lull you gently to sleep and then burn, baby, burn. I settled on the habaneros because I, for one, wanted the burn to last.

Next I turned my attention to the spices, herbs, and aromatics (onions, garlic, and the like). Allspice, the predominant spice in jerk, is so named because its flavor is reminiscent of several spices: clove, cinnamon, and nutmeg. It was a must, along with garlic. Onion was tasty but added too much moisture and inhibited browning on the grill; instead, I added scallions to get the oniony flavor without the excess moisture. After I included thyme for its robust aroma, my paste was potent but problematic: It was becoming a veritable town meeting of type-A spices, and they all wanted the floor.

Vegetable oil helped quiet the room, but my paste still lacked finesse. I had seen several recipes that called for molasses. Sure enough, its dark, smoky flavor subdued the other ingredients. Molasses also transformed my paste from dry and gritty to smooth and spreadable.

Some recipes call for marinating the chicken for days—a step I wanted to skip. But my first attempt at a "quick" two-hour marinade was disastrous. The thickly smeared paste burned and fell off as soon as the chicken hit the grill. Worse still, the meat below the skin was bland; a two-hour marinade wasn't enough. Letting the chicken marinate overnight helped—the jerk paste had time to work its magic on the meat—but most of the paste was still burning and falling off the skin.

I realized that if I wanted the paste to flavor the meat more quickly, I would have to lift up the skin and rub the spices directly on the meat. This technique produced dramatic results, cutting the minimum marinating time from 24 hours to two. (For even more flavor, I could still marinate the chicken overnight, but this step was now optional.)

I had one last problem: The skin was burning before the meat near the bone was cooking through. The solution was

Jerk chicken is an island favorite that travels well. Cool down the heat with some grilled pineapple.

on the side: COOL FRUIT SALSA

GRILLED BANANA AND RED ONION SALSA
MAKES ABOUT 3 CUPS

Grill the bananas and red onions alongside the chicken and then use them to make this salsa at the last minute. Slightly underripe bananas hold their shape especially well on the grill.

- 1 large red onion, peeled and cut into ½-inch rounds
- 3 bananas, peeled and halved lengthwise
- 2 tablespoons vegetable oil
- ½ teaspoon ground cumin
  Salt and pepper
- 2 tablespoons lime juice
- 2 tablespoons chopped fresh mint
- 1 tablespoon light brown sugar
- 1 tablespoon dark rum (optional)

This cool fruit salsa is the perfect accompaniment to fiery jerk chicken. The fresh fruit flavors make for a refreshing break from the chile burn, and the bracing acidity of the vinegar intensifies the smoke flavor of the grilled chicken. In this recipe, we like the starchy sweetness of bananas, but other thickly sliced tropical fruits, including mangoes, papayas, or even pineapple, will work as well.

1. Brush both sides of onion rounds and banana halves with oil and sprinkle with cumin and salt and pepper to taste. Grill onion over hottest part of grill, covered, until well browned, 3 to 4 minutes per side. Transfer onion to cooler part of grill and place bananas, cut side down, over hottest part of grill. Grill bananas, covered, until browned in spots, about 2 minutes per side. Transfer onion and bananas to cutting board and cool slightly.

2. Whisk together lime juice, mint, brown sugar, and rum (if using) in medium bowl until sugar has dissolved. Roughly chop onion and bananas, add to bowl, and toss to coat. Season salsa to taste with salt and pepper. Serve.

---

pretty simple: a two-level fire. I began by placing the chicken skin side down over the hot part of the grill (the part with more coals) to crisp the skin. This caused the jerk paste on the exterior of the bird to char slightly—just enough to create an authentic smoky flavor. After flipping the chicken to cook it skin side up for a few minutes, I slid the chicken over to the cooler part of the grill (with fewer coals) to finish cooking. Fifteen minutes later, I had perfectly cooked jerk chicken.

When serving the chicken, I passed around some lime wedges. The tart tropical flavor of the lime mingled with the jerk beautifully, proving that with great jerk (just like marriage) the whole is greater than the sum of its parts. **– Jeremy Sauer**

EASY JERK CHICKEN
SERVES 4

If you are averse to spicy foods, remove the seeds and ribs before processing the chiles. If you cannot find habaneros, substitute 4 to 6 jalapeño chiles. This recipe can easily be doubled, but, depending on the size of your cooking grate, you may have to grill the chicken in two batches.

- 1 bunch scallions, chopped
- 3 garlic cloves, peeled
- 2 teaspoons ground allspice
- 1 tablespoon dried thyme
- 2 teaspoons salt
- 2 tablespoons molasses
- 2–3 habanero chiles, stemmed
- ¼ cup vegetable oil
- 3 pounds bone-in, skin-on chicken thighs, legs, or breasts
- 1 lime, cut into wedges

1. Puree scallions, garlic, allspice, thyme, salt, molasses, chiles, and oil in food processor or blender until almost smooth, scraping down sides if necessary. Wearing latex gloves and working with one piece of chicken at a time, slide fingers between skin and meat to loosen skin, then rub 1 tablespoon spice mixture under skin of each piece and transfer chicken to gallon-sized zipper-lock bag. Pour remaining spice mixture over chicken, seal bag, and turn bag so that chicken pieces are covered with mixture. Refrigerate for at least 2 hours or up to 36 hours.

2. Light charcoal grill. When coals are covered with thin layer of gray ash, stack them 2 to 3 briquettes high on

one side of grill and in single layer on other side. Set cooking grate in place, cover grill, and let heat 5 minutes. (If using gas grill, preheat grill, covered, with all burners on high; once grill is hot, leave one burner on high and turn other burners to low. In step 3, cook chicken covered.)

3. Remove chicken from bag and arrange skin side down over hot part of grill. Cook chicken until well browned on both sides, 3 to 5 minutes per side. Transfer chicken to cooler part of grill and continue to cook, turning occasionally, until very dark and fully cooked, 15 to 22 minutes. Serve with lime wedges.

SWEET 'N' SMOKY JERK CHICKEN

Although not a traditional Jamaican ingredient, chipotle chiles create a variation with an appealing smokiness, which is balanced nicely by the sweetness from additional molasses.

Follow recipe for Easy Jerk Chicken, increasing molasses to ¼ cup and substituting 4 chipotle chiles in adobo sauce for habanero chiles.

GOOD MEALS IN ABOUT 30 MINUTES

A refreshing main-course salad with salmon and potatoes

ZESTY SALMON AND POTATO SALAD
SERVES 4

Thanks to the microwave, the salmon cooks up juicy and tender in just minutes.

- 1 pound small red potatoes, scrubbed and halved
  Salt
- 1½ pounds salmon fillet
  Pepper
- ¼ cup chopped red onion
- ¼ cup sour cream
- ¼ cup mayonnaise
- ¼ cup chopped fresh chives
- 2 tablespoons lemon juice
- 2 tablespoons prepared horseradish
- 1 head Bibb or romaine lettuce, torn into large bite-sized pieces

1. Cover potatoes with water, add 1 teaspoon salt, and water to boil in medium saucepan over high heat. Reduce heat to medium and simmer until potatoes are tender, about 10 minutes. Drain and rinse potatoes under cold water.

2. Meanwhile, place salmon in microwave-safe dish and season with salt and pepper. Microwave on full power until fish is cooked through and flakes easily with fork, 5 to 7 minutes. Using tongs, remove and discard skin. Transfer salmon to medium bowl and cool slightly. Use 2 forks to flake fish apart. Add cooked potatoes to bowl.

3. Whisk onion, sour cream, mayonnaise, chives, lemon juice, and horseradish together in small bowl. Toss 2 tablespoons dressing with lettuce in large bowl. Toss remaining dressing with salmon and potatoes. Adjust seasonings with salt and pepper.

4. Divide lettuce among 4 plates. Top with salmon and potatoes. Serve.

Fiesta Slaw

Bistro Slaw

Spicy Peanut Slaw

Casablanca Slaw

Sassy Summer Slaws

It's hard to imagine a backyard barbecue or summer picnic that doesn't include coleslaw. But many slaws can be pretty ho-hum, tasting like mayonnaise and nothing else. I wanted to deliver recipes with more punch—and more flavor.

Cabbage makes a great slaw, but there are other options. I tried a bunch of different vegetables (and even a few fruits) before I settled on my favorites. In addition to flavor, I made my selections based on color (I wanted slaws with plenty of eye appeal) and texture (slaws should be fairly crisp). I found that carrots, bell peppers, fennel, and apples all make crunchy, tasty slaws.

Regardless of the vegetable, I noticed a difference in slaws made with finely cut or grated vegetables and those containing thicker-cut vegetables. The thinner vegetables made better slaws—they absorbed dressings easily and were crisp without being hard and overly crunchy. Many vegetables can be shredded in a food processor, but it doesn't take too much time to slice them with a knife. Another option is an inexpensive plastic V-slicer (sometimes called a mandoline). One of these handy tools can turn a head of cabbage into a pile of slaw in just a minute or two.

For dressings, I turned to bold ingredients—everything from peanut butter to frozen orange juice concentrate. I stirred in fresh herbs, sugar, and spices to make savory, sweet, tart, and spicy slaws.

One more thing to keep in mind: Slaws shed a lot of liquid if they sit in the refrigerator for too long, which can make them soggy and waterlogged. These slaws are best served right after they are made.

–Rebecca Hays

FIESTA SLAW
SERVES 4 TO 6

Although a mix of red, orange, and yellow peppers will provide the prettiest appearance, this slaw can be made with just one type of bell pepper. For a spicier slaw, do not remove the inner flesh and seeds from the jalapeño. Very thin strips of bell pepper are essential for this recipe, so make sure your knife is plenty sharp.

- 2 tablespoons juice plus ¹/₂ teaspoon grated zest from 1 lime
- 1 tablespoon vegetable oil
- 1 small garlic clove, minced
- ¹/₂ medium jalapeño chile, seeded and minced
  Salt and pepper
- 4 medium bell peppers, seeded and cut into ¹/₄-inch strips
- ¹/₃ cup minced fresh cilantro

Whisk lime juice, zest, oil, garlic, jalapeño, ¼ teaspoon salt, and ⅛ teaspoon pepper together in large bowl. Add peppers and cilantro and toss well to combine. Adjust seasonings with salt and pepper. Serve.

BISTRO SLAW
SERVES 4 TO 6

It's important to slice the fennel very thin. Use the slicing disk on a food processor or a sharp chef's knife. A sweet, crisp apple, such as a Fuji, Gala, or Braeburn, works best in this recipe. To prepare the apples, quarter and core them, then cut into ¹/₄-inch slices and, finally, into ¹/₄-inch strips.

- ¹/₂ cup mayonnaise
- ¹/₄ cup cider vinegar
- 1 tablespoon sugar
  Salt and pepper
- 2 small fennel bulbs, sliced crosswise very thin (about 6 cups)
- 2 sweet apples, cut into ¹/₄-inch strips
- 2 tablespoons minced fresh tarragon

Whisk mayonnaise, vinegar, sugar, ¼ teaspoon salt, and ⅛ teaspoon pepper together in large bowl until sugar has dissolved. Add fennel, apples, and tarragon and toss well to combine. Adjust seasonings with salt and pepper. Serve.

SPICY PEANUT SLAW
SERVES 4 TO 6

Crunchy peanut butter lends a chunky texture to this slaw, but smooth peanut butter can be used in a pinch. Use a sharp knife or a food processor fitted with a slicing blade to shred the cabbage.

- ¹/₄ cup plus 1 tablespoon crunchy peanut butter
- 2 medium garlic cloves, minced
- 1 teaspoon finely grated fresh ginger
- 1 tablespoon light brown sugar
- 1 tablespoon rice vinegar
- ¹/₄ teaspoon red pepper flakes
- 3 tablespoons hot water
- ¹/₂ medium head red cabbage, finely shredded (about 6 cups)
  Salt
- 3 scallions, thinly sliced on bias

Whisk peanut butter, garlic, ginger, brown sugar, vinegar, pepper flakes, and water together in large bowl until dressing is creamy. Add cabbage and toss well to combine. Adjust seasonings with salt, and sprinkle scallions over slaw. Serve.

CASABLANCA SLAW
SERVES 4

To shred the carrots, use the large holes on a box grater or a food processor fitted with the shredding disk. Most preshredded packaged carrots are too thick and crunchy for this recipe.

- 3 tablespoons frozen orange juice concentrate, thawed
- 1 tablespoon lemon juice
- 2 teaspoons honey
- 2 tablespoons vegetable oil
- ¹/₂ teaspoon ground coriander
  Salt
- 1 pound carrots, peeled and finely shredded (about 5 cups)
- ¹/₃ cup currants or raisins

Whisk orange juice concentrate, lemon juice, honey, oil, coriander, and ¼ teaspoon salt together in large bowl. Add carrots and currants and toss well to combine. Adjust seasonings with salt. Serve.

Skillet Lasagna

Dear Cook's Country,

I love lasagna, but it's a real labor of love—something I make only once in a while. My friend mentioned an interesting lasagna recipe she heard about that's cooked on the stovetop instead of in the oven. Do you have a recipe you could share? It sounds so easy.

Tracey Barth, Boston, Mass.

Dear Tracey,

The premise is simple—combine all of the ingredients for the sauce in a skillet, add the uncooked noodles, cover, and "bake" on the stovetop. Once the sauce has reduced to the proper consistency and the noodles are tender, add cheese and you have the flavors of lasagna in a quick weeknight casserole.

But as I soon learned, skillet lasagna—at least a good one—isn't always that easy to execute. My first attempts yielded a scorched, pasty sauce and crunchy noodles. Another lasagna was so watery my friends in the kitchen called it lasagna soup.

After fussing with various brands of prepared tomato sauces, as well as different types of canned tomatoes, I finally figured out the best combination. A large can of diced tomatoes thinned out with a little extra water gave the sauce a nicely chunky and substantial texture—and there was just enough liquid to cook the pasta. A small can of tomato sauce fortified the tomato flavor and helped hold the lasagna together.

The rest of the sauce was easy to develop—sautéed onions, garlic, and red pepper, along with a pound of ground meat. Meatloaf mix (a combination of ground beef, pork, and veal sold in one package at most supermarkets) gave the sauce the most flavor, but any ground meat (even turkey) will work.

Once I got the sauce right, cooking the noodles was easy. I broke the noodles into rough 2-inch lengths, placed them on top of the browned meat and vegetables, then poured the tomatoes over the noodles. I prefer the slightly chewier texture and ruffled appearance of regular lasagna noodles (the kind you usually boil), but no-boil noodles worked, too.

To give my stovetop lasagna a boost of flavor, I used grated Parmesan instead of bland mozzarella. I also tried stirring ricotta into the lasagna just before serving, but the lasagna turned pink and grainy. Instead, I simply dotted tablespoons-ful over the top of the lasagna and allowed the cheese to heat through for several minutes.

Finished with a little fresh basil, this free-form skillet lasagna tastes like a "real" lasagna, except that it takes only about 45 minutes prepare (from start to finish). –Julia Collin Davison

SKILLET LASAGNA

SERVES 4 TO 6

Use a 12-inch nonstick skillet with a tight-fitting lid for this recipe.

- 1 (28-ounce) can diced tomatoes
  Water
- 1 tablespoon olive oil
- 1 medium onion, minced
  Salt
- 3 garlic cloves, minced
- 1/8 teaspoon red pepper flakes
- 1 pound meatloaf mix
- 10 curly-edged lasagna noodles, broken into 2-inch lengths
- 1 (8-ounce) can tomato sauce
- 1/2 cup plus 2 tablespoons grated Parmesan cheese
  Pepper
- 1 cup ricotta cheese
- 3 tablespoons chopped fresh basil

1. Pour tomatoes with their juices into 1-quart liquid measuring cup. Add water until mixture measures 1 quart.

2. Heat oil in large nonstick skillet over medium heat until shimmering. Add onion and 1/2 teaspoon salt and cook until onion begins to brown, about 5 minutes. Stir in garlic and pepper flakes and cook until fragrant, about 30 seconds. Add ground meat and cook, breaking apart meat, until no longer pink, about 4 minutes.

3. Scatter pasta over meat but do not stir. Pour diced tomatoes with juices and tomato sauce over pasta. Cover and bring to simmer. Reduce heat to medium-low and simmer, stirring occasionally, until pasta is tender, about 20 minutes.

4. Remove skillet from heat and stir in 1/2 cup Parmesan. Season with salt and pepper. Dot with heaping tablespoons ricotta, cover, and let stand off heat for 5 minutes. Sprinkle with basil and remaining 2 tablespoons Parmesan. Serve.

SKILLET LASAGNA WITH SAUSAGE AND PEPPERS

Follow the recipe for Skillet Lasagna, substituting 1 pound Italian sausage, removed from its casing, for meatloaf mix. Add 1 chopped red bell pepper to skillet with onion in step 2.

Tracey Barth has a full-time day job, and she is the coach of a women's basketball team. Despite her busy schedule, she always finds time to make her husband's favorite dish, lasagna.

Stovetop Secrets
BUILDING SKILLET LASAGNA

To cook all of the ingredients in one pan, a little attention to the ordering of the layers is necessary. It may not look like much as you begin the cooking process, but, after 20 minutes and an occasional stir, a layered lasagna appears almost as if by magic.

1. Start by sautéing onion, garlic, and meat in the skillet. Scatter the broken lasagna noodles over the meat.
2. Pour the diced tomatoes and tomato sauce over the noodles. **3.** Cover and cook for 20 minutes. Add Parmesan, dot with ricotta, cover the skillet, and let cheese soften off heat.

The Ultimate Steakhouse Burger

A burger worthy of the finest steakhouse—made with supermarket beef.

Because home-grilled burgers often turn out crumbly and dry, I saw merit in using a binder. Two popular candidates failed: bread crumbs were gritty, and oatmeal was mealy. Next I tried a technique common to meatball recipes: I soaked white bread in milk, mashed the bread to a paste, and mixed the paste with the ground beef. This gave me a less-intrusive binder that produced a tender, cohesive, and fine-textured interior.

To promote browning, many restaurants slather butter over steaks before cooking them. I was a bit skeptical about mixing fat into ground beef, which already has plenty of it, but it seemed worth a try. Sure enough, the crust browned beautifully. To my surprise, it also made the burgers more moist.

It occurred to me that bacon might add a welcome smokiness not offered by butter. I ground bacon in a food processor and mixed it with ground beef. The flavor was great, but the bits of half-cooked bacon in a rare burger were off-putting. I wanted the flavor, not the bacon itself. For my next test, I cooked the bacon, chilled the rendered fat, and mixed the fat into the beef. This test was a revelation. My burger was seriously juicy, its charred and smoky flavor was significantly enhanced, and the crust that formed from the added fat was extraordinary. This burger rivals the best any steakhouse can serve. –Eva Katz

Anna Fragakis hosts an annual Fourth of July cookout and is always looking for a mouth-watering burger recipe.

Dear Cook's Country,
I love a good steakhouse burger, charred and crusty on the outside, moist and juicy on the inside. My attempts to make such a burger on my grill are never as good. Am I missing something?

Anna Fragakis, Atlanta, Ga.

Dear Anna,
Seasoning ground beef with salt and pepper is sufficient for a good burger, especially if the burger is cooked on a very hot grill. But this bare-bones preparation is rarely memorable. I've eaten only a few great burgers, and it was never at home. These great steakhouse burgers all shared the same traits: a moist, fine-grained interior paired with a charred, flame-grilled crust. Like you, I wanted to take my burgers to the next level, but how?

3 Secret Ingredients Make a Better Burger

The addition of a little bread, milk, and bacon fat can turn even the leanest ground beef into a moist, rich burger. To make sure that the bread dissolves into the burgers, mash the milk and bread together with a fork until a smooth paste forms.

THE ULTIMATE HAMBURGER

SERVES 4

For this recipe, you want ground beef that is 85 percent to 90 percent lean. With the added bacon fat, 80 percent lean beef will make slightly greasy burgers. Crumble the cooked bacon slices over a salad, or use the slices as a burger topping.

- 8 **strips bacon**
- 1–2 **slices white sandwich bread, crusts removed and discarded, remaining bread cut into 1/2-inch pieces (about 1 cup)**
- 1/4 **cup milk**
- 1 1/2 **pounds ground beef (see note)**
- 1 **teaspoon salt**
- 1/2 **teaspoon pepper**
- 2 **large garlic cloves, very finely minced**
  Vegetable oil for grill rack

1. Fry bacon in large skillet over medium heat until crisp, about 8 minutes. Transfer bacon to plate lined with paper towels. Spoon 3 tablespoons bacon fat into heatproof bowl and place in refrigerator while preparing other ingredients.

2. Place bread in small bowl, add milk, and let mixture sit until saturated, about 5 minutes. Using fork, mash bread and milk until it forms smooth paste. Break up beef into small pieces in medium bowl. Season with salt and pepper, then add garlic, bread paste, and reserved bacon fat. Using fork or hands, lightly knead together so that ingredients are well incorporated and mixture forms cohesive mass. Divide meat into 4 equal portions. Using hands, toss each portion of meat back and forth to form loose ball, then gently flatten each ball into 3/4-inch-thick patty.

3. Oil cooking grate and grill burgers over very hot fire, without pressing down on them, until well seared on both sides, 7 to 10 minutes. Serve, topped with bacon, if desired.

Burger-Building Contest

We asked readers how they embellish burgers at home and received hundreds of ideas. Here are our favorites. Our hearty congratulations to our grand-prize winner, Karen Nash, who will receive $500. All 12 runners-up will receive a complimentary one-year subscription to the magazine.

Our Grand-Prize Winner!

Crabby Patty
Sometimes being crabby is a good thing! **Karen Nash** of Bishopville, Md., puts a regional spin on her burgers, topping them with melted fontina cheese, lump crab-meat sautéed in butter and parsley, sliced onion, and a sprinkle of Old Bay seasoning.

My Thai
Turning to Southeast Asia for inspiration, **Janna Denig** of Oakland, Calif., tops her burgers with sliced cucumber, peanut sauce, shredded carrot, and sesame seeds.

Hawaii Five-O
Shari Hoffman of Federal Way, Wash., brushes teriyaki sauce on burgers before removing them from the grill, then tops them with grilled ham and pineapple before serving.

Truck Stop
Mark Drapa of Westford, Vt., enjoys breakfast anytime with his favorite burger, topped with cheddar cheese, fried egg, bacon, hash browns, and Tabasco sauce.

Caprese
Kathlene Gover of Glendale, Ariz., turns a classic Italian salad into a burger garnish. She tops burgers with a slices of fresh mozzarella cheese, ripe tomato, whole basil leaves, and pesto.

Reuben
Meg van Meter of Ambler, Pa., substitutes a burger for the corned beef to create an untraditional Reuben sandwich, complete with Thousand Island dressing, Swiss cheese, sauerkraut, and caraway seeds.

My Big Fat Greek Burger
Deb Schneider of Glouster, Ohio, garnishes her burgers with roasted red pepper mayonnaise (combine 1 part chopped roasted red peppers with 2 parts mayonnaise in a blender until smooth), kalamata olives, feta cheese, and fresh parsley.

California Dreamin'
Jill Sersen may live in Hoboken, N.J., but she makes a classic California burger. Her simple recipe: Top burgers with avocado slices, sprouts, tomato slices, and baby greens.

Yankee Doodle
Lindsay Mustard of Waltham, Mass., pairs Vermont cheddar cheese and apple slices—a perfect match for the cranberry horseradish ketchup recipe we got from **Carole Resnick** of Cleveland, Ohio. We made a quick version with 3 tablespoons canned whole cranberry sauce, 2 tablespoons ketchup, and 1 teaspoon horseradish.

Mama Mia
Instead of putting hamburger on your pizza, how about putting pizza on your hamburger? **Laura Polach** of Barnhart, Mo., gives it a whirl by topping her burgers with pizza sauce, shredded mozzarella, pepperoni, fresh oregano, and grated Parmesan cheese.

Red, Hot, and Blue
Scott Ireland of Penfield, N.Y., borrows this classic combination for chicken wings from nearby Buffalo. When his burgers come off the grill, he brushes them with a mixture of 1 part melted butter and 2 parts Tabasco sauce, then tops them off with celery slices, blue cheese dressing, and any remaining sauce.

Boca Grande
You'll definitely need a *boca grande* (big mouth) for **Jodi Spoor's** take on a local favorite from her hometown of San Antonio, Texas. She melts pepper Jack cheese on her burgers, spreads them with refried pinto beans, and finishes things off with salsa,guacamole, pickled jalapeño peppers, and crushed corn chips.

When Things Go Wrong in the Kitchen

READERS SHARE FUNNY STORIES ABOUT COOKING MISHAPS

A LASTING IMPRESSION

Three years ago, my husband's college roommate was in town visiting his girlfriend. Wanting to see our friend (and check out his new girl), we offered to have them over for dinner. I had every burner on our small gas stove going at once in our teeny kitchen. I noticed that the asparagus was finished, so I placed my oven mitt on top of a pot lid while I turned to clear a space in the sink to drain the boiling water.

When I turned back to the stove, I noticed that the pots weren't the only things steaming! My oven mitt was also emitting some steam. I laughed to myself, feeling lucky that I had noticed the mitt before it caught fire and turned into a real disaster. I quickly folded the oven mitt in half, smacked it a few times to extinguish any spark, threw it on the bedroom floor, and closed the door.

When we sat down to eat I was feeling mighty smug, having prepared the entire meal with no major problems. As we sipped our wine and poked at the food, I could still smell smoke, but I couldn't determine why. By the end of dinner there was no denying that something was burning. My mind jumped to the oven mitt on the bedroom floor. I threw open the door and smoke came pouring out. On the floor, smoldering like old newspaper in a fireplace, were the remains of my mitt. I grabbed it and ran into the bathroom, small black flakes of mitt material flying off all around me. I threw the mitt in the bathtub and started the shower to put out any remaining sparks. Just then my husband called to me from the bedroom. The parquet wood floor was still smoking, a perfect mitt print burned right into it.

You could say that I had made a lasting impression not only on our dinner guests but also on the floor. For months after, we would tell the story to friends and take them into the bedroom, where the evidence lay, black as night.

Becky Joyce Danville, Calif.

KITCHEN ART

My first preheating disaster occurred when I was 8 years old. My parents were away, and my cousin and I decided to make cookies. We turned the oven on to preheat and, unfortunately, did not check the inside of the oven first. We had no idea that my dad was storing last night's big Tupperware bowl of potato chips in there. When we were ready to put the cookies in the oven, we were met with an oven full of fire. The good news is that my mom was finally able to get the new oven she had been wanting.

Sadly, I forgot this lesson later in life. Recently, I turned on the oven to preheat without checking inside—where I had been storing a fancy appetizer tray borrowed from my sister-in-law. After fanning the fumes away from the smoke alarm and peeling the melted plastic tray from my oven rack, I was left with a rather pretty, wavy, bubbly clump of plastic. As a reminder to myself to check the oven before turning it on, I displayed the tray in my kitchen for several weeks. The funny part is that I received many compliments on my beautiful piece of "art." Maybe I should think about becoming a preheating artist!

Elizabeth Vance Seattle, Wash.

A CASE OF THE CHOCOLATE MEASLES

I saw a wonderful-looking chocolate dessert on TV—tulip-shaped chocolate cups filled with ice cream—and decided I would try the recipe for a large dinner party.

I had to dip balloons into melted chocolate to shape the "tulips." I dipped the first balloon halfway into the chocolate to form the tulip cup. Wow, I thought, this was going to be beautiful. I set the four chocolate-dipped balloons aside to cool, and, as I was ready to dip the fifth—boom!—the first balloon exploded, followed by all the others.

There was chocolate on the ceiling, walls, floors, cabinets, and all over my kitchen as well as on my face! I found chocolate for a week afterward in places you would never imagine. When I tell this story I have to laugh, as you would have, had you seen me covered in chocolate measles!

Dianna Villani Collegeville, Pa.

PUMPKIN HEAD

When I was new to cooking, I decided to make a pumpkin pie. The recipe called for "cooked pumpkin," so I opened a can of pumpkin and put it on the stove to cook. Then I left the kitchen to answer the phone and got carried away with my conversation.

Imagine my surprise when I began hearing plops, pings, and loud gurgles coming from my kitchen. I ran to see what was going on, only to find that the walls, ceilings, and floor were covered with large orange spots and the pumpkin was burning on the stove. In the process of trying to get to the stove and remove the pan, I was hit with some plops, but they came from the ceiling, so I did not get burned. I finally managed to get the kitchen cleaned up, and the ceilings, walls, and floors sparkled.

When my husband got home from work he gave me a kiss and a hug, running his hand up the back of

my head into my hair. He pulled away with a funny expression on his face and pulled his hand from my hair. It contained a large plop of pumpkin! It was sometime before I got up the nerve to tell anyone about how I learned that pumpkin is already cooked when you take it from a can!

Nancy Sparks Morrison Via e-mail

THE CHICKEN BLUES

Years ago, when experimenting with different recipes, I decided to try chicken chow mein. It called for Chinese cabbage, but I figured any kind would work and so used red cabbage instead. Well, the chicken pieces turned a lovely shade of blue, and the rest of the dish was purple. It tasted fine, but my family could not get past the color and refused to even try it. Everyone still talks about my blue chicken, and that was over 25 years ago!

Carol Spangenberg Philadelphia, Pa.

THE LAST BITE

When my son, Paul, was about 8 years old and I was a single mom, he told me he wanted to know what lobster tasted like. I decided to make a special dinner for two, and we went to pick out our lobsters at the local market. He pressed his little face against the glass as he searched for two perfect lobsters. When he pointed to the ones he wanted, the counter clerk pulled them out for us.

When we got home, I placed the live lobsters in the kitchen sink and Paul just sat on the counter examining them. While I was busy getting things prepared for these two sea creatures, Paul had decided to have a countertop lobster race, and one of the lobsters fell harmlessly to the floor. But the band broke off one of its huge claws, and this maverick lobster now had plans other than becoming our dinner.

There we were, scrambling around in our flip-flops, trying to make sure that our fingers and toes were out of the way as we tried to get hold of the lobster, which was turning and pinching every which way until it finally caught my son's toe with its claw. The lobster seem distracted by my son's toe and screaming, so I was able to grab it and put it safely back into the sink. Paul was laughing and crying at the same time. When he finally regained some of his composure, he simply stated: "This will be the one that I eat, to have the last bite back."

Carolann Garwood High Point, N.C.

Send us your funniest kitchen disaster stories. Please write to us at Kitchen Disasters, Cook's Country, P.O. Box 470739, Brookline, MA 02447. If you'd like to use e-mail, write to us at kitchendisasters@bcpress.com.

Notes from Our Test Kitchen

TIPS, TECHNIQUES, AND TOOLS FOR BETTER COOKING

< Grill Brushes FOILED AGAIN

Hardly a week goes by that we don't fire up at least one of our grills. And with all this use comes a need for constant cleaning. A good grill brush is the best tool for the job, but most brands wear out so quickly that we often make our own "brush." Associate editor Keri Fisher demonstrates, using a crumpled wad of aluminum foil held in a pair of long tongs to scrape stuck-on food off a hot grill grate. Once the grate is clean, we toss out the foil and use the tongs to flip the food as it cooks.

PANS FOR PENNIES

There's no need to break the bank when it comes to buying a square baking pan like the one used to make our Reduced-Fat Crumb Coffee Cake (page 8). During the course of our testing, we observed that the Baker's Secret Nonstick 8-Inch Baking Pan and the Pyrex 8-Inch Square Glass Cake Pan gave us evenly baked cakes with perfect lift every time. As if that wasn't reason enough to buy either of these pans, we found that they were easy on the wallet, too—just $5 each. Better than fancy pans and at a fraction of the price? Sounds almost too good to be true. But it gets better. You can purchase these pans almost anywhere—in most hardware stores and kitchen shops and even in some supermarkets.

Pyrex 8-Inch Square Glass Cake Pan

Baker's Secret Nonstick 8-Inch Baking Pan

STRAWBERRY YIELDS FOREVER

It just wouldn't feel like summer without a couple of quarts of fresh strawberries in our refrigerator. But when these heavy, juicy fruits are kept in their original basket, the berries on top crush those on the bottom. In the test kitchen, we safely store strawberries—or any delicate berry—by spreading them out on a dinner plate lined with paper towels, which absorb any excess moisture. The plate goes into the refrigerator, and we've got smush-free berries at the ready.

FREEZE AND BAKE

Sometimes you want just one or two fresh-baked cookies, not a whole batch. No problem. With a little help from the freezer, you can bake as many—or as few—cookies as you like. After making a batch of dough, portion it out as if for baking on parchment-lined baking sheets or on large plates and place in the freezer until completely frozen, at least 30 minutes. Remove the frozen unbaked cookies from the sheet, arrange them in layers in an airtight storage container (use the same parchment sheets to separate the layers), and place the sealed container back in the freezer. When you've got a craving for a just-baked cookie, preheat the oven and bake according to the recipe. You may need to increase the baking time by a minute or two, but no defrosting is necessary, and you can keep the frozen cookies for up to two months. This method works with most cookies, including our Washboards (page 9) and Triple-Chocolate Cookies (page 17).

SHOPPING with the TEST KITCHEN

TEATIME During development of our recipes for flavored iced teas (page 20), we went through a lot of tea bags. We noticed that two brands, Twinings Ceylon Orange Pekoe Tea and Red Rose Tea, delivered an unpleasant glass of bitter iced tea, while the generic market brand from our local Stop & Shop was practically undrinkable. Three brands won our thumbs up. Tetley Classic Blend and Salada tea bags both produced smooth-flavored iced tea, but our favorite was Lipton. With a smooth, rich flavor, this familiar brand is our top choice for tea, whether iced or not.

Our Top Choice

KETCHUP PHOTOGRAPH: ROSS DURANT/PICTURE ARTS/FOODPIX

Kitchen Creations
Playing Ketchup

While making burger toppings (see page 27), we were so inspired by Carole Resnick's cranberry horseradish ketchup that we decided to create a few flavored ketchups of our own.

PASSAGE TO INDIA KETCHUP
Combine 1/4 cup ketchup, 1/4 cup mango chutney, and 1/2 teaspoon curry powder.

VERY BERRY KETCHUP
Combine 1/4 cup ketchup, 3 tablespoons raspberry jam, and 1/4 teaspoon cinnamon.

FIVE-ALARM KETCHUP
Combine 1/4 cup ketchup, 3 tablespoons minced pickled jalapeño slices, and 1/2 to 1 teaspoon Tabasco sauce.

SPICY, SMOKY KETCHUP
Combine 1/4 cup ketchup, 2 tablespoons molasses, and 1 minced chipotle chile.

MONGOLIAN KETCHUP
Combine 1/4 cup ketchup, 1/4 cup plum jam, 1 teaspoon grated ginger, and 1/2 teaspoon five-spice powder.

How to Make
AN OVERSIZED OMELET
Our eight-egg Denver Omelet (page 21) calls for a special cooking method that requires a nonstick skillet and lid.

1. The outside rim of an omelet always cooks quickly. To cook the omelet evenly, pull the cooked edges of egg toward the center of the pan and allow raw egg to run to the edges. **2.** When the omelet is set on the bottom but still very runny on the top, it's time to cover the skillet and turn the heat down to low. **3.** After the top of the omelet begins to set, sprinkle with the cheese and let the omelet rest off heat until the cheese has partially melted. **4.** After using a rubber spatula to push half of the omelet out onto a platter, tilt the skillet so that the omelet folds over itself to make the traditional half-moon shape.

Food Shopping

CHOCOLATE ICE CREAM: Are Premium Brands Best?

Do premium ice creams—the kind sold in small pint- or quart-sized packages—taste better than mass-market brands sold in half-gallons tubs? Should be an easy question to answer, right? But it's not—even though the differences between the two styles are pretty clear.

When ice cream is churned, air is incorporated. If no air were added, the ice cream would be hard and stiff, like an ice cube. Manufacturers can control the amount of air added to the ice cream mixture before it freezes. This air, called overrun, can increase the volume of the ice cream by as little as 20 percent (this is typical of premium brands) or as much as 100 percent (typical of mass-market brands). More overrun produces a fluffy, light ice cream with more air and less of everything else, including fat. Less overrun produces a creamy, dense ice cream with little air and a lot of fat. So when you buy a fluffy ice cream packed in a large tub, you're buying a fair amount of air. But this may not be as bad as it sounds.

When we conducted a blind tasting of seven best-selling brands, two reigned over the rest—one brand, as it turned out, for each style of ice cream. Fans of premium ice cream praised Ben & Jerry's for having a dense, creamy texture and an intense flavor they found reminiscent of fine bittersweet chocolate. Meanwhile, tasters who preferred mass-market Edy's Grand liked it for its fluffy texture and sweet, milk-chocolaty flavor. The other five brands weren't bad—we're talking about ice cream, after all. But tasters did downgrade them for weak flavor and/or icy texture. The ice creams are listed below in order of preference. –Erika Bruce

Top Picks

1. BEN AND JERRY'S Chocolate Ice Cream
$3.79 for 1 pint; 16 grams of fat per ½-cup serving
Described by numerous tasters as "creamy" and "rich," this chart-topper has twice the fat of mass-market ice creams. Tasters admired the "very dense" texture that they also described as "fudge-like" and "almost chewy." The chocolate flavor was judged to be "intense" but not overly aggressive.

2. EDY'S Grand Chocolate Ice Cream
$5.29 for 1.75 quarts; 8 grams of fat per ½-cup serving
Several tasters recommended this as the best choice for families with kids. "Like something you'd get from the ice cream truck, but better." Short on richness, Edy's was admired for its "milk chocolate" flavor. It's less dense that the premium brands, but, unlike the other modestly priced varieties, it's not icy.

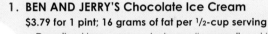

Runners-Up

3. BREYERS Chocolate Ice Cream $5.29 for 1.75 quarts; 8 grams of fat per ½-cup serving
Favored by tasters who preferred an "old-fashioned" or "nostalgic" taste, Breyers was likened to a Fudgsicle. Its "not-too-rich" flavor earned points with some, while others insisted that it "could have been creamier." A few tasters called the texture "icy" and "grainy."

4. TURKEY HILL Philadelphia Style Chocolate Ice Cream $5.29 for 1.75 quarts; 10 grams of fat per ½-cup serving
Tasters focused on the texture of this brand, calling it "smooth," "fluffy," "not dense," and "creamy, like a milkshake." The flavor was "malty," "milk chocolaty," and, for some, "too sweet."

5. BLUE BELL Dutch Chocolate Ice Cream $5.49 for 2 quarts; 8 grams of fat per ½-cup serving
Blue Bell was likened to a "Milky Way candy bar," a virtue for some tasters but approaching "too sweet" for others. Although appealingly "fluffy," according to one taster, others deemed it too "airy" and "wispy."

6. HÄAGEN-DAZS Chocolate Ice Cream $5.69 for 1 quart; 18 grams of fat per ½-cup serving
With the highest amount of fat per serving, it was surprising that Häagen-Dazs failed to pull in more points. But its attractively "smooth," "creamy" texture couldn't make up for a "boring" flavor, variously called "light chocolate," "dusty," and "a little acidic."

7. BLUE BUNNY Chocolate Ice Cream $4.85 for 2 quarts; 7 grams of fat per ½-cup serving
While one taster liked Blue Bunny for a "chocolate taste that stands out," another downgraded it for tasting like a "brownie mix." Still other tasters detected "bubble-gum sweetness" and a "minty aftertaste." The texture was described as "fluffy" and "wispy."

Buyer's Guide
Ice Cream Cones

Once available only in ice cream parlors, specialty cones now take up significant shelf space in supermarkets. We decided to eat more ice cream, this time in cones, to see if we could make some recommendations about six widely available styles.

We quickly came to the conclusion that there is no such thing as a bad ice cream cone. Although our all-around favorite was the sugar cone, we found something to like in each of the cones we tasted. The cones are listed in order of preference, but each style had its fans.

NABISCO
Comet Sugar Cones
$2.59 for 12
These "crunchy" cones have a "strong vanilla flavor." Be prepared for drips and leaks, but this cone "never gets soggy."

KEEBLER
Waffle Cones
$2.59 for 12
These "light," "crunchy" cones taste almost like cake. "The most like homemade."

JOY
Ice Cream Cups
$1.29 for 12
While some tasters complained about a "Styrofoamy" texture, fans praised these cones for being "light" and "crispy." Another plus: Their sturdy, flat base resists leaks.

NABISCO
Oreo Chocolate Cones
$2.29 for 12
These "very crunchy" chocolate sugar cones have "good flavor" and are "not too sweet."

KEEBLER
Waffle Bowls
$3.45 for 10
Technically not a cone, but the "neat shape" and "good homemade flavor" are a winning combination.

KEEBLER Fudge Shoppe
Fudge-Dipped Ice Cream Cups
$2.59 for 12
While dipping a cone in chocolate is great for flavor, the texture is "soft," even "a bit stale."

Equipment Roundup

BLENDERS: Aren't They All the Same?

At first glance, you might think all blenders are alike. But after testing nine inexpensive models, I can tell you they are not. Pureed soup with stringy bits of broccoli, strawberry smoothies with hidden "icebergs," and pesto that refused to come together were some of the problems I encountered.

TAPERED JARS WORK BEST: Blade design, size, and sharpness were similar in all nine models; it's in the way the food reaches the blade that they differed. While it's easy to ladle hot soup into a blender jar with a wide mouth, if the base of the jar is just as wide, you have a large gap (up to an inch) between the blade tip and the side of the jar, where food seeks refuge. A blade elevated above the jar bottom creates a similar safe haven for stray bits of food. The best blenders leave no room for ingredients to hide and have a tapered, funnel-shaped jar that guides the ingredients to the blade.

HEAVY GLASS BEATS PLASTIC: The three bargain-basement blenders in the lineup were disappointing. A few extra dollars will get you a better blender—one that includes a heavy glass jar. Plastic jars are prone to scratching and are more likely to retain color and odor over years of use.

DIAL CONTROLS TOP BUTTONS: Buttons, which clutter most base units, and the crevices surrounding them, can be difficult, if not impossible, to clean. Dial controls wipe clean easily. Another drawback of the button design is that it's too easy to go straight for high speed; do so and you get an eruption of food. Patient cooks will punch their way up from low speed to high, but I did not do this once and paid the messy price. With the dial, I had no choice but to rev up through the speeds, a much easier and neater proposition.

'PULSE' IS ESSENTIAL: High speed, in which nearly all blending takes place, was essentially the same in all of the blenders. An 18-speed blender merely offers 17 "medium" speeds that most of us will never use. The pulse feature, however, is worth having. It gets the food moving and begins to break it down; high speed takes care of the rest.

SUMMING UP: What did I learn about blenders after making such a mess of the test kitchen? The best ones have a funnel-shaped glass jar and an easy-to-clean dial. Braun's PowerMax ($49) fits the bill, and dialing through the five speeds keeps things tidy. But just in case you make a mess anyway, it's nice to know that all parts are dishwasher-safe.

–Garth Clingingsmith

Highly Recommended
BRAUN PowerMax MX2050
Price: $49.00
Comments: Reduced ice cubes to a powder in less than 10 seconds and produced an ultra-smooth (nearly emulsified) pesto in 30 seconds. A smoothie passed the test of passing through a strainer cleanly, and pureed soup was almost—but not quite—perfect. The only blender with all dishwasher-safe parts.

Recommended
OSTER Classic Beehive Design 4119 Price: $48.89
Comments: The quickest blender with pesto, an able ice crusher, and the top performer when pureeing soup. Not the smoothest of smoothies, but perfectly drinkable. No pulse feature, but easy-to-use dial-type control, which has just two speeds, makes pulsing easy to manage with just a twist of the dial.

OSTER 12-Speed Osterizer 6663
Price: $39.99
Comments: Same test results as the Oster Classic, but this model has a button control panel, which, predictably, was nearly impossible to clean. The 12 speeds on the panel, which also has a pulse button, don't compensate for the advantages of the easier-to-use and clean Classic.

BLACK & DECKER ProBlend BL600
Price: $36.00
Comments: High marks on three of four tests, but the B&D faltered with pesto. The top three blenders performed other tasks better and faster. A safety feature that lets you lock the jar to the base seems unnecessary.

Recommended with Reservations
HAMILTON BEACH BlendMaster 50159 Price: $19.99
Comments: The price is right, but little else. While this was the best contender under $30, it has a plastic jar, sports push buttons that bear a comparison to loose teeth, and produced chunky results across the board. We wouldn't call that a bargain.

CUISINART SmartPower Basics 18-Speed Blender CB-18
Price: $39.95
Comments: It's easy to pour soup into this blender's short, squat jar, but the shape also makes for less than perfect purees. There's plenty of room for the food to hide from the blade in the ample space between it and the jar wall. The result? Ice is merely roughed up. Same design flaw makes it nearly impossible to make pesto.

Recommended with Reservations
HAMILTON BEACH BlendSmart 18-Speed Blender 56406
Price: $43.33
Comments: The silly one-touch "BlendSmart" feature starts the blade slowly. Using it produced results that were never as good as those produced by simply turning the blender on high or using the pulse button. The broad-bottomed jar made it impossible to attain a smooth pesto or evenly crushed ice.

Not Recommended
FARBERWARE Special Select 10-Speed Blender FSB100
Price: $25.00
Comments: A good option for pureeing, especially soup, but stumbled with a thicker smoothie. Other tasks were impossible to accomplish—as was prying the handle-less lid off the jar.

PROCTOR SILEX 8-Speed Blender 5717R8 Price: $18.88
Comments: The only blender to fail the smoothie test, and it struggled with other tasks. The flimsy push buttons and lightweight plastic jar don't inspire confidence.

Gadgets & Gear
Magic Bullet

If you've watched enough television, you've likely heard of the Magic Bullet. According to the infomercial, this multipurpose tool can "peel, chop, mix, blend, whip, grind, and more." Can something that looks like a small blender really do all that?

To find out, we ran the Magic Bullet through a dozen tests, from grinding coffee to blending a microwaved Alfredo sauce. It performed well when grinding dry items, such as spices, coffee, and Parmesan cheese, but most every other test proved problematic. Attempts to chop onions yielded a flood of juice. Cream whipped so quickly that stopping anytime before stiff peaks was nearly impossible. That Alfredo sauce? The Magic Bullet managed it, but a whisk could have done the same.

In the end, this $99 "countertop magician" is not able to deliver on its laundry list of promises. In addition, storing the unit's 23 pieces is a nightmare, and the motor emits an eardrum-bursting noise that makes a regular blender seem downright quiet. We'll take our favorite blender—at half the price—any day. We'll just stick with a whisk, knife, or coffee grinder when the need arises. –G.C.

Is the Magic Bullet a silver bullet for kitchen multitasking?

Thanks for the Memories

The Chocolate Pudding Date

Lynn Ness Bakersfield, Calif.

Thirty years ago, the man who is now my husband was just my "new boyfriend." We attended the University of Florida, and one day, when we were studying together at the campus library, he told me that he missed homemade chocolate pudding more than anything. "You know," he said with a wink, "the way to a man's heart is through his stomach." I eagerly told him that I would make him chocolate pudding that night. He warned me that he could tell if it was burned or scorched.

That night, I felt more pressure than a great chef in the world's biggest cook-off. My first effort burned and was so lumpy it could have passed for very bad gravy. I put that pot aside, grabbed a clean one, and hurriedly started again. This time I stirred the pudding constantly to make sure there were no lumps, but I could definitely smell scorched milk. "No," I told myself, "that won't do." I put the second pot aside and started all over in a new pot. I lowered the heat and stirred more often. This time the cooking was a total success. But, just as I was patting myself on the back, I saw my unused cup of sugar sitting on the counter by the stove.

I had run out of pots and was cooking my fourth batch of pudding in a skillet when the doorbell rang. I quickly poured the pudding into pudding cups and yelled, "Just a minute!" I started toward the door when my eyes fell on the three pots with failed puddings on the counter. I quickly hid the pots in the cabinet under my kitchen sink.

My chocolate pudding was a great success, so much so that my boyfriend insisted on washing the dirty dishes. I told him that the dishwashing soap was under the sink. When he started laughing, it hit me that he had found my stash of burnt pudding pots. He was so touched by my efforts that he washed all of my dishes—the burnt pudding pots, too.

Thirty years later, my husband still kids me about our pudding date. Once in a while, he'll go into the kitchen and rattle around under the kitchen sink and say he's "just looking for some chocolate pudding."

The Pie with a Hex

David R. Winkles Las Cruces, N.M.

My father's mother used to make a chess pie that was famous. The recipe, which is 100 to 200 years old, seems simple—it contains cream, butter, eggs, sugar, and vanilla. But, apparently, the recipe has a "hex" on it. When anyone makes it for the first time, the pie comes out green and pockmarked, with a filling that has the consistency of stiff rubber. The second time you make the pie, and all times thereafter, the recipe never fails. All of my aunts have verified that this was their experience.

I loved the pie and made my first one when I was 11. My mother never had the nerve to try it, but my grandmother gave me the recipe. She had not mentioned the hex, so when I opened the oven door, I was overcome with dismay. The pie resembled my idea of a Martian who had not quite succumbed to smallpox. It was quickly placed in the trash.

Several months lapsed before I had the nerve to try this recipe again. This time, the pie looked and smelled just like my grandmother's. In fact, my father came home as the pie was cooling on the rack. He asked, "Where's Mother?" referring to my grandmother. My mother said she wasn't there, to which my father replied, "I know she's here. That's her pie and only she can make it." I'm not sure what he thought when he found out that his son had made it, but he was happy to eat it.

Blue in the Face

Arthur H. Richardson, Jr.
East Bridgewater, Mass.

Back in the mid-1940s, my family lived in New Hampshire, where my uncle owned 75 acres of woods and fields. I remember one summer when the blueberries were especially plentiful. From my aunt and uncle's home, if you looked across the street and all the way down the dirt road that led to the sandpit, the bushes had a distinct bluish hue. In fact, those blues were so plentiful that between my aunt, my mother, and me, we canned 110 quarts that summer. That's not a misprint!

Besides the canning that seemed to go on daily, we ate blueberries with milk, blueberries with ice cream, blueberries on our morning cereal, blueberry pancakes, blueberry waffles, and, every so often, a mysterious blueberry "witches' brew" prepared by my aunt. My skin must have had a bluish tinge when I went back to school that September.

Grandmother's Meat Market

Philip Murphy Via e-mail

My grandmother came to Boston from Ireland after the potato famine. She was a housemaid and saved her pennies so that she could train at the Fannie Farmer cooking school. She eventually became a cook and worked in private homes into her nineties, and she always bought the very best food.

As a child, I would go to the downtown marketplace with my mother every Saturday morning, and we'd always visit a shop with a green and gold sign that read "Swann Newton and Co./Provisioners to the Trade." It was the prime beef and lamb supplier for my grandmother, and my mother and I were their legacy customers. I remember the perilous trip down the polished stairs, the sweet smell of new sawdust, the swaying of the hanging halves and hindquarters, and the aroma of fine beef. The old market was "improved," and prime beef has been systematically downgraded, but the memory of Swann Newton still takes me back to better days.

Batter Up and Fry

Marc Wheeler Juneau, Alaska

Last Thanksgiving, I deep-fried my first turkey, and it was succulent and tasty. Later that afternoon, my friends and I remembered one of the DVD extras from the film *Supersize Me*. The "extra" portrayed a fry shop in England that fries all kinds of foods, including Twinkies. Idle minds and a potful of 350-degree oil are a dangerous combination. We couldn't resist the temptation to plunge a few Twinkies of our own into the bubbling grease. We were a little disappointed when the Twinkies turned into hot, creamy, viscous logs.

Not being faint of heart, we turned to other readily available items. Fried Power Bars were not very good. We came very close to battering and frying a slice of pumpkin pie, but some shred of respect for tradition held us back. We finally had some success with deep-fried chocolate. Oozy, hot Dove chocolate surrounded by a crunchy fried batter was a delight.

Sunday Pasta with Nonna

Linda Cotroneo Burlington, Mass.

My grandmother is long gone now, but I have saved her wooden pasta board and rolling pin, which are common in the Lemarche region of Italy, where she was born. I remember the gentle "snap" of the rolled pasta sheets, which, to a young child, looked like fine, thin tablecloths of dough. My grandmother's hands moved swiftly and deftly as she rolled out the ball of dough with the large rolling pin, always teaching with a smile on her face. She used a doughnut cutter, minus the hole (it was removable!) to cut round circles from the dough. The filling was always ricotta, spinach, and eggs seasoned with nutmeg. My job was to place the filling on the circles and fold the dough over to form the shape of a half-moon. Then we would dip our forks in flour and press along the edges to seal them. Now that I am a Nonna, I hope that I, too, can pass along happy memories to my grandchildren.

Send us your food memories. Write to us at Food Memories, Cook's Country, P.O. Box 470739, Brookline, MA 02447. If you'd like to use e-mail, write to us at foodmemories@bcpress.com. If we publish your story, you'll receive a complimentary one-year subscription to *Cook's Country*.

Postcards from Home

COOK'S COUNTRY READERS SHOW US WHAT'S COOKING AT HOME

Pancake Potluck Adriana Valencia Oakland, Calif.

Adriana writes: "I have been throwing a semi-annual pancake breakfast potluck in my driveway since 1999. My 12th Semi-Annual Pancake Breakfast Potluck was on the same day as my 29th birthday, and I asked friends to bring a topping or drink. I spent the night or two before my potluck making waffles and freezing them. I also put together about 20 pounds of homemade pancake mix and stored it in a large sealable bucket. I prepare the pancake batter in a 5-gallon bucket the morning of the breakfast. I invite everyone I know—friends from school, cycling buddies, childhood friends I haven't seen in years, and (I make this a rule) at least one person I've met only once. A good mix of people always shows up."

The Dream Life of a Dog
Cathleen Cahill St. Louis, Mo.

Cathleen writes: "I found Sooner in Telequah, Okla., starving and eating out of a garbage can. I nursed him back to health, and he has repaid me many times, as when he alerted me to a burglar who was 'shopping' in our garage. He has also learned to enjoy the good things in life. Both my husband and I love to cook and share meals with friends. Sooner always joins us in the kitchen. As you can see, the aroma from the oven sends him off into dreamland!"

Onion Fever Janna Hughes Abrams, Wis.

Janna asked us if we had any onion soup recipes, and we can see why. She writes: "My husband, Greg, is the gardener in our house. He tills, plants, weeds, and harvests, without much help from me. Each year he harvests a good-sized crop, with onions the size of softballs. One onion is enough for a large pot of onion soup."

Really Cooking from Scratch
Matt Sherman Gainesville, Fla.

Matt writes: "Homemade pizza from scratch blessed our family last week. We did everything from grinding the wheat for the dough to carefully chopping and assembling the tomatoes and spices for the sauce. We also roasted the red and orange bell peppers ourselves before soaking them in oil and garlic and adding them to the pie. Working together keeps our family close."

a Reader Worth Meeting

Dana Sly is just 12 years old, but she's already an accomplished cook. She recently wrote to us about the vegan cornbread recipe she developed following our rigorous testing methods. She even sent pictures along to document each stage of her recipe development process. It turns out that Dana's cornbread won a purple Grand Champion ribbon at the Woodbury County Fair in Iowa. We arranged for Dana and her parents to come to our test kitchen for the day. She taught some of the "old" hands in the kitchen a trick or two. Thanks, Dana!

Galley Cook
Regina K. DeBadts Cocoa, Fla.

Regina writes, "In 2003 I moved aboard a sailboat! I have enclosed a picture of myself cooking on our small Pearson Ariel, a 26-footer named *Althea*. In the photo, I am preparing a dish on the Foreman Grill, which we use begrudgingly when the weather outdoors is not conducive to grilling!"

From left to right: Dana shows senior editor Bridget Lancaster how to make her vegan cornbread recipe. Proud parents Dave and Lin look on in the test kitchen. It wasn't all work for Dana—she also got to taste-test chocolate cakes.

We'd love to see what you're growing, cooking, and eating at home. E-mail your photos to postcards@bcpress.com or send them to Postcards, Cook's Country, P.O. Box 470739, Brookline, MA 02447. If we publish your photo, you will receive a complimentary one-year subscription to *Cook's Country*. Make sure to include your name, address, and daytime phone number along with your photo. And tell us a little bit about what makes your photo special.

Recipe Index

main courses

Antipasto Heroes RC
Apricot-Glazed Chicken Breasts 15
Easy Jerk Chicken 23
    Sweet 'n' Smoky Jerk Chicken
**Grilled Spicy Lime Chicken with Black Bean
    and Avocado Salad** 11
Luau Kebabs RC
Memphis BBQ Spareribs 14
**Pan-Fried Pork Cutlets with Orange and
    Green Olive Salsa** 21
Shanghai Chicken Salad RC
Shrimp Piccata Pasta RC
Skillet Lasagna 25
    Skillet Lasagna with Sausage
    and Peppers
"Texas Red" Chili con Carne 11
The Ultimate Hamburger 26
Zesty Salmon and Potato Salad 23

dip, dressings, salads, salsa, and sides

Dressed-Up Ketchups 29
    Five-Alarm Ketchup
    Mongolian Ketchup
    Passage to India Ketchup
    Spicy, Smoky Ketchup
    Very Berry Ketchup
French Dip 18
Grilled Banana and Red Onion Salsa 23
Mediterranean Couscous Salad RC
Roasted German Potato Salad RC
Salad Dressings 18
    All-American French Dressing
    Creamy French Dressing
Sautéed Zucchini and Corn with Chives RC
Special Sauce 18
Spinach Orzo 21
Summer Slaws 24
    Bistro Slaw
    Casablanca Slaw
    Fiesta Slaw
    Spicy Peanut Slaw

breakfast

Family-Style Denver Omelet 21

sweet treats and teas

Fresh Strawberry Desserts 6–7
    Quick Strawberry Trifle
    Strawberry-Pineapple Tart
    Strawberry Pretzel Bars
    Strawberry Scones
Marshmallow Treats 12–13
    Amazing Mousse
    Chocolate Fluff Cookies
    Confetti Kebabs
    Rocky Road Bark
Reduced-Fat Crumb Coffee Cake 8
Simple Syrup for Iced Tea 20
    Cinnamon Syrup
    Orange, Lime, or Lemon Syrup
Summer Berry Bake RC
Sweet Iced Tea 20
    Apple Pie Iced Tea
    Cherry Lime Rickey Iced Tea
    Nantucket Iced Tea
    Orangeade Iced Tea
    Raz-Ma-Tazz Iced Tea
Triple-Chocolate Cookies 17
Washboard Cookies 9

RC = Recipe Card

Cook's Country

AUGUST/SEPTEMBER 2005

Beer-Can Chicken
Tricks from the BBQ Circuit

Rating Kitchen Knives
Cheaper Brand Wins

Grilled Flank Steak
How to Stuff and Roll

WHISKEY-GLAZED PORK CHOPS
Secrets to Sauce That Sticks

BOSTON BAKED BEANS
No-Stir Recipe for Slow Cooker

TOMATO BUYING GUIDE
Are Heirlooms Worth Eating?

LOW-FAT CHOCOLATE CAKE
Take Out Fat, Not Flavor

BETTER MACARONI SALAD
Creamy, But Not Heavy

LEMONADE TASTE TEST
Is Store-Bought Any Good?

SALAD BAR STIR-FRY
Let the Supermarket Prep Your Veggies

FRESH CORN FRITTERS
Ready in Just 15 Minutes

$4.95 U.S./$6.95 CANADA

Our Great American Sundae Contest Winner!
Rachel Billings of Somerville, Mass., won our $500 grand prize for her **Mississippi Mud Pie Sundae,** made with coffee ice cream, chocolate sauce, crushed frozen sandwich cookies, and halved chocolate-covered almonds. See page 26 for her recipe, along with 11 other first-rate sundaes.

Cook's Country

Dear Country Cook,

It wasn't that long ago in America that we all had some fun with our food. I remember one dinner in particular when my mother served the courses in reverse. We started with dessert, then the main course, and, finally, the radish/celery tray. Of course, she also walked backwards, coming in and out of the kitchen heel first.

Every August, my family visits Vermont's Washington County Fair. My favorite exhibit, the display of vegetable art, includes cabbage faces and squash monsters. The kids and I also check out the pie-baking contest—a mile-high slice of lemon meringue usually wins the blue ribbon.

These days, food is too often examined, researched, tested, exalted, portioned, analyzed, and marketed. It is a subject worthy of philosophers, scientists, politicians, and calorie-crunching nutritionists. But, lest we forget, food is also eaten, baked, decorated, given to neighbors, taken on a picnic, and even thrown. As a kid, I even sat on a pie, the one I had hidden in my bed, quickly forgetting where I had put it.

Food is fun. And it tastes pretty good, too.

Christopher Kimball
Founder and Editor, Cook's Country Magazine

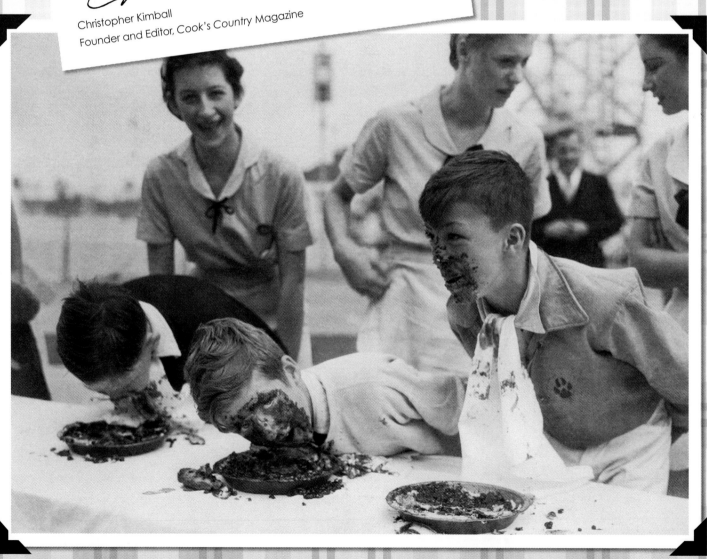

Favorites in Pie-Eating Contest Early leaders in the John R. Thompson Pie-Eating Handicap held at the Chicago World's Fair, September, 7, 1934, are shown as they lapped the field. They are (left to right) Richard Ness, Morton Dunn, and Seymour Kaplan. Image: © Bettmann/CORBIS.

Cook's Country

departments

RECIPE CONTEST: **Chicken Salads** **4**

RECIPE MAKEOVER: **Chocolate Sheet Cake** **6**

SLOW COOKING: **Boston Baked Beans** **7**

LOST RECIPES: **Orange Drop Doughnuts** **8**

FUN FOOD: **Watermelon Desserts** **10**

ON THE SIDE: **Corn Fritters** **13**

GETTING TO KNOW: **Tomatoes** **15**

EASIER THAN YOU THINK: **Quick Pickles** **19**

REGIONAL FAVORITES: **Creole Crab Cakes** **21**

FOR YOUR CONVENIENCE: **Salad Bar Stir-Fry** **23**

EASIER THAN YOU THINK: **Blue-Ribbon Fudge** **23**

FOOD SHOPPING: **Lemonade** **30**

EQUIPMENT ROUNDUP: **Chef's Knives** **31**

features

12 Whiskey-Glazed Pork Chops
A whiskey glaze shouldn't taste like sweet barbecue sauce. But it shouldn't burn your throat either.

14 Tomato Salads
Four simple salads let the tomatoes keep the starring role but offer some flavorful support.

17 Cool and Creamy Macaroni Salad
This picnic classic is all about finding the right consistency for a salad that's neither dry nor greasy.

18 Barbecued Beer-Can Chicken
We uncover the secrets to this barbecue cook-off classic.

20 Summer Garden Potato Salad
Potato salad dressed with vinaigrette—not mayonnaise—and tossed with green beans sounds appealing. But not if the vegetables are soggy and the dressing pools in the bowl.

22 How to Stuff Flank Steak
This recipe promises big flavors. But butterflying the meat is tricky, and grilling a stuffed flank steak requires perfect timing.

24 Rescuing Zucchini Bread
Come August, baking zucchini bread for friends and family seems like a good idea. But most loaves are too soggy and bland to give away—even to pesky neighbors.

25 Shaking Up Smoothies
Yogurt and fruit smoothies can be icy punishments handed out only to dieters. Could we create creamy smoothies that deliver a healthy blast of fruit flavor?

26 The Great American Sundae Contest
Twelve readers reinvent this summer classic.

27 Foolproof Ice Cream Sauces
Use these never-fail sauces to make our award-winning sundaes or to quickly dress up a plain bowl of ice cream.

in every issue

2 Kitchen Shortcuts

9 Ask Cook's Country

16 I'm Looking for a Recipe

16 Quick Cooking

28 Notes from Our Test Kitchen

32 When Things Go Wrong . . .

Founder and Editor Christopher Kimball
Executive Editor Jack Bishop
Senior Editor Bridget Lancaster
Test Kitchen Director Erin McMurrer
Copy Chief India Koopman
Associate Editors Keri Fisher, Eva Katz
Assistant Editor Melissa Baldino
Test Cooks Stephanie Alleyne
Katie Henderson
Jeremy Sauer
Assistant Test Cooks Meredith Butcher
Cali Todd
Kitchen Assistant Nadia Domeq
Contributors Matthew Card,
Lauren Chattman, Garth Clingingsmith,
Julia Collin Davison, Sean Lawler,
Diane Unger-Mahoney, Sandra Wu
Proofreader Dawn Carelli

Design Director Amy Klee
Designer Heather Barrett
Staff Photographer Daniel J. van Ackere

Vice President Operations James McCormack
Production Manager Mary Connelly
Project Manager Anne Francis
Production Assistants Jeanette McCarthy
Jennifer Power
Christian Steinmetz
Systems Administrator Richard Cassidy
Internet Technology Director Aaron Shuman

Chief Financial Officer Sharyn Chabot
Controller Mandy Shito
Staff Accountant Maya Santoso
Office Manager Saudiyah Abdul-Rahim
Receptionist Henrietta Murray
Publicity Deborah Broide

Vice President Marketing David Mack
Marketing Assistant Connie Forbes
Circulation Director Bill Tine
Circulation Manager Larisa Greiner
Fulfillment Manager Carrie Horan
Circulation Assistant Elizabeth Dayton
Products Director Steven Browall
Direct Mail Director Adam Perry
Customer Service Manager Jacqueline Valerio
Customer Service Representative Julie Gardner
E-Commerce Marketing Manager Hugh Buchan

Editorial Office: 17 Station Street, Brookline, MA 02445; 617-232-1000; fax 617-232-1572. Subscription inquiries: 800-526-8447.
Postmaster: Send all new orders, subscription inquiries, and change-of-address notices to Cook's Country, P.O. Box 8382, Red Oak, IA 51591-1382.

ON THE COVER: PHOTOGRAPHY: Rob Fiocca/PictureArts/Foodpix ILLUSTRATION: John Burgoyne.
IN THIS ISSUE: COLOR FOOD PHOTOGRAPHY: Keller + Keller. STYLING: Mary Jane Sawyer. ILLUSTRATION: Lisa Parett.

Cook's Country magazine (ISSN 1552-1990), number 04, is published bimonthly by Boston Common Press Limited Partnership, 17 Station Street, Brookline, Mass., 02445. Copyright 2005 Boston Common Press Limited Partnership. Application to mail at periodical postage rates pending at Boston, Mass., and additional mailing offices. POSTMASTER: Send address changes to Cook's Country, P.O. Box 8382, Red Oak, IA 51591-1382. For subscription and gift subscription orders, subscription inquiries, or change-of-address notices, call 800-526-8447 in the U.S. or 515-247-7571 from outside the U.S., or write us at Cook's Country, P.O. Box 8382, Red Oak, IA 51591-1382.. PRINTED IN THE USA

Visit with us at www.cookscountry.com!
Go online to ask questions, share kitchen tips, and enter recipe contests. You can also take a sneak peek at what we've got cooking for upcoming issues.

Kitchen Shortcuts

Egg Retrieval

I have found it handy to use a pronged pasta spoon when retrieving hard-cooked eggs from hot water. Most pasta spoons have the depth to securely hold the egg, and there are slots in the spoon to drain away excess water.

Juliet Muller
Phoenix, Ariz.

Peppercorn Transfer

None of my funnels are big enough to let peppercorns pass through, so refilling my pepper grinder has always been a circus act. I pour peppercorns into my hand or a sheet of paper, then try to slip the peppercorns into the grinder. Inevitably, random peppercorns drop and bounce all over my kitchen—or, on my more lucid days, into the sink. Last week, when I was about to leap into the void once again, I looked up and saw the solution sitting a few inches away: a disposable coffee filter. My number 4 folded coffee filter funneled the peppercorns perfectly. Not one was lost.

GOOD IDEA

Loretta Chen
San Francisco, Calif.

Keep It Simple
Chile Press

Instead of using a knife to chop canned chile peppers (such as pickled jalapeños), I use my garlic press. Works great—and really makes sense if you need minced garlic in the recipe, too.

Barbara Erskine
via e-mail

Keeping Your Kitchen Cool

Keeping your kitchen cool is of paramount importance in southern Texas. One little trick I use is to keep a teakettle filled with cold water on my electric cooktop. When I'm finished using a burner and turn it off, I put the filled teakettle on top; the heat goes into the water in the kettle instead of the room. It is amazing how much difference this makes.

Gayle Longoria via e-mail

Better Way to Make Rice

When I am making white long-grain rice, I simmer it with the lid off. Once the water boils down, I reduce the heat, place a paper towel on top of the pot, and then slide the lid in place. The paper towel absorbs the excess steam, and my rice comes out fluffy.

Barbara Cardeli-Arroyo
via e-mail

Getting That Last Drop of Maple Syrup

After struggling with upside-down bottles of sticky syrup, I discovered that a few seconds in the microwave makes the syrup thin enough to dispense easily. I remove the lid and microwave the plastic or glass container for a few seconds at a time until the syrup reaches a pourable consistency. This works with corn syrup and honey, too.

Marge Poling
Hagerstown, Md.

Short-Order Bacon

When cooking bacon, I cut the unopened package in half vertically to make each slice half as long. I then bake these short slices on a cookie sheet in a 350-degree oven. The slices bake up nice and flat and are easy to add to sandwiches. It's also easier to turn the slices because they don't flop around as much as the full-length ones.

Lia Soscia
North Bellmore, N.Y.

Oil (Container) Change

I often purchase vegetable and olive oils at warehouse clubs to save money, but they come in large containers that are hard to handle when you want just a dribble of oil. So I change the containers, transferring the oil to 24-ounce water bottles with squirt tops. These bottles are much lighter, and it's a snap to squeeze out just enough oil to coat a pan.

Karen Johnson
Silverthorne, Colo.

The Quick Chill

When I make a large pot of something hot (chili, stew, chicken in a slow cooker) and want to cool it down quickly, I open a bag of frozen vegetables and toss them in. They also add color, flavor, and fiber. Frozen corn is great with chili, peas with stew, and mixed vegetables with chicken. The possibilities are endless.

Bob Sabean
Barrington, N.H.

No-Stir Tomato Sauce

My family loves slow-simmered spaghetti sauce, but I don't have the patience to stand in the kitchen all day stirring to make sure the sauce doesn't burn. Instead, I preheat my oven to 300 degrees while I brown the meat, onions, and celery in a large ovensafe pot. After I've added the tomatoes and seasonings, I put the lid on the pot and put the pot in the oven. The sauce turns out beautifully every single time, whether I take a moment to stir it or not.

Ruth Hallows
Davenport, Iowa

Organizing Cookie Sheets

To organize my cookie sheets, I use plain metal bookends. They help to keep the cookie sheets upright and in place.

Christine Claypoole
Cambridge, Mass.

A Better Way to OJ

I recently bought a case of Florida juice oranges to support a local young women's rugby team, but I don't have a juicer! A glass hand citrus juicer was too small to adequately wring the juice out of the oranges, and I didn't want to spend the money on an expensive electric juicer. To my delight, a ricer worked extremely well. I washed the oranges, sliced them in half, and put a single half cut side down in the ricer. One squeeze, perfect juice, and no seeds!

Jonathan Frishtick
Norwich, Vt.

If you'd like to submit a tip, please send a letter to Kitchen Shortcuts, *Cook's Country*, P.O. Box 470739, Brookline, MA 02447. Or e-mail us at shortcuts@bcpress.com. Include your name, address, and phone number. If we publish your tip, you will receive a one-year subscription to *Cook's Country*.

Makeshift Steamer

Instead of steaming vegetables with an expandable basket insert (lost in a move across country), I balance a wire-mesh strainer across the rim of a deep saucepan. With water boiling down below the lowest point of the strainer and the saucepan lid holding the strainer securely in place, my cut-up vegetables steam perfectly.

Meredith McNabb
Decatur, Ga.

Chopped Vegetable Transfer

Few utensils can transfer a large amount of chopped vegetables to a pot on the stove. I use a small dustpan (reserved for just this purpose) to do the job.

Leon Gilner
Victoria, Texas

No-Waste Tomato Paste

When I am making my famous Italian sauce, I always add a can of tomato paste to the pot. Nothing like digging the tomato paste out of the can to make cooking a joy! I have found that by opening both ends of the can with a can opener and using one cut end to push the paste through, all of my tomato paste ends up in the sauce rather than stuck in the bottom of the can.

Fran Ferlazzo
Pleasanton, Calif.

Parchment for Pizza

When making bread or pizza on a baking stone, I used to put flour or cornmeal on the peel. Often the flour would burn or the cornmeal would get too crunchy. My solution was to put parchment paper on the peel instead. I then place the pizza or bread on top and trim away the excess parchment, leaving just a small border of paper to grab. I then slide the parchment, pizza and all, right onto the stone with ease.

Vincent Marano
Feasterville, Pa.

Good to the Last Drop

Whenever I want to get every last drop of batter off the beaters on my hand mixer, I use a tiny hors d'oeuvre spreader. (You know the kind. It looks like a miniature butter knife, and mine has a carrot-shaped handle.) The small steel blade works great and takes the place of tiny spatula—something I don't have.

Gwen Mancini
Utica, N.Y.

Baby Your Zester

I use the smallest holes on my grater for zesting limes, lemons, and oranges, but I hate cleaning it. I recently started using a baby-bottle brush, which gets into the smallest holes on the grater, making cleaning easier.

Christine Claypoole
Cambridge, Mass.

Foiling Grease

To dispose of grease, I line a soup bowl with aluminum foil and pour the drained grease into the bowl. After the fat hardens, I lift out the foil and toss the grease in the garbage.

Laura Lee
Colfax, Ind.

Corked

I use pushpins to post recipes or general kitchen reminders, and I store the pins in my uten-sil drawer. After getting stuck by more than one pin while reaching around in the drawer, I figured out a way to safeguard my fingers: I just push the pins into old wine corks. Now every time I pull out a pin, it brings back a memory of a great bottle of wine.

Doris B. Miller
York, Pa.

Flour Cap

When sifting flour with a turn-handle sifter, flour seems to fly out and make a mess. I've found that covering the top with an elasticized plastic bowl cover keeps the flour in the sifter, and I'm able to sift faster without worrying about getting flour all over my counters.

Dan Geskie
Valley Stream, N.Y.

Quicker Picker-Upper

When browning meat, the easiest way to drain the fat is to wipe the inside of the pan with paper towels. They absorb grease quickly and make cleanup a breeze since there's no messy grease to drain.

Celine Swieboda
Naperville, Ill.

Nonstick Rice Krispie Treats

After mixing the marshmallow and Rice Krispies, I spray my hands with cooking spray. That keeps them from sticking to the mixture when I press it into the pan.

Shelly Hagood
Newman Lake, Wash.

Putty Knife to the Rescue

I keep a 2-inch plastic putty knife in the kitchen for damage-free scraping of pans with stuck-on food and for cleaning my glass cooktop. They are available at most hardware stores.

George Meier Charlotte, N.C.

Hot Tip!
Bread-Dough Warmer

My kitchen is on the cold side, so bread dough is slow to rise. I use my microwavable herbal comfort pack (the kind  used for backaches and found at the drugstore) as an insulator for the bowl of dough. A thick towel also helps to hold the heat in.

Karen Wilson
Springfield, Ore.

Dressing Jar

LESS MESS

I use empty spice jars to make vinaigrette. I drop in a pinch of salt, a tablespoon of vinegar, some pepper, and 3 or 4 tablespoons of oil. Then I put the lid on and shake to make an emul-sion. I also mark the jar in tablespoon gradations for easy measuring. No messing with whisks or measuring spoons.

Jacqueline Lucas
Port Chester, N.Y.

Neat Trick
Sticky Spoons

Stirring sticky or pasty ingredients like cream cheese or honey into dry ingredients (or vice versa) can make a lumpy, half-mixed mess. I spray my wooden spoons with non-stick spray before stirring, and they release these ingredients quickly and easily, making for more even mixing.

Melisa Apye-Mose
Woodbine, Md.

DOUBLE DUTY

Shear Genius

I give my pie crusts a unique look by cutting the dough with pinking shears. The shears can be used to cut lattice strips or to cut around the edges of the pie dough instead of fluting it by hand.

Michaela Rosenthal
Woodland Hills, Calif.

The flavors of Southern California inspire our grand-prize winning recipe.

Our $500 Grand-Prize Winner!

Dawn Forsberg San Diego, Calif.

We invited readers to send us their favorite twists on traditional chicken salad and received nearly 150 recipes. Dawn Forsberg of San Diego, Calif., submitted a recipe that was deceptively simple (with just eight ingredients) yet inspired. Dawn explains, "The flavors in my chicken salad represent the local cuisine in Southern California. Cilantro and jalapeño are ingredients that you find in abundance here." By using pickled jalapeños, Dawn added a bracing acidity and some heat, which helped balance the richness of the mayonnaise.

We asked Dawn how she came up with her recipe. It turns out she's a vendor at the Hillcrest Farmers Market in San Diego and has been selling out of her Cilantro-Jalapeño Tuna Salad every weekend. "I tried my tuna salad with chicken and loved it," says Dawn. We think what's good for tuna is even better with chicken. Thanks to Dawn and all of the readers who sent us recipes.

JALAPEÑO CHICKEN SALAD
MAKES ABOUT 5 CUPS

Pickled jalapeños can be found in the international aisle at the supermarket, near the taco fixings.

2/3	cup mayonnaise
1	tablespoon lime juice
3	cups shredded cooked chicken
1/2	medium celery rib, chopped fine
1/2	small red onion, chopped fine
1/2	red bell pepper, seeded and chopped fine
2	tablespoons chopped fresh cilantro
1/4	cup sliced pickled jalapeños, chopped fine
	Salt and pepper

Mix mayonnaise and lime juice in small bowl until combined. Toss chicken, celery, onion, bell pepper, cilantro, and jalapeños in large bowl. Add mayonnaise mixture and toss until evenly coated. Season with salt and pepper to taste. Serve or cover and refrigerate for up to 2 days.

NOTE: To make tortilla bowl in photo, spray both sides of large flour tortilla with nonstick cooking spray. Toast tortilla in nonstick skillet over medium heat until spotty brown on both sides but still soft, about 3 minutes. Using tongs, drape tortilla over small overturned bowl. Place second overturned bowl over tortilla and cool completely.

Pickled jalapeños and cilantro freshen up this easy chicken salad created by a reader in California.

Recipe Contest Runners-Up

Apricot Chicken Salad

Curried Chicken Salad

Waldorf Chicken Salad

Chinese Chicken Salad

Susan Calhoun
Alpharetta, Ga.

Mary Frye
Mount Airy, Md.

Michele Ferrier
San Francisco, Calif.

Alice Chigas
Las Vegas, Nev.

APRICOT CHICKEN SALAD
MAKES ABOUT 5¹/₂ CUPS

Susan writes: "The addition of preserves makes this recipe special. I always ask people what they think the secret ingredient is, and no one ever guesses! I prefer to use 'no sugar added' preserves when making this salad. The spicy cayenne pepper balances the sweetness of the jam—so don't leave it out. This salad is more flavorful if made several hours before serving."

- ¹/₃ cup mayonnaise
- ¹/₄ cup apricot or peach preserves
- 1 tablespoon lemon juice
- ¹/₄ teaspoon cayenne pepper
- 3 cups shredded cooked chicken
- ¹/₂ cup red grapes, halved
- ¹/₂ cup slivered almonds, toasted
- 2 tablespoons chopped fresh tarragon
  Salt

Mix mayonnaise, preserves, lemon juice, and cayenne in small bowl until combined. Toss chicken, grapes, almonds, and tarragon together in large bowl. Add mayonnaise mixture and toss until coated. Season with salt to taste. Serve or cover and refrigerate for up to 2 days.

CURRIED CHICKEN SALAD
MAKES ABOUT 6 CUPS

Mary writes: "This salad began with a recipe that my godmother, Marnie, gave me for basic chicken salad with curry powder and grapes. Over the years, it has gradually evolved along with my exposure to new foods."

- ²/₃ cup mayonnaise
- 1 tablespoon lime juice
- 1¹/₂ tablespoons curry powder
- ¹/₂ teaspoon ground cumin
- ¹/₂ teaspoon ground coriander
- 3 cups shredded cooked chicken
- 1 large celery rib, chopped fine
- ¹/₂ medium onion, chopped fine
- 1 cup fresh or canned diced pineapple
- ¹/₂ cup currants
- ¹/₂ cup pistachios, toasted and chopped
  Salt and pepper

Mix mayonnaise, lime juice, curry powder, cumin, and coriander in bowl until combined. Toss chicken, celery, onion, pineapple, currants, and pistachios together in bowl. Add mayonnaise mixture and toss until coated. Season with salt and pepper to taste. Serve or cover and refrigerate for up to 2 days.

WALDORF CHICKEN SALAD
MAKES ABOUT 6 CUPS

Michele writes: "My mother always put orange segments in her Waldorf salad. It was a nice complement to the apples and chicken. The oranges, however, did make the salad a little watery, so I now add my own twist to her recipe by using zest and a little orange juice."

- ¹/₂ cup raisins
- ¹/₄ cup juice plus 1 tablespoon grated zest from 1 large orange
- ²/₃ cup mayonnaise
- 3 cups shredded cooked chicken
- 1 large sweet apple, cored and chopped
- 1 large celery rib, chopped
- ³/₄ cup walnuts, toasted and chopped
  Salt and pepper

Stir raisins and orange juice together in bowl and plump for 10 minutes. Mix orange zest and mayonnaise together in separate bowl until combined. Toss chicken, apple, celery, and walnuts in large bowl. Add raisin and mayonnaise mixtures and toss until coated. Season with salt and pepper to taste. Serve or cover and refrigerate for up to 2 days.

CHINESE CHICKEN SALAD
MAKES ABOUT 5¹/₂ CUPS

Alice writes: "This recipe was inspired by a dish that I had at a restaurant in Palo Alto, Calif., 25 years ago. My three sons always request it, so I usually make the recipe times four or five to feed the boys and their friends. I serve it at our annual Christmas Eve party and at our covered-dish suppers and picnics. The ingredients are easy to prepare ahead of time and can then be transported in plastic bags. If you do make this salad ahead, dress it directly before serving."

- ¹/₃ cup vegetable oil
- 1 tablespoon toasted sesame oil
- 3 tablespoons rice or white vinegar
- 2 tablespoons sugar
- 1 tablespoon soy sauce
- 3 cups shredded cooked chicken
- ¹/₂ head iceberg lettuce, shredded
- 4 scallions, sliced thin
- ¹/₄ cup dry-roasted peanuts
- 2 tablespoons sesame seeds, toasted
  Salt and pepper
- ¹/₂ cup chow mein noodles

Whisk vegetable oil, sesame oil, vinegar, sugar, and soy sauce in small bowl until sugar dissolves. Toss chicken, lettuce, scallions, peanuts, and sesame seeds together in large bowl. Add dressing and toss until coated. Season with salt and pepper to taste. Sprinkle chow mein noodles over top and serve immediately.

We are looking for creative sandwich recipes for an upcoming contest. Please submit entries by September 1, 2005. Write to Recipe Contest, Cook's Country, P.O. Box 470739, Brookline, MA 02447, or e-mail us at recipecontest@bcpress.com. Either way, please make sure to include your name, address, and daytime phone number, and tell us what makes your recipe special. The grand-prize winner will receive $500. All entries become the property of Cook's Country. We look forward to reading (and tasting) your recipes!

ROAST CHICKEN BREASTS FOR SALAD YIELDS 6 CUPS SHREDDED COOKED CHICKEN

Use leftover cooked chicken in any of these salads, or try our roasting method to make chicken specifically for salad. If you're going to roast chicken for salad, we think it makes sense to roast a good amount. This recipe makes twice as much chicken as you'll need for each salad. If you don't want to make that much chicken, simply halve this roast chicken recipe. If you make the full recipe, you can double any of the chicken salad recipes or freeze the leftover shredded chicken for up to 1 month.

- 2 large whole, skin-on, bone-in chicken breasts (at least 1¹/₂ pounds each)
- 1 tablespoon vegetable oil
  Salt and pepper

1. Adjust oven rack to middle position and heat oven to 400 degrees. Cover rimmed baking sheet with foil.

2. Dry chicken with paper towels, rub skin with oil, sprinkle with salt and pepper, and place skin side up on baking sheet. Roast until thermometer inserted in thickest part of breast registers 160 degrees, 35 to 40 minutes. Let chicken cool to room temperature, remove and discard skin, and cut breasts from bone. Divide each breast into 2-inch pieces and shred by hand.

Recipe Makeover CHOCOLATE SHEET CAKE

We wanted a sheet cake with great taste and texture, but not much fat. Unfortunately, every low-fat recipe we tried was bland, spongy, or dry.

Layer or sheet, Bundt or jellyroll, most every chocolate cake will make me break into a toothy, chocolate-crumb-covered smile. With one exception, that is. In my experience, low-fat chocolate cakes, always bland and spongy, never chocolaty, are simply not worth eating.

But recently, a waistline-watching chocoholic friend begged me to come up with a lighter version of her favorite sheet cake: moist and tender, packed with undeniably chocolate flavor, and topped with a creamy chocolate frosting.

None of the early recipes I tried were even remotely worth the reduced calories, and it seemed that the more desperate the recipe writers got, the goofier the ingredients became. Cakes made with canned beets and Marshmallow Fluff were particularly bad.

To give my cake as much deep chocolate flavor as possible, I began by replacing some of the flour with cocoa powder, which contains a lot of flavor but not much fat. With cocoa powder in my recipe, I was able to use just 3 ounces of melted chocolate instead of the 6 to 8 ounces common in most regular chocolate cake recipes. To intensify the chocolate flavor, I borrowed a professional baker's trick and mixed in a bit of instant coffee.

Efforts to replace the butter entirely with common low-fat substitutes like applesauce, sour cream, or yogurt were unsuccessful. The cakes made with these replacements were unappealingly dense and gummy. Instead of eliminating the butter entirely, I just used less—6 tablespoons instead of the two sticks found in most recipes. Low-fat buttermilk added flavor and moisture with a minimal amount of fat.

The flavor of my cake was now very good, but its texture was slightly dry and crumbly. What to do? As I scoured the test kitchen for ideas, I unwittingly found my answer while glancing over at a coworker who was developing a chocolate smoothie recipe: Hershey's chocolate syrup!

To keep things simple, I decided to stick with a traditional butter and confectioners' sugar frosting. Instead of going with the usual whole stick of butter, I used half that and made up the rest of the moisture with skim milk for a slightly looser—though still creamy—frosting. For the chocolate flavor, I used just 1 ounce of melted unsweetened chocolate (the flavor of semisweet didn't come through enough here) and replaced some of the confectioners' sugar with cocoa powder. A bit of instant coffee helped things along.

In the end, I was able to trim about one-third of the calories and more than half of the fat from my friend's recipe. And I had fooled many of my skeptical coworkers with a cake that produced chocolaty smiles instead of grimaces.

–Sandra Wu

REDUCED-FAT CHOCOLATE SHEET CAKE SERVES 20

- 3 ounces semisweet chocolate, chopped
- 3/4 cup cocoa powder
- 2 tablespoons chocolate syrup
- 1 1/2 cups all-purpose flour
- 1 teaspoon baking powder
- 1 teaspoon baking soda
- 1/4 teaspoon salt
- 6 tablespoons unsalted butter, softened but still cool, cut into 1-inch pieces
- 1 1/4 cups sugar
- 2 large eggs
- 1 teaspoon vanilla extract
- 2 teaspoons instant coffee granules
- 1 1/2 cups low-fat buttermilk
- 1 recipe Reduced-Fat Creamy Chocolate Frosting (follows)

1. Adjust oven rack to center position and heat oven to 350 degrees. Coat 13 by 9-inch baking pan with cooking spray, line bottom with parchment, and spray again. Melt chocolate with cocoa until smooth and whisk in chocolate syrup. Whisk together flour, baking powder, baking soda, and salt in bowl.

2. Place butter in large bowl and beat with electric mixer at medium speed until smooth, about 1 minute. Add sugar and continue to beat until well incorporated, 1 minute longer, stopping mixer as necessary to scrape down bowl. Add melted chocolate mixture and beat until mixture looks thick and grainy, about 1 minute. Add eggs, vanilla, and instant coffee. Beat at medium-high until fluffy and pale brown, 2 minutes. With mixer on low, add one-third flour mixture, followed by half of buttermilk.

And the Numbers...
All nutritional information is for one serving.

TRADITIONAL HOMEMADE
Chocolate Sheet Cake with Chocolate Frosting
CALORIES: 374
FAT: 23 g
SATURATED FAT: 14 g

COOK'S COUNTRY
Reduced-Fat Chocolate Sheet Cake
CALORIES: 269
FAT: 9 g
SATURATED FAT: 6 g

Repeat, ending with flour mixture. Scrape down bowl, increase speed to medium, and beat until creamy and without lumps, about 30 seconds. Give batter final stir.

3. Pour batter into prepared pan and smooth top. Bake until toothpick inserted into center of cake comes out with a few crumbs attached, 25 to 30 minutes. (See page 29 for more information on checking for doneness.) Cool on wire rack 20 minutes. Run knife around pan perimeter to loosen. Invert cake onto second rack, peel off parchment, and reinvert onto lightly greased rack. Cool completely (at least 1 hour), frost cake, and serve.

REDUCED-FAT CREAMY CHOCOLATE FROSTING
MAKES 2 CUPS

- 4 tablespoons unsalted butter, cut into 4 pieces
- 1 ounce unsweetened chocolate, chopped
- 1/4 teaspoon salt
- 1/4 teaspoon instant coffee granules
- 3/4 cup cocoa powder
- 3 cups confectioners' sugar
- 1 cup skim milk

1. Melt butter and chocolate together until smooth. Stir in salt and coffee granules until dissolved, then transfer to medium bowl to cool, 10 minutes.

2. Whisk cocoa and confectioners' sugar in medium bowl. Using electric mixer at low speed, gradually add cocoa mixture to melted chocolate mixture (mixture will appear grainy). Gradually add milk, beating until milk is completely incorporated. Increase speed to medium-high and beat until light and creamy, about 1 minute.

Say goodbye to bland low-fat cakes and hello to one with real chocolate flavor.

Secret Ingredient
Although unconventional, a mere 2 tablespoons of chocolate syrup gives our cake extra moisture and flavor—without adding any fat.

Slow Cooking BOSTON BAKED BEANS

My grandmother baked (and stirred) her beans all day. I wanted to dump my beans in a slow cooker and forget about them, but they kept on coming out tough, not creamy and soft like my grandmother's.

My memories of Boston baked beans date back to my grandmother's kitchen, where I watched her spoon the mahogany beans from her stoneware bean pot. She fussed over the beans for hours, stirring every half-hour or so, as her tiny Maine home filled with the aroma of salt pork, onion, brown sugar, and molasses. She didn't seem to mind the fuss. There were plenty of other kitchen chores to keep her occupied in between stirrings.

Unlike my grandmother, I have to be out the door by 7:30, clutching an oversized travel mug of coffee and the keys to my aging Explorer. I have found that baked beans don't require much attention, but they do require some, and so I worried that a "dump and forget" strategy using a slow cooker might not yield the rich, creamy baked beans I was after.

My concerns were well founded. The beans turned out pale and watery, and, even after cooking for 12 hours, they sounded like hail when they hit my dinner plate. After more tests, I hit on two partial solutions. First, these beans—just like my grandmother's—would need an overnight soak. Second, they would need an additional 15-minute parboil; this seemed to soften the beans to the point where my slow cooker could take over and finish the job.

To my surprise, even after taking both steps, undercooked beans were still a problem. I did some research and found that baking soda is often added to beans to soften the skins. When I added the soda to the slow cooker, the beans turned mushy. The better solution was to parboil the beans with a little baking soda, then to throw out the cooking water before adding the beans to the slow cooker.

The sauce proved trickier. When I bake beans in the oven, I take the lid off the pot during the final hours of cooking, which allows the sauce to thicken. But take the lid off a slow cooker and you lose all of the heat. I started with 8 cups of water (the amount used in many recipes) but clearly needed less, because with the slow cooker evaporation was not an issue. A mere 2 cups was the right amount for 1 pound of beans!

Per Grandma's recipe, I browned the salt pork (to render some fat) and the onion (to maximize the flavor). If I skipped this step, the beans were greasy and lacking in flavor.

To brighten the flavor, I added a bit more molasses just before serving. Mustard and vinegar perked things up, too; they are always best added at the end of cooking because their acidity can toughen the beans.

Finally, Boston baked beans that were rich, creamy, and every bit as good as those served for Saturday-night suppers in Maine—even though I had spent the day at work, not stirring the pot.

–Diane Unger-Mahoney

BOSTON BAKED BEANS SERVES 4 TO 6
Don't use dark or blackstrap molasses, which will become bitter tasting in the slow cooker.

- 1 **pound navy beans, picked over and soaked in cold water for 8 to 12 hours**
- 1/2 **teaspoon baking soda**
- 2 **bay leaves**
- 4 **ounces salt pork, rind removed**
- 1 **medium onion, minced**
- 1/4 **cup plus 2 tablespoons mild molasses**
- 1/4 **cup packed dark brown sugar**
- 2 **cups boiling water**
- 1 **tablespoon Dijon mustard**
- 2 **teaspoons cider vinegar**
  Salt and pepper

1. Set slow cooker to high to preheat. Drain beans and transfer to large Dutch oven. Add 8 cups water, baking soda, and bay leaves. Bring to boil over medium-high heat, then use wide spoon to skim off any foam that rises to top. Boil 15 minutes. Drain beans and transfer to slow cooker insert, discarding bay leaves.

2. While beans are cooking in Dutch oven, score fatty side of salt pork and cut into 2 pieces. Place scored side down in medium nonstick skillet over medium heat and cook until fat is rendered, 8 to 10 minutes. Turn salt pork over, add onion, and cook until lightly browned, about 5 minutes. Transfer to slow cooker insert. Stir 1/4 cup molasses, brown sugar, and boiling water into slow cooker insert.

3. Cover beans with piece of aluminum foil, then cover slow cooker with lid. Set slow cooker to low and cook until beans are tender and creamy, 10 to 12 hours. (Alternatively, cook on high for 5 to 6 hours.)

4. Turn off slow cooker and remove lid and aluminum foil. Stir in remaining 2 tablespoons molasses, mustard, and vinegar and season with salt and pepper to taste. Cover slow cooker with lid and let beans sit until sauce has slightly thickened, 15 to 20 minutes. Serve.

Speeding Up SLOW-COOKER BEANS

Slow cookers are notorious for failing to soften baked beans. Placing a layer of foil directly on the beans helps to keep the heat at the bottom of the pot—and in the beans—rather than letting it rise to the lid. This step shaves hours off the cooking time.

The American Table:
The Great Boston Molasses Flood

On January 15, 1919, around lunchtime, Beantown suffered an experience that would stick in Boston's collective memory for years to come. A giant holding tank containing more than 2 million gallons of molasses exploded and sent a near tidal wave of the stuff up to 15 feet high through the streets of the city's North End. Twenty-one people were killed as the molasses demolished everything in its path.

Given the relative obscurity of molasses in today's economy, it's hard to imagine a tank filled with 2 million gallons of it. But a century ago, molasses, remained an important commodity. From colonial times onward, it was distilled into rum, enjoyed by the colonists, and exported to Europe. But molasses, a byproduct of the cane-sugar-refining process imported from the Caribbean and West Indies, could also be used to make industrial-grade alcohol. This was in turn used to manufacture gunpowder and other munitions, both in great demand during World War I. But with the end of the war in late 1918, the demand for industrial alcohol fell, and the coming of Prohibition signaled the end of the legal manufacture of drinking alcohol. In fact, the day after the great molasses flood, the state of Nebraska ratified the 18th Amendment to the Constitution, and Prohibition became the law of the land. Molasses never regained its importance in the New England economy.

Lost Recipes ORANGE DROP DOUGHNUTS

U.S. Soldier Eating Doughnuts (circa 1910–1920). Photographer unknown. Library of Congress, Prints & Photographs Division, LC-USZ62-106755.

FOOD HISTORY: *The American Red Cross became associated with doughnuts during World War I. At the height of World War II, Red Cross workers served doughnuts at a rate of 400 per minute to American GIs.*

These old-fashioned "drop and fry" doughnuts couldn't be easier, but making them lighter and rich with orange flavor was a challenge.

Dear Cook's Country,
I'm an 82-year-old army veteran, and during my long military career my family moved often, and my wife, Sally, never complained. To show my gratitude, I started a ritual of making her breakfast in bed. Sally loved my homemade doughnuts, but these were no ordinary doughnuts. They were from a recipe that I clipped out of one of Sally's ladies' magazines (which I lost long ago) and were made by dropping spoonfuls of batter into hot fat. They tasted of fresh orange and were incredibly brown and crisp.

We'll be celebrating our 60th wedding anniversary in November, and I'd love to surprise her with a batch of hot doughnuts. Anything you can do for an old romantic?

Charlie "Spider" McKinnon, Ashtabula, Ohio

Dear Charlie,
Sounds like Sally is one lucky woman. Yeast-raised, jelly-filled, cake, cruller, bear claw, ring, or hole, I've never met a doughnut I didn't like. Since your orange-flavored, crispy confection had yet to cross my path, I was determined to introduce myself.

Cake doughnuts (a relative of your batter-dropped doughnuts) are an all-American phenomenon that started in the late 1800s, thanks to the availability of baking powder. Many 19th-century cookbooks show these quicker doughnuts being rolled and stamped out, just like their yeasted brethren. Eventually, savvy doughnut makers realized that dropping spoonfuls of cake batter into hot oil meant that fresh doughnuts could be on the table in minutes, without the fuss of rolling and stamping.

Drop doughnuts caught on like wildfire, and soon there were flavors of every kind—spiced, chocolate, and even your orange doughnut. In the late 1940s and into the 1950s, the name "orange drop doughnuts" started to appear in Betty Crocker cookbooks and magazines. I

tried these recipes, and, truth be told, they were pretty good. With a little more work, I hoped to make a super-orangey doughnut worthy of breakfast in bed.

Some recipes use nearly 3 cups of flour for two dozen doughnuts, but these heavy (yet tasty) lead balloons fell straight to the bottom of my belly. Two cups of flour—paired with 2 teaspoons of baking powder—worked much better. Two eggs and a little melted butter made these doughnuts properly rich.

As for liquid ingredients, some recipes call for milk as well as orange juice. But diluting the orange flavor just seemed wrong, so I added only juice. For even more orange flavor, I added a whopping tablespoon of grated zest to the batter— far more than the teaspoon or so found in older recipes.

Finally, I took a cue from a few recipes and rolled the hot doughnuts in a batch of homemade orange-flavored sugar. The pleasant aroma of citrus wafted through the test kitchen, and I saw my fellow doughnut hounds line up.

Happy anniversary. And I hope Sally enjoys the doughnuts. –Bridget Lancaster

ORANGE DROP DOUGHNUTS
MAKES 24 TO 30
You'll need 3 oranges for the zest and juice. See page 28 for information about monitoring the temperature of frying oil.

Orange-Sugar Coating
1/2	cup sugar
1	teaspoon grated orange zest

Doughnuts
	About 2 quarts vegetable oil
2	cups all-purpose flour
2	teaspoons baking powder
1/4	teaspoon salt
2	large eggs
1/2	cup sugar
1	tablespoon grated orange zest
1/2	cup orange juice
2	tablespoons unsalted butter, melted

1. For the coating Pulse sugar and zest in food processor until blended, about 5 pulses. Transfer to medium bowl. (If making by hand, toss zest and sugar in medium bowl using fork until evenly blended.)

2. For the doughnuts Heat 3 inches of vegetable oil in 4-quart saucepan until temperature reaches 350 degrees. Whisk flour, baking powder, and salt together in medium bowl. Whisk eggs, sugar, and orange zest in large bowl. Whisk in orange juice, then butter, until well combined. Stir in flour mixture until evenly moistened.

3. Using two dinner teaspoons, carefully drop heaping spoonfuls of batter into hot oil. (You should be able to fit about 6 spoonfuls in pan at one time. Do not overcrowd.) Fry, maintaining temperature between 325 and 350 degrees, until doughnuts are crisp and deeply browned on all sides, 3 to 6 minutes. Using slotted spoon, transfer doughnuts to plate lined with paper towels. Drain for 5 minutes. Add doughnuts to bowl with orange sugar and toss until well coated. Place on serving plate and repeat with remaining batter, regulating oil temperature as necessary. Doughnuts are best served warm.

**How to Make
ORANGE DROP DOUGHNUTS**

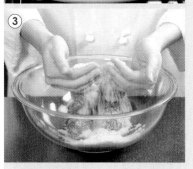

1. To avoid splashes of oil, use two dinner teaspoons to "drop" the doughnut batter carefully into the oil. **2.** When the doughnuts are deep brown and float to the top of the oil, use a slotted spoon to transfer them to a plate lined with paper towels. **3.** Let the doughnuts drain for 5 minutes, then transfer them to the orange sugar and toss until coated.

Looking for a lost recipe?
We can help. Drop us a line and tell us about the recipe you want to find. Write to Lost Recipes, Cook's Country, P.O. Box 470739, Brookline, MA 02447. Or e-mail us at lostrecipes@bcpress.com.

The zest and juice from three oranges flavor these simple (and addictive) baking powder doughnuts.

Ask Cook's Country

WE TRY TO ANSWER ANY QUESTION YOU THROW AT US!

THE $30 MIS-STEAK

My wife and I recently sat down to what we hoped would be a great dinner of two grilled porterhouse steaks that cost me $30. But I overcooked them—and I was using a thermometer! What went wrong?

Noah Reed San Jose, Calif.

Location, location, location! You might assume that the sensor on your thermometer is right at the tip, but on some models it is in fact an inch or two up. To find out where the sensor is on your thermometer, bring a pot of water to a boil and slowly lower your thermometer into the pot until it registers 212 degrees (adjusting, of course, for high altitudes). Knowing the location of the sensor is only half the battle, however. Now you have to insert the thermometer into the steak so that the sensor is right in the middle. We have found that the easiest way to do this (no matter where the sensor is located) is to use tongs to lift the steak off the grill (or out of the pan) and insert the thermometer through the side of the steak. Make sure the thermometer is not touching any bone, which will throw off the reading. And make sure to check each steak—some will cook faster than others depending on their thickness and their location on the grill (or in the pan).

GREEN GARLIC

My garlic often sprouts before I can use it. Can I still use it, even when green shoots are coming out of the cloves?

Andrew Marks Las Vegas, Nev.

Many people believe that those green shoots have a bitter taste. To find out for ourselves, we used raw garlic in mayonnaise and cooked garlic in pasta with olive oil and tried each recipe with the shoots removed before mincing the garlic as well as with the shoots left in. In both applications, tasters could clearly identify a more bitter, unpleasant taste in the batch made with the shoots left in. No need to dump your sprouted garlic, however, you can simply cut out and discard the shoots.

POISON APPLE

I've heard that apple seeds contain cyanide. Is that true? Should I be concerned?

Sparky Patterson Fort Myers, Fla.

Yes, it's true, and no, you shouldn't be concerned. Apple seeds contain amygdalin, which releases hydrogen cyanide when digested. But there are two reasons why you shouldn't be concerned: First, the human body can detoxify small amounts of cyanide. Second, apple seeds have a tough outer coating

Are apple seeds dangerous?

that is largely impervious to digestive juices. In other words, you would have to chew and swallow the seeds from several pounds of apples to be in any real danger.

COOKWARE MEASURES UP

Can you tell me what, exactly, is a "large" skillet or a "medium" saucepan? Are there general guidelines for what to use?

Sophie Shepherd Germantown, Pa.

Many recipe writers (ourselves included) find it simpler to call for a "large skillet" than to specify a measurement; we don't want you to feel that you can't make the recipe if you don't have a skillet that is exactly the right size. In general, a large skillet is about 12 inches (they can be as large as 14 inches, but we find these pans too large for most home burners), medium around 10 inches, and small 8 inches or less. (Skillets are measured across the top from rim to rim.) For saucepans, large is 3 to 4 quarts, medium 2 to 3 quarts, and small 1 to 2 quarts. A large Dutch oven (the only kind worth owning) holds 6 to 8 quarts.

OUT, DAMN STAIN!

While cutting up roasted beets for a salad, I seem to have stained my cutting board. Is there a way to remove stains from a plastic cutting board, or am I doomed to have a pink board forever?

Erika Belle Pomona, N.Y.

If your board won't fit into the dishwasher (several runs through will remove most stains), or if you are among the (weary) many who don't own one, try our time-honored method of an overnight bleach soak. Fill your kitchen sink halfway with water and add 1 teaspoon of bleach for each approximate quart of water (6 to 7 tablespoons for 5 gallons of water, which would fill a typical 10-gallon kitchen sink halfway). Immerse the board in the solution, dirty side up. When it rises to the surface, drape one or two clean kitchen towels (that you're not afraid of bleaching) over the surface and splash the towel(s) with another ¼ cup bleach. A sparkling-clean (and sanitized) board will await you in the morning.

ELECTRIC A-PEEL

My family loves apple pie, so I find myself peeling pounds of apples every week. I saw a battery-operated peeler advertised on TV and thought it might give my cramped hands a break. Then again, it might just be a waste of 10 bucks. Have you tried it?

Kimberly Chisholm Worcester, Mass.

We had heard about this gadget, so we ordered one to see what it could do. We had our reservations from the start—how hard is it to peel an apple anyway?—but we

Do you know how to measure your cookware?

pushed them aside and tested the Speedy-Peel with an open mind, using it on carrots and ginger as well as apples. We should have trusted our instincts. The Speedy-Peel had a dull blade, was uncomfortable to hold, and emitted an irritating shriek that reminded one test cook of a dentist's drill. The peeler vibrated so violently you could still feel it in your hand for more than an hour after use. We just couldn't see how maintaining a grip on a vibrating blade was any easier than applying the pressure needed to peel an apple manually (even with the Speedy-Peel, you must drag the peeler back and forth over the surface of whatever you are peeling). The bottom line? Save your money—the Speedy-Peel has no appeal.

A SALTIER SALT?

I've been hearing a lot about kosher salt lately. Is it true that it's "saltier" than table salt?

Rachel Hilly Boulder, Colo.

Kosher salt is a coarse salt that gets its name from its use in the preparation of meat according to Jewish dietary guidelines. The coarse texture is useful in koshering, which is intended to draw blood out of the meat. With their large surface area, crystals of kosher salt do this more effectively than the small, compact crystals of table salt. Kosher salt is often perceived as being saltier than table salt because the large, flaky crystals dissolve more quickly on the tongue. But the truth is that salt is salt; 1 pound of kosher salt contains just as much sodium chloride as 1 pound of table salt. In fact, because kosher salt weighs less than table salt by volume (that is, when measuring with a spoon), more kosher salt must be used to get the same salty effect.

Not all kosher salt is the same.

The two most popular brands of kosher salt are made differently and therefore measure differently: If substituting Morton's Kosher Salt for table salt in specific recipes, increase the measurement by 50 percent (for example, from 1 teaspoon to 1½ teaspoons); if using Diamond Crystal Kosher Salt, increase by 100 percent (from 1 teaspoon to 2 teaspoons).

Send your cooking questions to Ask Cook's Country, P.O. Box 470739, Brookline, MA 02447. If you prefer to use e-mail, write to askcookscountry@bcpress.com. See if you can stump us!

Fun Food

Make a Splash with Watermelon!

Chase away the dog days of summer with these four refreshing watermelon treats. We scoop it, chill it, freeze it, and mold it to create playful desserts with everyone's favorite summer fruit. Who knew that cooling down could be so much fun?

RECIPES BY LAUREN CHATTMAN

TUTTI-FRUTTI WATERMELON BOATS SERVES 2

Threading the kiwi slices through skewers and then placing each skewer into a melon ball gives this fruit salad the look of a boat in full sail. This recipe can be doubled, tripled, or quadrupled.

- 2 ripe medium bananas, peeled and cut in half lengthwise
- 1/2 small seedless watermelon
- 2 tablespoons sliced almonds, toasted
- 2 tablespoons sweetened, flaked coconut, toasted
- 1 kiwi, peeled and cut crosswise into 6 thin rounds

1. Make boats Place 2 banana halves in each of 2 banana split dishes or medium shallow bowls, placing rounded sides against outside of dishes to form cradle for melon. Using small ice cream scoop, scoop 3 balls watermelon into each dish, nestling melon balls into banana halves.

2. Garnish Sprinkle with almonds and coconut.

3. Make sails Thread skewer through each kiwi slice and stick one end of skewer into each melon ball. Serve.

WATERMELON CITRUS PUNCH SERVES 8 TO 10

If necessary, trim the bottom of the melon half so it can rest on a flat base. To keep the punch ice-cold, refrigerate the hollowed-out watermelon for at least one hour prior to serving.

- 1/2 large seedless watermelon
- 1 (12-ounce) can frozen pink lemonade concentrate
- 1 (6-ounce) can frozen limeade concentrate
- 5 cups chilled seltzer
- 1 lemon or lime, sliced thin
- 1 pint lemon or lime sherbet

1. Hollow out melon Scoop out watermelon until only pale green interior shows; refrigerate shell.

2. Make punch Puree 4 cups watermelon pulp in batches in blender until smooth and transfer to large bowl. Stir lemonade and limeade concentrates into bowl with melon puree until completely melted. (Mixture can be covered with plastic wrap and refrigerated overnight.)

3. Add fizz and garnish When ready to serve, gently stir seltzer into punch. Pour punch into watermelon shell (refrigerating any excess) and float lemon or lime slices on top.

4. Serve with sherbet Ladle punch into glasses, then float small scoop of sherbet on top of each glass. Serve.

WATERMELON ICE POPS MAKES 12 POPS

The melon mixture must be partially frozen before the chocolate chip "seeds" can be suspended in it.

- 1/2 small seedless watermelon
- 1/2 cup sugar
- 1/4 cup mini chocolate chips
- 1 pint lime sherbet, softened

1. Make watermelon ice Scoop out and measure 5 cups watermelon pulp. Puree watermelon and sugar in batches in blender until smooth. Push puree through mesh strainer into medium bowl. Cover and freeze until puree is slightly slushy but not yet solid, 2 to 3 hours. Remove from freezer and stir well, scraping any slush from sides of bowl. Stir in chocolate chips.

2. Freeze pops Place twelve 3-ounce disposable cups in shallow baking pan. Spoon watermelon puree into cups (puree will come to within ½ inch of rims). Place pan in freezer until puree is solid but not rock hard, 1 to 2 hours.

3. Add "rind" Spread softened sherbet on top of each portion of watermelon puree so that it comes up to edge of cup; smooth sherbet with back of spoon. Cover each cup with plastic wrap and cut small slit in center of plastic. Insert Popsicle stick into pop so that it almost reaches bottom of cup. Freeze until solid, at least 5 hours and up to 2 days.

4. Unmold Let pops sit at room temperature for 1 minute, then gently pull out from cups. (Alternatively, paper cups can be peeled away from pops.) Serve.

POLKA-DOT MINTY MELON MOLD SERVES 6

For a festive appearance, use a small melon baller to make the polka dots in this gelatin dessert. Alternatively, you can cut 1-inch cubes from the melons, making this a "confetti" melon mold instead.

- 2 cups water
- 2 envelopes unflavored gelatin
- 2 cups packed fresh mint leaves
- 1 1/4 cups sugar
- 1 1/2 cups 1-inch seedless watermelon balls or cubes
- 1 1/2 cups 1-inch honeydew balls or cubes
- 1 1/2 cups 1-inch cantaloupe balls or cubes

1. Soften gelatin Place ½ cup water in small bowl and sprinkle gelatin over water. Let gelatin stand until softened, about 10 minutes.

2. Make mint syrup Bring mint, sugar, and remaining 1½ cups water to boil in small saucepan. Reduce heat to low and simmer 5 minutes. Pour through mesh strainer, pressing on mint to extract as much flavor as possible. Gradually whisk gelatin into hot syrup. Cool to room temperature.

3. Make mold Toss watermelon, honeydew, and cantaloupe in large bowl until jumbled. Transfer melon to 1½-quart bowl, using slotted spoon to leave any accumulated juices behind. Pour cooled mint mixture over melon. Cover with plastic wrap and refrigerate until completely set, at least 6 hours and up to 1 day.

4. Unmold Dip bottom of bowl in hot water for 30 seconds. Place serving plate over bowl, invert, and tap gently to unmold. Slice and serve.

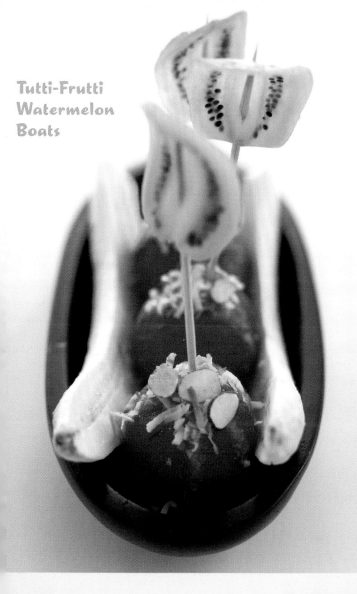

Tutti-Frutti
Watermelon
Boats

Watermelon Ice Pops

Watermelon Citrus
Punch

Polka-Dot
Minty Melon Mold

Whiskey-Glazed Pork Chops

A whiskey glaze shouldn't taste like sweet barbecue sauce. But it shouldn't burn your throat either.

Dear Cook's Country,
Whenever we eat out, my boyfriend, Dave, wants to go to the neighborhood chain restaurant so he can order off of the "Jack Daniel's" menu of steaks, ribs, and chops glazed with a thick, brown sauce. The food always looks pretty good, but the glaze tastes like a sweet barbecue sauce—there's no whiskey flavor at all. I'd like to make a recipe for Dave at home that would actually taste like Jack Daniel's. Then maybe when we eat out, we could go somewhere else!

Ricky Fossil, Sarasota, Fla.

Dear Ricky,
Pairing the earthy, smoky flavor of whiskey with mild pork is a great idea. And, evidently, there's more than one way to go about it. I found recipes that put whiskey into sticky glazes, overnight marinades, flaming pan sauces, flavored butters, and more. Which of these approaches, I wondered, would be the best way to create a happy marriage of flavors?

I started by testing recipes that exposed the pork chops to the whiskey for a long time, via overnight marinades and long, slow simmers. I figured more time would equal more flavor. These avenues were dead ends. The chops that soaked overnight had a sour, medicinal flavor, while the long-simmered chops were dried out (think shoe leather) and devoid of any flavor at all, whiskey or otherwise. The notion of marinating the chops for an hour or so was promising (and something I wanted to explore later on), but it was clear that for a real hit of whiskey flavor, I would have to make a sauce.

I chose widely available center-cut chops and used the test kitchen's basic technique for sautéing chops in a hot pan filmed with oil. My first thought was to add a shot of booze to a finished sauce. This backfired badly—the harsh taste of raw alcohol came through, with none of the deeper, more desirable flavors. Using the whiskey as the base for the sauce, then cooking it down for a few minutes, was much more promising. As the whiskey reduces, the pungent alcohol cooks off and the sugars and other subtler, mellower flavors are concentrated. This type of sauce also develops an attractive, rich brown color, aided by the dissolved crusty bits left over from searing the chops.

Developing a tasty pan sauce was a simple matter of finding the right ingredients to complement the charred, woodsy flavor (and surprising sweetness) of the reduced whiskey. Cider vinegar and cayenne pepper added acidity and heat, mustard helped to thicken the sauce, as did brown sugar, which also brought a welcome hint of molasses. Cutting the whiskey with an equal amount of apple cider helped to mellow its smokiness. I tried adding a bit of vanilla extract (a common ingredient in dessert sauces made with whiskey) and liked the way it paired with the spicy cayenne in particular.

As much as I liked the pan sauce, I was not ready to abandon the idea of infusing some of that flavor into the meat itself. In earlier tests, a one-hour marinade had added flavor to the meat, but I didn't want to make a separate marinade and sauce. Could I take a portion of the sauce ingredients and use them as a marinade? Sure enough, my marinade

The pork chops are marinated and glazed with the same spicy/sweet mix of flavors—Jack Daniel's, cider, brown sugar, cayenne, and vanilla.

really improved the flavor of the chops, which were now getting that great whiskey flavor from two sources—a marinade and a pan sauce.

It was time to plate these pork chops. But rather than just pour the sauce over them, I decided to reduce it even further, concentrating the flavors, until it resembled a thick, syrupy glaze. Then I returned the chops to the pan and let them sit off the heat for a few minutes, until the glaze cooled just enough to coat them thoroughly.

I hope these flavorful chops will keep your boyfriend happy until your next dinner out, when you get to pick the place!
–Sean Lawler

TENNESSEE-WHISKEY PORK CHOPS SERVES 4

Refrigerate the marinating chops in a shallow bowl in case the zipper-lock bag leaks. Watch the glaze closely during the last few minutes of cooking—the bubbles become very small as it approaches the right consistency.

1/2	cup Jack Daniel's Tennessee whiskey or 1/2 cup bourbon
1/2	cup apple cider
2	tablespoons light brown sugar
1	tablespoon Dijon mustard
1/8	teaspoon cayenne pepper
1/2	teaspoon vanilla extract
4	teaspoons cider vinegar
4	bone-in, center-cut pork chops, about 1 inch thick
2	teaspoons vegetable oil Salt and pepper
1	tablespoon unsalted butter

1. Whisk whiskey, cider, brown sugar, mustard, cayenne, vanilla, and 2 teaspoons vinegar together in medium bowl.

Transfer 1/4 cup whiskey mixture to gallon-sized zipper-lock plastic bag, add pork chops, press air out of bag, and seal. Turn bag to coat chops with marinade and refrigerate 1 to 2 hours. Reserve remaining whiskey mixture separately.

2. Remove chops from bag, pat dry with paper towels, and discard marinade. Heat oil in large skillet over medium-high heat until just beginning to smoke. Season chops with salt and pepper and cook until well browned on both sides and a peek into thickest part of a chop using paring knife yields still-pink meat 1/4 inch from surface, 3 to 4 minutes per side. Transfer chops to plate and cover tightly with foil.

3. Add reserved whiskey mixture to skillet and bring to boil, scraping up any browned bits with wooden spoon. Cook until reduced to thick glaze, 3 to 5 minutes. Reduce heat to medium-low and, holding on to chops, tip plate to add any accumulated juices back to skillet. Add remaining 2 teaspoons vinegar, whisk in butter, and simmer glaze until thick and sticky, 2 to 3 minutes. Remove pan from heat.

4. Return chops to skillet and let rest in pan until sauce clings to chops, turning chops occasionally to coat both sides, and a peek into thickest part of a pork chop using paring knife shows completely cooked meat (145 degrees on instant-read thermometer), about 5 minutes. Transfer chops to platter and spoon sauce over. Serve.

Break Out the Good Stuff

Bourbon was fine, but we loved the deep, caramel-flavored glaze we got when using Jack Daniel's in this recipe.

on the side: CORN FRITTERS

Nothing quite beats ears of fresh summer corn that are simply boiled and buttered. At least that holds true for the first half of corn season. But after weeks of eating boiled corn as the vegetable side dish for dinner, my family wants a change of pace. Corn fritters are a surprisingly simple way to turn fresh ears of corn into something truly memorable.

Now, you might think fritters are heavy, but the opposite is true. Good fritters are actually quite light—ideally, little corn pancakes that are creamy in the middle and crisp on the outside. After spending a week last summer making stacks (and stacks) of hot fritters, I found that the amount of flour in the batter has the greatest effect on texture. Many recipes use 1 cup of flour or more, but my batter has just 3 tablespoons, so these fritters are especially light.

There's just no such thing as too much corn in a corn fritter. Because I wanted to see the corn as well as taste it, I cut some kernels

whole off the cob with a knife and grated the rest of the corn on a box grater. And to make sure that I extracted every last bit of flavor from every cob, I used a knife to scrape out any remaining corn pulp. I packed in still more corn flavor by adding a little cornmeal to the batter.

These fritters taste like a hot, buttered ear of corn, but they are sturdy enough to dip into salsa, sour cream, or maple syrup—my personal favorite. **–Bridget Lancaster**

FARMSTAND CORN FRITTERS
MAKES 12 FRITTERS

Serve these crisp corn fritters with almost anything from the grill. The batter can be covered and refrigerated up to 4 hours.

1 1/2	pounds fresh corn (2 large or 3 to 4 medium ears), husks and silk removed
1	large egg, beaten lightly
3	tablespoons all-purpose flour
3	tablespoons cornmeal
2	tablespoons heavy cream
1	small shallot, minced
1/2	teaspoon salt
	Pinch cayenne
1/2	cup corn oil or vegetable oil, or more as needed

1. Using chef's knife, cut kernels from 1 to 2 ears corn and place in bowl (you should have about 1 cup whole kernels). Grate kernels from remaining 1 to 2 ears on large holes of box grater (you should have generous 1/2 cup grated kernels) into bowl with cut kernels. Using back of knife, scrape any pulp remaining on all cobs into bowl. Stir in egg, flour, cornmeal, cream, shallot, salt, and cayenne.

2. Heat oil in large heavy-bottomed, nonstick skillet over medium-high heat until shimmering. Drop 6 heaping tablespoonfuls batter in pan. Fry until golden brown, about 1 minute per side. Transfer fritters to plate lined with paper towels. If necessary, add more oil to skillet and heat until shimmering; fry remaining batter. Serve fritters immediately.

Kitchen Wisdom TURNING FRESH CORN INTO FRITTERS

For a mix of textures, cut whole kernels from some ears of corn (left) and grate kernels from the remaining ears (center). And for maximum flavor, use the back of a knife to scrape the pulp from all of the cobs (right).

FOOD FACT: *People once placed tomatoes on mantels in new homes, believing they would guarantee prosperity or ward off evil spirits. If ripe tomatoes were unavailable, pincushions made to look like tomatoes were used. Today, pincushions are still most often red.*

Tomato Salads

You could argue that all a truly perfect tomato needs is a sharp knife and a sprinkle of coarse salt. Some of us have even been known to snack on sweet, tiny Sun Gold tomatoes as if they were candy. But where's the inspiration in that? These salads succeed by pairing tomatoes with complementary, flavorful ingredients like smoky bacon, crunchy fennel, creamy avocado, tangy feta cheese, and sweet corn. The secret is to let the tomatoes shine rather than bury them under a cloak of goopy dressing or lose them in an everything-but-the-kitchen-sink mess of ingredients.

Just about any good tomato will work in these recipes. Use the glossary on page 15 for suggestions and guidance, but keep in mind acidity level when making your selection. While a highly acidic tomato would nicely complement the fat in bacon and avocado, it would be too much in a salad with a buttermilk dressing. Yellow and orange tomatoes tend to be the least acidic, while green varieties (not to be confused with unripe red tomatoes) are generally the most acidic. Red tomatoes usually fall somewhere in between. **–Keri Fisher**

'IT'S ALL GREEK TO ME' TOMATO SALAD SERVES 4

If you prefer, use the sweeter-tasting red bell pepper instead of the more traditional green pepper in this salad.

- 2 tablespoons extra-virgin olive oil
- 1 tablespoon red wine vinegar
- 1 tablespoon lemon juice
- 1/2 teaspoon dried oregano
  Salt and pepper
- 1 pound tomatoes, cored and cut into 1-inch chunks (or 1 pound cherry or grape tomatoes, cut in half)
- 1/2 seedless cucumber, halved lengthwise and cut crosswise into 1/4-inch slices
- 1/2 green bell pepper, seeded and cut into thin strips
- 3/4 cup pitted kalamata olives, chopped
- 1 1/2 cups crumbled feta cheese

Whisk oil, vinegar, lemon juice, oregano, and salt and pepper to taste in small bowl. Place tomatoes, cucumber, pepper, and olives in large bowl. Add vinaigrette and toss until evenly coated. Gently toss in cheese and adjust seasonings. Serve.

'BRING HOME THE BACON' TOMATO SALAD SERVES 4

Drain the bacon on paper towels after it is cooked to keep any extra bacon fat from diluting the dressing once the salad is mixed.

- 1 tablespoon plain yogurt
- 1 tablespoon mayonnaise
- 1 tablespoon milk
- 1/2 small garlic clove, minced
  Salt and pepper
- 1 pound tomatoes, cored and cut into 1-inch chunks (or 1 pound cherry or grape tomatoes, cut in half)
- 1 ripe but still firm avocado, diced
- 8 slices bacon, cooked until crisp and crumbled
- 1 head Bibb lettuce, leaves separated but left whole

1. Whisk yogurt, mayonnaise, milk, garlic, and salt and pepper to taste in small bowl. Place tomatoes, avocado, and bacon in large bowl. Add dressing and toss until evenly coated. Adjust seasonings.

2. Line serving bowl with lettuce leaves and fill with salad. Serve.

'FIT AS A FENNEL' TOMATO SALAD SERVES 4

Remove any dried-out portions of the fennel bulb before slicing it.

- 1/4 cup mayonnaise
- 1/2 cup grated Parmesan cheese
- 1 tablespoon milk
- 1/2 small garlic clove, minced
  Salt and pepper
- 1 pound tomatoes, cored and cut into 1-inch chunks (or 1 pound cherry or grape tomatoes, cut in half)
- 1/2 fennel bulb, trimmed and sliced thin
- 1/2 medium red onion, sliced thin
- 1/4 cup thinly sliced fresh basil
- 2 ounces thinly sliced deli ham, cut into 1/4-inch strips

Whisk mayonnaise, Parmesan, milk, garlic, and salt and pepper to taste in small bowl. Place tomatoes, fennel, red onion, and basil in large bowl. Add dressing and toss until evenly coated. Gently toss in ham and adjust seasonings. Serve.

'RHAPSODY IN BLUE CHEESE' TOMATO SALAD SERVES 4

Tossing the blue cheese into the salad after it's dressed helps keep the cheese from breaking apart too much.

- 2 ears corn, kernels removed
- 2 tablespoons extra-virgin olive oil
- 2 tablespoons balsamic vinegar
  Salt and pepper
- 1 pound tomatoes, cored and cut into 1-inch chunks (or 1 pound cherry or grape tomatoes, cut in half)
- 1 cup arugula, torn into 1 1/2-inch pieces
- 4 scallions, sliced thin
- 2/3 cup crumbled blue cheese

1. Bring 2 quarts water to boil in large saucepan. Add corn and simmer 2 minutes. Drain and let cool.

2. Whisk oil, vinegar, and salt and pepper to taste together in small bowl. Place tomatoes, arugula, scallions, and corn in large bowl. Add vinaigrette and toss until evenly coated. Gently toss in cheese and adjust seasonings. Serve.

'It's All Greek to Me'

'Bring Home the Bacon'

'Fit as a Fennel'

'Rhapsody in Blue Cheese'

Getting Them Ripe

Ripe tomatoes are deep in color, smell sweet, and yield gently to pressure. Do not refrigerate tomatoes; the cold destroys flavor and retards ripening. Tomatoes will continue to ripen at room temperature. To speed up the process, place the tomatoes in a paper bag (tomatoes release ethylene as they ripen, which speeds the ripening process when contained in a bag). A paper bag can do only so much, however; hard green tomatoes will not develop full tomato flavor no matter how long they sit on your counter; skip the paper bag and just fry them up instead.

Getting to Know Tomatoes

Confused by the colorful array of tomatoes now available at farmstands? So were we—until we rated dozens of varieties in a big tomato taste test. We were looking for a balance between sugar and acid. Here are our tasting notes on 15 popular conventional and heirloom varieties.

Brandywine
MISS POPULARITY

This popular Amish heirloom from the late 1800s is prized for its strong tomato flavor. Tasters praised it as sweet tasting, with a lot of juice, "barely any seeds, and "a good balance of acid."

Orange Tomato
SUN KISSED

These tomatoes tend to be sweeter and less acidic than red tomatoes. Common varieties include Pineapple, Orange Strawberry, and Striped German, which is streaked with red.

Red Cherry
BEST IN WINTER

"Very sweet and watery," with deep color and "tough" skins. Your best bet during the winter months, they should generally be passed over in favor of more flavorful varieties in the summer.

Ugly Ripe
INNER BEAUTY

Developed in response to the bland supermarket tomato, Ugly Ripes take their name from the pleats near the stem, known as cat facing or monkey facing. Despite the name, these tomatoes are sweet, juicy, and tender, with "good balance."

Zapotec Pleated
SHOWSTOPPER

Originally grown by the Zapotec Indians of Mexico, this heirloom tomato has a mild, sweet flavor with an almost hollow interior. Pleats turn to scalloped edges when sliced, which is why the Zapotec is prized more for its looks than its flavor.

Garden Peach
PRETTY AS A . . . TOMATO

Very pale yellow, with a faint pink fuzzy blush, this 100-year-old heirloom variety resembles a peach in color and texture. Our tasters found this tomato to be "mildly acidic," sweet, and juicy.

Supermarket Red
STYLE, NO SUBSTANCE

Not really a variety, the supermarket tomato is valued for its firmness, color, and ability to ship without bruising. We found it to have a mild, slightly sweet, "sturdy" flavor and to have "deep red color inside and out."

Green Zebra
BRIGHT AND TANGY

This beautiful heirloom fruit has a well-balanced, "real tomato flavor" that tasters loved. Flavor is "tangy" and "sweet." Ripe fruits are amber green with darker stripes.

Sun Gold Cherry
SWEET CANDY

"Vastly better" than the somewhat larger red cherry tomatoes, these golden beauties have an extremely high sugar content, which makes them perfect for snacking out of hand or tossing in a colorful salad.

Wonder Light
YELLOW FOR COOKING

Also known as Plum Lemon, this golden plum tomato should be used for cooking, not slicing. Not a lot of juice (which is what you want from a cooking tomato) and "hardly any flavor."

Grape
ONE-DIMENSIONAL

"Mild and tough," with deep color and low moisture, grape tomatoes are oval in shape and small in size, like round cherry tomatoes. Sweet year-round, but without the characteristic tang of a good ripe tomato.

Vintage Wine
STRIPED STUNNER

Pale pink with golden stripes, this heirloom tomato is prized by gourmet grocers for its visual appeal. Tasters described the flavor as mild and "slightly sour" yet "well balanced," while the texture was mealy and "a bit grainy."

Yellow Pear Cherry
OUTER BEAUTY

Small and vibrant, these beautiful pear-shaped tomatoes may look terrific, but they don't have much flavor to back them up. Described as "mild" and "somewhat sweet." Prized for their color and shape.

Roma
BEST FOR COOKING

Their meaty texture makes these supermarket staples great for cooking. What "little flavor" Romas have "tastes refrigerated," however, so don't use these tomatoes in salads. Also called plum tomatoes.

Purple Cherokee
BALANCING ACT

Tasters loved this very juicy tomato with "big sweetness" balanced by "slight bitterness" and great acid tang. Very meaty, with few seeds, it turns deep purple-brown when ripe.

I'm Looking for a Recipe

READERS HELP READERS FIND RECIPES

Tangerine Dinner Rolls

My father keeps telling me about these dinner rolls that his grandmother used to make. They were sweet dinner rolls with a tangerine section folded inside and a sugar coating on top. I would love to surprise my father and make them for him.

Tawnya Rivera
via e-mail

Milwaukee Cheesecake

I had a house fire and it took out my kitchen. One recipe, which I had been saving since 1974, was for Milwaukee Cheesecake. Made with marshmallows, heavy cream, and, of course, cream cheese, it was wonderfully creamy. It also had a graham cracker crust.

Chris Sroka
Minneapolis, Minn.

Buccellato

I grew up in Chicago, where there used to be a bakery called Fontana Brothers. They made an anise-flavored bread called *buccellato*.

Pam Ziarko
Buffalo Grove, Ill.

Persimmon Cake

Many years ago I bought a box of Fuyu persimmons at a farm and was given a recipe for persimmon cake. I made the cake and really enjoyed it. This year, I tried making the same cake from memory, but it didn't turn out right.

Charles Woo
Sacramento, Calif.

Italian "Scotch"

My grandmother used to make a recipe that my family calls Scotch (I don't know the correct spelling). I know that it was made with pizza dough, stuffed with some kind of parsley mixture, and then baked.

Jennifer Kunz
Forked River, N.J.

Swedish Flop Coffee Cake

Years ago I worked in a bakery called Heck's that was located on North Avenue in Chicago but has since gone out of business. The bakery made a Swedish Flop Coffee Cake that had an almost pastry-like consistency, a cream filling, and a streusel topping.

Donna Raysby
Lombard, Ill.

We've Got Mail

Several readers sent us recipes for the Burnt Sugar Cake requested by Jacquelyn Clymer in our April/May issue. We really liked Sister Delores Crosby's recipe (below). To see our notes on this recipe (as well as more details on cooking times and procedures), go to **www.cookscountry.com** and click **Looking for a Recipe**. You'll find dozens more recipes submitted by other readers who responded to this page in other issues of *Cook's Country*.

Boiled Cake

When I was a child, my grandmother used to make a "boiled cake" that included cinnamon, raisins, and, occasionally, pecans. It was a very dark, moist, dense cake that was absolutely delicious. The unusual thing was that she started cooking the batter on the stovetop. She would then pour it into a large cast-iron skillet and bake it in the oven. We never iced this cake; we ate it like a snack cake.

Vickie L. Hurst
Dallas, Texas

Orange Alaska Chiffon Cake

Back in the 1950s, a friend's mother made Orange Alaska Chiffon Cake. I didn't have the foresight to get the recipe, but I still dream of this treat. It consisted of sponge cake layers with orange filling and a browned meringue frosting that was drizzled with orange sauce.

Barb Glinski
Garden City, Mich.

Yugoslavian Potica

I am of Yugoslavian descent, and my grandmother used to make a cake called *potica*. I remember as a little girl watching her roll out the dough on her dining room table. It would take her the whole day to make this cake.

Jen McNabb
Westford, Mass.

Potato Kugel

My mother made her potato kugel with grated potatoes, oil, matzo meal, and beaten eggs and then baked it in a greased 13 by 9-inch casserole pan. There may have been some leavening in the recipe, as my mother didn't make it for Passover.

Alexandra Hans
Newton Centre, Mass.

Cream Cheese Mints

A friend of mine once gave me her recipe for cream cheese mints, but she has since moved out of state, and I lost touch with her. If I remember correctly, she used butter, cream cheese, and powdered sugar. She then used a frosting tube to form the mints. They had an almost frosting-like consistency, but they hardened slightly when refrigerated.

Nancy Ellingson
Waldorf, Minn.

BURNT SUGAR CAKE   Sister Dolores Crosby, Brier, Wash.

When my twin and I were growing up in Spokane, Wash., our mother used to make a Burnt Sugar Cake on special occasions. This was in the late 1940s or early 1950s. Here is her recipe. I still have the card that she typed up and sent to me. This cake NEVER failed!

1/2	cup butter	INSTRUCTIONS: Cream butter, add sugar
1 1/2	cups sugar	gradually. Add egg yolks, warm water, and flour
3	egg yolks	(2 cups). Beat 5 minutes. Add burnt sugar, then
1	scant cup warm water	beaten egg whites. Lastly, add the 1/2 cup flour that
2	cups flour	has the baking powder mixed in. Bake in layers and
	Burnt sugar*	use favorite icing or frosting with a little of the burnt
3	egg whites, beaten but	sugar in.
	not too light	
1/2	cup flour with 1 1/2	*As I recall, we simply put sugar into a cast-iron pan
	teaspoons baking	and stirred it until it caramelized and became a
	powder mixed in	heavy liquid. We always made extra for the next time.

Are you looking for a special recipe? Let other readers help. Just send us your requests, and we will print as many of them as we can. Write to Looking for a Recipe, Cook's Country, P.O. Box 470739, Brookline, MA, 02447, or send an e-mail to lookingforarecipe@bcpress.com. If you can help with one of the above requests, contact us at the same postal or e-mail address.

Quick Cooking

MAIN-COURSE RECIPES
READY IN ABOUT 30 MINUTES

Grilled Pork Tenderloin with Salsa

Grilled Swordfish with Eggplant Salad

Grilled Steak and Onion Salad

Zesty Shrimp Pasta Salad

Mahogany Chicken

Avocado Crab Louis

Open-Faced Sausage Sandwiches

Cheesy Broccoli Calzones

Find the Rooster! A tiny image of the rooster on the front cover has been hidden somewhere in the pages of this issue. If you find it, write to us with its location (plus your name and address), and you will be entered into a random drawing. The first winning entry drawn will receive the Forschner Victorinox Fibrox Chef's Knife (the winner of our equipment roundup on page 31), and each of the next five winners will receive a complimentary one-year subscription to *Cook's Country*. To enter the contest, write to us at Rooster, Cook's Country, P.O. Box 470739, Brookline, MA 02447, or e-mail us at rooster@bcpress.com. Entries are due September 1, 2005.

Did you find the rooster in the June/July 2005 issue? It was hidden in the Shanghai Chicken Salad recipe card. Dean Everett of Lawrenceville, Ga., spotted it and won the Braun PowerMax Blender.

GRILLED PORK TENDERLOIN WITH PEACH SALSA

GRILLED SWORDFISH WITH EGGPLANT SALAD

GRILLED STEAK AND ONION SALAD

ZESTY SHRIMP PASTA SALAD

GRILLED SWORDFISH WITH EGGPLANT SALAD SERVES 4

Halibut or salmon steaks can be substituted for the swordfish.

- 1 cup packed fresh cilantro leaves
- 1/2 medium red onion, coarsely chopped
- 4 medium garlic cloves, peeled
- 1 teaspoon cumin
- 1 teaspoon paprika
- 1/4 teaspoon cayenne pepper
- 1/8 teaspoon cinnamon
    Salt
- 3 tablespoons lemon juice
- 6 tablespoons olive oil
- 2 swordfish steaks, each about 1 pound and 1 to 1 1/4 inches thick
    Pepper
- 1 large eggplant, sliced crosswise into 1/2-inch rounds
- 1 cup cherry tomatoes, cut in half or in quarters if large
- 1 (15-ounce) can chickpeas, drained and rinsed

1. Process cilantro, onion, garlic, cumin, paprika, cayenne, cinnamon, 1/2 teaspoon salt, lemon juice, and 3 tablespoons oil in food processor or blender until smooth.

2. Cut each swordfish steak in half and place in baking dish. Coat with 1/2 cup cilantro mixture. Brush eggplant slices with remaining 3 tablespoons oil and season with salt and pepper.

3. Grill swordfish and eggplant over hot fire until fish is cooked through and eggplant is grill-marked and soft, 5 to 6 minutes per side for fish and 3 to 4 minutes per side for eggplant.

4. Transfer fish to serving platter. Chop eggplant into 1-inch chunks and place in medium bowl. Add tomatoes, chickpeas, remaining cilantro mixture, and salt and pepper to taste. Serve fish with eggplant salad.

GRILLED PORK TENDERLOIN WITH PEACH SALSA
SERVES 4

The brown sugar in the rub used on the pork has a tendency to burn, so watch the tenderloins closely as they cook.

- 2 peaches, peeled, pitted, and chopped fine
- 1/2 small red onion, chopped fine
- 1 tablespoon lime juice
- 2 tablespoons chopped fresh mint
- 1/2 jalapeño chile, seeds and ribs removed, then minced
    Salt and pepper
- 2 tablespoons cumin
- 1 tablespoon coriander
- 2 teaspoons brown sugar
- 3/4 teaspoon cayenne pepper
- 2 pork tenderloins, 1 1/2 to 2 pounds total
- 2 tablespoons olive oil

1. Combine peaches, onion, lime juice, mint, and chile in medium bowl. Season with salt and pepper to taste.

2. Combine cumin, coriander, brown sugar, cayenne, 1/2 teaspoon salt, and 1 teaspoon pepper in small bowl. Coat tenderloins with oil and rub evenly with spice mixture.

3. Grill meat over hot fire until browned on all four sides and internal temperature reaches 145 degrees, about 3 minutes per side. Transfer to platter, cover with foil, and let rest 5 minutes. Slice pork into 1-inch-thick pieces and serve with peach salsa.

ZESTY SHRIMP PASTA SALAD SERVES 4 TO 6

The spicy pesto flavors this room-temperature pasta salad. The pesto can be prepared a day in advance and refrigerated until needed.

- 1/4 cup walnuts, toasted
- 2 medium garlic cloves, peeled
- 2 cups packed fresh cilantro leaves
- 1 cup packed fresh basil leaves
- 3 anchovy fillets, rinsed and patted dry
- 1/2 cup extra-virgin olive oil
- 1 teaspoon grated zest plus 3 tablespoons juice from 2 limes
- 1/2 jalapeño chile, seeds and ribs removed
    Salt
- 1 pound fusilli or other short, curly pasta
- 1 pound cooked medium shrimp, peeled
- 1 pint grape or cherry tomatoes, cut in half

1. Bring 4 quarts water to boil in large pot.

2. Meanwhile, process nuts, garlic, cilantro, basil, anchovies, 7 tablespoons oil, zest, juice, and chile in food processor or blender until smooth, stopping to scrape down bowl as necessary. Transfer to small bowl and season with salt to taste. Cover with plastic wrap.

3. Add 1 tablespoon salt and pasta to boiling water. Cook until al dente. Reserve 1/4 cup cooking water, drain pasta, and transfer to large serving bowl. Stir in reserved cooking water and remaining 1 tablespoon oil and cool to room temperature. When cooled, toss with pesto, shrimp, and tomatoes. Serve.

GRILLED STEAK AND ONION SALAD SERVES 4

Any salad mix, including baby spinach, can be used in place of the arugula.

- 1 1/2 tablespoons balsamic vinegar
- 1 small garlic clove, minced
- 4 tablespoons olive oil
    Salt and pepper
- 1 large red onion, cut crosswise into 1/2-inch-thick rounds
- 2 boneless strip or rib-eye steaks, each 12 ounces and 1 1/2 inches thick
- 11 cups lightly packed stemmed arugula
- 1/2 cup crumbled blue cheese

1. Whisk vinegar, garlic, and 3 tablespoons oil together in small bowl. Season with salt and pepper to taste.

2. Brush onion with remaining 1 tablespoon oil. Season onion and steaks with salt and pepper.

3. Grill over hot fire until steaks are well browned on both sides and internal temperature registers 125 degrees, 5 to 7 minutes per side, and onions are charred and soft, about 4 minutes per side. Transfer to cutting board and let steaks rest 5 minutes. Slice steaks thinly across grain.

4. Toss arugula with 1/4 cup dressing in large bowl and season with salt and pepper to taste. Divide arugula among 4 individual plates or place on one large platter. Arrange steak and onions on top. Drizzle remaining dressing over steak and onions and scatter cheese on top. Serve.

MAHOGANY CHICKEN

AVOCADO CRAB LOUIS

OPEN-FACED SAUSAGE SANDWICHES

CHEESY BROCCOLI CALZONES

AVOCADO CRAB LOUIS SERVES 4

This light salad is perfect when it's just too hot to cook. You'll need one hard-cooked egg to make this recipe.

- 1/3 cup mayonnaise
- 1 1/2 tablespoons chili sauce
- 2 tablespoons chopped scallions
- 1/4 teaspoon Worcestershire sauce
- 8 teaspoons lemon juice
- Hot pepper sauce
- Salt and pepper
- 1 large tomato, cored, seeded, and finely diced
- 4 ounces lump crabmeat
- 2 avocados, each halved, pitted, slipped from skins, and cut in half again
- 1 hard-cooked egg

1. Whisk mayonnaise, chili sauce, 1 tablespoon scallions, Worcestershire sauce, 2 teaspoons lemon juice, and hot pepper sauce to taste together in small bowl. Season with salt and pepper to taste.

2. Combine tomato, crabmeat, remaining 1 tablespoon scallions, and 2 teaspoons lemon juice in medium bowl.

3. Place 2 avocado wedges on each of 4 plates. Season with salt and pepper and drizzle avocado on each plate with 1 teaspoon lemon juice. Spoon some dressing over avocado, then mound some crab mixture on top. Using large holes of box grater, grate egg over top of crab. Serve.

MAHOGANY CHICKEN SERVES 4

A splatter screen (or a large, inverted strainer/colander) is helpful for reducing the mess when browning the chicken. Serve with plain steamed rice. Mirin is sweetened Japanese rice wine sold in the international aisle at many supermarkets, usually near the soy sauce.

- 8 bone-in, skin-on chicken thighs (5 ounces each), trimmed of excess fat
- Pepper
- 2 teaspoons vegetable oil
- 1/2 cup soy sauce
- 1/4 cup sugar
- 2 tablespoons mirin, sweet sherry, or white wine
- 2 teaspoons grated fresh ginger
- 1 medium garlic clove, minced
- 1/2 teaspoon cornstarch
- 2 scallions, sliced thin on diagonal

1. Dry chicken thoroughly with paper towels and season with pepper. Heat oil in large nonstick skillet over medium-high heat until shimmering. Cook chicken, skin side down (thighs will fit into pan snugly), until skin is deep brown and crisp, 15 to 20 minutes. (Chicken should be moderately brown after 10 minutes. If too browned, reduce heat; if pale, increase heat). Turn chicken over, reduce heat to medium, and cook until second side is brown and meat is thoroughly cooked, about 10 minutes.

2. Meanwhile, whisk soy sauce, sugar, mirin, ginger, garlic, and cornstarch together in small bowl.

3. Transfer chicken to plate and pour off fat. Add soy mixture to skillet and return to medium heat. Return chicken to skillet, turn to coat with sauce, and simmer, skin side up, until sauce is thick and glossy, about 2 minutes. Transfer chicken to serving platter and sprinkle with scallions. Pour remaining sauce into small bowl and pass separately. Serve.

CHEESY BROCCOLI CALZONES SERVES 4 TO 6

We had good results with Pillsbury refrigerated pizza dough, but ready-made dough from your local pizzeria is an even better choice. If you use the Pillsbury dough, simply unroll it and use the rectangular shape. If you like, serve the calzones with your favorite basic tomato sauce.

- 2 1/2 tablespoons olive oil
- 3 cups shredded mozzarella cheese
- 1 cup crumbled feta cheese
- Salt
- 1 pound frozen broccoli florets
- 2 garlic cloves, minced
- Pepper
- Flour for rolling out dough
- 2 (1-pound) balls ready-made pizza dough

1. Adjust oven racks to upper-middle and lower-middle positions and heat oven to 475 degrees. Brush two baking sheets with 1 1/2 teaspoons oil each. Combine cheeses in small bowl.

2. Bring 1 cup water and 1/2 teaspoon salt to boil in large skillet over high heat. Add broccoli, cover, and simmer until broccoli is just tender, 3 to 5 minutes. Drain thoroughly and roughly chop. Wipe skillet dry, add remaining 1 1/2 tablespoons oil and garlic, and cook over medium heat until fragrant, about 1 minute. Toss in broccoli and season with salt and pepper to taste.

3. On lightly floured counter, roll out one ball of dough to 12-inch round. Transfer to one baking sheet. Roll out second dough ball and place on second baking sheet. Mound half of cheese on one side of each dough round, leaving 1-inch border around edges. Top each with half of broccoli. Brush dough edges with water, fold over filling, press edges to seal, and cut 5 slits in top of dough. Bake until golden, 15 to 20 minutes. Serve.

OPEN-FACED SAUSAGE SANDWICHES SERVES 4

Look for a large round loaf of Italian bread, which will produce substantial slices. Use spicy or sweet sausage or a mix of both.

- 2 tablespoons red wine vinegar
- 1 small garlic clove, minced
- 1/2 teaspoon Dijon mustard
- Salt and pepper
- 1/3 cup extra-virgin olive oil
- 2 large red bell peppers (or 1 red and 1 green pepper), seeded and cut into 1 1/2-inch pieces
- 1 large red onion, cut into 1 1/2-inch pieces
- 1 pound Italian sausage, cut into 1-inch pieces
- 8 slices Italian peasant bread, cut 1 inch thick
- 1 (7-ounce) package ready-mix salad greens

1. Whisk vinegar, garlic, mustard, and salt and pepper to taste together in small bowl. Whisk in oil. Toss peppers and onions with 2 tablespoons dressing in bowl and season with salt and pepper. Thread onion, pepper, and sausage onto four 12-inch metal skewers.

2. Grill over medium fire, turning skewers as needed, until sausage is well browned, about 9 minutes. Add bread slices to grill and cook until grill-marked, about 1 1/2 minutes per side. Remove bread and skewers from grill.

3. Drizzle each bread slice with 1/2 teaspoon dressing. Toss greens with remaining dressing in large bowl and season with salt and pepper to taste. Place 2 slices grilled bread on each of 4 plates. Mound salad over and around bread. Place one skewer on each plate. Serve.

Cool and Creamy Macaroni Salad

This picnic classic is all about finding the right consistency for a salad that's neither dry nor greasy.

Dear Cook's Country,

To tell you the truth, I feel sort of silly asking this, but do you have a good recipe for macaroni salad? By the time any backyard party is over, what's left of my macaroni salad—unfortunately, there's usually a lot left—is chalky and dry. I've tried adding more mayonnaise, but that doesn't seem to help. Any advice? I'm a good cook, and this recipe is supposed to be so easy.

Christopher Speed, Needham, Mass.

Dear Christopher,

It's often the simplest dishes that cause us the most trouble in the test kitchen. Macaroni salad is usually thrown together for a barbecue or block party without much thought. Everyone knows the recipe—cooked macaroni and mayonnaise tossed with chopped vegetables and seasonings. Although serviceable, this formula often makes a dry, bland salad. And that's a shame, because a great macaroni salad shouldn't be any more difficult to prepare than a mediocre one.

Believe it or not, the secret to perfect macaroni salad is leaving the cooked pasta a bit wet.

The main problem is the macaroni, which soaks up the mayonnaise and leaves the salad very dry. Stirring in more mayonnaise makes the salad greasy. So how do you satisfy macaroni's thirst without using an excess of mayonnaise?

My first attempt to solve this problem was to make sure that the macaroni was fully cooked, so that it would not be able to absorb any more moisture. But rather than fixing the problem, this made it worse. The pasta still soaked up the mayonnaise, but now it was also mushy.

Next I tried cooking the macaroni only till it still had some bite left and rinsed it under cold water before tossing it with the mayonnaise. The rinsing cooled the macaroni immediately, and the cooled macaroni soaked up less mayonnaise. But after 10 to 15 minutes, the salad still tended to dry out.

I finally hit upon a novel idea: What if I didn't drain the pasta so thoroughly? If the pasta was wet, perhaps it would absorb water rather than mayonnaise. At first even this idea seemed bound to fail. A salad made with damp macaroni looked pretty watery. But after a few minutes the macaroni absorbed the extra water, and the consistency of the salad became perfect. If left for a long time, this salad, too, will dry out a bit, but simply stirring in a few tablespoons of water restores its original creamy consistency.

As for flavorings, I tried combinations of various herbs, vegetables, and spices but found that the obvious choices—onion, celery, parsley, Dijon mustard, cayenne, and lemon juice—worked best. The one somewhat unusual ingredient that my tasters liked was garlic powder. Although raw garlic was too harsh, the powder rounded out the flavor of the salad in a really nice way.

My last thought was that if the macaroni soaked up water, maybe it would also soak up the flavor of the seasonings. After making two salads side by side—one in which the seasonings were tossed with the pasta and allowed to sit briefly before the mayonnaise was added, the other in which everything was tossed together at once—I was surprised by the difference. The pasta tossed with the seasonings first, then the mayonnaise, tasted fresher and brighter.

Finally, a word on mayonnaise. Regular mayonnaise tastes best (no surprise here), but low-fat mayonnaise isn't bad in this salad. Nonfat mayonnaise and Miracle Whip should be avoided, though, because of their candy-sweet flavor.

–Julia Collin Davison

COOL AND CREAMY MACARONI SALAD

SERVES 8 TO 10

Don't drain the macaroni too well before adding the other ingredients—a little extra moisture will keep the salad from drying out. If you've made the salad ahead of time, simply stir in a little warm water to loosen the texture.

	Salt
1	pound elbow macaroni
1/2	small red onion, minced
1	celery rib, minced
1/4	cup minced fresh parsley
2	tablespoons lemon juice
1	tablespoon Dijon mustard
1/8	teaspoon garlic powder
	Pinch cayenne
1 1/2	cups mayonnaise
	Pepper

1. Bring 4 quarts water to boil in large pot. Add 1 tablespoon salt and macaroni and cook until nearly tender, about 5 minutes. Drain in colander and rinse with cold water until cool, then drain briefly so that macaroni remains moist. Transfer to large bowl.

2. Stir in onion, celery, parsley, lemon juice, mustard, garlic powder, and cayenne, and let sit until flavors are absorbed, about 2 minutes. Add mayonnaise and let sit until salad texture is no longer watery, 5 to 10 minutes. Season with salt and pepper to taste. Serve. (The salad can be covered and refrigerated for up to 2 days. Check consistency and seasonings before serving.)

Barbecued Beer-Can Chicken

Could we uncover the secrets to this barbecue cook-off classic?

Dear Cook's Country,
I recently attended a local barbecue cook-off and thought something called beer-can chicken was the best in show. It was smoky, spicy, crispy, and juicy—the best chicken I've ever eaten. I watched this young guy as he barbecued chickens on beer cans, but he was not sharing any secrets. Here's what I saw: He propped up whole birds on open beer cans and cooked them in a covered charcoal grill with wood chips. Can you fill in the blanks?

Augus McDuffie, Sumter, S.C.

Dear Augus,
Beer-can chicken is a barbecue-circuit trick that's been around for years. The beer can is placed inside the cavity of the chicken and acts as both stand and steamer. The dry heat of the grill attacks the chicken from all sides, rendering the skin to a crackly crunch. Meanwhile, the beer steams happily away on the inside, ensuring especially moist meat.

O r at least that's how things are supposed to work. But if you cook a whole chicken directly over hot coals, things can get ugly real quick. Unless cooked with indirect heat, drippings from the chicken cause unwelcome flare-ups and char the skin. To make room for the upright bird, I placed it in the center of the grill and banked the coals on the sides. Now I had an empty space below the chicken and radiant heat to brown the bird front and back. After adding some soaked wood chips to the coals, I had even heat, lots of smoke, and enough room on the grill to cook two small chickens at once.

With the fire under wraps, it was time to start piling on the flavor. I saw the beer can as my workhorse, capable of pulling triple duty, not only as stand and steamer but as flavor container. By itself, the beer didn't provide much more flavor than plain water, but a few crumbled bay leaves added to the can did the trick, infusing the meat with potent herbal flavor.

Now that I had the smoke from the grill and the flavorful steam from the can, it was time to spice things up. I knew from past experience that certain seasonings perform better under fire (some spices taste worse when subjected to heat, while others taste better), so I turned to five with a definite affinity for barbecue: black pepper, cayenne, paprika, salt, and sugar (light brown tasted best).

Next I wondered how to achieve cracklin' crisp chicken skin. I tried oiling the chickens before rubbing on the spices, but these birds ended up flabby and flavorless. I tried patting the chicken dry with paper towels before rubbing on the spices, and this time I rubbed them not just on the skin but under it and inside the chicken cavity. This was a big improvement, although the skin was still turning out a bit on the thick side, especially around the thighs.

Hoping to help drain the excess fat, I used a skewer to poke holes all over the skin. This worked perfectly, rendering out the fat in those hard-to-reach places and leaving an extra-crispy skin. An unexpected benefit of this technique was that the skewer captured and deposited small amounts of the rub deep into the meat—in essence, the skewer was injecting the seasonings into the chicken, making for a full-on flavor invasion.

The final step was to make a quick glaze with beer, ketchup, vinegar, and sugar. The glaze was tasty, but after I added some of the spice rub and a couple splashes of hot sauce, it was great. I applied the glaze about 20 minutes before the chicken was finished cooking (any earlier and it might char), and when I lifted the lid off the grill, these birds looked amazing and tasted even better.

–Jeremy Sauer

BBQ BEER-CAN CHICKEN

MAKES 2 CHICKENS, SERVING 4 TO 6
Look for chickens that weigh between 3 and 3$^1/2$ pounds; if they are significantly larger, you may have trouble fitting the lid on the grill.

Spice Rub
- 2 tablespoons packed light brown sugar
- 2 tablespoons paprika
- 1 tablespoon salt
- 1 tablespoon black pepper
- 1 teaspoon cayenne pepper

Glaze
- 2 tablespoons packed light brown sugar
- 2 tablespoons ketchup
- 2 tablespoons white vinegar
- 2 tablespoons beer
- 1 teaspoon hot sauce

Beer and Chicken
- 2 (12-ounce) cans beer
- 4 bay leaves, crumbled
- 2 whole chickens (3 to 3$^1/2$ pounds each), patted dry
- 4 cups wood chips

1. For the spice rub Mix brown sugar, paprika, salt, black pepper, and cayenne in bowl.

2. For the glaze Stir brown sugar, ketchup, vinegar, beer, and hot sauce together in medium bowl. Add 1 tablespoon spice rub.

3. For the rest Measure out 1 cup beer from each can; take 2 tablespoons from measured beer and add to ketchup glaze. Prepare beer cans as shown in photo 1 at top of page 19, and add 2 crumbled bay leaves to each can.

No doubt about it—grilling a spice-rubbed chicken on top of a beer can looks odd. But if the result is crackling crisp skin and moist, juicy meat, why not give it a try?

4. Prepare chickens as shown in photos 2 through 4.

5. Soak wood chips in bowl of water to cover for 15 minutes. Light large chimney starter filled with charcoal briquettes (about 90 coals) and burn until charcoal is covered with fine gray ash. Place 13 by 9-inch disposable aluminum roasting pan in center of grill. Pour half of coals into pile on each side of grill, leaving pan in center. Scatter wood chips evenly over coals, set cooking grate in place, cover, and let grill heat up 5 minutes.

6. Place chickens (on cans) on center of grate, using drumsticks to stabilize them. Cover and grill until skin is well browned and very crisp, 40 to 60 minutes. Brush with ketchup glaze and grill, covered, until thigh meat registers 170 degrees on instant-read thermometer, about 20 minutes longer. Wearing oven mitts or using wad of paper towels, transfer chickens (still on cans) from grill to cutting board and let rest for 10 minutes. Hold base of can with oven mitt or wad of paper towels, insert tongs into neck cavity of chicken, and pull chicken off can. Carve and serve.

BBQ BEER-CAN CHICKEN ON A GAS GRILL
To hold the wood chips, you will need a small disposable aluminum tray.

Prepare recipe for BBQ Beer-Can Chicken through step 4. Soak wood chips in bowl of water to cover for 15 minutes, then place chips in small aluminum tray and place tray directly on primary burner. Turn all burners to high and close lid, keeping grill covered until wood chips begin to smoke, about 15 minutes. Leave primary burner on high, and turn off all other burners. Place chickens (on cans) on cool part of grill and proceed with recipe from step 6.

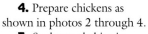
Essential Steps for
FLAVOR THAT'S MORE THAN SKIN DEEP

From its crisp, spiced skin to its moist meat, beer-can chicken is flavored through and through. Here's how to get the ultimate beer-can chicken experience from your grill.

1. Use a church key can opener to punch holes in the top of the can; this will allow the maximum amount of steam to escape. **2.** Loosen the skin on the breasts and thighs of the chicken by sliding your fingers between the skin and the meat.

3. Massage the spice mixture on the skin, under the skin, and inside the cavity. **4.** Using a skewer, poke the skin all over to render as much fat as possible.

Gadgets & Gear
DISPOSABLE ALUMINUM PANS

Place a disposable aluminum roasting pan in the bottom of the grill. Add hot coals on either side of the pan, which will catch fat from the chickens as they barbecue.

Fun Flavors: BEYOND BEER
Don't want to use beer? Try flavoring the chicken with the warm flavors of apple cider, cinnamon, and cloves instead.

APPLE HARVEST CIDER-CAN CHICKEN
Follow recipe for BBQ Beer-Can Chicken, making these changes: For rub, replace cayenne with 1/4 teaspoon ground cinnamon and 1/4 teaspoon ground cloves. For glaze, substitute 2 tablespoons maple syrup for brown sugar, 2 tablespoons cider vinegar for white vinegar, and 2 tablespoons apple cider for beer. Use 2 empty 12-ounce beer or soda cans to hold 1/2 cup cider each. Instead of bay leaves, sprinkle 1/4 teaspoon ground cinnamon and 1/4 teaspoon ground cloves into each can.

Easier Than You Think:
Quick Pickles

Quick pickles are salted for 1 hour, then cooked in vinegar for just 5 minutes.

Most people would sooner wear white after Labor Day than make pickles. That's a shame, because homemade pickles are bushels better than store-bought. And making them doesn't have to be a weekend-long affair. Though traditional pickles must be brined, canned, and fermented, often with special additives or ingredients, quick pickles are salted for an hour and then cooked briefly in vinegar. The result? Flavorful, crunchy pickles ready to eat in less than four hours. If they don't disappear the first day, these pickles will keep for up to two weeks. **–Keri Fisher**

'KOSHER' DOUBLE-DILL PICKLES MAKES ABOUT 16
Garlic is said to make dill pickles "kosher," and the double dose of dill—fresh and dried—packs in extra flavor. Don't overcook the cucumbers; they will lose their big crunch.

- 1 **pound pickling (Kirby) cucumbers, each sliced lengthwise into 4 spears**
- 1 **tablespoon kosher salt**
- 1 **tablespoon black peppercorns**
- 1 **tablespoon dried dill weed**
- 6 **garlic cloves, smashed**
- 1/2 **cup plus 1 tablespoon fresh chopped dill**
- 1 1/2 **cups distilled white vinegar**
- 1/2 **cup ice**

1. Toss cucumbers with salt in colander set over bowl. Let stand 1 hour. Discard liquid.

2. Place peppercorns, dill weed, garlic, and 1/2 cup fresh dill in paper coffee filter or several layers of cheesecloth and tie tightly with kitchen twine. Bring spice bag and vinegar to boil in medium saucepan. Reduce heat to low and add cucumbers. Cover and cook until cucumbers turn dull olive-brown, about 5 minutes. Discard spice bag.

3. Transfer cucumbers and liquid to glass bowl, add ice, and stir until melted. Stir in remaining 1 tablespoon fresh dill. Refrigerate, uncovered, at least 1 hour before serving. (Pickles can be refrigerated in covered container for up to 2 weeks.)

See another recipe on page 20

continued from page 19

FOOD FACT: *The average American eats 139 pounds of potatoes every year. Think that's a lot? In Ireland, annual per capita potato consumption is more than 300 pounds.*

BREAD-AND-BUTTER PICKLES MAKES 1 QUART

There's no consensus on how these sweet pickles got their name. Some claim the pickles are (like bread and butter) good enough to eat at every meal, others say it's because they are often eaten on or with sandwiches. Another theory is that they took their name from the word *smorgasbord*, which translates literally as "bread and butter table." It's not surprising that pickles often appear as part of this Swedish buffet.

1	pound pickling (Kirby) cucumbers, sliced crosswise into ¹/₈-inch disks
1	medium onion, halved and sliced thin
1	tablespoon kosher salt
1	cup cider vinegar
³/₄	cup sugar
¹/₂	teaspoon yellow mustard seeds
¹/₄	teaspoon celery seeds
¹/₈	teaspoon ground turmeric

1. Toss cucumbers, onion, and salt in colander set over bowl. Let stand 1 hour. Discard drained liquid.

2. Bring vinegar, sugar, mustard seeds, celery seeds, and turmeric to boil in large saucepan. Reduce heat to low, add cucumbers and onion, and press to submerge in liquid. Cover and cook until cucumbers turn dullish olive-brown, about 5 minutes.

3. Transfer entire pan contents to glass bowl. Refrigerate, uncovered, at least 2 hours before serving. (Pickles can be refrigerated in covered container for up to 2 weeks.)

Making a Good Vinaigrette

Use good vinegar. Wine vinegars (white, red, balsamic, or sherry) are the first choice in the test kitchen.

Use good oil. Extra-virgin olive oil is the most flavorful choice.

Know the right ratio. For every tablespoon of vinegar, add 3 to 4 tablespoons of oil, depending on how much vinegar punch you want to taste.

Season well. Salt and pepper are a must, and fresh herbs are better than dried.

Whisk, stir, or shake. It doesn't matter how you combine dressing ingredients—an old jelly or spice jar with a lid is just fine.

Summer Garden Potato Salad

Cook the beans and potatoes separately and dress each right away so that the hot vegetables can soak up the flavor of the vinaigrette.

Potato salad dressed with vinaigrette, not mayonnaise, and tossed with green beans? Sounds appealing. But not if the vegetables are soggy and the dressing pools in the bowl.

Because this dish gets its flavor from the vinaigrette, I started there. Extra-virgin olive oil, white wine vinegar, and minced shallots produced a winning combination, and Dijon mustard won out over contenders such as whole grain and spicy mustard for its clean appearance and tangy bite.

When dressing a leafy salad in the test kitchen, we use 2 tablespoons of vinegar for every ½ cup of oil. But my tasters wanted a dressing with more punch—after all, potatoes are pretty bland. I ended up adding an extra tablespoon of vinegar to satisfy their request.

After considering typical cooking methods, I decided that boiling both vegetables in the same pot would be the most efficient approach. But I soon learned that cooking the vegetables together meant one was almost sure to overcook. I decided to cook the beans first, lift them out of the pot with a slotted spoon, and then add the potatoes. I dropped the beans into a bowl of ice water to keep them from overcooking, but when I then tossed the cooled beans with the vinaigrette, the beans just sat there and the vinaigrette fell to the bottom of the bowl. Maybe hot beans would better absorb the dressing. They did. The best method proved to be just undercooking the beans, drying them (so as not to dilute the dressing), and immediately transferring them

Dear Cook's Country

We recently attended my son Ronnie's Little League potluck supper. The coach's wife, Becky, brought a green bean potato salad dressed with oil and vinegar—a welcome (and delicious) change from the creamy mayonnaise salads that usually appear. Becky told me how to make her salad, but when I tried the recipe at home it was terrible. The vegetables were overcooked and flavorless and the dressing puddled in the bottom of the bowl. I'm too embarrassed to tell her what happened. Where do you think I went wrong?

Clara May Hoke, Thurmont, Md.

Dear Clara May,

The recipe you describe sounds like a French garden potato salad with a mustard-based vinaigrette. Infusing the vegetables with the flavors of the dressing is the key to making this salad. While a creamy mayonnaise dressing will cling to potatoes no matter what, a thin vinaigrette can just sit there. When that happens, the salad is bland.

to the vinaigrette. As the beans cooled, they continued to soften slightly and soak up the flavorful vinaigrette.

In the test kitchen, we use red potatoes for salad because they hold their shape better than other types of potatoes. Skins are often a topic of debate when making potato salad. In this case, I found that leaving the skins on the cut potatoes helped them remain intact as they cooked. The rosy color of the skin also made the salad more attractive. As with the green beans, warm potatoes did a better job of absorbing the dressing than cooled potatoes; 10 minutes was enough time for the warm potatoes to soak up the vinaigrette and to nearly cool down.

I finished the salad with a generous handful of fresh herbs. My tasters liked the classic combination of parsley, basil, and chives.

While this salad was nearly perfect when first made, I noticed that it became dry as it sat around, even for just half an hour. And the color of the herbs faded, too. To solve the problem, I borrowed a trick I use when making mayonnaise-based potato salad. I reserved a portion of the dressing (along with all of the herbs) to add at serving time. The salad was now moist and the herbs bright green. I hope it measures up to Becky's! –Cali Todd

GARDEN POTATO SALAD
SERVES 6

The key to infusing this summer-fresh salad with flavor is dressing the green beans and potatoes while they are hot. The salad can be made up to 1 day in advance. Just bring the salad back up to room temperature and add the fresh herbs and reserved dressing before serving.

- 1/2 cup extra-virgin olive oil
- 3 tablespoons white wine vinegar
- 1 1/2 tablespoons Dijon mustard
- 1 small shallot, minced
- 1/2 teaspoon pepper
- 8 ounces green beans, ends trimmed and cut into 1 1/2-inch pieces
- 2 tablespoons salt

- 2 pounds red potatoes, scrubbed and cut into 1 1/2-inch pieces
- 1/4 cup chopped fresh parsley
- 2 tablespoons chopped chives
- 2 tablespoons chopped fresh basil

1. Whisk oil, vinegar, mustard, shallot, and pepper together in large bowl. Reserve 1/4 cup dressing in measuring cup.

2. Bring 6 cups water to boil in large saucepan. Add green beans and salt. Cook, uncovered, until green beans are slightly tender but still crisp, about 4 minutes. Using slotted spoon, transfer beans to plate lined with paper towels to drain briefly, then add to bowl with dressing. Toss to coat.

3. Add potatoes to still simmering water. Bring back to boil and cook until paring knife can be inserted into potatoes with no resistance, 7 to 10 minutes. Using slotted spoon, transfer potatoes to colander and drain briefly. Add hot potatoes to bowl with beans and dressing. Toss gently to combine and let sit at least 10 minutes.

4. Add parsley, chives, basil, and reserved dressing to bowl. Toss gently to combine and serve.

DILLY GARDEN POTATO SALAD

The familiar combination of lemon and fresh dill makes this potato salad a natural side for grilled fish. Salmon is an especially good choice.

Follow recipe for Garden Potato Salad, substituting 3 tablespoons lemon juice for vinegar and 2 tablespoons chopped fresh dill for basil.

POTATO SALAD 'DU JARDIN'

Tarragon and orange flavor this potato salad with the taste of southern France.

Follow recipe for Garden Potato Salad, replacing 1 tablespoon vinegar with 1 tablespoon orange juice. Substitute 2 tablespoons chopped fresh tarragon for basil and add 1 teaspoon grated orange zest along with herbs.

Regional Favorites: *Creole Crab Cakes*

A mix of spices and aromatic vegetables flavors these crab cakes, and heavy cream adds a touch of richness.

In Louisiana, most dishes, including the crab cakes, are flavored with green bell pepper, onion, and celery. Plenty of fresh garlic, dry mustard, and cayenne add even more Creole flavor. And a little heavy cream adds richness (because no Louisiana dish isn't rich). Of course, for crab cakes that actually taste like crab, you need to start with a healthy dose of lump crabmeat and keep the binder (in this case saltines) to a minimum. Serve with our quick version of classic rémoulade (a mayonnaise-based sauce) for an additional Creole kick.
–Keri Fisher

CREOLE CRAB CAKES SERVES 4
You'll need about 30 saltines; crush them until most have turned to dust, with a few larger pieces no bigger than a small pebble. Serve these crab cakes hot with lemon wedges and Quick Rémoulade (below). See page 28 for tips on buying crabmeat.

- 2 teaspoons plus 3 tablespoons vegetable oil
- 1/2 small onion, chopped fine
- 1/2 green bell pepper, seeded and chopped fine
- 1 celery rib, chopped fine
- 1 tablespoon minced garlic
- 1 1/2 pounds lump crabmeat, picked over for any shells
- 1 1/4 cups crushed saltine crackers
- 1/4 cup mayonnaise
- 1 large egg
- 2 tablespoons heavy cream
- 1 tablespoon dry mustard
- 1/4 teaspoon cayenne pepper
- 1 tablespoon Worcestershire sauce

1. Heat 2 teaspoons oil in medium skillet over medium heat. Add onion, bell pepper, celery, and garlic and cook until soft, about 5 minutes. Transfer to plate and refrigerate 5 minutes.

2. Transfer vegetables to large bowl. Stir in crabmeat and 3/4 cup cracker crumbs, being careful not to break up large pieces of crab. Whisk mayonnaise, egg, heavy cream, mustard, cayenne, and Worcestershire together in small bowl. Using spatula, fold into crab mixture. Divide into 8 portions and shape each into 1 1/4-inch-thick cake. Transfer to plate, cover, and refrigerate until well chilled, at least 30 minutes or up to 1 day.

3. Heat remaining 3 tablespoons oil in large nonstick skillet over medium-high heat until shimmering. Meanwhile, dredge crab cakes in remaining 1/2 cup cracker crumbs and press to adhere crumbs to cakes. Cook 4 crab cakes until well browned on both sides, about 5 minutes per side. Transfer to plate lined with paper towels and repeat with remaining crab cakes. Serve immediately.

QUICK RÉMOULADE
MAKES ABOUT 1 1/2 CUPS
This simple sauce can be refrigerated for up to 3 days.

- 1 cup mayonnaise
- 1 tablespoon whole-grain mustard
- 1/4 cup chopped dill pickles
- 1 scallion, sliced thin
- 1 tablespoon lemon juice
- 1/4 teaspoon cayenne pepper
- Salt and pepper

Stir mayonnaise, mustard, pickles, scallion, lemon juice, cayenne, and salt and pepper to taste together in small bowl. Refrigerate until ready to use.

Secret Ingredient
Saltine crackers add more flavor than other binders and—unlike bread crumbs—won't make crab cakes pasty.

How to Stuff Flank Steak

The Best Way to STUFF FLANK STEAK

This recipe promises big flavors for a crowd. But butterflying the meat can be tricky, and grilling a rolled, stuffed flank steak requires perfect timing.

Dear Cook's Country,
My supermarket sells rolled flank steak stuffed with ham, cheese, and herbs. The package says "great for grilling," but I can never seem to get the timing right. Do you have any hints on cooking stuffed flank steak? And I wouldn't mind learning how to stuff the meat myself.

Whitney Cox, Evanston, Ill.

Dear Whitney,
Stuffed flank steak has its roots in Italian-American cooking. The filling typically includes prosciutto, cheese, and fresh herbs. Most recipe writers praise this combination for its potent flavors and economy—a stuffed flank steak will feed eight people, maybe more. But no one talks about the big problem with this recipe: cooking the meat.

A regular flank steak is less than an inch thick. You can just nick the meat with a knife and take a peek inside to tell when it's done. But when stuffed and rolled, a flank steak becomes several inches thick, and this method won't work. And once you slice the meat, you can't really put it back together—so it better be done. Unfortunately, most recipes we tested yielded charred exteriors and raw centers. We figured we needed to start at the beginning to understand this recipe.

The first step is *butterflying*, which is just a fancy term for cutting something almost in half to make it thinner. I wasn't having much success though, ending up with ragged-looking meat. I got much better results when I put the meat in the freezer for about 20 minutes, which helped to firm it up before I cut into it.

Imported prosciutto was on the ingredient list, but I wanted to use a widely available domestic ham—Black Forest ham from the deli proved the best substitute. While I was at the deli counter, I also picked up some thinly sliced provolone. Tasters liked its strong flavor, and the cheese melted nicely, too.

For the bread-crumb mixture, I tossed dried crumbs with a little minced garlic and a handful of chopped parsley. A few briny capers cut through the richness of the meat and cheese. Finally, I mixed in chopped roasted peppers.

It was time to tackle the biggest challenge when making this recipe: grilling it to perfection. I thought a hot fire would sear the steak and cook it through, but the steak's exterior charred long before the interior was ready. A lower-temperature fire, however, didn't brown the steak very well. In the end, I banked all of the hot coals on one side of the grill. I seared the steak over the hot coals, then moved the meat over to the cool side (without coals) and covered the grill to finish cooking.

The interior of the steak was juicy and tender, but the exterior was a bit leathery after being on the grill for more than half an hour. I brushed the next steak with olive oil before putting it on the grill and then again when I moved the meat to the cool side of the grill. The slick of oil kept the exterior moist and tender.

–Matthew Card

STUFFED FLANK STEAK
SERVES 8 TO 10
An instant-read thermometer is a must for this recipe.

1	cup plain bread crumbs
3/4	cup coarsely chopped roasted red peppers
1/2	cup extra-virgin olive oil
2	tablespoons drained capers
1/4	cup chopped fresh parsley
2	garlic cloves, minced
1/4	teaspoon red pepper flakes
	Salt and pepper
1	flank steak (about 2 pounds), frozen for 20 minutes
8	ounces thinly sliced Black Forest deli ham
8	ounces thinly sliced deli provolone cheese

1. Mix bread crumbs, roasted peppers, 2 tablespoons oil, capers, parsley, garlic, red pepper flakes, and ½ teaspoon salt together in medium bowl.

2. Season steak with salt and pepper and position so that long side faces you. Butterfly steak (see photo 1). Layer ham, cheese, and seasoned crumbs over steak (photo 2). Starting with short side, roll and tie steak (photos 3 and 4). Season with salt and pepper, brush with 2 tablespoons oil, and refrigerate while heating grill. (Steak can be wrapped and refrigerated for 1 day.)

3. Light large chimney starter filled with charcoal briquettes (about 90 coals) and burn until covered with thin coating of ash. Empty coals into grill and spread into even layer over half of grill. Set cooking grate in place, cover, and let heat for 5 minutes.

4. Grill steak over fire until browned on all four sides, about 12 minutes. Move steak to cool side of grill and brush with 2 tablespoons oil. Cover grill and cook until instant-read thermometer inserted into center of steak registers 120 degrees, 20 to 30 minutes, rotating and brushing steak every 10 minutes with 1 tablespoon oil.

5. Transfer steak to cutting board, tent with foil, and let rest 10 minutes. Remove twine and slice steak crosswise into ½-inch-thick slices. Serve.

STUFFED FLANK STEAK ON A GAS GRILL
Follow recipe for Stuffed Flank Steak through step 2. Heat all burners on high for 15 minutes. Grill steak until browned on all four sides, about 12 minutes. Leave primary burner on high and turn off all other burners. Move steak to cool side of grill and proceed as directed in step 4, cooking steak with lid down.

1. Slice the chilled steak horizontally, opening the steak as if it were a book. Split the steak to within 1/2 inch of the edge.
2. Layer ham and cheese over the steak, then cover with the bread-crumb mixture, leaving a 1-inch border around the edges of the steak. Pat crumbs to adhere.
3. Starting with a short edge, roll up the steak tightly. **4.** Use kitchen twine to tie the steak at 1-inch intervals. Loop a piece of twine around both ends of the steak to keep the filling from falling out.

For Your Convenience

SMART SHORTCUTS FOR EASIER EVERYDAY COOKING

Say goodbye to tedious chopping.
Use the supermarket salad bar as your prep cook.

SALAD BAR STIR-FRY SERVES 4

Although stir-frying is quick, the vegetable preparation can be tedious. Thanks to the local supermarket salad bar, you can cut out most of the work. Choose vegetables from each category in the box at right. If you like, instead of pork you can use flank steak or boneless chicken breasts cut into thin, 2-inch-long slices.

³/₄	pound pork tenderloin, cut into ¹/₃-inch rounds, then into ¹/₃-inch strips
3	tablespoons soy sauce
1	tablespoon dry sherry
2	tablespoons plus ¹/₃ cup water
5	tablespoons oyster sauce
1	teaspoon toasted sesame oil
1	tablespoon light brown sugar
1	teaspoon cornstarch
6	medium garlic cloves, minced
1	tablespoon minced fresh ginger
3	tablespoons peanut or vegetable oil
1¹/₂	pounds salad bar vegetables

1. Combine pork and soy sauce in medium bowl. Cover and refrigerate for 10 minutes. Meanwhile, whisk sherry, 2 tablespoons water, oyster sauce, sesame oil, brown sugar, and cornstarch in measuring cup. Combine garlic, ginger, and 2 teaspoons peanut oil in small bowl.

2. Heat 2 teaspoons peanut oil in large nonstick skillet over medium-high heat until just smoking. Drain meat, add to skillet, and break up any clumps. Cook, without stirring, for 1 minute, then stir and cook until browned around edges, about 30 seconds. Transfer meat to clean bowl.

3. Add 1 tablespoon peanut oil to skillet and heat until just smoking. Add batch 1 vegetables (see list at right) and cook 30 seconds. Add ¹/₃ cup water, reduce heat to medium, cover, and cook until crisp-tender, about 2 minutes. Drain vegetables on paper towels.

4. Add remaining 2 teaspoons oil to skillet, increase heat to medium-high, and heat until just smoking. Add batch 2 vegetables and cook, stirring frequently, until spotty brown, 1½ to 3 minutes.

5. Clear center of skillet and add garlic and ginger. Cook for few seconds, return meat and cooked vegetables to skillet along with batch 3 vegetables, and toss to combine. Add sauce and toss until thick and evenly distributed, about 30 seconds. Serve immediately.

Batch Those Veggies

Vegetables cook at different speeds, so they must be added to the stir-fry pan at different times.

BATCH 1: Cook under Cover
- broccoli or cauliflower florets

BATCH 2: Stir-Fry Quickly
- shredded: cabbage, carrots
- sliced: celery, mushrooms, onions, bell peppers
- whole: baby corn

BATCH 3: Add at the Last Minute
- bean sprouts
- spinach leaves

Easier Than You Think: Blue-Ribbon Fudge

For a smooth and creamy texture every time, we rely on evaporated milk and Marshmallow Fluff.

Although candy making is usually best left to professionals, homemade fudge is surprisingly easy to prepare—if you know a few tricks. Conventional recipes call for heavy cream, which can separate when heated. We found that evaporated milk is much more stable. And for a fluffy, light texture, we add Marshmallow Fluff, which eliminates the tedious beating of the fudge that standard recipes require. The Fluff also prevents any crystallization of the sugar, so the texture of this fudge is creamy and smooth, never grainy. Finally, the combination of bittersweet and unsweetened chocolates gives this fudge its intense chocolate flavor. Use a candy thermometer to monitor the temperature of the sugar mixture as it cooks. Once it reaches 234 degrees, it's done. (At higher temperatures, the fudge will turn crumbly.) And wait to add the chocolate until the sugar mixture has cooled to 200 degrees. If added right away, the chocolate can separate. **–Diane Unger-Mahoney**

BLUE-RIBBON FUDGE MAKES ABOUT 5 POUNDS

Stir the fudge constantly to prevent scorching. This fudge can be made in either a glass or metal baking dish.

4	cups sugar
1	(12-ounce) can evaporated milk
16	tablespoons (2 sticks) unsalted butter
2	cups walnuts or pecans, toasted and chopped coarse
1	(8-ounce) jar Marshmallow Fluff
2	teaspoons vanilla extract
12	ounces bittersweet chocolate, chopped
8	ounces unsweetened chocolate, chopped

1. Line 13 by 9-inch baking dish with two pieces of foil, placed perpendicular to each other; let edges of foil overhang pan.

2. Bring sugar, evaporated milk, and butter to boil in large, heavy-bottomed Dutch oven over medium-high heat, stirring constantly. Reduce to simmer and cook, stirring constantly, until mixture is light tan in color and registers 234 degrees on instant-read or candy thermometer, 7 to 12 minutes.

3. Take pan off heat; stir in walnuts, Marshmallow Fluff, and vanilla until uniformly combined. Let mixture cool to 200 degrees, about 7 minutes.

4. Stir in chocolates until smooth. Pour mixture into prepared pan and refrigerate, uncovered, until firm, about 4 hours. Using foil overhang, remove fudge from pan and cut into squares. (Fudge can be refrigerated in airtight container for up to 1 month.)

Rescuing Zucchini Bread

Come August, baking zucchini bread for friends and family seems like a good idea. But most loaves are too soggy and bland to give away—even to pesky neighbors.

Dear Cook's Country,
Every summer, I turn the abundance of zucchini in my garden into loaves I give out to neighbors and friends. My zucchini bread is fine but never great. It's the summertime equivalent of fruitcake. This year I'd like to bake a gift that everyone really wants to receive.

Jason Turim, San Francisco, Calif.

Dear Jason,
The problem with zucchini bread dates back to the health food craze of the 1960s and 1970s, when oil-based vegetable and fruit loaves became popular. While carrot cake and banana bread are usually pretty good, zucchini bread starts with two big deficits: Zucchini, by its nature, is very bland and very watery.

In my experience, some loaves are so tasteless and gummy that they're a waste of otherwise good ingredients. Other recipes use a heavy hand with sugar and spices to cover up the problem, but the resulting loaf is more like zucchini cake. But it doesn't have to be this way. Zucchini bread can be moist, lightly sweetened, and gently spiced.

Part of the appeal of zucchini bread is its simplicity. The technique couldn't be much easier: Stir the dry ingredients (flour, leavener, spices, and salt) together in one bowl, stir the wet ingredients and sweetener (oil, eggs, sugar, and often yogurt or sour cream) together in a second bowl, and then fold the dry ingredients into the wet, while adding grated zucchini.

After grating up the first batch of zucchini, I noticed an awful lot of water in the bowl. Merely draining off the water had little effect. Loaves without the liquid were still pretty soggy. Other watery vegetables, such as cabbage and eggplant, are sometimes salted before cooking. Taking a cue from this technique, I sprinkled the grated zucchini with a little sugar instead of salt and set it in a colander to drain. This method was evidently too successful—the bread was now much too dry. I needed to try something else.

If zucchini is a water-filled sponge, I figured, then why not treat it that way? I placed grated zucchini in a kitchen towel and wrung out every drop of moisture I could. The texture of the bread made with squeeze-dried zucchini was much better. But everyone still complained about the bland flavor.

Because zucchini bread is supposed to be "healthy," many recipes call for oil rather than butter. It wasn't hard to imagine that melted butter would make a tastier loaf. Sure enough, butter beat oil hands down.

Most zucchini bread recipes also call for either sour cream or yogurt. Tasters liked them both for the tangy flavor they added to the bread (in fact, I decided to add a little lemon juice for even more zip), but they preferred the lighter, cakier texture of the loaf made with yogurt. The sour cream version was dense and heavy by comparison.

Finally, I tackled the spices and sugar, which, in my opinion, are often used too freely. Tasters liked the simple combination of cinnamon and allspice. As for sugar, I saw recipes that called for anywhere from 1 to 3 cups. My final recipe ended up near the low end of the scale at just 1½ cups.

My zucchini bread is pretty good. Now if only I could find a fruitcake recipe that everyone likes. **–Stephanie Alleyne**

ZUCCHINI BREAD

MAKES ONE 9-INCH LOAF
Cut large zucchini in half lengthwise and scoop out the seeds with a spoon before shredding.

1	pound zucchini
2	cups all-purpose flour
1	teaspoon baking soda
1	teaspoon baking powder
1	teaspoon ground cinnamon
1	teaspoon ground allspice
½	teaspoon salt
1½	cups sugar
¼	cup plain yogurt
2	large eggs
1	tablespoon lemon juice
6	tablespoons unsalted butter, melted and cooled

1. Adjust oven rack to middle position and heat oven to 375 degrees. Generously coat 9 by 5-inch loaf pan with cooking spray.

2. Following photos (below left), shred and squeeze zucchini. Whisk flour, baking soda, baking powder, cinnamon, allspice, and salt in large bowl. Whisk sugar, yogurt, eggs, lemon juice, and butter in bowl until combined.

3. Gently fold yogurt mixture and zucchini into flour mixture using spatula until just combined. Transfer batter to prepared pan.

4. Bake until golden brown and skewer inserted in center comes out with a few crumbs attached, 45 to 55 minutes. Cool for 10 minutes, then turn out onto wire rack to cool at least 1 hour. (Bread can be wrapped in plastic and stored at room temperature for 3 days.)

FRUITY ZUCCHINI BREAD
Stir ¾ cup golden raisins or chopped dried apricots into batter along with zucchini.

NUTTY ZUCCHINI BREAD
Stir ½ cup toasted sliced almonds and ½ cup toasted and chopped pistachios into batter along with zucchini.

Squeezing out the liquid from the zucchini and using butter (not oil) are the secrets to zucchini bread so good you won't want to give any loaves away to friends or neighbors. For five quick cream cheese spreads, see page 29.

Kitchen Secrets THE GRATE SQUEEZE

Zucchini is more than 95 percent water, so it's no wonder that zucchini bread is notoriously soggy. This technique rids the zucchini of much of its moisture and concentrates the flavor at the same time.

1. Using the coarse holes on a box grater, grate the zucchini, peel and all. **2.** Place the grated zucchini in a clean dish towel and wring out as much liquid as possible.

Forget the ice and freeze the fruit for chilly smoothies with intense flavor.

Shaking Up Smoothies

Yogurt and fruit smoothies can be icy punishments handed out only to dieters. Could we create creamy smoothies that deliver a healthy blast of fruit flavor?

Dear Cook's Country,
I try to drink a yogurt smoothie every morning for breakfast (to make me feel better about all the not-so-healthy food I eat during the rest of the day), but if I see one more banana smoothie, I'll cry. Any ideas for interesting smoothies that will be easier to swallow?

Becky Farmer, Arlington, Mass.

Dear Becky,
I've tried to get on the smoothie wagon numerous times, only to fall off after my umpteenth "Banana Blast." Ice, yogurt, and bananas may make something healthy, but this classic combination is also pretty bland. I was up for your challenge to create more exciting smoothies, but first I needed to figure out some smoothie basics.

A great yogurt smoothie clearly begins with yogurt, but it also needs something frozen to give it body and slushiness. Our tasters nixed ice and gave the go-ahead to frozen fruit, which provides the body, coldness, and slushiness of ice without the watery ice crystals. Frozen fruit is also quick (washed and trimmed and ready to go), cheap, and of much better quality than most fresh fruit during the off-season. As for juice, just ½ cup (for 1½ cups yogurt and 2 cups frozen fruit) made the smoothie thin enough to pass the straw test but not so thin that you forgot you were drinking a smoothie.

I found that bananas are a must because they add body and creaminess. Just don't go overboard—two small bananas were enough to create a creamy consistency without getting in the way of the other fruit flavors. A hit of honey (just 2 tablespoons) added a hint of sweetness and balanced the tartness of the yogurt.

Now that I had the formula for a great smoothie, I headed to the freezer case for inspiration. Mixed frozen berries are an obvious choice, but frozen cherries and pineapple work, too. With the pineapple I used coconut milk instead of juice for a tasty piña colada smoothie. To the cherries I added chocolate syrup for a smoothie that tasted just like chocolate-covered cherries. Though I couldn't find frozen oranges, frozen orange juice concentrate provided just the right consistency and sweetness for a Creamsicle smoothie—just add vanilla. And I channeled The King himself and combined frozen bananas and peanut butter for a smoothie Elvis would have loved. These smoothies are great for breakfast (or anytime really) and easy as Strawberry Cream Pie (frozen strawberries and vanilla). **–Keri Fisher**

VERY BERRY MAKES 5½ CUPS

- 2 cups frozen mixed berries
- 2 small bananas, roughly chopped (about 1½ cups)
- 1½ cups plain yogurt
- ½ cup apple juice
- 2 tablespoons honey

Mix all ingredients in blender until smooth.

PIÑA COLADA MAKES 6 CUPS

- 2 cups frozen pineapple chunks
- 2 small bananas, roughly chopped (about 1½ cups)
- 1½ cups plain yogurt
- 1 cup unsweetened coconut milk
- 2 tablespoons honey

Mix all ingredients in blender until smooth.

THE ELVIS MAKES 5 CUPS

While we can't claim that Elvis drank this smoothie, we're certain that The King would have liked it, considering his fondness for grilled peanut butter and banana sandwiches.

- 3 medium bananas, roughly chopped (about 2½ cups) and frozen for at least 2 hours
- ¼ cup creamy peanut butter
- 1½ cups plain yogurt
- ½ cup apple juice
- 2 tablespoons honey

Mix all ingredients in blender until smooth.

CREAMSICLE MAKES 5½ CUPS

- 1 (12-ounce) can frozen orange juice concentrate
- 2 small bananas, roughly chopped (about ½ cups)
- 1½ cups vanilla yogurt
- ½ cup orange juice
- 1 teaspoon vanilla extract

Mix all ingredients in blender until smooth.

TAKES TWO TO MANGO MAKES 6 CUPS

- 2 cups frozen mango
- 2 small bananas, roughly chopped (about 1½ cups)
- 1½ cups plain yogurt
- ¾ cup pineapple juice
- 2 tablespoons honey

Mix all ingredients in blender until smooth.

STRAWBERRY CREAM PIE MAKES 5½ CUPS

- 2 cups frozen strawberries
- 2 small bananas, roughly chopped (about 1½ cups)
- 1½ cups vanilla yogurt
- ½ cup apple juice
- 2 tablespoons honey
- 1 teaspoon vanilla extract

Mix all ingredients in blender until smooth.

CHOCOLATE-COVERED CHERRY MAKES 6 CUPS

- 2 cups frozen cherries
- 2 small bananas, roughly chopped (about 1½ cups)
- 1½ cups plain yogurt
- ½ cup apple juice
- ¼ cup chocolate syrup

Mix all ingredients in blender until smooth.

The American Table:
What's in a Name?

In 1904, the word *smoothie* (a variation of *smoothy*) made its first appearance in the Merriam-Webster dictionary, which defined it as "a smooth-tongued person." In the 1930s, it became a trade name for a company's line of girdles and brassieres. By the 1950s, it was automotive paint. The health craze of the 1960s welcomed blended fruit drinks called smoothies, but it wasn't until 1973 that *smoothie* entered the vernacular as a frozen fruit drink. That's when the Smoothie King franchise made its debut in Louisiana.

Smooth Moves

Trying to save a few calories? Low-fat yogurt works well, but nonfat yogurt just doesn't cut it—tasters found it "gritty."

Flash freeze. Frozen fruit adds flavor and body without iciness and is often better than fresh during the off-season. If you've got great fresh fruit on hand, freeze it for 2 to 3 hours before using.

Unripe bananas taste as green as they look. Buy the ripest bananas you can find—and don't worry about a few brown spots.

Improvising. Our formula: 2 cups frozen fruit, 1½ cups yogurt, ½ cup juice, 2 bananas, and 2 tablespoons honey.

Serving size. These recipes yield three to four breakfast-sized servings. Smoothies do not hold, but the recipes can be halved.

The Great American Sundae Contest

Twelve readers reinvent this summer classic, and our test kitchen provides recipes for six easy sauces.

Our $500 Grand-Prize Winner!

Rachel Billings
Somerville, Mass.

Mississippi Mud Pie
Rachel builds her sundae with frozen crushed Oreo Double Stuff cookies, coffee ice cream, chocolate sauce, and halved chocolate-covered almonds.

2nd Place

Mary Janet Maxwell
Fairmont, N.C.

Black Forest Brownie
Mary spoons chopped chocolate-covered cherries and cubed brownies into her sundae dish and then adds vanilla ice cream and cherry sauce.

3rd Place

Jean Clevenger
Foothill Ranch, Calif.

Chocolate-Orange Explosion
Jean hollows out an orange and fills it with chocolate sorbet. The sorbet is then topped with chocolate sauce, crumbled chocolate biscotti, chopped oranges, and orange zest.

After-Dinner Mint
Michele Ferrier of San Francisco, Calif., pours Junior Mints into a sundae dish and tops them with mint chocolate chip ice cream. A drizzle of crème de menthe, whipped cream, and fresh mint finishes things off.

Taste of Paradise
Lanette Van Wagenen of Dimondale, Mich., tops vanilla ice cream with halved pineapple slices, blueberries, sliced bananas, diced strawberries, toasted coconut, and macadamia nuts.

Coffee and Doughnuts
Sallie Barrett of Kinston, N.C., starts with a glazed doughnut and adds a scoop of coffee ice cream, a dollop of whipped cream, and a dusting of ground instant coffee.

Kahlúa Tiramisu
Jenna Bryan Misencik of Huntersville, N.C., pours chocolate sauce into a dish lined with halved ladyfingers. She drops vanilla ice cream inside the ladyfingers, drizzles with Kahlúa, and finishes with whipped cream, chocolate shavings, and a raspberry.

Triple-Peanut Punch with Chocolate
Rebecca Hart of Havertown, Pa., layers crushed Nutter Butter cookies, chocolate ice cream, peanut butter sauce, and crushed peanut brittle to make this peanut lover's sundae.

Lemon Meringue Pie
Charlotte West of Falmouth, Mass., tops lemon sorbet with prepared lemon curd and toasted Marshmallow Fluff. Cinnamon graham crackers finish this fanciful sundae.

S'mores
Mary Ann Lee of Clifton Park, N.J., puts broken graham crackers in her sundae dish, tops them with a scoop of vanilla ice cream, another graham cracker, marshmallow sauce, chocolate sauce, and chopped chocolate.

Strawberry Cheesecake
Lillian Julow of Gainesville, Fla., mixes 1 part cream cheese with 4 parts strawberry ice cream, spoons this mixture over crushed Pecan Sandies, and tops off the lot with whipped cream and strawberry sauce.

Maple Walnut Waffle
Janet Eliades of Nashua, N.H., uses toasted waffles as a bed for maple walnut ice cream, which she then tops with maple syrup, toasted walnuts, and whipped cream.

Foolproof Ice Cream Sauces

Use these never-fail sauces to make our award-winning sundaes or to quickly dress up a plain bowl of ice cream.

You don't need to be a soda jerk to make a good ice cream sauce. And you don't need a lot of time. With 20 minutes (or less) and ingredients you already have on hand, you can prepare top-quality sauces that outshine anything you can buy in a jar.

What's the secret to successful sauces for ice cream? Good ingredients are a must, but the right texture is important, too. You want dessert sauces that will stick to the ice cream, not just run to the bottom of the bowl. In many cases, this means heating sauce ingredients—even if the sauce is best served at room temperature. Slow and low is best when simmering sugary sauces—you don't want anything to scorch. And remember that sauces will continue to thicken as they cool.

–Stephanie Alleyne

STRAWBERRY SAUCE

MAKES 4 CUPS

Jam gives this sauce a thick, glossy sheen. This recipe makes a lot of sauce, but it can easily be cut in half.

- 16 ounces frozen strawberries, coarsely chopped
- 1/2 cup sugar
- 1 cup strawberry jam
- 2 tablespoons lemon juice

Bring strawberries, sugar, jam, and lemon juice to boil in medium saucepan over medium heat. Simmer until sauce coats back of spoon, about 15 minutes. Remove from heat and cool until sauce begins to thicken, at least 30 minutes. Serve at room temperature.

CHOCOLATE SAUCE

MAKES 2 CUPS

- 1/2 cup heavy cream
- 8 tablespoons (1 stick) unsalted butter
- 1/2 cup light corn syrup
- 1/2 cup confectioners' sugar
- 9 ounces bittersweet chocolate, chopped
- 1 teaspoon vanilla extract

Bring cream, butter, corn syrup, and confectioners' sugar to boil in medium saucepan over medium heat. Remove from heat and stir in chocolate and vanilla until sauce is smooth. Serve warm.

BUTTERSCOTCH SAUCE

MAKES 2 CUPS

- 8 tablespoons (1 stick) unsalted butter
- 1 cup packed light brown sugar
- 1/2 cup heavy cream
- 2 teaspoons light corn syrup
- 1 teaspoon vanilla extract

Heat butter and sugar in medium saucepan over medium heat until sugar dissolves, about 3 minutes. Remove from heat and slowly stir in cream. Stir in corn syrup and vanilla. Serve warm.

PEANUT BUTTER SAUCE

MAKES 2 CUPS

Make sure to cook the sauce over low heat; with too much heat, the peanut butter will cause the sauce to break. For a special treat, pour over ice cream along with the chocolate sauce.

- 1 cup sugar
- 3/4 cup evaporated milk
- 8 tablespoons (1 stick) unsalted butter
- 1/2 cup creamy peanut butter
- 1 teaspoon vanilla extract
- 1/8 teaspoon salt

Bring sugar, milk, butter, peanut butter, vanilla, and salt to simmer in medium saucepan over medium heat. Reduce heat to low and cook, stirring often, until sauce is smooth and thick, about 3 minutes. Serve warm.

CHERRY SAUCE

MAKES 2 1/2 CUPS

Look for the cherries to begin to break down before adding the cornstarch.

- 2 (15-ounce) cans pitted Bing cherries, drained
- 1/2 cup sugar
- 1/4 cup light corn syrup
- 1 tablespoon lemon juice
  Pinch salt
- 2 teaspoons cornstarch dissolved in 1 tablespoon water

Bring cherries, sugar, corn syrup, lemon juice, and salt to boil in medium saucepan over medium-high heat. Simmer until cherries begin to break down, about 10 minutes. Remove from heat and stir in cornstarch mixture. Return to high heat and boil until sauce coats back of spoon, about 1 minute. Remove from heat and cool until sauce begins to thicken, at least 30 minutes. Serve at room temperature.

MARSHMALLOW SAUCE

MAKES 3 1/2 CUPS

- 1 (16-ounce) jar Marshmallow Fluff
- 3 tablespoons water

Stir Marshmallow Fluff and water together in medium saucepan over medium-low heat until smooth, about 2 minutes. Cool and serve at room temperature.

Corn syrup helps our chocolate sauce cling to ice cream.

AUGUST/SEPTEMBER 2005 • COOK'S COUNTRY **27**

---

is that so?

Ouch! What Causes Brain Freeze?

Watch out: Slurp your smoothie too fast and you'll fall victim to brain freeze, aka ice cream headache, that sharp pain between your eyes that comes on fast and furious when you eat something too cold too quickly. What's happening? When something very cold hits the roof of your mouth, the blood vessels above it constrict; the pain you feel is the effects of those same blood vessels dilating as your body tries to send more blood to the area to warm things up. The pain lasts only about 30 seconds or so, but if you want to get rid of it sooner, try pressing your (warm) tongue to the roof of your mouth. Or avoid it altogether by keeping the cold stuff away from that area in the first place. Thankfully, an article in the *British Medical Journal* by Joseph Hulihan ("Ice Cream Headache," May 10, 1997—yes, people do scientific studies on such things) concluded that "Ice cream abstinence is not indicated."

Ready When You Are

These sauces can be refrigerated for at least a week. If the sauce is best served at room temperature, let it warm up on the counter. If the sauce is best served warm, pour it into a medium saucepan and heat over low heat, stirring frequently, until warm and smooth. To reheat a sauce in the microwave, pour it into a microwave-safe bowl and heat, uncovered, for 20 seconds. Stir and repeat in 15- to 20-second increments until the sauce is warm and smooth.

Notes from Our Test Kitchen

TIPS, TECHNIQUES, AND TOOLS FOR BETTER COOKING

< Why Is Cali Smiling? She's probably thinking about our tasty Orange Drop Doughnuts (page 8). When we deep-fry in the test kitchen, we use an instant-read thermometer to monitor the temperature of the oil. Read on to find out what to do if you don't have one of your own.

NO THERMOMETER, NO PROBLEM

When deep-frying, heating the oil to just the right temperature is essential. Properly heated oil ensures that food will become crisp and browned. Oil that's too cool (the most common mistake made by home cooks) will yield pale, greasy food. A good candy thermometer or instant-read thermometer that registers high temperatures is a great tool, but with a little observation you can tell if the oil is ready for frying by making a test run of sorts.

Heating oil to the proper frying temperature (usually between 325 and 375 degrees—recipes will vary) takes a few minutes, depending on the amount of oil in the pot. When you think the oil might be ready, drop a small piece of bread (with the crust removed) or a small spoonful of batter (perfect if you're making our Orange Drop Doughnuts on page 8) into the hot oil.

If the bread or batter sizzles and fine bubbles appear (middle photo), the oil is just right and you can add your first batch of food. If there's no action in the pan and your bread or batter just sits there (left photo), the oil isn't hot enough. Remove the bread or batter using a slotted spoon, wait a minute or two, and try again with more bread or more batter.

If the oil bubbles furiously or the bread or batter colors almost instantly (right photo), the oil is much too hot. Take the pan off the heat and wait a few minutes before adding the first batch of food.

WHEN TO CHOP HERBS

During summer, when herbs are at their very best, we throw them into just about any dish. But while most herbs can be chopped a few hours ahead with no ill effect, some are best prepared just before use. Cilantro becomes soapy tasting if chopped in advance. Basil becomes slimy and blackens once chopped. A chopped scallion (not a true herb but often used like one) starts to release a noticeably slimy residue as it sits and, like cilantro, can develop a soapy flavor. It's best to use each of these three immediately after chopping.

MUFFIN TIME

Like most quick breads, our zucchini bread (page 24) doesn't have to be baked in a loaf pan. A muffin tin is another good option. In addition to being cute and easy to eat, muffins have the advantage of baking up in half the time of bread. To make zucchini muffins, coat a 12-cup muffin tin with cooking spray, fill each cup three-quarters full, and bake on the middle rack of a preheated 375-degree oven until a skewer inserted into the middle of a muffin comes out with a few crumbs attached, 22 to 27 minutes. These muffins are best served warm. Try them with one of the cream cheese spreads on page 29.

TOO COOL
No Bubbles

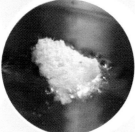

JUST RIGHT
Some Bubbles

TOO HOT
Lots of Buubles

One Great Tool CHIMNEY STARTER >

We remember when the prospect of lighting a charcoal grill on a windy day would fill us with dread. Dousing the coals with lighter fluid (and choking on its fumes) was the only surefire method—that is, until the chimney starter became standard issue in our test kitchen. Reminiscent of a beer stein, the chimney starter features a cylindrical chamber that holds charcoal and a lower basket-type area that holds newspaper. To get the coals going, all you have to do is place the chimney on the bottom rack of your grill, stuff a couple of pages of newspaper in the bottom basket, fill the upper tube with the desired amount of charcoal briquettes, and light the newspaper. In about 15 minutes you've got gray, ashy coals that are ready to be dumped into the grill. And thanks to the stay-cool handle on the side of the chimney starter, even the dumping of coals is a safe procedure.

You can find chimney starters at most hardware stores or wherever grills are sold, but it pays to think big and buy an extra-large model that will hold 5 or 6 quarts of charcoal. Sears offers an extra-large Weber Brand Chimney Starter for $12.99 (Sears item #07110139000, Weber Manufacturers model #87886). Order it by visiting www.sears.com or calling 800-349-4358. No matter which brand you buy, chimney starters make lighting charcoal a breeze—even when there is a breeze.

SHOPPING with the TEST KITCHEN

BUYING CRABMEAT

While we engineered our recipes for Creole Crab Cakes (page 21) and Avocado Crab Louis (recipe card) to work with several of the different kinds of crabmeat available at the supermarket, we did find big differences in the quality of packed crabmeat and formed a few preferences.

Unless otherwise labeled, crabmeat starts with cooked Atlantic blue crabs. If money's no object, try lump crabmeat. Usually packed in plastic containers available in the refrigerator near the fish counter, this product features big, tender chunks of crabmeat. It has the best texture and freshest flavor.

Most lump crabmeat is pasteurized to extend its shelf life. If you find fresh crabmeat from just-cooked crabs (available locally when crabs are in season), it will taste even sweeter. Whether fresh or pasteurized, lump crabmeat is pricey, anywhere from $19.99 to $23.99 per pound.

Backfin crabmeat has a more shredded texture. Although we missed the large chunks found in lump crabmeat, the backfin tasted sweet and fresh and cost a little less than lump—roughly $10.99 to $16.99 per pound.

Pouched crabmeat is a relatively new option. Similar to tuna in a pouch, this shelf-stable product features pasteurized lump crabmeat at a lower cost—just $6.99 for 12 ounces. The quality was OK (our tasters found it a bit watery), but it was not as good as the refrigerated lump or backfin crabmeat.

There is one product you should avoid. Imitation crabmeat, made of pollock that has been dyed orange, does not taste anything like crab. In fact, it doesn't taste like anything, period. Don't be tempted by the seemingly low price. A 6-ounce can may cost just $5, but that works out to a price of about $14 per pound. In this case, imitation is not the sincerest form of flattery.

< Kitchen Know-How AVOIDING A STICKY SITUATION

Before you throw those swordfish steaks on the grill (see our recipe card), you'll want to take every precaution to keep them from sticking to the cooking grate. In the test kitchen, we've found that nonstick cooking spray (which should be applied when the grate is still cool) works only some of the time and that fish baskets keep fish from developing a proper sear. Our preferred method for fish-proofing a grill involves a wad of paper towels dipped in vegetable oil. After the grate gets nice and hot, grab the wad of oiled paper towels with long-handled tongs and run them over the grate to grease well. Now you can grill up that costly piece of swordfish without fear of losing half to the cooking grate.

Jeremy demonstrates the best way to oil a hot grill grate. Grease the grate with oiled paper towels before cooking anything likely to stick, especially fish or burgers.

MEASURING FROZEN FRUIT

Though we usually reserve liquid measuring cups for liquids, we find it easier to measure chunky frozen fruit for smoothies (page 25) and other recipes in a 2-cup glass measure instead of traditional dry measuring cups. To measure 2 cups of frozen fruit, fill the cup to the top with fruit and then gently press down so it spreads somewhat to the edges of the glass. Once pressed, the top of the fruit should sit just slightly above the 2-cup mark.

IS IT DONE YET?

It's an old kitchen maxim: Don't remove a cake from the oven until a toothpick inserted in the center comes out with no crumbs attached. Many of us in the test kitchen have followed this directive for years, but recently we've discovered that finding a few crumbs sticking to the toothpick (not raw batter, mind you) isn't such a bad thing. In fact, a few crumbs can be the sign of a moist and tender cake. That's because residual heat continues to bake the cake once it is removed from the oven. If you wait until a toothpick comes out perfectly clean, the cake may be dry and crumbly by the time it cools.

Our "few crumbs attached" maxim is especially apt when baking low-fat cakes such as our Reduced-Fat Chocolate Sheet Cake (page 6). Without a healthy dose of fat to keep it moist, this cake will become chokingly dry if overbaked. In general, we think it's best to check all cakes a few minutes before the earliest baking time recommended in the recipe. You can always test the cake again if it's not done, but once a cake is overbaked there's no going back.

To determine whether a cake is done, insert a toothpick into the center and look for just a few moist crumbs to adhere (top). Raw batter (bottom) means the cake needs more time. If the toothpick is completely clean, the cake may have overbaked.

Do You Really Need This? VERTICAL CHICKEN ROASTER

The beer-can chicken craze has moved out of the barbecue circuit and into pop culture, but at a price. Entrepreneurs are out in full force to make a buck by selling vertical roasters that are supposed to make beer-can chicken easier to prepare. Most vertical chicken roasters consist of a simple metal cage and a set of instructions that reads: "Place beer can in cage. Place cage in chicken. Roast as directed for 'authentic' beer-can chicken flavor." Not bad for $17.99 (beer can not included), plus shipping and handling, right? Wrong. It's much easier to use a plain old beer can—forget the roaster. At that price, you could afford to fill your beer can with single-malt scotch.

AN ALTERNATIVE TO STRAINERS

Straining soups, stocks, and sauces is one way to remove solid ingredients. But it's not the only way. Instead of carrying large pots over to the sink, we often wrap herbs (and sometimes vegetables) in cheesecloth. When the dish is done, we simply lift out and discard the cheesecloth, along with its contents, which have given up their flavor to the liquid. When making our Quick Pickles (page 19), you can wrap the spices in cheesecloth so that they are easily removed from the brine. Cheesecloth is rarely a must (for pickles, you can just wrap the spices in a paper coffee filter), but it is nice to have on hand. Some craft-supply stores carry cheesecloth by the yard. Jo-Ann Stores, a fabric retailer, sells 100 percent cotton cheesecloth by the yard or in bulk on the Web at www.joann.com.

Kitchen Creations
Cream Cheese Spreads

Our zucchini bread (page 24) is good enough to stand on its own, but a slather of cream cheese makes it even better. Flavor that cream cheese with jam, spices, or citrus zest and you have something memorable. These spreads will keep in a covered container in the refrigerator for a week.

ZESTY APRICOT SPREAD
With rubber spatula, combine 8 ounces cream cheese, at room temperature, with 1/3 cup apricot jam, 2 tablespoons confectioners' sugar, and 1 tablespoon grated lemon zest in bowl until smooth.

MAPLE-CINNAMON SPREAD
With rubber spatula, combine 8 ounces cream cheese, at room temperature, with 2 tablespoons maple syrup, 1 tablespoon brown sugar, and 1/2 teaspoon ground cinnamon in bowl until smooth.

LEMON-GINGER SPREAD
With rubber spatula, combine 8 ounces cream cheese, at room temperature, with 1/3 cup ginger preserves, 1 tablespoon grated lemon zest, and 1/2 teaspoon ground ginger in bowl until smooth.

OH-SO-ORANGE SPREAD
With rubber spatula, combine 8 ounces cream cheese, at room temperature, with 1/3 cup orange marmalade, 2 tablespoons confectioners' sugar, and 1 tablespoon grated lemon zest in bowl until smooth.

SWEET PINEAPPLE SPREAD
With rubber spatula, combine 8 ounces cream cheese, at room temperature, with one 8-ounce can crushed pineapple, drained, and 2 tablespoons brown sugar in bowl until smooth.

Food Shopping

LEMONADE: What's the Secret to Great Flavor?

Lemonade is a wolf in sheep's clothing, a seemingly natural, kid-friendly alternative to soda with about the same sugar content as Coca-Cola, which has 27 grams of sugar in every 8 ounces of cola. Of course, that is probably why it is so popular with young and old alike. Youngsters love the sweetness, and grown-ups like to think they're drinking something somewhat healthy (it's juice!). But given the reality—lemonade is a treat—it better taste pretty good. We held a blind tasting of nine popular brands of frozen concentrate and prepared lemonades (skipping the powdered mixes) and found that despite the near-equivalent sugar content among the brands (26 to 28 grams per 8 ounces), flavor differences were vast.

At their core, all brands contain lemon juice, water, and sugar, though never in that order and not always in those forms; high-fructose corn syrup, lemon juice concentrate, and natural lemon flavors made numerous appearances. The well-rated Florida's Natural was the purest of the bunch, with a short ingredient list of just water, lemon juice, sugar, and grapefruit pulp. Compare that with the ingredients in our lowest-rated brand, Snapple: water, high-fructose corn syrup, citric acid, lemon juice from concentrate, gum acacia, natural lemon flavor with other natural flavors, salt, ascorbic acid (Vitamin C), and beta carotene (for color). No wonder one taster described it as "not lemonade-y." Tasters clearly wanted a "natural" lemon flavor.

But great lemon flavor alone isn't enough; there's a reason why we drink lemonade and not lemon juice. Winning brands were consistently described as "sweet/tart," with a "middle-of-the-road blend of sweet and sour," while low-ranked lemonades were "unbalanced," "too tart," or "sickly sweet." Brands with too much or too little lemon flavor also failed the test. Lemonades are listed in order of preference. –Keri Fisher

① ② ③ ④ ⑤ ⑥ ⑦ ⑧ ⑨

Top Picks

1. **NEWMAN'S OWN Old Fashioned Roadside Virgin Lemonade** $2.29 for 64-ounce carton
   Comments: Praised for its "natural-tasting lemon flavor" and "good balance of sweet and tart," this brand was deemed "just right."

2. **FLORIDA'S NATURAL Lemonade** $2.00 for 64-ounce carton
   Comments: Many found this brand to be the "most drinkable," with "nice balance." A handful thought it was "too sweet."

3. **MINUTE MAID Premium Frozen Concentrated Lemonade** $1.49 for 12-ounce can
   Comments: Fans of this frozen concentrate found it "light, clean, and tart," with "good flavor," though some found it "not lemony enough."

Don't Bother

4. **MINUTE MAID Premium Lemonade** $2.00 for 64-ounce carton
   Comments: Despite the strong showing of its frozen cousin, this refrigerated version was deemed "totally muted and boring" as well as "artificial."

5. **NANTUCKET NECTARS Squeezed Lemonade** $1.59 for 17.5-ounce bottle
   Comments: "That's not lemonade!" complained one taster of this "artificial" brand that was so tart it "makes you wince!"

6. **ODWALLA Pure Squeezed Lemonade** $4.99 for 64-ounce jug
   Comments: Several tasters found this "painfully sweet" lemonade to taste "like apple juice," while others complained of an "odd aftertaste."

7. **TROPICANA Lemonade** $2.00 for 64-ounce carton
   Comments: The lemonade made by the company renowned for its orange juice was panned as "not lemony enough" and "candy-like." Or, as one taster put it simply: "Ick, ick."

8. **CASCADIAN FARM Organic Lemonade Frozen Concentrate** $3.39 for 12-ounce can
   Comments: "Blech!" wrote one taster of the lone organic brand. Most others agreed, including one who asked, "What was that? That wasn't lemonade."

9. **SNAPPLE Lemonade** $1.35 for 16-ounce bottle
   Comments: Panned by all as "very bad," "sickly sweet," and "fake," with one taster going as far as to compare it to "the smell of rubber boots left in the sun."

Taste Test
Whipped Toppings

Either you grew up eating prepared whipped toppings or you didn't. That's what we learned when we held a blind tasting of Cool Whip, Reddi-wip, and Dream Whip. Tasters who grew up on these toppings had no trouble picking out their childhood favorite: "The fact that I know this is Reddi-wip tells me I eat too much whipped cream." "I know my Dream Whip when I see (and taste) it!" "Cool Whip. It is what it is." Moreover, if you're familiar with these whips, tasting them side by side is equivalent to comparing apples and oranges: You just can't do it.

That's why, despite clear preferences among individual tasters, the overall scores for the three toppings were very close. Dream Whip, a powder that is whipped with milk, edged out a slight win over frozen Cool Whip and aerosol Reddi-wip (the only topping that actually contains cream).

We held a second tasting and this time included homemade whipped cream, which handily beat the packaged substitutes. In fact, the other contenders in this tasting took such a whipping that many tasters said they would sooner skip whipped cream than swallow a supermarket substitute. For the rest of us, keeping a prepared topping on hand for emergencies (hot fudge sundae—we need whipped cream, stat!) isn't a bad idea. Dream Whip lasts indefinitely in the cupboard, while Cool Whip and Reddi-wip will keep for several months in the freezer and refrigerator, respectively. The choices are listed in order of preference.

THE REAL THING
(Home-whipped heavy cream)
$2.19 for 16 ounces of heavy cream
(yields about 4 cups)
"Perfect."

DREAM WHIP
$2.59 for 2.6-ounce box with
2 envelopes, each making 2 cups
"Certainly not dreamy," wrote one taster of this topping; its "light, fluffy texture" won some fans despite its "strange aftertaste."

COOL WHIP
$1.69 for 8-ounce tub
(yields about 3 1/2 cups)
More than one taster compared this "way too sweet" topping to "melted marshmallows."

REDDI-WIP
$3.09 for 7-ounce canister
(yields about 3 cups)
This topping deflated quickly, leading tasters to describe it as "a little too loose," though some found it "real creamy."

Equipment Roundup

CHEF'S KNIVES: Is There a Bargain Out There?

Our test kitchen is stocked with knives that cost $100 or more. These knives are pretty good—and for that price, they ought to be. But could we find a decent knife for less than $50? To find out, we rounded up nine 8-inch chef's knives (the best size for most cooks).

STRENGTH MATTERS When we cut butternut squash in half, more than one of our nine test knives (including the Henckels International) felt dangerously flimsy. Others managed this task but cut crookedly as the blade bent (such as the Oxo). A few knives (especially the top-rated Forschner and Wüsthof) completed this task without a hitch.

ROUNDED IS RIGHT We chopped onions and minced parsley with all nine knives. These tasks were much easier to perform if the cutting edge was curved rather than perfectly straight. Try this test to understand why: Start with the knife tilted up on its tip, with the heart of the blade sitting on the food to be cut. From there, slide the knife forward while lowering the handle until the knife sits flat on the cutting board. If the edge is rounded, the knife almost "rocks" back to the starting position when you lift it; a flat blade (like those on both Henckels knives tested) falls to the board with a rhythm-breaking thump and doesn't "rock" back up.

SHARPER IS BETTER All nine knives started out sharp enough to slice a tomato. At the end of testing, several knives were dull, especially the Chicago Cutlery and Farberware. Our recommended knives remained sharp throughout our tests.

A SURE GRIP IS SAFER Smooth, polished handles became dangerously slick when we tried cutting up a chicken, but textured handles helped us keep a good grip. Blades on some knives were so narrow that our testers' knuckles kept crashing into the cutting board. At the store, hold the knife in your hand. If the handle is too smooth or if there doesn't seem to be enough clearance room for your knuckles, move on to another knife.

SUMMING UP The Forschner Victorinox, which cost just $25, was the clear winner in these trials, and it rivals the best of the pricey knives in our test kitchen. **–Garth Clingingsmith**

Highly Recommended
FORSCHNER Victorinox Fibrox Chef's Knife
Price: $25.33
Comments: One tester summed it up: "Premium-quality knife at a bargain price." Knives costing four times as much would be hard pressed to match its performance. The blade is curved and sharp; the handle comfortable. Overall, "sturdy" and "well balanced."

Recommended
WÜSTHOF GOURMET Cook's Knife
Price: $49.99
Comments: Best suited for cooks with smaller hands. Testers with large hands complained that their knuckles hit the board before the blade did. The spine of the knife was thought to be "unnecessarily sharp," but this knife performed well in all tests.

MAC Chef Series Chef's Knife
Price: $47.50
Comments: This "ultra-light" knife is also "ultra-sharp," although the "skinny" handle doesn't fill a palm very well and the thin blade is too flexible to chop up squash or chicken bones. If you use a cleaver for those tasks, this knife could be a "nimble" addition to your collection.

Recommended with Reservations
J. A. HENCKELS Twin Signature Chef's Knife
Price: $29.95
Comments: Described as hefty but bulky, this knife also comes with a contoured handle that can get slippery and "didn't feel comfortable" in all testers' hands. The blade borders on being "too flat."

Not Recommended
CALPHALON Contemporary Cutlery Chef's Knife
Price: $31.99
Comments: A dead ringer for expensive German knives, but the thick blade on this knife is heavy enough to tax even the strongest cook. "Feels more like an ax" than a kitchen knife.

OXO Good Grips Chef's Knife
Price: $12.99
Comments: A delicate knife not suited for even the most delicate tasks. The blade bowed and twisted even when used to chop parsley, and it bent permanently when faced with strenuous jobs such as splitting squash.

J. A. HENCKELS International Fine Edge Pro Chef's Knife
Price: $11.40
Comments: We found nothing to like about the cheapest knife of the bunch. This "overgrown paring knife" left no room for knuckles. The perfectly flat blade and shiny, slick handle make this contender a shoe-in for the junk drawer.

FARBERWARE Pro Forged Chef's Knife
Price: $19.99
Comments: This knife feels unfinished, and the rough seams between blade and handle are uncomfortable. Forget slicing—we could only "bruise" onions.

CHICAGO CUTLERY Walnut Tradition Chef's Knife
Price: $13.05
Comments: The "shaggy" wooden handle needs some sanding. While dull knives bruise vegetables, this one doesn't even scratch the surface. One tester realized, "This is why folks get cut."

Gadgets & Gear Flexible Cutting Mats

In the test kitchen, we avoid cross-contamination (passing bacteria from one food to another) by using different cutting boards for meat, poultry, seafood, and produce. Restaurants often do the same, but having a cupboard at home devoted to four cutting boards seems excessive—and expensive.

Flexible cutting mats (also called chopping mats) are a perfect supplement to a single cutting board. They are thin enough to be rolled up like a newspaper yet sturdy enough to withstand the strike of a blade. At home, I use one to cut up chicken for a stir-fry, toss it out of the way in the sink, and then proceed, safely, with the veggies. Flexible mats are also great for transferring ingredients: Simply roll up the mat and funnel food right into the pan.

A set of two of flexible cutting mats can cost as little as $5, but we like Progressive International's $10 Food Safety Chopping Mat Set, which contains four 15 by 11-inch mats, each a different color, and two 11 by 7½-inch mats for smaller jobs. All six mats are dishwasher-safe, and they are thicker (and stronger) than the competition. **–G.C.**

Flexible mats are handy supplements to a regular cutting board.

When Things Go Wrong in the Kitchen

READERS SHARE FUNNY STORIES ABOUT COOKING MISHAPS

KITCHEN WISDOM

A few years ago, I received the *Joy of Cooking* daily calendar as a gift, and it had a quote by Irma Rombauer that caught my fancy. It said: "When cooking, be nonchalant and proceed with an attitude of victory over all difficulties, imaginary or otherwise." I put this calendar page on my refrigerator and often thought of it when I encountered challenges in the kitchen. One day, I was preparing dinner and opening a can of tomatoes. When my can opener broke the seal, the can exploded, and its contents were sprayed all over my kitchen—even on the calendar page on the refrigerator door. Now a spattered mess, the page remains on my fridge as a reminder to cheerfully carry on in the face of culinary disaster.

Alison Wood via e-mail

BREAD OR BISCUIT?

A year after my husband, Jim, and I were married, I thought I would surprise him and bake bread. After all, how hard could this be? Well, the dough did not rise properly, but I baked it anyway. The bread, of course, turned out flat. I decided to throw it out and not mention it. Later that afternoon, Jim said he wanted to show me something. We walked to where his dog happened to be tied up. Jim looked at the dog and said, "Get it!" Immediately the dog began to dig. The dog looked quite pleased with himself as he held my loaf of bread in his mouth. Maybe I can't bake bread, but I do make a mean dog biscuit.

Barb Murphy Iowa City, Iowa

AN APPEALING CAKE

My first foray into baking something all by myself took place when I was about 11. I spread the thick, smooth apple cake batter into the buttered baking pan and topped it with a generous amount of nutmeg- and cinnamon-spiced sugar. The final step was to "peel and core apple; place on top of cake." I carefully peeled and cored the apple, placed the naked apple in the refrigerator, and laid the peels on top of the sugar mixture.

When my dad came home from work and made his customary peek into the fridge, he said, "What happened to this apple?" Only then did it dawn on me. I checked the oven and found shriveled black curls atop a sandy mass of sugar. All was forgiven, and now we call this disaster Amy's Apple Peel Cake.

Amy Turim Takoma Park, Md.

THE CLEANEST CHICKEN

My wife and I were members of a ski club in Lincoln, N.H., for 24 years. One year, one of our newer members, who was a chef, decided to make this incredible chicken dish. He had bought at least 30 pounds of chicken breasts and spent a considerable amount of time precisely skinning and boning them. To marinate the breasts, he put them into a large stockpot along with lots of garlic, a curious mixture of herbs and spices, and about 3 cups of olive oil from a half-gallon jug.

Meanwhile, he started his sauce. Fifteen minutes into the sauce, he took a peek at the chicken and cried out, "Look at the chicken, it's disintegrating!" Well, a sniff made it clear that instead of grabbing for the olive oil, he had grabbed the jug of Pine-Sol that someone had left on the counter.

John G. Roberts Shapleigh, Maine

PEANUT BRITTLE PAVEMENT

My mother encouraged us to help out in the kitchen, but there was one cardinal rule: Do not cook if Mom is not around to make sure that nothing catches fire. After a couple of years of cooking by her side, I was pretty sure that I had outgrown the rule. To prove it, I decided to whip up a big batch of my mother's favorite candy, peanut brittle, while she was out shopping.

According to the recipe, I was supposed to melt the sugar in a double boiler; not only did we not have a double boiler, but I had no idea what it was. I decided to use my mother's favorite frying pan. Before long, there was a nice thick stew of what could have become peanut brittle, but I left the mixture in too long and the brittle practically turned into concrete, adhering to the inside of that pan as if it were new pavement laid down on an old sidewalk. I thought I might fix this minor problem by turning up the heat and melting the brittle off the pan, but it only stuck more stubbornly. I then tried to cool the pan by submerging the bottom in water. The pan cracked and sizzled, but the brittle stayed where it was.

By now, my heart was pounding so loudly I could no longer hear the ticking of the clock. My mother would be back soon. I grabbed my father's hammer and a screwdriver. As my brother held the pan, I hammered away at the peanut brittle. I was about halfway done when my mother walked in. As I surveyed the broken brittle pieces, the dented pan, and the astounded look on my mother's face, I had to face facts: My first solo culinary adventure had been an utter flop. "At least nothing caught fire, Mom," I offered. She wasn't amused.

Diane MacEachern Takoma Park, Md.

THE CRYING MOUSSE

Years ago, when I was still a young bride and trying to impress my mother-in-law, I decided to demonstrate my fledgling culinary skills. Mama Naomi, as I affectionately called her, had been home for only a few days following her seventh back surgery, and her spirits were low. Naomi was not a big eater, so the main meal was rather simple. I was planning to dazzle her with dessert. I chose a recipe for chocolate mousse and worked diligently, following the recipe to the letter—or so I thought!

After clearing away the dishes for the main course, I carried the mousse into the dining room. I was so pleased with how rich and dark the dessert looked. Mom took the serving spoon and plunged it into the dish, and there it stayed. It seems the spoon had become stuck. Try as she might, she could not get the spoon out. I was mortified. Mom looked at the spoon, looked at me, and burst into laughter. She laughed so hard that tears trickled down her cheeks. I soon joined her in the laughter.

My husband came in to see what was going on, but we were laughing too hard to explain. All we could do was point to the dish. He gripped the spoon and tried to pull it out, sending us into another round of laughter. I had accomplished my goal of cheering up Mama Naomi, but not in the manner I had intended.

Vicki Hutnik Houston, Texas

THE BEST SALT COOKIES

My mother first allowed me to bake on my own when I was 7 or 8. I decided to make sugar cookies and was told to call her when they were ready to go into the oven. My mother put the cookies in the oven and we waited for the first batch to bake. She sampled one first and ate the entire cookie, telling me how wonderful it was. Imagine my surprise when I ate one myself and discovered that I had substituted the hearty measurement of sugar with salt! Only a mother would eat "salt cookies" and claim how much she liked them. I can't wait till my daughters, now ages 3 and 5, are old enough to bake up their own surprises.

Maria Lockheardt Andover, Mass.

Send us your funniest kitchen disaster stories. Please write to us at Kitchen Disasters, Cook's Country, P.O. Box 470739, Brookline, MA 02447. If you'd like to use e-mail, write to us at kitchendisasters@bcpress.com. If we publish your story, you'll receive a complimentary one-year subscription to *Cook's Country*.

Postcards from Home

COOK'S COUNTRY READERS SHOW US WHAT'S COOKING AT HOME

A Tasty Barnyard Birthday Cake
Abby Hall La Crosse, Wis.
Abby tells us: "I made this cake to celebrate the first birthday of our daughter, Grace. The barnyard and the barn were made out of almond pound cake and frosted with rum buttercream. The silo was made out of round cookies, and I made the animals using royal icing."

Our Youngest Reader
Julie Sexten Mt. Vernon, Ill.
Julie writes: "Macie, my 18-month-old daughter, enjoys looking through my cooking magazines and was quite excited when your charter issue arrived in the mail. The 'I-meam' (translation = ice cream) recipes were her favorite."

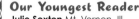

Super-Size Cake
Linden Staciokas Fairbanks, Alaska
Linden writes: "My husband works hard to control his love of fast food, so for his last birthday, I agreed to make him a Big Mac cake. It took four cake recipes to make it. Good thing there were guests!"

"Pick" of the Month

Saute'n Sophie
Kevin Stein
Stone Mountain, Ga.
Kevin writes: "This photo is of my daughter, Sophie. We call it 'Saute 'n' Sophie.' Please note that the burner is not on!"

Wild Mushroom Harvest
Debbie Mrazek Camas, Wash.
Debbie hunts wild mushrooms with her family in Washington's Columbia Gorge. Her 5-year-old son even pitches in. Debbie writes: "He is great at finding chanterelles and loves to eat them cooked in butter sauce." She took this photo of their "find" after a day of mushroom hunting.

Pepper Relish Day
Michael Hall
Dracut, Mass.
Michael writes: "Years ago, my grandmother started a fall tradition that we call Pepper Relish Day. The entire family would get together at her house and pitch in to make enough pepper relish to last through the year. This day brought all the aunts, uncles, and cousins together, and everyone had a job to do. I remember going with my father and sister to pick out fresh peppers at local farms. My grandmother is no longer with us, but she had 10 children, and they carry on the tradition. Today, my father, sister, and I make the pepper relish each fall and supply our families and friends with the coveted jars."

Cooking Club
Jennifer Schmidt Norton, Mass.
Jennifer writes: "This photo was taken during one of our cooking-club get-togethers. Kit is serving a chocolate-pear torte to Tina."

First Florida Fish
John Frates Englewood, Fla.
John recently moved to Florida and sent us this photo of his very first redfish, which he caught from his kayak. He writes: "This catch was very special to me, and I wanted to prepare it in a special way. I was looking for something that was not too spicy in order to enjoy more of the natural flavor of the fish. I found a simple and delicious recipe posted on a public forum for Florida kayak anglers."

We'd love to see what you're growing, cooking, and eating at home. E-mail your photos to postcards@bcpress.com or send them to Postcards, Cook's Country, P.O. Box 470739, Brookline, MA 02447. If we publish your photo, you will receive a complimentary one-year subscription to *Cook's Country.* Make sure to include your name, address, and daytime phone number along with your photo. And tell us a little bit about what makes your photo special.

Recipe Index

main courses
Avocado Crab Louis RC
BBQ Beer-Can Chicken 18
   Apple Harvest Cider-Can Chicken
Boston Baked Beans 7
Cheesy Broccoli Calzones RC
Chicken Salad 4
   Apricot
   Chinese
   Curried
   Jalapeño
   Waldorf
Creole Crab Cakes 21
Grilled Pork Tenderloin with Peach Salsa RC
Grilled Steak and Onion Salad RC
Grilled Swordfish with Eggplant Salad RC
Mahogany Chicken RC
Open-Faced Sausage Sandwiches RC
Salad Bar Stir-Fry 23
Stuffed Flank Steak 22
Tennessee-Whiskey Pork Chops 12
Zesty Shrimp Pasta Salad RC

salads, sides, spreads, and sauce
Cool and Creamy Macaroni Salad 17
Cream Cheese Spreads 29
   Lemon-Ginger
   Maple-Cinnamon
   Oh-So-Orange
   Sweet Pineapple
   Zesty Apricot
Farmstand Corn Fritters 13
Garden Potato Salad 21
   Dilly Garden Potato Salad
   Potato Salad "du Jardin"
Quick Pickles 19
   Bread and Butter
   "Kosher" Double-Dill
Quick Rémoulade 21
Tomato Salads 14
   "Bring Home the Bacon"
   "Fit as a Fennel"
   "It's All Greek to Me"
   "Rhapsody in Blue Cheese"

sweet treats and smoothies
Blue-Ribbon Fudge 23
Ice Cream Sauces 27
   Butterscotch
   Cherry
   Chocolate
   Marshmallow
   Peanut Butter
   Strawberry
Orange Drop Doughnuts 8
Reduced-Fat Chocolate Sheet Cake 6
Smoothies 25
   Chocolate-Covered Cherry
   Creamsicle
   Piña Colada
   Strawberry Cream Pie
   Takes Two to Mango
   The Elvis
   Very Berry
Watermelon Desserts 10
   Polka-Dot Minty Melon Mold
   Tutti-Frutti Watermelon Boats
   Watermelon Citrus Punch
   Watermelon Ice Pops
Zucchini Bread 24
   Fruity
   Nutty

RC = Recipe Card

Cook's Country

OCTOBER/NOVEMBER 2005

Oven-Fried Chicken
Corn Flakes Make Crunchiest Coating

Sunday-Best Roast Beef
Turn a Cheap Cut into a Champ

Cheesiest Potato Casserole
With Super-Crisp Crust

12 QUICK APPETIZERS
Easy Recipes for Four Parties

APPLE TURNOVERS
Extra-Easy and Extra-Flaky

SLOW-COOKER BEEF STEW
Learn the Secrets to Big Flavor

PECAN PRALINE PIE
Foolproof Southern Classic

EASY ROAST PORK LOIN
Two-Ingredient Glaze Browns Roast Beautifully

GREAT GRILLED CHEESE
A Cake Pan Is Key!

RATING INDOOR GRILLS
One Model Torches the Rest

$4.95 U.S./$6.95 CANADA

0 74470 05251 7
1 1>

Our Quick Pasta Sauce Contest Winner!
Elaine Sweet of Dallas, Texas, won first place with a recipe that starts with basil from her garden and adds tomatoes, capers, anchovies, and lemon juice. See page 4 for her **Garden Pesto Sauce.**

Cook's Country

Dear Country Cook,

The first Saturday of every month, our family often attends the Pawlett Community Church fundraiser for the new steeple. Pork, applesauce, Jell-O salad, mashed potatoes, corn, green beans, gravy, stuffing, iced tea, and, usually, a choice of yellow or chocolate cake. If you don't get there well before 5 P.M., they are already working on the second seating.

In small towns like ours, no public event is without a good feed, whether it's coffee hour at our lightly attended Methodist church, a wake, Old Home Day, the August fireman's parade, or the Christmas celebration at the town hall, complete with lasagna and brownies.

The first time I cooked for a covered-dish supper, I realized that this was something special. The food is a "Nice to Know You," a "Welcome to Our Town," and a "Hope to See You Again Soon" all wrapped up in a dozen biscuits or a Dutch oven filled with BBQ beans.

Some folks say it with flowers, others with fancy presents. A cook says it with a tin of sugar cookies or an applesauce cake. It's still the best way to say hello and make a few friends that I've ever tried.

Christopher Kimball
Founder and Editor, Cook's Country Magazine

Getting ready to serve dessert at the Pie Town, N.M., Fair, October 1940. Photographer: Russell Lee.
Library of Congress, Prints & Photographs Division, FSA-OWI Collection LC-USF351-366

OCTOBER/NOVEMBER 2005

Cook's Country

departments

RECIPE CONTEST: **Quick Pasta Sauces** 4

SLOW COOKING: **Hearty Beef Stew** 7

LOST RECIPES: **Quaker Bonnet Biscuits** 8

RECIPE MAKEOVER: **Oven-Fried Chicken** 9

FUN FOOD: **Halloween Treats** 10

DRESSING UP: **Pork Roast** 14

LEFTOVERS: **French Dip Sandwiches** 21

REGIONAL FAVORITES: **Dirty Rice** 22

ON THE SIDE: **Quick Dinner Muffins** 22

EASIER THAN YOU THINK: **Bread Pudding** 25

EASIER THAN YOU THINK: **Split-Pea Soup** 26

GETTING TO KNOW: **Winter Squash** 27

FOOD SHOPPING: **Packaged Stuffing** 30

EQUIPMENT ROUNDUP: **Indoor Grills** 31

features

12 Classic Cornbread and Sausage Dressing
Can stuffing be baked outside the bird and still taste great?

13 Quick and Easy Apple Turnovers
Store-bought puff pastry makes quick work of homemade apple turnovers, but we had to solve two problems: soggy pastry and leaky filling.

15 The Best Grilled Cheese Sandwiches
Mom's grilled cheese may have been good, but we'll bet she didn't use a grater or cake pan to make it even better.

17 Cleaning Up Sloppy Joes
This cafeteria classic is often little more than a sweet, greasy dumping ground for third-rate burger meat. Is there a not-so-Sloppy Joe waiting to be discovered?

18 Four Easy Appetizer Parties
Hundreds of readers sent in recipes for their favorite quick party foods. Our test kitchen selected the top 12 and put them together in four simple menus.

20 Sunday-Best Garlic Roast Beef
Could we infuse an inexpensive cut of beef with rich garlic flavor while keeping the harsh, bitter notes at bay?

23 The Cheesiest Potato Casserole
Scalloped potatoes can be bland, starchy, and greasy. We wanted a simple recipe that also delivered big, nicely balanced flavors.

24 Southern Pecan Praline Pie
What's the secret to a pecan praline pie with a smooth and sliceable filling?

26 How to Roast Winter Squash
Roasted, glazed squash can be creamy, with a crackling, sweet exterior. Or it can be soggy, stringy, and burnt. How do you make sure to get the former, not the latter?

in every issue

2 Kitchen Shortcuts

6 Ask Cook's Country

14 Reader Mailbag

16 I'm Looking for a Recipe

28 Notes from Our Test Kitchen

32 When Things Go Wrong . . .

Founder and Editor Christopher Kimball
Executive Editor Jack Bishop
Senior Editor Bridget Lancaster
Test Kitchen Director Erin McMurrer
Copy Chief India Koopman
Associate Editors Keri Fisher, Eva Katz
Assistant Editor Melissa Baldino
Test Cooks Stephanie Alleyne
Katie Henderson
Jeremy Sauer
Assistant Test Cooks Meredith Butcher
Cali Rich
Kitchen Assistant Nadia Domeq
Contributors Lauren Chattman,
Garth Clingingsmith,
Diane Unger-Mahoney
Recipe Tester Barbara Atkins

Design Director Amy Klee
Marketing Designer Julie Bozzo
Designer Heather Barrett
Staff Photographer Daniel J. van Ackere

Vice President Operations James McCormack
Production Manager Mary Connelly
Project Manager Anne Francis
Production Assistants Jeanette McCarthy
Jennifer Power
Christian Steinmetz
Systems Administrator Richard Cassidy
Internet Technology Director Aaron Shuman

Chief Financial Officer Sharyn Chabot
Controller Mandy Shito
Staff Accountant Maya Santoso
Office Manager Saudiyah Abdul-Rahim
Receptionist Henrietta Murray
Publicity Deborah Broide

Vice President Marketing David Mack
Circulation Director Bill Tine
Fulfillment Manager Carrie Horan
Circulation Assistant Elizabeth Dayton
Products Director Steven Browall
Direct Mail Director Adam Perry
Customer Service Manager Jacqueline Valerio
Customer Service Representative Julie Gardner
E-Commerce Marketing Manager Hugh Buchan

Vice President Sales Demee Gambulos
Marketing Assistant Connie Forbes

Editorial Office: 17 Station Street, Brookline, MA 02445; 617-232-1000; fax 617-232-1572. Subscription inquiries: 800-526-8447.
Postmaster: Send all new orders, subscription inquiries, and change-of-address notices to Cook's Country, P.O. Box 8382, Red Oak, IA 51591-1382.

ON THE COVER: PHOTOGRAPHY: Loftus/Stockfood. ILLUSTRATION: John Burgoyne.
IN THIS ISSUE: COLOR FOOD PHOTOGRAPHY: Keller + Keller. STYLING: Mary Jane Sawyer. ILLUSTRATION: Lisa Parett.

Cook's Country magazine (ISSN 1552-1990), number 5, is published bimonthly by Boston Common Press Limited Partnership, 17 Station Street, Brookline, MA., 02445. Copyright 2005 Boston Common Press Limited Partnership. Application to mail at periodical postage rates pending at Boston, Mass., and additional mailing offices. POSTMASTER: Send address changes to Cook's Country, P.O. Box 8382, Red Oak, IA 51591-1382. For subscription and gift subscription orders, subscription inquiries, or change-of-address notices, call 800-526-8447 in the U.S. or 515-247-7571 from outside the U.S., or write us at Cook's Country, P.O. Box 8382, Red Oak, IA 51591-1382.. PRINTED IN THE USA

Visit us at www.cookscountry.com!
Go online to ask questions, share kitchen tips, and enter recipe contests. You can also take a sneak peek at what we've got cooking for upcoming issues.

Kitchen Shortcuts

Quick Dry for Cookie Cutters

Towel-drying metal cookie cutters to keep them from rusting is tedious. To get around this, once the last batch of cookies is done, I put the washed cookie cutters on a baking sheet and pop it in the oven for a few minutes. Even with the oven turned off, the residual heat dries the cookie cutters thoroughly in no time.

Mary Kibler, Atlanta, Ga.

Lemons Cut through Grease

DOUBLE DUTY

After juicing a lemon, I turn the halves inside (inner flesh side) out and use them for the initial scrubbing of greasy pans. When I switch to a soapy sponge or scrubber to finish the job, most of the grease is already gone. Now my sponges and scrubbers last longer, and my hands smell like lemons!

Cindy Stern
Moorpark, Calif.

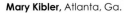

Catchall for Corn Cob Kernels

I use an angel food cake pan to cut corn off the cob. The end stands up nicely in the hole (especially if some of the stalk is still attached) and the pan catches all the kernels. I can do 36 cobs in no time!

Kathy Courtney
Calgary, Alberta, Canada

An Unsticky Solution
Freezing Plastic Wrap
To keep plastic wrap from sticking to itself, store it in the freezer. When unwrapped, it will not cling to itself and returns to room temperature in a matter of seconds.

Amy Lewis Gurnee, Ill.

Plastic Makes Perfect

I find it easier to cut lettuce with a knife than to tear it by hand. The problem is that a metal knife can cause the cut leaves to brown. Now I use a plastic knife. It's just as easy to use as a metal one and won't turn the leaves brown.

Marlene Lee
McMinnville, Ore.

Spin Away Extra Dressing

If you add too much dressing to your salad, there's an easy way to fix it. Just spin the dressed salad in your salad spinner; much of the excess dressing comes off.

Royce and Rachel Hayes
Via e-mail

Keep Vanilla Beans Soft

Because dried-out vanilla beans are nearly impossible to split and scrape, I store whole beans in a jar filled with vodka, bourbon, or brandy. They stay soft, making it easy to scrape out every last bit of vanilla. As a bonus, the liquor makes a fine vanilla extract.

Judy Conger
West Lafayette, Ind.

Separating Coffee Filters

Before I make my first cup of coffee, the last thing I want to do is struggle with a stack of paper filters to remove just one. Then I realized that simply blowing across the outer layers of the stack separates the filters easily. This trick works with muffin liners, too!

Jim Barton
Chesapeake, Va.

Spray-On Soap

Pouring dish soap from a bottle onto a sponge seems wasteful to me. To save on dish soap, I fill a spray bottle one-quarter full, top it off with water, give the mixture a quick stir, then close the bottle. Spraying this formula on dishes cuts grease fast as well as saving me a little money.

Kyoko Claire Murata
Carrollton, Ga.

Easy Garlic Peeling

If I have more than a clove or two of garlic to peel, I zap them in the microwave for five to 10 seconds. Once the cloves cool for a minute or two (they can get really hot), it's incredibly easy to slip off the skins.

Pennie Foster
Gainesville, Fla.

Getting under the Skin

I learned this trick from a friend when we were making deep-fried turkey. He'd always had the problem of tearing the turkey skin with his fingers when trying to apply a spice rub underneath it. Then he thought to try a wooden spoon with a long, thin handle. The handle slides right under the skin and easily reaches all around the bird. This technique works with whole chickens, too.

Keena Golden
San Francisco, Calif.

Steam the Mess Away

Anyone who bakes much bread ends up with some dough stuck to the counter. An easy way to remove it is to wet a kitchen towel with hot water and place it on the work area. In five or 10 minutes, the mess will lift off easily with a bench scraper or nylon scouring pad.

Tim Knight
Monterey, Calif.

Hook before You Cook

Nothing will spoil my appetite faster than a vein left behind in a cooked shrimp. After shelling shrimp, I use a medium-size crochet hook to remove the vein. Not only does it slide easily into the space, but the hook end can be used to pull the vein out so you never have to touch it.

Christine Bock
Schaumburg, Ill.

If you'd like to submit a tip, please send a letter to Kitchen Shortcuts, Cook's Country, P.O. Box 470739, Brookline, MA 02447. Or e-mail us at shortcuts@bcpress.com. Include your name, address, and phone number. If we publish your tip, you will receive a one-year subscription to Cook's Country.

Cooling Down the Counter
To keep my countertop cool when rolling out pastry or cookies or when making candy, I chill it with homemade ice packs. I make the packs out of gallon-size freezer bags filled halfway with water. I force out as much air as possible, seal them, and place them in the freezer on a flat surface (a cookie sheet works well), which lets me stack them and so saves space. They also make good ice packs for picnics.

Lyn Hite
Harveysburg, Ohio

Cleaning Your Disposal
To keep my garbage disposal clean, I throw a few cubes of ice down the drain a couple of times a week and run the disposal. The hard ice breaks up any food clinging to the blade and gets rid of lingering odors.

Kim Hoffmann
Chicago, Ill.

Creative Pancake Shapes
The best method I've found to make pancakes personalized with initials is the fat-separating pitcher. The long spout is easy to control, and the cup holds lots of batter.

Norine A. McQueeney
New Boston, N.H.

Easier Egg Whites
When mixing a batter that calls for stiffly beaten egg whites, I beat the whites first and then use the same beaters to mix the rest of the batter before folding in the whites. This saves me from having to clean and dry the beaters, where residual fat might ruin the whites.

Estee Lichter
Far Rockaway, N.Y.

Shake 'n' Bake French Fries
Straight from the frozen food aisle, most french fries taste pretty bland. To spice things up, I buy the fries that come in a resealable bag and sprinkle salt, pepper, paprika, and garlic powder directly into the bag. After a quick shake, the fries are coated evenly and will taste just like the seasoned fries served in restaurants.

Patrice A. Perez
Lancaster, Calif.

Lump-Free Gravy
When you're in a hurry to make gravy, try this: Pour some of the pan juices into a jar with a wide mouth and a screw top (a large jelly jar works well). Add flour, close the top, and shake vigorously. This will incorporate the flour quickly without a lot of work. Pour the jar contents back into the pan and finish your lump-free gravy.

Brian Mathes
West Roxbury, Mass.

Stabilizing Whipped Cream
I add a small amount of instant vanilla pudding instead of sugar while whipping cream. It stabilizes and sweetens the cream at the same time.

Niko Okamoto
Seattle, Wash.

Recycling Newspaper Bags
While cooking breakfast, I use the plastic bag used to deliver the morning newspaper to hold vegetable peelings, egg shells, coffee grounds, and more. The bag is made from sturdy plastic and does not tear easily. When finished, I just tie the end in a knot and throw the bag away.

Susan Trantham
Lufkin, Texas

WD-40 in the Kitchen
Nothing is more aggravating than scratching a new pot or pan when trying to remove the manufacturer's sticker. To solve the problem, my husband came up yet another use for WD-40: Just spray some on the sticker, wait a few minutes, then wipe off the sticker with a paper towel. It comes off cleanly, without leaving any scratches.

Deborah Setser
Prestonsburg, Ken.

Carve Your Squash
When it comes to splitting acorn squash, I don't reach for a cleaver but for that incredibly cheap saw blade that comes in pumpkin-carving kits. It takes very little time and almost no power to cut an acorn squash with this little saw. A carving kit can be had for practically nothing—try looking in a dollar store.

Monica Stephens
Austin, Texas

Thrifty Gifts
Whenever I go to thrift stores or garage sales, I always find single pieces of china plates. Because they are singles, you can always pick them up very inexpensively—sometimes for 5 or 10 cents! I use these dishes to give away cookies and candies to friends and neighbors. They always look wonderful, and I never have to worry about getting the plate back.

Janice Anello
Hammond, Ind.

Vinegar Kills Weeds, Too
Here's another use for the hot vinegar left when you clean an iron or a coffee pot: Pour it on weeds. White vinegar is an herbicide, and boiling water also kills weeds.

Dale Dow Eugene, Ore.

Oil-Temperature Test for Pan-Popped Corn
Pan-popped corn is the best, but it's difficult to tell when the oil temperature is just right. To ensure perfect popping every time, put three kernels in the pot with the cold oil and turn up the heat to full blast. When you have heard them all pop, dump in the rest.

Bennet K. Langlotz
Genoa, Nev.

Saving Tomato Paste
After opening a fresh can of tomato paste, put whatever you don't use in a small freezer bag, press out the excess air, flatten it until about 1/8 inch thick, and seal. Once the paste is frozen, you can break off a piece whenever you need it.

Renee Amodeo
Grand Rapids, Mich.

Neater Grating
As if my Microplane grater weren't handy enough, I've discovered that if I use it upside down, it contains the grated zest or cheese, making it easier to judge the amount. This method cuts down on the mess, too.

Daniel C. Perkin
Denver, Colo.

Easy-Bake Pie Crust
Prebaking a pie shell usually means baking it with pie weights, then removing the shell from the oven to take out the weights, and returning it to the oven to let it brown. I found a way to get a golden, flaky crust with only one trip to the oven: Just twist two pieces of parchment paper and use them to hold up the sides of the crust. Bake at the specified temperature and watch the bottom and edges of the crust brown evenly.

Linda Honneffer
Lakewood, N.J.

A Fresh Take on Pesto Wins Our Grand Prize

Our $500 Grand-Prize Winner!

Elaine Sweet Dallas, Texas

What's for dinner? Evidently, pasta, based on the avalanche of entries we received for this contest. Many of these recipes would pass muster at anyone's family supper, but the following five are exceptional. Best of all, they can be prepared in about the time it takes to cook the pasta.

Our grand-prize-winning recipe, from Elaine Sweet of Dallas, Texas, is a potent variation on traditional pesto. Elaine writes: "Texas summers are hot and wet, so the basil in my garden grows like a weed. The capers and anchovies contribute a natural salty taste, and the fresh lemon juice keeps everything tasting bright."

Elaine always makes a double recipe. The extra pesto keeps in the refrigerator for several days or in the freezer for several months. Everyone in the test kitchen loved this brash, flavorful sauce. It was great on pasta, but we also used leftover sauce to perk up steamed fish, sandwiches, pizzas, rice, and more.

Basil teams up with almonds, capers, anchovies, and tomatoes for a new twist on an old favorite.

GARDEN PESTO SAUCE MAKES ENOUGH TO SAUCE 2 POUNDS OF PASTA

Pesto works with most pasta shapes—everything from linguine to penne. As with traditional pesto, this one is quite thick, so make sure to reserve some of the pasta cooking water to help thin it out.

- 1/3 cup slivered almonds, toasted
- 2 cups packed fresh basil
- 1/2 cup packed fresh parsley
- 1 pound plum tomatoes, cored and seeded
- 1/4 cup drained capers
- 3 anchovy fillets, rinsed and drained
- 3 garlic cloves, peeled
- 1/2 teaspoon red pepper flakes
- 1/2 cup finely grated Pecorino cheese
- 1 tablespoon lemon juice
- 1/3 cup extra-virgin olive oil
  Salt and pepper

1. Pulse almonds in food processor or blender until finely chopped. Add basil, parsley, tomatoes, capers, anchovies, garlic, pepper flakes, and Pecorino and blend until smooth. With machine running, add lemon juice, then add oil in steady stream until emulsified. Season with salt and pepper.

2. Toss pesto with cooked pasta and reserved pasta cooking water, if necessary (see "How to Cook Pasta," page 29), and serve.

Cindy Szerlip
Redondo Beach, Calif.

Patricia Lohrey
Port Ludlow, Wash.

Mary Shivers
Ada, Okla.

Janet Gradwohl
Trophy Club, Texas

CREAM SAUCE WITH SAUSAGE AND PEAS MAKES ENOUGH TO SAUCE 1 POUND OF PASTA

Cindy writes: "This sauce came about after one of our weekly trips to the farmers market. After a little collaboration with my kids, I came up with a light pasta sauce that we all love." Cindy's recipe also works well with frozen peas. Farfalle (butterfly-shaped pasta) or small shells do a fine job of cradling the crumbled sausage and peas.

1 pound hot or mild Italian sausage, casings removed and meat crumbled
1 tablespoon olive oil
1/2 medium onion, chopped fine
1 garlic clove, minced
1/2 teaspoon red pepper flakes
1/3 cup white wine
3/4 cup low-sodium chicken broth
1 cup plus 2 tablespoons heavy cream
2 cups fresh or frozen peas
1/2 cup finely grated Parmesan cheese
Salt and pepper

1. Brown sausage in large skillet over medium heat, 6 to 8 minutes. Using slotted spoon, transfer sausage to plate lined with paper towels. Pour off grease in pan. Add oil and heat over medium heat until shimmering. Add onion and cook until softened, 3 to 5 minutes. Add garlic and pepper flakes and cook until fragrant, about 30 seconds. Add wine and simmer until almost evaporated, 1 to 3 minutes. Add broth and 1 cup cream; simmer until sauce reaches consistency of light cream, 6 to 9 minutes. Stir in peas and sausage and cook until flavors meld, about 2 minutes. Remove from heat, stir in cheese, and season with salt and pepper.

2. Toss sauce and remaining 2 tablespoons cream with cooked pasta and serve.

ROASTED RED PEPPER AND BACON SAUCE MAKES ENOUGH TO SAUCE 1 POUND OF PASTA

Patricia writes: "When our son returned home from college refusing to eat red meat, I really had to get creative. This sauce was a lifesaver. It's terrific without the bacon as well. Simply substitute 1 tablespoon olive oil for the bacon fat used to sauté the onion." You'll need a 10-ounce jar of roasted red peppers for this recipe. The sauce works well with spaghetti.

1 1/2 cups jarred roasted red peppers, drained
1 (14.5-ounce) can diced tomatoes
1 teaspoon dried oregano
1/4 teaspoon cayenne pepper
2 tablespoons red wine
2 tablespoons olive oil
6 slices bacon, chopped
1/2 medium onion, chopped fine
2 garlic cloves, minced
1 cup heavy cream
Salt and pepper

1. Puree red peppers, tomatoes, oregano, cayenne, wine, and oil in food processor or blender until smooth.

2. Cook bacon in large skillet over medium heat until crisp, about 7 minutes. Using slotted spoon, transfer bacon to plate lined with paper towels. Pour off all but 2 teaspoons fat from pan and return to medium heat. Add onion and cook until softened, about 3 minutes. Add garlic and cook until fragrant, about 1 minute. Add red pepper mixture to skillet and bring to simmer. Reduce heat, cover, and simmer until flavors meld, 10 to 15 minutes. Remove from heat and stir in cream and half the bacon. Season with salt and pepper.

3. Toss sauce with cooked pasta and serve, sprinkling bowls with remaining bacon.

ARTICHOKE ALFREDO SAUCE MAKES ENOUGH TO SAUCE 1 POUND OF PASTA

Mary writes: "I had never eaten many artichokes, but after enjoying an artichoke dip at my niece's house I started cooking with them more often. Soon after, I happened to be making fettuccine Alfredo. Remembering the dip, I added artichokes. Since then, I have made the recipe for family and friends as a main dish, but we also enjoy it with a grilled steak." Don't let this sauce simmer after adding the sour cream, or the mixture will curdle. This take on the classic Italian Alfredo sauce pairs perfectly with fettuccine.

4 tablespoons unsalted butter
1 small onion, chopped fine
1 garlic clove, minced
2 (8-ounce) cans artichoke hearts, drained, rinsed, and chopped coarse
1/2 cup sour cream
1 1/4 cups heavy cream
1/2 cup finely grated Parmesan cheese
1/2 teaspoon grated zest plus 1 tablespoon juice from 1 lemon
Salt and pepper
1/4 cup chopped fresh parsley
2 tablespoons chopped fresh basil

1. Melt butter in large skillet over medium heat. Add onion and cook until softened, 3 to 5 minutes. Add garlic and cook until fragrant, about 1 minute. Increase heat to medium-high, add artichokes, and cook until slightly browned, 3 to 5 minutes. Remove from heat and stir in sour cream, 1 cup heavy cream, Parmesan, and lemon zest and juice. Cook over low heat (do not boil) until ingredients are heated through, about 2 minutes. Season with salt and pepper.

2. Toss sauce, remaining 1/4 cup cream, parsley, and basil with cooked pasta and serve.

SPICY TUNA SAUCE MAKES ENOUGH TO SAUCE 1 POUND OF PASTA

Janet writes: "I had never thought of adding tuna to a sauce until my husband, Bill, was served a similar dish at Lake Lugano, Switzerland. This recipe works great on a weeknight because I always have the ingredients on hand and it's very quick to cook. I just add a salad and garlic bread and, voilà, I have one of Bill's favorite meals." Serve this chunky sauce with penne or ziti.

2 tablespoons extra-virgin olive oil
2 garlic cloves, minced
1/4 teaspoon cayenne pepper
1/4 teaspoon red pepper flakes
2 (6-ounce) cans water-packed tuna, drained
1/3 cup drained capers
1 cup pitted kalamata olives, chopped
1 (28-ounce) can diced tomatoes
2 teaspoons sugar
Salt and pepper
1/4 cup chopped fresh basil

1. Heat oil, garlic, cayenne, and pepper flakes in large skillet over medium heat until fragrant, 2 to 3 minutes. Add tuna, capers, and olives and toss to combine. Stir in tomatoes and sugar, cover, and simmer over medium-low heat until flavors are blended, about 20 minutes. Season with salt (sparingly) and pepper.

2. Toss sauce and basil with cooked pasta and serve.

We are looking for chicken soup recipes for an upcoming contest. Send us entries by November 1, 2005. Write to us at Recipe Contest, Cook's Country, P.O. Box 470739, Brookline, MA 02447, or e-mail us at recipecontest@bcpress.com. Either way, please make sure to include your name, address, and daytime phone number, and tell us what makes your recipe special. The grand-prize winner will receive $500. All entries become the property of Cook's Country. We look forward to reading (and tasting) your recipes.

Ask Cook's Country

PUTTING THE SQUEEZE ON LEMONS

Are there any tricks (that actually work!) to get the most juice out of lemons?

Trudy Gorman Woodstock, Ga.

We squeezed a dozen lemons—cold, rolled, and warm—and found that each yielded the same amount of juice. The only difference was that warm and room-temperature lemons were softer and therefore easier to squeeze than the cold lemons. When you use a tool like a reamer or juicer, this doesn't come into play as much, but if you're juicing by hand, we recommend room-temperature lemons. To quickly warm a cold lemon, you can heat it in the microwave until it is warm to the touch.

When purchasing lemons at the supermarket, choose large ones that give to gentle pressure; hard lemons have thicker skin and yield less juice. To quickly juice a lemon, we prefer a wooden reamer with a sharp tip that can easily pierce the flesh. Plastic reamers with rounded tips didn't work as well in our tests. Plastic and glass juicers (which sit on the counter and collect juice) are better suited to oranges and grapefruits than lemons.

When it comes to lemons, thin skins are best.

SHOPPING FOR PORK CHOPS

I recently made pork chops that were spongy and left a pool of juice on the plate. The label said the pork was "enhanced." I beg to differ. What have they done to my pork?

Carsen Jorgensen Seattle, Wash.

Because today's pork is so lean, it is also somewhat bland tasting and becomes dry if overcooked. Enter enhanced pork, which has been injected with a solution of water, salt, varying flavoring agents, and chemicals such as sodium phosphate, sodium lactate, potassium lactate, and sodium diacetate; all boost flavor and juiciness. (Pork containing any additives must be labeled with a list of the ingredients.) After several taste tests, we have concluded that while enhanced pork is indeed juicier and more tender than unenhanced pork, the latter has more genuine pork flavor. Some tasters picked up unappealing artificial, salty flavors in enhanced pork, and many found the ultra-tender texture bordered on spongy. Though unenhanced pork can be hard to find, we recommend it. Just don't overcook it, or the meat will be dry. A final temperature (after resting) of 145 to 150 degrees leaves the meat with a hint of pink and some juice. Because the temperature rises as meat rests, chops should come off the heat at 140 to 145 degrees, thicker roasts at 135 to 140 degrees.

TREACLE FOR HARRY POTTER FAN

My son is having a Harry Potter–themed birthday party, and I'd like to make him treacle tart, just like they eat in the books. I found a recipe in an English cookbook, but I can't find treacle anywhere and I'm not even sure what it is. Is there a substitute?

Jim Smith Portland, Maine

Treacle is sugar cane syrup, a British staple that most sources say is similar to molasses or corn syrup. There are two types of treacle: light (known more commonly as golden syrup) and black. We purchased both and made tarts with these British ingredients as well as with molasses, light corn syrup, and dark corn syrup. Tasters overwhelmingly chose the golden syrup tart, which was praised for its "nice sweetness and flavor." The black treacle tart, on the other hand, was universally panned as "bitter," "brutal," and "burnt." Both light and dark corn syrups were found to be suitable substitutes for golden syrup (and can be used in the same ratio), but molasses had a strong "malty" flavor that tasters rejected. Lyle's Golden Syrup is the most popular brand in Britain and can be ordered online at www.britshoppe.com. A 1-pound jar costs $4.99.

Create a "magic" tart with this British staple.

CHOPPED OR WHOLE NUTS

Does it matter if I buy whole or chopped nuts at the supermarket?

Linda Bates Meredith, N.H.

We prepared batches of banana bread (in which the nuts are mixed into the batter) and brownies (the nuts are sprinkled on top) using both whole nuts we chopped in the test kitchen and packaged chopped nuts. The results were mixed, with tasters showing only a slight preference for the fresh-chopped nuts. So go ahead and use the packaged chopped nuts—you won't be able to taste the difference.

THE BEST WAY TO COOK RICE

Is there a simple formula for cooking rice? The package directions always seem to turn out rice that is either chewy or mushy.

Lauren Hirsch Wynnewood, Pa.

We checked the package directions on several brands of long-grain white rice and found vastly different ratios, ranging from 1½ cups to 2¼ cups water for 1 cup of rice. We got the best results—separate grains of rice that retained a bit of chew—with 1½ cups water for 1 cup rice along with 1 teaspoon oil or butter, which helped keep the grains separate, and

½ teaspoon salt. The best method was to combine all of the ingredients in a pot, bring them to a boil, reduce the heat to low, cover, and simmer until all of the liquid was absorbed (about 15 minutes). We then let the rice sit, covered and off heat, for 5 minutes longer so it could finish steaming. A quick fluff with a fork and the rice was ready to serve. To make 2 cups of rice, use 2½ cups water, 2 teaspoons oil or butter, and 1 teaspoon salt. The cooking time is the same. (See page 29 for tips on rinsing rice.)

CANNED VERSUS DRIED BEANS

When can I substitute canned beans for dried beans?

Alan Krasnick West Chester, Pa.

Most recipes that call for dried beans are soups or stews that require the beans to cook slowly with the other ingredients so that that they release their starches and thicken the dish. When you replace the dried beans with canned beans and shorten the cooking time (cooking canned beans for the same amount of time as dried beans would cause the beans to disintegrate), you sacrifice both the flavor and texture of the finished dish. On some occasions (such as for a salad or quick pasta dish), a recipe might call for dried beans to be cooked, drained, and then added. In these instances, you can safely substitute canned beans. A general rule of thumb is that 1 cup of dried beans equals 3 cups of canned beans.

WHAT IS WHITE CHOCOLATE?

I read somewhere that white chocolate isn't really chocolate. Is that true? If it's not chocolate, what is it?

Claire Murphy Watertown, Mass.

For chocolate to qualify as a true chocolate, it must contain cocoa butter and cocoa solids. Because white chocolate contains only cocoa butter and no solids, it doesn't qualify. What's more, some so-called white chocolate doesn't qualify as true white chocolate because it doesn't contain at least 20 percent cocoa butter by weight. That's why you're more likely to find white "morsels" or "chips" in your supermarket.

In a blind tasting, we found that cocoa butter isn't crucial to great flavor—evidently, any fat will do. Our tasters preferred Guittard Choc Au Lait White Chips ($2.79 for 12 ounces), which had more fat (33 percent) than the other five brands we tasted but not much cocoa butter.

These chips may be white, but are they really made from chocolate?

To ask us a cooking question, write to Ask Cook's Country, P. O. Box 470739, Brookline, MA 02447. If you prefer e-mail, write to askcookscountry@bcpress.com. See if you can stump us!

Beef stew and a slow cooker make a perfect match—if you can keep the vegetables from turning to mush.

A grilling trick turns out to be the secret to beef stew with perfectly cooked vegetables.

The typical slow-cooker recipe for beef stew has many drawbacks. Ingredients are usually just dumped into the pot and left to their own devices, which means no browning and little flavor. The meat and vegetables heat up, but the flavors never really marry, producing a dish that is watery and flavorless. Who would want to marry those vegetables anyway? They're usually cooked to the point of exhaustion. Potatoes take on an unappetizing brown color, and carrots and parsnips assume the texture of baby food.

I wanted a rich, substantially thick and beefy stew, with lots of root vegetables that would taste the way nature intended. I didn't mind a bit of kitchen prep before I headed off to work in the morning (or the night before), but I didn't want to have to fuss with dinner too much once I got home.

I started with generous pieces of beef chuck (a cut that is ideal for long, slow cooking) and browned them well for maximum flavor. With the browned meat off to the side, I browned onions and added tomato paste—a chef's secret for adding color and flavor to many soups, stews, and sauces.

The stew that resulted from these efforts was pretty good, but not good enough; the color was washed out, and it lacked truly meaty flavor. After several failed attempts, I hit upon an unusual solution: a splash of soy sauce. No one could identify this mystery ingredient,

but everyone in the kitchen appreciated the rich brown color and intense savory flavor it gave the stew.

To thicken the stew, I tried flour, cornstarch, and even potato flakes, but I had the best results with another unlikely ingredient, Minute Tapioca, which is most often used to thicken fruit pies. It withstood the test of time in the slow cooker and thickened the stew without giving it a starchy aftertaste.

The last problem to solve was that of the drab and mushy vegetables. At first I tried roasting them separately and adding them to the pot just before serving. The roasted vegetables tasted great, but an hour of chopping and roasting vegetables pushed the family meal closer to bedtime than dinnertime. Stealing a trick often used in grilling, I made a "hobo pack" by wrapping the vegetables in foil. Then I placed the pack on top of the beef in the slow cooker. It may have looked like a flying saucer, but when I unfolded the foil the aroma of sweet, earthy vegetables filled the kitchen. Frozen peas turned gray in the pack, so I added them to the stew itself at the last minute.

Finally, it was time to test this recipe on my family, who gathered around the table for what was one of the best beef stews we had eaten in a long time. The meat was fork-tender, the broth rich and just thick enough to coat a spoon, and the vegetables were perfectly cooked. I'd trade this stew for the stovetop version any time. –Diane Unger-Mahoney

HEARTY BEEF STEW

SERVES 6 TO 8

If you're going to be away from your slow cooker for more than 10 hours, cutting the vegetables into larger, 1 1/2- to 2-inch pieces will help them retain their texture.

- 5 pounds boneless beef chuck-eye roast, trimmed and cut into 1 1/2-inch cubes
  Salt and pepper
- 3 tablespoons vegetable oil
- 4 medium onions, chopped fine
- 1 (6-ounce) can tomato paste
- 2 cups low-sodium chicken or beef broth
- 3 tablespoons soy sauce
- 1 pound carrots, peeled and cut into 1-inch pieces
- 1 pound parsnips, peeled and cut into 1-inch pieces
- 1 pound red potatoes, cut into 1-inch pieces
- 1 1/2 teaspoons minced fresh thyme
- 2 bay leaves
- 2 tablespoons Minute Tapioca
- 2 cups frozen peas, thawed

1. Dry beef with paper towels, then season with salt and pepper. Heat 1 tablespoon oil in large nonstick skillet over medium-high heat until just smoking. Add half of beef and brown on all sides, about 8 minutes. Transfer to slow-cooker insert and repeat with remaining beef (you shouldn't need more oil).

2. Add 1 tablespoon oil, onions, and 1/4 teaspoon salt to empty skillet and cook until golden brown, about 6 minutes. Add tomato paste and cook, stirring well, for 2 minutes. Add broth and soy sauce, bring to simmer, and transfer to slow-cooker insert.

3. Toss carrots, parsnips, potatoes, 1/2 teaspoon thyme, and remaining 1 tablespoon oil in bowl. Season with salt and pepper. Wrap vegetables in foil packet that will fit in slow cooker. Stir bay leaves and tapioca into slow-cooker insert; set vegetable packet on top of beef.

4. Set slow cooker to high, cover, and cook for 6 to 7 hours. (Or cook on low for 10 to 11 hours.) Transfer vegetable packet to plate. Carefully open packet (watch for steam) and stir vegetables and juices into stew. Add remaining 1 teaspoon thyme and peas and let stand until heated through. Season with salt and pepper to taste and serve.

Beef Stew Secrets

Beef stew made in a slow cooker tends to have three big problems: It's watery, it's bland, and the vegetables are cooked to mush. Here's how we solved these problems.

TO THICKEN THE STEW without giving it a starchy texture, use Minute Tapioca.

FOR BIG BEEFY FLAVOR, slip in a few tablespoons of soy sauce.

FOR PERFECTLY COOKED VEGETABLES, steam them on top of the stew in a "hobo pack" (see below).

How to Make A HOBO PACK

To make the pack, place the vegetables on one side of a large piece of heavy-duty aluminum foil. Fold the foil over, shaping it into a packet that will fit into your slow cooker, then crimp to seal the edges.

Make Ahead

You can do most of the prep for this recipe the night before the ingredients go into the slow cooker. Prepare the recipe through step 2 and refrigerate the browned beef and onion mixture in separate containers. In the morning, just transfer everything to the slow cooker and proceed with step 3. The cooking time will run to the high end of the ranges given in the recipe.

Nearly a century ago, Mary Midleton collected farmers' recipes, including one for Quaker bonnet biscuits, during a visit to her aunt and uncle in Bucks County, Pa.

Photo from Edith M. Thomas, *Mary at the Farm and Book of Recipes*, courtesy of Project Gutenberg at www.gutenberg.org.

An old-fashioned recipe turns out to combine the convenience of biscuits with the soft texture and yeasty flavor of good dinner rolls.

A few years ago, I sampled some biscuits at a Pennsylvania farm-stand. They tasted like rich dinner rolls and were called Quaker bonnet biscuits. The best thing about them was their shape— tiny replicas of a woman's bonnet viewed from the back.

A recipe for bonnet biscuits was hard to find—until I started searching through old Quaker journals and recipe collections. My best lead came from a 1915 book titled *Mary at the Farm and Book of Recipes Compiled during Her Visit among the "Pennsylvania Germans,"* by Edith M. Thomas.

With a lot of guesswork (Mary's original recipe called for "a quick but not too hot oven"), I prepared this recipe and it provided a darn good biscuit. But the recipe needed some updating.

I started by cutting it in half to make a more reasonable number of biscuits. Using butter in place of a combination of butter and lard made the rolls taste better, but my kitchen colleagues wanted more butter. In the end, I used the same amount of fat called for in Mary's original recipe but just half the flour. Mary's recipe didn't call for salt and sugar, but the rolls tasted better when I added modest amounts of each.

I knew that rapid-raise yeast would speed up the rising time. (It's also more widely available than the cake yeast called for in the original recipe.) After an hour, the dough had doubled in size (the usual sign that a yeast dough is ready), so I patted it out and stamped out biscuits. After giving the cut biscuits a second rise, I popped them in the oven, and a few minutes later I had yeasty biscuits that were nice and flaky.

I wanted to shave even more time off of this already-shortened recipe. Mary might have had all morning to make them, but I wanted to whip up a batch of these tender biscuits after work for dinner. I was now down from four hours to around two; could I do better?

During my research, I ran across several super-quick Southern yeast biscuit recipes, including Alabama biscuits and angel biscuits, that skipped the initial rising time. As soon as the dough came together, it was rolled out, cut, allowed to rise, and baked. Could a Southern recipe speed up the preparation of these Pennsylvania biscuits?

Judging from the way my tasters tore into them, I'd say they approved of these "once-raised" Quaker bonnet biscuits. And if I let the cut biscuits rise

in a warm oven, the rising time was just half an hour. I had great biscuits in just an hour—start to finish. That sounds like a recipe that belongs in any modern kitchen. **–Bridget Lancaster**

QUAKER BONNET BISCUITS
MAKES 18

To make these biscuits without a food processor, freeze the sticks of butter until hard and then grate them into the dry ingredients using the large holes of a box grater. Toss gently with your hands to evenly distribute the butter, and proceed with the recipe.

- 1 **cup whole milk**
- 1 **large egg**
- 1 **package rapid-rise or instant yeast**
- 4 **cups all-purpose flour, plus extra for work surface**
- 2 **tablespoons sugar**
- 1½ **teaspoons salt**
- 8 **tablespoons (1 stick) unsalted butter, cut into ½-inch pieces and chilled, plus 1 tablespoon unsalted butter, melted (for assembling biscuits)**

1. Adjust oven racks to upper-middle and lower-middle positions and heat oven to 200 degrees. Once oven reaches 200 degrees, maintain temperature for 10 minutes, then turn off oven.

2. Stir milk, egg, and yeast together in large measuring cup until combined.

3. Process flour, sugar, and salt in food processor until combined. Add chilled butter and pulse until mixture looks like coarse cornmeal, about fifteen 1-second pulses. Transfer to large bowl.

4. Stir in milk mixture until dough comes together. Turn dough out onto lightly floured work surface. Briefly knead to bring dough together, about 1 minute, adding more flour if necessary. Following steps 1 through 4 (right), roll, cut, and assemble biscuits on parchment-lined baking sheets. Cover with kitchen towels and place in warm oven. Let rise until doubled in size, 25 to 35 minutes.

5. Remove baking sheets with biscuits from oven and heat oven to 375 degrees; return baking sheets to oven once it is fully preheated. Bake biscuits until golden brown, about 15 minutes, rotating and switching baking sheets halfway through baking time. Serve hot or warm.

This old-fashioned "biscuit" looks like a bonnet but tastes like a rich dinner roll.

How to Make QUAKER BONNET BISCUITS

1. Roll the dough into a 12-inch round. Cut out eighteen 2½-inch circles, ¾ inch thick, and place them on parchment-lined baking sheets.

2. Re-roll the remaining dough out to a thickness of ½ inch, then cut out eighteen 1¼-inch rounds.

3. Lightly brush larger dough rounds with melted butter.

4. Place one smaller round slightly off center on top of each larger round.

Recipe Makeover OVEN-FRIED CHICKEN

Could Southern-style deep-fried chicken be slimmed down without sacrificing flavor, crunch, or happiness?

No fryer needed for this extra-crisp chicken.

My husband's favorite dinner begins (and ends) with crispy, crunchy deep-fried chicken. The impish twinkle in his eye as he munches on piece after piece is truly adorable (even if you're not married to him).

But it's no secret that classic fried chicken is laden with calories (a whopping 552 per piece) and fat (34 grams to be exact). Before subjecting my husband to a lifetime of grilled chicken-breast dinners, I decided to try my hand at a low-fat, "oven-fried" version of his ultimate meal. A daunting task, I can assure you, since it would have to pass not only professional muster with my fellow test cooks but also domestic muster in the man-food taste test at home.

Many recipes called for dipping boneless, skinless chicken breasts in beaten egg whites or low-fat mayonnaise to help adhere dried bread crumbs or fine-ground cornmeal. But chicken worth eating was the goal here, not spa food.

No self-respecting fried-chicken lover would dream of using anything other than bone-in chicken parts. My first concessions were to use bone-in breasts (which have fewer calories and less fat than dark meat) and to remove the skin. I knew that removing the skin would cost me flavor and moistness, so I borrowed a tried-and-true fried-chicken trick and soaked the parts in robustly seasoned buttermilk. Buttermilk also happens to be low in fat, so I had no worries about tacking on extra calories.

In search of a tasty coating, I tested some "creative" options offered by writers of "healthy" recipes, including grated Parmesan cheese, dry Cream of Wheat, pulverized shredded wheat, bran flakes, Weetabix cereal, crushed pretzels, packaged stuffing mix, and even ground-up low-fat popcorn. Unfortunately, these ideas solicited little more than amusement from my tasters.

Luckily, a mixture of crushed corn flakes and fresh bread crumbs was pretty close to perfect. The bottom of each chicken piece was a bit soggy, but baking the chicken on a wire rack solved this problem and eliminated the need for turning. Because the coating was still a bit dry, I mixed in a modest 2 tablespoons of oil, which gave the baked chicken a genuine "fried" texture.

My coating now had great crunch, but it needed more flavor. Salt, pepper, and garlic powder picked up on the seasonings I'd added to the buttermilk marinade. I tossed in cayenne for heat and paprika for color. Still not completely satisfied, I recalled the ground poultry seasoning (a humble mixture of ground sage, thyme, and bay leaves) that always worked wonders for my mother's roast chicken, so I added some to the coating for a savory jolt.

My gamble had paid off. The flavorful, craggy, deeply golden brown coating of this batch was a far cry from the lackluster coating found on most "oven-fried" recipes. But the acid test awaited me at home, with my husband. When he proclaimed my recipe both "crispy" and "crunchy," I knew my work was done.

–Stephanie Alleyne

OVEN-FRIED CHICKEN SERVES 8
To crush the corn flakes, place them inside a plastic bag and use a rolling pin to break them into pieces no smaller than 1/2 inch.

    2   cups buttermilk
    2   tablespoons Dijon mustard
  2 1/4 teaspoons salt
  1 1/2 teaspoons garlic powder
  1 1/2 teaspoons black pepper
    1   teaspoon hot pepper sauce
    8   split bone-in chicken breasts (10 to
        12 ounces each), skin removed and
        ribs trimmed with kitchen shears
  2 1/2 cups crushed corn flakes
   3/4 cup fresh bread crumbs
   1/2 teaspoon ground poultry seasoning
   1/2 teaspoon paprika
   1/8 teaspoon cayenne pepper
    2   tablespoons vegetable oil

1. Whisk buttermilk, mustard, 2 teaspoons salt, 1 teaspoon garlic powder, 1 teaspoon black pepper, and hot sauce together in large bowl. Add chicken, turn to coat well, cover, and refrigerate at least 1 hour or overnight.

2. Adjust oven rack to upper-middle position and heat oven to 400 degrees. Line rimmed baking sheet with foil, set wire rack on sheet, and coat rack with nonstick cooking spray.

3. Gently toss corn flakes, bread crumbs, remaining 1/2 teaspoon garlic powder, remaining 1/2 teaspoon black pepper, remaining 1/4 teaspoon salt, poultry seasoning, paprika, and cayenne in shallow dish until combined. Drizzle oil over crumbs and toss until well coated. Working with one piece at a time, remove chicken from marinade and dredge in crumb mixture, firmly pressing crumbs onto all sides of chicken. Place chicken on prepared rack, leaving 1/2 inch of space between each piece. Bake until chicken is deep golden brown, juices run clear, and instant-read thermometer inserted deep into breast away from bone registers 160 degrees, 35 to 45 minutes.

FIERY OVEN-FRIED CHICKEN
Follow recipe for Oven-Fried Chicken, increasing hot pepper sauce to 1 tablespoon. Replace 1/4 teaspoon salt in crumb mixture with 1/2 teaspoon chili powder and increase cayenne to 1/4 teaspoon.

And the Numbers...
All nutritional information is for one serving.

TRADITIONAL HOMEMADE Fried Chicken
CALORIES: **552**
FAT: **34g**
SATURATED FAT: **10g**

COOK'S COUNTRY Oven-Fried Chicken
CALORIES: **216**
FAT: **9g**
SATURATED FAT: **4g**

The Crunchiest Choice
After testing a dozen options, tasters decided that corn flakes made the crispiest coating for our Oven-Fried Chicken.

🕐 **NO TIME TO SPARE?** Want to serve Oven-Fried Chicken after work? Marinate the chicken in the buttermilk mixture and combine the dry ingredients in a zipper-lock bag (all but the oil) the night before or in the morning before heading out. When you come home, all you'll have to do is heat the oven, toss the crumb mixture with oil, coat the chicken, and bake.

Fun Food

New Tricks for Halloween Treats

If you're trying to figure out what to do with all of that leftover Halloween candy, try one of these five clever recipes. RECIPES BY LAUREN CHATTMAN

PEANUT BUTTER CUP ICE CREAM AND SNICKERS BAR SAUCE SERVES 4

To soften vanilla ice cream quickly, turn it into a large bowl and cut it into large chunks. As soon as you can work the ice cream with a rubber spatula, fold in chopped Reese's or other peanut butter cups and refreeze.

- 1 pint vanilla ice cream, softened
- 10 mini peanut butter cups, chopped coarse
- 10 mini Snickers bars, chopped coarse
- 1/4 cup heavy cream

1. Make peanut butter ice cream Stir ice cream and peanut butter cups together in large bowl until combined. Return to freezer until firm, at least 30 minutes.

2. Make Snickers sauce Combine Snickers bars and cream in small saucepan over low heat, stirring frequently, until melted into chunky sauce. Remove from heat.

3. Serve Scoop ice cream into four bowls and spoon warm sauce over it. Serve.

CARAMEL TURTLES MAKES 12

Toast the nuts in a 350-degree oven until fragrant, 5 to 7 minutes.

- 60 pecan halves, toasted and cooled
- 12 soft caramel candies
- 1 (1 1/2-ounce) bar milk chocolate, broken into 12 squares

1. Bake turtles Adjust oven rack to middle position and heat oven to 350 degrees. Line baking sheet with parchment paper. Arrange pecans on baking sheet in clusters of 5, 1 for turtle head, 2 for arms, 2 for legs. Flatten each caramel piece with your hand so that it measures 1¼ inches square. Lightly press flattened caramel on top of each cluster. Bake until caramel is soft and shiny but not yet runny, 3 to 4 minutes.

2. Add chocolate Remove baking sheet from oven and place 1 piece of chocolate on top of each caramel. Return to oven until chocolate begins to melt, about 30 seconds. Remove from oven and smooth chocolate over caramel with small spoon. Cool completely on baking sheet.

3. Chill Refrigerate turtles until chocolate hardens, about 15 minutes, and serve. (Turtles can be stored in airtight container at room temperature for up to 3 days.)

CANDY-COATED CARAMEL APPLES MAKES 6

Freezing the caramels for 10 minutes will make it easier to remove their wrapping.

- 2 cups crushed Kit Kat, Twix, or Heath candy bars
- 6 small apples
- 1 (14-ounce) bag soft caramel candies
- 1/4 cup heavy cream

1. Prepare apples and candy bars Line baking sheet with parchment paper. Place crushed candy bars in shallow bowl. Insert craft stick into stem end of each apple.

2. Melt caramels Heat caramels and heavy cream in medium saucepan over medium-low heat, stirring constantly, until smooth.

3. Coat apples Holding 1 apple with stick over pot of caramel, spoon sauce over apple to coat, allowing excess to drip back into pot. Roll apples in crushed candy, pressing to help candy adhere. Place apple, stick up, on parchment paper. Repeat with remaining apples and serve. (Apples can be refrigerated for several days; bring to room temperature before serving.)

M&M CLUSTERS MAKES ABOUT 30

This recipe works with milk chocolate, too.

- 2 cups small pretzels, broken into 1-inch pieces
- 1 cup salted dry-roasted peanuts
- 8 ounces white chocolate, melted but warm
- 1/2 cup mini M&M candies

1. Mix clusters Line baking sheet with parchment paper. Combine pretzels and peanuts in medium bowl. Stir in white chocolate until combined.

2. Shape clusters Spoon tablespoonfuls onto prepared baking sheet. Sprinkle 4 or 5 M&Ms over each cluster. Refrigerate until chocolate hardens, about 15 minutes, and serve. (Once hardened, clusters can be stored in airtight container at room temperature for up to 2 days.)

PEPPERMINT-SURPRISE BROWNIE BITES

MAKES 36

Cut the cooled brownies into squares or use a cookie cutter for alternate shapes (we like stars and crescents).

- 8 tablespoons (1 stick) unsalted butter
- 2 ounces unsweetened chocolate
- 3/4 cup all-purpose flour
- 1/2 teaspoon baking powder
- 1/4 teaspoon salt
- 1 cup sugar
- 2 large eggs
- 1 teaspoon vanilla extract
- 16 (1 1/2-inch) York Peppermint Patties or other chocolate-covered peppermint candies

1. Prepare pan Adjust oven rack to middle position and heat oven to 350 degrees. Line 8-inch-square baking pan with heavy-duty aluminum foil, making sure that foil is tucked into all corners and that at least 1 inch overhangs top on all sides.

2. Make batter Melt butter and chocolate together. Set aside to cool slightly. Combine flour, baking powder, and salt in small bowl. Whisk sugar and eggs together in large bowl. Stir chocolate mixture and vanilla into egg mixture. Stir in flour mixture until just incorporated.

3. Assemble Set 1 cup brownie batter aside. Pour remaining batter into prepared baking pan. Arrange Peppermint Patties on top of batter, leaving about ½ inch between each piece. Smooth reserved 1 cup batter over candy.

4. Bake Bake until just set in center, 30 to 35 minutes. (Cake tester won't work because of candy.) Cool completely in pan on wire rack, about 2 hours. Grasp overhanging foil on sides of pan and transfer brownies to cutting board. Cut into 36 pieces and serve. (Brownies will keep at room temperature in airtight container for up to 3 days.)

Peppermint-Surprise
Brownie Bites

M&M Clusters

Caramel Turtles

Candy-Coated
Caramel Apples

Classic Cornbread and Sausage Dressing

Sausage and chicken broth give this stuffing a meaty flavor, even though it's baked outside of the turkey.

Every year I've got two Thanksgiving specialties: cornbread stuffing and dry turkey. A friend recently told me that cooking the stuffing inside the turkey is the problem, since it increases the roasting time. Should I bake the stuffing separately? —Betsy Carlson, New Britain, Conn.

Kitchen Wisdom
DRYING CORNBREAD

Although cornbread gives stuffing great flavor, it also adds a lot of moisture, making a soggy baked mess. If you have the time, cube the cornbread, spread it out on baking sheets, and let it sit overnight on the counter. If you're in a hurry (and who isn't around the holidays), pop the baking sheets holding the cornbread into a 400-degree oven until slightly crisp, 15 to 20 minutes.

When cooked inside the bird, stuffing reaches a safe temperature (165 degrees) only after the breast meat is overcooked and dry. The flip side, of course, is that the stuffing tastes great, having been basted with the juices from the roasting turkey. Baking the stuffing separately does solve the dry white meat problem, but, as most home cooks know, that stuffing will be a bit dry and bland. Welcome to the perpetual Thanksgiving dilemma.

One thing I knew from past experience is that if you're going to bake the stuffing separately, cornbread is a better choice than regular white bread simply because it is tastier to start with. To replace the meaty flavor supplied by the turkey's

juices, I turned to sausage, browned on the stovetop to cook it through and bring out the flavor. I started by testing crumbled bulk, breakfast, and Italian sausage, none of which worked well (too sweet, too greasy, or too outspoken). Kielbasa and chorizo were good, but andouille, a smoky, spicy Southern sausage, was the test kitchen favorite. As for vegetables, I went with onions and celery (also cooked on the stovetop before being added to the stuffing) but omitted carrots because of their sweetness. (Cornbread can be sweet.) To perk things up, I added garlic, sage, and a healthy dose of black pepper.

To add moisture, many recipes turn to dairy products (half-and-half and milk are popular) and eggs. But each of these made the stuffing too cakey. Both water and wine gave the stuffing a washed-out flavor. I had the most success with chicken broth, which replaced some of the missing poultry flavor without overpowering the taste of the cornbread.

If the stuffing is to absorb this liquid, the cornbread must be dry. Fresh cornbread is much too soft to use as is—unless you like gluey, dense stuffing. Some recipes call for stale cornbread. Sure enough, I found that day-old cornbread holds its shape better and is the best choice for stuffing. But I had equally good results with cornbread that I quickly "staled" in a 400-degree oven for 20 minutes.

As for baking the stuffing, a half-hour in a 400-degree oven did the trick. You can even bake the stuffing after taking the roasted turkey out

of the oven. It will cook in the time it takes for the bird to rest. This will guarantee that both the stuffing and the turkey will be steaming hot and moist when they hit the table.
–Jeremy Sauer

CORNBREAD AND SAUSAGE STUFFING
SERVES 10 TO 12

Spicy andouille sausage from Louisiana is the test kitchen's favorite in this recipe, but chorizo or kielbasa work well, too. For the cornbread, try our recipe at www.cookscountry.com or use your own.

12	cups prepared cornbread cut into 3/4-inch cubes (crumbs included)
1 1/2	pounds andouille sausage, halved lengthwise and sliced into 1/4-inch-thick half-moons
2	tablespoons unsalted butter
2	small onions, chopped fine
3	celery ribs, chopped fine
2	tablespoons minced fresh sage
3	garlic cloves, minced
1	teaspoon salt
1	teaspoon pepper
4	cups low-sodium chicken broth

1. Adjust oven racks to upper-middle and lower-middle positions and heat oven to 400 degrees. Spread cornbread evenly over two baking sheets. Bake until slightly crisp, 15 to 20 minutes; cool. Using oven mitts, remove upper-middle rack from oven.

2. Lightly brown sausage in Dutch oven over medium-high heat, 5 to 7 minutes, and transfer to plate lined with paper towels. After pouring off residual fat in pot, melt butter, add onions and celery, and cook until soft, about 5 minutes. Stir in sage, garlic, salt, and pepper and cook until fragrant, about 1 minute. Add broth and sausage to pot and scrape bottom with wooden spoon to release any browned bits. Add cornbread and gently stir until liquid is absorbed. Cover Dutch oven with lid and set aside 10 minutes. (Stuffing can be refrigerated overnight. Let sit at room temperature for 30 minutes before baking.)

3. Uncover Dutch oven and bake until top of stuffing is golden brown and crisp, about 30 minutes. Serve.

CORNBREAD AND BACON STUFFING

Replace sausage with 1 pound bacon, chopped; replace celery with 3 cups fresh or frozen corn kernels; and replace sage with 3 scallions, sliced thin.

Are Cornbread Mixes Any Good?

With all the cornbread mixes on the market, we wondered if we could get from-scratch quality out of a box. We gathered seven brands and prepared them according to the package instructions. None could compete with homemade—which isn't much harder to prepare. All of the cornbreads made from a mix were bland, and most were dry and gritty. Although these flaws were fatal when we tasted the cornbreads plain, when used in stuffing, the best two mixes—Betty Crocker and Jiffy—were acceptable. Store-bought cornbread will also make do in a pinch.

Quick and Easy Apple Turnovers

Although I can bake a great apple pie, I've yet to master the apple turnover. I have two problems: soggy pastry and leaky filling.

—Trish Estepp, Butler, Tenn.

Frozen puff pastry from the supermarket makes turnovers easy to prepare, but it doesn't ensure success. The recipes I tested were mushy, messy, and mediocre.

Most recipes called for either sliced or shredded apples, but I found both to be unappealing. Slices were undercooked (unless paper-thin, a real kitchen headache), and shredded apples looked like little worms. Searching for a happy medium, I pulsed the apples and sugar in the food processor until the apples were roughly chopped. The random chunkiness of the processed apples was great for texture, but now they gave off too much liquid and waterlogged the pastry.

I tried straining the apple mixture, but this left the filling too dry and grainy. What I needed was a binder to create a cohesive filling. Cooking some of the apples would do the trick, but I didn't want to complicate a simple recipe. Could I get away with a shortcut—store-bought applesauce—to produce that "cooked apple" texture? Sure enough, the applesauce combined with the strained apple mixture made for just the right consistency and boosted the apple flavor. With a little lemon juice and a pinch of salt, my filling was just right.

Over the years, I've learned that puff pastry works well as long as you play by its rules. For the perfect puff, the pastry must be cold and the oven hot. After assembling the turnovers, I placed them in the freezer for 15 minutes just to firm them up. When cooked in a 400-degree oven, the pastry layers puffed perfectly—well, almost.

Most of the turnovers split at the seams while they baked. What I needed was some sort of "glue" to brush over the edges of the pastry before sealing. After glancing over at the draining apple mixture, I realized that I could use the juice from the apples; I'd been planning to throw it out anyway! The sticky, sugary juice made a great sealant. Getting a little apple crazy, I brushed more of the apple juice over the top of the turnovers. This helped them to brown, and a sprinkle of cinnamon sugar made them look as good as they tasted. –Jeremy Sauer

EASY APPLE TURNOVERS
MAKES 8

If you don't have a food processor, grate the peeled and cored apples on the coarse side of a box grater before mixing them with the lemon juice, sugar, and salt. This recipe is easily cut in half. For more information on puff pastry, see page 29.

- 3/4 cup sugar
- 1 teaspoon ground cinnamon
- 2 Granny Smith apples, peeled, cored, and chopped coarse
- 1 tablespoon lemon juice
- 1/8 teaspoon salt
- 1/2 cup applesauce
- 2 sheets (9 by 9 1/2 inches) frozen puff pastry, thawed overnight in refrigerator
  Flour for dusting work surface

1. Adjust oven racks to upper-middle and lower-middle positions and heat oven to 400 degrees. Combine 1/4 cup sugar and cinnamon in small bowl.

2. Pulse apples, remaining 1/2 cup sugar, lemon juice, and salt in food processor until chopped into pieces no larger than 1/2 inch. Allow to sit for 5 minutes, then drain in fine-mesh strainer set over bowl. Reserve juices. Transfer apple mixture to medium bowl and stir in applesauce.

3. Unfold 1 sheet puff pastry onto lightly floured work surface and roll into 10-inch square. Cut into four 5-inch squares and fill each turnover with 2 tablespoons apple mixture, brush edges with reserved apple juice, then fold and crimp (see photos at right). Place turnovers on plate and freeze until firm, about 15 minutes. Repeat with remaining sheet puff pastry and filling.

4. Line two rimmed baking sheets with parchment paper.

Make Ahead
You can fill, fold, and freeze the unbaked turnovers up to 1 month in advance. Freeze them on a baking sheet, then transfer to a zipper-lock freezer bag. Before baking, allow the turnovers to sit at room temperature for 20 minutes, then proceed with the recipe as directed.

With turnovers still on large plate, brush tops with reserved apple juice and sprinkle with cinnamon sugar. Place 4 turnovers on each baking sheet and bake until well browned, 20 to 26 minutes, rotating sheets halfway through baking time. Transfer turnovers to wire rack and let cool slightly. Turnovers can be served warm or at room temperature.

SUGAR AND SPICE APPLE TURNOVERS

Reduce cinnamon to 1/2 teaspoon and add 1/2 teaspoon ground ginger, 1/4 teaspoon ground nutmeg, and a pinch ground cloves to cinnamon sugar.

Recipe Keys
PERFECT TURNOVERS

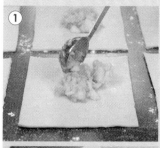

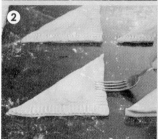

1. Place 2 tablespoons of the apple mixture in the center of each 5-inch square of pastry. Brush edges of pastry with reserved apple juice.
2. Bring one corner over pastry to meet opposite corner to form a triangle. Use a fork to crimp the edges and seal turnovers.

Store-bought puff pastry makes great turnovers if the dough is rolled thin, kept cold, and sealed tightly.

Reader Mailbag

Thanks for the Memories: BAKING BUNGALOW

Sue Mega, Attleboro, Mass. When I was a child, we lived in a small bungalow with large heating vents on the bottom of the walls in each room. Every few months, my mother would bake bread. She would prepare the dough and place it in front of one of the vents to rise. With nothing to do while she waited, and since she had the yeast and flour sitting out, she would prepare more dough for cinnamon rolls or Danish pastries. Before long, half the vents in the house would have bowls sitting in front of them. By the time the baking was finished, my mother would be exhausted and would swear never to do it again. Fortunately, she always forgot that vow.

Creepy, Colorful Cookies

Tazio Hilbert of Brooklyn, N.Y., sent us this photo of herself making Halloween cookies.

Not Your Average Wedding Cake

Kachina and Alex Allen live in New York City, but they are originally from Australia. Kachina tells us: "In Australia, the redback spider is well known as one of the most venomous. The top tier of our wedding cake celebrated this Australian creature with two redback spiders holding hands. The cake was especially appropriate as we met on the Internet, otherwise known as the Web."

Thanks for the Memories: GRITTY BREAD

Trish Estepp, Butler, Tenn. My grandmother, affectionately called Mamma, used to make the most wonderful bread that we all called gritty bread. Mamma and Pappa lived in a pre–Civil War log cabin on the Kentucky River. Every summer, Pappa would create a new grater for Mamma. He would remove the bottom from an empty coffee can, lay it flat, and create a series of holes in the can using a 16-penny nail. This created a surface for "gritting" corn. Mamma would "grit" whole ears of corn on the grater and then use it to make gritty bread, which was moist, somewhat chewy, and had a wonderful taste of fresh corn. I can almost taste it now.

Dressing Up: Pork Roast

Roast pork can be dry and usually needs gravy. Or does it?

A boneless pork roast requires almost no prep. And if you add vegetables to the roasting pan, you've got a complete meal. More often than not, though, pork roasts are dry and poorly browned, and the vegetables are steamed, not roasted. You could brine the pork (that is, soak it in a saltwater solution for an hour) to add moisture and brown the pork in a skillet to develop a caramelized crust, but these steps take time. How about a quicker, easier solution?

After some testing, I found that coating the pork with a flavorful glaze does the trick on both counts: It adds moisture and gives the pork a deep golden crust as it caramelizes in the oven. Two other easy steps can minimize the problem of dry meat. The first is to remove the pork from the oven once a thermometer inserted into the very center registers 140 degrees. (This seems like a low temperature, but the residual heat in the roast will cause the temperature to climb to about 150 degrees.) The second is to let the roast rest on a cutting board for 10 minutes before slicing it. This resting time reduces the loss of juices during carving.

And what about those vegetables? For a true roasted flavor, they need more time in the oven than the meat. Once the meat starts to rest on a cutting board, crank up the oven heat, spread out the vegetables, and keep on roasting them. –Eva Katz

MARMALADE-GLAZED PORK ROAST WITH PARSNIPS AND ONIONS
SERVES 6

For best results, avoid using enhanced pork (pork injected with a solution of water, salt, and chemicals); it causes the pork to exude excess liquid as it cooks, inhibiting the caramelization of the vegetables.

- 1 boneless pork loin roast (2½ to 3 pounds)
  Salt and pepper
- ⅓ cup orange marmalade
- 1 tablespoon chopped fresh rosemary
- ½ cup orange juice
- 1 tablespoon olive oil
- 1 pound parsnips, peeled and cut into 3-inch pieces
- 2 medium red onions, peeled and cut into 1-inch wedges

1. Adjust oven rack to middle position and heat oven to 375 degrees. Place pork in center of large roasting pan and season liberally with salt and pepper.

2. Combine marmalade and rosemary in large bowl. Spread half of marmalade mixture on pork. Add orange juice and olive oil to remaining marmalade mixture. Toss parsnips and onions with 2 tablespoons mixture and season with salt and pepper. Arrange vegetables around pork. Roast until instant-read thermometer inserted in thickest part of meat registers 120 degrees, 30 to 45 minutes. Pour remaining marmalade mixture over pork, increase oven temperature to 450 degrees, and roast until instant-read thermometer registers 140 degrees, 15 to 20 minutes.

3. Transfer roast to cutting board and tent with foil. Toss vegetables and juices and redistribute evenly over pan bottom. Roast until juices thicken and vegetables caramelize, about 10 minutes. Slice pork and serve with roasted vegetables, pouring pan juice over meat.

A two-ingredient glaze creates a browned crust on the pork and flavors the vegetables, too.

Better Than Your Mother's Grilled Cheese

As a kid, I got hooked on my mother's grilled cheese. Her recipe is simple and delicious. Now that I'm over 30, I'd like to try something more adventurous. –Elizabeth Speed, Needham, Mass.

The memory of Mom's crisp yet gooey toasted sandwich is still sacred to everyone here at *Cook's Country*. But spending all day in a test kitchen gets one thinking: "Gee, maybe even a grilled cheese sandwich is worth a second look." So with the image of a crisp, golden crust and a molten cheese center in mind, I started testing.

First I tested the bread. Flimsy white bread made soggy sandwiches. Sturdy sliced bread with a fine, dense crumb (such as Arnold or Pepperidge Farm) was much, much better. To avoid burning the bread, I found that a steady medium-low heat produced consistently golden brown crusts. The slow cooking also ensured an evenly melted interior.

Butter beat out contenders such as oil, mayonnaise, and cooking spray by a landslide because of its flavor. Melting the butter in the skillet and then adding the sandwiches produced poor results. The first side of the sandwiches had a fairly even layer of butter, but the second side was left high and dry. Melted butter brushed onto the outer sides of the bread (before the sandwiches were assembled) made for much more even cooking.

While turning out one grilled cheese after another, I couldn't help but think how much I like sandwiches made in an Italian panini press. Could I create a mock sandwich press using common kitchen equipment? A lightweight cake pan, used to lightly press the sandwiches, fit the bill. The metal pan serves as a heat conductor that helps to keep the top of the sandwich crisp while the bottom forms its own thick, brown crust.

What about Mom's grilled cheese? Her sandwiches are still tops in my book because she made them, but I'm sure she wouldn't mind my adding these dressed-up versions to my repertoire. –**Cali Rich**

CLASSIC GRILLED CHEESE SANDWICHES SERVES 4

In the test kitchen, we like the tang of sharp cheddar tempered by the mild, smoothly melting Monterey Jack.

- 1⅓ **cups grated sharp cheddar cheese**
- ⅔ **cup grated Monterrey Jack cheese**
- 8 **slices hearty white sandwich bread**
- 4 **tablespoons unsalted butter, melted**

1. Combine cheeses in bowl. Brush top side of each slice of bread with melted butter. Flip 4 slices over, sprinkle with cheese, and compact cheese lightly with hand. Cover with remaining bread slices, buttered side up.

2. Heat large nonstick skillet over medium-low heat for 1 minute. Place 2 sandwiches in pan and weight with round cake pan, pressing lightly. Leave cake pan on top and cook until first side is golden brown, 3 to 5 minutes. Flip sandwiches, press again with cake pan, and cook until golden brown, about 2 minutes. Repeat with remaining 2 sandwiches.

WINDY CITY GRILLED CHEESE SANDWICHES

If you like a Chicago hot dog, you'll love this sandwich. Press the relish with paper towels to remove excess moisture.

Use 2 cups grated Swiss cheese. Layer ¼ cup cheese, 1 very thin slice red onion (with rings separated), 1 thin slice bologna, 2 teaspoons Dijon mustard, 1 tablespoon dill pickle relish, another slice bologna, ¼ cup prepared sauerkraut (rinsed and drained), and ¼ cup cheese into each sandwich.

LITTLE ITALY GRILLED CHEESE SANDWICHES

The olive spread (sometimes labeled tapenade) is optional but delicious.

Use 1⅓ cups grated provolone cheese and ⅔ cup grated mozzarella cheese. Combine 1 cup jarred roasted red peppers, drained and chopped, with ¼ cup jarred pepperoncini, drained and minced. Layer ¼ cup cheese, 2 thin slices salami, one quarter of pepper mixture, 2 additional thin slices salami, 2 teaspoons kalamata olive spread, if using, and ¼ cup cheese into each sandwich.

GRILLED PIMENTO CHEESE SANDWICHES

Press the tomato slices between paper towels to remove moisture.

Mix 1⅓ cups grated cheddar cheese and ⅔ cup grated Monterey Jack cheese with 2 tablespoons mayonnaise, 2 tablespoons jarred pimentos, drained and chopped, 2 teaspoons minced yellow onion, ½ teaspoon hot pepper sauce, and ¼ teaspoon pepper. Layer each sandwich with cheese mixture and 2 thin slices tomato.

MONTEREY MELTS

Turkey, bacon, and avocado flavor this California classic.

Use 2 cups grated Monterey Jack cheese mixed with ¼ cup canned pickled jalapeño chiles, minced. Layer ¼ cup cheese-chile mixture, 2 slices deli turkey, 3 strips cooked bacon, several avocado slices, and ¼ cup cheese-chile mixture into each sandwich.

Use grated rather than sliced cheese for quick, even melting.

Steps to GREAT GRILLED CHEESE

1. Brushing melted butter on the bread guarantees even coverage and better browning. **2.** A round metal cake pan performs double duty as a press to compact the filling ingredients and as a heat conductor to crisp the crust.

> ### Cooking for a Crowd
> Grilled cheese sandwiches are best cooked two at a time. If you want to keep the first batch hot, place a baking sheet in the oven and heat the oven to 250 degrees. When the first batch is done, slide the sandwiches onto the hot baking sheet to keep them crisp and warm.

I'm Looking for a Recipe

READERS HELP READERS FIND RECIPES

We've Got Mail For months readers have been sending us recipes in response to the request for Apple Pie in a Bag (April/May 2005 issue). We particularly liked the letter and recipe sent by Eden Kuhlenschmidt (at right). To read our notes on this recipe (with details on cooking times and procedures), go to **www.cookscountry.com** and click **Looking for a Recipe.** You'll find dozens more recipes submitted by other readers who responded to this page in other issues of *Cook's Country.*

PAPER BAG APPLE PIE — Eden Kuhlenschmidt Sellersburg, Ind.

We have been using this recipe in our family for Thanksgiving for at least 45 years. In fact, it is such a favorite that I cross-stitched the recipe with a picture of an apple pie, framed it, and hung it in the kitchen so I wouldn't lose the recipe. My mother says that paper bags today aren't as thick as older bags and are more likely to burn or even catch fire if placed too close to heat coils. Since the mid-1990s, we've been double-bagging the pie, and that seems to keep the same flavor locked in.

		INSTRUCTIONS:
3–4	apples, peeled and sliced	Mix apple slices in sugar, nutmeg, and flour. Place
½	cup sugar	apple mixture in unbaked pie shell. Crumble topping together and
½	teaspoon nutmeg	sprinkle on top of pie. Place pie in paper bag (or doubled bag).
2	tablespoons flour	Fold edges and clip together.* Bake at 425 degrees for 1 hour,
1	unbaked pie shell	depending on your oven, it may take a little more or a little less time.
Topping		*Over time, we have tried various methods of sealing the paper
½	cup sugar	bag, from staples to tape, but in recent years have placed the
½	cup flour	sealed pie on a cookie sheet and folded the end of the bag
½	cup butter	between the cookie sheet and the oven shelf.

Plum Pudding Pie

My great-aunt Ida used to make a plum pudding pie for me when I was a small boy. She wouldn't give anyone the recipe because she had won a lot of blue ribbons for it at the state fair. It was as rich as pecan pie and had damson plums and walnuts in it. I remember it having a tall meringue, but that might be because I was quite small at the time.

Carl Early Gillespie
Independence, Mo.

Chicago-Style Italian Beef

I am originally from Chicago, but I now live in the Boston area. One of the foods that I miss the most is Italian beef. It involved marinating a roast overnight; it was then cooked and sliced thinly.

Michelle Zeamer
Holliston, Mass.

Pastelon

As a child, I remember eating a dish called *pastelon*. If I recall correctly, it is a lasagna-like dish made in Puerto Rico with ground beef, spices, and fried yellow plantains. I have tried to re-create this dish several times without success.

Lucy Diaz
Brooklyn Park, Minn.

Steam Pudding

Every summer, my paternal grandmother used to make what she called steam pudding, with whatever fruit was abundantly available in central Pennsylvania, usually black raspberries or peaches. The fresh fruit was mixed throughout, not just on top or as a garnish. The pudding was more like a sweet bread or gummy cake in texture, and it had a glossy top but no icing. The pudding was cut into large squares and eaten deep-dish style with a spoon, with added milk and granulated sugar. It was served with the main course rather than for dessert.

Peggy Morrissette
Dunkirk, Md.

Fleskapolse

My husband is looking for a Norwegian recipe for pork sausage called *fleskapolse*. The sausage has a ring of solidified grease just inside the casing and is precooked so you can spread it on rye bread.

Judy Benson
Morton Grove, Ill.

Polish Butter Cookies

When I was a kid, my aunt had a friend from Lansing, Ill., who made butter cookies every Christmas. They were the best butter cookies I have ever tasted. I remember her saying that the cookies contained liquor—possibly brandy? I know she was Polish, and I do believe it was a Polish butter cookie recipe.

'Littlesiskin'
Via e-mail

Poppin' Fresh Pie

Back in the mid-1970s I lived in Minneapolis, where there was a place called the Poppin' Fresh Pie Shop that made sour cream raisin pie. I have tried without success to find this recipe. It was a custard pie with whipped cream and sour cream folded in and then chilled.

Debbie Chapman
Via e-mail

Deep-Fried Sauerkraut Balls

In the early 1970s I baby-sat for a family that hosted great cocktail parties. After the parties, I got to clean up and nosh on the leftovers. I particularly remember deep-fried sauerkraut balls. They were tangy, crunchy, and slightly creamy.

Roxane Hoey
San Francisco, Calif.

Salt-Rising Bread

In Oklahoma City in the 1940s and 1950s, the Crescent Bakery used to make the most fragrant, intensely flavored bread called salt-rising bread. I have tried different recipes, but what I make never tastes as intense.

Covar Dabezies
Lubbock, Texas

Chrusciki

I have been searching for a recipe for *chrusciki* (Polish bow ties). I remember most of the ingredients—egg yolks, vanilla, flour, sour cream, and rum—but can't remember the measurements.

Dolores Doerflein
Arenel, N.J.

Crow's Nest Apple Cake

Every fall, my grandmother would make an apple cake that she called crow's nest. The apple slices were mixed right in the batter and also laid on the bottom of the pan, like an upside-down cake. This cake was delicious, and fall just hasn't been the same without it.

Deborah Barr
Via e-mail

Fruit Fluff

In the 1950s, my grandmother used to make a raspberry or strawberry "fluff" that she would put in a graham cracker crust. I believe the recipe also used something similar to Cool Whip.

Karen Morse
Prescott, Ariz.

Prune Cake

Until she passed away at the age of 97, my grandmother would make a prune cake for my birthday every year. It was a spice cake with stewed prunes added to make a moist, heavily flavored, decadent cake. I ate a cake similar to hers at the New Hampshire Shaker Village restaurant a few years ago. I suspect it is an Amish or Pennsylvania Dutch recipe.

James M. Sutton, Jr.
Rancho Mirage, Calif.

Banana-Bread Pudding

My mother is looking for a bread pudding recipe that uses leftover banana bread. She saw it on one of the public television shows a few years ago. It also calls for a chocolate glaze or sauce.

Joy Clarendon
Austell, Ga.

Australian Oat Cookies

While I was visiting San Francisco, I purchased the best cookie at a corner café. It was called an Australian oat cookie. I found the cookie again in the airport just before I departed. I cannot find this cookie in any of my cookbooks, and I even e-mailed a request to the Sydney Tourism Bureau, which did not respond. This cookie was so good.

Susan Smith
Auburn, Ala.

Golden Walnut Treasure Bars

My sister passed away in 1982, and I regret that I did not take her recipe box to remember her by. I would like to find her recipe for golden walnut treasure bars. The batter and the icing contain instant coffee, and the recipe also calls for sherry. The flavor matures when the bars are eaten a day or two later and is unbelievably delicious. It would be so lovely to taste them one more time.

Charlotte Bell
Gainesville, Fla.

Are you looking for a special recipe? Let other readers help. Just send us your requests, and we will print as many of them as we can. Write to Looking for a Recipe, Cook's Country, P.O. Box 470739, Brookline, MA, 02447, or e-mail us at lookingforarecipe@bcpress.com. If you can help with one of the above requests, contact us at the same postal or e-mail address. We will post responses on www.cookscountry.com.

Find the Rooster! A tiny version of this rooster has been hidden somewhere in the pages of this issue. If you find it, write to us with its location (plus your name and address), and you will be entered into a random drawing. The first winning entry drawn will receive the Krups indoor grill (see our test winner on page 31), and the next five winners will each receive a free one-year subscription to *Cook's Country.* To enter the contest, write to us at Rooster, Cook's Country, P.O. Box 470739, Brookline, MA 02447, or e-mail us at rooster@bcpress.com. Entries are due by November 30, 2005. We'll announce the winner of the contest from the August/September 2005 issue in our December/January issue. The winner will receive a Forschner Chef's Knife.

CHICKEN CUTLETS WITH BACON, ROSEMARY, AND LEMON

CHEESY RAVIOLI BAKE

HEARTY FISHERMAN'S STEW

HARVEST SUPPER SALAD WITH SMOKED TURKEY AND APPLES

CHEESY RAVIOLI BAKE SERVES 4 TO 6

Look for fresh ravioli near the cheese counter at the supermarket. Don't overcook the ravioli. We found that cooking times varied between 4 to 7 minutes, depending on the brand.

- 3 tablespoons unsalted butter
- 2 garlic cloves, minced
- 1 (28-ounce) can diced tomatoes
- 2 tablespoons coarsely chopped fresh basil
- 1/3 cup heavy cream
  Salt
- 2 (8-ounce) packages fresh cheese ravioli
- 1 (6-ounce) bag baby spinach
- 1 cup shredded mozzarella cheese

1. Bring 4 quarts water to boil in large pot for cooking pasta. Meanwhile, adjust oven rack to center position and heat oven to 450 degrees. Grease shallow 2-quart baking dish with 1 tablespoon butter.

2. Melt remaining 2 tablespoons butter in large skillet over medium heat. Add garlic and cook until fragrant but not brown, about 30 seconds. Add tomatoes, increase heat to high, and cook until thickened and almost dry, about 10 minutes. Stir in basil and cream and simmer until sauce thickens, about 2 minutes. Season with salt.

3. Add 1 tablespoon salt and ravioli to boiling water and cook until al dente. Add spinach to pot with pasta and stir until wilted, about 30 seconds. Drain pasta and spinach, return to pot, and stir in tomato sauce. Transfer mixture to baking dish, sprinkle with cheese, and bake until top is golden, about 10 minutes. Cool 5 minutes before serving.

CHICKEN CUTLETS WITH BACON, ROSEMARY, AND LEMON SERVES 4

- 5 slices bacon, chopped
- 1/4 cup all-purpose flour
- 4 boneless, skinless chicken breasts, trimmed
  Salt and pepper
- 1 tablespoon unsalted butter
- 4 garlic cloves, sliced thin
- 1 tablespoon chopped fresh rosemary
- 1/8 teaspoon red pepper flakes
- 1 cup low-sodium chicken broth
- 2 tablespoons lemon juice

1. Fry bacon in large skillet over medium-high heat until crisp, about 5 minutes. Transfer bacon with slotted spoon to plate lined with paper towels. Spoon off all but 2 tablespoons bacon fat.

2. Meanwhile, place flour in shallow dish. Season chicken with salt and pepper, dredge in flour, and shake to remove excess. Add butter to reserved bacon fat in skillet and heat over high heat, swirling to melt butter. When foam subsides, reduce heat to medium-high and cook chicken until browned on both sides, 3 to 4 minutes per side. Transfer chicken to plate (leaving fat in skillet) and cover loosely with foil.

3. Reduce heat to medium and add garlic, rosemary, and pepper flakes. Cook until garlic is browned and crisp, about 2 minutes. Add broth and lemon juice, scrape up browned bits from bottom of skillet with wooden spoon, and simmer until slightly thickened, about 4 minutes.

4. Return chicken and bacon to pan and simmer, turning chicken once or twice, until sauce is thick and glossy, 2 to 3 minutes. Adjust seasonings and serve.

HARVEST SUPPER SALAD WITH SMOKED TURKEY AND APPLES SERVES 4

If you like, walnuts can be used in placed of almonds in this main-course salad.

- 2 teaspoons honey
- 1/4 cup red wine vinegar
- 2/3 cup dried cherries or cranberries
- 6 tablespoons extra-virgin olive oil
  Salt and pepper
- 2 small heads red or green leaf lettuce, torn into bite-sized pieces
- 2 cups shredded red cabbage
- 1 apple, cored and cut into 2-inch strips
- 4 thick slices smoked deli turkey, cut into 2-inch strips
- 1 1/2 cups crumbled blue cheese
- 1/3 cup slivered almonds, toasted

1. Whisk honey and vinegar in medium microwave-safe bowl. Add cherries, cover with plastic wrap, cut several steam vents in plastic, and microwave on high until cherries are plump, about 1 minute. Whisk in oil, 1/4 teaspoon salt, and 1/8 teaspoon pepper. Cool dressing to room temperature.

2. Toss lettuce, cabbage, and apple with dressing in large bowl. Divide salad among individual plates and top each with portion of turkey, cheese, and nuts. Serve.

HEARTY FISHERMAN'S STEW SERVES 4

Cod is our favorite fish in this stew, but halibut and swordfish are also good choices. Use only the white and light green parts of the leeks. Slice leeks in half lengthwise, wash well, and then cut crosswise into thin slices. If you can't find chorizo, use hot Italian sausage. Serve this stew with thick slices of crusty bread.

- 2 tablespoons olive oil
- 1/2 pound chorizo sausage, cut into 1/2-inch pieces
- 2 leeks, sliced thin
- 1 red bell pepper, seeded and cut into thin strips
- 4 garlic cloves, minced
- 1/2 cup white wine
- 2 (14.5-ounce) cans diced tomatoes
- 1 (8-ounce) bottle clam juice
- 1 (14-ounce) can cannellini beans, drained, rinsed, and lightly mashed with fork
  Salt and pepper
- 1 1/2 pounds firm, thick boneless white fish fillets, cut into 2-inch chunks
- 1/3 cup chopped fresh parsley

1. Heat oil in Dutch oven over medium-high heat until just shimmering. Add sausage and cook until browned, 5 to 7 minutes. Add leeks, red pepper, and garlic and cook until soft, about 5 minutes. Add wine and simmer until reduced by half, about 1 minute. Add tomatoes, clam juice, and beans. Bring to boil, reduce heat to maintain gentle simmer, and cook, uncovered, for 10 minutes to blend flavors. Season with salt and pepper.

2. Gently stir in fish and parsley, cover, and simmer until fish is cooked through, about 5 minutes. Serve.

EASY TORTILLA CASSEROLE

SPICY BAKED SHRIMP

SPICY BEEF AND NOODLES

COUNTRY FRENCH PORK CHOPS

SPICY BAKED SHRIMP SERVES 4

For this recipe, we prefer the softer texture of fresh bread crumbs. To make bread crumbs, tear 3 slices of good-quality sandwich bread into quarters and grind in a food processor.

- 6 tablespoons unsalted butter
- 4 garlic cloves, minced
- 2 teaspoons lemon juice, plus 1 whole lemon, quartered
- 1½ tablespoons hot pepper sauce
  Salt and pepper
- 2 pounds jumbo shrimp, peeled and deveined, tails intact
- 2 teaspoons paprika
- ⅛ teaspoon cayenne pepper
- 2 teaspoons Dijon mustard
- 1 cup bread crumbs, preferably fresh (see note)
- 2 tablespoons chopped fresh parsley

1. Adjust oven rack to middle position and heat oven to 500 degrees. Coat large baking sheet with cooking spray.

2. Melt butter in small saucepan over medium heat. Add garlic and cook until fragrant, about 1 minute. Add lemon juice and hot sauce and season with salt and pepper. Remove from heat.

3. Toss shrimp, paprika, cayenne, mustard, ¼ teaspoon salt, and ⅛ teaspoon pepper together in large bowl. Add 2 tablespoons butter mixture. Place bread crumbs in shallow bowl.

4. Dip one side of each shrimp in bread crumbs, pressing to adhere crumbs. Place shrimp breaded side up on baking sheet, spacing them slightly apart. Spray shrimp with cooking spray and bake until just cooked through and bread crumbs are golden and crisp, 8 to 9 minutes. Rewarm butter mixture and stir in parsley. Serve shrimp with butter mixture and lemon wedges.

EASY TORTILLA CASSEROLE SERVES 4

You can find crisp tostada shells alongside other Mexican ingredients at many supermarkets. Sturdy corn tortillas chips make a fine alternative.

- 1 (28-ounce) can diced tomatoes, drained
- 1 small onion, chopped coarse
- 2 garlic cloves, peeled
- 2 canned chipotle chiles
- 2 tablespoons vegetable oil
- 2 cups shredded rotisserie chicken
- ¾ cup low-sodium chicken broth
- ¼ cup chopped fresh cilantro
  Salt and pepper
- 15 (5-inch) corn tostadas or 8 cups corn tortilla chips, broken into 2-inch pieces
- 1½ cups shredded Monterey Jack cheese
- 1 cup sour cream, for serving

1. Adjust oven rack to middle position and heat oven to 425 degrees. Grease 2-quart casserole dish. Puree tomatoes, onion, garlic, and chiles in blender until smooth, about 1 minute.

2. Heat oil in medium saucepan over medium heat until shimmering. Add tomato sauce, bring to simmer, and cook until slightly thickened, 5 to 7 minutes. Add chicken, broth, and cilantro and season with salt and pepper to taste.

3. Place half of chips in prepared dish; top with half of sauce and chicken mixture and half of cheese. Repeat with second layer. Using fingers, expose several chips on top layer so they can crisp in oven. Bake until bubbly and cheese begins to brown, 12 to 15 minutes. Serve with sour cream.

COUNTRY FRENCH PORK CHOPS SERVES 4

This recipe pairs nicely with mashed potatoes and wilted spinach.

- 4 bone-in rib or center-cut pork chops, about 1 inch thick
  Salt and pepper
- 2 teaspoons vegetable oil
- ¾ cup low-sodium chicken broth
- 2 tablespoons brown sugar
- 2 tablespoons red wine vinegar
- ½ cup pitted prunes, chopped coarse
- ½ cup pitted green olives, chopped coarse
- 1 tablespoon unsalted butter
- 2 tablespoons chopped fresh parsley

1. Pat pork chops dry with paper towels and season with salt and pepper. Heat oil in large skillet over medium-high heat until just smoking. Cook chops until well browned on both sides but still pink in center, 3 to 4 minutes per side. Transfer chops to plate and cover tightly with foil.

2. Add broth to skillet and bring to boil, scraping up any browned bits with wooden spoon. Add brown sugar, vinegar, prunes, and olives and simmer until sauce thickens, 4 to 5 minutes. Whisk in butter and parsley and season with salt and pepper to taste.

3. Reduce heat to medium-low and return chops and accumulated juices to skillet. Simmer, turning chops once or twice, until sauce clings to chops and meat is completely cooked (145 degrees on instant-read thermometer), 3 to 5 minutes. Transfer chops to platter and spoon sauce over them. Serve.

SPICY BEEF AND NOODLES SERVES 4 TO 6

If your market carries fresh Chinese egg noodles, use two 9-ounce packages in place of the ramen noodles.

- 1 pound boneless shell sirloin steak
  Salt and pepper
- 1 teaspoon plus 2 tablespoons vegetable oil
- 4 cinnamon sticks
- 4 whole cloves
- 4 garlic cloves, sliced thin
- 1 (1½-inch) piece fresh ginger, peeled and cut into thin strips
- 2 cups low-sodium chicken broth
- 1 teaspoon red pepper flakes
- 2 tablespoons soy sauce
- 4 packages instant ramen noodles (seasoning packets discarded)
- 1½ pounds fresh spinach, stem ends trimmed

1. Season steak with salt and pepper. Heat 1 teaspoon oil in large skillet over medium-high heat until just smoking. Add steak and brown on both sides, about 3 minutes per side. Transfer steak to plate and cover with foil.

2. Reduce heat to medium and add remaining 2 tablespoons oil, cinnamon, and cloves. Stir-fry until cinnamon sticks unfurl, about 1 minute. Add garlic and ginger and cook until soft, 1 to 2 minutes. Add broth, pepper flakes, and soy sauce, increase heat to high, and simmer until reduced by half, about 8 minutes. Discard cinnamon and cloves.

3. Meanwhile, cook noodles in large pot of water until almost tender, about 2½ minutes. Stir in spinach and cook until wilted, about 30 seconds. Reserve ⅓ cup noodle water; drain and return noodles and spinach to pot. Add sauce and reserved water (if needed) and cook over medium-low heat until flavors meld, about 1 minute. Divide noodles among individual bowls. Slice meat thinly against grain and place on top of noodles. Serve.

Cleaning Up Sloppy Joes

My family loves Sloppy Joes, even though most of the recipes I've tried are more like "meat candy on a bun." Is there any way to make this recipe less sweet but still delicious and easy?

—Hannah Protzman Brookline, Mass.

This cafeteria staple is often little more than a sweet, greasy dumping ground for third-rate burger meat. But I figured there was a not-so-Sloppy Joe waiting to be discovered.

Since the sauce is often so problematic, I started there. Ketchup is a must, but too much made the sauce saccharine. Most recipes also called for excessive amounts of sugar, which just made things worse. In search of an alternative to "meat candy on a bun," I tested just about every tomato product I could get my hands on.

Heinz chili sauce was the right consistency, but it contained flecks of horseradish that turned the sauce bitter. Canned crushed tomatoes needed lengthy cooking, while tomato paste made the sauce dry and stiff. Tomato puree, however, added the strong tomato flavor I was looking for. When mixed with ketchup and just a teaspoon of brown sugar, it produced a sauce that was first and foremost about tomatoes, with a gentle sweetness that everyone (even the naysayers in the test kitchen) liked.

Besides being too sweet, most published recipes were also too greasy. After much

trial and error, I decided that a middle-of-the-road choice—85 percent lean ground beef—was the best way to cut down on the slick factor.

I also discovered that the way I cooked the meat was just as important as its fat content. Most recipes say to brown the meat completely before adding the liquid ingredients. But each time I did so, my Sloppy Joes turned out tough and crumbly. I eventually stumbled on the key to soft, tender meat: Cook it until just pink (no further) and then add the remaining ingredients.

In the test kitchen, we are never content to leave good enough alone. My colleagues liked my recipe so much that they wanted variations. I found I could substitute ground turkey for the beef as long as I followed the same cooking procedure—that is, cook the meat until just pink (no further) before adding the sauce. And for Sloppy Joes with a south-of-the-border twist, I added more spices, chiles, and black beans and served the concoction in taco shells. For my final variation, I replaced the ketchup with barbecue sauce to create a smoky version of this family classic. **–Stephanie Alleyne**

A combination of tomato puree, ketchup, and mild spices creates a filling that's familiar but not too sweet.

Make Ahead

If you find yourself with leftover Sloppy Joes or just feel like making a double batch, the meat mixture freezes well for up to one month. To return the meat mixture to its original consistency, you may need to add a little water when it is reheated.

SLOPPY JOES SERVES 4

Be careful not to cook the meat beyond pink in step 1; if you let it brown at this point it will end up dry and crumbly. The meat will finish cooking once the liquid ingredients are added. Serve, piled high on a bun, with your favorite pickles.

- 2 tablespoons vegetable oil
- 1 medium onion, chopped fine
- ½ teaspoon salt
- 2 garlic cloves, minced
- ½ teaspoon chili powder
- 1 pound 85 percent lean ground beef
  Pepper
- 1 teaspoon brown sugar
- 1 cup tomato puree
- ½ cup ketchup
- ¼ cup water
- ¼ teaspoon hot pepper sauce
- 4 hamburger buns

1. Heat oil in large skillet over medium-high heat until shimmering. Add onion and salt and stir until coated with oil. Reduce heat to medium, cover, and cook, stirring occasionally, until onion is soft, about 10 minutes (if onion begins to burn after 5 minutes, reduce heat to low). Add garlic and chili powder and cook, uncovered, stirring constantly, until fragrant, about 30 seconds. Add beef and cook, breaking up meat with wooden spoon, until just pink, about 3 minutes.

2. Add ¼ teaspoon pepper, brown sugar, tomato puree, ketchup, water, and hot sauce. Simmer until Sloppy Joe sauce is slightly thicker than ketchup, 8 to 10 minutes. Adjust seasonings. Spoon meat mixture onto hamburger buns and serve.

Joe's Sloppy Cousins

SLOPPY JANES

For a slightly lower-fat version, substitute 1 pound ground turkey for the ground beef. The turkey should also be cooked till just pink.

SLOPPY JOSÉS

For a spicy twist, increase the chili powder to 1 tablespoon and add 2 tablespoons ground cumin and ¼ teaspoon cayenne pepper along with the garlic and chili powder. Add 1 chipotle chile, minced, and 1 (15-ounce) can black beans, drained and rinsed, with the other ingredients at the start of step 2. Substitute 4 taco shells for the hamburger buns.

SMOKY JOES

For this smoky version, replace the ketchup with an equal amount of barbecue sauce. Serve on soft deli-style onion rolls instead of hamburger buns.

Four Easy Appetizer Parties

Hundreds of readers sent in recipes for their favorite quick party foods. Our test kitchen selected the top 12 recipes and put them together in four simple menus.

CRISPY MEXICAN BITES
MAKES 36 PIECES
Angela Hines Defiance, Ohio
Make-Ahead Note: The cream cheese mixture can be refrigerated for 3 days. Fill the scoops up to 1 hour before serving.

- 4 ounces cream cheese, at room temperature
- 1/3 cup sour cream
- 1 garlic clove, minced
- 1/2 teaspoon dried oregano
- 1/2 teaspoon chili powder
- 36 Tostitos Tortilla Scoops
- 1 cup drained canned black beans
- 1 cup chunky salsa, drained
- 6 scallions, chopped fine

Stir cream cheese, sour cream, garlic, oregano, and chili powder together in bowl until smooth. Fill each tortilla scoop with black beans, salsa, cheese mixture, and scallions. Serve within 1 hour.

STUFFED JALAPEÑOS
MAKES 24 PIECES
Paula Sue Pekar Shiner, Texas
Make-Ahead Note: The stuffed jalapeños can be refrigerated up to 1 day. Let them sit at room temperature for 20 minutes before baking.

- 12 medium jalapeño chiles (preferably with stems attached)
- 8 ounces cream cheese, at room temperature
- 1/2 cup shredded cheddar cheese
- 4 thin slices Black Forest ham, chopped fine
- 1 tablespoon lime juice
- 1 teaspoon chili powder
- 2 scallions, chopped fine
- 1/2 teaspoon salt

Adjust oven rack to middle position and heat oven to 350 degrees. Cut each jalapeño lengthwise through stem (you should end up with 2 complete halves) and remove ribs and seeds. Combine cream cheese, cheddar, ham, lime juice, chili powder, scallions, and salt in bowl. Fill each jalapeño half with cheese mixture. Place jalapeños on parchment-lined baking sheet. Bake until filling is hot, about 20 minutes. Cool slightly and serve warm.

FRESH PINEAPPLE SALSA
MAKES ABOUT 3 CUPS
Elizabeth O'Shea
Needham, Mass.
Make-Ahead Note: This sweet and spicy salsa tastes even better after at least 1 hour in the refrigerator and can be made up to 1 day in advance.

- 1 fresh pineapple, peeled, cored, and chopped coarse (about 3 1/2 cups)
- 1 red bell pepper, seeded and chopped coarse
- 2 jalapeño chiles, seeds and ribs removed, chiles chopped coarse
- 1 garlic clove, minced
- 1/2 red onion, chopped coarse
- 1/4 cup packed fresh cilantro or parsley
- 2 tablespoons lime juice
  Salt and pepper
  Plantain or blue corn chips

Working in 2 batches, pulse pineapple, bell pepper, jalapeños, garlic, onion, and cilantro in food processor or blender until coarsely chopped to salsa-like consistency. Stir in lime juice and salt and pepper to taste. Serve with chips.

Adjust oven rack to middle position and heat oven to 350 degrees. Spoon 1/2 teaspoon jelly into each filo cup. Place 1 piece of Brie in each cup and sprinkle with 1/4 teaspoon almonds. Place filo cups on parchment-lined baking sheet. Bake until cheese is melted and jelly is bubbly, about 15 minutes. Cool slightly and serve warm.

CREAMY BEET SPREAD WITH ENDIVE LEAVES
MAKES ABOUT 3 CUPS
Danielle Carbeneau
Washington, D.C.
Make-Ahead Note: This creamy spread gets better as it sits and can be made up to 1 day in advance. To prevent discoloration, cut the endive as close as possible to serving time.

- 1 (15-ounce) can whole beets, drained and chopped fine
- 1 cup crumbled blue cheese,
- 1/4 cup walnuts, toasted and chopped
- 2 tablespoons chopped fresh basil or tarragon
- 2 tablespoons balsamic vinegar
- 3 tablespoons extra-virgin olive oil
  Salt and pepper
- 2 heads endive, cut in half lengthwise, leaves of each half separated

Combine beets, cheese, walnuts, basil, vinegar, oil, and salt and pepper to taste in bowl. Cover and refrigerate until flavors meld, at least 30 minutes. Serve with endive spears as scoops, or spoon mixture onto endive.

Elegant Evening

ROAST BEEF CANAPÉS
MAKES 12 PIECES
Mark Welton Salisbury Mills, N.Y.
Make-Ahead Note: The canapés can be refrigerated for up to 4 hours. Bring to room temperature before serving.

- 4 slices dark pumpernickel or rye bread, crusts removed
- 1/2 cup garlic-flavored Boursin cheese, at room temperature
- 4 thin slices deli roast beef, cut into quarters
- 1/2 cup jarred roasted peppers, cut into 1/4-inch strips
- 3 tablespoons chopped fresh dill or tarragon

Cut bread slices into quarters. Spread each piece with 2 teaspoons cheese and top with 1 piece roast beef. Top with 2 pepper strips and sprinkle with dill or tarragon. Serve.

BAKED BRIE CUPS
MAKES 30 PIECES
Melissa Boudreau
Via e-mail
Make-Ahead Note: The filled cups will keep up to 2 days in the refrigerator or 1 month in the freezer. If frozen, defrost for 20 minutes before baking.

- 1/3 cup red currant jelly
- 2 (2.1-ounce) boxes frozen mini filo cups
- 1 (8-ounce) wheel firm Brie, rind trimmed, cheese cut into 1/2-inch cubes
- 1/4 cup coarsely chopped smokehouse almonds

A Light Beginning

STUFFED CHERRY TOMATOES

MAKES ABOUT 24 PIECES

Christopher Speed New York, N.Y.
Make-Ahead Note: This easy appetizer can be refrigerated for up to 1 day. Garnish with parsley just before serving.

- 1 pint cherry tomatoes
- 4 ounces plain goat cheese
- 2 tablespoons prepared green or black olive tapenade
- 2 tablespoons minced fresh parsley

Cut ¼-inch slice off top of each tomato and gently scoop out seeds. Stir goat cheese and tapenade together in bowl until smooth. Transfer cheese mixture to small zipper-lock plastic bag and press cheese into one corner. Twist bag tightly around cheese, squeezing out as much air as possible. Snip off corner tip of plastic bag, insert tip into each tomato, and squeeze to fill each tomato. Transfer to platter and garnish with parsley. Serve.

Asian Flavors

SESAME CHICKEN BITES

MAKES 24 PIECES

Inez Shuman Grantsville, W.V.
Make-Ahead Note: After the chicken tenders are skewered and brushed with hoisin sauce (do not sprinkle with sesame seeds), they can be refrigerated, tightly wrapped, for up to 1 day.

- 1 pound boneless, skinless chicken breasts, cut into 2-inch pieces
- ¼ cup soy sauce
- 2 tablespoons grated fresh ginger
- 2 garlic cloves, minced
- ¼ cup hoisin sauce
- ¼ cup sesame seeds
- 4 scallions, chopped fine

1. Adjust oven rack to upper-middle position and heat oven to 400 degrees. Combine chicken, soy, ginger, and garlic in bowl. Cover and refrigerate 15 minutes.
2. Thread chicken onto wooden skewers, brush with hoisin sauce, and sprinkle with sesame seeds. Place on baking sheet and cover exposed skewer ends with foil to keep from burning. Bake until chicken is cooked through, about 20 minutes. Sprinkle with scallions and serve.

GINGERED SHRIMP TOASTS

MAKES ABOUT 36 PIECES

Annette Hoppe Lexington, Va.
Make-Ahead Note: The cream cheese spread can be refrigerated for up to 2 days. The seasoned shrimp can be refrigerated for up to 1 day.

- 1 thin baguette, sliced into ½-inch-thick rounds
- ½ cup extra-virgin olive oil
- 1 tablespoon grated fresh ginger
- 1 garlic clove, peeled
- ¼ small onion
- 4 ounces cream cheese, at room temperature
- ½ teaspoon plus 1 tablespoon lemon juice
  Salt

SMOKED SALMON PINWHEELS

MAKES 48 PIECES

Shawn Dean Jersey City, N.J.
Make-Ahead Note: The cream cheese and salmon spread can be refrigerated for up to 2 days. After preparing the pinwheels, refrigerate them until ready to serve, no more than 3 hours.

- 8 ounces cream cheese, at room temperature
- 4 tablespoons butter, at room temperature
- 8 ounces smoked salmon
- 3 tablespoons lemon juice
- 4 tablespoons drained capers
- 6 tablespoons fresh dill
  Salt and pepper
- 1 loaf (about 24 slices) thinly sliced soft black bread, crusts removed

1. Process cream cheese, butter, smoked salmon, lemon juice, capers, 4 tablespoons dill, and salt and pepper to taste in food processor until smooth.
2. Use rolling pin to roll bread slices flat on both sides. Spread 1 tablespoon salmon mixture over each slice of bread. Roll into tight cigar shape and slice in half diago-

- ½ pound cooked medium shrimp, each sliced in half lengthwise
- 1 tablespoon chopped fresh basil
- 1 tablespoon chopped fresh chives
  Pepper

1. Adjust oven rack to middle position and heat oven to 350 degrees. Brush bread slices with ¼ cup oil. Bake on baking sheet until golden brown, about 10 minutes.
2. Process ginger, garlic, and onion in food processor until smooth. Add cream cheese, ½ teaspoon lemon juice, and ½ teaspoon salt and process until smooth. Toss shrimp, remaining oil, 1 tablespoon lemon juice, basil, chives, and salt and pepper to taste in bowl.
3. Spread each toast with cream cheese mixture and top with 1 sliced shrimp. Serve.

CHUTNEY CHEESE ROUNDS

MAKES 36 PIECES

Marcia Pittleman Denver, Colo.
Make-Ahead Note: Unbaked and tightly wrapped, the

nally. Transfer to platter and place angled side up. Garnish with remaining 2 tablespoons dill. Serve.

ASPARAGUS PUFFS

MAKES 24 PIECES

Renee Pokorny Ventura, Calif.
Make-Ahead Note: The puffs can be made ahead. Skip the step of brushing the tops with egg and sprinkling with cheese. Wrap the baking sheet tightly in plastic and freeze for up to 1 month (once completely frozen, the puffs can be transferred to a storage bag). When ready to bake, let the puffs sit at room temperature for 20 minutes, then brush with egg, sprinkle with cheese, and bake as directed.

- 1 cup ricotta cheese
- 1 cup grated Parmesan cheese
- ¾ pound asparagus, trimmed, blanched, dried, and chopped fine
- ¼ cup minced fresh chives
- 2 tablespoons lemon juice
  Salt and pepper
- 1 (1-pound) box frozen puff pastry, thawed in refrigerator overnight
  Flour for dusting work surface
- 1 large egg, lightly beaten

1. Adjust oven rack to middle position and heat oven to 375 degrees. Combine ricotta, ¾ cup Parmesan, asparagus, chives, lemon juice, and salt and pepper to taste in bowl.
2. Unfold both pieces puff pastry on lightly floured surface and roll out to flatten bumps or creases. Using 2½-inch round cookie cutter, cut out 24 rounds. Brush rounds with egg. Place 1 tablespoon cheese mixture slightly off center on each round. Fold round over cheese and crimp edges with fork. Place on parchment-lined baking sheet. Brush tops with egg and sprinkle with remaining Parmesan.
3. Bake until puffed and golden brown, about 20 minutes. Cool slightly and serve warm.

assembled rounds will keep in the refrigerator for 1 day or in the freezer for 1 month. If frozen, let sit at room temperature for 10 minutes before baking.

- 1½ cups grated sharp cheddar cheese
- 4 ounces cream cheese, at room temperature
- 1 tablespoon Dijon mustard
- ¼ teaspoon salt
  Pinch cayenne
- ¼ cup mango chutney
- ¼ cup chopped crystallized ginger
- ¼ cup finely chopped pecans
- 36 white Melba toast rounds
- ¼ cup minced fresh mint

1. Adjust oven racks to upper-middle and lower-middle positions and heat oven to 400 degrees. Combine cheddar, cream cheese, mustard, salt, and cayenne in bowl. Combine chutney, ginger, and pecans in second bowl.
2. Spread heaping teaspoon of cheese mixture onto each Melba cracker. Using spoon, make well in center of cheese mixture and place ½ teaspoon chutney mixture in well. Place crackers on 2 parchment-lined baking sheets. Bake until cheese is bubbly, about 10 minutes. Sprinkle with mint and serve immediately.

Sunday-Best Garlic Roast Beef

I always get good results when I choose an expensive roast but was wondering if there was some way to dress up a cheaper cut. Maybe something flavored with garlic? –Annie O'Dowd, Chicago, Ill.

A trio of garlic preparations turns a cheap roast into something worthy of a special meal.

SUNDAY-BEST GARLIC ROAST BEEF
SERVES 6 TO 8

Look for a top sirloin roast (see photo below) that has a thick, substantial fat cap still attached. The rendered fat will help to keep the roast moist. When making the jus, taste the reduced broth before adding any of the accumulated meat juices from the roast. The meat juices are well seasoned and may make the jus too salty. A heavy-duty roasting pan with a dark or nonstick finish or a broiler pan is a must for this recipe.

Beef
- 8 large garlic cloves, unpeeled
- 1 (4-pound) top sirloin roast, with some top fat intact

Garlic-Salt Rub
- 3 large garlic cloves, minced
- 1 teaspoon dried thyme
- 1/2 teaspoon salt

Garlic Paste
- 12 large garlic cloves, peeled, cloves cut in half lengthwise
- 2 sprigs fresh thyme
- 2 bay leaves
- 1/2 teaspoon salt
- 1/2 cup olive oil
  Pepper

Jus
- 1 1/2 cups low-sodium beef broth
- 1 1/2 cups low-sodium chicken broth

1. For the beef: Toast unpeeled garlic cloves in small skillet over medium-high heat, tossing frequently, until spotty brown, about 8 minutes. Set garlic aside. When cool enough to handle, peel cloves and cut into 1/4-inch slivers.

2. Using paring knife, make 1-inch-deep slits all over roast. Insert toasted garlic into slits.

3. For the garlic-salt rub: Mix minced garlic, thyme, and salt together in small bowl. Rub all over roast. Place roast on large plate and refrigerate, uncovered, at least 4 hours or preferably overnight.

Good cooks know that tenderloin and prime rib require very little, other than a nice fat bank account. Preparing a cheaper cut is another matter. These roasts tend to have more gristle, more connective tissue, and flavors that are often sour or livery.

So I began with a bit of testing to find out which cuts are best and identified three widely available inexpensive roasts (see box, right). The top sirloin was an all-around crowd pleaser: tender, juicy, and beefy tasting.

Our test kitchen has found that large beef roasts cook more evenly at low temperatures. In a hot oven, the outer portions of the roast tend to overcook by the time the middle is done. However, roasting at a low temperature allows for little flavor development on the exterior of the roast. To ensure a nicely browned exterior, the roast must first be seared.

To simplify matters, I chose not to sear the meat on the stovetop but in a hot oven, turning down the heat once the outside browned. My first try didn't produce enough browning, though, and I thought it might be the stainless steel pan I was using. Taking a hint from baking—where darker, nonstick surfaces produce darker cakes because of better heat absorption—I tried a nonstick roasting pan, and it did a much better job. (You can use a broiler pan in a pinch.)

Your suggestion of using garlic with a cheaper roast is a good one. Tests with slivers of raw garlic inserted into the meat were unsuccessful, as the garlic was harsh tasting. Toasting unpeeled garlic cloves in a skillet took the nasty bite out of them. To get even more garlic flavor, I rubbed the meat with a garlic-salt mixture and then refrigerated it. The flavor improved after four hours, but I got the best results when I let a roast rest overnight. The one problem was that the garlic rub was burning and turning bitter during the high initial heat of searing. To solve the problem, I simply wiped off the rub before searing.

Things were going well, but I still wanted a touch more flavor and so I applied a cooked garlic paste to the meat after searing. Cooking the garlic in oil over low heat for half an hour took the bite out of it and made it sweet.

In the end, it was the triple garlic whammy that won over the test kitchen. I think this roast can compete with that fancy, high-priced Christmas prime rib any day of the year.

–Katie Henderson

Three Cheap Cuts
We tested three popular inexpensive roasts and found one champ, one solid pinch-hitter, and one roast that you definitely do not want in your line-up.

BEST BET
Top Sirloin Roast

This cut from the hip area tasted incredibly meaty and had plenty of marbling, which made for a succulent roast. It can also be labeled as top butt, top sirloin butt, center-cut roast, or spoon roast.

SECOND CHOICE
Blade Roast

This roast from the shoulder was beefy and juicy, and its shape made it very easy to slice. A thin line of sinew was the only unpleasant distraction.

STEER CLEAR
Bottom Round Roast

This roast from the rump area was tough and lacking in flavor. Even worse was the absence of fat and marbling, which made the meat very dry.

4. For the garlic paste: Heat halved garlic cloves, thyme, bay leaves, salt, and oil in small saucepan over medium-high heat until bubbles start to rise to surface. Reduce heat to low and cook until garlic is soft, about 30 minutes. Cool completely. Strain, reserving oil. Discard herbs and transfer garlic to small bowl. Mash garlic with 1 tablespoon garlic oil until paste forms. Cover and refrigerate paste until ready to use. Cover and reserve garlic oil.

5. Adjust oven rack to middle position, place nonstick roasting pan or broiler pan bottom on rack, and heat oven to 450 degrees. Using paper towels, wipe garlic-salt rub off beef. Rub beef with 2 tablespoons reserved garlic oil and season with pepper. Transfer meat, fat side down, to preheated pan and roast, turning as needed until browned on

all sides, 10 to 15 minutes.

6. Reduce oven temperature to 300 degrees. Remove roasting pan from oven. Turn roast fat side up and, using spatula, coat top with garlic paste. Return meat to oven and roast until internal temperature reaches 125 degrees on instant-read thermometer, 50 to 70 minutes. Transfer roast to cutting board, cover loosely with foil, and let rest for 20 minutes.

7. For the jus: Drain excess fat from roasting pan and place pan over high heat. Add broths and bring to boil, using wooden spoon to scrape browned bits from bottom of pan. Simmer, stirring occasionally, until reduced to 2 cups, about 5 minutes. Add accumulated juices from roast and cook 1 minute. Pour through fine-mesh strainer. Slice roast crosswise against grain into ¼-inch slices. Serve with jus.

A GARLIC TRIPLE WHAMMY

Not one, not two, but three garlic preparations are used to give our roast beef full garlic flavor without any of that harsh garlic burn. Here's how we do it.

① Toasted Garlic

Toast unpeeled garlic cloves. Peel and sliver the cloves and insert the slivers into slits cut into the roast.

② Garlic-Salt Rub

Combine minced garlic with herbs and salt. Rub garlic salt over roast and refrigerate at least 4 hours.

③ Garlic Paste

Poach halved garlic cloves and herbs in oil. Strain garlic and mash into paste. Rub garlic paste over browned roast.

What to Do with Leftovers: *French Dip Sandwiches*

In the test kitchen, our cooks often tire of dishes during the testing process. Chocolate cake, again? Garlic roast beef did not suffer this fate, in part because the leftovers are easily transformed into tasty French dip sandwiches. Just layer thinly sliced roast beef and cheese (we like provolone, but Swiss cheese works, too) into buttered sub rolls, broil, and you've got a satisfying lunch. The most important element in this sandwich is the jus, which is used to moisten the beef and is served with the sandwiches for dipping. More often than not, no jus is left over. I came up with an easy solution to make a full-flavored jus in no time, even without pan drippings. **–K.H.**

FRENCH DIP SANDWICHES SERVES 4

If you have leftover jus from the roast, use it. Otherwise, make the Quick Jus that follows.

- 1 teaspoon olive oil
- 1 onion, halved and sliced thin
- 4 (6-inch) sub rolls
- 2 tablespoons unsalted butter, softened
- 4 cups thinly sliced leftover roast beef
- 1 cup jus, heated in small saucepan
- 4 slices provolone cheese, cut in half

1. Position oven rack 6 inches below heating element and heat broiler. Heat oil in small nonstick skillet over medium-high heat until shimmering. Add onion and cook, stirring frequently, until browned, about 7 minutes.

2. Meanwhile, slice rolls in half lengthwise and spread interior of both sides with butter. Place on baking sheet, buttered side up, and broil until golden, 1 to 3 minutes. Remove top half of each roll.

3. Using tongs, dip beef slices into hot jus and place about 4 slices beef on bottom half of each roll. Spoon onions over beef and arrange provolone on top. Broil until cheese has melted. Set top half of each roll in place and serve with extra jus for dipping.

QUICK JUS MAKES 1 CUP

- 1 teaspoon olive oil
- 1 cup leftover roast beef trimmings
- ¼ cup minced onion
- 1 teaspoon all-purpose flour
- 2 cups low-sodium beef broth

Heat oil in medium skillet over medium-high heat until just smoking. Add beef and cook until dark brown, about 1 minute. Reduce heat to medium, add onion, and cook until slightly softened, about 1 minute. Add flour and cook, stirring constantly, until fragrant and toasty, about 1 minute. Whisk in broth, scraping up browned bits with wooden spoon. Simmer until liquid is reduced by half, about 10 minutes. Pour through fine-mesh strainer and serve.

Leftover roast beef is reborn in this tasty sandwich with sautéed onions, melted provolone, and our Quick Jus for dipping.

Regional Favorites: Dirty Rice

Authentic recipes use giblets to enrich this Cajun classic. We wanted to keep the richness but skip (most of) the giblets.

Like frugal cooks everywhere, Cajun cooks from generations past found plenty of ways to use every part of the animals they raised. Traditionally, chicken "giblets"—the gizzard, heart, kidneys, and liver—were used to flavor rice, at the same time turning it brown and so giving rise to the name "dirty." But dirty rice isn't just about appearances—it's about turning a bland white grain into a rich, meaty side dish.

After trying everything from bacon and sausage to hamburger meat, I found that ground pork came closest to producing the flavor I'd gotten when I made a batch of dirty rice with giblets. But this dish was still a long way from the real thing. Because chicken livers are still widely available, I wondered if this one member of the original four-some would do the trick. Sure enough, my tasters agreed that rice made with both chicken livers and ground pork lived up to the name "dirty."

–Jeremy Sauer

To keep the rice light and fluffy, cook the "dirty" ingredients separately and drain off their fat.

DOWN 'N' DIRTY RICE SERVES 4 TO 6

Pass hot pepper sauce at the table for a real taste of Louisiana.

- 1 tablespoon vegetable oil
- 8 ounces ground pork
- 1 medium onion, chopped fine
- 1 rib celery, chopped fine
- 1 red bell pepper, seeded and chopped fine
- 3 garlic cloves, minced
- 4 ounces chicken livers, rinsed, trimmed of fat, and chopped fine
- 1/4 teaspoon dried thyme
- 1/4 teaspoon cayenne pepper
  Salt
- 2 1/4 cups low-sodium chicken broth
- 2 bay leaves
- 1 1/2 cups long-grain white rice, rinsed (see page 29)
- 3 scallions, sliced thin

1. Heat oil in Dutch oven over medium heat until shimmering. Add pork and cook until browned, about 5 minutes. Stir in onion, celery, and bell pepper and cook until softened, about 10 minutes. Add garlic, chicken livers, thyme, cayenne, and 1 teaspoon salt and cook until browned, 3 to 5 minutes. Transfer to fine-mesh strainer set over bowl and cover with foil.

2. Increase heat to high and add chicken broth, bay leaves, and rice to empty pot. Scrape bottom of pot with wooden spoon to remove browned bits. Bring to boil, reduce heat to low, cover, and cook until rice is tender, 15 to 17 minutes. Remove from heat, discard bay leaves, and fluff rice with fork. Gently stir in drained meat and vegetable mixture (discarding any accumulated juices) and sprinkle with scallions. Serve immediately.

---

on the side: QUICK DINNER MUFFINS

Replace sugar with cheese for an easy alternative to rolls.

For a double dose of flavor, the cheese is baked into the muffins and sprinkled on top.

Muffins aren't just for breakfast. Replace the sugar with cheese, spices, and scallions and you have an easy alternative to dinner rolls or biscuits. Dinner muffins don't require rising time or fussy shaping—just combine the flour and dry ingredients in one bowl, whisk the milk, melted butter, and egg in a second bowl, and then gently stir the dry and wet ingredients together. The batter will be ready in the time it takes to preheat the oven.

A few key points about the ingredients in this recipe. I found that sour cream makes these muffins especially rich and moist. It also adds a slight tang that works well with the cheese. Although you could add almost any kind of cheese, my tasters liked the combination of pungent blue cheese tempered with nutty Parmesan. Sprinkling the grated Parmesan over the batter after it has been portioned into the greased muffin tin ensures that the muffin tops will be especially cheesy, browned, and crisp. One caution: These muffins taste best when served warm. –Eva Katz

SAVORY CHEESE MUFFINS
MAKES 12

For a big cheese presence, shred the Parmesan on the large holes of a box grater. Use both the white and green parts of the scallions. If you prefer, use an equal amount of shredded cheddar in place of the blue cheese.

- 3 cups all-purpose flour
- 1 tablespoon baking powder
- 1 teaspoon salt
- 1/4 teaspoon cayenne pepper
- 1/8 teaspoon black pepper
- 1 cup crumbled blue cheese
- 2 scallions, chopped
- 1 1/4 cups milk
- 3 tablespoons unsalted butter, melted
- 1 large egg, beaten
- 3/4 cup sour cream
- 1/2 cup shredded Parmesan cheese

1. Adjust rack to middle position and heat oven to 350 degrees. Coat regular 12-cup muffin tin with nonstick cooking spray.

2. Whisk flour, baking powder, salt, cayenne, and pepper together in large bowl. Mix in blue cheese and scallions, breaking up any clumps, until cheese is coated with flour. Whisk milk, butter, egg, and sour cream together in medium bowl. Using rubber spatula, gently fold wet ingredients into dry ingredients until just combined (batter will be heavy and thick). Divide batter among muffin cups. Sprinkle Parmesan over batter in each cup.

3. Bake until light golden brown and toothpick inserted in center of muffin comes out with a few crumbs attached, 25 to 30 minutes. Cool in pan on wire rack for 5 minutes. Run knife around muffins to loosen, invert pan, and remove muffins. Cool slightly, about 10 minutes. Serve warm.

The Cheesiest Potato Casserole

I used to fight with my brother for extra helpings of the crisp, browned crust on my mother's scalloped potatoes. But no one fights over the scalloped potatoes that I make.

–Debbie Irving, Houlton, Maine

Every country cook knows the basic recipe for scalloped potatoes: Layer thinly sliced potatoes and cheese in a shallow casserole dish, cover with liquid, and bake. In the best of all worlds, the potatoes form dense layers, the liquid reduces to a creamy, flavorful sauce, and the cheesy crust is golden and crisp. But scalloped potatoes are often heavy and bland.

Using just cream makes the dish too rich and greasy. But leaner dairy choices can curdle in the oven. My solution was to cut the heavy cream with a little chicken broth. Simmering fresh thyme and garlic with the cream and broth made the sauce taste better. As for the cheese, I decided to pair Gruyère or Swiss (for both their meltability and their flavor) with Parmesan (for its browning ability and its flavor).

Russets, all-purpose, and Yukon Gold potatoes all worked well, although the russets, with their tender bite and earthy flavor, were my favorite. More important than the type of potato used is the way the potatoes are sliced—very thin, if they are to cook evenly. Unless you have excellent knife skills, a mandoline is recommended.

A top layer of golden, bubbly cheese was nice, but I wanted a topping worth fighting for. I remembered a savory bread pudding with crisp bread cubes poking out of the custard. Unconventional as it might seem, a bread topping looked great on my scalloped potatoes, and its tasty crunch kept everyone in the kitchen coming back for more. –Eva Katz

For even coverage, toss the potato slices with the sauce and then spoon the mixture into the casserole dish.

CHEESY POTATO CASSEROLE SERVES 8 TO 10

If you're making the casserole ahead to bring to a potluck supper, see page 29 for tips on keeping it warm.

- 4 garlic cloves, 1 clove cut in half lengthwise, remaining cloves minced
- 1 tablespoon unsalted butter, softened
- 1 cup shredded Gruyère or Swiss cheese
- 1 cup coarsely grated Parmesan cheese
- 1½ cups heavy cream
- 1½ cups low-sodium chicken broth
- 2 teaspoons chopped fresh thyme
- ⅛ teaspoon nutmeg
- ¾ teaspoon salt
- ⅛ teaspoon pepper
- 2½ pounds russet potatoes (4 to 5 medium), peeled and sliced ⅛ inch thick
- 4–5 slices hearty white sandwich bread, crusts removed and torn into pieces (about 4 cups)

1. Adjust oven rack to middle position and heat oven to 350 degrees. Use cut side of halved garlic to rub sides and bottom of 2-quart shallow baking or gratin dish. Allow garlic in dish to dry briefly, about 2 minutes, then coat dish with softened butter. Combine cheeses in small bowl.

2. Bring minced garlic, cream, broth, thyme, nutmeg, salt, and pepper to boil in large saucepan over medium-high heat. Reduce heat to medium-low and simmer until liquid is reduced to 2½ cups, about 5 minutes. Remove from heat and gently stir in potatoes.

3. Spoon half of potato mixture into prepared dish. Sprinkle with half of cheese, add remaining potato mixture, and press with spatula to compact. Following photo, press bread pieces into casserole. Bake 40 minutes. Sprinkle remaining cheese on top and continue baking until golden and bubbling, 25 to 30 minutes. Remove from oven and let rest 20 minutes before serving.

Make Ahead

This casserole can be assembled (leave off the bread) and refrigerated up to 24 hours. When ready to bake, add bread topping and bake according to the recipe. If you're cooking for a crowd, double the ingredients and use two baking dishes of similar size.

Gadgets & Gear
MANDOLINES

PYREX SLICER: Best Buy

A mandoline is a hand-operated slicer, specifically designed for firm vegetables. The adjustable blade is capable of cutting paper-thin slices, eliminating the need for well-honed knife skills. We tested five models and found three good choices. The Progressive Mandoline ($27.99) was easy to use and clean, whereas the New Benriner ($32.95) scored highest in comfort and durability. Although the safety guard that holds the food on the Pyrex Kitchen Slicer ($5.99) did not glide easily, it's easy to overlook this flaw given the low price.

–Meredith Butcher

Surprise Topping
SANDWICH BREAD

For an extra-crisp crust, press roughly torn pieces of sandwich bread into the casserole right before it goes into the oven.

Southern Pecan Praline Pie

Last Thanksgiving, I made my grandma's pecan praline pie, but it turned out gritty, taffy-like, and boozy. Her pies were perfect. Can you help?

—Virginia Cole, Macon, Ga.

Having spent much of my life in the South, I found the notion of a pecan praline pie (with a nip of bourbon) right up my alley. This pie should turn out buttery, dark, and rich, nothing like chewy taffy.

I knew a plain old pie crust wouldn't do for a pie like this, so I began to build the praline flavor there. Instead of using the granulated white sugar and butter/shortening mix typical of American pie crusts, I used dark brown sugar and all butter. The pie was off to a good start.

Next came the filling. I uncovered two approaches to it in my research. One was inspired by the praline part of the recipe and followed traditional candy-making technique, cooking brown sugar, pecans, butter, and cream. The other was modeled on pecan pie fillings, cooking brown sugar, pecans, butter, corn syrup, and eggs.

As I soon learned, praline may be a great candy, but it's a lousy recipe for pie filling; it's much too hard. And no matter how I cooked the core ingredients on the stovetop, the filling was gritty.

I had better luck with recipes that followed the pecan pie approach. Using corn syrup rather than cream made the filling less likely to seize or become gritty. And the eggs ensured that the filling set up in the oven while still remaining soft enough to slice. Now all I had to do was tweak the flavors. I wanted something darker and richer than the test kitchen's favorite pecan pie filling.

My first thought was to use dark corn syrup rather than the light corn syrup called for in most pecan pie recipes. The candy-like flavor of dark corn

syrup was perfect, if a bit sweet. An extra dose of salt kept the filling from being too cloying. For more richness, I increased the amount of butter. With 2 tablespoons of bourbon (or 4 if you want a more potent pie), the filling was perfect.

—**Bridget Lancaster**

SOUTHERN PECAN PRALINE PIE SERVES 8 TO 10

Chopping the pecans with a knife will produce a fine dust that can cloud the resulting pie. Instead, use a rolling pin to gently break the pecans into small, 1/2-inch pieces. Be sure to remove the pie from the oven when the center is set but still wobbly; residual heat will finish the job.

Dough

- 1 1/4 cups all-purpose flour, plus extra for dusting
- 2 tablespoons dark brown sugar
- 1/2 teaspoon salt
- 8 tablespoons (1 stick) unsalted butter, cut into 1/4-inch pieces and chilled
- 3–4 tablespoons ice water

Filling

- 8 tablespoons (1 stick) unsalted butter, cut into 1-inch pieces
- 3/4 cup packed dark brown sugar
- 1 teaspoon salt
- 3 large eggs
- 3/4 cup dark corn syrup
- 1 tablespoon vanilla extract
- 2 tablespoons bourbon
- 2 cups whole pecans, toasted, cooled, and broken into small pieces (see note)

1. For the dough: Pulse flour, brown sugar, and salt in food processor until blended. Add butter and pulse until flour is pale yellow and resembles coarse cornmeal, ten to fifteen

For extra-neat slices, chill the pie thoroughly, cut slices, and then let the pieces come back to room temperature before serving.

How to FORM A SINGLE CRUST

Sure, it will taste good no matter how it looks, but an attractively crimped or edged pie crust will showcase all of your hard work.

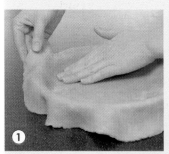

1. Lift up the edges of the dough and ease it down into the pie plate. Press lightly to adhere the dough to the sides of the pie plate. **2.** Use a pair of scissors to trim the dough overhang to within 1/2 inch of the outer lip of the pie plate. Roll the trimmed overhang under so that it is even with the lip of the pie plate. **3.** Use fingers to create fluted edges.

1-second pulses. (To do this by hand, grate frozen butter into flour using large holes of box grater, then rub flour-coated pieces between your fingers until flour turns pale yellow and coarse.) Turn mixture into medium bowl.

2. Using rubber spatula, fold 3 tablespoons water into flour mixture, then press against side of bowl (if mixture doesn't hold together, add up to 1 more tablespoon water). Squeeze dough together and flatten into disk. Dust with flour, wrap in plastic, and refrigerate at least 30 minutes or up to 2 days before rolling.

3. Remove dough from refrigerator and let stand until dough is malleable enough to roll out but still cool, 10 to 20 minutes. Adjust oven rack to middle position and heat oven to 375 degrees. Roll dough on lightly floured surface into 12-inch circle. Roll dough over pin and unroll it evenly into 9-inch Pyrex pie plate. Fit dough into pie plate and flute edges (see photos on page 24). Refrigerate for 40 minutes, then freeze for 20 minutes.

4. Line pie shell with two 12-inch pieces aluminum foil, fitting foil so that it hangs over edges of crust. Distribute 2 cups pie weights (see page 28) over foil, then bake until dough under foil dries out, 20 to 25 minutes. Carefully remove foil and weights, then continue to bake until crust is firmly set and lightly browned, 10 to 15 minutes. Remove pie

shell from oven and set aside. (Shell can be cooled, wrapped tightly in plastic, and stored at room temperature for 1 day.)

5. For the filling: Lower oven temperature to 275 degrees. Place pie shell in oven if not still warm.

6. Cook butter, brown sugar, and salt together in medium saucepan over medium heat until sugar is melted and butter is absorbed, about 2 minutes. Remove from heat and whisk in eggs, one at a time; whisk in corn syrup, vanilla, and bourbon. Return pan to medium heat and stir constantly until mixture is glossy and warm to touch, about 4 minutes. (Do not overheat; remove pan from heat if mixture starts to steam or bubble. Temperature should be about 130 degrees.) Remove pan from heat and stir in pecans.

7. Pour mixture into warm shell and bake until center feels set yet soft, like gelatin, when gently pressed, 45 to 60 minutes. Cool pie completely on rack, at least 4 hours. (Pie can be refrigerated for up to 1 day.) Serve pie at room temperature (or warm it briefly in oven), topped with whipped cream or vanilla ice cream.

AFTER-HOURS SOUTHERN PECAN PRALINE PIE
The extra bourbon in this pie will please the adults at the table.

Add 2 more tablespoons bourbon to pie along with pecans in step 6. Proceed with recipe as directed.

The American Table:
A Slice of Humble Pie

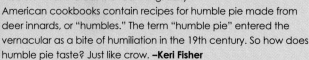

We've all been forced to eat humble pie at some point upon suffering embarrassment. Chances are you wouldn't want to eat the real thing. Early American cookbooks contain recipes for humble pie made from deer innards, or "humbles." The term "humble pie" entered the vernacular as a bite of humiliation in the 19th century. So how does humble pie taste? Just like crow. **–Keri Fisher**

Easier Than You Think: *Bread Pudding*

Bread pudding should be simple, but does it have to be plain?

Bread pudding should be a simple affair. After all, this recipe was intended as nothing more than a quick and easy way to use stale leftover bread. But somewhere along the way, things got complicated—at least if you follow the recipes printed in most modern cookbooks. First, there is a trip to a bakery for specialty breads such as brioche or challah. After that, the crusts are removed and the bread is cubed and left overnight to stale. Then there is the two-hour soaking of the bread in the custard. Finally, many recipes insist on baking the pudding in a roasting pan filled with steaming hot water. All this left me wondering if bread pudding might be simplified—greatly.

Here is the good news. Bread pudding can indeed be as simple as it was first intended. Firm, hearty sliced white bread from the supermarket, such as Arnold or Pepperidge Farm, works perfectly well. (Squishy sliced bread doesn't.) There's no need to cut off the crusts or to wait for the bread to stale. Soaking the bread in the custard for 20 minutes is sufficient, and a water bath is definitely not necessary—the pudding will bake up nice and creamy as long as you keep the oven temperature low.

Having made this recipe so simple, I wondered if I might spend some of the time I'd saved jazzing up the bread and egg custard. Inspired by the oversized cappuccinos served in big white porcelain cups at my local coffee shop, I decided to flavor the custard with coffee, add chopped bittersweet chocolate to the pudding, and then bake individual portions in large coffee cups. Just before serving, I topped the baked puddings with whipped cream to create something that looks fancy enough to serve at a dinner party but is in reality easy enough to prepare when you get home from work. **–Eva Katz**

INDIVIDUAL MOCHACCINO BREAD PUDDINGS SERVES 4
Use a wide, hearty loaf of sandwich bread—a smaller loaf may not provide enough bread. Top with whipped cream just before serving.

- Butter for greasing coffee cups
- 2 large eggs
- 1/3 cup sugar, plus 1 1/2 tablespoons for topping
- 1 cup milk
- 1 cup heavy cream, plus 3/4 cup for topping
- 1 1/2 tablespoons instant espresso or coffee powder
- 1 teaspoon vanilla extract
- 4–5 slices firm white bread, cut into 1 1/2-inch squares (5 cups)
- 3/4 cup chopped bittersweet chocolate (4 ounces)
- Cocoa powder for dusting tops

1. Adjust oven rack to middle position and heat to 325 degrees. Butter four 1-cup, ovensafe coffee cups or ramekins.

2. Whisk eggs and 1/3 cup sugar together in large bowl. Whisk in milk, 1 cup heavy cream, instant espresso, and vanilla. Transfer custard to large measuring cup.

3. Arrange 4 bread squares in bottom of each coffee cup, overlapping pieces so they fit snugly. Sprinkle 1 heaping tablespoon chocolate on top of bread in each cup. Make second layer using 4 bread pieces, then top with remaining chocolate. Pour custard over bread and chocolate. Transfer coffee cups to rimmed baking sheet and set aside for 20 minutes.

4. Bake until puddings are set but still a bit wobbly when shaken, 25 to 30 minutes. Cool for at least 30 minutes (we like to serve these warm) or to room temperature. (Puddings can be refrigerated overnight; bring to room temperature, then warm in microwave, checking progress every 30 seconds.)

5. With electric mixer, beat remaining 3/4 cup cream and 1 1/2 tablespoons sugar to soft peaks. Spoon whipped cream over each pudding. Sprinkle with cocoa and serve immediately.

Bake and serve these mocha-flavored bread puddings in large coffee cups.

Easier Than You Think:

Split-Pea Soup

Don't have a leftover ham bone? No problem. Just buy a precooked ham steak.

Most folks avoid making split-pea soup because classic recipes call for a ham bone. The simple substitute is a ham steak (they are sold precooked), which offers plenty of meat to eat along with the split peas. Others shy away from split-pea soup because it's so often boring and bland. I wanted a simple recipe that was also full of flavor.

In reviewing the ingredients in a typical recipe, I found garlic and bay leaf, as well as onions and carrots, to be subtle but necessary flavor boosters. But most of the other ingredients—like potatoes, salt pork, celery, leeks, thyme, and red pepper flakes—were unnecessary, masking the flavor of the ham and split peas rather than enhancing them. Cooking the vegetables in butter added richness to the soup, and a pinch of sugar balanced the saltiness of the ham. It turns out that for great ham and split-pea soup, less is more. **–Keri Fisher**

SPLIT-PEA SOUP WITH HAM MAKES ABOUT 3 QUARTS

The ham steak is very salty, so you probably won't need to add salt to the soup. If you have any leftover roast ham in your refrigerator, feel free to use it in place of the ham steak (though you may need to adjust the seasonings).

- 3 tablespoons unsalted butter
- 1 medium onion, chopped medium
- 2 carrots, peeled and chopped medium
- 3 large garlic cloves, minced
- 1 pound ham steak, chopped fine
  Pinch sugar
- 1 pound dried split peas, picked over and rinsed
- 6 cups low-sodium chicken broth
- 2 cups water
- 1 bay leaf
  Pepper

Melt butter in large stockpot over medium heat. Add onion, carrots, garlic, ham, and sugar; cover and cook until vegetables are soft, 8 to 10 minutes. Add peas, broth, water, and bay leaf; increase heat to high and bring to boil. Reduce heat to medium-low and simmer until peas are soft, about 40 minutes. Discard bay leaf and add pepper to taste. Serve.

Make Ahead

Split-pea soup can be refrigerated for several days or frozen for a month. Because split peas continue to soak up liquid over time, the soup may be dense when reheated. If the soup is too thick, stir in 1/4 cup water at a time until the consistency is to your liking. Simmer over medium-low heat until the soup is hot.

FOOD FACT: *The word* squash *comes from the Narragansett Indian word* askutasquash, *which, translated loosely, means "eaten raw." Though thin-skinned summer squash can be eaten raw, winter squash are best cooked.*

How to Roast Winter Squash

Roasted, glazed squash can be creamy, with a crackling, sweet exterior. Or it can be soggy, stringy, and burnt. How do you make sure to get the former, not the latter?

Some dishes are so easy that most home cooks don't even use a recipe. Roasted winter squash brushed with some sort of sweet glaze is one of those side dishes that most of us simply prepare without thinking. After all, what can go wrong? Well, a lot.

Simply brushing a glaze on squash halves and then throwing them in a hot oven—the method recommended in many recipes—was a no-go; the topping dried and charred long before the squash was cooked. Covering the squash with aluminum foil for some or all of the cooking time turned out a steamed watery topping and soggy squash. Cooking the squash uncovered and adding the glaze at the end of the cooking process did solve the burning problem but did nothing for the texture of the squash, which was now too dry. I finally hit upon an easy solution. I started roasting the squash flesh side down. (It turned out that a preheated pan prevented the squash from sticking and also shaved a few minutes from the cooking time.) Then, once the squash was cooked through, I flipped it and added the glaze.

I knew that broiling would be my best bet for developing a crackly brown coating, but when I put the squash directly under the broiler, it scorched around the edges. I lowered the oven rack and found that I got good results—both during the initial baking and the subsequent broiling—with the rack in the upper-middle position (6 to 8 inches from the heating element). The glaze was golden brown and crisp, with no burnt edges. **–Keri Fisher**

BROWN-SUGAR-GLAZED WINTER SQUASH
SERVES 4 TO 6

Don't mix the brown sugar and butter ahead of time; it will crystallize and separate. Butternut squash can be stringy when undercooked, so if you're not sure, err on the side of overcooking.

- 2 medium butternut or buttercup squash (about 2½ pounds each)
- 5 tablespoons unsalted butter, melted
- 5 tablespoons dark brown sugar
  Salt and pepper

Adjust oven rack to upper-middle position, place baking sheet on rack, and heat oven to 400 degrees. Split squash in half lengthwise and scrape out seeds. Remove baking sheet from oven and position squash cut side down. Return quickly to oven and roast until tender and flesh is easily pierced through skin with skewer, 40 to 50 minutes. Remove from oven, turn cut side up, and set oven to broil. Whisk butter and sugar together in small bowl, brush mixture on squash, sprinkle with salt and pepper, and broil until browned and crisp, about 5 minutes. Serve.

VARIATION FOR SMALL WINTER SQUASH

Smaller winter squash—such as acorn, delicata, and sweet dumpling—will cook more quickly and require less glaze.

Follow recipe for Brown-Sugar-Glazed Winter Squash, using 2 medium acorn, delicata, or sweet dumpling squash (1 to 1½ pounds each). Reduce roasting time to 20 to 30 minutes and reduce butter and brown sugar to 3 tablespoons each.

How to ROAST AND GLAZE SQUASH

1. Starting the squash facedown on a preheated baking sheet will yield a lightly browned exterior and a smooth, creamy interior.

2. Applying the glaze to the squash just before it is broiled lets it caramelize without burning.

Getting to Know Winter Squash

Winter squash range in flavor from bitter to super-sweet, and their texture can be fibrous or creamy. The big problem is that looking at the thick skin doesn't tell you much about what's underneath. That's why we held a taste test of 12 varieties. While some varieties are worth seeking out at farmstands, others are best used as porch decorations.

Blue Hubbard
BIG AND TASTY

Though daunting in size (it can run upward of 15 pounds), the blue hubbard was a big hit with our tasters, who liked the "intense squash flavor" and "creamy" texture of the pale orange flesh. Look for smaller pieces wrapped in plastic at the supermarket.

Red Turban
SUPERFICIAL BEAUTY

Striking in appearance but "vegetal" in flavor, this squash is best used for decorative purposes. Our tasters found its flavor "bitter" and akin to "canned asparagus."

Buttercup
SWEET AND CREAMY

Dark green on the outside and deep orange inside, this sweet squash was deemed "creamy" and "milder than butternut." While the texture can be a bit dry, buttercup was a favorite with tasters.

Sweet Dumpling
SWEET AS CUSTARD

This small squash with pale yellow flesh was universally liked. Tasters praised its "sweet" and "nutty flavor" and its "creamy," "custardy" texture. To make the most of its small size, we like to serve it halved with the skin on.

Golden Hubbard
BLUE IS BETTER

Not as common as its blue cousin, the golden hubbard was described as "more assertive" and "not as sweet." Some found it "slightly bitter" and "a bit dry."

Butternut
OLD RELIABLE

Butternut is prized for its "mildly sweet," nutty flavor and "lovely smooth texture." It can be "a little fibrous" but generally lives up to its name as "very buttery." The thin skin can be easily removed with a sharp vegetable peeler.

Carnival
SWEET BUT STRINGY

This festive squash was praised for its "very fresh," "sweet" flavor, though many tasters found it "too watery," "stringy," and "not very exciting."

Spaghetti
BLAND AND BORING

When cooked, the flesh of this squash forms translucent strands that resemble spaghetti. "Mild" and "vegetal," spaghetti squash is usually sauced; it tends to be "bland on its own."

Acorn
IDEAL FOR STUFFING

This popular squash was praised by tasters as "very sweet" and "nutty," though many found it "a little watery" and "starchy, like a russet potato." Its small size makes it a perfect candidate for stuffing.

Delicata
BEAUTIFULLY SWEET

Tasters liked the "nutty" flavor of this "sweet," "creamy" squash, which also goes by the name sweet potato or bohemian squash. The thin skin is edible, if a bit tough. Definitely worth seeking out.

Kabocha
DRY AND STARCHY

Though it resembles a pumpkin in shape (but not color) and is just as sweet, the kabocha has "dense flesh" and a "mealy," "starchy" texture that makes it more like a sweet potato. Interesting, but not a favorite.

Golden Nugget
TOO BLAND

Sweet and slightly bland, golden nuggets resemble pumpkins inside and out. With an extra-thick skin and small amount of flesh, this squash requires a lot of work for a low yield. There are better choices.

Notes from Our Test Kitchen

TIPS, TECHNIQUES, AND TOOLS FOR BETTER COOKING

< It's Not All Fun and Games It may be seem like "working" in the test kitchen is just one long party. The day we sampled 30 finalists in our Quick Appetizer Contest did feel like a party. We received hundreds of entries before picking the 12 winners on pages 18 and 19.

HOW TO THAW A FROZEN TURKEY

Although we think fresh turkeys taste best, many cooks (including some who work in the test kitchen) buy frozen birds on occasion. Although you might think a frozen bird is easier (no need to put in an order for a fresh bird from the butcher), a frozen turkey requires some planning, unless you want to deal with a rock-hard bird on Thanksgiving morning.

- **Several days before Thanksgiving:** Always defrost a turkey in the refrigerator—never on the counter. Count on 1 day of defrosting for every 4 pounds of bird. That means 3 days for a 12-pound bird, 4 days for a 16-pound bird, and so on. Make sure to defrost the bird in a large disposable roasting pan to catch any juices.
- **Day before Thanksgiving:** Didn't plan ahead and the turkey is still rock-solid on Wednesday? Don't panic, you can defrost the frozen turkey in a bucketful of cold tap water. Plan on about 30 minutes per pound. To avoid bacterial growth, change the water every 30 minutes. Given the hassle involved with this method, it pays to plan ahead. **–Jeremy Sauer**

KEEPING BISCUIT CUTTERS SAFE AND SOUND

Our recipe for Quaker Bonnet Biscuits (page 8) calls for two different-sized biscuit (or cookie) cutters to make the biscuits' quirky hat-like shape. Because these thin metal cutters are easily damaged once let loose in a drawer, the test kitchen likes to buy them in a set that comes nested in a protective tin. A Cook's Wares (www.cookswares.com, 800-915-9788) carries a set of 11 cutters from Ateco for $14.99. The cutters range in size from ¾ inch to 3⅝ inches. **–Bridget Lancaster**

These cutters come with a handy carrying case.

EASIER CHEESE GRATING

Although the creamy texture of Monterey Jack is perfect for our Classic Grilled Cheese Sandwiches (page 15), it can be difficult to shred on a box grater. Try freezing the packaged cheese for 30 minutes before attempting to grate it. You will have fewer clumps of broken cheese. **–Cali Rich**

PIE DOUGH GETS WET

Most cooks we know struggle when it comes to rolling out pie crust. The most common problem is dough that cracks or crumbles because it's too dry. Many older recipes promoted the idea of adding very little water to the dough. But using a good amount of water is key to easy rolling. How do you know when you've added enough? The dough should come together easily when pinched. If it feels dry, keep adding ice water. Once the dough feels right, shape it into a disk, wrap it tightly in plastic, and chill for at least one hour. Besides making the dough easier to handle, chilling gives the dough time to absorb the water evenly.

What should you do if the dough still seems dry and crumbly when you roll it out? Just break the dough back into clumps, place it in a large bowl, and gradually work in more ice water, 1 tablespoon at a time, with your hands. Shape the dough into a disk, wrap it in plastic, and chill thoroughly before attempting to roll it out again. **–Bridget Lancaster**

BAKING BLIND

Our Southern Pecan Praline Pie (pages 24–25) doesn't bake long enough for the crust to cook through, so prebaking the pie shell is a must—unless you like a soggy crust. Baking an unfilled pie shell, called "blind baking" by the experts, can be a challenge. Without the weight of the filling to hold the dough in place, it can balloon or, worse, shrink dramatically. How, then, can you make sure that your pie shell comes out of the oven looking the same as is went in—only browner?

After years of pie making in the test kitchen, we've found that the unbaked pie shell should be refrigerated for 40 minutes and then frozen for 20 minutes before baking. In the refrigerator, the dough relaxes and so is less likely to shrink when heated. Once chilled, freezing ensures that the fat in the dough is very cold and melts more slowly in the oven, which promotes flakiness. Finally, to keep the dough from ballooning in

EQUIPMENT in the TEST KITCHEN

A Tapered Rolling Pin

You probably grew up in a home with an American-style rolling pin. You know—the kind with ball bearings and handles. This heavy pin is fine for beating yeasted bread dough into submission, but it's not our first choice for most tasks. Our test cooks prefer a more delicate French-style tapered pin. A tapered pin is usually quite long (18 inches or more), so it can handle any job. The tapered ends allow for easy pivoting of the pin and increase the odds of turning out a perfectly round circle of dough. Because a tapered rolling pin is handle-free, you can apply pressure just where you need it; pressing down on the handles of an American-style pin applies pressure evenly across the entire pin. All of this adds up to pie dough of even thickness from edge to edge. And because a tapered rolling pin is so thin and light, it's easy to flip dough onto the pin and ease it into a pie plate. Sur La Table (www.surlatable.com, 800-243-0852) sells a 19½-inch tapered rolling pin (item #19440) for $12.95. **–Bridget Lancaster**

the oven, you need to weight it. If you don't own metal or ceramic pie weights, pennies work just as well to conduct the heat from the oven to the crust as well as to weight it. And pennies are far better than the dried beans or rice used by many home cooks.

–Bridget Lancaster

Pennies make great pie weights. Store them in a doubled-up ovenproof cooking bag, which can be placed in and lifted out of the pie plate and used over and over again, eliminating the customary step of lining the pie dough with a doubled layer of aluminum foil.

Timing the Perfect Turkey

Anyone who's cooked a turkey knows that timing the bird is tricky. No one wants to serve dinner in the middle of the football game, and a midnight supper is no good either. Use the chart below to help plan your meal. For absolute precision, gauge doneness according to the internal temperature—the thickest part of the thigh should register 170 to 175 degrees on an instant-read thermometer. If cooking a big bird—18 to 22 pounds—you may decide it's too heavy to rotate; in that case, roast it breast side up for the entire cooking time.

TURKEY WEIGHT	12–15 lbs	15–18 lbs	18–22 lbs
SERVINGS	10–12	14–16	20–22
OVEN TEMPERATURE	400°	400°	425°, reduced to 325° after 1 hour
ROASTING TIME Breast Side Down Breast Side Up	45 min 50–60 min	45 min 1 hour, 15 min	1 hour 2 hours
RESTING TIME	30 min	30 min	35–40 min

Test Kitchen Basics: How to Cook Pasta

OK, you probably don't need a recipe for cooking pasta, but these test kitchen tricks will guarantee *perfect* pasta every time.

- **Use 4 quarts of water for every pound of pasta.** You'll need a very large pot, but this large amount of water will ensure that the pasta cooks evenly and won't clump.

- **Forget about adding oil to the pot, but use plenty of salt.** Adding oil to the boiling water does not prevent sticking. Frequent stirring does. Skip the oil but make sure to add salt—roughly 1 tablespoon for 4 quarts of water—or the pasta will taste bland.

- **Taste the pasta early and often for doneness.** Reading the instructions on the box is a good place to start, but for al dente pasta you may need to shave a few minutes off the recommended time.

- **Wait! Before you drain that pasta . . .** Take a liquid measuring cup and retrieve about 1/2 cup of the cooking water from the pasta pot. Then go ahead and drain the pasta for just a few moments before you toss it with the sauce. (Don't let your pasta sit in the colander too long; it will get very dry very quickly.) When you toss your sauce with the pasta, add some (or all) of this reserved pasta water to help spread the sauce.

Don't forget to save some water!

MAKING RICE FLUFFY

We may like our rice dirty (see recipe on page 22), but gummy is another story. Rinsing the rice removes much of the exterior starch, thereby preventing the grains from sticking together. The resulting rice cooks up light and fluffy, making it perfect for dirty rice, rice pilafs, or even cool rice salads.

Rinsing rice washes away excess starch and ensures a light texture in pilafs and salads.

To rinse rice, place it in a bowl, cover with cold water, and swish to release the starch. Change the water until it remains nearly clear. Alternatively, place the rice in a fine-mesh strainer set over a large bowl. Run water over the rice and use your hands to swish the rice around to release excess starch. Pour off the water and repeat until the water is no longer cloudy.

–Jeremy Sauer

BAKE, CARRY, AND SERVE

Ever wonder how you're going to transport a hot casserole to a potluck party without spilling it all over your car? And what about keeping it hot and ready to serve? While developing our Cheesy Potato Casserole (page 23), we ran across the CorningWare AnyWare, an ensemble that includes a 13 by 9-inch (3-quart) baking dish, a secure-fitting lid, a hot/cold pack, and an ergonomic bag that functions as a carrying case and insulated warmer (or

The CorningWare AnyWare is perfect for transporting casseroles to potluck suppers.

cooler). After 1½ hours in the insulated case, the casserole was still quite warm and moist. However, because the casserole was covered with a plastic lid hot from the oven, the crispy golden topping became a bit soggy. Fortunately, this problem was easily remedied—five minutes in a 450-degree oven restored the topping to its original glory. The AnyWare casserole dish is deeper than the 2-quart baking dish called for in the recipe, but the cooking times were not affected. You can find the AnyWare at many kitchen supply stores and at Bed Bath & Beyond (www.bedbathandbeyond.com, 800-462-3966) for $29.99. –Eva Katz

PUFF PASTRY LOVES THE FRIDGE

Given the huge amount of work that homemade puff pastry requires, no sane cook makes this dough from scratch. Luckily, with puff pastry available in the frozen foods section of nearly every grocery store (we use Pepperidge Farm), the hard work has been eliminated. Still, store-bought puff pastry can present the uninitiated with some minor obstacles, particularly when it comes to temperature.

For the perfect puff, the pastry should never come to room temperature. Most cooks thaw puff pastry on the counter, but it can quickly get too warm. We recommend letting the pastry defrost slowly in the refrigerator, where it can't overheat. When rolling or cutting the pastry on the counter, do so as quickly as possible. If the dough becomes too soft, return it to the refrigerator for five minutes or so to firm up. Once the puff pastry has been shaped, make sure to chill the dough thoroughly before baking—15 minutes in the freezer or 30 minutes in the refrigerator will do the trick. –Jeremy Sauer

GRAPPLE WITH THIS

What do you get when you cross a grape with an apple? A Grapple, of course. And they've been popping up on supermarket shelves. Grapples are not some odd hybrid of apple and grape; they're just plain old Washington Fuji apples dipped in a Concord grape flavoring solution. We found the artificial, bubblegum flavor distressing. The dollar-plus price tag (for each Grapple) was a shock, too.

–Jeremy Sauer

A dollar plus change is a lot to pay for an apple that tastes like bubblegum.

> Inside the Test Kitchen The Turkey Does a Flip

Roasting a turkey isn't all that difficult, but producing the picture-perfect bird can be a challenge. Luckily, the test kitchen has come up with a trick that will give you a turkey that's both golden brown and juicy every time. We call it "the flip," and it calls for rotating—or flipping—the turkey roughly halfway through the cooking time.

Start the turkey breast side down in a V-shaped rack lined with foil. By cooking the bird upside down, the delicate breast is shielded from direct oven heat and is less likely to dry out. The juices run down into the breast, which also helps keep it moist. In order to brown the skin, you need to flip the turkey right side up. Two wads of paper towels or two clean towels—along with some kitchen confidence and a friend—will get the job done.

Food Shopping

PACKAGED STUFFING: Taste versus Convenience

Each year, Americans spend almost $300 million on packaged stuffings. We figured that these products, much like frozen pie crusts, are purchased for the sake of convenience, shoppers knowing all the while that they're sacrificing taste and texture. But $300 million is a serious vote of consumer confidence, so we decided to hold a blind tasting to judge the quality of these stuffings fairly.

We purchased eight popular brands of herb-flavored stuffing, and it was immediately clear from the ingredient list that fresh, natural flavors had been discarded for the usual suspects: MSG, high-fructose corn syrup, yeast, partially hydrogenated soybean and/or cottonseed oil, caramel color, BHT, propyl gallate, and the like. Chicken stock appeared in just three brands, and flavorful herbs were few and far between. Only Arnold contained herbs other than parsley (rosemary, thyme, sage, and basil), but they came in at the bottom of the ingredient list. Although the labeling on the Kellogg's bag promised that its contents were seasoned with "five savory herbs," only "spices" were listed as an ingredient.

So how did they taste? Well, every brand was a far cry from the real thing. In addition to poor flavor (from "bland" and "murky" to "strongly objectionable"), the stuffings suffered from textural extremes—all were panned as either "pasty" and "gummy" or "dry" and "chewy." Why not buy a packaged stuffing and doctor it up with fresh, high-quality ingredients? A nice idea in theory, but why try to fix something that is so obviously broken? With just a little extra work, you can a make stuffing from scratch that will turn out a lot better. (See our recipe on page 12.)

In the end, the stuffings that made it to the top of our list were put there not because of their great flavor or texture but because they were "not objectionable." As one taster wrote, "The best, but so what?" The stuffings are listed in order of preference.

–Keri Fisher

Passable in a Pinch

1. **STOVE TOP Stuffing Mix Savory Herbs** $1.69 for 6 ounces
   Comments: "Not objectionable," wrote one taster of this familiar staple, and others agreed, with some going so far as to say it "tastes fairly homemade." Many, however, were turned off by the "bad artificial aftertaste."

2. **BELL'S Traditional Stuffing** $2.79 for 16 ounces
   Comments: More than one taster praised the "balanced herb flavor," though many found this stuffing "too wet" and "mushy." Most agreed that this stuffing was simply "OK."

① ②

③ ④ ⑤ ⑥ ⑦ ⑧

Don't Bother

3. **ARNOLD Herb Seasoned Premium Stuffing** $2.79 for 14 ounces
   Comments: Most tasters found this "basic" stuffing "too dry and chewy," though a few praised it as "not too mushy." "Holy poultry seasoning!" wrote one taster, and others agreed, noting the overpowering "artificial herb flavor."

4. **KELLOGG'S Stuffing Mix** $2.19 for 6 ounces
   Comments: "Is this Elmer's?" asked one taster of this "mushy," "paste-like" stuffing. Though some tasters liked the "nice meaty flavor," the best most tasters could say was that it was "not terrible."

5. **PEPPERIDGE FARM Cubed Herb Seasoned Stuffing** $2.79 for 14 ounces
   Comments: "Tastes fake," wrote one taster of this "average," "one-dimensional" stuffing that was "chalky and very wet at the same time."

6. **PEPPERIDGE FARM One Step Stuffing Garden Herb Mix** $1.99 for 6 ounces
   Comments: Tasters agreed that this "dry and chewy" stuffing "needs some help." The bread pieces were "too fine," and there was "not much flavor other than bread."

7. **MANISCHEWITZ Homestyle Stuffing Stove Top Mix** $3.69 for 6 ounces
   Comments: This matzo-based stuffing was described as "overcooked oatmeal" and "funky, and not in a good way." Most agreed with the taster who described it as "nothing like stuffing."

8. **ZATARAIN'S New Orleans Style French Bread Stuffing Mix** $2.00 for 6.6 ounces
   Comments: "Tastes like the Oodles of Noodles flavoring packet," wrote one taster of this bright yellow, "strangely sweet" stuffing that was deemed "fake in every way."

Taste Test Boneless Chicken Breasts

It used to be that there was only one kind (or brand) of chicken breast in the market. Today, most markets offer several choices, and you need a dictionary to decipher the terms on the packages. Are natural, free-range, or kosher birds any better than the supermarket chicken we've been eating all these years?

To find out, we held a blind tasting of four types of boneless, skinless chicken breasts represented by natural Bell & Evans, free-range Eberly's, kosher Empire, and supermarket staple Perdue.

It turns out that what people look for in chicken is tenderness and juiciness. Our top-rated birds were described as both, while the lower-rated chickens were consistently described as "dry and chewy." As one taster wrote of the low-rated free-range chicken: "I will have pieces of this stuck in my teeth for weeks."

All samples were seasoned with salt and pepper (adjusting for the kosher chicken's inherent saltiness) and broiled. Chickens are listed in order of preference; prices are what we paid in Boston-area stores. **–Keri Fisher**

Kosher $6.69/pound
The koshering process includes salting the birds to draw out impurities; this process is similar to brining and adds flavor and moisture. Kosher birds are slaughtered not by machine but by hand, a fact that some believe leads to fewer blood clots and cleaner-tasting, more tender meat. Our tasters favored the kosher chicken as "nicely seasoned and juicy." As one taster put it, "a chicken I can get on board with!"

Natural $5.99/pound
The U.S. Department of Agriculture (USDA) defines "natural" as chicken given no antibiotics or hormones and fed a vegetarian diet. Tasters found our sample "moist" and "tender" but "a little lacking in flavor."

Free-Range $7.99/pound
The USDA definition of "free-range" requires only that chickens have "access" to the outdoors. The amount of access—five minutes or five hours—is not determined. Theoretically, free-range chickens get more exercise and so can be tougher and more flavorful than other birds. Tasters found the bird we sampled to be "juicy" but also a bit "chewy" and "fibrous." Some found it "bland."

Supermarket $4.99/pound
Supermarket birds tend to be bred for a higher meat-to-bone yield, which results in large breasts and skinny legs. Though praised by many for its "strong chicken flavor," the supermarket chicken was also faulted for its "stringy texture."

Equipment Roundup

INDOOR GRILLS: Does the Champ Reign Supreme?

Thanks largely to George Foreman's Lean Mean Fat Reducing Grilling Machine (55 million Foreman grills have been sold since 1995), indoor electric grills have become common kitchen appliances. But the champ now has plenty of competition, so we brought seven models, all priced under $80, into the test kitchen for some culinary sparring with burgers, salmon, zucchini, grilled cheese sandwiches, and thick Cubano panini (roast pork, ham, and cheese on sub rolls).

FAT RESERVOIRS ARE OVERRATED: Fat drainage is one of the popular selling points for many indoor grills, but in our tests the removable reservoirs on four models never filled with much, if any, fat. The moats surrounding the other three grills never overflowed, even after two batches of hamburgers.

FIXED GRILL PLATES ARE BEST: The grills with removable plates (the George Foreman Next Generation, both Hamilton Beach models, and the Black & Decker) had noticeable hot spots or a top plate that ran hotter than the bottom. The grills with fixed plates (Krups, George Foreman Hot Metals, and Villaware) produced even heat across their grilling surfaces.

FASTER IS NOT ALWAYS BETTER: With both a top and bottom heat source, an indoor grill will take roughly half the time of conventional stovetop cooking. However, aside from the speed, hamburgers and salmon didn't gain anything other than some attractive grill marks. With a few extra minutes, a skillet could have done just as well and offers more possibilities (like deglazing the pan to make a sauce). On the other hand, indoor grills made shatteringly crisp sandwiches and panini.

BIGGER IS BETTER: The size of the cooking surfaces ranged from 62 square inches on both Hamilton Beach grills to 110 square inches on the Krups. While the Krups grill could accommodate five burgers or two large panini, the smaller grills could handle just two burgers or one panini at a time.

LOOK AT THE RIDGES: Using an infrared thermometer to measure the temperature of preheated cooking surfaces was tricky; like an oven, they cycle up and down through a range of temperatures. A better gauge of performance was the width of the ridges (the portion of the cooking surface that actually touches the food) and the distance between those ridges. With the Krups (with wide, closely spaced ridges) nearly half of the cooking surface is in contact with the food. The narrow, widely spaced ridges on both Hamilton Beach grills meant that just a fraction of the cooking surface was in contact with the food, and browning suffered.

SUMMING UP: Krups is a must-have if you like grilled sandwiches, but for burgers and fish a heavy pan is just as good.

–Garth Clingingsmith

Highly Recommended
KRUPS Universal Grill and Panini Maker FDE312
Price: $79.95
Comments: The largest grill and the only one to pass all of our tests with flying colors. Burgers and salmon were deeply browned, zucchini was evenly cooked, and sandwiches were golden and crisp. Spaciousness and performance make the extra cleanup associated with the fixed grill plates worth the bother.

Recommended
GEORGE FOREMAN Hot Metals Family Size Grill GR26SBTMR
Price: $58.88
Comments: Second only to the Krups in size. Tops of burgers and salmon browned a little more than the bottoms. Top plate floated above thin pieces of zucchini, which colored only on the bottom. Cool-touch exterior is a plus.

Recommended with Reservations
VILLAWARE Uno Two-Way Grill 2030
Price: $68.99
Comments: The reservoir cup takes away from the grilling surface area, so even two burgers were crowded. Salmon and sandwiches turned out fine. Good for a one- or two-person household.

Recommended with Reservations
BLACK & DECKER Grill and Wafflebaker G48TD
Price: $49.88
Comments: Reversible plates transform this grill into an able waffle iron. The other side is a flat griddle (not grill), so forget about grill marks. Large items, if not relatively flat, kept the lightweight "lid" off kilter, resulting in lopsided sandwiches.

Not Recommended
GEORGE FOREMAN Next Generation with Removable Plates GRP4
Price: $59.99
Comments: Removable plates make cleanup easy, but performance pales, literally, in comparison with the top-rated grills. Browning was faint in all of our tests, especially at the front half of the narrow, elongated grill. The grill's front-heavy "lid" made for asymmetric sandwiches.

Not Recommended
HAMILTON BEACH Grill/Griddle with Removable Grids 25295
Price: $49.99
Comments: We had better luck with the griddle, or flat, grates, but that isn't saying much. Sandwiches ended up soggy and burgers and salmon looked more steamed than grilled. The performance of the second set of grill grids was even worse.

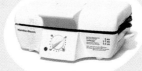

Not Recommended
HAMILTON BEACH Grill with Removable Grids 25285
Price: $39.99
Comments: The tall, sharp ridges on the cooking surface cut into both grilled cheese sandwiches and sturdy hamburgers. Browning was pale, and the sandwiches weren't as crisp as they should have been.

Gadgets & Gear Lodge Grill Press

A few frugal test cooks dubbed our favorite indoor grill a "glorified sandwich maker" and scoffed at the idea of shelling out up to $80 for this convenience. Instead, this vocal test kitchen minority heralded the humble grill press—a flat, heavy weight used in diners to cook everything from bacon and burgers to sandwiches—as a cheaper way to go.

Lodge Manufacturing's Grill Press (model LPG3, $21.95 at www.lodgemfg.com) is a perfect candidate. Cast iron is nearly indestructible, so it can be tossed onto a burner (or over the coals) without concern and will retain plenty of heat. Once heated, the press can be placed over any food as it cooks in a heavy skillet.

On the downside, a grill press doesn't make grill marks on food. Also, even when preheated, the press isn't sufficient to cook the top of the food—we still had to flip burgers, salmon, and sandwiches to cook the second side. The grilled sandwiches were excellent, although the Lodge Grill Press can handle only one large sandwich at a time. In contrast, the Krups indoor grill can cook two panini at once, and there's no flipping involved. If you want to make sandwiches for a crowd (or if grill marks on sandwiches and other foods are important to you), the Krups indoor grill might be worth the extra $60. **–G.C.**

Can you save some money by using an old bacon press?

When Things Go Wrong in the Kitchen

READERS SHARE FUNNY STORIES ABOUT COOKING MISHAPS

A SURPRISE DINNER GUEST

One year I grew so much broccoli that I had to freeze some. When my grandmother came over for dinner, I pulled out a package of broccoli and boiled it. My grandmother was the first to get the buttered broccoli. She took some and passed it on. My son got it next and my husband took it just before me. He thought that I must have added bacon bits to the broccoli until he noticed that the bacon bits had feet! My grandmother had removed her worm and quietly placed it in her paper napkin. I was so embarrassed.

Margo Seegrist Shelton, Wash.

CREATIVE HOLIDAY COOKING

The first time I invited my in-laws over for Thanksgiving, I really wanted to impress my mother-in-law. I started the day by baking a mincemeat pie. But when the pie was only partially baked, I realized that I should have put the turkey in first because it would need more time. As I took the pie out, I burned my arm on the oven door and the pie flipped upside down in the oven! I salvaged as much as I could, but I didn't do a very good job of cleaning out the pie scraps. Once the turkey had been roasting for a while, my mother-in-law commented on how smoky the kitchen was. I thought for a second and told her I had decided to make "smoked" turkey. After the turkey was done, I pressed the pie scraps into a pie plate and finished baking the pie. It looked peculiar, so I put a thick layer of whipped cream over it. My mother-in-law said she had never seen anything like the dessert I served. I told her it was mincemeat jumble.

Elaine Shipman Scappoose, Ore.

HEAVY-DUTY PANCAKES

I was living in a small mountain village outside of Beirut, Lebanon, back in 1974. I was just 20 years old, but thanks to my dad I had been cooking since I was 7. I had come across some big fat berries in the local market and thought I would whip up a batch of pancakes for my housemates. We had recently moved, and most of our kitchen stuff was still in boxes, but I managed to find all of the ingredients, including a small bag of what I thought was flour. The texture seemed a bit odd, but I figured it must be "Lebanese" flour. I mixed up the batter, added the berries, and started cooking. The first few pancakes were very heavy and hard. I started feeling a bit queasy after tasting them, so I asked one of my housemates to finish cooking the pancakes while I rested a bit. A few minutes later, I heard loud guffaws coming from the kitchen and went to see what all the laughing was about. Apparently, I had used plaster of Paris in place of flour. We took the remaining batter, poured it into a glass jar to harden, and kept it as a memento.

Connie Ledlow Fairbanks, Alaska

THE SWEETEST MASHED POTATOES

When asked what dish they want at a family feast, my nieces and nephews consistently reply, "Uncle Layne's mashed potatoes." Little do they know just how wrong a batch of mashed potatoes can go! Some years ago, while preparing dinner, everything was ready except for the potatoes. I added butter, salt, and pepper and gave the potatoes their first mashing before adding the milk. "Milk? Where's the milk? We can't be out of milk!" I thought. I checked for evaporated milk, powdered milk, Coffee-Mate, and buttermilk, but we had nothing. "Why not vanilla ice cream?" I thought.

I served dinner and waited, with anticipation, for my wife to taste the potatoes. "What have you done to the potatoes?" she exclaimed. I had to agree that they tasted very, very bad. (The flecks of vanilla bean weren't helping either.) To this day, whenever someone in the family clamors for Uncle Layne's mashed potatoes, I can't help but glance over at my wife, knowing the twinkle I'll find in her eyes.

Layne Carruth Cordova, Tenn.

HOW NOT TO IMPRESS YOUR FUTURE MOTHER-IN-LAW

The first holiday I spent with my future husband, Dan, and his family, I was eager to impress his mother with my culinary skills. I buttered the rolls with gusto, placed them in the oven, and watched them like a hawk. I wrapped a dish towel around my hand and attempted to remove the pan of golden brown rolls, but the dish towel dropped onto the glowing red oven coil and caught fire! With my back to my future mother-in-law, I started waving the flaming towel frantically to put out the fire. By the time I was done, the rolls had charred and the dish towel had a huge black hole burned through the middle. To her credit, and my relief, Dan's mother simply laughed and gave me a hug. Every Christmas since, I give her some new dish towels!

Beth Harris-Murphree Tyler, Texas

MY CO-WORKERS WILL EAT ANYTHING

Many years ago, I was at a friend's house one evening after work and we were chatting away while she made banana bread. Once the bread came out of the oven, we tasted it, and it was quite clear that she had forgotten to add the sugar. It was beyond awful—truly inedible. Our big joke at the time was that our co-workers would eat anything, so we decided to bring the banana bread into work the next day and see what would happen. We sliced up the bread, put it next to the coffee machine in the hallway, and hid in my office, peeking out the door from time to time to monitor the progress of the banana bread. We doubled up in laughter as the bread disappeared in a flash and people came back for seconds.

Deirdre Nicholson
South Burlington, Vt.

MAGIC OVEN

I've had a number of kitchen disasters, especially around the holidays, but the funniest one happened on Thanksgiving when my son was about 11. We have a small house in San Francisco, and the kitchen has a small JennAir electric oven. That year, I had a fairly big turkey, around 15 pounds, large enough so that the heating element was fairly close to the turkey. For some reason, I had decided to baste the turkey with brandy. We were close to—but fortunately not in front of—the oven when it exploded. The door opened and a large ball of flame issued forth. As quickly as that happened, a vacuum was created and the door slammed itself shut. My son was impressed. "Wow, Mom," he said. "Do it again!"

Diane K. Martin San Francisco, Calif.

A SECRET INGREDIENT

Early on in my marriage, I wasn't always the most accomplished chef. One time, I invited a co-worker and her husband over for dinner. I prepared most of the meal in advance, including a loaf of garlic bread. Everything turned out fine, except we all couldn't help but wonder what was that crunchy stuff on top of the bread. We pondered it for some time, until it dawned on me that I had forgotten to take the plastic wrap off the bread before putting it into the oven!

Kendra Fletcher Denair, Calif.

Send us your funniest kitchen disaster stories. Write to us at Kitchen Disasters, Cook's Country, P.O. Box 470739, Brookline, MA 02447. If you'd like to use e-mail, write to us at kitchendisasters@bcpress.com. If we publish your story, you'll receive a complimentary one-year subscription to *Cook's Country*.

Brown-Eyed Susan

In the 1950s, garden-themed cakes started cropping up in cookbooks like wildflowers and took on names such as chrysanthemum and pink azalea. The Brown-Eyed Susan Cake, with the flavors of orange and chocolate, is one of our favorites from this period.

To make this cake you'll need:

- 1   recipe yellow cake batter for two 9-inch pans*
- 5   ounces unsweetened chocolate, melted
- 2   teaspoons grated zest plus 1 tablespoon juice from 1 orange
- 4   cups vanilla buttercream frosting*
      Yellow food coloring (optional)
      Semisweet chocolate chips
      Candied orange peel

For the cake layers: Divide batter between two bowls. Stir 2 ounces melted chocolate into one bowl and orange zest into second bowl. Drop batter by spoonfuls into two greased 9-inch cake pans, alternating between chocolate and orange batters. Bake on middle rack in 350-degree oven until toothpick inserted in center comes out with a few crumbs attached, 20 to 25 minutes. Cool for 5 minutes, then turn layers out onto racks to cool completely.

For the frosting: Divide frosting between two bowls. Stir remaining 3 ounces melted chocolate into one bowl and orange juice into second bowl. Add 2 drops yellow food coloring (if using) to bowl with orange frosting.

To assemble: Spread chocolate frosting between cake layers and on sides of cake. Coat top of cake with orange frosting and decorate with chocolate chips and candied orange peel to resemble flowers.

*Yellow cake and vanilla frosting recipes are available at www.cookscountry.com, but feel free to use your own.

Recipe Index

appetizers and quick breads
Quaker Bonnet Biscuits 8
Quick Appetizers 18–19
  Asparagus Puffs
  Baked Brie Cups
  Chutney Cheese Rounds
  Creamy Beet Spread with Endive Leaves
  Crispy Mexican Bites
  Fresh Pineapple Salsa
  Gingered Shrimp Toasts
  Roast Beef Canapés
  Sesame Chicken Bites
  Smoked Salmon Pinwheels
  Stuffed Cherry Tomatoes
  Stuffed Jalapeños
Savory Cheese Muffins 22

main courses
Cheesy Ravioli Bake RC
Chicken Cutlets with Bacon, Rosemary, and Lemon RC
Country French Pork Chops RC
Easy Tortilla Casserole RC
Harvest Supper Salad with Smoked Turkey and Apples RC
Hearty Beef Stew 7
Hearty Fisherman's Stew RC
Marmalade-Glazed Pork Roast with Parsnips and Onions 14
Oven-Fried Chicken 9
  Fiery Oven-Fried Chicken
Pasta Sauces 4–5
  Artichoke Alfredo Sauce
  Cream Sauce with Sausage and Peas
  Garden Pesto Sauce
  Roasted Red Pepper and Bacon Sauce
  Spicy Tuna Sauce
Spicy Baked Shrimp RC
Spicy Beef and Noodles RC
Split-Pea Soup with Ham 26
Sunday-Best Garlic Roast Beef 20

sandwiches
Classic Grilled Cheese 15
  Grilled Pimento Cheese
  Little Italy Grilled Cheese
  Monterey Melts
  Windy City Grilled Cheese
French Dip Sandwiches 21
Sloppy Joes 17
  Sloppy Janes
  Sloppy Josés
  Smoky Joes

side dishes
Brown-Sugar-Glazed Winter Squash 26
Cheesy Potato Casserole 23
Down 'n' Dirty Rice 22
Cornbread and Sausage Stuffing 12
  Cornbread and Bacon Stuffing

desserts
Easy Apple Turnovers 13
  Sugar and Spice Apple Turnovers
Halloween Treat Makeovers 10
  Candy-Coated Caramel Apples
  Caramel Turtles
  M&M Clusters
  Peanut Butter Cup Ice Cream and Snickers Bar Sauce
  Peppermint-Surprise Brownie Bites
Mochaccino Bread Puddings 25
Southern Pecan Praline Pie 24–25
  After-Hours Southern Pecan Praline Pie

RC = Recipe Card

Cook's Country

DECEMBER/JANUARY 2006

Easy Holiday Menu
Our Old-Fashioned Favorites

Prize-Winning Cookies
4 Inspired Christmas Recipes

Crispiest Roast Chicken
Cornstarch Adds Crunch!

PECAN COFFEE CAKE
Extra-Moist and Extra-Nutty

BEEF & VEGETABLE SOUP
Turn Canned Broth into a
Rich Soup

EASY CHICKEN PARMESAN
Skillet Recipe Saves
Time and Fuss

RATING TOASTERS
$20 Model Beats Competition

CREAMY PARTY DIPS
Leaner, Fresher, Better

CHOCOLATE TASTE TEST
Are Nestlé Chips
Still a Winner?

CHEESY BISCUITS
No-Fail Recipe

$4.95 U.S./$6.95 CANADA

0 74470 05251 7   01>

Our Christmas Cookie Contest Winner!
Mary Hay Glass of Arlington, Va., won first place with a recipe that coats buttery toffee cookies with melted semisweet chocolate and chopped pecans. See page 4 for her **Chocolate Toffee Butter Cookies.**

Cook's Country

Dear Country Cook,

I learned to cook at the hands of Marie Briggs, our local Vermont baker. Much like the girl in this photo, I learned by watching as Marie kneaded bread, baked cookies, and rolled out pie dough. With my head just high enough to see down the work table, I slowly learned what food was supposed to look and taste like.

But Marie, in the manner of all country folks, taught me a great deal more. Instead of reprimanding or chastising, she led by example, whether that meant standing beside me rolling out a pie the right way (after I had failed) or feeding one more unexpected dinner guest. She also taught me that a job well done is its own reward. (Vermonters don't give compliments.)

Marie is long gone, but I still dream about her and her kitchen. I'd like to stand beside her just one more time and watch her knead anadama bread, her powerful forearms stroking the soft folds of dough, or watch as she expertly stuffs the Thanksgiving turkey. Marie taught me how to cook, but I often wonder, in my late middle years, how much more I might have learned at her side.

Christopher Kimball
Founder and Editor, Cook's Country Magazine

Preparing the Thanksgiving turkey, 1925. Image: © Bettmann/CORBIS.

DECEMBER/JANUARY 2006

Cook's Country

departments

RECIPE CONTEST: **Christmas Cookies** — 4
RECIPE MAKEOVER: **Hot Party Dips** — 7
SLOW COOKING: **Beef Short Ribs** — 8
LOST RECIPES: **Tipsy Squire** — 9
FUN FOOD: **Peppermint Desserts** — 10
GETTING TO KNOW: **Spices** — 15
DRESSING UP: **Pan-Seared Steak** — 18
ON THE SIDE: **Salad with Roasted Pears** — 21
EASIER THAN YOU THINK: **Cheese Biscuits** — 27
FOOD SHOPPING: **Chocolate Chips** — 30
EQUIPMENT ROUNDUP: **Toasters** — 31

features

12 Test Kitchen's Favorite Holiday Menu
We reached back into our mothers' (and grandmothers') recipe boxes to create a classic menu for the holidays.

14 Old-Fashioned Mulled Cider
Joe Cataldo of Hudson, N.Y., wants a more balanced holiday beverage that tastes like apples rather than potpourri.

17 Nuttiest-Ever Coffee Cake
Sarah Willmore of Abilene, Texas, asks for a pecan coffee cake that positively shouts "Nuts!"

19 Not Just Plain Peas
They may be frozen, but peas need not be humble.

20 Crispy Roast Chicken and Potatoes
Daniel Smith of Berlin, Conn., likes to roast chicken and potatoes together, but he wants the chicken crispier and the potatoes less greasy.

22 A Better Breakfast Casserole
Claudia Coleman of Mobile, Ala., likes the idea of a casserole assembled before bedtime but wants something not too heavy and not at all bland.

23 Waking Up Winter Fruit Salads
A simple, sweet dressing is the secret to a superior fruit salad.

24 Skillet Chicken Parmesan
Lucille Arena of Collegeville, Pa., says her kids love this dish, but it's a lot of work for something that usually turns out soggy.

25 Cheesy, Creamy Carbonara
When Jane Edney of Fairhope, Ala., makes carbonara at home, it turns out dry and pasty instead of creamy and cheesy. We offer to help.

26 Really Good Beef and Vegetable Soup
Quality restaurants use homemade beef stock. Is there a way to create something almost as good with canned broth?

in every issue

2 Kitchen Shortcuts
6 Ask Cook's Country
16 I'm Looking for a Recipe
24 Reader Mailbag
28 Notes from Our Test Kitchen
32 When Things Go Wrong . . .

Founder and Editor Christopher Kimball
Executive Editor Jack Bishop
Senior Editor Bridget Lancaster
Test Kitchen Director Erin McMurrer
Copy Chief India Koopman
Associate Editors Keri Fisher, Eva Katz
Assistant Editor Melissa Baldino
Test Cooks Stephanie Alleyne
Katie Henderson
Jeremy Sauer
Assistant Test Cooks Meredith Butcher
Cali Rich
Kitchen Assistant Nadia Domeq
Contributors Lauren Chattman,
Diane Unger-Mahoney
Recipe Tester Barbara Akins

Design Director Amy Klee
Marketing Designer Julie Bozzo
Designer Heather Barrett
Staff Photographer Daniel J. van Ackere

Vice President Operations James McCormack
Project Manager Anne Francis
Production Assistants Jeanette McCarthy
Christian Steinmetz
Systems Administrator Richard Cassidy
Internet Technology Director Aaron Shuman

Chief Financial Officer Sharyn Chabot
Controller Mandy Shito
Staff Accountant Maya Santoso
Office Manager Saudiyah Abdul-Rahim
Receptionist Henrietta Murray
Publicity Deborah Broide

Vice President Marketing David Mack
Circulation Director Bill Tine
Fulfillment Manager Carrie Horan
Circulation Assistant Elizabeth Dayton
Products Director Steven Browall
Direct Mail Director Adam Perry
Customer Service Manager Jacqueline Valerio
Customer Service Representative Julie Gardner
E-Commerce Marketing Manager Hugh Buchan

Vice President Sales Demee Gambulos
Marketing Assistant Connie Forbes

Editorial Office: 17 Station Street, Brookline, MA 02445; 617-232-1000; fax 617-232-1572.
Subscription inquiries: 800-526-8447
Postmaster: Send all new orders, subscription inquiries, and change-of-address notices to Cook's Country, P.O. Box 8382, Red Oak, IA 51591-1382.

ON THE COVER: PHOTOGRAPHY: Loftus/Stockfood. ILLUSTRATION: John Burgoyne.
IN THIS ISSUE: COLOR FOOD PHOTOGRAPHY: Keller + Keller. STYLING: Mary Jane Sawyer, Marie Piraino. ILLUSTRATION: Lisa Parett.

Cook's Country magazine (ISSN 1552-1990), number 6, is published bimonthly by Boston Common Press Limited Partnership, 17 Station Street, Brookline, MA., 02445. Copyright 2006 Boston Common Press Limited Partnership. Application to mail at periodical postage rates pending at Boston, Mass., and additional mailing offices. POSTMASTER: Send address changes to Cook's Country, P.O. Box 8382, Red Oak, IA 51591-1382. For subscription and gift subscription orders, subscription inquiries, or change-of-address notices, call 800-526-8447 in the U.S. or 515-247-7571 from outside the U.S., or write us at Cook's Country, P.O. Box 8382, Red Oak, IA 51591-1382.. PRINTED IN THE USA

Visit us at www.cookscountry.com!
Go online to ask questions, share kitchen tips, and enter recipe contests. You can also take a sneak peek at what we've got cooking for upcoming issues.

Kitchen Shortcuts

READERS SHARE CLEVER TIPS FOR EVERYDAY COOKING CHALLENGES

Peel Off the Fat

I find that placing plastic wrap directly on top of newly made stock before refrigerating it makes it easier to skim off the fat the next day. I just peel away the wrap, and the fat comes right off with it!

Carol Smith
Tucson, Ariz.

NEAT IDEA

Steaming Tortillas

Whether it's a simple bean-and-cheese roll-up or a breakfast burrito, my son and I have a great love for all things rolled in a flour tortilla, and I've figured out a great way to heat them up: Boil a bit of water in a large skillet and cover with a wire-mesh splatter guard. Place the cheese-topped tortilla on the splatter guard and cover lightly with a lid or some aluminum foil. The steam warms and softens the tortillas so they're easy to roll up, and it melts the cheese, too.

Charlie Metcalf
Portland, Ore.

Sharp Idea!
Storing Tools Safely

Here's a safe way to store or transport sharp items such as knives, rasp-type graters, and vegetable peelers: Take the tube from an empty roll of paper towels. Flatten it out, staple one end closed, and staple one side to keep it flat. Slide your knife or grater into the makeshift sheath and voilà—no more nicks and cuts!

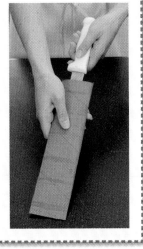

Mrs. Dae M. Thompson
Marietta, Ga.

Bubbles to the Rescue

LIGHT AND FLUFFY WAFFLES

When I use a store-bought mix to make waffles, I substitute club soda, ounce for ounce, for the milk. The carbonation in the club soda gives the waffles a lighter, fluffier texture than milk does, so I don't get that I-just-ate-a-pile-of-waffles feeling of fullness.

Kate Finley Orange Park, Fla.

MEAT MUFFINS?

I've become pretty well known for my special version of meatloaf. I use a ½ cup ice cream scoop to make meatloaf balls and place one in each hole of a greased muffin tin. The "muffins" bake quickly—30 minutes as opposed to an hour for a regular meatloaf. Everyone gets their own "muffin" (or two) for supper, and if there are leftovers I just put them in a container and freeze.

Linda Martin
Redding, Calif.

PERFECT PATTIES

When I make burgers, I usually make a large batch and freeze the extras. To shape the patties quickly, I use an old jar lid with a much larger sheet of plastic wrap placed over it. (The ring from a wide-mouthed canning jar or the lid from a mayonnaise or peanut butter jar will do.) Cover with one corner of the plastic wrap, put the meat in, then fold the opposite corner of the wrap over the top and press the meat into a round flat shape. This really speeds up the job and makes large, uniform patties.

Tamara Malczewska
Victoria, BC, Canada

NO MORE RAW ONION FLAVOR

I dislike the harsh taste of raw onion in potato salad, and I've come up with an easy way to eliminate it. I chop the onions while the potatoes are boiling, put the onions in a colander in the sink, and, when the potatoes are done, pour the boiled potatoes and hot water into the colander. I then let the potatoes sit until cool enough to handle. The boiling water and piping-hot potatoes cook the onions just enough to remove the raw taste without wilting them or causing them to lose their freshness.

Nancy Jo Leachman
Salina, Kan.

SECRET SAUCE

My secret meatloaf ingredient is a can of Sloppy Joe sauce. It adds just the right punch to an old family recipe. A game of refrigerator hide-and-seek often ensues to claim the leftovers—if there are any.

Betsy Race
Strongsville, Ohio

FREEZING CHICKEN CUTLETS

You can't beat the prices on bulk packs of chicken breasts at warehouse clubs. But because on any given night I never knew whether I'd be feeding the whole family or just myself, I was never sure how many to put in a freezer bag. I took to pounding the breasts into cutlets between sheets of plastic, then stacking them (still in the plastic) and putting the whole batch in a freezer bag. I place them flat in the freezer until they are solid. Then I can easily pry off as many (or as few) as I require.

Shawn Harvell
New Castle, Del.

PLIABLE CABBAGE LEAVES

I used to have a problem with cabbage leaves splitting and cracking when I rolled them to make stuffed cabbage. Then I found that freezing the cabbage first—the whole head—solved the problem. As the cabbage thaws, the leaves become easy to peel off and are pliable enough to roll without tearing.

Sami Klein
Columbia, Md.

BETTER BEAN SOUP

If you're making a quick bean soup from canned beans and it looks a bit thin, add a can of refried beans to the simmering soup. It will look like it's been cooking for hours!

Rebecca Silvestri
Palm Bay, Fla.

A FLAKY WAY TO THICKEN SOUP

I hate to admit to having instant mashed potato flakes

If you'd like to submit a tip, please send a letter to Kitchen Shortcuts, Cook's Country, P.O. Box 470739, Brookline, MA 02447. Or e-mail us at shortcuts@bcpress.com. Include your name, address, and phone number. If we publish your tip, you will receive a one-year subscription to *Cook's Country*.

in the house, but I found that a sprinkle or two gives stews, soups, and pot pies that "second day" thickness and flavor I like—instantly.

Susan Scarborough
Amelia Island, Fla.

LINING PANS WITH FOIL

When lining a pan with aluminum foil, turn the pan upside down and mold the foil over the outside. Remove the foil, turn the pan right side up, and the foil will fit inside the pan perfectly, with no tearing or bunching.

Arlene J. Wineman
Crystal Lake, Ill.

A QUICK ICING

Some cake and brownie mixes, while not bad, can certainly benefit from a little icing. I make a quick icing by melting five or six small peppermint patties in the microwave for 30 seconds and then mixing in about ⅛ cup milk. I then pour the icing over the cake and tilt the pan to allow for an even coating. It's delicious (and even better with toasted coconut on top).

Rachel Perdue
Oakland, Calif.

STAY ORGANIZED

Whenever I purchase a new item for the kitchen, whether a blender, food processor, or stove, I staple the sales receipt inside the booklet accompanying the product. The booklets are all stored together in a kitchen drawer. If there is any problem with a warranty or I need to order a new part, I have easy access to the necessary information. I can also check the age of a product if it begins to malfunction.

Mary Ellen Looney
Hooksett, N.H.

MAGNETIZE YOUR RECIPES

We covered the back of one of our kitchen cabinet doors with pieces of galvanized steel. Using magnetic clips, we can now hang recipes at eye level, right above our counter workspace.

Sandy and Marge Coyman
Berlin, Md.

FOOD-PROCESSOR-PULLED CHICKEN

I poach and shred several pounds of chicken at a time and freeze it in portions to use in tortilla soup, enchiladas, tacos, chicken salads, pasta sauces, soups, and chicken pot pies. But shredding chicken is a messy, tedious job. My solution is to put cut-up, poached chicken in the food processor with the plastic "dough" blade and pulse several times. I get perfectly shredded chicken in seconds.

Diana Beutner
Minneapolis, Minn.

LEMON-FRESH MICROWAVE

The best way to clean a microwave and make it smell good at the same time is as follows: Cut a lemon in half, squeeze the juice into a 4-cup Pyrex measuring cup, and add the squeezed lemon halves. Add water to the measuring cup until it's about an inch from the top. Microwave on high until boiling and then microwave for three minutes more. Leave the door closed and let sit for 10 minutes. Take out the measuring cup (be careful, the lemon water will still be hot), and wipe down the inside. It will be sparkling clean and fresh smelling.

Susan Maxwell
Rogue River, Ore.

SAVE YOUR CEREAL BOX LINERS

Save the glassine-type bags that your cereal is packed in and use them for pounding chicken or meat. Just place the item inside the bag and pound away with your meat mallet. These bags are tougher than plastic wrap—and so won't tear—and they're free!

Russell Niermeyer
The Villages, Fla.

SUPER-THIN CUKES

When I need really thin slices of cucumber (for cucumber sandwiches or salads), I use a vegetable peeler to remove the skin and then use it again to shave the cucumber into super-thin circles. It's very quick!

Cristina Hamill
Annapolis, Md.

MASH AND MEASURE

When mashing bananas for baking, I place the peeled bananas directly in a 4-cup Pyrex measuring cup and mash them with a potato masher (I use the type with a "zigzag" design). The flat bottom of the measuring cup makes for a much better mashing surface than the curved bottom of a bowl, and when I'm done I can measure the volume of the bananas right in the cup—no need to dirty two bowls.

Yi Wen Liu
San Jose, Calif.

Marching to the Mixer

A BATTALION OF BUTTER

I have been baking a lot with the holidays approaching and have come up with a good way to soften butter. Instead of laying the sticks down on the counter, I stand them up on their ends, like little soldiers. More surface area is exposed to the (relatively) warm air, so the butter softens a bit more quickly.

Al Bottari Westbury, N.Y.

A Cheap Solution!

Disposable Pizza Peels

Pizza peels are hard to find, cumbersome to store, and, most of all, expensive. That's why I use something that I always have on hand—a large pizza-delivery box. Cut the box in half at the hinge and you've got two peels. Just flour the cardboard lightly before assembling the pizza, and the pizza slides right onto the baking stone.

Jess Rehr, Seattle, Wash.

Get a Grip

DOUBLE DUTY

Whenever I can't get the top off of a jar, I place a thick rubber band around the lid. (The supermarket bands used on bunches of asparagus and broccoli work well.) The extra traction makes it easy to open anything from a sticky jar of molasses to a stubborn jar of pickled jalapeños.

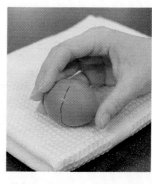

Lisa McKeown
Bohemia, N.Y.

Careful Egg Cracking

I'd been trying to figure out a way to crack eggs without getting pieces of shell in the bowl, and one day I tried it on a kitchen towel set on the counter. The towel acted like a shock absorber, so the egg split much more evenly when opened into the bowl. You can crack eggs rather firmly in this way, and they won't fall apart.

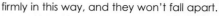

Mary Germain, Manlius, N.Y.

Neat Rolling!

Shaping Slice-and-Bake Cookies

When I'm preparing cookie dough that needs to be chilled or frozen, I wrap the dough in plastic and then place it in a cardboard paper towel tube that I've sliced open to form a large semicircle. This keeps the soft dough from conforming to the shape of the cookie sheet or the refrigerator shelf. The bottom of the dough retains a nice round shape that yields perfect cookies.

Charlotte Neises Dubuque, Iowa

Our $500 Grand-Prize Winner!

Mary Hay Glass Arlington, Va.

Prize-winning cookies put new twist on favorite flavors.

When we receive Christmas cookies from friends and relatives, we always look forward to that special cookie—the one we'd never make ourselves. As we baked hundreds of recipes from our readers, we searched for the unique and found four inspired creations. Although made with familiar ingredients—toffee, eggnog, lemon, and peppermint—these cookies are as distinctive as the readers who created them.

It was tough to pick a grand-prize winner, but tasters kept coming back to Mary Hay Glass and her Chocolate Toffee Butter Cookies. Mary describes them as "delicious and attractive." That's a hard combination to beat.

CHOCOLATE TOFFEE BUTTER COOKIES
MAKES 5 DOZEN COOKIES

Two kinds of Heath Toffee Bits are sold at the market. Make sure to buy the ones without chocolate.

- 2¹/₃ cups all-purpose flour
- ¹/₂ teaspoon baking powder
- ¹/₂ teaspoon salt
- 16 tablespoons (2 sticks) unsalted butter, softened but still cool
- 1 cup packed light brown sugar
- 1 large egg
- 1 teaspoon vanilla extract
- 1 cup Heath Toffee Bits (without chocolate)
- 1¹/₂ cups semisweet chocolate chips
- 1 tablespoon vegetable oil
- ²/₃ cup pecans, toasted and chopped fine

1. Whisk flour, baking powder, and salt together. With electric mixer, beat butter and brown sugar on medium speed until fluffy, about 3 minutes. Add egg and vanilla and beat until combined, about 30 seconds. Reduce speed to low, add flour mixture in two batches, and mix until incorporated. Stir in toffee bits. Divide dough in half and roll each piece into log about 9 inches long and 1¹/₂ inches in diameter. Flatten logs until 2¹/₂ inches wide. Wrap and refrigerate until firm, about 1¹/₂ hours.

2. Adjust oven racks to upper-middle and lower-middle positions and heat oven to 350 degrees. Line 2 baking sheets with parchment paper.

3. Using chef's knife, cut dough into ¹/₄-inch slices; transfer to baking sheets, spacing 1 inch apart. Bake until just browned around edges, 10 to 12 minutes, rotating rack position and direction of baking sheets halfway through baking time. Cool cookies completely on baking sheets. Use remaining dough to make second batch of cookies.

4. Transfer baked cookies to wire rack set in baking sheet. Melt chocolate and mix with oil in bowl until smooth. Dip part of each cookie into melted chocolate or drizzle chocolate over cookies with spoon. Sprinkle pecans over cookies. Don't touch until chocolate sets, about 1 hour.

Depending on how you apply the chocolate and pecan garnishes, these toffee-flavored butter cookies can look quite different.

Lisa Renshaw
Kansas City, Mo.

Emerson London
Washington, D.C.

Allison Heaton
Austin, Texas

MACADAMIA EGGNOG CREAMS

MAKES 5 DOZEN 3-INCH STAR COOKIES

Lisa says: "Every Christmas, I bake the same 12 cookie varieties for my family. This cookie is a favorite. I created the recipe as a spinoff on the traditional sugar cookie with an eggnog flavor. They remind me of my childhood holidays." You can use cutters of various sizes and shapes for this cookie, but, like Lisa, we prefer stars.

- 3½ cups all-purpose flour
- ½ teaspoon baking soda
- ½ teaspoon ground nutmeg
- ½ teaspoon salt
- ½ cup plus 2 tablespoons eggnog
- 1 large egg
- 16 tablespoons (2 sticks) unsalted butter, softened but still cool
- ¾ cup granulated sugar
- ¼ cup packed light brown sugar
- 1 tablespoon rum
- 1 cup confectioners' sugar
- 1 cup whole macadamia nuts, toasted and chopped

1. Whisk flour, baking soda, nutmeg, and salt together in medium bowl. Whisk ½ cup eggnog and egg together in measuring cup. With electric mixer, beat butter and granulated and brown sugars together on medium speed until fluffy, about 3 minutes. Add flour mixture and eggnog mixture alternately, in two batches, beating after each addition until incorporated. Divide dough into quarters and wrap and refrigerate until firm, about 1 hour.

2. Adjust oven racks to upper-middle and lower-middle positions and heat oven to 375 degrees. Line 2 baking sheets with parchment paper.

3. Using rolling pin, roll each dough quarter into 12-inch round about ⅛ inch thick. Cut with 3-inch star cutter and transfer to prepared baking sheets (scraps can be re-rolled once). Bake until lightly browned around edges, 8 to 10 minutes, rotating rack position and direction of baking sheets halfway through baking time. Cool cookies completely on baking sheets. Use remaining dough to make second batch of cookies.

4. When cookies have cooled, whisk remaining 2 tablespoons eggnog and rum together in medium bowl. Whisk in confectioners' sugar until smooth. Spoon glaze over cookies and sprinkle with nuts. Do not touch until glaze sets, about 30 minutes.

MOLASSES SPICE LEMON SANDWICH COOKIES

MAKES ABOUT 3 DOZEN COOKIES

Emerson says: "These cookies have been made for three generations in my family, although I added the lemon filling. Even my mother admits they are better than the original recipe."

- 2 cups all-purpose flour
- 2 teaspoons baking soda
- 1 teaspoon ground cinnamon
- 1 teaspoon ground ginger
  Salt
- ¼ teaspoon ground cloves
- 2 cups granulated sugar
- ¼ cup dark molasses
- 1 large egg
- 15 tablespoons unsalted butter, 12 tablespoons melted and cooled, 3 tablespoons softened
- 3 tablespoons lemon juice
- 2 cups confectioners' sugar

1. Whisk flour, baking soda, cinnamon, ginger, ¾ teaspoon salt, and cloves together in medium bowl. In separate bowl, stir 1½ cups granulated sugar, molasses, egg, and melted butter together until combined. Add dry mixture to butter mixture in three batches, stirring after each addition. Cover bowl with plastic and refrigerate until dough is firm, about 1 hour.

2. Adjust oven racks to upper-middle and lower-middle positions and heat oven to 375 degrees. Line 2 baking sheets with parchment paper.

3. Place remaining ½ cup granulated sugar in small bowl. Shape dough into ¾-inch balls. Roll balls in granulated sugar, then transfer to prepared baking sheets, spacing balls 2 inches apart. Bake until tops are just beginning to crack, 8 to 10 minutes, rotating rack position and direction of baking sheets halfway through baking time. Cool cookies on baking sheets for 3 minutes, then transfer to wire rack to cool completely. Use remaining dough to make second batch of cookies.

4. Whisk remaining 3 tablespoons softened butter, lemon juice, and pinch of salt together in medium bowl. Whisk in confectioners' sugar until smooth. Turn half of cooled cookies over (bottom side up) and spread each with 1 teaspoon lemon filling. Sandwich with another cookie.

CHRISTMAS MERINGUE KISSES

MAKES ABOUT 4½ DOZEN COOKIES

Allison says: "Christmas in our house isn't complete without these little puffs of heaven, and we even find ourselves making them in the middle of the summer to satisfy our cravings." Try to work as quickly as possible when shaping the kisses; they will deflate if left too long before baking. These cookies will keep for at least a week if stored in an airtight container.

- 2 large egg whites
- ⅛ teaspoon salt
- ⅛ teaspoon cream of tartar
- ½ teaspoon vanilla extract
- ⅔ cup sugar
- 2 cups mini semisweet chocolate chips
- 3 tablespoons crushed peppermint candies
- 2 teaspoons vegetable oil

1. Adjust oven racks to upper-middle and lower-middle positions and heat oven to 275 degrees. Line 2 baking sheets with parchment paper.

2. With electric mixer, beat whites in large bowl until foamy. Add salt and cream of tartar and continue beating until soft peaks form, about 3 minutes. Add vanilla and sugar, 1 tablespoon at a time, and continue beating until mixture is glossy and stiff, about 2 minutes. With spatula, fold in 1 cup chocolate chips and peppermint candies.

3. Using piping bag with plain tip or teaspoon, pipe or dollop teaspoon-sized dots of batter onto prepared baking sheets. Bake until cookies begin to crack and are light gold, 25 to 30 minutes, rotating rack position and direction of baking sheets halfway through baking time. Let cool on baking sheets for 5 minutes, then transfer cookies to wire rack to cool completely.

4. Melt remaining 1 cup chocolate chips and mix with oil in small bowl. Dip bottoms of cooled kisses into chocolate and place, chocolate side up, on wire rack until chocolate sets, about 30 minutes.

We are looking for holiday side dishes for an upcoming contest. Send us entries by January 31, 2006. Write to us at Recipe Contest, Cook's Country, P.O. Box 470739, Brookline, MA 02447, or e-mail us at recipecontest@bcpress.com. Include your name, address, and daytime phone number, and tell us what makes your recipe special. The grand-prize winner will receive $500. All entries become the property of Cook's Country. For more information on this and other contests, go to www.cookscountry.com.

Ask Cook's Country

KEEPING GARLIC FRESH

I'd like to buy garlic in bulk from one of those big discount chains, but I'm afraid it will go bad before I can use it. What's the best way to store garlic?

Josh Roth Staten Island, N.Y.

As garlic ages, the cloves sprout green shoots. These sprouts contain more of the bitter compounds found in garlic and must be removed and discarded before the garlic can be used. The best storage method, then, is one that staves off sprouting. To find out which method is best, we placed garlic heads in bowls, baskets, and paper bags in a dark cabinet, on the counter, and even in the refrigerator and freezer. We also spent $10 for a "garlic keeper," a lidded ceramic vessel with holes that allow for airflow. The flavor of the frozen and refrigerated garlic deteriorated after only one week, though it showed no signs of sprouting. On the counter and in the cabinet, the garlic didn't sprout as long as two conditions were

This ceramic garlic keeper prevents garlic from sprouting, but so does a paper bag or a basket placed in a cabinet.

met: The garlic had to be stored away from light and allowed some airflow. So we can recommend three options: storing garlic in a paper bag or garlic keeper on the counter or placing it in a basket in a cabinet.

BLEACHED VS. UNBLEACHED FLOUR

Are there general guidelines as to when to use bleached flour and when to use unbleached?

Silvia M. Toth-Fernandez Katy, Texas

Over the course of several months, the color of unbleached flour will turn from beige to white. To expedite this process, many companies "bleach" flour with chemicals, most often chlorine gas or benzoyl peroxide. These chemicals lower the protein content of the flour and make it more likely to yield tender baked goods. Some critics claim that bleaching also imparts an off flavor.

To judge any flavor or textural differences for ourselves, we prepared batches of biscuits with unbleached and bleached flour and held a blind tasting. Though some astute tasters detected a faint "raw," "artificial" flavor in the batch made with bleached flour, most people agreed that both batches of biscuits were acceptable. (Note that even our pickiest tasters couldn't detect any differences between bleached and unbleached flour in yellow cake or chocolate chip cookies, recipes where other ingredients overwhelm the flavor of the flour.) Based on these tests, we have a slight preference for

unbleached flour (which is what we use in the test kitchen), but bleached flour is fine, too.

TO PEEL OR NOT TO PEEL?

I made the Creamy Potato Casserole (charter issue), and it was really yummy. But I was wondering why the recipe calls for cooking the potatoes with their skins on and then peeling them. It was an extra step that made the recipe just a little more difficult to make.

Julie Schaeffer Northbrook, Ill.

For mashed potatoes, we generally boil whole unpeeled potatoes and then peel them for a texture that is light and fluffy. When potatoes are peeled and cut before boiling, the flesh both absorbs some of the cooking water and loses some starches and flavor to the water. We assumed the same would hold true for our Creamy Potato Casserole. But when we got your letter, we decided to revisit the issue. We held a blind tasting and found that tasters had a hard time differentiating between the casserole made with unpeeled whole potatoes and that made with peeled and cut potatoes. The many ingredients in the casserole—heavy cream, chicken broth, garlic, butter, and Parmesan and cheddar cheese—apparently mask the flavor and textural differences that can be detected in mashed potatoes. For this recipe, then, feel free to peel and cut the potatoes first.

MEASURING SHALLOTS

If a recipe calls for one shallot, does that mean the whole bulb or one clove?

Roni Sweet Tamarac, Fla.

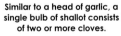 Shallots vary both in size and in the number of cloves they contain, so it can be confusing when a recipe calls for "one shallot." While we can't speak for other recipe writers, when we call for one shallot we are referring to the whole bulb. For greater accuracy, you can measure the shallot when minced. We have found that one medium shallot equals 3 tablespoons minced.

Similar to a head of garlic, a single bulb of shallot consists of two or more cloves.

FASTER BAKED POTATOES

Is it possible to make a decent "baked" potato in a microwave oven?

Bani Arora Ithaca, N.Y.

We held a tasting of oven-baked potatoes versus microwaved potatoes and found that tasters vastly preferred the crisp skin and fluffy texture of the oven-baked potatoes. But we don't always have time to bake potatoes (we like to bake them for 1 hour

and 15 minutes at 350 degrees) and so wondered if there was an easier, quicker way. We found it in a hybrid method whereby we first microwaved four potatoes for eight minutes, which cooked them about halfway, then finished them in a 450-degree oven for 20 minutes, which gave them that crisp skin we were after.

VINEGAR PRIMER

What's the difference between cider vinegar and distilled vinegar? Are they interchangeable for cooking and in salad dressings?

Anne Baselt Bremerton, Wash.

Vinegar is made by turning fermented liquid into acetic acid by adding certain bacteria to the liquid. Cider and distilled vinegars are made by the same process but start with different liquids: Cider vinegar begins with apple cider and distilled vinegar with ethyl alcohol (also known as grain alcohol).

 Although both vinegars are commonly used in pickle recipes (and are often substituted for each other), they do have distinctly different flavors. We like to use sweeter cider vinegar in sweet pickles, reserving white vinegar for applications such as sour pickles, where we want acidity without

Cider vinegar (left) is sweeter than distilled vinegar (right).

added flavor. While cider vinegar is fine in a sweet salad dressing, we don't think distilled vinegar adds much to any dressing. In general, we find that vinegars that start with wine are the best choice for salad dressings.

(NO) FEAR OF FRYING

I read that foods fried correctly absorb very little oil. Is this true?

Sandra Voswick Smyrna, Del.

We cooked up three batches of our Steak Fries (April/May 2005) and measured the oil before and after to see how much the fries had absorbed. On average, ¼ cup of oil was absorbed (some of which was blotted off with paper towels), which means that each serving had about 10 grams of fat—the same amount that's in 1 cup of soybeans, 1 cup of cottage cheese, or 1 ounce of cream cheese. Not a very high dietary price to pay for a great steak fry.

To ask us a cooking question, write to Ask Cook's Country, P. O. Box 470739, Brookline, MA 02447. If you prefer e-mail, write to askcookscountry@bcpress.com. See if you can stump us!

Recipe Makeover HOT DIPS

Could we re-create the creamy hot dips of our childhood but add more flavor and take away some of the fat?

As a kid, I knew company was coming when the creamy hot dips came out. Mom's artichoke dip, Aunt Sheila's crab dip, and Aunt Rita's spinach dip—bubbling and creamy, these dips varied in flavor but all shared the same crisp, buttery bread-crumb topping. Now that I'm old enough to entertain, I wanted to create lower-fat versions of these family favorites.

Most hot dips rely on a similar base—mayonnaise, sour cream, and/or cream cheese—to which flavorings are added. Mayonnaise (both nonfat and low fat) was too sweet and gloppy, nonfat sour cream was unappetizingly runny, and nonfat cream cheese tasted like cardboard. The best combination turned out to be a mix of low-fat sour cream and light cream cheese, two lower-fat products that are actually pretty good.

Cheese is a must in any hot dip. A little Parmesan was fine, but too much made the dip grainy. Most nonfat cheeses refused to melt in the oven (one wonders what they are really made of). I had better luck with low-fat cheddar, which melted nicely and added lots of flavor. Cooked onion and garlic tasted better than the onion powder and garlic salt found in many older recipes. Fresh herbs, lemon juice, and cayenne pepper added the necessary zip.

My favorite part of any hot dip is the buttery crumb topping. Parmesan and a shot of cooking spray added flavor and crispness—and with much less fat than butter. Once I added roasted artichoke

hearts (frozen are fine), lump crabmeat, or cooked frozen spinach, I had three great low-fat dips. I think Mom, Aunt Sheila, and Aunt Rita would dig right in.

–Stephanie Alleyne with Keri Fisher

LIGHT AND CREAMY HOT DIP
MAKES 4 CUPS, SERVING 12
Use this basic recipe to create three different dips flavored with artichokes, crab, or spinach.

Topping
- 1 slice hearty white sandwich bread
- 2 tablespoons grated Parmesan cheese

Creamy Base
- 1 cup light cream cheese, at room temperature
- 1/2 cup shredded low-fat cheddar cheese
- 1/4 cup low-fat sour cream
- 2 tablespoons grated Parmesan cheese
- 2 tablespoons lemon juice
- 2 tablespoons chopped parsley
- 1/2 teaspoon cayenne pepper
- 1 recipe prepared artichokes, crab, or spinach (recipes follow)
  Salt and pepper

1. Adjust oven rack to upper-middle position and heat oven to 375 degrees. Lightly spray 2-quart casserole dish with cooking spray.

2. For the topping Process bread and cheese in food processor until finely ground, about 15 seconds.

3. For the base Pulse cream cheese, cheddar, sour cream, Parmesan, lemon juice, parsley, and cayenne with prepared artichokes, crab, or spinach until coarsely chopped, about ten 1-second pulses. Season with salt and pepper. Scrape mixture into prepared dish. (Dip can be wrapped in plastic and refrigerated for up to 2 days. Bring back to room temperature before baking.)

4. Sprinkle topping over dip and lightly spray crumbs with cooking spray. Bake until browned and bubbly, about 20 minutes. Serve.

FOR LIGHT AND CREAMY HOT ARTICHOKE DIP

1. Toss 2 (9-ounce) packages frozen artichoke hearts (do not thaw) with 1 teaspoon olive oil, 1/2 teaspoon salt, and 1/4 teaspoon pepper on foil-lined rimmed baking sheet. Roast in 450-degree oven until browned around

edges, 20 to 25 minutes. Cool 10 minutes, then chop coarse.

2. Heat 2 teaspoons olive oil in large nonstick skillet over medium-high heat until shimmering. Add 1 medium onion, chopped fine, and cook until soft, about 6 minutes. Add artichokes and cook until beginning to brown and liquid evaporates, about 5 minutes. Add 2 minced garlic cloves and 2 teaspoons minced fresh thyme and cook until fragrant, about 1 minute.

FOR LIGHT AND CREAMY HOT CRAB DIP

Heat 2 teaspoons olive oil in large nonstick skillet over medium-high heat until shimmering. Add 1 medium onion, chopped fine, and 1 red bell pepper, seeded and chopped fine, and cook until soft, about 6 minutes. Stir in 2 minced garlic cloves and cook until fragrant, about 1 minute. Stir in 3/4 pound lump crabmeat (picked over) and 1 1/2 teaspoons Old Bay Seasoning.

FOR LIGHT AND CREAMY HOT SPINACH DIP

Heat 2 teaspoons olive oil in large nonstick skillet over medium-high heat until shimmering. Add 1 medium onion, chopped fine, and 1 red bell pepper, seeded and chopped fine, and cook until soft, about 6 minutes. Add 1 (16-ounce) package frozen spinach and cook until defrosted and liquid evaporates, about 10 minutes. Stir in 2 minced garlic cloves, 2 teaspoons minced fresh thyme, and 1 tablespoon lemon juice and cook until fragrant, about 1 minute.

One creamy base can be transformed into three flavorful hot dips—perfect for spreading on crackers or coating vegetables.

And the Numbers...
All nutritional information is for a serving of 1/3 cup.

	Before	After
ARTICHOKE DIP		
CALORIES:	226	110
FAT:	17g	6g
SATURATED FAT:	9g	3g
CRAB DIP		
CALORIES:	304	120
FAT:	27g	6g
SATURATED FAT:	10g	3.5g
SPINACH DIP		
CALORIES:	233	100
FAT:	22g	6g
SATURATED FAT:	7g	3g

Taste Test
CREAM CHEESE

One ounce of regular cream cheese contains 100 calories and 10 grams of fat. Philadelphia brand, the test kitchen's favorite, is available in three slimmer versions. How do they stack up to the real thing? Our test kitchen tasters found two good choices—and one terrible spread. In the end, we chose light cream cheese because it has less calories and fat.

Fat-Free Cream Cheese
"Objectionable flavor" and "gummy texture" make this product unacceptable. Just 30 calories per ounce (and no fat), but who cares?

Light Cream Cheese
"Good flavor" and "decent texture" are just fine in a creamy dip. A modest 60 calories and 4.5 grams of fat per ounce.

Neufchâtel 1/3 Less Fat Cream Cheese
"Almost as good" as the real thing. Weighs in with 70 calories and 6 grams of fat per ounce.

Slow Cooking BEEF SHORT RIBS

Meaty short ribs are slow food; time and gentle heat turn this tough cut into a blue-ribbon dinner. So why not use a slow cooker?

NOT TOO BITTER Many of the beers we tested in our short ribs recipe turned bitter after 10 hours in the slow cooker. Newcastle Brown Ale had a good balance of sweet and bitter flavors and was the test kitchen's top choice. O'Doul's Amber Nonalcoholic Beer was surprisingly good, too—a bit sweet, but still with plenty of personality.

Short ribs are just what their name says—short pieces cut from any part of the beef ribs. Because they are rich with fat and connective tissue, they are perfect for slow cooking—a process that turns tough meat soft and also melts excess fat, which can be easily discarded. The problem is that I rarely have hours to tend a simmering pot. That's where I thought my slow cooker might come in. Armed with 50 pounds of short ribs (those bones weigh a lot), I marched into the kitchen.

For my first test, I simply tossed the ribs into the slow cooker, added onions and beer for flavor, turned on the cooker, and ran off to work. After 10 hours in the slow cooker, these ribs were pretty much a disaster. The sauce was bland and watery, an inch of fat floated on top, and the meat was gray.

My next efforts were all aimed at adding flavor to this dish. First I browned the short ribs in a skillet, and this helped to develop a beefy flavor (it also rendered quite a bit of fat). Next I tested combinations of beef and chicken broth with varying amounts of beer (both light and dark) and was continually disappointed. The sauce had no personality and little beer flavor. But when I used only dark beer—and no broth—the sauce was nicely enriched with its hearty flavor. Wanting an even more complex flavor, I tried an unlikely ingredient that I'd seen in another recipe: prunes. Melting into the sauce, they were detected by no one in the finished dish (not even by those who don't like prunes) yet magically sweetened it, adding deep color and flavor.

The onions were of course also crucial to flavor, and I found that I had to use a hefty 3 pounds, browning them in the skillet after browning and removing the ribs. A little tomato paste and soy sauce further punched up the flavor and color of the sauce, and tapioca worked like a charm to thicken the liquid as it cooked. (Flour and cornstarch imparted raw, starchy flavors that no one liked.)

The only remaining problem was the fat. Even after meticulous skimming, each dinner plate ended up with a slick of orange grease that challenged even the strongest dishwashing liquid. There was just one way to solve this problem: Make the ribs the night before I wanted to serve them, letting the slow cooker work while I slept. In the morning, I refrigerated the ribs and sauce separately and then just before dinner removed the fat that had solidified on top of the sauce. I then reheated the meat in the defatted sauce. **–Diane Unger-Mahoney**

BEER-BRAISED SHORT RIBS
SERVES 4 TO 6

The only way to remove fat from the braising liquid is to prepare this recipe a day or two before you want to serve it. Luckily, the short ribs actually taste better if cooked in advance and then reheated in the defatted braising liquid. See page 29 for tips on shopping for short ribs.

- 5 pounds English-style beef short ribs (6 to 8 ribs), trimmed of excess fat
  Salt and pepper
- 2 tablespoons vegetable oil
- 2 tablespoons unsalted butter
- 3 pounds yellow onions, halved and sliced thin
- 2 tablespoons tomato paste
- 2 (12-ounce) bottles dark beer
- 2 tablespoons Minute Tapioca
- 2 bay leaves
- 2 teaspoons minced fresh thyme
- 2 tablespoons soy sauce
- 12 pitted prunes
- 3 tablespoons Dijon mustard
- 2 tablespoons minced fresh parsley

1. Season ribs with salt and pepper. Heat oil in 12-inch skillet over medium-high heat until just smoking. Add half of ribs, meaty side down, and cook until well browned, about 5 minutes. Following photo 1, turn each rib on one side and cook until well browned, about 1 minute. Repeat with remaining sides. Transfer ribs to slow-cooker insert, arranging them meaty side down, as shown in photo 2. Repeat with remaining ribs.

2. Pour off all but 1 teaspoon fat from skillet. Add butter and reduce heat to medium. When butter has melted, add onions and cook, stirring occasionally, until well browned, 25 to 30 minutes. Stir in tomato paste and cook, coating onions with tomato paste, until paste begins to brown, about 5 minutes. Stir in beer, bring to simmer, and cook, scraping browned bits from pan bottom with wooden spoon, until foaming subsides, about 5 minutes. Remove skillet from heat and stir in tapioca, bay leaves, 1 teaspoon thyme, soy sauce, and prunes. Transfer to slow-cooker insert.

3. Set slow cooker on low, cover, and cook until ribs are fork-tender, 10 to 11 hours. (Alternately, cook on high for 4 to 5 hours.) Transfer ribs to baking dish and strain liquid into bowl. Cover and refrigerate for at least 8 hours or up to 2 days.

4. When ready to serve, use spoon to skim off hardened fat from liquid. Place short ribs, meaty side down, and liquid in Dutch oven and reheat over medium heat until warmed through, about 20 minutes. Transfer ribs to serving platter. Whisk mustard and remaining teaspoon thyme into sauce and season with salt and pepper. Pour 1 cup sauce over ribs. Sprinkle with parsley and serve, passing remaining sauce separately.

For a sauce that's long on flavor, we add prunes (yes, prunes) to our short rib recipe.

Know-How RIB RULES

1. The ribs taste best if fully browned before going into the slow cooker. Brown the meaty side of the ribs, then turn them on each side to finish browning (you can lean the ribs against each other if they won't stand on their own). **2.** Place the browned ribs in the slow cooker with the meaty side facing down and the bones facing up. This placement will ensure that the meat stays submerged throughout the long cooking time.

Lost Recipes TIPSY SQUIRE

What's the secret to a great trifle? According to an old-fashioned American recipe, the answer is stale cake, jam (not fruit), and a stiff shot of sherry.

Trifle, that familiar tower of cake, cream, custard, and fruit, is quite the looker on the holiday buffet table, but beneath that fragile facade there is often little more than soggy cake, grainy custard, and fruit strewn about helter-skelter.

So when I faced yet another spiffy-looking trifle at a Christmas party last year, I took the smallest helping possible (the hostess was eagle-eyeing all takers) and headed off to a corner to hide my disappointment. Disappointment never came. The cake, although soft, was still sturdy; the custard was light, fluffy, and nearly crumb-free; and there was plenty of sweet sherry. Even better, save for the top, there were no forlorn pieces of fruit, just a layer of jam sandwiched inside the pieces of cake. I went back to the table to have another, and yet another helping, before finally asking just what I was eating. "Tipsy Squire," the hostess replied. Tipsy indeed. After a long cab ride home, it was time for a little investigation.

I scoured cookbooks from Great Britain, home of the trifle. Books from the 19th century were packed with concoctions from the straightforward Tipsy Cake (a sherry-soaked sponge cake filled with cream) to the more whimsical Tipsy Hedgehog (a booze-laden sponge cake covered with cream and studded with sliced almond "spikes"). I turned to American cookbooks. Miss Drucy Harris offered her rendition of Tipsy Charlotte in the Dayton, Ohio, *Presbyterian Cookbook* (1873). She made it by stuffing a large, hollowed-out sponge cake with sherry and vanilla cream. Tipsy Pudding—sherry-spiked custard poured over sponge cake—appeared in a number of American cookbooks, including Fannie Farmer's *Boston Cooking-School Cook Book* (1896).

But I finally found a recipe for Tipsy Squire (the name referring to the effect this dessert might have on a teetotaling man of importance) in a classic American cookbook by Mrs. S. R. Dull called *Southern Cooking* (first published in 1928, this popular book was updated and released again in 1941 and 1968). This Southern specialty was well known in Georgia, and it was definitely a trifle. It carried all of the tipsy traits: lots of sherry, layers of custard, and sponge cake. While this recipe tasted good, it was still soggy—until I incorporated a technique from the other

tipsy recipes I found in 19th-century cookbooks: stale sponge cake. Why is that important? Like the Tipsy Squire I enjoyed at the Christmas party, the recipe I made with stale cake produced a tidy trifle with distinct components; the modern trifles made with fresh cake all turned into a gloppy mess.

Stale sponge cake may have been commonplace a century ago (there were plenty of leftovers), but today few home cooks make sponge cake (never mind having any leftover pieces). Luckily, most good bakeries offer high-quality sponge cake. After some serious cake staling, which requires an overnight sit (unwrapped) on the countertop or three hours in a 200-degree oven, it was time to build the tipsy.

No matter how soaked with sherry (very soaked) or buried beneath layers of custard (deeply), the cake retained some of its texture, and the custard was fresh and fluffy. The test kitchen gobbled it up and then, just like me, went back for seconds and then thirds. **–Bridget Lancaster**

TIPSY SQUIRE SERVES 10 TO 12

The beauty of this trifle is that most of the components can (if not should) be made in advance. Once assembled, Tipsy Squire actually improves after an overnight stay in the fridge. You'll need a 3-quart trifle dish to make this impressive dessert. Bake shops sell sponge cake in various sizes; just trim larger cakes to suit this recipe. To stale cake rounds, leave them uncovered on the counter overnight or place them on a wire rack over a baking sheet in a 200-degree oven for 3 hours.

- 2 (8-inch) round stale sponge cakes (each about 1 1/2 inches thick), homemade or store-bought
- 1 1/2 cups cream sherry
- 1 cup seedless raspberry jam
- 2 cups heavy cream
- 1 recipe Easy Custard (recipe follows)
- 40 small almond macaroons or amaretti cookies, homemade or store-bought
- 1 cup fresh raspberries

1. Slice each cake round in half horizontally. Brush each cut side of one cake with 1/4 cup sherry, then spread with 1/4 cup jam.

Stack 2 cut sides together (resulting in jam sandwich). Repeat with second cake to make second jam sandwich. Cut each cake into 5 long slices, then cut 5 more slices crosswise. (Reserve small jam cakes for nibbling; you will need 30 to 40 of the larger jam cakes for step 3.)

2. Beat cream and 1/4 cup sherry with electric mixer at medium-high speed to soft peaks. Reduce speed to low, gradually add custard, and mix well, about 1 minute. Toss macaroons with remaining 1/4 cup sherry in large bowl.

3. Arrange 12 to 14 (depending on size) macaroons in single layer to cover bottom of 3-quart trifle bowl. Spoon 2 cups custard mixture evenly over macaroons. Arrange 15 to 20 jam cakes in single layer on custard. Top with 2 cups custard mixture. Repeat layering of cookies, custard mixture, jam cakes, and custard mixture once more. Arrange remaining 12 to 16 macaroons in circle midway between rim of bowl and center of trifle, so that they stick up slightly like a crown. Cover tightly with plastic wrap and refrigerate at least 12 hours or up to 2 days. When ready to serve, pile raspberries inside macaroons.

EASY CUSTARD MAKES 3 1/2 CUPS

- 2 cups heavy cream
- 1/2 cup sugar
  Pinch table salt
- 5 large egg yolks
- 3 tablespoons cornstarch
- 4 tablespoons cold unsalted butter, cut into 4 pieces
- 1 1/2 teaspoons vanilla extract

1. Heat cream, 6 tablespoons sugar, and salt in heavy saucepan over medium heat until simmering, stirring occasionally to dissolve sugar. Meanwhile, whisk egg yolks in medium bowl until thoroughly combined. Whisk in remaining 2 tablespoons sugar until sugar begins to dissolve. Whisk in cornstarch until mixture is pale yellow and thick, about 30 seconds.

2. When cream mixture reaches full simmer, gradually whisk half into yolk mixture to temper. Return mixture to saucepan, scraping bowl with rubber spatula; return to simmer over medium heat, whisking constantly, until 3 or 4 bubbles burst on surface and mixture is thickened, about 1 minute. Off heat, whisk in butter and vanilla. Transfer mixture to bowl, press plastic wrap directly on surface, and refrigerate until set, at least 3 hours or up to 2 days.

CLASSIC COOKBOOK A mainstay in Southern kitchens for several generations, *Southern Cooking* (1928) was written by Henrietta Stanley Dull, home economics editor of the *Atlanta Journal* for many years.

This treasured Southern recipe actually tastes as good as it looks.

Fun Food PEPPERMINT DESSERTS

Get into the holiday spirit with four easy sweets that pair peppermint with chocolate.

No need to say bah, humbug, when it comes to making holiday desserts. Yes, you're busy, but there's still time for dessert if you follow one of these four simple recipes that team up peppermint with chocolate. The yule log cake may look like an all-day project, but this dessert doesn't require any baking. Our white chocolate candy bark is festive enough for gift giving but requires just three ingredients and 10 minutes of effort. And for something even simpler, try a mug of peppermint hot chocolate or mini ice cream sandwiches made with chocolate doughnuts and crusted with peppermint candies. –**Lauren Chattman**

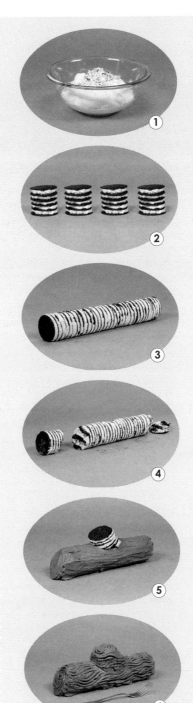

(1)

(2)

(3)

(4)

(5)

(6)

ICEBOX PEPPERMINT YULE LOG CAKE
SERVES 4 TO 6

If you prefer, place the peppermint candies in a zipper-lock plastic bag and crush them with a rolling pin or heavy skillet. For the chocolate wafers, a 9-ounce box will give you enough for this recipe.

20	round red- and white-striped hard peppermint candies
2¾	cups heavy cream
½	cup confectioners' sugar
½	teaspoon vanilla extract
¼	teaspoon peppermint extract
36	Nabisco Famous Chocolate Wafers
¼	cup cocoa powder, sifted
	Candy spearmint leaves and Red Hots for garnish

1. Make peppermint cream Process candies in food processor until crushed but not ground. With electric mixer, beat 1½ cups cream, ¼ cup sugar, vanilla, and peppermint extract in large bowl until soft peaks form. Using rubber spatula, fold crushed candy into peppermint cream.

2. Make cookie stacks Spread 1 tablespoon peppermint cream on chocolate wafer. Top with another wafer and repeat 4 more times to produce stack of 6 wafers with cream in between each cookie. Make 6 stacks, each with 6 wafers. Spread 1 tablespoon peppermint cream on top of 5 stacks, leaving 1 stack plain.

3. Make log Lay cookie stacks on sides and press together end to end, making one 16-inch log (plain stack without cream on top wafer should be placed at end). Wrap log in plastic and freeze until firm, at least 5 hours or up to 1 week.

4. Trim log With electric mixer, beat remaining 1¼ cups cream, remaining ¼ cup sugar, and cocoa in large bowl until stiff peaks form. Cut thin piece diagonally from one end of frozen log and discard. Cut 2-inch piece diagonally from other end of frozen log and set aside.

5. Make bump Transfer frozen cake to serving platter. Spread all but ½ cup cocoa cream evenly over top, sides, and ends of log. Press reserved 2-inch piece on top of log to make bump, placing it several inches from one end of log. Cover bump with remaining cocoa cream.

6. Decorate log Drag tines of fork down length of log to simulate bark. Freeze until firm, at least 3 hours or up to 2 days. Before serving, let stand at room temperature for 20 minutes. Garnish platter with candy spearmint leaves and red hot candies.

MUG O' MINTY HOT CHOCOLATE SERVES 4
This recipe can be doubled to serve a crowd.

4	cups whole or low-fat milk
6	ounces semisweet chocolate, chopped fine
1	tablespoon cocoa powder
½	teaspoon peppermint extract
	Whipped cream
8	small candy canes

Bring milk just to simmer in medium saucepan over medium-high heat. Reduce heat to low and whisk in chocolate and cocoa powder until chocolate is melted and cocoa powder is dissolved. Remove from heat and stir in peppermint extract. Pour into 4 mugs and garnish each mug with whipped cream and 2 candy cane stirrers.

PEPPERMINT ICE CREAM SANDWICHES
MAKES 8 MINI SANDWICHES
These little ice cream sandwiches are great for after-school snacks as well as a fun family dessert.

8	round red- and white-striped hard peppermint candies, crushed in food processor
1	pint vanilla ice cream, slightly softened
8	chocolate-glazed mini doughnuts, split in half horizontally

Place crushed candy on small plate. Sandwich 3 tablespoons ice cream between cut sides of 2 doughnut halves, pressing halves so that ice cream extends just a bit beyond edges. Roll ice cream edges in peppermint to coat, sprinkle more peppermint in doughnut hole, then transfer sandwiches to large plate in freezer. Repeat with remaining doughnuts, ice cream, and candy. Freeze until firm, at least 2 hours. Wrap individually in plastic wrap and freeze for up to 1 week.

WINTERMINT BARK MAKES ABOUT 1 POUND
The red, green, and white colors of this simple confection make it a perfect holiday gift. Unsalted pumpkin seeds can be substituted for the pistachio nuts.

1	cup unsalted pistachios
1	pound white chocolate, melted
12	round red- and white-striped hard peppermint candies, crushed in food processor

1. Make candy Line 8-inch-square baking pan with heavy-duty aluminum foil, making sure that foil is tucked into all corners and that there is at least 1 inch overhanging top of pan on all sides. Stir pistachios into melted chocolate, scrape mixture into prepared pan, and smooth top. Sprinkle peppermint candies on top and refrigerate until firm, about 1 hour.

2. Cut into pieces Grasping foil overhang, lift out candy and transfer to cutting board. Peel away and discard foil. Cut bark into rough chunks with chef's knife. Layer pieces between waxed paper in airtight container and refrigerate for up to 2 weeks.

Minty Hot Chocolate

Peppermint Ice Cream Sandwiches

Yule Log Cake

Wintermint Bark

Test Kitchen's Favorite Holiday Menu

Our test kitchen staff held a cook-off with favorite heirloom recipes from our mothers and grandmothers. We've put the best of these dishes together in an easy menu for your family to share.

Cook's Country Holiday Menu

First Course
Italian Spinach and
Radicchio Salad

Dinner
Dr. Pepper–Glazed Ham
Cranberry-Apple-Orange Relish
Braised Brussels Sprouts with
Bacon and Pecans
Savory Corn Pudding
Sweet Potato Casserole

Dessert
Western-Slope Pear Cake with
Ginger Cream

ITALIAN SPINACH AND RADICCHIO SALAD SERVES 8 TO 10

My Italian grandmother always made sure we had radicchio and fennel on the holiday table. She would tell us that crimson radicchio looked festive. As for the fennel, she was a firm believer in its healing powers. "Eat the fennel and it will make room for the rest of the big meal," she would tell my siblings and me. I suspect this was just a trick to get us to eat a salad with vegetables, but it worked.
–Jack Bishop

2 (6-ounce) bags baby spinach
  (about 18 loosely packed cups)
2 medium heads radicchio, torn into
  bite-sized pieces (about 6 cups)
6 tablespoons extra-virgin olive oil
1 large red onion, halved and sliced thin
2 small fennel bulbs, sliced very thin
  Salt
6 tablespoons balsamic vinegar
  Pepper

1. Toss spinach and radicchio together in large bowl. Heat oil in large skillet over medium-high heat until shimmering. Add onion, fennel, and ¾ teaspoon salt and cook, stirring occasionally, until vegetables are softened and browned, 6 to 8 minutes. Stir in vinegar and pepper to taste and cook until syrupy, about 30 seconds.

2. Scrape fennel mixture into bowl with spinach and radicchio. Toss until salad greens wilt slightly, about 1 minute. Serve immediately.

DR. PEPPER-GLAZED HAM
SERVES 20 TO 30

Never one to shy away from the possibility of failure, Mom always experimented with traditional Christmas recipes—even when it came to the ubiquitous spiral-sliced ham. This adventurous (and successful) attempt to dress up the holiday ham with a Dr. Pepper glaze may seem strange at first glance, but the combination of flavors from the fruity soda, fresh orange juice, and mustard give this ham an unbeatable sweet tang that's pure genius. Use of an oven bag gets the ham on the table in record time and ensures that it's moist through and through. This ham is more than enough to serve a crowd and still have some leftovers. **–Bridget Lancaster**

½ cup Dr. Pepper
¾ cup light brown sugar
2 tablespoons fresh orange juice
2 teaspoons Dijon mustard
1 spiral-sliced, bone-in half ham
  (7 to 10 pounds), preferably shank end

1. Bring Dr. Pepper, sugar, orange juice, and mustard to boil in medium saucepan. Reduce heat to medium-low and simmer until mixture is syrupy and measures ¾ cup, about 8 minutes. (Glaze can be refrigerated for up to 2 days; reheat when needed.)

2. Remove ham from packaging and discard plastic disk that covers bone. Place ham in plastic oven bag, tie bag shut, and trim excess plastic. Set ham cut side down in 13 by 9-inch baking dish and cut 4 slits in top of bag. (If you don't have an oven bag, place ham cut side down in baking dish and wrap tightly with foil.) Let stand at room temperature for 1½ hours.

3. Adjust oven rack to lowest position and heat oven to 250 degrees. Bake ham until center registers about 100 degrees on instant-read thermometer, 1½ to 2½ hours (about 14 minutes per pound if using plastic oven bag, about 17 minutes per pound if using foil), depending on weight of ham.

4. Remove ham from oven and roll back sides of bag to expose ham. Brush ham liberally with glaze and return to oven briefly until glaze becomes sticky, about 10 minutes. Remove from oven,

An Italian-inspired salad (bottom left) starts our favorite holiday meal. Glazed ham (top) is an easy centerpiece and works well with a no-cook cranberry relish (bottom right).

Bacon turns braised Brussels sprouts (left) into a crowd pleaser. Corn pudding (right) is creamy and cheesy.

brush entire ham again with glaze, loosely cover with foil, and let rest for 30 to 40 minutes before carving.

CRANBERRY-APPLE-ORANGE RELISH MAKES 2 CUPS

No matter what else was on the dinner table, it just wasn't Christmas without my mom's relish. Sweet, sour, bitter, and a bit spicy, the relish was enjoyed by each member of the family in his or her own way. Dad had it with his ham, Mom liked it on buttermilk biscuits, and my brother mixed into his mashed sweet potatoes. As for me, I just spooned a big pile onto my plate and ate it straight up, like a side dish. –Jeremy Sauer

1 large sweet apple, peeled, cored, and roughly chopped
1 (12-ounce) bag cranberries
1 whole orange, cut into quarters (including rind)
3/4 cup sugar
1 teaspoon ground ginger
Pinch salt

Pulse all ingredients in food processor until mixture resembles coarse meal. Refrigerate for 1 to 2 days for flavors to fully develop. Serve.

BRAISED BRUSSELS SPROUTS WITH BACON AND PECANS

SERVES 8 TO 10

When I was a kid, I thought bacon could make anything taste good—even Brussels sprouts. Now that I'm all grown up, I realize the secret to this recipe from my great-aunt Carole is the braising technique, which ensures that the Brussels sprouts are tender without being mushy or waterlogged, as is usually the case when these little cabbages are boiled. –Stephanie Alleyne

8 strips bacon, chopped
2 large shallots, chopped fine
2 garlic cloves, minced
2 pounds fresh Brussels sprouts, trimmed and halved through stem ends
1 cup low-sodium chicken broth
2 teaspoons minced fresh thyme
4 teaspoons sherry vinegar
2 tablespoons unsalted butter

Salt and pepper
1/2 cup pecans, toasted and chopped

1. Fry bacon in skillet over medium heat until crisp, 8 to 10 minutes. Transfer to paper-towel-lined plate. Pour off excess grease but do not wipe skillet clean.
2. Cook shallots in same skillet over medium heat until soft, about 10 minutes. Add garlic and cook until fragrant, about 30 seconds.
3. Toss Brussels sprouts with shallots and garlic, add broth, and reduce heat to medium-low. Cover and cook, tossing once or twice, until paring knife can be inserted into sprouts without resistance, 13 to 18 minutes.
4. Stir in thyme, vinegar, butter, reserved bacon, and salt and pepper to taste. Transfer to serving bowl. Sprinkle pecans on top. Serve immediately.

SAVORY CORN PUDDING

SERVES 8 TO 10

My mother's sweet corn pudding was my favorite part of any holiday meal. It was so decadent I would forego the pecan pie and have a second helping of corn pudding for dessert. My sweet tooth has been tamed (a bit), so I now put a savory corn pudding on my holiday table. This version is creamy and rich, like Mom's, but the addition of cheese and herbs makes it decidedly part of dinner, not dessert.

–Cali Rich

1 tablespoon unsalted butter, softened, for greasing casserole dish
Salt
6 cups frozen corn
1 1/2 cups heavy cream
6 large eggs, lightly beaten
1 1/2 cups shredded sharp cheddar cheese
1 tablespoon sugar
1/4 teaspoon cayenne pepper
3 tablespoons chopped fresh basil

1. Adjust oven rack to middle position and heat oven to 350 degrees. Grease 2-quart casserole dish with butter. Bring large kettle of water to boil for water bath. Bring 2 quarts water to boil in large saucepan for corn.

2. Add 1 tablespoon salt and corn to boiling water and cook for 1 minute. Drain in colander and dry with paper towels. Pulse 4 cups corn in food processor until rough puree forms, about ten 1-second pulses. Transfer to large bowl and stir in remaining whole corn, 1 teaspoon salt, cream, eggs, cheese, sugar, cayenne, and basil until combined.
3. Pour corn mixture into casserole and transfer dish to roasting pan. Pour boiling water from kettle into roasting pan until it comes halfway up sides of casserole dish. Place roasting pan in oven and bake until pudding is set and a few brown spots appear around edges, 40 to 45 minutes. Remove casserole from water bath, transfer to wire rack, and let set for 5 to 10 minutes before serving.

Make Ahead: The corn can be cooked, processed, and mixed with the whole corn, salt, cream, cheese, sugar, and cayenne up to 2 days in advance. Refrigerate until ready to use, then stir in the eggs and basil when ready to cook.

SWEET POTATO CASSEROLE

SERVES 8 TO 10

My favorite Thanksgiving dish was my mother's sweet potato "pie," which wasn't really a pie at all but a casserole of canned yams and apple pie filling topped with marshmallows. This is my (slightly) more grown-up version. Be careful when broiling the topping, as it quickly goes from underdone to burnt. –Keri Fisher

4 pounds sweet potatoes (about 4 large potatoes), scrubbed and dried
5 tablespoons unsalted butter, melted
5 tablespoons dark brown sugar
Salt and pepper
2 cups applesauce
2 cups mini marshmallows

1. Adjust oven rack to upper-middle position, place baking sheet on rack, and heat oven to 400 degrees.

2. Cut potatoes in half lengthwise. Place them flesh side down on hot baking sheet and roast until flesh is easily pierced through skin with skewer, 25 to 35 minutes. Remove potatoes from oven and set oven to broil. Whisk together butter and sugar. Flip potatoes flesh side up and brush with butter mixture. Sprinkle with salt and pepper to taste and broil until top is glazed, about 5 minutes. Remove from oven and cool.

3. While sweet potatoes are cooking, place applesauce in fine-mesh strainer and press lightly to drain off excess liquid (you should have 1 1/4 cups solids). Transfer solids to large bowl. Scoop cooled sweet potato pulp out of skin and add to bowl with applesauce. Mash apples and sweet potato together until combined. Transfer to 2-quart casserole dish, top with marshmallows, and broil until melted, 1 to 2 minutes. Serve.

Make Ahead: The sweet potato and applesauce mixture can be mashed and refrigerated up to 2 days in advance. Heat the mixture in a medium saucepan or microwave until warm before transferring it to a casserole dish and topping with marshmallows.

WESTERN-SLOPE PEAR CAKE WITH GINGER CREAM

SERVES 10 TO 12

This recipe survived on a scrap of paper found in my grandmother's recipe box. I have fond memories of her and my mother making it when I was a child. My mom always said that the pears from Paonia, Colo., were delicious in this cake, but I've found that canned pears work just as well.

–Pat O'Connor

Editor's note: This recipe from a reader in Denver, Colo., so impressed everyone in the test kitchen that we just had to include it in our menu. Thanks, Pat.

(continued on page 14)

Sweet potato casserole (left) gets a boost from applesauce. Our holiday dinner finishes up with a simple pear cake (right) made with canned fruit.

1 cup all-purpose flour
1/2 teaspoon baking powder
3/4 teaspoon ground ginger
1/4 teaspoon salt
7 tablespoons unsalted butter,
6 tablespoons softened but
still cool, 1 tablespoon melted
2/3 cup plus 2 tablespoons
packed light brown sugar
2 large eggs
1 teaspoon minced fresh
ginger
1 cup heavy cream
1 (15-ounce) can pear halves
in syrup, drained and cut into
1/4-inch slices
1 tablespoon confectioners'
sugar

1. Adjust oven rack to middle position and heat oven to 350 degrees.

2. Whisk flour, baking powder, 1/2 teaspoon ground ginger, and salt together in medium bowl. Beat 6 tablespoons butter and 2/3 cup brown sugar with electric mixer at medium speed until pale and fluffy, about 3 minutes. Beat in eggs, one at a time, until incorporated. Beat in fresh ginger and 1/4 cup cream until incorporated. Reduce speed to low and add dry ingredients in two batches.

3. Pour batter into greased 9-inch cake pan. Arrange pear slices in fan-shaped pattern on top of batter and lightly press slices into batter. Scatter remaining 2 tablespoons brown sugar on top of pears and drizzle with 1 tablespoon melted butter. Bake until toothpick inserted in center of cake comes out with a few crumbs attached, 35 to 40 minutes. Let cake cool in pan for 10 minutes, invert onto cutting board, and invert again onto wire rack to finish cooling.

4. When ready to serve, whip remaining 3/4 cup cream, confectioners' sugar, and remaining 1/4 teaspoon ground ginger to soft peaks. Slice cake and serve with whipped cream.

Make Ahead: This cake tastes better if made a day in advance. Just wrap tightly in plastic and store at room temperature. Whip the cream close to serving time.

Old-Fashioned Mulled Cider

I like the idea (and aroma) of mulled cider, but it takes so long and often ends up tasting like potpourri. Can you come up with a quicker recipe that actually tastes like apples? –Joe Cataldo, Hudson, N.Y.

The process of mulling has long been used to hide flaws in mediocre wine. Assertive spices make even the worst red wine drinkable. (Think sangría for wintertime.) But mulled cider starts with cider—and cider usually tastes pretty good. When mulling cider, the goal should be to accent the honest apple flavor with spices, not overwhelm it.

In choosing spices, I decided to adopt a "less is more" philosophy, but before I ruled anything out, I wanted to see if ground or whole spices would work best. I made a batch with each and let them simmer for an hour, standard procedure in most mulled cider recipes. The results were immediately evident. The ground spices floated on top of the cider, making every sip gritty and chalky. Although it wasn't horrible, this batch tasted dusty compared with the cider made with whole spices that I had toasted beforehand to bring out their flavor.

To pare down the variety (and avoid the "potpourri" problem), I kept cinnamon and cloves for their classic holiday flavor and coriander for its floral characteristics. A surprise came in the form of black peppercorns, which offered a welcome subtle bite. I tried a variety of fresh and dried fruits, and my tasters liked the fruity perfume of orange peel. Mulled cider requires a little sweetener, and my tasters preferred the caramel notes of brown sugar to plain white sugar.

After about 20 tests, I was beginning to tire of waiting an hour for the cider to simmer before I could taste it. Could I trim some time from the recipe without sacrificing flavor? I tried turning up the heat to a boil, but that just made the cider cloudy and the spices bitter. I went back down to a bare simmer and tried simply reducing the total time. To my surprise, my tasters preferred the fresher flavor of the cider simmered for just 30 minutes.

Given the minimal ingredient list and short simmering time, I could now mull cider even for the unexpected guest. That's what I call getting into the holiday spirit.

–Jeremy Sauer

FIRESIDE MULLED CIDER
MAKES ABOUT 2 QUARTS
Use a meat mallet or heavy saucepan to break the cinnamon stick into several pieces. See page 28 for more information on straining mulled cider.

1 stick cinnamon, broken into
pieces
1/2 teaspoon whole coriander
seeds
1/2 teaspoon black
peppercorns
1/4 teaspoon whole cloves
2 quarts apple cider
4 strips orange zest (each
about 2 inches long)
1–3 tablespoons light or dark
brown sugar (to taste)

Toast spices in large saucepan over medium heat, shaking pan occasionally, until fragrant, 1 to 3 minutes. Add cider, orange zest, and sugar and bring to a boil. Reduce heat to low and simmer for 30 minutes, using wide, shallow spoon to skim away foam that rises to surface. Pour cider through fine-mesh strainer lined with coffee filter and discard spices and orange zest. Serve. (Mulled cider can be refrigerated in airtight container for up to one week. Reheat before serving.)

MULLED CIDER À LA PUMPKIN PIE
Pumpkin pie flavors work well with cider.

Follow recipe for Fireside Mulled Cider, using 2 sticks cinnamon and substituting 1/2 teaspoon whole allspice berries and 1/8 teaspoon fresh ground nutmeg for coriander and peppercorns. Replace zest with 1 vanilla bean, split in half and seeds scraped out, adding bean and seeds to pot.

MULLED APPLE 'CHAI'-DER
The flavors of *chai*, the Indian concoction of milk, tea, and spices, inspired this variation.

Follow recipe for Fireside Mulled Cider, substituting 1 star anise pod and 1/2 teaspoon crushed cardamom pods for coriander. Replace orange zest with 4 strips lemon zest.

Less is more when it comes to mulling cider.

How to TOAST SPICES, NUTS, AND SEEDS

Toasting whole spices, nuts, and seeds helps to release essential oils, bringing out their full flavor and aroma. Spices need only be toasted until they become fragrant, usually 1 to 3 minutes, while nuts and seeds should be toasted until they begin to darken slightly in color, generally 3 to 5 minutes.

Toast whole spices, nuts, or seeds in a skillet (without any oil) set over medium heat, shaking the pan occasionally to prevent scorching.

Getting to Know Spices

Any kitchen worth its salt (and pepper) has a cabinet lined with a colorful array of spices. But what does each one really taste like? To find out, we held the test kitchen's first-ever spice "sniffing" by steeping 16 often-used spices in boiling water and inhaling the aromatic vapors.

Allspice
MULTIPLE PERSONALITIES
This purple-black berry is the fruit of an evergreen tree native to the Southern hemisphere. It is named "allspice" because it tastes like a combination of cinnamon, nutmeg, and cloves, with a touch of brown sugar and dried fruit.

Caraway Seeds
THE RYE GUY
Similar in shape and color to cumin seeds and also from a plant in the parsley family, caraway seeds are warm and floral, with just a hint of licorice.

Cardamom
FLOWER POWER
Each of these football-shaped pods contains about 20 small seeds that possess a pungent, floral aroma and a sweet, citrusy flavor.

Cinnamon
LIKE CHRISTMAS ON A STICK
This sweet-hot spice is the bark of a species of evergreen tree. Cinnamon comes in two types: Ceylon, which is light brown and sweet, and cassia, which is much darker and slightly bitter. Most U.S. markets sell cassia.

Cloves
USE ONLY A PINCH
One of the most distinctive and powerful spices, cloves are unopened flower buds from a species of evergreen. Once dried, these tiny reddish-brown spices have a sweet, peppery flavor. Use sparingly.

Coriander
BABY CILANTRO
This light brown spherical seed is the dried fruit of the herb cilantro, a member of the parsley family. Coriander possesses a sweet, almost fruity flavor with just a hint of the soapy-metallic character of mature cilantro.

Cumin Seeds
PUNGENT AND PEPPERY
Like caraway seeds and coriander, these tiny, elongated seeds belong to a plant in the parsley family. Their flavor is earthy and warm, but it's their pungent, almost musty aroma that sets them apart from other warm spices.

Fennel Seed
GOOD & PLENTY
Fennel seeds come from a bulbless variety of the fennel plant. They exhibit a heavy anise flavor reminiscent of black jelly beans and an earthy, butterscotch-like aroma.

Juniper Berries
HALLMARK OF GIN
These dark purple berries come from the juniper shrub, native to both North America and Northern Europe. They are best known as the primary flavoring agent in gin, but their clean, sweet, piney aroma also enhances various meats and cabbage dishes.

Mace
NUTMEG'S BLANKET
This spice begins as the bright red membrane covering the nutmeg seed. Most often found in its ground form, mace tastes similar to nutmeg but is slightly more astringent and has just a touch of sweetness. Mace can be substituted for nutmeg in most recipes.

Mustard Seed
SHARP AND COLORFUL
These acrid seeds are typically yellow, brown, or black, the brown and black varieties being prized for their stronger flavor. Mustard seeds have almost no aroma, but their flavor is earthy and sharp, with a strong peppery kick.

Nutmeg
WARM AND WOODSY
This large, oval spice is the seed of a tree. Nutmeg's flavor is warm and woodsy but assertively spicy. Nutmeg loses its aroma quickly, so it's best to grate whole nutmeg for recipes in which it's the star, such as eggnog.

Peppercorns
MOST POPULAR
Green peppercorns possess a mild herbal flavor. They are soft, underripe, and typically sold pickled in brine. Piquant black peppercorns are slightly underripe but dried. White peppercorns are fully ripe, but their skin is removed before drying, making them less pungent than black peppercorns.

Pink Peppercorns
PINK PRETENDER
Not a true peppercorn, this spice is the dried berry from the *Baies* rose plant. These berries hail from Madagascar and are pungent and floral in flavor, with a distinctly sweet aftertaste. Although they are typically sold whole, they can be ground and used in much the same way as true peppercorns.

Saffron
PACKS A PUNCH
Pound for pound the most expensive spice in the world, saffron is the stigma from a variety of crocus flower. Just the slightest pinch lends a raisin-like flavor and a vibrant orange hue to many dishes. When buying saffron, look for dark red threads devoid of yellow or orange.

Star Anise
THE STAR OF THE SHOW
This star-shaped staple of Asian cookery is harvested in China from a variety of evergreen tree. Though it's best known for its role in Chinese five-spice powder, its warm licorice flavor also lends itself to various soup broths, teas, jams, jellies, cookies, and liqueurs.

I'm Looking for a Recipe

READERS HELP READERS FIND RECIPES

We've Got Mail

For months readers have been sending us recipes in response to the request for boiled cake (August/September 2005 issue). We really liked the letter and recipe sent by Billie Hall (at right). For the test kitchen's notes on this recipe (with more details on cooking times and procedures), go to www.cookscountry.com and click Looking for a Recipe. You'll find dozens more recipes submitted by readers who responded to recipe requests in other issues of *Cook's Country*.

BOILED CAKE Billie Hall, Jericho, Vt.

The boiled cake recipe requested in your August/September 2005 issue sounds very much like my grandmother's eggless, milkless cake. This recipe was particularly useful during World War II, when eggs and many other items were rationed. This cake does turn out heavy, but it is very moist. We ate Grandma's cake plain, but it was also very good with some whipped cream on top.

1	(15-ounce) box raisins	1	teaspoon salt
2	cups sugar	1	teaspoon cinnamon
2	heaping tablespoons vegetable shortening	3	cups flour
		1	teaspoon nutmeg
2	cups water	1	cup walnut meats (optional)
1	teaspoon baking soda	1/2	teaspoon cloves
1	teaspoon baking powder		

INSTRUCTIONS: Boil together the first 4 ingredients for 5 minutes in a good-sized pot. Let cool. Mix the remaining ingredients into the same pot. Place in 2 greased and floured small bread pans or 1 large bread pan. Bake for 45 minutes at 350 degrees.

Brown Derby Cake

My mother loved to go to bakeries, especially one in Manchester, Conn., that sold Brown Derby Cake. My mom has been gone for many years now, but I have many fond memories of eating Brown Derby Cake with her.

Becky Grose
Palm Beach Gardens, Fla.

Candy Chicken

I am trying to find a recipe called either candy chicken or candied chicken. My mom used to make it back in the 1970s from a recipe on the Tang jar. I know there was honey in the sauce. I would love to be able to make that childhood dish and revisit those happy times.

Maria Piszek
Steelton, Pa.

Dutch Girls

In Southern California, VandeKamps Bakery used to make the best cookies called Dutch Girls. They were rectangular, crispy, very light brown, and covered with a crunchy layer of large sugar crystals. I've tried a few recipes from the Internet, but I end up with cookies that are too tough or too soft. The originals tasted buttery and sweet and their texture was crumbly and tender.

Cecilia Schreyer
Corona del Mar, Calif.

Chuy's Jalapeño Dip

I've been to Houston a few times on business, and there's a Tex-Mex restaurant chain there called Chuy's. Their food is ubiquitous Southwestern fare except for one special item that I've never seen anywhere else. It's a creamy, pale-green, spicy dip for tortilla chips and I could it eat by the bucketful!

Melissa Hayman
Wilmington, Del.

Oatmeal Brownies

Back in the late forties or early fifties, my mother and I made oatmeal brownies from a recipe that was on the Hershey's cocoa can. The brownies were delicious, especially with chopped pecans or flaked coconut.

David Sewell
Wichita Falls, Texas

Wheat Germ Bars

Our family has lost a favorite recipe: wheat germ bars with chocolate. We inherited the recipe from friends in the early 1970s, but it was lost during one of our international moves. It is basically a bar made of wheat germ that is baked and topped with melted chocolate chips.

Thomas P. Flannery
Lexington, Mass.

Avocado Ice Cream

When I was a child growing up in the 1940s, my mother used to make avocado ice cream in an old-fashioned hand-cranked machine. It reminded me of pistachio ice cream. Over the years, the recipe has disappeared, much to my dismay.

Sharon Betts
Rollins, Mont.

Lemon Chess Pie

About 40 years ago, I spent a month in Blytheville, Ark., while my husband was in training as a flight engineer on Boeing bombers. My 18-month-old daughter and I stayed in a Best Western motel there. Across the highway was a small, locally owned café that served a lemon chess pie that was rich and smooth, with a strong and distinctive lemon flavor, almost like lemon curd made with fresh lemon. In the recipes that I've tried, the lemon flavor was not tart enough.

Gina Bryant
Sun City West, Ariz.

Tootie's Pie Crust

My husband and I used to buy the most wonderful pies from Tootie Pies in Medina, Texas. The owner has since closed her little shop and sold her closely guarded family recipes to the Texas Heritage Provisions Co. Although there were many different fillings, the pie crust was what made her pies special. The crust was rich, sweet, flaky, a little puffy, and almost shortbread-like.

Sandy Connor
El Paso, Texas

Rhubarb Kugel

During a visit with my 96-year-old grandmother in Bismarck, N.D., one of her friends invited my family to lunch. We had a delightful time and thoroughly enjoyed all of the food, especially the rhubarb kugel. The dear old lady who made us the kugel gave new meaning to the word "hospitality"—she was blind! Both she and my grandmother have since passed on, but every time I bake bread, I remember those ladies in North Dakota.

Brea McClain
Summerfield, N.C.

Prune Relish

In the late 1970s, my mentor at the Parsons School of Design made a wonderful relish from prunes. She worked on some advertising for the Prune Board of California, and I believe the recipe came from them. I think it also had onions and green peppers. It was terribly addictive and I could eat it right out of the pot!

Karen Rusch
West Stockbridge, Mass.

Black Walnut Cake

I would love to find this old recipe that my grandmother made. It was a black walnut cake, and I used to help her shell the walnuts because she always told me it made a better cake if I helped her. I think it was just a way of keeping me out of her hair at the time. This two-layer cake was very moist and it was frosted.

Pearl Kern
Lacey, Wash.

Memorable Tamales

Years ago, when I was living in Burlington, Vt., there was a wonderful restaurant on Riverside Avenue called Tortilla Flat. I always ordered the open-faced tamale—corn husks topped with a thick layer of masa dough, spicy cooked beef, and shredded cheddar cheese. The tamale was brought to the table piping hot right from the oven. It was so good that I still think about it 25 years later.

Lillian Julow
Gainesville, Fla.

Secret Fruit Bread

My sister-in-law makes fruit bread that is similar to an Irish soda bread, but it is sweeter tasting and more yellow in color when you cut into it. She will not give me the recipe as it is a secret recipe from her mother. The only fruit it contains are the raisins; the other ingredients are flour, butter, eggs, sugar, baking powder, and milk. I do not know what makes it yellow, but I would love to be able to make something like it.

Dorothy Drislane
Carmel, N.Y.

Are you looking for a special recipe? Let other readers help. Just send us your requests, and we will print as many of them as we can. Write to Looking for a Recipe, Cook's Country, P.O. Box 470739, Brookline, MA, 02447. Or e-mail us at lookingforarecipe@bcpress.com. If you can help with one of the above requests, contact us at the same postal or e-mail address. We will post responses on www.cookscountry.com.

Find the Rooster! A tiny version of this rooster has been hidden somewhere in the pages of this issue. If you find it, write to us with its location (plus your name and address), and you will be entered into a random drawing. The first winning entry drawn will receive a Farberware toaster (our test winner—see page 31), and the next five winners will each receive a free one-year subscription to *Cook's Country*. To enter the contest, write to us at Rooster, Cook's Country, P.O. Box 470739, Brookline, MA 02447, or e-mail us at rooster@bcpress.com. Entries are due by January 31, 2006. Did you find the rooster in the August/September 2005 issue? It was hidden in the photo of the chimney starter on page 28. Shirley Thomas of Sherwood, Ore., spotted it, and she won a Forschner chef's knife.

SPAGHETTI WITH SAUSAGE MEATBALLS

BAKED COD WITH CRUNCHY LEMON-HERB TOPPING

RUSTIC POTATO SOUP

PORK CHOPS WITH SPICY ORANGE GLAZE

BAKED COD WITH CRUNCHY LEMON-HERB TOPPING
SERVES 4

Haddock, halibut, or bluefish fillets are good alternatives to cod. If some of the fish pieces are very thin, fold them in half to make thicker pieces. If you like, substitute dill or basil for the parsley.

- 1 tablespoon unsalted butter
- 24 Ritz crackers, crushed into coarse crumbs (about 1 cup)
- 2 tablespoons minced fresh parsley
- 3 tablespoons mayonnaise
- 2 small garlic cloves, minced
- 1 teaspoon grated zest plus 1 tablespoon juice from 1 lemon
- 4 skinless cod fillets (about 2 pounds)
  Salt and pepper
  Lemon wedges for serving

1. Adjust oven rack to middle position and heat oven to 450 degrees. Grease baking sheet with butter. Toss cracker crumbs and 1 tablespoon parsley together in medium bowl. Mix remaining 1 tablespoon parsley, mayonnaise, garlic, lemon zest, and lemon juice together in small bowl.

2. Pat fish dry with paper towels, then season with salt and pepper. Place on buttered baking sheet, spacing pieces about 1/2 inch apart. Brush tops and sides of fish with mayonnaise mixture, then press cracker crumbs into mayonnaise.

3. Bake until crumbs are golden brown and fish flakes apart with fork, about 15 minutes. Serve with lemon wedges.

SPAGHETTI WITH SAUSAGE MEATBALLS SERVES 4

- 2 slices white sandwich bread, crusts discarded, torn into small pieces
- 1/2 cup buttermilk
- 1 pound sweet Italian sausage, casings removed
- 1 large egg, lightly beaten
- 2 tablespoons extra-virgin olive oil
- 3 garlic cloves, minced
- 1 (28-ounce) can crushed tomatoes
- 1 (14.5-ounce) can diced tomatoes
- 1 tablespoon minced fresh basil
  Salt and pepper
- 1 pound spaghetti
  Grated Parmesan cheese

1. Bring 4 quarts of water to boil in large pot. Adjust oven rack to middle position and heat oven to 475 degrees. Line baking sheet with foil.

2. Soak bread in buttermilk in bowl for 5 minutes. Using fork, mash until smooth. Mix in sausage and egg until combined. Form mixture into 1 1/2-inch meatballs and place on baking sheet. Spray meatballs with cooking spray. Bake until deeply browned, 17 to 20 minutes.

3. Meanwhile, heat oil and garlic in large skillet over medium heat until garlic is golden, about 3 minutes. Add tomatoes, increase heat to medium-high, and simmer until sauce thickens, 15 to 20 minutes. Stir in basil and salt and pepper to taste. Toss in meatballs.

4. Add 1 tablespoon salt and pasta to boiling water. Cook pasta until al dente. Reserve 1/4 cup cooking water, drain pasta, and return pasta to pot along with reserved water. Ladle some tomato sauce (without meatballs) over spaghetti and toss well. Divide pasta among bowls and top with more sauce and meatballs. Serve, passing Parmesan at table.

PORK CHOPS WITH SPICY ORANGE GLAZE SERVES 4

Starting the pork chops in a cold skillet allows them to heat up slowly and hold on to their interior moisture—a method that works best with thin chops. If using an electric stove, turn the burner to medium just before seasoning the chops in step 1.

- 4 bone-in rib or center-cut pork chops, 1/2 to 3/4 inch thick
- 1 teaspoon plus 1 tablespoon olive oil
  Salt and pepper
- 1 teaspoon ground cumin
- 1/2 teaspoon sugar
- 2 garlic cloves, minced
- 1/8 teaspoon red pepper flakes
- 3/4 cup orange juice

1. Rub each chop with 1/4 teaspoon oil and sprinkle with salt, pepper, and cumin. Sprinkle one side of each chop with 1/8 teaspoon sugar.

2. Place chops, sugared side down, in large nonstick skillet and press meat into pan. Cook, without moving, over medium heat until lightly browned, 6 to 9 minutes. Turn chops, reduce heat to low, cover, and cook until center of chops registers 145 to 150 degrees on instant-read thermometer, 3 to 6 minutes. Transfer chops to platter, tent with foil, and let rest while making sauce.

3. Add remaining tablespoon oil, garlic, and pepper flakes to empty pan and cook over medium heat until fragrant, about 30 seconds. Add juice and simmer until slightly thickened, about 5 minutes. Tip accumulated juices from platter with chops into skillet, cook 1 minute, season with salt and pepper, and pour sauce over chops. Serve.

RUSTIC POTATO SOUP SERVES 4 TO 6

Let the potatoes simmer in the broth while you prep and cook the remaining ingredients. Because the kielbasa is quite salty, no added salt is necessary.

- 6 cups low-sodium chicken broth
- 2 pounds red potatoes, peeled and cut into 3/4-inch cubes
- 1 bay leaf
- 2 tablespoons unsalted butter
- 1 pound kielbasa, cut into 1/2-inch pieces
- 2 large leeks, white and light green parts only, cut in half lengthwise, then sliced thin crosswise
- 1/2 bunch kale, stems removed and leaves cut crosswise into 1/4-inch strips (about 4 packed cups)
  Pepper

1. Bring broth, potatoes, and bay leaf to boil in large saucepan over medium-high heat. Reduce heat to medium-low and simmer until potatoes are tender, about 10 minutes. Discard bay leaf. Using potato masher, coarsely break up potatoes, leaving some large chunks.

2. Meanwhile, melt butter in Dutch oven over medium heat. Cook kielbasa, stirring frequently, until lightly browned in spots, about 4 minutes. Add leeks and cook until soft, about 4 minutes.

3. Add potato mixture and kale to Dutch oven and simmer until kale is tender, about 5 minutes. Season with pepper and serve.

CHICKEN WITH MUSHROOMS AND LEEKS

TACO SALAD

STIR-FRIED BEEF WITH SNOW PEAS AND CASHEWS

BROILED PAPRIKA CHICKEN

TACO SALAD SERVES 4 TO 6

For a spicier taco salad, add a pinch of cayenne to the meat mixture. If you like, top this salad with diced avocados, shredded pepper Jack or cheddar cheese, minced red onion, or sour cream.

- 2 tablespoons lime juice
- 3 garlic cloves, minced
- 1 1/2 teaspoons ground cumin
- 1/3 cup plus 1 teaspoon olive oil
  Salt and pepper
- 1 pound 90 percent lean ground beef
- 1 tablespoon chili powder
- 1 tablespoon tomato paste
- 1/2 cup water
- 2 hearts romaine lettuce, shredded
- 2 tomatoes, cored, seeded, and chopped
- 4 cups corn tortilla chips, broken into 1-inch pieces
- 1/4 cup roughly chopped fresh cilantro

1. Combine lime juice, 1 teaspoon minced garlic, 1/2 teaspoon cumin, 1/3 cup olive oil, and salt and pepper to taste in small bowl.

2. Heat remaining teaspoon oil in large skillet over medium heat until shimmering. Add beef and cook, breaking up clumps with wooden spoon, until lightly browned, about 5 minutes. Add remaining garlic, remaining 1 teaspoon cumin, and chili powder and cook until fragrant, about 30 seconds. Stir in tomato paste and water and simmer until thickened, about 3 minutes. Remove from heat, season with salt and pepper, and cover to keep warm.

3. Toss lettuce, tomatoes, and chips with lime juice dressing in large bowl. Divide salad among individual plates and top each portion with some meat mixture. Sprinkle with cilantro and any additional toppings (see suggestions above). Serve.

CHICKEN WITH MUSHROOMS AND LEEKS SERVES 4

Start browning the chicken before you prepare the vegetables. Goat cheese makes the sauce creamy and tangy.

- 8 bone-in, skin-on chicken thighs (about 2 1/2 pounds), trimmed of excess fat
  Salt and pepper
- 1 teaspoon vegetable oil
- 1 tablespoon unsalted butter
- 10 ounces white mushrooms, wiped clean and sliced thin
- 2 leeks, white and light green parts only, chopped into 1/4-inch pieces
- 1/3 cup white wine
- 3/4 cup low-sodium chicken broth
- 1 1/2 tablespoons minced fresh tarragon
- 1 cup crumbled goat cheese

1. Adjust oven rack to middle position and heat oven to 400 degrees. Dry chicken thoroughly with paper towels and season with salt and pepper. Heat oil in large nonstick skillet over high heat until shimmering. Cook chicken skin side down (thighs will fit into pan snugly) until skin is deep brown and crisp, 10 to 15 minutes. Turn chicken over, reduce heat to medium-high, and cook until second side is lightly browned, about 3 minutes. Transfer chicken to baking dish and place in oven while making sauce. Bake chicken until cooked through, 6 to 8 minutes.

2. Meanwhile, discard fat in skillet. Melt butter in empty skillet over high heat until foaming. Add mushrooms and leeks and cook until mushroom liquid evaporates, about 5 minutes. Add wine and cook until almost evaporated, about 1 minute. Add broth and 1 tablespoon tarragon and simmer until slightly thickened, about 5 minutes. Whisk in goat cheese and simmer until thickened, about 1 minute. Add remaining tarragon and season with salt and pepper.

3. Return chicken to skillet and turn to coat with sauce. Serve.

BROILED PAPRIKA CHICKEN SERVES 4

Broilers vary in heat output, so cooking times can vary dramatically. When you are broiling chicken, it is best to use an instant-read thermometer or cut into the thickest part of the breast to check for doneness.

- 2 tablespoons unsalted butter, softened
- 3 garlic cloves, minced
- 1 tablespoon paprika
  Salt and pepper
- 4 bone-in, skin-on split chicken breasts (about 3 pounds)

1. Adjust one oven rack to lowest position (rack should be 13 inches away from broiler element) and second oven rack to highest position (about 5 inches away from broiler element) and heat broiler. Line bottom of broiler pan with foil and fit with slotted broiler-pan top.

2. Mash butter, garlic, 2 teaspoons paprika, 1/4 teaspoon salt, and 1/4 teaspoon pepper together in small bowl to form paste. Using fingers, carefully loosen skin from meat. Spoon about 2 teaspoons of butter mixture under skin of each breast, then work butter evenly under skin. Rub both sides of chicken breasts with remaining 1 teaspoon paprika, 1/2 teaspoon salt, and 1/4 teaspoon pepper. Place chicken skin side down on broiler-pan top.

3. Broil on lower rack until just beginning to brown, 12 to 16 minutes. Turn chicken skin side up and continue to broil on lower rack until skin is slightly crisp and thickest part of meat registers 160 degrees on instant-read thermometer, 10 to 16 minutes. Move pan to upper rack and broil until skin is spotty brown and crisp, about 1 minute. Serve.

STIR-FRIED BEEF WITH SNOW PEAS AND CASHEWS SERVES 4

Put the raw flank steak in the freezer for 15 minutes to make slicing easier. Working with the grain, cut the steak into three long strips, then cut each strip across the grain into 1/8-inch-thick slices. Serve with steamed rice.

- 1 1/4 pounds flank steak, cut into thin slices (see note)
- 2 tablespoons soy sauce
- 1/3 cup hoisin sauce
- 1/3 cup water
- 1/2 teaspoon red pepper flakes, or more to taste
- 2 tablespoons peanut or vegetable oil
- 1/2 pound snow peas, stem ends trimmed
- 4 garlic cloves, minced
- 1 tablespoon minced fresh ginger
- 1/2 cup unsalted roasted cashews, chopped

1. Combine steak and soy sauce in medium bowl, cover, and refrigerate while preparing other ingredients. Whisk hoisin sauce, water, and pepper flakes together in small bowl.

2. Heat 2 teaspoons oil in large nonstick skillet over high heat until just smoking. Add half of steak, break up clumps with wooden spoon, and cook, without stirring, for 1 minute. Toss steak until browned around edges, about 30 seconds. Transfer to clean bowl. Heat 2 teaspoons oil in skillet until just smoking and repeat with remaining beef.

3. To now-empty skillet, add remaining 2 teaspoons oil and heat until just smoking. Add snow peas and cook, stirring once or twice, for 2 minutes. Clear center of pan and add garlic and ginger. Cook, mashing garlic mixture with back of spatula, until fragrant, about 45 seconds. Stir garlic mixture into snow peas, then toss in steak. Whisk hoisin sauce mixture to recombine, pour into pan, and cook until thickened, about 1 minute. Stir in cashews and transfer to platter. Serve.

Nuttiest-Ever Coffee Cake

I love pecan coffee cake, but you can barely taste the nuts in my recipe, and the cake is dry. I'd like a recipe that shouts 'Nuts!' –Sarah Willmore, Abilene, Texas

Most coffee cakes are nothing more than plain old yellow cake hiding under a crumb topping. They are light and fluffy when they should be moist and rich. And even when the texture is right, often the flavor is not. Why bother with a coffee cake that just whispers (instead of shouts) "nuts"?

A Bundt pan is the traditional choice for coffee cake. Besides producing an attractive, sculptured cake, the pan's shape helps bake the cake from the inside, which is essential when you've got a heavy batter.

Most cake recipes follow the same technique: Cream butter and sugar, beat in eggs, and alternate additions of dry ingredients and milk. This method requires five to eight minutes of mixer action and whips a fair amount of air into the batter—perfect for a fluffy yellow cake but all wrong for my idea of coffee cake, which should be rich, moist, and luxurious. I tried a variety of other methods without success until I remembered a little-known cake-mixing method in which softened butter is beaten with some of the liquid ingredients directly into the flour mixture for just two minutes. The butter coats the flour, making the cake rich and tender. And without all of the whipping action, the batter is both more dense (a good thing) and more rich (an even better thing). The cake was still on the dry side, though, and the solution was to replace the milk with sour cream.

My favorite element in any coffee cake is the streusel layer swirled through the middle. But I could add only so much streusel before it sank to the bottom. To intensify the flavor of the streusel, I toasted the nuts (a step omitted by most recipe writers), but the cake was still lacking in nut flavor.

I tried a variety of techniques, from lining the cake pan with ground nuts to adding whole and roughly chopped nuts to the batter. The winning technique, which made this recipe go from good to great, emerged when I finely ground toasted pecans and added them directly to the flour mixture, making something like a "pecan flour." Now every bite—not just the streusel—was shouting "Nuts!" –Katie Henderson

Ground pecans pull double duty as an ingredient in both the cake and the swirl of sweet streusel. A glaze—Tropical Orange is pictured here—makes the perfect finishing touch.

PECAN SOUR CREAM COFFEE CAKE

SERVES 12 TO 16

Very soft butter (see photo, above right) can be incorporated into the cake easily, whereas cold or even cool butter will form unblended nuggets in the batter. You can toast, cool, and grind the nuts for both the streusel and cake together. See page 14 for tips on toasting nuts.

Streusel

- 1/2 cup pecans, toasted, cooled, and ground fine
- 3 tablespoons dark brown sugar
- 1 tablespoon all-purpose flour
- 1 teaspoon ground cinnamon

Cake

- 16 tablespoons (2 sticks) unsalted butter, cut into 1/2-inch pieces, at room temperature, plus 1 tablespoon softened butter for greasing pan
- 6 large eggs
- 1 3/4 cups sour cream
- 1/4 cup maple syrup
- 1 1/2 tablespoons vanilla extract
- 3 cups all-purpose flour
- 1/2 cup pecans, toasted, cooled, and ground fine
- 1 1/4 cups granulated sugar
- 1 1/2 tablespoons baking powder
- 1 1/4 teaspoons baking soda
- 1 teaspoon salt
- 1 recipe glaze (see page 28)

(continued on page 18)

Getting It Right
OH-SO-SOFT BUTTER

Our coffee cake requires room-temperature butter. You'll know the butter is soft enough when the weight of a dinner knife causes the blade to glide right through the butter with no resistance.

Getting It Right
A VERY FINE GRIND

Because some of the nuts are added directly to the cake batter, they must be ground very finely. Use a food processor to grind the toasted and cooled nuts until they are sandy. But do not overprocess the nuts, either, or they will form a paste and clump together. In a pinch, you can use a knife to chop the nuts very finely, but don't stop until you get the proper texture, as shown in the photo.

Toasted Pecans

Ground Pecans

Coffee Cake

continued from page 17

1. For the streusel Combine pecans, brown sugar, flour, and cinnamon in small bowl and set aside.

2. For the cake Adjust oven rack to lowest position and heat oven to 350 degrees. Grease 12-cup nonstick Bundt pan with 1 tablespoon softened butter. Whisk eggs, sour cream, maple syrup, and vanilla together in medium bowl.

3. With electric mixer, mix flour, pecans, sugar, baking powder, baking soda, and salt on lowest setting in large bowl until combined. Add room-temperature butter and half of egg mixture and beat on lowest setting, taking care not to splatter ingredients, until mixture starts to come together, about 15 seconds. Scrape down sides of bowl, add remaining egg mixture, and beat on medium speed until batter is light and fluffy, about 2 minutes (scrape down sides of bowl again after 1 minute).

4. Add 5 cups batter to prepared Bundt pan, using rubber spatula to smooth out surface. Sprinkle streusel evenly over batter and then cover with remaining batter, spreading it out evenly.

5. Bake until skewer inserted into middle of cake comes out with a few crumbs attached, about 60 minutes. Cool cake in pan on wire rack for 30 minutes, then invert onto wire rack to cool completely before glazing, about 1 hour.

6. Using fork or whisk, drizzle glaze over top and sides of cake. Slice and serve.

Make Ahead

The finished cake can be wrapped in plastic and stored at room temperature for up to 3 days. If you want to plan ahead even further, wrap the cooled but unglazed cake in two layers of plastic and then one layer of foil and freeze the cake for several weeks. Defrost the wrapped cake overnight on the counter, glaze, and serve.

Dressing Up: Pan-Seared Steak

Caramelized onions dress up a simple pan-seared steak, but they need to cook for a long, long time—or do they?

My favorite steakhouse serves my favorite steak (a strip steak) with a pile of caramelized onions. Glossy and rich, the onions turn a simple seared steak into something special enough to command $28. I had to wonder: Could I buy a good strip steak for about $6 and some onions with pocket change and replicate this dish at home?

Probably. But I realized there was one pretty big obstacle: Caramelizing onions takes lots of time and requires patience. At a restaurant, some unlucky prep cook gets to peel, slice, and caramelize bags of onions in the morning. I don't mind peeling and slicing onions at home, but it seemed silly to spend 40 minutes browning onions to sauce a steak that cooks in just eight minutes.

After several false starts in the test kitchen, I hit upon a shortcut. I cooked the onions for about 10 minutes, or until lightly browned, and then added balsamic vinegar to the pan. Two minutes later the onions were soft and fully browned. How can two minutes of cooking time with vinegar eliminate 30 minutes of caramelizing time?

Well, I'm relying on some culinary sleight of hand here. The sugar in the vinegar (enhanced by the addition of a little brown sugar) speeds up the browning process, and the steam generated by the simmering vinegar softens the onions in a flash. Finally, the vinegar tints the onions brown. My balsamic onion sauce may not taste exactly like caramelized onions, but it's pretty close.

Finally, some pointers on pan-searing steaks. For a nicely browned and flavorful crust, pat the steaks dry with paper towels, use enough heat (medium-high is best), and don't fuss with the steaks as they cook (just one turn will do). You need a heavy skillet and must get it (and some oil) good and hot. Finally, choose steaks between 1 and 1¼ inches thick; they will cook through evenly without burning on the exterior. Sounds simple . . . because it is. **–Stephanie Alleyne**

PAN-SEARED STEAKS WITH BALSAMIC ONIONS

SERVES 4

The cooking times here yield medium-rare steaks. Because the sauce is so rich, we think three steaks (the maximum you can fit comfortably in a large skillet) will feed four people when sliced thin.

- 3 tablespoons vegetable oil
- 2 large red onions, peeled and cut into ½-inch rounds, rings separated
  Salt and pepper
- 3 boneless 8- to 10-ounce strip steaks, 1 to 1¼ inches thick
- 3 garlic cloves, minced
- ½ cup plus 1 tablespoon balsamic vinegar
- 1 teaspoon minced fresh rosemary
- 1 tablespoon light brown sugar

1. Heat 2 tablespoons oil in large skillet over medium heat until shimmering. Add onions and ½ teaspoon salt and cook, stirring frequently, until lightly browned, about 10 minutes. Transfer onions to bowl. Wipe out skillet with paper towels.

2. Add remaining 1 tablespoon oil to skillet and cook over medium-high heat until just smoking. Meanwhile, pat steaks dry with paper towels and season with salt and pepper. Cook steaks, without moving, until browned on first side, 4 to 5 minutes. Flip steaks and continue to cook until browned on second side, 3 to 4 minutes more. Transfer steaks to plate and wrap with foil.

3. Discard fat in skillet, return onions to pan, and set over medium heat. Add garlic and cook until fragrant, about 30 seconds. Add ½ cup vinegar, rosemary, and brown sugar and cook, scraping up browned bits with wooden spoon, until thick and syrupy, about 2 minutes. Pour any accumulated steak juices into pan along with remaining 1 tablespoon vinegar. Season with salt and pepper.

4. Slice steaks crosswise into ¼-inch slices and transfer to platter. Spoon onions and sauce over steak. Serve.

Balsamic vinegar helps to brown the onions and enhances the flavor of a four-minute pan sauce.

Steak Lexicon

Confusing labels and multiple names make a trip to the meat counter a challenge, even for our intrepid shoppers. Use this guide to our favorite boneless steaks (all suitable for pan-searing) to make sure nothing gets lost in translation.

Strip Steak

Aliases: Top Loin Steak, Shell Steak, Sirloin Strip Steak, New York Strip Steak, Kansas City Strip Steak
Tasting Notes: Big beefy flavor with a nice chew. Fat is mostly around the perimeter.

Rib-Eye Steak

Aliases: Spencer Steak, Delmonico Steak
Tasting Notes: Fine, smooth texture and rich flavor. Noticeable pockets of fat throughout the meat.

Tenderloin Steak

Aliases: Filet Mignon, Châteaubriand, Tournedo
Tasting Notes: Very tender and extremely mild. The leanest of the premium steaks.

Not Just Plain Peas

They may be frozen, but peas need not be humble.

Although we think most vegetables are better fresh than frozen, peas are an exception. Their natural sugars turn to starch within hours after being picked, which means that fresh peas are mealy unless cooked the same day they are harvested. Frozen peas are harvested, cooked, and frozen within hours of being picked, which locks in their sweet flavor.

What's the best way to bring frozen peas back to life at home? Most cooks dump the peas into a pot of salted water or microwave them. Once tender, the peas are drained and tossed with butter and seasonings. This simple method isn't bad, but could I do better?

My first thought was to cook the peas in something more flavorful than salted water; I hoped the cooking liquid could also work as a sauce. So I piled ingredients into a saucepan and brought the liquid to a boil. Unfortunately, by the time the liquid reduced to a saucey consistency, the peas turned army green. I had better luck when I added the peas (still frozen) to an almost-finished sauce. By the time the peas were tender, they had soaked up plenty of flavor, and the sauce was the perfect consistency.

You can use almost any liquid (orange juice, cream, or chicken broth) and add spices, herbs, toasted nuts, or ham to jazz things up. One last secret: Whatever seasonings you choose, add a pinch of sugar to enhance the flavor of the peas. –Stephanie Alleyne

For a side dish worthy of a holiday table, cook peas in a flavorful sauce, like this one with ham steak, onion, and cream.

CREAMY PEAS WITH HAM AND ONION SERVES 4 TO 6

Because the cream is reduced to the proper consistency before the peas are added to the pan, the peas should be cooked with the cover on. The ham and onion add plenty of sweetness, so this recipe doesn't require any sugar.

- 2 tablespoons unsalted butter
- 6 ounces ham steak, cut into ½-inch pieces
- 1 red onion, halved and sliced thin
- ⅔ cup heavy cream
- 1 tablespoon chopped fresh tarragon or parsley
  Salt and pepper
- 1 pound frozen peas, not thawed

1. Melt butter in large skillet over medium-high heat. Add ham and cook until browned, about 5 minutes. Add onion and cook until soft and beginning to brown, about 5 minutes.

2. Add cream, tarragon, and salt and pepper to taste. Bring to simmer and cook until cream just begins to thicken, about 3 minutes. Stir in peas, cover, and cook until tender, about 5 minutes. Adjust seasonings with salt and pepper and serve.

SMASHED MINTY PEAS
SERVES 4 TO 6

Be careful not to overprocess the peas. They can go from smashed to pureed in seconds.

- ½ cup low-sodium chicken broth
- 1 pound frozen peas, not thawed
- 2 cups chopped Boston or Bibb lettuce
- 2 tablespoons chopped fresh mint
- 4 tablespoons unsalted butter
- ½ teaspoon sugar
  Salt and pepper

1. Bring broth, peas, lettuce, mint, butter, sugar, and salt and pepper to taste to simmer in medium saucepan over medium-high heat. Cover and cook until peas are tender, 8 to 10 minutes.

2. Transfer to food processor and pulse until coarsely mashed, about ten 1-second pulses Adjust seasonings with salt and pepper and serve.

DILLY PEAS AND CARROTS SERVES 4 TO 6

Because carrots require more cooking time than peas, they get a head start in this recipe.

- 2 cups baby carrots, cut crosswise into thirds
- ½ cup juice plus 1 tablespoon grated zest from 2 oranges
  Salt
- 1 pound frozen peas, not thawed
- 2 tablespoons unsalted butter
- ½ teaspoon sugar
- 1 tablespoon chopped fresh dill

Bring carrots, orange juice, and ½ teaspoon salt to simmer in medium saucepan over medium-high heat. Cover and cook until carrots are crisp-tender, about 4 minutes. Add peas, orange zest, butter, sugar, and dill, increase heat to high, and cook, uncovered, until peas are tender and liquid is syrupy, about 5 minutes. Adjust seasonings with salt and serve.

CURRIED PEAS
SERVES 4 TO 6

If you don't have regular yogurt or sour cream on hand, whole milk or low-fat yogurt will also work in this recipe.

- 2 tablespoons olive oil
- 1 red onion, chopped fine
  Salt
- 2 garlic cloves, minced
- ½ teaspoon curry powder
- 1 teaspoon ground cumin
- ½ cup low-sodium chicken broth
- ½ teaspoon light brown sugar
- 1 pound frozen peas, not thawed
- 1 cup sliced almonds, toasted
- ⅓ cup yogurt or sour cream
- 2 tablespoons chopped fresh cilantro
  Pepper

1. Heat oil in large skillet over medium-high heat until shimmering. Add onion and ½ teaspoon salt and cook until soft and beginning to brown, about 5 minutes. Add garlic, curry powder, and cumin and cook until fragrant, about 1 minute. Add broth and brown sugar and bring to boil.

2. Stir in peas and almonds and cook, uncovered, until peas are tender, about 5 minutes. Off heat, stir in yogurt, cilantro, and salt and pepper to taste. Serve.

Crispy Roast Chicken and Potatoes

I love the idea of roasting a chicken together with potatoes, but how do you get the chicken really crispy while keeping the potatoes from getting really greasy? –Daniel Smith, Berlin, Conn.

We'll take our chicken and potatoes extra crispy, please.

The Secret Is in the Starch

After searching in vain for a foolproof recipe for crispy roast chicken, we stumbled upon a secret ingredient: plain old cornstarch. Sprinkling just 2 teaspoons of cornstarch over the chicken before putting it into the oven helped to form a crispy, golden crust. How does this work? Before sprinkling the bird with cornstarch, we used a skewer to poke holes in the skin. In the oven, the fat escapes through these holes, mixes with the starch, and creates an extra-crisp coating.

CORNSTARCH
Not just for thickening.

At first glance, roasting chicken and potatoes together seems easy enough. Just toss some potatoes in the roasting pan with a whole bird, right? Well, that's exactly what I did, and I ended up with soggy, greasy potatoes. I also ended up with overcooked breast meat, having roasted the chicken breast side up at 400 degrees, the temperature most recipes recommend.

The test kitchen, having roasted thousands of chickens over the years, has come up with a slightly fussy method (calling for high heat, a V-rack, and three turns in the oven) that keeps the breast meat from overcooking. This method also produces fairly crisp skin. But I wanted *really* crisp skin.

I noticed a curious phenomenon during roasting: The rendered fat was literally boiling beneath the skin. I figured that this liquid would keep the skin from getting truly crispy, no matter how high the heat. Maybe poking holes in the skin would release this fat and allow for better crisping. This technique did let the fat seep out from beneath the skin, but it actually left the skin soggy and greasy. Perhaps dredging the chicken in flour, just as is done for fried chicken, would help. Nope. The flour simply turned gummy. On my next try I replaced the flour with a sprinkling of cornstarch, a trick used in many Asian stir-fry recipes. By the time I had flipped the chicken breast side up, I knew I was on the right track. The cornstarch was sizzling in the rendering fat and creating an extra-crunchy coating. For one last test, I cranked the oven up to 475 degrees. This super-hot oven made for an even more superior bird, its skin deeply browned and crisp, its meat moist and tender.

To solve the problem of the soggy, greasy potatoes, I tried giving them less oven time: Instead of starting the potatoes along with the chicken, I added them to the roasting pan when I turned the chicken for the third (and last) time. To keep the fat from smoking in this very hot oven, I lined the roasting pan with foil. Then, just before I added the potatoes, I gathered the corners of the foil and discarded the rendered fat (often as much as ¼ cup) that had collected over the first 30 minutes of cooking time. After discarding the fat and foil, I spread the potatoes, cut side down, in the bottom of the hot roasting pan, replaced the V-rack (with the chicken breast side up), and returned the pan to the oven. No more greasy potatoes!

Two minor problems to solve and I would be done. The first was that fat was pooling around the thighs as the chicken cooled on the V-rack. This problem was easily solved by placing the roasted chicken on an angel-food-cake pan insert for cooling (sitting the bird on an empty soda can also worked). Granted, the chicken looked a bit odd standing upright on the counter, but this was the best way to allow excess fat and juices to drain. The second problem was that a number of folks in the test kitchen thought that the potatoes were lacking in flavor (chicken flavor, that is). To add chicken flavor, I simply poured the juices from the cavity of the chicken (as I was moving it for resting) onto the potatoes and popped them back in the oven to finish cooking. Ten minutes later, they were deep brown and infused with chicken flavor, minus the fat.

Not the simplest roast chicken in the world, perhaps, but by far the best roast chicken and potatoes I've ever tasted!

–Jeremy Sauer

CRISPY ROAST CHICKEN AND POTATOES SERVES 4

If you have it, a nonstick roasting pan works best here. If using a chicken larger than 4 pounds, the oven time will need to be lengthened slightly.

- 2 teaspoons cornstarch
  Salt
- 1 whole chicken (3½ to 4 pounds), giblets discarded, skin patted dry with paper towels
- 2 pounds small red potatoes, scrubbed and halved
- 2 teaspoons vegetable oil

1. Line roasting pan with foil, letting foil come up sides of pan. Adjust oven rack to middle position (8 to 10 inches from broiler element), place roasting pan on rack, and heat oven to 475 degrees. Coat V-rack with cooking spray.

2. Combine cornstarch and 2 teaspoons salt in small bowl. Use skewer to poke holes all over chicken skin. Rub cornstarch mixture evenly over chicken.

3. Remove roasting pan from oven. Place chicken, wing side up, in V-rack, then place V-rack in roasting pan (see photo 1). Roast chicken 15 minutes. Remove roasting pan from oven and, using wad of paper towels, flip chicken so that other wing is facing up. Roast 15 minutes.

4. Meanwhile toss potatoes, oil, and ½ teaspoon salt in medium bowl. Remove roasting pan from oven and, with potholder, carefully transfer V-rack with chicken to rimmed baking sheet. Gather up foil by its corners, capturing any fat and juices, and discard. Arrange potatoes, cut side down, in roasting pan. Using wad of paper towels, flip chicken breast side up in V-rack. Place V-rack back in roasting pan (photo 2) and roast chicken until instant-read thermometer inserted into thickest part of thigh registers 170 degrees, about 20 minutes.

5. Using wad of paper towels, remove chicken from V-rack and pour juices from cavity into roasting pan with potatoes. Place chicken on angel-food-cake pan insert or empty soda can to rest upright for 10 to 15 minutes. Meanwhile, toss potatoes in chicken juices (photo 3), return to oven, and cook until well browned and crisp, 10 to 15 minutes. Carve chicken and serve with potatoes.

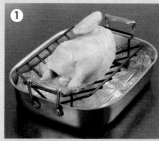

Roasting Secrets
TURNING THE BIRD

1. Place the chicken, wing side up, in a greased V-rack. Place the V-rack in a preheated roasting pan lined with foil and roast for 15 minutes. Flip the chicken so that the other wing faces up and roast for another 15 minutes.

2. Remove the V-rack from the roasting pan, discard the foil and grease, add the potatoes to the empty roasting pan, turn the chicken breast side up, and return the V-rack to the pan. Roast for another 20 minutes or until done.

3. Remove the roasting rack and chicken, tipping the juices from the cavity back into the roasting pan. Toss the potatoes with the chicken juices and return to the oven to finish cooking.

---

on the side: GREEN SALAD WITH ROASTED PEARS

In my house, salads are not optional, at least when it comes to dinner. I usually just put a big bowl of greens on the table and everyone is happy. But once in a while, I want something more interesting. Salad can be fun, right?

One obvious choice—a recipe that is served at many restaurants these days—is a roasted pear and blue cheese salad. Yes, it's more work than throwing some bagged lettuce in a bowl and adding bottled dressing, but it seems worth the small amount of trouble.

I first had to decide which varieties of pear would be best. I found that Bosc pears were generally mealy and flat tasting after roasting; Anjou and Bartlett were much better choices (see page 28 for more information on pear varieties). It also became clear that roasting ripe pears is a mistake—they become mushy before they brown and just fall apart in the salad bowl. The good news is that this recipe works best with harder pears, the type most often available in the supermarket.

But I learned that even rock-hard pears can turn to mush if roasted incorrectly. At lower oven temperatures, the pears had the texture of baby food by the time they were browned. For nicely caramelized pears with some bite, I found that a hot oven was key; I even had to preheat the baking sheet to expedite browning. Tossing the pears with a little maple syrup helped, too.

Fancy food writers would wax eloquent about pairing the sharp flavor of blue cheese and assertive greens like watercress with the sweet flavor of roasted pears. Whatever. This salad tastes great, it's easy to make, and your family or your lucky guests will think that you snagged the recipe from a restaurant chef. Not bad for a few rock-hard pears and a hot oven! –Eva Katz

Finally, a use for those rock-hard pears sold in most supermarkets. Roasting the pears unlocks their sweetness and makes them the star in this simple salad.

GREEN SALAD WITH ROASTED PEARS AND BLUE CHEESE SERVES 4 TO 6

Pears can be roasted up to three hours in advance, but keep them at room temperature until ready to serve.

- ¼ cup maple syrup
- 1 tablespoon grated fresh ginger
- 3 firm pears, preferably Anjou or Bartlett (see page 28)
  Salt and pepper
- 2 tablespoons cider vinegar
- 1 small shallot, minced
- 3 tablespoons extra-virgin olive oil
- 2 bunches watercress, thick stems removed (8 cups)
- 1 head Bibb lettuce, torn into bite-sized pieces (6 cups)
- 1 cup crumbled blue cheese

1. Line rimmed baking sheet with foil. Adjust oven rack to lower-middle position, place baking sheet on rack, and heat oven to 500 degrees. Whisk syrup and ginger together in bowl. Peel and quarter pears lengthwise. Core pears, then halve each quarter lengthwise.

2. Toss pears with 3 tablespoons syrup mixture. Spread pears on preheated baking sheet and season with salt and pepper. Roast until browned on bottom, about 15 minutes. Flip each slice and roast until tender and deep golden brown, about 5 minutes. Let pears cool on baking sheet while preparing salad.

3. Whisk vinegar, shallot, oil, and salt and pepper to taste into remaining syrup mixture. Combine watercress and lettuce in large serving bowl. Gently toss with vinaigrette. Scatter pears and blue cheese on top and serve.

A Better Breakfast Casserole

When developing our breakfast casserole recipe, we found that a corner or two of waffle often wouldn't fully absorb the custard, and some unlucky test cook would end up with a mouthful of dry waffle. To remedy the situation, we weighted the casserole and then waited some more (refrigerating the casserole for at least one hour). We found two easy ways to weight the assembled casserole before baking.

A. Press plastic wrap directly onto the surface of the casserole, top with another 8-inch-square baking dish, then weight with heavy canned goods. **B.** Press plastic wrap directly onto the surface of the casserole, then place two 1-pound boxes of brown sugar on the plastic wrap and top with a cast-iron pan.

Because it can be assembled the night before, I love the idea of a breakfast casserole. But my recipe is too heavy and sort of bland. Can you come up with something that's lighter and tastier? –Claudia Coleman, Mobile, Ala.

In its simplest form, a breakfast casserole consists of day-old bread soaked in custard (eggs and cream) and then baked until golden and fluffy. Most recipes also add sausage and cheese. The finished dish is so rich you have to let out your belt before breakfast even begins. This recipe should be lighter and—here's the catch—tastier.

After making several over-the-top recipes, I was convinced that the custard was obliterating the other flavors. I could barely taste the sausage and cheese—they added heaviness but not much else. I knew I needed to lighten the custard. Most recipes are in the range of four to eight eggs and two to three cups of cream. I couldn't do much about the eggs—I found that six was the right number—but I quickly concluded that this dish was best made with far less cream—just 1½ cups.

But did I really need cream? To my surprise, a casserole made with whole milk was actually preferred to one made with cream. (Low-fat milk wasn't bad either, but skim milk didn't work.) There was still plenty of fat in my working recipe (from the sausage and cheese), but now you could taste those ingredients instead of just the dairy richness of the custard.

To pump up the flavor even further, I had some other tricks to try. I tested four types of breakfast sausage (sage, hot, maple, and regular). Tasters liked the touch of sweetness added by the maple sausage. As for the cheese, cheddar and Monterey Jack are the standards, but cheddar is far more flavorful and got the thumbs up in the test kitchen.

Up until this point, I had been using white sandwich bread (as most recipes suggest); I wondered if a change might be in order. I tried French and Italian loaves as well as ciabatta and brioche, but they were all too chewy or too strongly flavored. Challah, a slightly sweet, egg-rich Jewish bread, was better but still not perfect. My tasters liked its sweet yeasty flavor but not its dense texture.

After scouring the bread aisle for something sweet but not too heavy, I wandered into the frozen food section and found what I was searching for: frozen waffles. Their airy, fluffy texture made the casserole much lighter than challah or even sandwich bread. And the flavor combination of the waffles and the maple sausage was such a hit with tasters that I decided to replace some of the milk in the custard with maple syrup.

–Jeremy Sauer

Company coming? Wake up to this make-ahead casserole that calls for frozen waffles instead of the typical white bread.

MAPLE SAUSAGE AND WAFFLE CASSEROLE
SERVES 6

Depending on their size and shape, you will need 6 to 8 waffles. Belgian-style frozen waffles are too thick for this recipe. To double the recipe, use a 13 by 9-inch baking dish and increase the baking time by 30 to 40 minutes.

6–8	frozen waffles (½ inch thick)
12	ounces maple breakfast sausage, crumbled
	Unsalted butter (for dish)
1½	cups shredded cheddar cheese
6	large eggs
1¼	cups whole or low-fat milk
¼	cup maple syrup
¼	teaspoon salt
⅛	teaspoon pepper

1. Adjust oven rack to middle position and heat oven to 375 degrees. Arrange waffles in single layer on baking sheet. Bake until crisp, about 10 minutes per side.

2. Brown sausage in nonstick skillet over medium heat, breaking it apart with spoon, 8 to 10 minutes. Drain on paper-towel-lined plate.

3. Butter 8-inch-square baking dish. Add half of waffles in single layer. Add half of sausage and ½ cup cheese. Repeat layering of waffles, sausage, and ½ cup cheese. Whisk eggs, milk, maple syrup, salt, and pepper in medium bowl until combined. Pour egg mixture evenly over casserole. Following photos A or B (above left), cover baking dish with plastic wrap and place weights on top. Refrigerate for at least 1 hour or overnight.

4. Adjust oven rack to middle position and heat oven to 325 degrees. Let casserole stand at room temperature for 20 minutes. Uncover casserole and sprinkle remaining ½ cup cheese over top. Bake until edges and center are puffed, 45 to 50 minutes. Cool 5 minutes. Cut into pieces and serve.

Taste Test: Frozen Waffles

Although we typically make our waffles from scratch, the use of store-bought waffles in our Maple Sausage and Waffle Casserole had us wondering which brand was best. We corralled eight brands of frozen waffles ranging from ordinary (Pillsbury Homestyle) to organic (Lifestream Hemp Plus) and tasted them topped with our winning maple syrup (see page 30). Eggo Homestyle was the undisputed winner. These waffles were praised for their buttery, eggy flavor and crisp exterior.

EGGO The best of the eight brands of frozen waffles we tasted.

Waking Up Winter Fruit Salads

A simple, sweet dressing is the secret to a superior fruit salad.

Paradise Found

There's no need for fruit salads to hibernate just because it's winter. Supermarkets carry an array of tropical fruit at this time of year, and even good berries and grapes can be found in most stores.

But most fruit salads—even those made with great summer fruit—are disappointingly dry and bland. The problem? Many cooks just toss fruit together in a bowl. What's needed to add both moisture and flavor is a dressing.

Our dressing consists of a "simple syrup" made from nothing more than cooked sugar and water. Flavor is added by way of citrus zest, chopped crystallized ginger, vanilla, nuts, coconut, and even fresh herbs. Because fruits can vary in their sweetness, the recipes call for a range in the amount of simple syrup. If the fruit tastes sweet on its own, use the smaller amount; if it's tart, use the larger amount. –Eva Katz

PARADISE FOUND SERVES 4 TO 6
Toast the coconut in a small skillet over medium heat, stirring it occasionally, until the shreds are lightly browned, about 6 minutes.

- 1/2 **small ripe pineapple, peeled, cored, and cut into 1/4-inch chunks**
- 2 **ripe mangos, peeled, pitted, and cut into 1/4-inch slices**
- 1 **cup unsalted macadamia nuts, chopped**
- 1/4 **cup sweetened shredded coconut, toasted**
- 2–4 **tablespoons Simple Syrup (see box)**

Layer pineapple and mango in serving bowl. Top with nuts and coconut and drizzle with syrup. Toss and serve.

Make Ahead
With the exception of recipes that use banana, fruit salads can be layered in a serving bowl, covered with plastic wrap, and refrigerated for several hours. When ready to serve, drizzle with syrup and toss to combine.

BAHAMA MAMA SERVES 4 TO 6
Because the banana will start to discolor pretty quickly, this salad should be served as soon as it is ready.

- 1 **tablespoon grated lime zest**
- 1 **tablespoon dark rum (optional)**
- 2–4 **tablespoons Simple Syrup (see box)**
- 1/2 **small ripe pineapple, peeled, cored, and cut into 1-inch chunks**
- 2 **medium ripe papayas, halved, peeled, and seeded, flesh cut into 1-inch chunks**
- 2 **large ripe bananas, peeled and cut into 1/4-inch-thick rounds**

Mix zest, rum, and syrup in small bowl and let sit 10 minutes. Layer pineapple, papaya, and banana in serving bowl. Drizzle with syrup. Toss and serve.

HOLLYWOOD HILLS SERVES 4 TO 6
Star fruit dresses up a simple berry salad. Look for crystallized ginger in the spice aisle at the supermarket.

- 2 **tablespoons crystallized ginger, chopped fine**
- 2–4 **tablespoons Simple Syrup (see box)**
- 2 **cups blueberries**
- 1 1/2 **cups blackberries**
- 1 1/2 **cups raspberries**
- 1 **star fruit, cut into 1/4-inch slices**

Mix ginger and syrup in small bowl and let sit 10 minutes. Layer berries in serving bowl. Arrange star fruit on top and drizzle with syrup. Toss and serve.

LOVERS' LANE SERVES 4 TO 6
When shopping for passion fruit, look for specimens that yield to gentle pressure. Firm fruit are not ripe.

- 1/2 **teaspoon vanilla extract**
- 2–4 **tablespoons Simple Syrup (see box)**
- 2 **ripe mangos, peeled, pitted, and cut into 1/4-inch slices**
- 1/2 **ripe papaya, peeled, seeded, and cut into 1/4-inch slices**
- 2 **ripe passion fruit, cut in half and seeds and soft, juicy flesh scooped out**

Mix vanilla and syrup in small bowl. Layer mango and papaya in serving bowl

Bahama Mama

Hollywood Hills

SIMPLE SYRUP
MAKES ABOUT 3/4 CUP, ENOUGH TO DRESS 3 TO 6 SALADS
Simple syrup keeps well in the refrigerator for up to 2 months.

- 1/2 **cup sugar**
- 1/4 **cup water**

Bring sugar and water to simmer in small saucepan over medium heat and cook until sugar dissolves, about 3 minutes. Transfer syrup to airtight container and refrigerate until needed.

and spoon passion fruit on top. Drizzle with syrup. Toss and serve.

THE GREEN MONSTAH
SERVES 4 TO 6
A fruity tribute to the Boston Red Sox, our hometown heroes.

- 1 **small honeydew melon, halved, seeded, and flesh scooped out with melon baller**
- 2 **cups green seedless grapes, halved**
- 2 **ripe kiwis, peeled, halved lengthwise, and cut into 1/4-inch-thick slices**
- 2–4 **tablespoons Simple Syrup (see box)**
- 2 **tablespoons thinly sliced fresh mint**

Layer melon, grapes, and kiwis in serving bowl. Drizzle with syrup and sprinkle with mint. Toss and serve.

MIAMI VICE SERVES 4 TO 6
For tips on peeling and sectioning citrus fruits, see the step-by-step photos on page 29.

- 1 **tablespoon grated lime zest**
- 2–4 **tablespoons Simple Syrup (see box)**
- 3 **grapefruit, peeled and sectioned**
- 3 **navel or Valencia oranges, peeled and sectioned**
- 3 **clementines or tangerines, peeled and sectioned**

Mix zest and syrup in small bowl and let sit 10 minutes. Layer grapefruit, oranges, and clementines in serving bowl. Drizzle with syrup. Toss and serve.

Lovers' Lane

The Green Monstah

Miami Vice

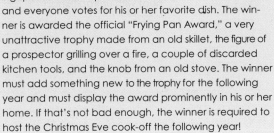

Christmas Eve Cook-Off

Debie Farris, San Jose, Calif. My family's Christmas Eve smorgasbord has turned into a cook-off. A noncooking spouse makes up a formal ballot, and everyone votes for his or her favorite dish. The winner is awarded the official "Frying Pan Award," a very unattractive trophy made from an old skillet, the figure of a prospector grilling over a fire, a couple of discarded kitchen tools, and the knob from an old stove. The winner must add something new to the trophy for the following year and must display the award prominently in his or her home. If that's not bad enough, the winner is required to host the Christmas Eve cook-off the following year!

Home, Sweet Home

Rose Bishop, Sag Harbor, N.Y.
My sister and I helped my mom make this pretty gingerbread house. It has all our favorite candies: Necco wafers for the roof, bubble gum shutters, spearmint leaves as shrubs, jelly beans to make a walkway, a chocolate cookie fence, and rock candy lollipops for trees. My mom even found a black licorice candy that looks like our dog.

A Chocolate Factory

Yvonne Berkovich, Seattle, Wash.
For the past 40 years, my extended family has gathered in Edmonton, Alberta, to hand-dip chocolates for the Christmas season. Not only is it a wonderful time to catch up on family news, but our efforts result in a delicious memory. We create approximately 180 pounds of chocolates, about 5,000 pieces. Cream-based, flavored fondants are made in advance, and we dip up to 15 flavors.

Thanks for the Memories:

New Year's Eve around the World

Michelle Guenard, Montreal, Quebec My favorite food memory is courtesy of my mom. She grew up in Holland and somehow ended up falling in love with a country boy from Canada. We didn't have a lot of money, but every New Year's Eve Mom would take my brothers and me to the same exotic food store. This was the one and only time that we were allowed to put anything we wanted in the shopping cart, as long as we'd never tasted it before! Thanks to this tradition we got to taste frogs legs, escargot, blue cheeses, and more. I think this was Mom's way of bringing other cultures to the prairies of Alberta.

We've re-engineered chicken Parmesan by breading the chicken after it is cooked—not before.

Skillet Chicken Parmesan

My kids love chicken Parmesan, but it's a lot of work for a dish that's usually soggy, bland, and greasy. –Lucille Arena, Collegeville, Pa.

Most recipes for chicken Parmesan are casserole-like creations that bury breaded cutlets in a puddle of sauce and a blanket of cheese. The soggy chicken, greasy breading, and bland cheese are rarely appealing. I figured that the only way to keep the breading from becoming soggy was to separate it from the chicken. Unconventional? Yes. But worth a try.

I browned chicken cutlets, added a quick tomato sauce and cheese, and then sprinkled toasted bread crumbs on the finished dish. The crumbs were crispy and no longer greasy. In fact, they were a bit dry and bland. I remedied this with a little olive oil, fresh basil, and Parmesan. Without breaded cutlets, the dish looked different, but the flavors were the same—maybe better because of the bread crumbs.

Rather than preparing tomato sauce in a separate pan, I wondered if I could just simmer the sauce ingredients with the chicken. Since the cutlets weren't breaded, there was no crisp coating to protect. This

worked better than I expected, with the chicken picking up the flavors of garlic, basil, and tomatoes from the sauce. My recipe now required just one pan and was ready in about 30 minutes.

My tasters still had one complaint—the cheese was bland. Despite its name, chicken Parmesan recipes invariably call for more mozzarella than Parmesan. When I tried the opposite, I found out why: Parmesan cooked up tough and dry. I had better luck when I replaced some of the bland mozzarella with provolone. The cheese was now gooey *and* flavorful. –Keri Fisher

SKILLET CHICKEN PARMESAN SERVES 4

To make fresh bread crumbs, grind 2 to 3 slices hearty white sandwich bread in the food processor.

1½	cups fresh bread crumbs
3	tablespoons olive oil
1¼	cups grated Parmesan
¼	cup chopped fresh basil
2	garlic cloves, minced
1	(28-ounce) can crushed tomatoes
	Salt and pepper
½	cup all-purpose flour

4	boneless, skinless chicken breasts (1½ pounds), halved horizontally (see page 28)
3	tablespoons vegetable oil
¾	cup shredded mozzarella
¾	cup shredded provolone

1. Toast bread crumbs in large nonstick skillet over medium-high heat until browned, about 5 minutes. Transfer to bowl. Toss with 1 tablespoon olive oil, ¼ cup Parmesan, and half of basil. In separate bowl, combine remaining olive oil, ¼ cup Parmesan, remaining basil, garlic, tomatoes, and salt and pepper to taste.

2. Place flour in dish. Season chicken with salt and pepper and coat with flour. Heat 2 tablespoons vegetable oil in now-empty skillet over medium-high heat until shimmering. Add 4 cutlets and cook until golden brown on both sides, about 5 minutes total. Transfer to plate and repeat with remaining cutlets and vegetable oil.

3. Reduce heat to medium-low and add tomato mixture to empty skillet. Return cutlets to pan in even layer, pressing down to cover with sauce. Sprinkle mozzarella, provolone, and remaining Parmesan over chicken. Cover with lid and cook until cheese is melted, about 5 minutes. Sprinkle with bread crumb mixture and serve.

FOOD FACT: *Spaghetti is America's favorite kind of pasta, with 40% of those surveyed by the National Pasta Association putting it at the top of their list. Runners-up include lasagna (12%), macaroni and cheese (6%), fettuccine (6%), linguine (3%), and angel hair (2%).*

Cheesy, Creamy Carbonara

I love pasta carbonara, but every time I make it at home, it turns out dry and pasty instead of creamy and cheesy. What am I doing wrong? –Jane Edney, Fairhope, Ala.

The Daily Grind

Preground pepper gave our carbonara a timid, dusty flavor. We switched to freshly ground, but it still wasn't assertive enough. Instead of increasing the heat with untraditional ingredients such as cayenne pepper or red pepper flakes, we opted to "bloom" the heat out of the black pepper by toasting it in rendered bacon fat before adding it to the pasta. This technique brought out the pepper's earthy complexity as well as more than enough heat.

Freshly ground pepper is a must for carbonara.

Carbonara is fast (it takes just 20 minutes to prepare) and convenient (it relies on staples most cooks always have on hand). When properly executed, steaming hot pasta marries with fresh eggs and cheese to create a sauce that drapes like a soft white blanket. Add to that some salty, chewy bacon, minced garlic, and a good hit of black pepper and you can't possibly go wrong. Or so I thought.

The results of my first test kitchen experiments would have worked better as wallpaper paste than pasta sauce. After starting out promisingly creamy, they seized up into a tangle of noodles so thick that I had to cut individual portions out of the serving dish with a knife. The problem? Cooked pasta is like a sponge. When I tossed the hot pasta with the eggs and cheese, the pasta quickly absorbed all of the liquid, leaving me with dry noodles strewn with chunks of cheese.

I added white wine, an ingredient in some traditional recipes. The wine did help to keep things moist and also added a touch of acidity to balance the richness of the eggs and cheese. But I couldn't add too much wine or the sauce would be boozy. A bit of heavy cream helped, but my sauce was still too thick. More heavy cream (often added in Americanized recipes) deadened the other flavors. The solution turned out to be right in the pasta pot. A ½ cup of reserved pasta cooking water loosened the sauce to just the right consistency.

Next on my list was selecting the type of cheese and bacon to use. Pecorino Romano, a sharply flavored sheep's milk cheese, was pre-

ferred over the milder-tasting Parmesan (you can use Parmesan in a pinch); the Pecorino melted more smoothly, making for a creamier texture. As for the bacon, the more authentic choice, pancetta (unsmoked Italian bacon), was outdone by American thick-cut bacon, as tasters welcomed its salty-smoky-sweet pork flavor.

Raw minced garlic was deemed overpowering, even after the heat of the pasta had mellowed its bite, so I decided to cook the garlic briefly in the bacon drippings before adding it to the pasta. As for the pepper, tasters preferred fresh-ground to preground. I added it to the pan along with the garlic to bring out its flavor and heat.

This sauce was much creamier and more flavorful than any of my first attempts, and it was just as easy to prepare.

–Jeremy Sauer

CREAMY CARBONARA

SERVES 4 TO 6

Although we call for spaghetti in this recipe, you can substitute any long thin pasta, such as linguine or fettuccine. Parmesan cheese can be substituted for the Pecorino Romano, though the sauce will not be as creamy or as flavorful. To avoid curdling the eggs, be sure to whisk constantly when adding the hot ingredients to the egg mixture. If you like your food extra-peppery, increase the pepper to 1¹/₂ teaspoons.

- 3 large eggs
- 1 cup grated Pecorino Romano cheese
- 2 tablespoons heavy cream
- ¹/₂ pound thick-cut bacon, cut into ¹/₂-inch pieces
- 3 garlic cloves, minced
- 1 teaspoon pepper
- ¹/₂ cup white wine
- 1 tablespoon salt
- 1 pound spaghetti

1. Bring 4 quarts water to boil in large pot.

2. Whisk eggs, cheese, and cream together in medium bowl. Meanwhile, fry bacon in large skillet over medium heat until crisp, about 7 minutes. Using slotted spoon, transfer bacon to small bowl. Pour off all but 2 tablespoons of bacon fat. Add garlic and pepper to skillet, return to medium heat, and cook until fragrant, about 30 seconds. Slowly whisk garlic mixture into bowl with eggs.

3. Return skillet to medium heat, add wine, and simmer, scraping bottom of pan with wooden spoon to remove browned bits, until reduced by half, about 5 minutes. Slowly whisk wine mixture into egg mixture.

4. While wine is reducing, add salt and pasta to boiling water. Cook until al dente. Reserve 1 cup cooking water, drain pasta, and return to pot. Immediately pour egg mixture over pasta and toss well to combine with ½ cup reserved cooking water. Add bacon and thin sauce with remaining cooking water as necessary. Serve.

Bacon, eggs, and cheese deliver big flavor in this easy-to-prepare pasta dish.

Really Good Beef and Vegetable Soup

I know good restaurants use homemade beef stock in their soups. Is there a way to create something almost as good with canned broth? –Katherine Geddes, New York, N.Y.

The right cut of meat turns canned broth into a satisfying bowl of soup.

The Beefiest Cut

We tested a variety of cuts before landing on the right choice—blade steaks.

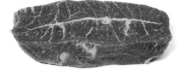

BLADE STEAK

Using homemade beef stock is a guaranteed method for producing great beef and vegetable soup, but most of us buy broth in a can and then try to doctor it up. Unfortunately, most of these quick fixes are ultimately unsatisfying. Could I start with canned broth and create a really good soup with tender, flavorful chunks of beef, a meaty broth, and perfectly cooked vegetables?

After some disappointing tests with meaty bones and canned broth, I realized this approach would take hours to yield good results. A restaurant might have all day to coax flavor from inexpensive bones, but I wanted something faster. I needed meat—and lots of it.

Because I didn't want the soup to cost a fortune, I focused on reasonably priced cuts that could serve a dual purpose—first as broth enhancer and later as soup ingredient. My plan was as follows: Brown the meat to build flavor, pour off any rendered fat, add the canned broth, simmer until the meat was tender and the broth flavorful, and, finally, shred the beef and add it back to the pot with some vegetables to make soup.

Lean cuts from the round yielded tasteless broth and chewy bits of overcooked beef. Cuts from the chuck tasted better but were too greasy. Boneless blade steaks, which are very beefy but not terribly fatty, were just the thing. Three pounds' worth made a good broth and provided enough meat for a hearty soup.

My broth was now meaty, but there was no disguising the faint tinny taste of the canned beef broth. Cutting the beef broth with a little water helped, as did a spoonful of tomato paste, but the best solution was to add several cups of chicken broth. Doctoring beef broth with chicken broth might seem strange, but it works.

As for the other soup ingredients, I added the onion and carrots (along with some drained canned tomatoes) once the broth was finished cooking so that the broth would taste like meat, not sweet vegetables. Herbs and garlic fared better when added to the broth as it cooked. My tasters liked a combination of bay leaves and thyme, along with a whole head of garlic. Although this sounds like a lot of garlic, it became surprisingly mellow when simmered for so long.

I found that other vegetables—everything from potatoes and parsnips to peas and spinach—could be added directly to the finished broth. You just need to time the addition of each vegetable correctly. I created a handy chart (on page 27) that will help you customize my soup with the vegetables you like best. Now that's great homemade beef and vegetable soup (and nobody will guess you used canned broth)!

–Katie Henderson

HEARTY BEEF AND VEGETABLE SOUP MAKES ABOUT 3 QUARTS, SERVING 6 TO 8

Follow the chart on page 27 to add other ingredients to this soup.

Broth
- 3 pounds beef blade steaks (about 8 steaks) Salt and pepper
- 2 tablespoons vegetable oil
- 1 tablespoon tomato paste
- 4 cups low-sodium chicken broth
- 4 cups low-sodium beef broth
- 2 cups water
- 1 garlic head, top third cut off and discarded, loose outer skins removed
- 2 bay leaves
- 1/2 teaspoon dried thyme

Soup
- 1 tablespoon unsalted butter
- 1 medium onion, chopped fine
- 2 medium carrots, peeled, halved lengthwise, and cut into 1/4-inch half-moons
- 1 (14.5-ounce) can diced tomatoes, drained Salt and pepper Chopped fresh parsley

1. For the broth Season blade steaks with salt and pepper. Heat 1 tablespoon oil in Dutch oven over medium-high heat until shimmering. Add half of steaks and cook until well browned on both sides, about 8 minutes. Set steaks aside on plate. Repeat with remaining tablespoon oil and steaks.

2. Pour off fat from Dutch oven and return to medium-high heat. Add tomato paste and cook, mashing paste with wooden spoon, for 30 seconds. Add chicken broth, beef broth, and water, and scrape browned bits from bottom of pot with wooden spoon. Return steaks and any accumulated juices to pot. Add garlic, bay leaves, and thyme and bring to simmer, using wide, shallow spoon to skim off foam or fat that rises to surface. Reduce heat to medium-low and simmer gently (do not boil) until meat is tender, about 2 hours.

3. Transfer steaks and garlic head to rimmed plate to cool. Once cool enough to handle, shred meat into bite-sized pieces, discarding any fat. Using tongs, squeeze garlic cloves into small bowl. Mash with fork until paste forms. Pour broth through fine-mesh strainer. Return shredded beef and garlic paste to broth. (Broth can be refrigerated for 3 days or frozen for 2 months.)

4. For the soup Melt butter in clean Dutch oven over medium heat. Add onion and carrots and cook until onion is softened but not browned, about 5 minutes. Add tomatoes and broth. Bring to simmer, reduce heat to medium-low, and cook until carrots are tender, about 20 minutes.

5. To serve, adjust seasonings with salt and pepper and sprinkle with parsley.

Customize Your Soup

It may be impossible to please all of the people all of the time, but that doesn't mean you can't try. Our Hearty Beef and Vegetable Soup is easily customized, letting you use vegetables you like and/or have on hand. Feel free to mix and match, but don't add more than 2 cups *total* vegetables, pasta, noodles, or rice. The vegetables can cook right in the soup pot, but pasta, noodles, and rice should be precooked separately so they don't make the broth too thick.

LONG COOKING

VEGETABLE	PREPARATION	AMOUNT	WHEN TO ADD
RED POTATOES	Scrubbed, then diced	up to 2 cups	With broth in step 4
PARSNIPS	Peeled, then diced	up to 1/2 cup	With broth in step 4
SWEET POTATOES	Peeled, then diced	up to 2 cups	With broth in step 4
TURNIP	Peeled, then diced	up to 1/2 cup	With broth in step 4

LAST MINUTE

VEGETABLE	PREPARATION	AMOUNT	WHEN TO ADD
FROZEN LIMA BEANS	None	up to 1/2 cup	5 minutes before soup is done
FROZEN PEAS	None	up to 1 cup	2 minutes before soup is done
BABY SPINACH	None	up to 2 cups	1 minute before soup is done

PASTA, EGG NOODLES, OR RICE: Cook and drain. Add up to 2 cups just before serving.

Easier Than You Think: *Cheese Biscuits*

Is there a way to add big cheese flavor to a simple biscuit recipe?

There is nothing quite like fresh-from-the-oven cheese biscuits. And while getting there doesn't take long, good results are far from guaranteed. We think cream biscuits are the best bet for beginners. Simply pouring heavy cream into the bowl replaces the challenging step of cutting cubes of butter into flour. Could I add cheese to this simple recipe?

After my first attempts, I would have answered no. When your colleagues in the kitchen are using words like "flat," "gummy," and "greasy" to describe your biscuits, you know you're in trouble. After some head scratching, I realized that excess moisture and

fat from the cheese were the culprits. It was pretty easy to solve the moisture issue. I just avoided wet cheeses, such as feta and goat, in favor of cheddar, Jack, Swiss, and Parmesan.

With drier cheeses in the mix, my biscuits were no longer flat—but they were still greasy and gummy in the center. After several tests, I found that my dough could handle no more than 1/2 cup to 3/4 cup of shredded cheese without suffering textural problems (the amount varied based on the fat content of the specific cheese). Unfortunately, this wasn't enough to make really cheesy biscuits.

My first thought was to top each biscuit with extra cheese prior to baking. Unfortunately, the added weight of the cheese kept the biscuits from rising properly, and the cheese burned before the biscuits were fully cooked. My ultimate (and somewhat unconventional) solution was to sprinkle extra cheese on each biscuit halfway through baking, when I rotated the baking sheet. –**Meredith Butcher**

CHEDDAR BISCUITS

MAKES 8 BISCUITS

Bake the biscuits immediately after cutting them. Allowing them to stand for any length of time can decrease the leavening power of the baking powder and prevent the biscuits from rising properly in the oven

2	cups all-purpose flour
2	teaspoons sugar
2	teaspoons baking powder
1/2	teaspoon salt
3/4	cup shredded extra-sharp cheddar cheese
1 1/2	cups heavy cream

1. Adjust oven rack to upper-middle position and heat oven to 425 degrees. Line baking sheet with parchment paper.

2. Whisk flour, sugar, baking powder, and salt together in medium bowl. Stir in 1/2 cup cheese. Add 1 1/4 cups cream and stir with wooden spoon until dough forms, about 30 seconds. Transfer dough from bowl to countertop, leaving dry, floury bits in bowl. In 1-tablespoon increments, add up to 1/4 cup cream to dry bits in bowl, mixing with wooden spoon after each addition, until moistened. Add moistened bits to rest of dough and knead by hand just until smooth, about 30 seconds.

3. Pat dough into 8-inch circle, cut into wedges (see page 29), and place on prepared baking sheet. Bake until just beginning to brown, 7 to 9 minutes. Remove baking sheet from oven, sprinkle 1 1/2 teaspoons remaining cheese on each biscuit, and return to oven, rotating baking sheet from front to back. Bake until golden brown and cheese topping has melted, 7 to 9 minutes. Serve warm.

JALAPEÑO-JACK BISCUITS

Replace cheddar with 3/4 cup shredded pepper Jack cheese. Add 1 tablespoon minced jalapeño, 1 tablespoon finely chopped chives, and 1/4 teaspoon cayenne to dry ingredients. Proceed as directed, increasing first and second baking times to 9 minutes.

SWISS CARAWAY BISCUITS

Replace cheddar with 1 cup grated Swiss cheese. Add 3/4 cup cheese and 1 tablespoon toasted caraway seeds to dry ingredients. Proceed as directed, sprinkling remaining cheese over biscuits halfway through baking.

PARMESAN-GARLIC BISCUITS

Replace cheddar with 1 cup grated Parmesan cheese. Add 3/4 cup cheese, 2 minced garlic cloves, and 1/2 teaspoon pepper with dry ingredients. Proceed as directed, sprinkling remaining cheese over biscuits halfway through baking.

Cutting biscuit dough into scone-like wedges is faster than punching out traditional rounds and re-rolling the scraps.

Notes from Our Test Kitchen

TIPS, TECHNIQUES, AND TOOLS FOR BETTER COOKING

FROZEN PEA TASTE TEST

Yes, frozen peas really do taste better than the "fresh" peas you can buy at the supermarket. Those fresh peas probably started out tasting great, but within hours of harvest the natural sugars in peas turn to starches. By the time you get "fresh" supermarket peas home, they are mealy and bland. In fact, in a blind taste test against three leading brands of frozen peas (Birdseye, Green Giant, and Cascadian Farm), fresh peas came in last. All three brands of frozen peas were sweet and tasty—no doubt because they were cooked and frozen the day they were harvested, which locked in their sweetness and held off their quick march to starchy and bland. –Stephanie Alleyne

Kitchen Creations
Cake Glazes

Our **Pecan Sour Cream Coffee Cake** (page 17) is good on its own but looks and tastes even better with a drizzle of sweet glaze running down its sides.

TROPICAL ORANGE

Whisk together 1 cup confectioners' sugar, 2 tablespoons orange juice, and 1 teaspoon grated orange zest.

MUST BE MAPLE

Whisk together 1 cup confectioners' sugar, 2 tablespoons milk, and 1 tablespoon maple syrup.

JAVA JOLT

Whisk together 1 cup confectioners' sugar and 1 teaspoon instant espresso or coffee dissolved in 2 tablespoons milk.

CINNAMON TOAST

Whisk together 1 cup confectioners' sugar, 2 tablespoons milk, and 1/2 teaspoon ground cinnamon.

STRAINED BREW

Unlike most fruit juices, apple cider contains residual solids from the cidering process, and we found these solids to be cause for concern when developing the recipe for our **Mulled Cider** (page 14). As the cider is heated, these impurities coagulate and cloud the cider. Although they don't make the cider taste much different, their grainy appearance and texture aren't very appetizing. To clear up the situation, we lined a fine-mesh strainer with a coffee filter (a few layers of cheesecloth or paper towels also work) and poured the cider through the strainer before serving. The fine weave of the coffee filter helps to remove most of the apple solids, making the mulled cider look much cleaner. If you're making the cider ahead of time, you can simply set the cider aside in the refrigerator overnight. Once the solids settle to the bottom, the clear cider can be carefully poured off and reheated. –Jeremy Sauer

CUTTING CUTLETS

Chicken Parmesan (page 24) is traditionally made with thin chicken cutlets. To make them, we recommend cutting boneless chicken breasts in half horizontally rather than pounding them flat. To make cutting the soft meat a little easier, you can freeze the chicken breasts until firm but not completely frozen, about 20 minutes. To cut, use the palm of your hand to hold the chicken breast in place, keeping your fingers straight and parallel to the breast. Using a sharp chef's knife, start at the thickest part of the breast and slice it in half horizontally, producing two even cutlets. –Keri Fisher

Making your own cutlets is easy.

Bath Time Crème brûlée, cheesecake, and even some savory custard-based dishes, such as our **Savory Corn Pudding** (page 13), can benefit from the use of a water bath during baking (the dish of food is placed in a larger pan containing hot water). The water lowers the temperature surrounding the dish (even if it boils, the water temperature will be cooler than the oven temperature) and prevents uneven cooking. Using a water bath can be slippery business, though, as the baking dish can slide around in the water-filled pan, potentially sloshing and spilling scalding water. Assistant test cook Meredith Butcher demonstrates a safe way to use a water bath. She lines the larger pan lengthwise with a kitchen towel, then places the food-filled dish on top of the towel before pouring in the hot water. The towel not only prevents potential slips and slides but also moderates the heat between the bottom of the baking dish and the pan containing the water.

Meet the 'Pear'ents

Although there are dozens of pear varieties, the most common choices in the supermarket are Bosc, Anjou, and Bartlett. We decided to find out which varieties were best for roasting, poaching, and eating out of hand.

Easily recognizable for their dull, brownish skin, Bosc pears are very sweet when ripe and have a hearty (some would say mealy) texture. We found that Boscs were best poached. The moist heat softened their texture and made them more appealing. In contrast, roasting emphasized their mealy qualities.

Anjou pears, with their light yellow-green hue, are creamy, tender, and incredibly juicy when ripe. They can be eaten out of hand and are great for roasting; the hot oven concentrates their mild flavor.

Bartletts are our favorite. Yellow when underripe, these pears turn a beautiful greenish-yellow when ready to eat. Their sweet, flowery flavor becomes more powerful when they are roasted, making Bartletts our top choice for **Green Salad with Roasted Pears and Blue Cheese** (page 21). –Eva Katz

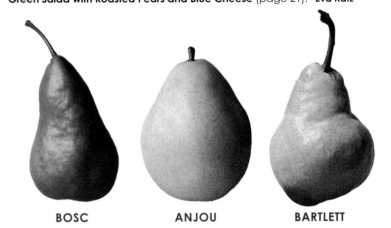

BOSC   ANJOU   BARTLETT

Kitchen Tip: MAKESHIFT V-RACK

An inexpensive V-rack does a great job of elevating roasts and birds to ensure even cooking. Caught without a V-rack and you want to make our **Crispy Roast Chicken and Potatoes** (page 21)? If you have a gas stovetop, you can improvise. Take two grates from the stovetop and place them in a V-position in a roasting pan. Place the chicken on top and roast away. –Jeremy Sauer

Shopping with the Test Kitchen SHORT RIBS

When it comes to choosing a cut of meat for our **Beer-Braised Short Ribs** (page 8), you have two options, both of which will deliver good results. English-style short ribs are cut from a single rib bone and feature a long flat bone with a rectangle of meat attached. Flanken-style ribs are cut across several bones and contain two or three small pieces of bone surrounded by pieces of meat. Because flanken-style ribs are more expensive and less widely available, we prefer English style. **–Diane Unger-Mahoney**

ENGLISH-STYLE RIB

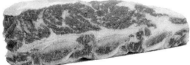

FLANKEN-STYLE RIB

SMART COOKIE

In the test kitchen, we've baked tens of thousands of cookies. Along the way we've come up with a few tips and techniques to keep the cookie-making process rolling along. **–Cali Rich**

- **The Warm-Up:** For easiest mixing, use room-temperature butter and eggs. Quickly warm up cold butter by cutting it into tablespoon-sized pieces, placing them flat on a plate, and microwaving on the lowest setting for 10 seconds at a time, until the butter is still waxy (not greasy) and bendable. Take the chill off eggs by placing them in a bowl of warm water for five minutes.
- **The Cool-Down:** To keep cookies from spreading and to make shaping easier, chill dough in the refrigerator for 30 minutes before using. If re-rolling cut-out scraps of dough, cover the scraps with plastic wrap and rechill before using them one more time.
- **The (Easy) Bake Oven:** Baking cookies one sheet at a time is a good idea, but if you've got an army's worth of cookies to bake you can double up by using the upper-middle and lower-middle oven racks and rotating the sheets halfway through baking. When you switch the sheets between top and bottom you should also turn them from back to front to safeguard against oven hot spots.
- **You Old Softie:** Cookies continue to bake and firm up on the hot baking sheet even after they are removed from the oven. For softer cookies, try underbaking by a minute or two, taking them out of the oven just as they begin to color around the edges. For chewier cookies, let them cool on the baking sheet rather than on a rack (unless specified otherwise in the recipe).
- **The Layered Look:** Once cooled, most cookies can be stored in an airtight container for at least 3 days. When storing decorated cookies (such as those on pages 4 and 5), slip sheets of waxed or parchment paper between layers of cookies to keep sticky glazes and fillings intact.

- **Shape Now, Eat Later:** If you would prefer to freeze the dough and bake the cookies later, simply cut out or roll the dough into balls and freeze on a baking sheet. When the dough has set, transfer the cutouts or balls to an airtight container and return to the freezer. Because the dough has already been portioned, there's no need for thawing; just add a couple of minutes to the baking time.

TWO GRINDERS ARE BEST

Freshly ground beans make the best coffee, so one coffee grinder is a must. Why own two grinders? We find that whole spices (page 15) often deliver better flavor than preground spices. In the test kitchen, we keep a dedicated spice and pepper grinder prominently labeled "FOR SPICES ONLY" (lest there be any doubt). To ensure an even grind, we gently shake the grinder during operation—think James Bond mixing a martini. Our favorite grinder is the Krups Fast-Touch Coffee Grinder, model 203, which retails for $19.99. You can pick one up at most department stores or through Amazon.com (item #203-42). **–Bridget Lancaster**

SIMMER, DON'T BOIL

The extra time required to "beef up" the canned broth in our **Hearty Beef and Vegetable Soup** (page 26) is well worth it. Although it's mostly a hands-off procedure, you do need to watch the pot. If the broth is allowed to boil, the fat and meat particles will get broken into smaller and smaller pieces that become suspended in the liquid. The resulting broth will be cloudy and greasy. For a clear, grease-free broth, make sure the broth simmers slowly. In this case, the notion that "a watched pot never boils" is a good one. For the clearest broth, use a wide spoon to skim the impurities that float to the surface in the first few minutes of cooking. **–Katie Henderson**

BOILED
Cloudy Broth

SIMMERED
Clear Broth

Inside the Test Kitchen
No-Roll Biscuits

Most biscuit recipes call for rolling out the dough, punching out rounds with a biscuit cutter, re-rolling the scraps, and punching out the remaining rounds. Hard work? No. Tedious? You bet. Besides calling for two specialized pieces of equipment (a rolling pin and biscuit cutter), the biscuits cut from the re-rolled scraps never rise as well as the fresh-cut biscuits. Is there an easier way?

Yes, as long as you're willing to sacrifice the traditional round biscuit shape. For our **Cheddar Biscuits** (page 27), we found that scone-like wedges were easier to cut and eliminated the scraps, so every single biscuit was a winner. Just press the dough into an 8-inch round shape—test cook Katie Henderson is using a cake pan to ensure a neat shape—and slice into wedges.

Kitchen Know-How
The Citrus Section

When slicing oranges, grapefruits, and other citrus fruits for salads, it's important to cut the sections free of the membranes, which are fibrous and bitter. Here's how we do this in the test kitchen.

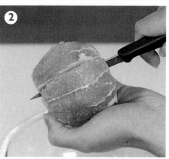

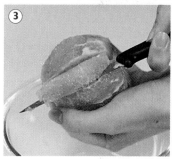

1. After cutting a thin slice from the top and bottom of the fruit, use a paring knife to slice off the rind, including the white pith, by cutting from the top to the bottom of the fruit. Try to follow the contour of the fruit as closely as possible.

2. Insert the blade of the paring knife just between the membrane and the section and slice to the center of the fruit. One side of the section will be separated.

3. Turn the blade of the knife so that it is facing outward. Slice along the membrane on the other side of the section until the section falls out. Repeat with the remaining sections.

Food Shopping

CHOCOLATE CHIPS: Can New Brands Compete with the Original?

Not so long ago, most markets had one—and only one—brand of chocolate chips, Nestlé Toll House Morsels. (Ruth Wakefield made the very first chocolate chip cookies at the Toll House Inn in Whitman, Mass., in 1930 and eventually sold the recipe to Nestlé.) Seventy-five years later, she would be amazed at the dozens of chips available in numerous flavors (raspberry, peanut butter, butterscotch) and shapes (mini, regular, and chunks). Are any of these chips better than the original? We tasted nine popular brands of semisweet chips, plain and in a chocolate chip cookie, to find out.

Chocolate chips contain less cocoa butter than bar chocolate. The lower fat content means that chips don't melt as readily, which is a good thing—they hold their shape better. Among the brands tested, the fat content hovered in a narrow range of 27 to 30 percent, and we found that the fat percentage did not correlate with tasters' preferences. Our tasters did pick up big differences in creaminess, awarding extra points to brands that were especially smooth melters. Smoothness is more a function of conching (the beating process used to turn unsweetened baking chocolate into eating chocolate) than cocoa butter content.

Chocolate chips contain more sugar than bar chocolate—in some cases, too much, according to our tasters. In general, the sweetest chips landed at the bottom of the rankings. Overall, tasters said the most important factor separating decent chips from great chips was chocolate flavor. Our top-rated chips were praised for their "intense" chocolate flavor; tasters complained about the "unremarkable" chocolate flavor in several low-rated brands.

So what's the chip of choice? According to our tasters, two relative newcomers. Guittard Classic Chips and Nestlé Toll House Chunks won points for their good chocolate flavor and moderate sweetness. The original Toll House morsels finished in a respectable third place. Brands are listed below in order preference. **–Keri Fisher**

Top Picks

1. GUITTARD Classic Semi-Sweet Dark Chocolate Chips
$2.79 for 12-ounce bag
Tasters loved the "buttery," "mellow chocolate flavor" and "lovely silky texture" of these chips, which were deemed "not too sweet, not too bitter." Though widely available throughout most of the country, availability in the Northeast is limited. See www.guittard.com for mail-order sources.

2. NESTLÉ Toll House Semi-Sweet Chocolate Chunks
$2.50 for 11.5-ounce bag
Though their unorthodox "rough-cut," "square" shape divided tasters, the "good chocolate flavor" and "nice blend of chocolate and sweet" helped these chips share top honors.

Runners-Up

3. NESTLÉ Toll House Semi-Sweet Chocolate Morsels $2.50 for 12-ounce bag
These familiar chips were praised for their "intense" chocolate flavor and "great creaminess," though some found them "almost too sweet," "like marshmallows."

4. GUITTARD Super Cookie Chips $2.79 for 10-ounce bag
Fans of these "big" chips praised the "good bitter/sweet balance" and "great chocolate flavor," though others found them "a little bland" and "more like milk chocolate."

5. BAKER'S Semi-Sweet Chocolate Chunks $2.85 for 12-ounce bag
"These aren't chips," complained one taster of these "solid" chunks that nonetheless won some fans with their "good balance" and "smooth" texture.

6. HERSHEY'S Semi-Sweet Chocolate Chips $2.29 for 12-ounce bag
These chips have a "rich, distinct flavor" that several detractors found "not very chocolaty" and "too sweet."

7. GHIRARDELLI Semi-Sweet Chocolate Chips $2.69 for 12-ounce bag
Many tasters liked the "rich flavor" of these chips, but some panned the "saccharine sweetness" that made them taste like a "caramel confection."

8. HERSHEY'S Special Dark Chocolate Chips $2.29 for 12-ounce bag
These new "dark" chips from Hershey's were criticized as "too sweet," with "unremarkable" chocolate flavor. A few tasters called them "pretty good."

9. MRS. FIELD'S Semi-Sweet Chocolate Chips $2.59 for 12-ounce bag
While some praised the "strong flavor" and "nice creaminess" of these chips, several tasters noted an odd "nutty" flavor. Most tasters deemed them "too sweet."

Taste Test Maple Syrup

According to the "experts" in the industry, grade A light amber—or "fancy," as it's called in Vermont—is the best maple syrup you can get. Honey gold and almost transparent, grade A light amber is typically made from the first sap of the season. (Maple syrup grades are determined by how much light passes through the syrup, which usually corresponds to when the syrup was made.) Next is grade A medium amber, which has a deeper color and stronger flavor. Close behind is grade A dark amber, which has a darker tawny color and more pronounced maple flavor. Grade B syrup, also known as cooking maple, is similar in color to grade A dark but has a more intense flavor that some say is better suited for cooking than for topping pancakes.

Because we're not ones to take experts at their word, we held a tasting to find out how these grades of syrup measured up in our kitchen. We chose the same brand of syrup (a test kitchen favorite) and ordered it in all four grades. We tasted the syrups plain (with waffles for dipping) and in a maple scone recipe.

While differences in flavor were harder to pick up in the scone, tasters still had clear preferences in both tests. They ranked grade A light amber (the so-called "best" syrup) last. Its flavor was too timid. The robust flavor of grade A dark amber was the clear favorite, but even grade B "cooking" syrup was preferred to light amber syrup. So much for conventional wisdom.

Below are our tasting notes on four grades of maple syrup, listed in order or preference. **–K.F.**

Grade A Dark Amber
Tasters were won over by the "natural," "rich, complex maple flavor" and "great depth" of this syrup. Though a few found it "too strong," most agreed that the "smoky flavor" provided a "hint of bitterness" that made it "yummy!"

Grade A Medium Amber
Fans of this syrup praised the "sweet and delicate" flavor and "mellow aftertaste." Some, however, complained that the color wasn't "deep enough" and found the flavor "a little thin" and "more sweet than mapley."

Grade B (Cooking Maple)
The most potent syrup you can buy, cooking syrup found fans with its "very strong and rich maple flavor" that more than one taster likened to "coffee." Others found it too strong, describing the flavor as "a little burnt."

Grade A Light Amber
It may be the "fanciest" of the lot, but our tasters found the light amber syrup "very mild" and only "vaguely maple-tasting." Others complained that there was "no depth" but suggested "this would be good for beginners."

Equipment Roundup

TOASTERS: Can You Buy Something Decent for Less Than $30?

Look in any fancy catalog and you'll see some pretty expensive toasters. For $250, you can buy a lot of features—pretty knobs, sleek design, vibrant color—but in our experience that money doesn't necessarily buy you a good slice of toast. With such a seemingly reasonable goal in mind, we selected 12 two-slot toasters that ranged in price from $15 to $30 and put them to the test.

HOW THEY WORK: Toasters use infrared radiation to toast bread. To produce that radiation, wires made of nichrome (an alloy of nickel and chromium) are wrapped around mica sheets on either side of the slot. The radiation is produced where the wire comes in contact with the mica sheet; the more wires, the more heat, the darker the toast. When you press the lever a timer is set; when the timer goes off, the slots are released and the toast pops out.

EVEN COVERAGE: The best toasters, we found, had a good number of wires (about nine per slot) that were evenly spaced, allowing for even toasting. Low-rated brands either had too few wires (which translated into spottily browned bread) or had wires that were clustered at the bottom of the toaster (which caused the bottom of the bread to burn).

CONSISTENT PERFORMANCE: Some models failed in this regard, turning out toast that was too dark immediately following a pair of perfectly toasted slices, or vice versa.

"SPECIAL" FEATURES: Do you really need a special setting for pastry or waffles? No. We were equally unimpressed with the "bagel" setting found on many toasters. We did like the defrost setting, which defrosted and then toasted bread in one cycle.

SUMMING UP: We learned that extra features and fancy designs don't make a good toaster. The Farberware FST200 ($19.99) may not be much to look at, but it consistently delivered evenly brown toast, which really shouldn't be too much to ask. Unfortunately, for most toasters it is. –Keri Fisher

Highly Recommended
FARBERWARE FST200
Price: $19.99

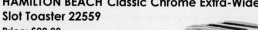

Comments: We were able to brown toast to five different shades, from no color to deep, dark brown. The plastic exterior stayed cooler than the exterior of any other toaster, and the defrost feature worked perfectly. One downside: With the controls on a long side, this toaster took up more counter space than most.

Recommended
SUNBEAM 6253 2-Slice Toaster
Price: $29.99

Comments: We were mostly unimpressed with the array of special features on this model (everything toasted just fine at the basic toast settings), though we did like "defrost" and "reheat," which warmed cold toast without adding more color.

OSTER 2-Slice Toaster 6325
Price: $29.99

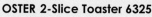

Comments: Though the slots on this model were long, we did have some trouble with thick bagels. Consistency was good at all but the highest setting, but the exterior of the toaster got very hot. The defrost setting, however, worked well, and the settings were mostly distinct.

BLACK & DECKER Classic Chrome 2-Slice Toaster T6000 Price: $29.99

Comments: We were disappointed with the defrost feature on this model, which left bagels cold in the middle at all but the highest setting. Consistency, however, was mostly good.

Recommended with Reservations
TOASTMASTER Cool Touch Bagel Perfect TT2CT
Price: $19.99

Comments: Consistency was an issue with this model, as the bread sometimes had wide strips of white at the top or was spottily browned. Still, we were able to produce five distinct shades of toast for the five settings. The slots were just a bit too short, causing the bread to catch sometimes on the way down.

HAMILTON BEACH Classic Chrome Extra-Wide Slot Toaster 22559
Price: $29.99

Comments: The higher settings of this model were much better than the lower ones, producing mostly consistent toast at varying shades of brown. The chrome got very hot, and the dial was difficult to read. Both "defrost" and "reheat," however, worked perfectly.

Not Recommended
PROCTOR SILEX Cool-Touch 2-Slice Toaster 22450
Price: $14.99

Comments: While consistency was good with this model, we simply couldn't get dark toast in one cycle. Even at the highest setting, the toast was only golden brown. In addition, the bread barely fit into the slots and sometimes needed a little help going down.

CUISINART Electronic Cool Touch 2-Slice Toaster CPT-120
Price: $29.95

Comments: Consistency was a serious problem with this model, which toasted bread more heavily on one side, and even that unevenness varied from batch to batch.

GE Classic 2-Slice Toaster 106808
Price: $24.83

Comments: We liked the large slots and excellent defrost and reheat features, but the toast was often spotty and uneven. Without a "cool-touch" feature, the exterior of this chrome model got very hot.

RIVAL Bagel Wide Cool Touch Toaster TT9270
Price: $17.97

Comments: The bread didn't quite fit into this toaster, so we often had to push it down to help it along. Three batches produced at the same setting were inconsistently toasted.

Gadgets & Gear Making Butter Spreadable

Try to spread cold butter on toast and you end up with a pile of crumbs. Thankfully, there are gadgets designed to make butter spread more easily. The top of the Norpro Butter Keeper ($7.99) is filled with butter and the base is then filled with water (which must be changed every few days). When the two pieces are put together, the water forms a seal around the butter, protecting it from light and air (which make good butter go bad). We found that butter kept in the Norpro tasted fresh for a month. The lid on the other butter keeper we tried—the Cook Street Butter Boat ($24.95)—formed only a loose seal, and the butter began to smell bad after a few days. The other gadgets we tried approached the problem from a different angle. The Cuisine International Butter Curler ($4.99), which strips thin curls of butter from a full stick, and the Max Space Butter Dispenser ($11.99), which turned a stick of butter into an ultra-thin ribbon, were both awkward to use. The Fox Run Craftsmen Butter Spreader ($1.99), essentially a plastic handle that holds a half-stick of butter, is great for buttering corn, not toast. –K.F.

The Norpro Butter Keeper was the best of the five gadgets designed to make butter more spreadable.

When Things Go Wrong in the Kitchen

READERS SHARE FUNNY STORIES ABOUT COOKING MISHAPS

"COFFEE" CAKE

Cooking is not my forte, but one year I decided to surprise my husband with a flourless chocolate cake for his birthday. I enlisted the help of a friend, and we set out to make cake. As we went through the list of ingredients, we read "1 cup of espresso." As no instructions for brewing the coffee were included in the recipe, we decided to go with ground beans. When we served the cake to my husband and a group of friends, however, I realized we had made a huge mistake. One friend looked up, smiled, and, showing lots of coffee grounds in her teeth, asked if she could have a cup of hot water to go with her coffee!

Kathryn Rudy Evanston, Ill.

DON'T TRUST WHAT YOU READ

I recently surprised my partner and several guests with a special brisket, using a recipe from a new cookbook by one of my favorite chefs. After the searing, sautéing, and simmering, the time came to "place the brisket in a large Dutch oven, cover with plastic wrap, cover yet again with foil, and place in the oven to bake on 350 degrees for several hours." Now, did I mention I went to culinary school for two years? I definitely paused, re-read, and thought, "No way." Then again, I had great faith in this accomplished chef. I proceeded to follow the instructions, assuming some magical occurrence would prevent the plastic wrap from melting all over the meat.

When the brisket was done, I was able to remove the foil, but the plastic wrap was nowhere to be found. I went ahead and sliced and served the brisket. As we started to eat, I could taste the not-so-slight flavor of plastic, which had permeated the meat and the sauce. "Stop!" I yelled. I told my guests that

cilantro can sometimes take on an "overpowering, plastic-like taste" when mixed with an acidic ingredient like the tomatoes that were used in the sauce. Everyone seemed to believe me. I then made spaghetti and we had a great time anyway.

Laurence Plotkin Venice, Calif.

A PICKY EATER'S REVENGE

I grew up poor during the Depression, and my mother and I lived in various rooming houses. When I was 3 or 4 years old, I was underweight and a very picky eater. One night, my mother made cornbread, one of my favorites. But when I tasted it, I spit it right out. That was a no-no during those hard times, and I was told to eat it. Then I began to cry. My mother wanted to know why. I told her it tasted like soap. Because I was such a picky eater, she didn't believe me and insisted that I eat the cornbread. I put up such a fight that she had to taste it for herself. After one bite, she went straight to the pantry and checked her box of yellow cornmeal. She found that someone in the rooming house had used her cornmeal and replaced it with Oxodyl, a laundry soap that looked exactly like yellow cornmeal. After that incident, whenever anything tasted funny to me, I didn't have to eat it.

Lois I. Peters Kent, Wash.

PEANUT BUTTER STIR-FRY

When we were first married, my wife used to make a peanut butter dip for chicken fingers. Anyway, she had to work late one evening, so I decided to surprise her by making her dinner. She likes Chinese food, so I whipped up a stir-fry, even though I had never made one before. I had no trouble browning the chicken or the vegetables, but when it came to the sauce, I had no idea what to put in. Then I remembered that peanut butter dip, made with apricot jam. I greeted my wife with a smile when she walked

in the door, but that smile quickly faded when I bit into my "peanut butter stir-fry." It was vile! To this day, when we try a new recipe that flops, you can bet you'll hear, "Well, at least it's better than that peanut butter stir-fry."

Matt Scott Jefferson City, Mo.

Send us your funniest kitchen disaster stories. Write to us at Kitchen Disasters, Cook's Country, P.O. Box 470739, Brookline, MA 02447. If you'd like to use e-mail, write to kitchendisasters@ bcpress.com. If we publish your story, you'll receive a complimentary one-year subscription to *Cook's Country*.

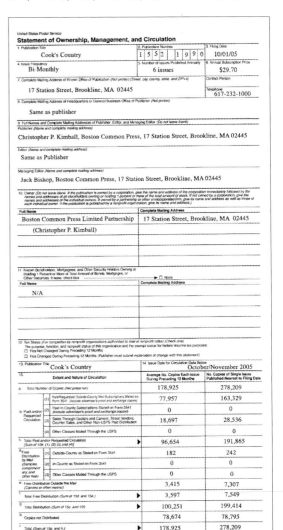

United States Postal Service
Statement of Ownership, Management, and Circulation

1. Publication Title: Cook's Country	2. Publication Number: 1 5 5 2 | 1 9 9 0		3. Filing Date: 10/01/05
4. Issue Frequency: Bi-Monthly	5. Number of Issues Published Annually: 6 issues		6. Annual Subscription Price: $29.70

7. Complete Mailing Address of Known Office of Publication (Not printer) (Street, city, county, state, and ZIP+4):
17 Station Street, Brookline, MA 02445

Contact Person:
Telephone: 617-232-1000

8. Complete Mailing Address of Headquarters or General Business Office of Publisher (Not printer):
Same as publisher

9. Full Names and Complete Mailing Addresses of Publisher, Editor, and Managing Editor (Do not leave blank)
Publisher (Name and complete mailing address):
Christopher P. Kimball, Boston Common Press, 17 Station Street, Brookline, MA 02445

Editor (Name and complete mailing address):
Same as Publisher

Managing Editor (Name and complete mailing address):
Jack Bishop, Boston Common Press, 17 Station Street, Brookline, MA 02445

10. Owner (Do not leave blank. If the publication is owned by a corporation, give the name and address of the corporation immediately followed by the names and addresses of all stockholders owning or holding 1 percent or more of the total amount of stock. If not owned by a corporation, give the names and addresses of the individual owners. If owned by a partnership or other unincorporated firm, give its name and address as well as those of each individual owner. If the publication is published by a nonprofit organization, give its name and address.)

Full Name	Complete Mailing Address
Boston Common Press Limited Partnership	17 Station Street, Brookline, MA 02445
(Christopher P. Kimball)	

11. Known Bondholders, Mortgagees, and Other Security Holders Owning or Holding 1 Percent or More of Total Amount of Bonds, Mortgages, or Other Securities. If none, check box. ☑ None

Full Name	Complete Mailing Address
N/A	

12. Tax Status (For completion by nonprofit organizations authorized to mail at nonprofit rates) (Check one)
The purpose, function, and nonprofit status of this organization and the exempt status for federal income tax purposes:
☐ Has Not Changed During Preceding 12 Months
☐ Has Changed During Preceding 12 Months (Publisher must submit explanation of change with this statement)

13. Publication Title: Cook's Country	14. Issue Date for Circulation Data Below: October/November 2005	
15. Extent and Nature of Circulation	Average No. Copies Each Issue During Preceding 12 Months	No. Copies of Single Issue Published Nearest to Filing Date
a. Total Number of Copies (Net press run)	178,925	278,209
b. Paid and/or Requested Circulation (1) Paid/Requested Outside-County Mail Subscriptions Stated on Form 3541 (Include advertiser's proof and exchange copies)	77,957	163,329
(2) Paid In-County Subscriptions Stated on Form 3541 (Include advertiser's proof and exchange copies)	0	0
(3) Sales Through Dealers and Carriers, Street Vendors, Counter Sales, and Other Non-USPS Paid Distribution	18,697	28,536
(4) Other Classes Mailed Through the USPS	0	0
c. Total Paid and/or Requested Circulation (Sum of 15b (1), (2), (3), and (4))	96,654	191,865
d. Free Distribution by Mail (Samples, complimentary, and other free) (1) Outside-County as Stated on Form 3541	182	242
(2) In-County as Stated on Form 3541	0	0
(3) Other Classes Mailed Through the USPS	0	0
e. Free Distribution Outside the Mail (Carriers or other means)	3,415	7,307
f. Total Free Distribution (Sum of 15d and 15e.)	3,597	7,549
g. Total Distribution (Sum of 15c. and 15f.)	100,251	199,414
h. Copies not Distributed	78,674	78,795
i. Total (Sum of 15g. and h.)	178,925	278,209
j. Percent Paid and/or Requested Circulation (15c. divided by 15g. times 100)	96.41%	96.21%

16. Publication of Statement of Ownership
☑ Publication required. Will be printed in the Dec/Jan 2006 issue of this publication. ☐ Publication not required.

17. Signature and Title of Editor, Publisher, Business Manager, or Owner

Date: 9/19/05

I certify that all information furnished on this form is true and complete. I understand that anyone who furnishes false or misleading information on this form or who omits material or information requested on the form may be subject to criminal sanctions (including fines and imprisonment) and/or civil sanctions (including civil penalties).

Instructions to Publishers

1. Complete and file one copy of this form with your postmaster annually on or before October 1. Keep a copy of the completed form for your records.
2. In cases where the stockholder or security holder is a trustee, include in items 10 and 11 the name of the person or corporation for whom the trustee is acting. Also include the names and addresses of individuals who are stockholders who own or hold 1 percent or more of the total amount of bonds, mortgages, or other securities of the publishing corporation. In item 11, if none, check the box. Use blank sheets if more space is required.
3. Be sure to furnish all circulation information called for in item 15. Free circulation must be shown in items 15d, e, and f.
4. Item 15h., Copies not Distributed, must include (1) newsstand copies originally stated on Form 3541, and returned to the publisher, (2) estimated returns from news agents, and (3), copies for office use, leftovers, spoiled, and all other copies not distributed.
5. If the publication had Periodicals authorization as a general or requester publication, this Statement of Ownership, Management, and Circulation must be published; it must be printed in any issue in October or, if the publication is not published during October, the first issue printed after October.
6. In item 16, indicate the date of the issue in which this Statement of Ownership will be published.
7. Item 17 must be signed.

Failure to file or publish a statement of ownership may lead to suspension of Periodicals authorization.

WHO COULD RESIST A HOT DUCK?

Some years ago, my fiancé and I were hosting two other couples for Christmas Eve dinner. I had cooked two ducks, and they were beautifully browned, with crisp skins. I put them on a platter in the oven to rest. When I went to retrieve them, I assumed the platter would no longer be hot. Unfortunately, I had forgotten to turn off the oven. I quickly dropped the platter, and one of the ducks fell onto the kitchen floor. My cocker spaniel got the duck in her mouth before I could say no. Using my sweetest voice, I called my fiancé, "Honey, could you please come into the kitchen, NOW!"

He managed to pry the duck from the dog's mouth, but because the meat was so torn up, we ended up carving in the kitchen. The ducks tasted great. Years later, as we were recounting this story to some friends, we realized that one of the couples who had eaten that duck was present, listening in horror.

Renate Coleshill Falls Church, Va.

Lady Baltimore

Statuesque Lady Baltimore Cake is dressed to impress, with three layers of tender white cake, stripes of dried fruit and nut filling, and mounds of sticky meringue-like icing. This cake was popularized by a writer, not a baker. Owen Wister named his 1906 romance novel after the cake. *Lady Baltimore* became a bestseller, and real bakers started making Lady Baltimore Cakes based on Wister's description. One-hundred years later, Lady Baltimore Cake is still popular, especially around Christmas.

To make this cake you'll need:

1   cup mixed dried fruits (any combination of cherries, dates, figs, pineapple, and raisins)
¼   cup pecans, toasted
2   tablespoons rum, bourbon, or water
6   cups seven-minute icing*
3   baked 8-inch white cake rounds*
     Sugared pecans*

For the filling: Process dried fruits and pecans in food processor until finely chopped. (Or chop very fine with knife.) Transfer to medium bowl and mix with rum. Stir in 2 cups icing.

To assemble: Place one cake round on serving platter. Spread half of fruit and icing mixture over cake. Repeat with another cake layer and remaining fruit and icing mixture. Top with remaining cake round. Spread remaining plain icing over top and sides of cake, using back of spoon to create attractive swirls and peaks. Decorate with sugared pecans.

*Recipes for white cake, icing, and sugared pecans are available at www.cookscountry.com, but feel free to use your own.

Recipe Index

beverages, biscuits, and breakfast

Cheddar Biscuits 27
    Jalapeño-Jack Biscuits
    Parmesan-Garlic Biscuits
    Swiss Caraway Biscuits
Fireside Mulled Cider 14
    Mulled Apple "Chai"-der
    Mulled Cider à la Pumpkin Pie
Maple Sausage and Waffle Casserole 22

starters, soups, salads, and sides

Braised Brussels Sprouts with Bacon and Pecans 13
Cranberry-Apple-Orange Relish 13
Green Salad with Roasted Pears and Blue Cheese 21
Hearty Beef and Vegetable Soup 26–27
Italian Spinach and Radicchio Salad 12
Light and Creamy Hot Dips 7
    Artichoke
    Crab
    Spinach
Peas Four Ways 19
    Creamy Peas with Ham and Onion
    Curried Peas
    Dilly Peas and Carrots
    Smashed Minty Peas
Rustic Potato Soup RC
Savory Corn Pudding 13
Sweet Potato Casserole 13
Winter Fruit Salads 23
    Bahama Mama
    The Green Monstah
    Hollywood Hills
    Lovers' Lane
    Miami Vice
    Paradise Found

main courses

Baked Cod with Crunchy Lemon-Herb Topping RC
Beer-Braised Short Ribs 8
Broiled Paprika Chicken RC
Chicken with Mushrooms and Leeks RC
Creamy Carbonara 25
Crispy Roast Chicken and Potatoes 21
Dr. Pepper–Glazed Ham 12
Pan-Seared Steaks with Balsamic Onions 18
Pork Chops with Spicy Orange Glaze RC
Skillet Chicken Parmesan 24
Spaghetti with Sausage Meatballs RC
Stir-Fried Beef with Snow Peas and Cashews RC
Taco Salad RC

sweet snacks and desserts

Cake Glazes 28
Holiday Cookies 4–5
    Chocolate Toffee Butter Cookies
    Christmas Meringue Kisses
    Macadamia Eggnog Creams
    Molasses Spice Lemon Sandwich Cookies
Lady Baltimore Cake (inside back cover)
Pecan Sour Cream Coffee Cake 17–18
Peppermint Desserts 10
    Icebox Peppermint Yule Log Cake
    Mug O' Minty Hot Chocolate
    Peppermint Ice Cream Sandwiches
    Wintermint Bark
Tipsy Squire 9
Western-Slope Pear Cake with Ginger Cream 13

RC = Recipe Card